THE UNITED STATES FORMALLY SIGNS THE UNITED NATIONS CHARTER

Edward R. Stettinius, Jr., then Secretary of State and Chairman of the United States Delegation, signs the UN Charter at San Francisco on June 26, 1945, as President Harry S. Truman stands near by.

United States

HISTORY

The Growth of Our Land

MERLE BURKE

ILLUSTRATED

1952

AMERICAN TECHNICAL SOCIETY · CHICAGO · U·S·A

PREFACE

This story of the United States of America has been written with a definite purpose in mind. It is only fair that you, the reader, should know what that purpose is.

Through a good many years of teaching social studies in high school, I have felt that one of the greatest handicaps to functional teaching has been the mass of detail with which most history textbooks are packed.

Students are often expected to memorize so much specific information that they frequently lose sight of the significant trends of history that are working themselves out in the events that occur.

It is my firm belief that a knowledge of the trends of history is infinitely more valuable than a memorized encyclopedia of specific facts. If one knows the over-all story, he can always search out the details that he may want from time to time. But if he has only masses of details that mean little or nothing to him, they will soon be forgotten, leaving him with nothing for his efforts.

Accordingly, in this book, I have made an effort to emphasize the trends —the direction of the broad sweep and tide of events as they have shaped our growth. I believe that a full knowledge of these trends is essential to an understanding of the forces that have made us what we are. These same forces are operating today both within and without this nation, and they bid fair to influence our future development.

For this reason I believe that the treatment of the subject in this text will be especially welcome to those who find in the study of our past an inspiring lesson for the living present and the future.

A great part of the history of the United States has been tied up with developments in other parts of the world. In order that our history as a nation may be seen in its full perspective against the background of the globe, considerable attention has been given in this book to world affairs that have so greatly influenced the course taken by the United States. You will also note that the treatment in this text has been two-fold in character—both chronological and topical. The approach in the first four units is chronological, taking events in the order of their occurrence. In the last four units, our study is topical, providing us with a fuller understanding of those events.

To help you in mastering your work, you will find at the close of each chapter a set of questions based upon the material covered in the chapter. You will also find a list of names and terms you should be able to identify and define. Also, to supply immediately some of the details you might want —and yet not clutter the text with them—I have placed at the end of each chapter a list of associated dates and have indicated the importance of each. At the end of each unit (the entire book is divided into eight units), you will find a selected list of related books which will make the further pursuit of your study of history both enjoyable and rewarding.

These aids to study have been carefully prepared with your needs uppermost in mind. In the organization of this text—designed not only for your benefit as a student but also for your reference as a responsible and well-informed citizen of your community—I am especially indebted for the helpful guidance of James McKinney, President; Dr. Edward C. Estabrooke, Educational Director; Allen Holbert, Principal of the High School; and the members of the History Department, Jack L. Cross, Robert Hennemeyer, Paul Owen, and Edward Parks, of the American School.

In writing the manuscript, I have tried to keep out my own feelings and opinions just as much as is humanly possible. However, I know that all of us tend to make decisions more on a basis of our emotions than our intelligence. I am vitally concerned that the future of the United States should be as bright as we can possibly make it. I believe we must go beyond a knowledge of facts and trends in preparing ourselves to take an active part in building America's future.

To this end, I have in certain places in the book departed from a factual presentation of material and have intentionally tried to outline some of the basic concepts and ideas which I believe must underlie our thinking if we are to build our future wisely and well. In each case I have stated that these are personal opinions and that you are not in any way bound to agree with them. I simply want you to do some thinking about them. For if we all think honestly and fairly on a background of what we know to be true of our past, together we can build a United States of America that will continue to prosper and flourish through the centuries to come. If we are to preserve American democracy, if we are to have government by the people, you and I are going to have to accept our responsibilities as citizens; we dare not permit others to do the job for us. This book is offered as a contribution toward the attainment of responsible and efficient and intelligent self-government. I hope you find it of service to you.

MERLE BURKE

CONTENTS

The New World
Is Discovered and Settled

INTRODUCTION

The early history of the New World had its roots in the old. The history of America began in the history of Europe. The crusades had served to awaken Western Europe from the long period of the "Dark Ages" that had followed the fall of the Roman Empire. They had acquainted the people of Western Europe with a far more advanced civilization that existed along the eastern shores of the Mediterranean Sea. They introduced new ideas that paved the way for the Renaissance (rebirth) in Western Europe.

The crusades also created a great new desire for trade with the East. In the attempt to find an all-water route from Western Europe to the East, the American continents were discovered.

Discovery was followed by exploration. The early explorers were Spanish, English, and French. In the beginning, they were looking for ways to get around the New World and on to the East. Later, they became more interested in the New World itself.

Exploration was followed rather naturally by colonization. The English, Spanish, French, and Dutch settled in different parts of North America, and for different reasons.

From the time of the crusades on, the struggle for colonies (empire-building) has made a great deal of both European and American history, clear down to the present. Part of that struggle was fought out in North America in the seventeenth and eighteenth centuries, particularly between Great Britain and France. The net result was to give Great Britain control of huge areas in North America and to make her the greatest colonial power of modern times.

This is the part of the story of America you will find covered in Unit One.

Chapter 1

America Appears on the World Map

EUROPEAN NAVIGATORS, SEARCHING FOR AN ALL-WATER ROUTE TO THE
EAST, STUMBLE UPON A NEW WORLD

Search for a New Trade Route. The Crusades were over. That long series—they lasted about 200 years—of religious-military expeditions from western Europe into the Near East had ended. They had been undertaken chiefly to free the Christian Holy Land (modern Palestine) from the Turks, who had so recently conquered it and had then denied Christian pilgrims the right to visit shrines there. But the Crusades had failed in their original purpose. True, Christian armies had captured Jerusalem and held it for 90 years. But when interest in fighting the war-loving Moslem-Turks had waned and the expeditions had ceased, the Turks were still in possession of the Holy Land.

The Crusades, however, like so many other enterprises that are oft-times called "failures," left in their wake a great many important consequences. Most of these concerned Europe principally and cannot be considered here. But one of them turned out to be of vital importance to what came to be known as the New World—America.

People who returned to western Europe from the Near East came back with newly acquired tastes for various products not to be found naturally in western Europe. The only way to satisfy these desires was to increase greatly the trade between the countries of western Europe and those of Asia.

Over the years two Mediterranean city-states gained a virtual monopoly of this growing trade. They were the Italian city-states of Venice and Genoa. These city-states were able to accomplish this because they possessed armies and navies capable of enforcing their monopoly.

This situation was especially hard on the countries of western Europe, for they—if they wanted the products of the East—had to buy them from the merchants of Venice and Genoa, who demanded high prices for these products. It was only natural for the countries that did the buying to dislike such an arrangement.

Out of this predicament in which the countries of western Europe found themselves grew the desire to find a new route to the East—one that would not pass through the Mediterranean, and one that was an all-water route, if possible.

Little Portugal took the lead in this new project. Prince Henry of Portugal was vitally interested in navigation. Sailors were not anxious, however, to sail out of the sight of land because of a triple fear: (1) they might get lost, (2) they might drop off the edge of what they believed to be a flat world,

2

and (3) they might be gobbled up by huge sea monsters which they believed inhabited the uncharted waters.

Then western Europe acquired two new gadgets that gave sailors courage. From China came an invention called the *compass,* which could tell them the directions; and from Greece came the *astrolabe* (an early version of the sextant), which could tell them their latitude and longitude. Equipped with these two new instruments, navigators sailed out into waters they had never visited before, determined to find a new all-water route to the East.

One such intrepid navigator, Bartholomew Diaz, pushing down the long west coast of Africa, was finally blown in a storm around the continent's southern tip (1487). He returned to Portugal (1488) calling that tip the Cape of Storms. But wise King John (Prince Henry had died shortly before this) changed the name to the Cape of Good Hope—hope that around this point might lie the all-water route for which they were searching.

And sure enough it did. In 1498 another Portuguese, Vasco da Gama, rounded the Cape of Good Hope, sailed up the eastern coast of Africa, and put in along the shore of what is now Ethiopia. There he picked up an Arab pilot and set sail again toward the northeast, finally dropping anchor in the harbor of Calicut,[1] on the south-

---

[1] This is not to be confused with Calcutta, an entirely different city built many years later by the British to serve as the capital of their holdings in India until 1912. Calicut was an important port from which were shipped great quantities of what has probably been India's greatest contribution to the world—cotton piece goods. So much of this product left Calicut that the port city gave its name to the goods—goods which your grandmother wore and called *calico.*

western coast of India. The all-water route from western Europe to the East had been discovered.

The Discovery of America. While this was going on, an Italian sailor named Christopher Columbus was making history. Columbus wanted to get a part of the wealth of the East for

Chicago Historical Society

CHRISTOPHER COLUMBUS

Portraits of Columbus vary greatly in their representation of his appearance. This picture was adapted from an original work by Antonio Moro, a Spanish Court painter who lived during the lifetime of Columbus.

himself. And he had a new idea about how to get to Cathay (China). Contrary to the accepted belief of the time, he thought the earth was a sphere and that by sailing due west he could eventually arrive at the East. This was not idle fancy either, for he had maps to support his contention. He had procured them from his father-in-law. (It has even been suggested that he may have married the girl just to get the maps.) Possessed of this idea, Columbus

DISCOVERY FLEET

Columbus and his men sailed across the Atlantic in three caravels—the flagship "Santa Maria," the "Pinta," and the "Niña." Caravels were small sailing vessels of the fifteenth and sixteenth centuries; they had broad bows and high afterdecks.

THE SHORES OF THE NEW WORLD IN VIEW

Columbus and his sailors had reason to rejoice upon seeing land after their Atlantic passage in 1492. The trip, including a stop at the Canary Islands, had taken more than two months. Much of the voyage had been across unknown ocean.

wandered about for twenty years trying to find someone interested enough in his idea to back him financially. Finally an interview was arranged with King Ferdinand and Queen Isabella of Spain. The result of this interview was that Columbus left with the promise of ships, men, and money. It is interesting to note that it was neither the desire to prove that the world was round nor the prospect of additional wealth from Cathay that won support for Columbus. Queen Isabella was a devoutly religious woman, and the possibility of spreading Christianity into new areas greatly appealed to her.

Columbus set out on August 3, 1492, with three ships: the "Santa Maria," of 100 tons; the "Pinta," of 50 tons; and the "Niña," of 40 tons. A total crew of 88 manned the three vessels. His course took him first to the Canary Islands and then westward across uncharted waters. Threatened with mutiny by his men, Columbus pushed on, and on the morning of October 12 land was sighted. Probably it was one of the Bahama Islands, but Columbus thought it was "the Indies" (India—the East). Accordingly, he called the natives *Indians*.

Someone has said that when Columbus left Spain, he didn't know where he was going; when he discovered land, he didn't know where he was; and when he got back home, he didn't know where he had been. Certainly it remained for subsequent voy-

ages (he reached the mainland in 1498) to disclose to Columbus that what he had reached in 1492 was not the Indies, but apparently a great new continent lying between western Europe and the coast of Cathay. Other explorers enlarged the fund of knowledge about this New World. One of them, Amerigo Vespucci, seemingly tried to perpetrate a fraud by claiming that he discovered the mainland in 1487—ahead of Columbus—and by writing about his explorations. His writings were so widely published that soon his name was given to the New World.

So it was that America appeared on the maps of the world.

AMERIGO VESPUCCI

Unwittingly or not, European mapmakers of the period gave Vespucci's name to the new lands across the sea, and it stuck.

FOR YOUR REVIEW

These Should Be Easy for You Now

1. Through what lands did the Crusades take place?
2. What was the original purpose of the Crusades? Judged by this purpose, were they successful?
3. What result of the Crusades is especially important to us? Why?
4. What two city-states came to control most of the traffic through the Mediterranean? What important search did this lead to?
5. What factors had a tendency to discourage open-sea navigation? What new inventions changed this?
6. Who discovered the Cape of Good Hope? Why was it so named?
7. Who discovered the all-water route to the East?
8. What was Columbus trying to do when he discovered the Americas? Why did Queen Isabella agree to help Columbus?
9. For whom was the New World named?

Associated Dates

1001—discovery of America by Leif Erickson
1095—start of the Crusades
1488—discovery of the Cape of Good Hope by Diaz
1492—discovery of the Americas by Columbus
1498—discovery of the all-water route to the East by Vasco da Gama
1499–1502—explorations in the New World by Amerigo Vespucci

Why Are These To Be Remembered?

Palestine	Bartholomew Diaz	Christopher Columbus
Venice and Genoa	Vasco da Gama	Ferdinand and Isabella
Prince Henry	Calicut	Amerigo Vespucci

Chapter 2

People Come To Explore the New World

BRAVE SOULS FROM THE OLD WORLD EXPLORE, CONQUER, AND CLAIM
PARTS OF THE NEW WORLD FOR EUROPEAN EMPIRE-BUILDING NATIONS

Motives for Exploring the New World. The discovery of America opened up a whole new era of world history. But the discovery was mostly a case of mistaken identity. Thoughts of the wealth of the Indies filled the minds of men of western Europe. Men who had believed the earth to be a sphere and who had made crude globes, had placed the westward location of China about six thousand miles closer to Europe than it actually is—a very fortunate mistake. Even after it became rather clear that the land Columbus had discovered was not China but a New World, interested people still considered it perhaps a fringe of Asia, an obstacle to be rounded before the riches of the East could finally be obtained. And of course, Columbus' discovery was at best a rediscovery; a fearless Norse navigator named Leif Ericson apparently came to North America from Greenland as early as the year 1000, and recent discoveries would appear to indicate that his fellow Scandinavians may have penetrated the continent as far as Minnesota. But colonization did not follow this early discovery, so Columbus gets the credit.

The Pope's Line. The Church had been the most powerful single organization in western Europe throughout the Middle Ages. Now, when the Portuguese and Spanish began to quarrel over the question of who had the right to explore where in the New World, the Portuguese appealed to the reigning Pope, Alexander VI, to divide the world between Portugal and Spain for the purpose of exploration and settlement. To accommodate, the Pope drew a "Line of Demarcation" (1493) north and south in the Atlantic Ocean about 600 miles west of the Azores and assigned all land west of the line to Spain and all east of it to Portugal. By a treaty the following year between the two countries, the line was moved farther west until it cut down through South America, resulting in Spain receiving practically all of that continent except Brazil.

Motive of Adventure. It took powerful motives to cause hardy but superstitious natives to leave their homelands to sail uncharted seas and explore unknown lands. Of course, the element of adventure was present; it has always been a powerful magnet to draw people away from the usual and customary into new experiences. It played its part here. But it alone was not enough.

Religious Motives. Religion played a major role in the lives and thinking of the people of western Europe during these times. The Church was an important institution. It was only natural that many should see in the natives of newly discovered lands an opportunity and a challenge to spread the Christian religion. Here were countless numbers of poor souls to be saved "out of the arms of the devil." The religious sincerity of many of the early explorers is not to be questioned.

Economic Motives. A larger and more important motive was economic. It reflected a pattern of the time which rapidly took shape. The prospect of the wealth of Cathay had opened the period of discovery. And was it not reasonable to expect the new lands to possess great riches also? Wherever riches were found, each discoverer claimed the land for the ruler under whose banner he happened to be sailing at the time. So the first western European empires were built. As you can imagine, considerable rivalry developed among the nations involved.

The early empire-building nations, particularly Spain, were interested in looting their colonies—in transporting tangible wealth to the homelands. Out of this fact grew the practice of exploitation that has been deplored so much in more modern times.

But in England the economic motive took a somewhat different form. England was rapidly becoming a manufacturing nation. She was producing, still by hand, it is true, more woolen goods than the people at home could buy. There was, therefore, a real need for export. Colonies were looked upon as the natural solution to the problem. They could help supply raw materials for England's growing industries and at the same time serve as markets for finished products. Later this whole program was accelerated by the invention in England of power machines— the beginning of the Industrial Revolution.

England was interested in colonies for still another reason. The growth of the woolen industry had caused much of England's agricultural land to be fenced in and turned to sheep grazing. As a result, many farmers were forced out of work, and, as usual, idleness brought a rise in crime. The prospect of colonies to which the unemployed might be "encouraged" to migrate appealed to those government officials who were bothered by the increasing problem at home. And to many others, the New World held out the hope of a better life than had ever been theirs in England.

For all these reasons, exploration and conquest in the Americas were pushed with considerable energy for quite a time. First came the Spanish, to be followed later by the French and the English, and, to a lesser extent, the Dutch. Let us stop here to take note of some of the better-known men who participated in these, to us, very important activities.

THE GREAT EXPLORERS

Balboa. Quickly, in the few years immediately following the discovery of America, Spain followed through on her initial advantage. She soon had occupied many of the islands of the West Indies, and made these her base of operations for further exploration and conquest. Out from Santo Domingo in 1510 went Vasco Nuñez de Balboa to establish and become governor of a colony at Darien, on the Isthmus of Panama. But things did not go well; Balboa got into political difficulty and in 1513 was ordered home by the king to face charges. Balboa reasoned that a new and important discovery would probably benefit him greatly before the king. From the Indians he had heard of a vast body of water that lay to the

IMPRISONING OF MONTEZUMA BY CORTES

According to the writings of Bernal Diaz, a member of Cortes' expedition, the Capital of Mexico was a city of splendor and the emperor was a magnificent personage. This picture is an artist's conception. Montezuma is at the left, his arms behind his back.

west; he set out to find it. On September 25, 1513, from a vantage point on a mountain on the Isthmus, he first saw the ocean we know as the Pacific. In four days he had reached it and claimed in the name of the King of Spain not only the ocean but all the lands it touched. Balboa called it the *Southern Ocean;* another explorer, Magellan, seven years later, gave it the name it bears today.

But Balboa was ill-fated. Back at Darien he had difficulty with the men he had left in charge while he was away. The trouble finally resulted in Balboa being charged with rebellion, convicted, and put to death in 1517.

Ponce de Leon. On his second voyage to the New World, Columbus had with him a man who was later to become a governor of Haiti and, after he had conquered it, of Porto Rico.[1] Here Juan Ponce de Leon heard rumors of a fabulous country to the north in which existed a "Fountain of Youth." He set out to find it, landing near the mouth of the St. John River in Florida on Easter Sunday in 1513. Easter Sunday in Spanish is called *Pascua Florida,* from which Ponce de Leon took his name for the new land. He thought he had discovered and claimed an island and returned in 1521 to explore it further, but was killed in a fight with hostile natives. His search for eternal youth had cost him his life.

[1] In 1932, Porto Rico was officially renamed Puerto Rico.

DISCOVERY OF THE MISSISSIPPI BY DE SOTO

De Soto wandered far and wide throughout what is now the southeastern United States—he sought to discover gold and riches, but instead discovered a great river.

Cortes. Like Balboa, Hernando Cortes got his start in Santo Domingo. From there he was sent out as second-in-command of an expedition to conquer Cuba. When word reached Cuba of a rich land to the west called Mexico, inhabited by highly civilized Indians, Cortes was made leader of a band to go there in search of gold. Eventually the little expedition landed on the shore of the Gulf of Mexico (1519), where Cortes founded the city of Vera Cruz. Here he burned his ten ships, so his men could not turn back to Cuba, and pushed inland with his little army of about 600 men and eighteen horses. (Thus was the horse introduced into North America.) The Aztec ruler, Montezuma, was outwardly friendly and received Cortes into his capital. But conquest was the Spanish purpose; Montezuma was seized and held as a hostage. Then the Aztec ruler died, and Cortes and his men were driven from the city by the enraged Indians. But with the determination and perseverance that marked the whole Spanish expansion program, the little band fought its way back in, conquering Mexico City island by island. (The city is made up of a group of islands in a huge lake, with roads connecting the islands.) Cortes spent several years in Mexico exploiting the land and the natives to make the conquest profitable. For years Spanish galleons crossed and recrossed the Atlantic carrying cargoes of gold and silver back to Spain.

BURIAL OF DE SOTO IN THE MISSISSIPPI

De Soto's end was a watery grave. His followers saw fit to bury him in the river he had discovered.

Pizarro. Another Spanish conqueror, whose name is often linked with that of Cortes because of the scope and savagery of his exploits, was Francisco Pizarro. In 1531 he arrived in Peru, in South America, home of the highly civilized Inca Indians. There he invited the Inca ruler to a banquet and then seized him as a captive. The Indians paid a huge ransom for their leader, but Pizarro killed him anyway and then proceeded to conquer the entire country. But villainy has its own reward. Pizarro and his partner in conquest, Almagro, quarreled, and Almagro was executed by Pizarro's brother. Then the son of Almagro invaded Pizarro's palace in the capital city he had built at Lima and murdered the ruthless Spaniard (1541). But Peru and most of South America had been brought into Spain's growing empire.

De Soto. After several years of exploring in Central America in search of a water connection between the Atlantic and Pacific Oceans, Hernando de Soto joined Pizarro in the conquest of Peru. Shortly thereafter he was appointed governor of Cuba and Florida by Charles V, who was then king of Spain. Not much was yet known about Florida, so in 1539 De Soto landed on Espiritu Santo Bay with a band of about 600 men. The little party pushed northward into the Carolinas, then west through Alabama to the Mississippi River, which De Soto had the honor of discovering. The Spanish explorer's chief objective was to find more gold and silver, and he showed no consideration for the natives in his search. This fact made his journey always hazardous and cost him the lives of more than 200 of his men in skirmishes with the Indians. De Soto fell ill and died in June of 1542 along the river he discovered. What were left of his little band found their way down the Mississippi to the Gulf of Mexico and eventually rejoined a Spanish settlement in 1543.

Coronado. Francisco Vásquez de Coronado, following the will-o'-the-wisp rumor of gold, led an expedition from Mexico in 1540 in search of the "seven wealthy cities of Cibola" that were supposed to exist to the north. The group wandered from Arizona to the Mississippi and pushed as far north as Kansas. They were the first white men ever to see the Grand Canyon of the Colorado River. Failing to find the riches for which they were looking, they returned to Mexico in 1542.

By this time the Spanish had pretty well gained control of the West Indies, Mexico, the southern part of what is now the United States, and all of South America except Brazil. This latter territory had been claimed for Portugal by Cabral, who, swinging far out into the Atlantic to get around the bulge of Africa on his way to India, had touched the eastern bulge of South America. In their territory the Spaniards had established perhaps as many as 200 settlements. One of these was St. Augustine in Florida (1565), the first permanent white settlement in what later became the United States.

Magellan. While many Spaniards were establishing themselves in the New World, other Spanish navigators and explorers were extending their interests in other parts of the world to make the Spanish empire a formidable

one. One of these men, Ferdinand Magellan, a Portuguese sailing for the King of Spain, led an expedition which sailed west from Spain, went all the way around the world and back to Spain (1519–1522), thus proving correct the theory which held that the earth was a sphere. Magellan himself

Chicago Historical Society

FERDINAND MAGELLAN

Fired by the idea of reaching the Indies by crossing the sea that Balboa had discovered, Magellan sailed westward and proved that the world was round. Only one of his fleet of five ships completed the voyage back to Spain—the starting place of the expedition.

was killed in a fight with natives in the Philippine Islands (named for King Philip of Spain), but several of his sailors managed to complete the history-making voyage.

Cartier. Spain was not the only European nation that was engaged in empire building and that was interested in the New World. The explorations of

CARTIER EXPLORING THE ST. LAWRENCE RIVER

When Cartier discovered the mouth of the St. Lawrence, he felt sure that he had found the long-sought gateway to the Orient. His later explorations up the great river disillusioned him on that score.

Jacques Cartier gave France her claim to land in North America. On his first voyage to the New World (1534), Cartier discovered the Gulf of St. Lawrence. He returned in 1536 to find and explore the St. Lawrence River. He sailed up the river as far as the present city of Montreal, which takes its name from the title Cartier gave to the hill on which it is located—Mount Royal, which in French is *Mont Réal*.

Champlain. The foothold Cartier gave France in North America was greatly extended by Samuel de Champlain. In fact, Champlain did so much for France in the New World that he has been called the "Father of New France." He was no newcomer in the New World when he made his first trip to the St. Lawrence area in 1603, for he had already made several voyages to the West Indies and Mexico. In 1608 he founded the present city of Quebec and in 1611 what is now Montreal. The beautiful lake which he discovered on the boundary between New York and Vermont still bears his name.

Cabot. England was drawn into competition for land in the New World in a rather roundabout manner. In 1497 John Cabot, an Italian sailing for England, had explored the eastern coast of North America and claimed it for England. But Cabot's efforts won him little favor with King Henry VII; he was awarded ten English pounds (£10) for his discovery, and no attempt was made to follow it up with colonization.

At home, England's economy was changing. Where she had formerly been an agricultural country, she was

Chicago Historical Society

CARTIER MEETING THE INDIANS

The picture depicts Cartier's first interview with the inhabitants of the land he named Canada. The event took place in 1535 at Hoche Laga, on the site of what is now Montreal.

becoming instead an industrial nation. There were no factories in the sense of the word today; power machines were still unknown. But during the winter months hand-driven machines in the little farm homesteads of the English countryside were busy turning the raw materials produced during the summer into quantities of manufactured goods. To find markets for these goods England embarked upon a course that was to make her for a considerable time the world's greatest political as well as economic empire.

Frobisher, Hawkins, and Drake. As England began to try for foreign trade, she found that Spain and Portugal had already gained a near-monopoly. In the beginning England's attempts to break that monopoly were little more than a private war of English adventurers against powerful Spain. Little Portugal had already "bitten off more than she could chew" and was no serious competitor. This chapter of history brings into the story such famous names as Martin Frobisher, John Hawkins, and Francis Drake. The latter two first clashed with the Spanish when they wedged their way into the lucrative slave trade in African Negroes. Drake's chief bid for fame was his pirating of Spanish ships loaded with gold on their way from the New World to Spain, and a plundering of Spanish settlements that finally took him completely around the world. To all this highhanded action Spain rightfully objected, but impulsive Queen Elizabeth's answer was to go personally to Drake's own ship and knight him on its deck.

Gilbert and Raleigh. As the struggle between England and Spain took on world-wide scope, England's interest in the New World rose. In 1578 Queen Elizabeth bestowed upon Sir Humphrey Gilbert exclusive right to explore and colonize the land claimed by John Cabot eighty years earlier. Gilbert planted a colony in Newfoundland, but it failed, and he was lost at sea on the return trip. Then his half-brother, Walter Raleigh, took over (1584) and explored the coastal region which he named Virginia for Elizabeth, Eng-

Chicago Historical Society

JOHN CABOT

John Cabot and his son, Sebastian, were both daring navigators who explored the shores of the New World while searching for Asia. They found little more than choice fishing grounds and a few refugee Spaniards.

land's Virgin Queen. But his attempts to colonize Virginia were unsuccessful.

One colony joined Drake on his way back to England on his trip around the

Chicago Historical Society

JOLIET AND MARQUETTE

During the sixteenth and seventeenth centuries, unattached Frenchmen traveled into the interior of the North American continent and laid the basis of French claims to territory. Joliet and Marquette were two such explorers.

world. Another just disappeared, and no trace was ever found of its members.

Then, by a stroke of fortune, England was able to break Spain's power once and for all. Henry VIII had changed England's religion from Catholic to Protestant. He wanted a divorce from his queen, Catherine of Aragon, and couldn't get it as long as he remained a member of the Roman church which refused to dissolve his marriage. After his death, his son, Edward VI, maintained the new Protestant religion, but Edward's half-sister Mary, who followed him, made England Catholic again. Mary was the wife of King Philip II of Spain. When she died, her half-sister Elizabeth came to the throne and promptly made England Protestant again. This change in religion, the af-

Chicago Historical Society

LA SALLE'S EXPEDITION ON THE MISSISSIPPI

La Salle journeyed back and forth between Montreal and the Illinois River and later down the entire length of the Mississippi when such travel was unthinkably difficult.

front to the memory of his wife, and English piracy on the high seas all brought Philip II, ardent champion of Catholicism, to send the Spanish fleet, the Great Armada, against England. But the little English ships, led by Sir Francis Drake, were more than a match for the bulky Spanish ships, and those the English didn't sink or capture were disposed of in a storm they encountered on their attempted flight home. Thus, in 1588 Spain's naval power was broken; England became mistress of the seas.

Marquette, Joliet, and La Salle. No record of early explorations, however sketchy, could omit the names of Marquette, Joliet, and La Salle. In 1666 Father Jacques Marquette, a Jesuit

missionary, came to Canada to administer to the Indians in the area north of the Great Lakes. In 1673 Marquette and Louis Joliet, a priest turned trader, made their way down the Wisconsin River to the Mississippi, and down it as far as the mouth of the Arkansas River. Here fear of the Spaniards, who had settled along the lower Mississippi, caused the party to turn back, by way of the Illinois and Chicago Rivers.

It remained for Robert La Salle to go all the way to the Gulf of Mexico. He had come to Canada in the same year as had Father Marquette (1666) and had gone into business for himself. But his love of adventure won out, and in 1681 he set out, with his faithful friend Tonti, to explore the Great River

Chicago Historical Society

LA SALLE CLAIMS THE MISSISSIPPI AND LOUISIANA FOR FRANCE

Several years after claiming Louisiana for his king, La Salle organized another expedition to establish a colony in the new empire, but was murdered by his own men before the task could be accomplished.

of which Joliet had written. From Lake Michigan they followed the Chicago River and the Illinois River to the Mississippi, and finally, on April 6, 1682, they reached the Gulf of Mexico. The friendly Indians gave La Salle to understand that he was the first white man to explore the river, so he claimed it and all the land along it for the King of France. In honor of his King he named the land Louisiana.

These, then, were the men who took a newly discovered and unexplored New World and made their slow way over it, here and there, wherever their fancy and their desire for treasure took them. And wherever they went, they claimed lands for the European empire-builders they represented and charted courses to make it easier for any who might follow them. Thus began European penetration of a new hemisphere.

FOR YOUR REVIEW

These Should Be Easy for You Now

1. Why did the first explorers come to America?
2. What was the purpose of the Line of Demarcation? Where was it drawn? Where was it later located?
3. For what three reasons did the later explorers come to America?

4. What did Spain expect to get from colonies? What did England expect to get from colonies?
5. Why is the voyage of Magellan's sailors important?
6. Why was the Spanish Armada sent against England? What was the principal result of its defeat by the British?
7. Make a list of the areas of the New World claimed by each of the following European nations: Spain, Portugal, France, England.

Associated Dates

1493—Line of Demarcation drawn
1497—eastern seacoast of North America claimed for England by John Cabot
1513—discovery of the Pacific Ocean by Balboa
1513—exploration of Florida by Ponce de Leon
1519–1521—conquest of Mexico by Cortes
1519–1522—voyage of Magellan's sailors around the world
1532—conquest of Peru begun by Pizarro
1534–35—Cartier's explorations along the St. Lawrence
1540–42—exploration of the southwestern part of North America by Coronado
1542—discovery of the Mississippi River by De Soto
1565—settlement of St. Augustine
1577–1580—voyage around the world by Sir Francis Drake
1588—defeat of the Spanish Armada
1608—Quebec founded by Champlain
1609—Henry Hudson explores along what came to be known as the Hudson River
1612—tobacco first grown in Virginia
1673—exploration along the Wisconsin, Mississippi, and Illinois rivers by Marquette and Joliet
1681–82—La Salle's explorations along the Mississippi River to the Gulf of Mexico

Why Are These To Be Remembered?

Leif Erickson
Pope Alexander VI
Vasco Nuñez de Balboa
Ponce de Leon
Hernando Cortes
Vera Cruz
Montezuma
Pizarro
Hernando de Soto
Cabral
St. Augustine
Ferdinand Magellan

Jacques Cartier
Samuel de Champlain
John Hawkins
Sir Francis Drake
Humphrey Gilbert
Sir Walter Raleigh
King Philip II
Queen Elizabeth
Father Marquette
Louis Joliet
Robert La Salle

Chapter 3

People Come To Colonize America

EUROPEAN PEOPLE, LOOKING FOR A CHANCE TO DETERMINE THE
COURSE OF THEIR OWN LIVES, COME TO AMERICA TO LIVE

Why People Came to America. Before we take up the story of the early settlements that were successfully planted in the New World, let us stop for a moment to consider the various reasons which caused people to leave an established existence for the relative insecurity and danger of life in a wild and untamed land.

Religious Reasons. Spain, as you have learned, was the first European country to become interested in the New World. Spain, more than any other country, was the champion of Catholicism in Europe. Many of her people who populated the Spanish settlements of Central America, South America, and the southern part of North America came to convert the Indians to Christianity. Their purpose was sincere, and they labored long and hard at their idealistic task.

But there was another kind of religious reason that brought many people over. The kind of religious freedom that we know in this country today did not exist in Europe in the sixteenth and seventeenth centuries. Then each ruler decided what religion his people were to have, and often those who wanted to practice a religion other than the ruler's choice were persecuted for their nonconformity. Under such circumstances, people from a good many European countries left their homelands for the opportunity of freedom of their convictions in a new land.

Political Reasons. Others came for political reasons. After the death of Elizabeth, the last of the Tudor ruling family in England, the throne passed to the Stuart family. James I was the first of the Stuarts to rule England. He was the son of Mary Stuart, Queen of Scots, whom Elizabeth had ordered executed after she fled to England and appealed to her cousin for protection. James had been ruling Scotland as James VI. When he became King of England, he brought an entirely new attitude to the government. You will read more about this attitude in Chapter 16. It is referred to in history as the "divine right" of kings to rule.

The fundamental idea behind this attitude was that kings received their authority direct from God. Therefore, they were able and prone to maintain that whatever they did was God's will. Since no subject dared question any act of a "divine right" monarch under severe penalty, kings could literally "get away with murder." James I and his successor, Charles I, were "divine right" monarchs. This type of government was something new to the English people, and its severity and unreasonableness were distasteful to them. The reaction against Stuart rule among an essentially freedom-loving people was

19

SEVENTEENTH CENTURY VESSELS ON A VOYAGE OF EXPLORATION IN
THE NEW WORLD

The sailing vessels that carried explorers across the Atlantic to America were pitifully small, slow, and fragile when compared to the modern steamships that are now used on the high seas.

enough to cause many to leave England to be able to do as they pleased in a new land. They came to the English colonies in America.

Again, some people came to America from Spain, Holland, France, and England because their governments wanted them to come. The countries of western Europe had been plunged into competition for colonies by the period of discovery and exploration that began near the end of the fifteenth century. Colonization was a necessary weapon in the struggle for an empire. No nation could hope to build a great empire unless it had the manpower to settle and hold the lands it claimed. This fact alone soon forced little Portugal out of the running. Most of the early settlers in America were Spanish, Dutch, French, or English, and each group vied with the others to see how much land it could occupy and defend as the struggle became more intense.

Economic Reasons. There were economic reasons that brought people to America also. As we have already pointed out, England was changing from an agricultural to a handicraft nation. As her people produced more and more goods, colonies became highly desirable for two economic reasons: (1) to serve as sources of raw materials for England's growing industry, and (2) to serve as markets for the finished goods England could not absorb at home.

The change from agriculture to industry meant England was becoming a land of large estates, as more and more of the small farms were thrown together to produce flax and such raw materials in greater quantities. Fewer people could earn a living at farming, and more and more were thrown out of work. As usual, unemployment produced not only economic, but moral and social security problems as well. Then someone had the happy thought that an easy way out of a rather complex difficulty would be to encourage and aid the unemployed people to migrate to the colonies and get a new start there. In many cases, it did not require a great deal of encouragement to get people to come to America, for their forced unemployment was contrary to their basic nature.

It was for these reasons, then, that settlers from western Europe began to make their slow way across the wide Atlantic to find new homes in the New World. It should be understood that these included people from Spain, Holland, and France, as well as England. But the remainder of this chapter will be used to tell briefly the stories of the founding of the thirteen English colonies along the eastern seacoast of North America. This is entirely proper, since these thirteen English colonies became the foundation upon which the United States was built.

Planting of the Thirteen English Colonies. The experiences of men like Sir Walter Raleigh, who had single-handedly attempted to plant colonies in the New World, had made clear one very important fact: the job of colonizing an undeveloped land was too big for individuals to handle alone. But at the outset of this period, governments had not become sufficiently interested in empire-building to undertake such projects. They were willing, however, to give official sanction to private trading companies organized for such a purpose. These private companies were given exclusive trading rights within a

designated area and were held responsible for the cost of government within that area.

The English government (James I, 1606) chartered two such companies for the New World: the London Company and the Plymouth Company. Most of the eastern seacoast of North America was divided between them. The London Company was granted colonizing rights between thirty-four and thirty-eight degrees north latitude and the Plymouth Company similar rights between forty-one and forty-five degrees, with the land between the two grants open to both companies.

A very important part of the charter creating the two companies was the provision that colonists "shall have and enjoy all Liberties, Franchises, and Immunities . . . as if they had been abiding and born, within this our Realm of England." Settlers were to remember this provision well and to demand that the mother country make good on it, an insistence that led finally to the American Revolution. The catch in the arrangement lay in the stipulation that, although the colonists were to have the right of local administration, the final governmental authority was reserved by the King of England.

The attempts of the Plymouth Company did not meet with success. The first expedition (sent out August 12, 1606) was captured by Spaniards. The following year a larger expedition settled along the Kennebec River in Maine, but the severity of the winter and the hardships of life in the New World caused the entire group to return to England in 1608.

Settlement of Jamestown. The London Company fared better. Its expedition left England on December 20,

Acme

THE FOUNDING OF JAMESTOWN

It cost the London Company a huge sum of money, and required dogged determination on the part of the English colonists to make Jamestown survive as a permanent settlement in America.

1606, and landed on Chesapeake Bay the following May. Three small ships brought 104 people, who founded a settlement on the James River. The new colony was called Jamestown, in honor of King James I of England.

The Jamestown settlers also found the going rough. The site selected for their colony was not a happy choice. It was a low, swampy, mosquito-infested peninsula which later was cut off completely into an island. Disease was prevalent, and the Indians, who by now had lost their wonder at the white man, were not friendly. The leaders of the new settlement were not wisely chosen, and their attitude toward the Indians did not help the situation.

The winter of 1607 was a hard one, and by spring only 40 people were left. In January a supply ship arrived from England with 110 new recruits and orders to bring back a paying load of produce for the company. Precious time was spent cutting lumber for shipment to England, and almost no crops were planted. In the fall, disease and famine again hit the little colony hard, and soon its number was reduced to 50 again. As if all this were not enough, another supply ship arrived and required loading for the return voyage.

If any man stood out in the midst of all this disaster, it was Captain John Smith, of Pocahontas fame. A strong-willed, practical man, Smith was better prepared by nature to meet the rigors of the new existence than the "gentlemen" who made up a goodly part of the population of the early settlement. As conditions became steadily worse, the people turned more and more to Captain John Smith for leadership. When other members of the local council died, Smith did not appoint men to take their places, and soon he was in sole command. His strong leadership was undoubtedly largely responsible for the fact that the colony lasted, particularly since he established friendly relations with the surrounding Indians.

In the fall of 1609, Captain John Smith went to England. The winter that followed, without his leadership, was called by the colonists "the starving time," and the population was reduced from 500 to 60. In the spring a new governor was sent out from England, and he decided to abandon the colony. The little band was already on the move when still another governor, Lord de la Warre, arrived with supplies and more settlers, and the entire group returned.

In 1609 a new charter was granted the London Company, which from then on was known as the Virginia Company. Under the old charter, most of the settlers had been but employees of the company, with little chance for personal advancement. The new charter provided a new incentive for people to come to America. Settlers were given shares of stock in the company, with the promise of land of their own and a share of the company's profits after seven years of faithful service in the colony.

The new charter also dissolved the council that had operated the colony and replaced it with a governor who

had the power virtually of a military dictator. Mild-mannered Lord de la Warre served in this capacity from 1609 to 1618, but in 1611 he returned to England and turned the actual work over to a deputy governor. From 1611 to 1616, this was Sir Thomas Dale, a harsh tyrant, but it can be said in fair-

From an old print

CAPTAIN JOHN SMITH

The man who kept Jamestown alive owed his life to the Indian maiden, Pocahontas. It was she who pleaded with her father, Chief Powhatan, to spare Smith's life when he was about to be executed by the Indians for an alleged assault against them.

ness that much of his severity probably was born of necessity. Experience, and the fact that there seemed to be no future for the colony, had made the settlers lazy and irresponsible. It took a firm hand to get a maximum of effort in an attempt to make the colony anything like a success.

In 1619 Sir George Yeardley took over as governor and immediately brought about an important change. From the outset, the venture had been operated on a communal basis, with all the produce going into a common store. Now the settlers had a new incentive to work; a small plot of land was given each one to farm as his own. The profit motive has always been an important factor in building America.

Another item that helped greatly in the development of Jamestown was the discovery (by John Rolfe, husband of Pocahontas, in 1612) that tobacco would grow easily in Virginia and could be sold readily in England for a good price. Soon this valuable crop was planted even in the edges of the little streets of Jamestown.

So the little colony caught, hung on, and grew. But as a financial investment, it was a complete failure. By 1624 it had cost the company £200,000 and had shown almost no return at all. Its importance to us is political. It was the first permanent English settlement in the New World and the cornerstone of British power in North America.

Settlement of Massachusetts. The settlement of Massachusetts grew out of religious difficulty in England. King Henry VIII, in order to be free to annul his marriage to Queen Catherine of Aragon, had forced Parliament to declare him head of the Church of England in place of the Pope. In this fashion Protestantism came to England. Under the remaining Tudor rulers, the three children of Henry VIII, the official religion fluctuated greatly. Henry VIII had made the change one of name principally; there were few differences at the outset between the Roman Catholic Church and the new Church of England (Anglican Church). But Edward VI, while preserving Protestant-

ism, widened the breach by instituting further changes. Mary Tudor, daughter of Catherine of Aragon, reinstated Catholicism as the official religion and earned the name of "Bloody Mary" for her persecution of Protestants. Elizabeth, who followed her, promptly changed the religion of England back to Protestant again.

All these changes in religion in England meant that two distinct religious groups were being created among the people. Many remained staunch Catholics, while others were just as staunch in their support of the new Protestantism. But since the religion of the king was supposed to be followed by the people, a serious problem was created. Protestants were not united either. There were many people in England who wanted the new church to swing further away from the practices and teachings of the Catholic Church than was the case under the moderate religion of Elizabeth and later of James I, the first of the Stuart ruling family. One group of these objected to the retention in the Church of England of the rites and ceremonies of Roman Catholicism. They wanted to purify the new church of these observances. Because of this, they were called Puritans. Another group felt that there was no chance of success in "purifying" the church and advocated separating entirely from it to form one of their own. These people were known as Separatists.

Both Elizabeth and James I persecuted the Separatists. James swore he would make them conform or drive them out of the country. Because they knew they would never submit, many Separatists left England voluntarily and went to the continent.

One of these bands of Separatists,

led by their pastor, John Robinson, located in Leyden, Holland (1609). But, after ten years there, they were not satisfied. Their economic condition was not improved, and their children were growing up with Dutch customs and speech. Wanting to get back onto English soil but not to England itself, the little band applied for permission to come to Virginia as colonists. Early in 1620 a patent was granted them by the Virginia Company. Seventy merchants in London put up £7,000 to finance the expedition. It was agreed that all the earnings of the new settlement should be pooled for seven years, and then divided among the shareholders. Each person who emigrated was to be given one share valued at £10.

The 102 people who left Holland on September 6, 1620, were not the entire settlement. Many could not leave because they were either too young or too old for such an experience. Some of those who did leave Leyden had not come from England but had been attracted to the religion of the group after it had come to the continent. Under the leadership of William Brewster, the emigrants embarked in a ship called the "Mayflower." Pastor Robinson remained behind.

Early in November the Pilgrims, as they were known, sighted land. But they were near Cape Cod, not Virginia. An attempt was made to push south, but difficulties were encountered, and the captain of the "Mayflower" refused to try further. After five weeks of exploring, the Pilgrims finally put ashore at Plymouth.

Before they landed, however, the colonists took care of what appeared to them an urgent matter. Since they had not reached Virginia, the terms of their original grant from the London (Virginia) Company did not apply, and some other basis of government had to be agreed upon. Such an agreement, called the Mayflower Compact, was drawn up and signed by all the men except the servants and the sailors. It provided for a democratic form of government for the new colony, but recognized the over-all control of the English crown. The Mayflower Compact served as the basis of government in the colony until it united with Massachusetts Bay in 1691.

As had been true in Virginia, the little colony found the going pretty tough at first, although their problems were softened somewhat by friendly relations with surrounding Indians. Frontier life called for the learning of new techniques for survival. Fish and game abounded, but the settlers did not know how to fish and to hunt and so could not make the greatest immediate use of the resources about them.

The original London (Virginia) Company patent had provided that all earnings of the colony should be put into one fund for seven years and then divided. The colonists tried to carry this out under the Mayflower Compact, but people became listless and lost initiative because they could not see how they were going to get ahead individually under this plan. To keep the colony from failure, Governor Bradford did away with the communal plan in 1623 and gave each family a parcel of land to be used for its own benefit. This restoration of individual initiative started the colony once more on the road to prosperity.

Religious life at Plymouth was very strict. The Separatists disliked the ceremonies of the established church, and

THE PILGRIMS

These resolute men and women braved a new life in the New World so that they could abide by their convictions.

for a time even marriages and burials were performed without the use of any religious services. In their deep religious belief, the people professed to see the hand of God in everything that happened to them. When the harvest turned out well in 1623, a special Thanksgiving Day was set aside. We usually trace our observance of Thanksgiving back to this day, although the colony had observed a similar occasion in 1621.

As Plymouth was settled largely by Separatists, so Massachusetts Bay was settled by Puritans. The first group, led by John Endicott, came out from England in 1628 and landed in Salem. In the beginning the religious motive was not dominant, but as the struggle between King Charles I and Parliament for political control of England became more severe, people who feared possi-

ble persecution left England in large numbers. Many Puritans asked permission, which was granted, to come to Massachusetts. There they settled in Boston and other towns along the coast, as well as in Salem, and took over, by virtue of their numbers, control of the entire colony.

With the Puritans in control, there was no religious toleration in Massachusetts; the colony was designed for Puritans and for Puritans only. People who were not Puritans were allowed in the colony only so long as they went about their affairs quietly and made no attempt to take part in the government of the colony. Church membership was made a prerequisite to having the right to vote. So determined was the thinking of the Puritans that nonconformists were frequently driven into exile, and even death was decreed for Quakers, some of whom had begun to filter into the colony.

In the settlement of Jamestown, England had taken firm hold of the southern part of the eastern coast of North America. The settlements of Plymouth and Massachusetts Bay gave her a hold on the northern part. The remaining English colonies were settled in the course of the following century.

Rhode Island. The settlement of the remaining New England colonies resulted largely from conditions that developed in Massachusetts Bay. As has been pointed out, the Puritans under Governor John Winthrop were determined that their little commonwealth should be operated entirely according to the will of God, and a few leaders were just as determined that they should be the interpreters of God's will. Many of the people who came to Massachusetts were not Puritans, and they objected seriously to the loss of both religious and political freedom which residence in the colony brought. Certain of them refused to surrender their rights; instead they chose to move elsewhere and settle. In some cases they were driven out. Apparently the Massachusetts leaders had forgotten their reasons for coming to America. Too often this pattern is followed where human rights are concerned: those who have fought to gain privileges are, in changed circumstances, unrelenting in denying those same privileges to others.

Roger Williams was one of the many who got into trouble over religious differences in Massachusetts. He had been pastor of churches at both Plymouth and Salem. He preached that the political government should have no right to dictate a person's religion—that church and state should be separated.

He preached that it was sinful to worship in the form of the established church and that all the land in America belonged to the Indians, not to the King of England. Immediately he was in all kinds of trouble. Before the general court he refused to disavow all he had said and was ordered exiled. Since it was winter, he was permitted to remain until spring under the provision that

SEAL OF THE MASSACHUSETTS BAY COLONY

Inscribed on this symbol of early government in the New World was an invitation to the Old World: "Come over and help us."

he would not preach to anyone. However, Williams violated the terms and, while plans were being made to send him to England, fled from the colony, finding refuge among the Narragansett Indians. There he founded (1636) a settlement at Providence (Williams' name for it) with some of his friends who followed him.

Another religious insurgent in Massachusetts was Mrs. Anne Hutchinson.

Mrs. Hutchinson appears to be the first person in America who advanced the idea that every person should have the right to interpret the will of God for himself even though his beliefs were in direct opposition to the doctrines of the church. Her punishment was banishment from Massachusetts. She and her followers journeyed southward and

Parker-Allston Associates, U.S. Fire Insurance Co.

ANNE HUTCHINSON

She rebelled against the church, was tried for her religious views by the General Court in Massachusetts, and was ordered expelled from the colony.

founded the settlement of Portsmouth (1638).

Rhode Island was composed of four settlements of religious dissenters from Massachusetts: Providence, Portsmouth, Newport, and Warwick. As might be expected, the colony became a champion for personal freedom. In 1643 Roger Williams obtained from Parliament a patent for Rhode Island which confirmed the settlers' land and their freedom. Later the terms of the

patent were included in a regular charter (1663).

Connecticut. Partly because of the religious situation in Massachusetts, partly because the richest soil in New England was there, and partly because the English wanted to offset the Dutch who were moving in, settlers began to locate south of Massachusetts and west of Rhode Island along the Connecticut River. Rev. Thomas Hooker and part of his congregation came from Cambridge (1636) and founded the towns of Hartford, Windsor, and Wethersfield. The next year trouble arose with the Pequot Indians, and the white settlers in the region banded together and massacred them into extinction. The resulting safety brought quick settlement of the Connecticut area. The colony finally received a charter from King Charles II in 1662.

Maine and New Hampshire. Settlements had been springing up in the area north of Massachusetts also. The land had originally been granted to Sir Ferdinando Gorges and Captain John Mason. In 1635 the area was divided, Mason taking New Hampshire and Gorges, Maine. Religious dissenters went north as well as south from Massachusetts and located in New Hampshire and Maine. Then, when Mason died and no strong leadership appeared in New Hampshire, Massachusetts extended its control over the colony and later did the same with Maine. In 1679 King Charles II separated New Hampshire from Massachusetts and gave the colony a charter. Maine continued as a part of Massachusetts until that state permitted a peaceful separation in 1820.

While Massachusetts Bay was thus responsible for the settlement of a large part of New England, Plymouth grew

Chicago Historical Society

HENRY HUDSON EXPLORING THE REGIONS ALONG THE RIVER NAMED FOR HIM

Hudson's ship, the "Half Moon," derived its name from its crescent-shaped design. The ocean-going vessel was made of wood and measured but sixty feet in length.

more slowly. In 1691, in a general re-organization, Plymouth and Massachusetts Bay were joined to form the colony of Massachusetts.

New York. We have already noted the presence of the Dutch in Connecticut. Their interest there dated from the discovery by Henry Hudson of the river named for him, which he explored as far as what is now Albany. Fur trade in the area grew, and in 1621 the Dutch West India Company was organized to compete with the Spanish in trade, and to settle colonies in Africa and in America. Beginning with a town on Manhattan Island, which the Dutch called New Amsterdam, the settlement of New Netherland was planted. The Dutch were unable to hold their claims in Connecticut against the English but off-

set this by seizing a Swedish colony that had established itself on the Delaware River.

It would have been wholly unrealistic to expect the Dutch to maintain New Netherland, surrounded as it was by growing English colonies, and especially since England was at war with Holland in Europe. After peace had been made in Europe, the King of England (Charles II, 1664) gave his brother, the Duke of York,[1] a grant of all land between the Connecticut and Delaware Rivers. That same year a naval force appeared before New Amsterdam, and the city fell without a shot being fired. Soon after, all the area was under the rule of the English, and

[1] Later he became James II as king of England.

New Netherland became New York. In 1673 the Dutch reconquered New York and named it New Orange, but the following year the English had it back again.

New Jersey. Before the Duke of York took over New Netherland, he had already given away part of his land. All the land between the Hudson and the Delaware Rivers he gave to his friends, Sir John Berkeley and Sir George Cartaret. To this land was given the name of New Jersey because Cartaret had once been governor of the island of Jersey in the English Channel. For a time the colony was divided into two parts— East New Jersey and West New Jersey —but in 1702 the proprietors gave up their interests, permitting the two parts to be joined into one as a royal province.

Maryland. When the Virginia Company fell in 1624, all of the Virginia grant reverted to the King of England. He cut off the north part of the territory and gave it to his favorite, George Calvert, Lord Baltimore, who had been a member of the Virginia Company. The land lay between the Potomac River and the fortieth parallel. Calvert obtained a charter to the land in 1632 and named the colony Maryland in honor of Queen Henrietta Maria.

The actual colonization was undertaken by Cecil Calvert after his father died. In 1634 the first settlement was made, consisting of a mixture of Catholics and Protestants. The Calverts themselves were Catholics, but they were broad-minded and liberal, and at a time when religious persecution was the trend in Massachusetts, religious toleration dominated in Maryland.

It had been hoped that many Catholics would migrate to Maryland from England, where they were suffering considerable persecution. But when the time came for settlement of the colony, conditions in England appeared on the way to becoming better, and not as many Catholics came as had been expected. Protestants were then encouraged to go to Maryland. Virginia did not like the loss of part of what she thought was rightfully her territory and began scheming to make trouble for Maryland to get it back. Almost from the beginning there was difficulty in the new colony, rising from a mixture of religious and political causes. When James II abdicated in 1688, and William and Mary came from Holland to rule England, the Protestants in Maryland revolted and set up their own government. William recognized the revolution and made Maryland a royal province. In 1715, when a Protestant came into the Baltimore title, Maryland was restored to the family and remained under proprietors until the time of the American Revolution.

The Carolinas. In 1663 Charles II granted the land between Virginia and Florida to eight nobles. The name Carolina was given to the area. A settlement had been planted nearly ten years earlier along Albemarle Sound by people who came from Virginia. Others followed and located in the same general area. It became a colony of small farms, noted for its democratic society. In sharp contrast was the aristocratic settlement located at Charleston in the southern part. Here rice became the chief product and did as much for the colony as tobacco did for Virginia. Instead of small farms, the southern division became a colony of large plantations with more Negro slaves than white masters. Soon the Albemarle set-

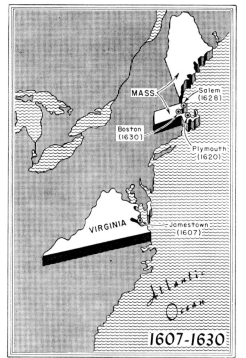

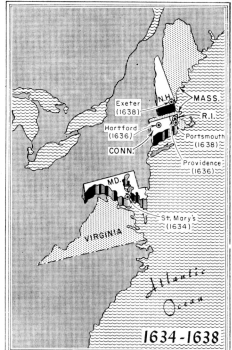

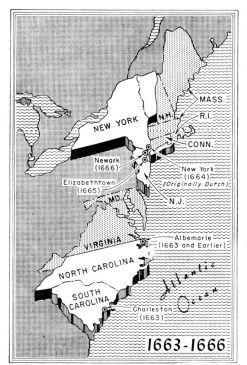

ENGLISH COLONIAL SETTLEMENTS IN THE TIME-ORDER OF THEIR FOUNDING
Outlines of the original thirteen colonies, in which local settlements were located, are drawn
to approximate present-day state boundaries.

tlements were known as North Carolina and the Charleston settlements as
South Carolina.

The proprietors of the Carolinas
never visited their colonies. They were
interested in profit, and profit was not
forthcoming. The aristocrats ruled the
more numerous poor people, but the
latter were becoming more and more
dissatisfied. Finally they refused to accept the rule of the proprietors any
longer and appealed to the King of
England to be taken over as a royal
province. This was done in 1729, at
which time the area was definitely divided into North and South Carolina.

Pennsylvania and Delaware. In
1681 William Penn received from King
Charles II a grant to land west of the
Delaware River. Apparently this land
was to satisfy a debt Charles II had
owed Penn's father, who had been an
admiral in the British navy. The King
himself called the land Pennsylvania, a
fact which embarrassed Penn greatly,
since he was a modest Quaker. To the
new colony, Penn invited all who were
thrifty and who worshiped God, and
offered them a large degree of self-rule.
Emigrants flocked to Pennsylvania, and
soon a large and prosperous colony had
been established. Penn's friendly and
fair treatment of the Indians (he made
treaties and bought from them the land
in his colony) made for peace and stability in Pennsylvania. In 1702 the
Lower Counties separated from the rest
of the colony and became Delaware.

Georgia. Georgia was the last of the
thirteen colonies to be founded. In the
England of the eighteenth century, people who could not pay their debts were
thrown into prison. General James
Oglethorpe, a member of Parliament,
sympathized with these imprisoned
debtors; he wanted to establish a colony to which they might go to get a
new start in life. He secured widespread support for his plan, and in 1732
the King of England granted Oglethorpe and his friends land between
South Carolina and Florida. The King's
willingness to do this came largely from
his desire to create a buffer colony between the Carolinas and Spanish Florida. The first settlement was planted at
Savannah in 1733 by Oglethorpe himself. Settlers came slowly; only a few
of them were the debtors for whom the
colony was planned. The regulations
were strict, as would be expected under the circumstances, and discouraged
many people. The original intention
was to prohibit slavery. But the settlers
saw how easy life was for their neighbors in Carolina who employed slave
labor. They therefore objected loudly
until the ban against slavery—along
with many other restrictions—was
lifted.

Thus the thirteen English colonies
were planted in the New World. English America stretched from French
Canada on the north, all the way
down the Atlantic seacoast to Spanish
Florida.

FOR YOUR REVIEW
These Should Be Easy for You Now

1. List and explain five reasons why people from Europe came to America to live.
2. What two companies did the British government charter to colonize in the New World? What important provision in their charters later was a basic cause of the American Revolution?

3. When the London Company became the Virginia Company in 1609, what inducement was included in the new charter to get more settlers to come to America?
4. Even though Virginia was a financial failure, why is it important to us?
5. Why was there religious difficulty in England? Who were the Puritans? The Separatists?
6. Who were the Pilgrims? Why did they come to America?
7. Why is the Mayflower Compact important?
8. What was the early colonists' experience with the communal plan?
9. How did the Puritans govern Massachusetts?
10. What factor was chiefly responsible for the settling of several other colonies in New England? What colonies were settled for this reason?
11. Where did the Dutch establish a settlement in North America? How did the English get control of it? What did they rename it?
12. How was New Jersey founded? Maryland? The Carolinas? Pennsylvania? Delaware?
13. For what specific purpose was Georgia established?

Associated Dates

1606—London Company and Plymouth Company chartered
1607—first settlement in Virginia (Jamestown)
1614—Dutch began to settle along the Hudson River
1619—first representative assembly in America (at Jamestown)
1620—first settlement in the Plymouth colony (landing of the Pilgrims at Plymouth)
1623—the first Thanksgiving Day
1623—first settlement in New Hampshire (Dover, Portsmouth)
1628—first settlement in Massachusetts Bay colony
1634—first settlement in Maryland (St. Marys)
1636—first settlement in Rhode Island by Roger Williams (Providence)
1636—first settlement in Connecticut
1638—first settlement in Delaware (by Swedes)
1655—Delaware taken by the Dutch
1664—Delaware taken over by New Jersey
1664—English take New Netherland; rename it New York
1665—first settlement in North Carolina
1670—first settlement in South Carolina (Charleston)
1681—first settlement in Pennsylvania
1682—Delaware given to William Penn
1688—"Glorious Revolution" in England; William and Mary brought to the throne
1691—Plymouth and Massachusetts Bay colonies join to make Massachusetts colony
1733—first settlement in Georgia (Savannah)
1820—Maine separated from Massachusetts; becomes a state

Why Are These To Be Remembered?

Mary Stuart	Sir George Yeardley	John Winthrop
James I	Puritans	Roger Williams
Charles I	Separatists	Thomas Hooker
London Company	Pilgrims	Henry Hudson
Plymouth Company	"Mayflower"	New Amsterdam
John Smith	William Brewster	George Calvert
Lord de la Warre	Mayflower Compact	William Penn
Sir Thomas Dale	John Endicott	James Oglethorpe

Chapter 4

Early America Is a Battleground for European Imperialism

HAVING CLAIMED LARGE AREAS OF THE NEW WORLD, EUROPEAN
EMPIRE-BUILDERS FIGHT ONE ANOTHER OVER THE SPOILS

Rivalry of England, France, and Spain. Three European nations had now established themselves on the North American continent. The English, as we have just seen, were entrenched along the eastern seaboard between Canada and Florida. The Spanish were settled in the West Indies and Mexico, and what is now Florida, Texas, and California—that is, in general, all the way across the southern part of the continent. By contrast, the French were in Canada, at the northern part of the continent, along the St. Lawrence River and south of it, along the Great Lakes, the Illinois, the Ohio, and the upper Mississippi Rivers. In 1699 the settlement of the province of Louisiana began in the lower Mississippi Valley.

The basic nature of the colonies of the three European countries differed markedly. The English settlements were built around the cultivation of the land; they were agricultural. The Spanish were conquerors who had come to loot; however, they were not too interested in organizing and ruling. The French wanted wealth in the form of furs; their colonies were built upon trapping and trading.

England, France, and Spain engaged in an almost continuous struggle for control of the rich lands of the New World, a struggle that lasted until long after the English colonies had won their independence. The rivalry between the English and the French was the most intense, partly because these two were long-time enemies and partly because their settlements were so located as to be in the way of each other's expansion.

CONFLICT BETWEEN FRANCE AND ENGLAND

King William's War. England and France were almost constantly at war for a period of about 125 years, from 1689 to 1815. It was a struggle for supremacy in Europe, for control of the seas, and for colonies. America became one of the battlegrounds of this imperialistic conflict. The early colonial wars in the New World were parts of what were really world wars of their time, fought in Europe and Asia as well as in America.

The first of these wars began in Europe.[1] Rivalries had developed among the ruling families of several of the more powerful countries of western Europe. Louis XIV of France, of the Bour-

[1] It was called the War of the Palatinate, the War of the Grand Alliance, or the War of the League of Augsburg (1689–1697).

34

bon family, was always looking for a chance to cripple the strength of the Hapsburg family, which had the center of its power in Austria. In 1688 he attempted to seize some of their land along the eastern border of France. War followed, and the next year England was drawn in, on the side against France. While this war was on in Europe, fighting also went on between the English and French colonists in America. The French plan in America was to take the Hudson Valley from the English and so divide their colonies. When the peace treaty was signed in 1697,[2] things were exactly as they had been when the war started. In the colonies the war was called King William's War because William III was King of England at the time.

Queen Anne's War. Peace did not last very long. In 1700 the Hapsburg King of Spain died and willed his throne to the grandson of Louis XIV of France. Louis was elated. "There are no more Pyrenees!"[3] he cried. But the Hapsburgs of Austria objected to this arrangement, and there were other nations in Europe, too, that did not want to see France and Spain united under the same ruler. Europe went to war again, and again England was on the side opposite France. When the war ended[4] in 1713, England had made some notable gains in America: (1) France ceded to her the colony of Acadia, which the English named Nova Scotia; (2) France gave up all claim to Newfoundland and the land around Hudson Bay; (3) England gained the right to trade, especially in slaves, with

the Spanish colonies in America. In Europe this was the War of the Spanish Succession (1702–1713); in America, Queen Anne's War.

King George's War. In 1744 the War of the Austrian Succession broke out in Europe. Charles VI of Austria had died and was succeeded by his daughter, Maria Theresa. There was some question of her right to the throne, and Frederick II of Prussia used this as an excuse to march against her and take the province of Silesia. England and Holland supported Austria against France and Spain and Prussia. The war lasted for four years and was fought in India, in Europe, in America, and on the seas. When it was over,[5] about the only result was that Frederick kept Silesia. The war in America was known as King George's War.[6]

French and Indian War. The treaty that ended King George's War did not bring peace to America. Treaties often do not really settle the differences that originally caused the war. They just give each side a breathing spell in which to get ready to start fighting again. So it was with England and France. Two rival powers were building empires; they were constantly extending their "spheres of influence." Since both wanted, in many instances, the same territory, trouble between the two was bound to continue until one or the other could prove itself strong enough to force the other to acknowledge her supremacy and withdraw its claims.

In America, the French wanted the Ohio Valley. Immediately after King George's War was over, they moved to establish their claim there. There

---

[2] The Treaty of Ryswick.
[3] Mountains on the border between France and Spain.
[4] Treaty of Utrecht, 1713.

[5] Treaty of Aix-la-Chapelle, 1748.
[6] George II was King of England.

weren't enough men available to build forts and settle the area. Instead of raising the French flag over settlements, the French buried lead plates all through the Ohio Valley as token of their claims. This brought the English-French tension to a new high, for Virginia already claimed the Ohio Valley as part of its original grant.

In 1754 the governor of Canada sent 1,000 men south to make French claims stronger. They built roads and forts in a manner that greatly disturbed the English. The governor of Virginia then sent a young fellow (he was twenty-one at the time) named George Washington with a letter to the French telling them to vacate. Instead, the French moved on southward and captured an English fort at the site of the modern city of Pittsburgh. Washington was forced to surrender to the French a rude defense he had built which he called Fort Necessity, but he and his men were permitted to march out with the honors of war. War between the two rivals had started again in America.

This struggle in the colonies is known as the French and Indian War (1754–1763). Various Indian tribes were allied with each side. In the New World the settlers had early learned to use the same tactics in fighting as the natives. This was hard on soldiers sent over from the continent who were trained in different methods. The classic example of this difference is the expedition of the English General Edward Braddock to try to retake Fort Duquesne (the French had named the fort at Pittsburgh for the governor of Canada) from the French. On the way he was ambushed by the enemy, but he stubbornly refused to adopt the frontier method of fighting from behind trees. The result was that more than two-thirds of his men were killed or wounded. Young George Washington, in charge of some Virginians with Braddock, saved the advance body from being completely wiped out.

Whenever or wherever war has occurred in history, the poor civilians (noncombatants we call them now) have always suffered. We have already pointed out how the British acquired Nova Scotia from the French. Naturally most of the settlers were French, and the English questioned their loyalty. The governor decided to force the Acadians (the French had called the province Acadia) to move south and settle in the English colonies. The tragedy of this separation of a people (in 1755) from their homes has been told most effectively in the poem *Evangeline,* by the American poet, Henry W. Longfellow.

Fighting between England and France had started in America two years before it began in Europe. Maria Theresa of Austria had not forgotten her loss of Silesia to Frederick II of Prussia a few years earlier. Now she set out to get it back (1756) and got France and Russia and later Spain to help her. Automatically, England joined with Prussia against France.

Up to this point the English in America had received very little help from England. The government there was doing a poor job of carrying on the war. Then William Pitt was put in charge, and things were different. The colonists respected Pitt, and the aid he sent gave them new confidence. Fort Duquesne was abandoned by the French when their Indian allies deserted them. The English renamed it Fort Pitt (hence Pittsburgh). The

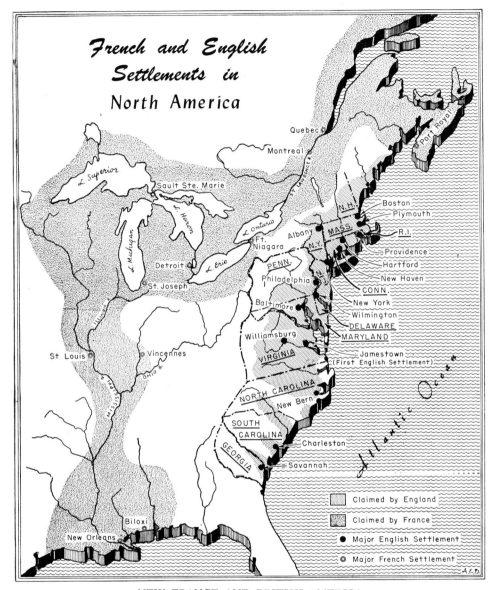

French and English Settlements in North America

NEW FRANCE AND BRITISH AMERICA

This map shows the territorial stakes of the two rival nations in North America prior to the French and Indian War.

French hold on the Ohio Valley was broken.

Gradually the French were pushed back into Canada, and soon a British expedition under James Wolfe appeared before Quebec. The French forces there were under the Marquis de Montcalm. Quebec had the reputation of being impregnable, and indeed it seemed so to the English, who had gotten nowhere after two months of bombardment. Winter was coming on,

BRADDOCK'S RETREAT

The British commander was mortally wounded in the July 9, 1755, engagement with the French at a place named Braddock's Field.

and Wolfe had to take the city quickly or give up. He decided to attack from the rear, and Montcalm arose one morning to find a British army drawn up on the Plains of Abraham ready to attack. He made the mistake of coming out to give battle. His unseasoned men were thrown into confusion, tried to retreat into the fort, and were completely routed by the English. Both Wolfe and Montcalm were killed. Today a single memorial in Quebec commemorates the valor of both. The English were able to hold Quebec against French attempts to retake it, and the following year the last French stronghold, Montreal, was surrendered. Canada was lost to France.

The treaty of Paris ended the war in 1763. France gave up Canada and all her land east of the Mississippi except the island of New Orleans to England, as well as most of her islands in the East Indies and the West Indies and in India itself. England received Florida from Spain and gave up Cuba, which she had seized.[7] By a secret agreement, France gave all her land west of the Mississippi (Louisiana and New Orleans) to Spain to repay her for the loss of Florida, but it was far from a generous gesture, for France had consistently lost money on Louisiana anyway.

William Pitt in England, James Wolfe in Canada, and Robert Clive,

[7] She also held the Philippine Islands for a time, but gave them up for a ransom.

England's "empire-builder" in India, had given England a great imperial victory over France. England emerged from this series of four wars not only undisputed mistress of the seas but also the greatest of all colonial powers.

England and France were to lock horns twice more in connection with America, as we shall see. Their struggle for influence in the New World was not completed until the final defeat of Napoleon in 1815.

FOR YOUR REVIEW

These Should Be Easy for You Now

1. In general, what parts of North America had been claimed and at least partly colonized by 1700 by the English, Spanish, and French? How did the colonies of the three differ in purpose? Why was the English-French rivalry the most intense?
2. What changes did King William's War bring in the colonies? Queen Anne's War? King George's War?
3. What part of America did the French especially want? How did this intensify the conflict with the English?
4. What part did George Washington play in the French and Indian War?
5. Who were the Acadians? How did the war affect them?
6. How did the English gain control of Canada?
7. What were the terms of the Treaty of Paris, 1763? How was the ownership of Louisiana changed secretly?
8. What were the general effects of the four wars England and France fought between 1689 and 1763?

Associated Dates

1689–1697—King William's War (War of the Palatinate)
1697—Treaty of Ryswick
1702–1713—Queen Anne's War (War of the Spanish Succession)
1713—Treaty of Utrecht
1744–1748—King George's War (War of the Austrian Succession)
1748—Treaty of Aix-la-Chapelle
1754–1763—French and Indian War (Seven Years' War)
1755—defeat of General Braddock
1755—French removal from Acadia
1758—English defeated at Ticonderoga
1759—victory of Wolfe over Montcalm at Quebec
1763—Treaty of Paris

Suggested Readings

Hough, C. S., *Leif the Lucky*
   Early Norsemen in America
Rolt-Wheeler, Francis, *In the Days before Columbus*
   Early America
Guerber, H. A., *Story of Our Civilization*
   What the Old World contributed to the New

Cooper, James Fenimore, *Last of the Mohicans*
   The struggle with the Indians in New York
Edmonds, Walter D., *Matchlock Gun*
   French and Indian War
Meadowcroft, Enid, *The First Year*
   The Pilgrims in America

Free Institutions Take Firm Root in the New Soil

INTRODUCTION

The English colonies in America found themselves part of the great British Empire. As such, they were subjected to the same kind of treatment as colonies elsewhere in the Empire. But the colonists felt they should be treated differently. Most of them had come from England, and for this reason they felt the American colonies were different from other colonies in the Empire that had native populations. And their original charters had guaranteed to them the same rights as Englishmen who lived in England.

But the British government did not see it that way. To the government, colonies existed for one purpose only: to be of assistance, in one way or another, to the mother country. This was the prevailing imperialist attitude of the time. When the colonists objected to the treatment they received, the government in London "cracked down" on them, just to show who had the authority. The increasing tension eventually led to war.

The American Revolution did not begin as a war for independence. But when it became clear that the American colonists could not win the liberties they wanted and remain a part of the British Empire, they struck out for complete freedom, and they won it.

The Articles of Confederation under which the new United States of America first operated were inefficient because the central government actually had less power than any of the states; and the states, therefore, were far from "united." To correct this situation, a group of colonial leaders met in Philadelphia and drew up the Constitution of the United States. We have been steadily realizing ever since what a good job they did.

Chapter 5

The English Colonists Are Dissatisfied

THE ENGLISH COLONISTS FIND THAT THREE THOUSAND MILES OF WATER
DO NOT PROTECT THEM FROM AUTOCRATIC GOVERNMENT

English Mercantilism. Let us stop here for a little while to examine the basic idea involved in imperialism—the grab for colonies, a struggle in which the English colonies in America found themselves involved. While it is true that in the early days of empire-building by the nations of western Europe there was some attention given to the desire to carry Christianity to the "heathen" (some early French and Spanish explorers came as missionaries), very soon the desire for profit overshadowed any other motive. The feudal system that operated in western Europe after the fall of the great Roman Empire, and served as a substitute for government in the absence of Rome's strong hand, had been broken down to make way for national states in the later Middle Ages. The competition that arose among the new nations led to undesirable results. The story of all history is the story of man's attempts to answer the question: Who shall have the power? And man's attempts to determine the answer have usually been selfish in nature; simple humanity too often has been completely disregarded.

All the European empire-builders thought that certain conditions regarding their own countries and the colonies were desirable. Each nation wanted to be as free as possible of all dependence upon other nations. Each wanted to provide for itself an adequate supply of food for its people. Each wanted to develop its own industry and provide employment for its people. Each wanted to export more than it imported: that is, to maintain a "favorable balance of trade." And each wanted to possess a large merchant fleet to carry its commerce and a big navy to protect its merchant ships.

This type of economic scheme for making a nation strong is called *mercantilism*. Clearly, under this plan the welfare of the colonies was of secondary interest to the mother country. To the empire-builders, colonies existed solely for the purpose of supporting the mother country. Colonies had two values: (1) to supply raw materials for the industries at home (remember industry was still in the hand production stage), and (2) to serve as markets for the finished products of that industry. While we are concerned chiefly with English mercantilism, we should remember that all the empire-builders were playing the same type of game.

The English government had from the outset looked upon the colonies in America from just this viewpoint. Not many years after the first colonies were founded, Parliament had passed some "Navigation Acts" for the purpose of making sure that the colonies played the role for which they were cast. These laws regulated colonial commerce completely. They provided that all goods being carried either to or from the colonies must be transported in English ships; that goods going to the colonies from another country must first pass through English ports and customs, thereby increasing their cost; and that certain goods produced in the colonies must be shipped only to England. England practiced other phases of mercantilism by paying extra for the production of those goods she needed most (these payments were called bounties) and putting high tariffs on those that were in competition with her own products. Also, she did all she could to discourage the development of industry in the colonies; her greatest need was for raw materials for her own industry.

Now, it should be pointed out that these laws did not bring great hardship to the American colonists. In many cases, they operated to the colonists' advantage. The chief thing in their favor, however, was the fact that the laws were not enforced.

People in the colonies continued to trade much as they pleased in spite of the laws. The English government closed its eyes to the situation. Sir Robert Walpole said, "Let sleeping dogs lie." Smuggling became the rule rather than the exception. Soon it was costing England £8,000 a year to collect £2,000 in customs duties in the American colonies.

The colonists were not hard hit, but they did not like the treatment they received. The English monopoly of trade increased prices; however, this wasn't the biggest source of irritation. A conflict was developing between two ideas that were firmly planted in the minds of the colonists. The first of these was that

Englishmen in America possessed the same rights as Englishmen in England; they were guaranteed by the original charters. The colonists remembered the Magna Carta, by which the nobles of England had made secure their rights against a stubborn King John in 1215. They remembered the Bill of Rights, which the English people made William and Mary accept in 1689—a document that gave Parliament greater power than the king. This brought them face to face with the second and conflicting idea. Englishmen everywhere have always respected the authority of Parliament. And it was Parliament that was passing the laws which the colonists disliked. To work out a satisfactory solution to this problem required more understanding and intelligence than the English government of that time possessed.

ENGLAND ADOPTS A NEW POLICY

England Tightens Controls. As we have said, the British government had been most lax in the enforcement of the Navigation Acts and other laws regarding the colonies. Then in 1763 its attitude changed. The French and Indian War was just over. It had cost the English greatly. They reasoned that the war had been fought for the benefit of the American colonies and that the colonists therefore should pay most of the bill. Also, said the English, further expenditures would undoubtedly be necessary to protect the colonists against the Indians. Already there had been an uprising of the Ottawa Indians under Chief Pontiac. The lack of unified action by the colonies in matters of defense seemed to put the task up to England. And England was willing to do the job; she believed in keeping close

THE RED MAN DISPOSSESSED

By the middle of the eighteenth century, the American Indians had lost vast tracts of land to onrushing white settlers.

control over her colonies. But she expected those colonies to bear the greater part of the expense.

Grenville's Imperial Policy. George III had recently become King of England. He was a headstrong, stubborn man who wanted all power for himself. He forced William Pitt and other good leaders out of office and made George Grenville prime minister. Grenville, believing firmly that the American colonies should provide more revenue, put through several new orders to bring this about.

The colonists in America were already irritated because of the British government's Proclamation of 1763. This decree ordered colonial governors not to grant to anyone land beyond the source of any river emptying into the Atlantic Ocean. The purpose of the order was to prevent further trouble with the Indians. The colonists looked upon it, however, as an attempt to prevent a westward movement and keep all settlers under the strict rule of the mother country.

Grenville's three measures (1763) didn't help matters at all. The first decreed that the Navigation Acts were to be strictly enforced; in addition, it provided for duties on more goods coming into the colonies. This measure showed Grenville's lack of knowledge of colonial trade; it operated to hurt England as much as the colonies. Much of the money to pay for goods imported into America from England came from colonial trade with Portuguese, Spanish, and French colonies. The new tariffs were so high that such trade became unprofitable. The final result was less goods bought from England.

Grenville's second act provided for

PATRICK HENRY

In 1765, ten years before the outbreak of the Revolutionary War, this fiery legislator delivered his "If this be treason . . ." speech before the Virginia Assembly.

a British army of 10,000 men to be stationed in the American colonies. Grenville said the purpose was to protect the colonists from attack. To the colonists it looked as if the soldiers were there to collect the taxes and keep them in line. They didn't like it at all.

The third measure was simply the threat of a tax in the form of stamps to be placed on all documents. The colonists' irritation flared into rage. Why, said they, if the mother country had the right to levy that tax, she could then proceed to all other kinds of taxes. Leaders expressed themselves freely, often in most ungentlemanly fashion. The cry "taxation without representation is tyranny" became common, even though sober reflection showed that

colonial representation in Parliament would have been too slight to prevent any action Parliament wanted to take.

It should be pointed out here that apparently England was entirely within her legal rights in the actions she took. And there is something to be said for the idea that colonies should help bear some of the expenses of the empire of which they were a part. Grenville had left the way open for the colonists to suggest some other method of contributing their share of the expense, but none was advanced. In 1765, when the Stamp Act was passed, requiring stamps on all legal documents, insurance policies, bonds, and newspapers, Grenville tried to ease the blow by providing that Americans rather than Englishmen should sell the stamps and that all money thus raised should be spent on the colonies.

The Americans were outraged. As usual, the more radical were heard most. Patrick Henry, the Virginia lawyer, uttered his first famous statement:[1] "Caesar had his Brutus, Charles the First his Cromwell, and George the Third (here there were cries of 'Treason, treason') . . . . may profit by their example! If this be treason, make the most of it." In the north, James Otis of Boston championed the colonial cause with similar speeches and writings. Speaking against the act in the English House of Commons, Colonel Isaac Barré had referred to Americans as "Sons of Liberty." Soon organizations of Sons of Liberty were formed in all the colonies, and rioting and destruction spread.

While the extremists were expressing themselves freely and often in an exaggerated fashion, the more conservative leaders were at work. A "Stamp Act Congress" met in New York in October, 1765, and drew up petitions to the King of England and statements of the colonists' version of their rights. They gave up the idea of representation as unworkable. They admitted Parliament's right to pass laws for colonial government and trade. But they insisted the right of taxation had been guaranteed to them in their charters and could not be taken from them. Boycotts of English goods soon had English merchants also urging the repeal of the Act.

Early in 1766 the Stamp Act was

repealed. It was obvious to the British government that the law could not be enforced. In fact, during the four and one-half months it had been in effect, only a few stamps had been sold in America.

American joy was unbounded. Demonstrations were staged in the colonies, and King George was toasted everywhere. Statues of King George were planned in Virginia and New York. The colonists felt their troubles were over.

The Townshend Acts. Actually, the colonists' troubles were just beginning. In their excitement, the Americans had overlooked the Declaratory Act, passed at the same time the Stamp Act was repealed. It was a simple statement of the right of Parliament to make laws for "the colonies and people of America, subjects of the crown of Great Britain, in all cases whatsoever." The Stamp Act was gone, but the British government was still insisting on the right that had produced the Stamp Act in the first place.

And England made other acts. The colonists were supposed to furnish quarters for the British troops in America. This was called the Quartering Act (1765). Sources of irritation multiplied. Then, in 1767, the British government passed three new acts pertaining to America. They were called the Townshend Acts for their originator, the Chancellor of the Exchequer (Secretary of the Treasury). The principal provision of the Townshend Acts were new duties on glass, lead, paper, and tea. It should be noticed that this was not a direct tax but an "external" tax— a kind the colonists had accepted as rightful. Passage in Parliament was easy; this body was controlled by the wealthy landowners who saw less taxes

---

[1] His second was his "Give me liberty or give me death" statement, made in St. John's Episcopal Church, Richmond, Virginia, before the Virginia Convention on March 23, 1775.

The Bloody Massacre perpetuated in King—Street BOSTON on March 5th 1770 by a party of the 29th REG.t

Unhappy Boston! see thy Sons deplore, | If scalding drops from Rage from Anguish Wrung | But know Fate summons to that awful Goal.
Thy hallow'd Walks besmear'd with guiltless Gore. | If speechless Sorrows lab'ring for a Tongue, | Where Justice strips the Murd'rer of his Soul
While faithless P—n and his savage Bands. | Or if a weeping World can ought appease | Should venal C—ts the scandal of the Land.
With murd'rous Rancour stretch their bloody Hands; | The plaintive Ghosts of Victims such as these; | Snatch the relentless Villain from her Hand.
Like fierce Barbarians grinning o'er their Prey. | The Patriot's copious Tears for each are shed, | Keen Execrations on this Plate inscrib'd,
Approve the Carnage, and enjoy the Day. | A glorious Tribute which embalms the Dead. | Shall reach a Judge who never can be brib'd

Copy Right Secured.

The unhappy Sufferers were Mess.rs Sam.l Gray, Sam.l Maverick, Jam.s Caldwell, Crispus Attucks & Pat.k Carr
Killed. Six wounded; two of them (Christ.r Monk & John Clark) Mortally

Engrav'd Printed & Sold by Paul Revere Boston

THE BOSTON MASSACRE

The historic engraving by Paul Revere depicts the bloody outcome of England's decision to station troops in Boston. The soldiers were to enforce obedience to the Townshend Acts—laws which the colonists found oppressive.

for themselves in more taxes for the colonies.

The Townshend Acts hurt trade in the colonies—in Massachusetts more than any other. Samuel Adams wrote a letter to the other colonies calling for joint action on this new and serious problem. The British Secretary for the colonies demanded that the letter be recalled. This the Massachusetts assembly refused to do.

Things were beginning to get out

of hand. Goods were being brought into the colonies without payment of duty in open violation of the law. Matters came to a head in Boston. Government officials asked that troops be sent to deal with the mob violence they were encountering there. For a year and a half, any major outbreaks of violence were avoided, although there were many personal flare-ups. Then, on March 5, 1770, British troops fired into a mob of Bostonians, killing four or five and injuring several. This incident has gone down in history as the "Boston Massacre." The next day, in a town meeting led by Samuel Adams and John Hancock, a wealthy merchant who had been engaging in smuggling to avoid payment of duties, the citizens of Boston demanded that the British troops be withdrawn. The governor gave in and ordered them to leave.

Boston Tea Party. This whole tax program was not working well for Great Britain. The cost of collecting the tax almost equaled the tax itself. On the very day of the "Boston Massacre" the government gave up the idea of taxing America for profit and substituted in its place the idea of taxing America on principle only—just to show it could be done. To accomplish this, all taxes were dropped except that on tea, and the price of tea in America was lowered so that colonists here could buy it for less than people in England, even including the tax.

The reaction in the colonies was good. Trade with England picked up again; it more than doubled in the next year. The conservatives were content with the removal of most of the taxes; the principle of the thing apparently didn't concern them very much. But there were others who felt

that as long as a single tax remained, the principle of taxation of the colonies without their consent remained alive, too. Men like Patrick Henry, Samuel Adams, and Thomas Jefferson continued to keep the matter constantly before the colonists.

Things might have gone on for some time without serious outbreak had it not been for the financial condition of the East India Company. The East India Company was losing money because the colonists wouldn't buy tea, one of its chief articles of trade. To try to get relief, it asked the British government for permission to send tea to the colonies without paying the tax of a shilling a pound (about 25 cents) that Parliament had levied on tea exported from England. In addition, the East India Company asked the government to remove the tax of threepence a pound (about six cents) on tea imported into America. This last the government refused to do; King George and his officials were determined to make the collection of this tax a test of the British government's authority over the colonies.

All of this was known to the colonists. When the ships loaded with tea arrived, the colonials refused to permit the tea to be cleared through customs. From several ports the ships turned back to England fully loaded. At Boston, the citizens would not permit the tea to be landed, and the governor would not permit the ships to leave for England; apparently he was going to force the issue. The colonists met it head on. Inspired by, and some say under the direction of Samuel Adams, a group of about fifty men, dressed as Indians, boarded the ships (on the night of December 16, 1773) and threw

THE BOSTON TEA PARTY

This escapade was the signal for a showdown between the British government and the people of the colonies. The issue at stake was whether or not England had the right to tax the colonists who had no representative in Parliament—whether or not the mother country was to have any money control over America.

into the sea 342 chests of tea valued at about $75,000.

The "Boston Tea Party" was without justification. It was condemned widely by the colonists. It can be defended only on the grounds that Samuel Adams, and those who felt as he did, believed things had gone so far as to make war certain and that they were simply forcing the inevitable.

The tea party had this effect. Parliament passed a series of five new laws (1774) which the colonists called the "Intolerable Acts." They brought more pressure than ever to bear upon Massachusetts. The Intolerable Acts provided that: (1) the port of Boston was to be closed until the tea was paid for and the citizens promised to pay the duty in the future; (2) the Massachusetts charter was altered to take away its liberal features, to have all the officials appointed by the king rather than elected by the assembly, and to permit town meetings only by permission of the governor; (3) government officials and soldiers charged with crimes could be taken to England for trial if the governor chose; (4) the act permitting the quartering of British troops in the colonies was revived and the commander of the troops, General Gage, was made Governor of Massachusetts; (5) the land between the Ohio River and the Great Lakes was added to the providence of Quebec. This was land to which Virginia, New York, Connecticut, and Massachusetts had laid claims and into which they hoped to expand. Probably the Quebec Act would have been passed anyway, but it came at a most unfortunate time.

The Colonists Unite. The die was cast. For the colonies there was only the choice of giving in to King George or resisting, and there was no thought of giving in. Where there had been friction among the colonies, the threat from the outside tended to unite them. The others felt that the challenge to Massachusetts was a challenge to all of them. Supplies poured in from outside Massachusetts to help the starving people there. Talk went around about a congress for all the colonies, something like the Stamp Act Congress of nine years earlier.

The First Continental Congress met in Philadelphia on September 5, 1774. All the colonies were represented but Georgia. The more radical element in the colonies were now in almost complete control. They had come to be known as "Whigs." The conservatives who favored giving in to the mother country were called "Tories."

There were varying opinions among the Whigs about what should be done. Some wanted to try for an arrangement that would give the colonies complete control of internal affairs and permit England to control trade outside America. Under this plan the colonies would have remained a part of the British Empire; this plan had no chance of success with the King.

The alternative was war. And in the minds of many, it would be war for independence. But such an idea was too bold to bring out into the open yet. Instead, the Congress decided to draw up a series of "Declarations and Resolves" to present the case of the colonies to the people of the colonies, of Canada, and of England, and then wait for public opinion to form. Also, the Congress adopted an agreement for a boycott of all trade from the colonies to any British port or from Britain to the colonies. This meant hardship, but plans were made to enforce it rigidly. Then the First Continental Congress adjourned, after arranging to meet again the following year.

Thus the American colonies came to the brink of revolution. As has been pointed out, there were various reasons for this. Back of them all was the empire system. England believed that her colonies should exist for her benefit, whether they liked it or not. For much of their early history the American colonists had been permitted to do about as they pleased. Then England acquired headstrong King George III who wanted to assert his power.

Another factor was that the sentimental tie to England was becoming thinner. It was strained in the beginning when some of the settlers came here because of their persecution at home. As other generations grew up who had no firsthand knowledge of the mother country, their loyalty became less and less. Many of the settlers in the English colonies in America had not come from England but from other European countries and had disliked England

JOHN HANCOCK'S HOUSE

Refinements of comfortable living were to be found in colonial America at the time of the Revolution. John Hancock's spacious and well-built house reflects buildings of the period—dwellings of well-to-do householders.

from the start. And all the colonists were aware of the Glorious Revolution in England in 1688 which had guaranteed the rights of people there by giving them the Bill of Rights. Englishmen in America believed they should have the same rights as Englishmen in England and they were willing to fight to get them, if necessary. Convictions and determination ran strong in America.

FOR YOUR REVIEW

These Should Be Easy for You Now

1. What is imperialism? What is mercantilism? What did imperialist nations consider the purpose of colonies to be?
2. What did the Navigation Acts provide for? How did they affect the colonists?
3. What two conflicting ideas were brought to the forefront of colonial thinking by the Navigation Acts?
4. Why did the English attitude concerning enforcement of laws in the colonies change after 1763?
5. Why did the Proclamation of 1763 irritate the colonists?
6. How were the Navigation Acts changed by Grenville? How did this change affect England? What were Grenville's other two acts that angered the colonists?

7. The colonists maintained that "taxation without representation is tyranny." But representation in the British Parliament would not have helped the colonies very much. Why?
8. What did the Stamp Act Congress do?
9. Why was the Stamp Act repealed? What new act was passed at the same time? What basic right did it attempt to establish?
10. What did the Townshend Acts provide for?
11. What situation brought on the "Boston Massacre"?
12. How did the British attitude of taxation change at this point? Why? What was the reaction in the colonies?
13. What situation led to the Boston Tea Party?
14. What did the Intolerable Acts provide? How did the colonies meet them?
15. What did the First Continental Congress do?
16. Summarize the conditions and situations that brought the American colonies to the brink of revolution against Great Britain.

Associated Dates

1215—Magna Carta signed
1651 and 1660—Navigation Acts
1689—English Bill of Rights accepted by William and Mary
1765—Stamp Act passed
      Stamp Act Congress
1766—Stamp Act repealed
      Declaratory Act passed
1767—Townshend Acts passed
1770—"Boston Massacre"
1773—Boston Tea Party
1774—Intolerable Acts
      First Continental Congress

Why Are These To Be Remembered?

Navigation Acts	Stamp Act	Samuel Adams
Magna Carta	Patrick Henry	"Boston Massacre"
Bill of Rights	James Otis	John Hancock
George III	Sons of Liberty	Intolerable Acts
George Grenville	Declaratory Act	First Continental Congress
Proclamation of 1763	Townshend Acts	

Chapter 6

The English Colonies Revolt

A REVOLUTION AGAINST AUTOCRATIC GOVERNMENT IS TRANSFORMED
INTO A STRUGGLE FOR INDEPENDENCE

Independence Declared. The situation in Boston was tense. General Thomas Gage, Governor of Boston, and a large force of British regulars which were under his command were virtual prisoners in a small area of the city. Throughout the winter the troops remained close to their quarters to prevent outbreaks of violence. But General Gage knew the spirit of rebellion was growing and that the coming of spring would make his task more difficult. So he seized the initiative and sent 800 of his men out on the evening of April 18, 1775, to go to Concord, 20 miles away, and destroy supplies that had been stored there by the colonists.

The Whigs were on the lookout for just such a move. By arrangement, a lantern hung in the steeple of the Old North Church signaled Paul Revere on the other side of the Charles River. Revere and William Dawes, on horseback, rode throughout the countryside arousing the people by calling, "The British are coming!" When the British reached Lexington the next morning, they found about sixty "Minutemen" waiting for them on the village commons. When the colonists would not withdraw, shots were fired, and eight of the colonial militiamen were killed and ten wounded.

The British troops went on to Concord and destroyed the supplies there.

When they started back to Boston, they found militiamen behind every tree and fence. With the aid of reinforcements sent out by General Gage, the British got back to Boston; but they lost 273 men on the way, almost three times as many as the Americans. The colonists followed, 16,000 strong, and laid siege to the city.

The war was on. If there had been any chance of a compromise solution of the difficulties that existed between the colonists and England, it was gone now. The decision would have to be made on the battlefield.

The story of what had happened at Lexington and Concord spread rapidly. By May 4 it had reached North Carolina. There, in Mecklenburg County, on May 20, a group of patriots adopted a series of resolutions declaring the commission of existing civil and military officers null and void and setting up a local government "until laws shall be provided for us by Congress." The Mecklenburg Resolutions were, in effect, a declaration of independence.

The Second Continental Congress. On May 10, 1775, the Second Continental Congress convened in Philadelphia. The New England militia were taken over as the Army of Congress (the Continental Army), and George Washington was appointed Commander-in-Chief. A statement of "the causes and

53

PAUL REVERE

This horseman did more than alert a band of colonists to meet an emergency—he called a new nation to the threshold of its existence.

THE BATTLE OF LEXINGTON

The American Revolution began when a ragged formation of colonists met serried ranks of British redcoats in an armed clash on Lexington Green in Massachusetts.

necessity for taking up arms" was drawn up; in it was the assertion that the colonists had no idea of separating from the mother country. Those who were thinking of independence were content to let events shape up the decision.

Battle of Bunker Hill. Events did just that. General Gage was in a bad spot in Boston. Around his position were hills, and he knew that if the Americans occupied these hills, he would be caught. And that was just what the Continental Army set out to do. On the night of June 16, 1775, Colonel William Prescott moved in and occupied Breed's Hill. He had intended to take Bunker Hill but got the wrong one in the dark. In the morning General Gage sent General Sir William Howe to retake the hill. The first attack up the hill fell back with great loss.[1] So did the second. On the third try the Americans retreated; their ammunition was gone. The British took the hill, but it cost them over 1,000 dead and wounded, against the colonial loss of 441. The Battle of Bunker Hill (as it is called) was, at least, a great moral victory for the new Continental Army.

George Washington in Command. In spite of this, the army was disheartened and demoralized when Washington arrived on July 2, 1775. His very presence gave the army new courage. Help came. Ethan Allen, of Vermont, and his "Green Mountain Boys" had taken Fort Ticonderoga on Lake Champlain and Seth Warner, leading a detachment of the group, had captured Crown Point. The supplies they captured were taken to Boston. The British didn't want to tackle the Americans on

THE MINUTE MAN

Groups of colonists pledged themselves to be ready to meet armed force whenever it should come. Each one of them was to become a soldier on a moment's notice.

another hill, so they agreed to spare the city and evacuate.

The British were busy elsewhere. Already at war in Europe and Asia, they had hired 22,000 Hessians (German soldiers) to put down the rebellion in America. All trade was stopped. The British fleet had burned Portland, Maine, and Norfolk, Virginia. But it failed in the South, where it suffered defeat at Charleston, as had an American expedition against Quebec.

The Great Declaration. All during this time the idea of independence was growing. There appeared in Philadelphia in January of 1776 a pamphlet

---

[1] Prescott had ordered his men not to fire "until you see the whites of their eyes."

Chicago Historical Society

BATTLE OF BUNKER HILL

The Revolution started in Massachusetts. However, Bunker Hill was the last battle of the war fought on the soil of the Bay Colony.

called *Common Sense.* At first it was thought to be the work of Benjamin Franklin, but later it was discovered that the author was Thomas Paine, an Englishman who had been in the colonies only about a year. It pointed out the foolishness of claiming loyalty to the king while carrying on a war against

him. It held that separation from Great Britain was the only logical solution. *Common Sense* was widely read.

On May 15, 1776, Virginia seized the initiative. There a convention declared the colony independent of Great Britain. And on June 7 Richard Henry Lee of Virginia proposed three resolu-

WASHINGTON ELM

The historic tree under which Washington first took command of the Continental Army.

tions in the Continental Congress. The resolutions declared (1) that "these colonies are and of right ought to be free and independent states"; (2) that the colonies should make alliances with foreign countries; and (3) that the colonies should band themselves together in a confederation.

Some of the delegates thought the last would be done first, but a committee was appointed to draw up a declaration of independence. On the committee were Thomas Jefferson, Benjamin Franklin, John Adams, Roger Sherman, and Robert R. Livingston.

The Congress voted in favor of independence on July 2, 1776, and two days

THOMAS PAINE

He gave eloquent expression to the growing spirit of independence.

FREEDOM WRITES IN A BIG, BOLD HAND

It was quiet in the big room. The weeks of talk were over. The moment of decision had come. The man picked up the pen. He'd let them know that he'd gone into it with all his heart . . . with a clear conscience . . . with the deep conviction of a man who does what is right. He smiled. The pen swept across the parchment, and the letters stood bold and clear: *John Hancock.*

later the written declaration was finally brought in before the delegates and formally adopted.

The Declaration of Independence was chiefly the work of Thomas Jefferson. It contained a long list of acts of oppression charged against the king. It asserted that "all men are created equal"; that all have the right to "life, liberty, and the pursuit of happiness"; that governments are established to secure these rights; that their right to rule is derived "from the consent of the governed"; that when a government ceases to guarantee these rights, the people should either alter it or abolish it and create one that will. From Lee of Virginia it adopted the statement that "these united colonies are and of right ought to be free and independent states." To support the declaration the signers pledged "our lives, our fortunes, and our sacred honor." The Declaration of Independence gave the name "United States of America" to the new nation.

INDEPENDENCE WON

Problems Faced by the Colonists.

Even after the Continental Congress had declared the American colonies free from England, the colonists were far from united. At the outset the Whigs who desired to separate from the empire were fewer than the Tories who wanted to stay in it. But as time went on and it became clear that the only way the colonists could gain the rights they wanted was to break away completely, the Whigs came to outnumber the Tories about two to one. Many colonists remained loyal to the end, however; there were about as many Tories fighting in the British army as there were soldiers in the Colonial army.

The Continental Congress was supposed to represent all of the colonies, but it didn't actually. There was a wide variety of interests between New England and the Carolinas that led sometimes to bitter rivalry and jealousy. There was little interest in any colony in providing troops for the Continental Army unless that colony itself was directly threatened. Sometimes Washington's little band dwindled to 2,000 men in all. The Congress found it difficult to provide arms, food, and clothing; it had no power to raise funds, and the people appeared about as opposed to taxation by their state governments as they had been to taxation by Parliament. Under the pressure of necessity, both the Congress and the states began to issue paper money. It had no backing and soon lost value until the phrase "not worth a Continental" became a byword. But it did help greatly to finance the war. Congress turned the job of raising funds over to the banker Robert Morris. Much of the support came from private contributions from

THE STATES ARE BORN

Here in this map are the boundary outlines of the colonies as they became the thirteen states of free America.

such people as Haym Salomon, a wealthy Jewish Philadelphia merchant.

Problems Faced by the British.

The British government bungled seriously in carrying on the war with America. Britain was engaged in a series of conflicts with France in Europe and Asia in their struggle for empire. At the outbreak of the war the British army numbered less than 40,000 men, and not near all of these could be sent to America. To make up the deficit, as we

HE MADE MONEY TALK FOR FREEDOM

Robert Morris had the gift of financial genius. At seventeen he had a boy's job with a big mercantile house in the Maryland colony. At twenty-one he was a partner in the business. At forty, he was one of the leading merchants in the colonies. When the Revolution broke out, Morris shouldered the heartbreaking job of raising money for the cause of independence. He dug deep into his own savings, borrowed from friends, pleaded with foreign bankers—and he got the money.

have said, George III hired Germans to fight in the British army. But, instead of setting up a single command in the colonies, England tried to run the war from London by orders sent to the generals at least six weeks away in the colonies. Also, British troops were not trained for frontier fighting and suffered unnecessary losses. Control of the seas was required to supply troops over here, and the loss of that control for a short time, as we shall see, spelled disaster.

British Attempt to Drive a Wedge. The British plan was to get control of the Hudson River Valley and cut New England off from the rest of the colonies. A British army under General William Howe landed at New York, and a British fleet under his brother lay offshore. Washington's army, rushed down from Boston, was forced to retreat across the Hudson into New Jersey and finally across the Delaware (August 27, 1776). Had the British followed up their advantage, the war

WASHINGTON CAPTURES THE HESSIANS AT TRENTON

In a daring maneuver that took his foe completely by surprise, General Washington conquered the Hessian force under Colonel Rall, who is shown surrendering his sword in this painting. The engagement was over in less than forty minutes, and American morale was given a tremendous boost at a dark period in the war for independence.

might have ended there. They didn't, and on Christmas night, 1776, Washington recrossed the Delaware and captured a Hessian force at Trenton. Then, leaving his campfires burning brightly to fool the enemy, Washington and his men slipped away in the night, and on the morning of January 3, 1777, defeated another column of the British army at Princeton. American morale, which had been low, was given a considerable boost.

The British made plans to try again. General John Burgoyne was to move down from Canada along Lake Champlain and the Hudson River. Colonel St. Leger was to advance along the Mohawk. General Howe was to come up the Hudson from New York. All three armies were to meet at or near Albany.

British tradition defeated the campaign. Lord George Germain, British colonial secretary, in a hurry to get away for the customary English weekend in the country, left Howe's orders in his desk. Howe, thinking he was on his own, decided to attack Philadelphia. Burgoyne, a member of Parliament and a writer of plays, found the going rough and supplies inadequate. St. Leger was met by New England militia and driven into Canada. After a series of defeats, Burgoyne finally surrendered at Saratoga on October 17, 1777.

Invasion of Philadelphia and Valley Forge. When Howe moved toward Philadelphia, Washington tried to stop him at Brandywine (September 11, 1777) but failed. The British entered the city on September 26. The British army was encamped at Germantown near by, and Washington resolved to try a surprise attack there. That failed, too. The Continental Army then set up headquarters for the winter at Valley Forge. There the men, poorly clothed and half starved, suffered great hardship, while near by, in Philadelphia, the British enjoyed themselves in the homes of the Tories. Pennsylvania farmers would not sell supplies to the American army for the depreciated Continental money. But, hard though it was, the winter at Valley Forge was put to good advantage. Baron von Steuben, a Prussian army officer who had come over to help the Americans, drilled Washington's men into a more effective fighting machine.

The Turning of the Tide. The British defeat at Saratoga was perhaps the turning point in the war. France soon came into the war openly on the side of the Americans. From the beginning the French people had been sympathetic, and many of them came over to fight in Washington's army. Most remembered of these was the young Marquis de Lafayette, who was made a major general in the Continental Army. Others who came were Johann de Kalb from France, and from Poland came Casimir Pulaski and Thaddeus Kosciusko, who planned the defenses at West Point.

Indirect assistance from the governments of both France and Spain had been coming to America since early in the war. Silas Deane had been in Paris buying supplies and shipping them to the colonies under the name of "Timothy Jones." He paid for his purchases

with money loaned to him by the kings of France and Spain. But not until Saratoga was the French government ready to come into the war openly. On February 6, 1778, the treaties were signed and France became an ally of the new United States.

Chicago Historical Society

MARQUIS DE LAFAYETTE

This French nobleman was a brilliant tactician who gave great service to the Revolutionary army. He was a personal friend of Washington.

It should be pointed out that the French government was not interested in American independence, as were the French people. The government merely saw an opportunity to strike a blow at England, France's old enemy. The alliance with France was of great benefit to the Americans, but the war left France in a weakened financial condition and helped to bring on the revolution there a few years later which overthrew the king and made France a republic.

A year after France came into the war, Spain declared war on England, independently and not as as ally of the United States. Spain did not approve of the Revolution but could not pass up the opportunity to oppose England.

War on the Frontier. When the Revolution started, both the British and the Americans tried to enlist the aid of the Indians in the land west of the colonies. The Indians apparently thought the British would win, for most of them fought on the British side. The result was a great deal of trouble for the frontier settlers who had already pushed over the mountains and on toward the Mississippi River.

Early in 1778 George Rogers Clark obtained permission from Governor Patrick Henry of Virginia to take a little band of men on an expedition against the British trading posts and forts in the area north of the Ohio River. Clark easily forced the surrender of the French settlements, now held by the British, at Kaskaskia and Cahokia on the Mississippi, and Vincennes on the Wabash. Thus all the settlements in the Illinois country came under Clark's control. The territory was organized as Illinois County, Virginia.

War in the South. England turned her attention now to the South. Savannah (December, 1778) and Charleston (May, 1780) were taken, and the British army marched back and forth across the Carolinas and Virginia doing about as it pleased. Finally, late in 1780, General Nathanael Greene managed to bring it in check in Carolina.

Yorktown—the End of the War. British General Charles Cornwallis then moved north to Virginia, where he took up a position on the coast near Yorktown. This gave Washington the opportunity he had been waiting for. He ordered the French fleet to shut off help from the sea, which it was able to do, and he and General Rochambeau and his French troops laid siege to the city on the land side. With supplies gone and no help in sight, Cornwallis surrendered on October 19, 1781. The war was over.

Important Figures of the Revolution. It has not been our purpose to tell the story of the war in great detail. Many of the battles were valiant stands and make fascinating reading. Detailed histories of the American Revolution are available in any library. We should take time here, however, to note a few of the people, not mentioned elsewhere, whose names are commonly associated with the story of the American Revolution. There was Nathan Hale, a spy for George Washington behind the British lines, whose last words before his execution are famous: "I only regret that I have but one life to lose for my country." The American navy had its beginning during the Revolution, with five small ships under the command of John Paul Jones, although most of the naval damage to Great Britain was done by privateers, operating with the consent of Congress. The biggest blot on American valor and honor during the struggle was placed there by Benedict Arnold. Arnold had been neglected and mistreated by Congress, and he tried to even the score by turning over to the enemy the plans for the fortifications at West Point.

The Treaty of Peace. The treaty to end the war was not signed until September 3, 1783. It recognized the independence of the United States and

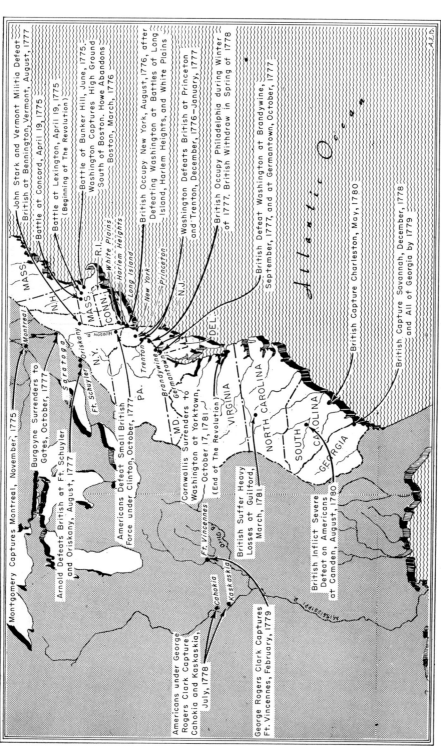

MILITARY ENGAGEMENTS OF THE REVOLUTIONARY WAR

How the fortunes of battle see-sawed back and forth are shown in this map. Though the British succeeded in enlisting Indian support on the frontier, the American forces won the area.

Montgomery Captures Montreal, November, 1775

Burgoyne Surrenders to Gates, October, 1777

Arnold Defeats British at Ft. Schuyler and Oriskany, August, 1777

Americans Defeat Small British Force under Clinton, October, 1777

Americans under George Rogers Clark Capture Cahokia and Kaskaskia, July, 1778

George Rogers Clark Captures Ft. Vincennes, February, 1779

Cornwallis Surrenders to Washington at Yorktown, October 17, 1781 (End of The Revolution)

British Suffer Heavy Losses at Guilford, March, 1781

British Inflict Severe Defeat on Americans at Camden, August, 1780

John Stark and Vermont Militia Defeat British at Bennington, Vermont, August, 1777

Battle at Concord, April 19, 1775

Battle at Lexington, April 19, 1775 (Beginning of The Revolution)

Battle of Bunker Hill, June, 1775. Washington Captures High Ground South of Boston. Howe Abandons Boston, March, 1776

British Occupy New York, August, 1776, after Defeating Washington at Battles of Long Island, Harlem Heights, and White Plains

Washington Defeats British at Princeton and Trenton, December, 1776—January, 1777

British Occupy Philadelphia during Winter of 1777. British Withdraw in Spring of 1778

British Defeat Washington at Brandywine, September, 1777, and at Germantown, October, 1777

British Capture Charleston, May, 1780

British Capture Savannah, December, 1778 and All of Georgia by 1779

Atlantic Ocean

Montreal

MASS.
N.H.
MASS.
CONN.
R.I.
White Plains
Harlem Heights
Long Island
New York
Trenton
Brandywine
Germantown
N.J.
Princeton
PA.
DEL.
MD.
N.Y.
Ft. Schuyler
Oriskany
Saratoga
Hudson
VIRGINIA
NORTH CAROLINA
SOUTH CAROLINA
GEORGIA
Ft. Vincennes
Cahokia
Kaskaskia
Ohio R.
MISSISSIPPI R.

A.E.D.

HE TALKED INDEPENDENCE IN A 21-GUN VOICE

At twelve he was a solemn boy when he left Scotland to go to sea, and the hard-fisted skippers soon showed him how tyranny tastes. John Paul Jones never liked that taste. But he was spunky and quick, and he got ahead—apprentice, mate, captain, owner. Even though John Paul Jones got ahead, he still wanted something else. He found it in America in 1775—the idea of freedom and independence! He joined the Revolution and fought for a free America on the high seas, mustering his own crews, paying them with his own money, pouring his health and strength into it. He was the first great skipper of the American navy.

placed the western boundary at the Mississippi River, which was to be used by both English and Americans. It permitted New Englanders to continue to fish in the coastal waters off Canada where they had been accustomed to fish before the war. In spite of British demands, the treaty made no real provision for giving back property seized from Tories during the Revolution or for the payment of debts owed to them.

The treaty was a very satisfactory one to the United States from a political standpoint, but it did not deal at all with commercial matters, a subject that was to cause more trouble with England at a later date.

One must not get the idea that the American Revolution was a co-operative movement of all the colonists. It was far from that. Few of the people fought in the Continental Army. Most

Chicago Historical Society

THE COMMANDER-IN-CHIEF RETIRES

After the close of the Revolutionary War, Washington bid farewell to his officers who had gathered at Fraunce's Tavern on December 4, 1783. A few weeks later, he resigned his commission to the Continental Congress, and returned to private life.

of them lived normal lives for the time, affected hardly at all by the war. In certain ways they became more resourceful, for the blockade of their trade forced them to produce more things for themselves. As is usual in time of war, some people made fortunes by selling supplies to the enemy, who had gold instead of Continental currency with which to buy.

The war put a new group of people into control of the government. The wealthy landowners, who made up the ruling class before the Revolution started, chose in the main to be loyal to the king. Their lands were seized, and many of them fled to Canada. Large estates were broken up into smaller farms. You will read more about these social and economic changes in later chapters.

English America was now free from the British Empire. Some problems were solved, but many more lay ahead. The going was to be quite rough for the new nation.

FOR YOUR REVIEW

These Should Be Easy for You Now

1. What events led to Paul Revere's famous ride? What resulted from it?
2. What did the Second Continental Congress do?

3. Why was the Battle of Bunker Hill a moral victory for the colonists? Why did the British evacuate Boston?
4. What colony first declared itself independent?
5. In addition to declaring the colonies free of Great Britain, what important ideas are incorporated in the Declaration of Independence? See Appendix.
6. What name was given to colonists who wanted to separate from England? To those who did not?
7. What difficulties did the Continental Congress experience in trying to carry on the war?
8. Show that the American Revolution was really part of a world war of its time.
9. What factors operated against the British and gave the Americans an advantage?
10. What was the British plan for the war? How did it work out?
11. Why is the Battle of Saratoga sometimes called the turning point of the war?
12. Why did France enter the war on the side of the Americans? How did the war affect France?
13. What was the importance of the expedition led by George Rogers Clark?
14. Describe the events that led to the surrender of Cornwallis.
15. What were the terms of the Treaty of Paris?

Associated Dates

1775—Battles of Lexington and Concord, April 19
 Second Continental Congress begins, May 10
 Mecklenburg Resolutions, May 31
 Battle of Bunker Hill, June 17
1776—Declaration of Independence signed, July 4
1777—Battle of Brandywine, September 11
 Surrender of Burgoyne at Saratoga, October 17
1778—France enters the war against England, February 6
1781—Surrender of Cornwallis, October 19
1783—Treaty of Paris signed, September 3

Why Are These To Be Remembered?

General Gage
Concord
Lexington
Paul Revere
Minutemen
Mecklenburg Resolutions
Breed's Hill
Bunker Hill
Ethan Allen
Hessians
Thomas Paine
Common Sense

Richard Henry Lee
Whigs
Tories
Robert Morris
Haym Salomon
General Howe
Saratoga
Valley Forge
Baron von Steuben
Lafayette
De Kalb
Pulaski

Kosciusko
George Rogers Clark
Kaskaskia
Cahokia
Vincennes
Nathanael Greene
Lord Cornwallis
Yorktown
General Rochambeau
Nathan Hale
John Paul Jones
Benedict Arnold

Chapter 7

Free America Becomes the United States

THE ENGLISH COLONIES, NOW FREE, ESTABLISH A GOVERNMENT OF
THEIR OWN

The new nation has many problems. Thus a new nation came into being. But it was a nation in name only. It was looked upon with the same lack of respect at home as it was abroad. The next eight years or so after the Revolution are often called the "critical period." It was a question whether the United States could survive or not.

One of the biggest problems was the debt created by the war. As we have pointed out, it was extremely difficult for the Continental Congress to raise money. Only the states could tax the people. Nearly eight million dollars had been borrowed abroad, in addition to the loans made here at home. Somehow or other, these debts had to be paid to keep the country's credit good. Also, there was all the paper money that had been issued by the Congress and by the states that had depreciated until $1,000 in Continental paper was worth only one dollar in gold. Something had to be done about it.

The army was restless, too. It hadn't been paid for some time. The feeling grew that the soldiers shouldn't go home until they had collected. Only Washington's personal popularity was able to command their continued loyalty.

States were jealous of one another. Most of them would not honor paper money issued by other states. Soon they were levying customs duties on goods brought across state lines. Problems piled up.

Then there was the matter of foreign trade. It had been greatly interrupted by the war and now must be restored. There was the problem of those colonists who had supported England during the war. Hatreds must have time to cool. A purely American society must be created.

Ratification of the Articles of Confederation. You will remember that the Continental Congress, at the time it was considering a declaration of independence, was also considering a plan for a confederation of the states. A scheme was finally agreed upon, and on November 17, 1777, the Congress adopted the Articles of Confederation and submitted them to the states to be ratified. This happened at the time when all were encouraged by the news of Burgoyne's surrender.

The Articles of Confederation was the first document of government under which the United States operated. It was little more than "a rope of sand." It did not establish a strong central government; it left with the states all powers not "expressly delegated to the United States." Those powers given to Congress were the ones the states could not readily handle themselves. Congress was to have an army of men provided by the states; it was to declare war and make peace, organize and equip a navy, to make treaties and alliances, to regulate coinage, to borrow money, and to operate a postal system. There was no provision for Congress to levy taxes.

The central government under the Articles consisted of Congress only. Its limited duties included those now shared by all three branches of our government. No provision was made for an executive to head the government. The Revolution was being fought against a headstrong executive, and the people didn't want anything like that to contend with again. Certain executive officers with specific and limited authority were to be appointed by Congress.

Representation in Congress was to be by states, but each state was to have only one vote, regardless of size, although the number of representatives varied. In important matters, nine votes were required for passage; others needed only a majority. Amendments had to be agreed to by all thirteen of the state legislatures. No federal courts were created.

Getting the Articles ratified by the states wasn't easy. The question of the western lands immediately came up. Seven states had claims to land from "sea to sea," based on their original charters. The six other states insisted that the western land should now belong to the United States and not to the individual states. Maryland said she would not ratify the Articles until the seven states had given up their claims. And the Articles could not go into effect until all the states had adopted them. But after Virginia and New York generously surrendered their claims and the other states had promised to do the same, Maryland ratified in 1781, and the new government was created. Later the other states gave up their claims, and the idea of common ownership through a central authority was established. It gave the government better standing.

Europe Predicts. Predictions abroad were that the new government could not succeed—in fact, that no government could unite thirteen selfish, bickering, sprawling states. It began to look as if this were true. During their period in the empire, the colonies were held together by one idea: allegiance to the King of England. During the Revolution another idea kept them united: independence. Now there was nothing, and each state went its own way, motivated by its own selfish interests.

The Evil Days of the Confederation. The greatest weakness in the Articles of Confederation was the lack of authority to levy and collect taxes. For money to run the country, Congress was dependent upon the generosity of the states. It could ask the states to collect taxes and turn the money over to Congress, but if the states didn't, there was nothing Congress could do about it. During the period the Articles operated, not even a fourth of the money asked for was ever paid by the states.

But every attempt to secure greater financial power for the central government was blocked by the states. The same thing happened whenever Congress tried to get authority to control commerce and regulate duties both at home and abroad.

Things were going from bad to worse. States fought among themselves over money, duties, and boundaries.

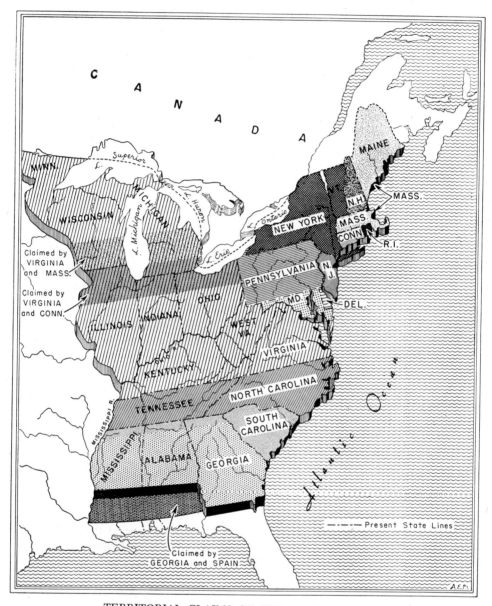

TERRITORIAL CLAIMS OF THE STATES IN 1781

When the Articles of Confederation were finally ratified, the idea of common ownership of land through a central authority was established.

What government there was seemed to be breaking down. In 1786 farmers in Massachusetts rose up in open revolt. Their leader was Daniel Shays, and the uprising is called Shays' Rebellion. The farmers could not pay their heavy taxes. When the courts ordered their property seized for payment, they stormed the courthouses at Northampton and Worcester and then headed for the arsenal at Springfield to get more weapons. The governor sent the militia out against them, and the rebellion was broken up. Clearly, something had to be done.

The Bright Light of the Confederation. It may appear from what we have said here that the Articles of Confederation were almost valueless. Such was not the case. While they were not adequate to solve the problems of the new nation, they were remarkable in that they were a long stride toward union and away from autocratic rule. They represented a necessary stage preliminary to the establishment of a strong central government. Really a great deal was accomplished under them.

The greatest accomplishment was the Northwest Ordinance of 1787. It was a set of laws providing for the government of the land northwest of the Ohio River. It set up a temporary rule under a governor, a secretary, and three judges, all appointed by Congress. When there were 5,000 free men who were of age living in the territory, an assembly elected by the people was to be added. Not more than five nor less than three states were to be made from this area. When any territory in the area had in it 60,000 free people, it could come into the Union, on the same basis as the other states. Personal rights were guaranteed to the people, including freedom of religion and trial by jury; slavery was prohibited.

The Northwest Ordinance of 1787 became the pattern for dealing with other lands that came under the rule of the United States. The new nation was building an empire. The land between the thirteen original states and the Mississippi was its first colony. The leaders of the government well remembered their experience as citizens of a colony in another empire; they recognized the importance of setting a precedent for granting to all citizens of territories owned by the United States the right of self-government and the opportunity to become a part of the United States. The new government refused to adopt the imperial principle that colonies exist solely for the purpose of supporting the mother country. The privileges stated in the Declaration of Independence and won by the Revolution were to be extended to all who wanted them.

The Spirit of Union. Within the thirteen states conditions were getting steadily worse. Interest in Congress diminished until in 1788 not even a quorum[1] could be mustered to do business, and the United States had no government at all except that of the states. More and more people were realizing that something had to be done.

The more people thought about the general condition of the country, the more they saw clearly that a strong central government was needed. And they realized that each state's refusal to give up any of its sovereignty was the chief stumbling block on the way to a strong central government. Even the states began to see the light. It appeared that the only law that was going to exist was whatever law each state could enforce for itself. The smaller states could see themselves being swallowed up by the larger ones. They began to see a value in surrendering some of their sovereignty to get security. All the while, men who favored a strong union were active at the job of shaping public opinion—men like George Washington, Alexander Hamilton, and James Madison of Virginia.

---

[1] Enough present to do business legally.

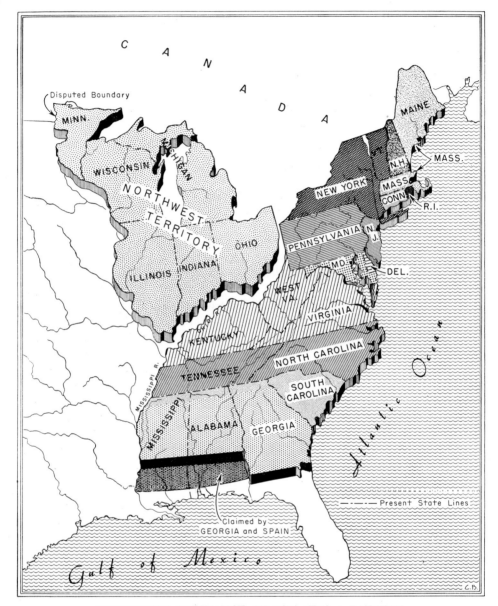

NORTHWEST ORDINANCE OF 1787 SETS A PATTERN

Creation of the Northwest Territory cut in half the land claims of the original states and provided a pattern for setting up the governments of future territories and states of the country.

It was the trouble over trade among the states that brought the first step toward "a more perfect union." Delegates from all the states were asked to meet at Annapolis (in 1786) to discuss trade problems. Only five states sent representatives, and Hamilton promptly got the convention to suggest another

LEADING ADVOCATE OF A STRONG UNION

George Washington's talents of leadership were employed in the service of his country in war and peace—toward the establishment of a "more perfect union" of the states.

meeting in Philadelphia in May, 1787, and then disband.

Congress didn't like too well what had happened, but since it appeared the convention was going to meet in Philadelphia whether or not Congress approved, Congress issued a call to all the states to attend the meeting there. Hamilton had stated the purpose of the coming Philadelphia meeting to be "to take into consideration the situation of the United States, to devise such further provisions as shall appear to them necessary to render the constitution of the federal (confederate) government adequate to the exigencies of the Union." Congress stated the purpose as simply "revising the Articles of Confederation."

UNITED STATES UNDER THE CONSTITUTION

The Constitutional Convention. Most of the states saw in the proposed Philadelphia convention a chance to make some badly needed adjustments in their newly created government. Accordingly, they picked their best men as delegates. It was a distinguished group that met in Philadelphia in May, 1787. But some of the men who had been most active in the Revolution were not there. Thomas Jefferson and Thomas Paine were out of the country at the time; Patrick Henry and Samuel Adams refused to come because they did not believe in what the convention proposed to do.

The Constitutional Convention met in Independence Hall in Philadelphia. This was the place where the Declaration of Independence was signed and where the Second Continental Congress had met. The sessions were secret; most of our knowledge about what went on is obtained from the detailed notes taken by James Madison.

Early in the convention the first big hurdle was cleared. It was decided that to try to revise the Articles of Confederation was useless and that the convention should start from the beginning and build an entirely new government. Some of the delegates who were not in favor of this went home at that point in the deliberations.

Two Opposite Plans. Two plans for the new government were brought before the convention. One was presented by Virginia. It proposed a congress of two houses; members of the lower house were to be elected by the states on the basis of population, and the members of the upper house were to be elected by the lower. The New Jersey plan called for a congress of one house only, with an equal number of representatives from each of the states.

Clearly the Virginia plan favored the large states because of their greater population. The New Jersey plan just as clearly gave the advantage to the smaller states. But there was another difference, too. The Virginia plan was an attempt to put the government of the country into the hands of the people; the New Jersey plan would keep it in the hands of the state governments. The real argument was whether

the government of the United States should be a strong national government by the people or a government in which the states would still hold the greater power.

The Birth of the Constitution. The argument between the supporters of the two plans went on for weeks. The threat was even voiced that the small states would look to some foreign country for help if they were not considered by the convention. Over the delegates hung the heavy realization that failure to produce a satisfactory government probably meant the end of the United States. Compromise finally prevailed. It was decided that Congress should have two houses. Membership in the lower, the House of Representatives, was to be based on the population of the states, with the representatives elected by the people; the upper house, the Senate, was to be composed of two senators from each state, to be elected by the state legislatures.

Another compromise had to be reached, this time on the slavery question. No attempt was made to abolish slavery, although some of the delegates would have favored doing so, because that would have surely prevented the Constitution from being adopted. The argument arose over whether or not slaves would be counted for purposes of representation in Congress and for taxation. The northern states felt slaves should not be counted as population, for they were neither citizens nor voters, but should be counted for taxation, since they were property. The southern states, of course, took the opposing view. The compromise reached provided that three-fifths of the slaves should be counted for both purposes, and that Congress should make no attempt to prevent any more slaves being brought into the country before 1808. Congress was given control of all other trade, both abroad and between the states, but all treaties had to be ratified by a two-thirds vote of the Senate.

The head of the new government was to be a president to be chosen for a four-year term by electors to be selected by each state in any way it should decide upon. Each state would have as many electors as it had senators and representatives.

A system of courts was also established, with a supreme court at its head. Judges of the courts were to be appointed by the President with the approval of the Senate.

The Founding Fathers had not forgotten their experiences with an autocratic government. They wanted to establish a strong government here but not one that would permit a single person, or even a few people, to gain the bulk of the power. They went back to the old Roman system of "checks and balances." They so divided the power among the Legislative Department (Congress), the Executive Department (the President), and the Judicial Department (the courts) that each would serve as a check upon the others at all times.

The Ratification of the Constitution. In September, 1787, the Constitution was finished, and thirty-nine of the fifty-five delegates signed it. Several had already left in disgust. It is doubtful if very many were entirely pleased with what they had done, but they felt the Constitution was better than the Articles of Confederation. They hoped that time would show up their mistakes and that the permit of amendment would correct them. It was decided that the Constitution should go into effect when nine of the thirteen states had adopted it.

Much interest was shown in the Constitution just as soon as it was published. Those delegates who favored it went home to campaign for its adoption. Organized opposition appeared, led by several famous men such as Patrick Henry and Samuel Adams. Those who favored adoption came to be known as the Federalists; those who opposed it, as Anti-Federalists.

The little states were pleased with the compromise about representation. Two of them were the first to ratify—Delaware and New Jersey. Then came Georgia. The first large state to accept the Constitution was Pennsylvania. Then came Connecticut, Massachusetts, Maryland, and South Carolina in order. Only one more was needed. New Hampshire became the ninth state to ratify on June 21, 1788. Virginia and New York soon followed. North Carolina came into the Union in 1789 and Rhode Island not until 1790.

The Bill of Rights. Many people felt the Constitution should contain a specific guarantee of those rights for which the colonists had fought in the Revolution. Several of the states submitted amendments at the time they ratified. At the first session the new Congress selected twelve of these amendments and submitted them to the states. Ten were adopted and declared in effect in 1791. These first ten amendments to the Constitution are usually referred to as our Bill of Rights. They guarantee such individual rights as freedom of religion, speech, and press; the right of states to have a militia; a regulation against the quartering of soldiers in people's homes without the consent of the householder;

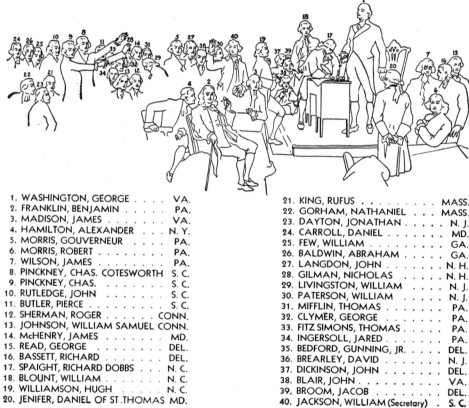

1. WASHINGTON, GEORGE . . . . VA.	21. KING, RUFUS . . . . MASS.
2. FRANKLIN, BENJAMIN . . . . . PA.	22. GORHAM, NATHANIEL . . . MASS.
3. MADISON, JAMES . . . . VA.	23. DAYTON, JONATHAN . . . . . N. J.
4. HAMILTON, ALEXANDER . . . N. Y.	24. CARROLL, DANIEL . . . . . . MD.
5. MORRIS, GOUVERNEUR . . . . PA.	25. FEW, WILLIAM . . . . GA.
6. MORRIS, ROBERT . . . . PA.	26. BALDWIN, ABRAHAM . . . . . GA.
7. WILSON, JAMES . . . . PA.	27. LANGDON, JOHN . . . . N. H.
8. PINCKNEY, CHAS. COTESWORTH S. C.	28. GILMAN, NICHOLAS . . . . . N. H.
9. PINCKNEY, CHAS. . . . . S. C.	29. LIVINGSTON, WILLIAM . . . . N. J.
10. RUTLEDGE, JOHN . . . . S. C.	30. PATERSON, WILLIAM . . . . . N. J.
11. BUTLER, PIERCE . . . . S. C.	31. MIFFLIN, THOMAS . . . . PA.
12. SHERMAN, ROGER . . . . . . CONN.	32. CLYMER, GEORGE . . . . PA.
13. JOHNSON, WILLIAM SAMUEL CONN.	33. FITZ SIMONS, THOMAS . . . . . PA.
14. McHENRY, JAMES . . . . MD.	34. INGERSOLL, JARED . . . . . . PA.
15. READ, GEORGE . . . . DEL.	35. BEDFORD, GUNNING, JR. . . . . DEL.
16. BASSETT, RICHARD . . . . . . DEL.	36. BREARLEY, DAVID . . . . N. J.
17. SPAIGHT, RICHARD DOBBS . . . N. C.	37. DICKINSON, JOHN . . . . DEL.
18. BLOUNT, WILLIAM . . . . . . N. C.	38. BLAIR, JOHN . . . . VA.
19. WILLIAMSON, HUGH . . . . . N. C.	39. BROOM, JACOB . . . . DEL.
20. JENIFER, DANIEL OF ST.THOMAS MD.	40. JACKSON, WILLIAM (Secretary) . S. C.

John M. Haass Lithography Co.

DELEGATES SIGN THE CONSTITUTION

This marked the beginning of the campaign for ratification. Of the fifty-five delegates to the Constitutional Convention, thirty-nine signed the Constitution and then returned home to vigorously urge adoption.

protection against unreasonable searching of property; protection against punishment without due process of law; the right to trial by jury; and protection against excessive bail and cruel punishment. These amendments are binding upon the federal government and must have given a much greater feeling of security to those states who feared that the federal government would become too strong.

The New Government at Work. New York City was selected as the meeting place for the new Congress and March 4, 1789, as the date. On that day not even a quorum was present, due chiefly to the very bad condition of the roads in winter. By April 6 enough members had arrived to do business, and the electoral votes were counted. George Washington was elected President unanimously, and John Adams Vice-President. Washington was aristocratic in his ways and was not a good public speaker, but no one could have been selected who commanded more respect and support from the people.

The new government got down to business at once. Three administrative departments were created. Thomas Jefferson of Virginia was appointed Secretary of State; Alexander Hamilton of New York, Secretary of the Treasury; and Henry Knox of Massachusetts, Secretary of War. These three men were Washington's advisers and came to be called the cabinet. Edmund Randolph of Virginia was made Attorney General and sat in on cabinet meetings although the Department of Justice was not formally organized until 1870. Congress created thirteen District Courts and three Circuit Courts (Judiciary Act of 1789) and provided that cases tried in lower courts could be appealed to

the Supreme Court for final decision. Washington appointed John Jay of New York as the first Chief Justice of the Supreme Court.

The financial condition of the country demanded immediate attention. There was the public debt to take care

Parker-Allston Associates, U.S. Fire Insurance Co.

HOW THE CONSTITUTION PROTECTS THE CITIZEN

Lambdin Milligan, a civilian, was imprisoned, convicted, and sentenced to be hanged in 1864 by United States military authorities. He petitioned the Supreme Court on the ground of illegal seizure and detention; he won a hearing and subsequent discharge.

of. The total debt, both national and state, was about $75,000,000. At home the national government owed about $42,000,000 and the states $21,000,000. The foreign debt of $12,000,000 was owed principally to France, Holland, and Spain. This doesn't sound like much today, but to the new government it was a huge problem.

Hamilton was determined that all

Smithsonian Institution

WHEN TRAVEL WAS SLOW AND UNCERTAIN

This early American stage coach is of the type that carried passengers between Philadelphia and other eastern cities during the early years of the Republic. Roads were bad and rides were uncomfortable.

the debt should be paid. The credit of the new government had to be maintained in good standing. Congress agreed with Hamilton on the national debt but balked when he proposed that the state debts should be taken over and paid by the national government. Many states couldn't see it because they had already paid their debts. The southern states were particularly opposed. It was at this point that the first political deal crept into the history of our federal government. In exchange for enough southern votes to pass his bill, Hamilton promised to get enough northern votes to locate the capital on the Potomac River, after it had existed for ten years in Philadelphia. Both bills were put through.

Hamilton also urged that a strong Bank of the United States be created. There was much opposition to this, too.

It was claimed that such a bank would be a monopoly and would provide unfair competition for private banks. But Washington sided with Hamilton, and the bank went into business in 1791.

The Secretary of the Treasury had gained the support of the business men of the country by getting Congress to agree to pay all of the debts of both the nation and the states, for they held most of the bonds. Now he moved to bring the authority of the government home to the farmers, too. He advocated an excise tax on distilled liquors as part of a higher tariff to raise money for current government expenses. Again opposition arose, but the bill finally passed and became the Tariff Act of 1792. Many farmers had been converting their grain into whiskey because it was more easily carried to market. An uprising occurred in Pennsylvania in 1794,

Chicago Historical Society

THE FIRST CAPITOL BUILDING OF THE U.S. IN WASHINGTON, D.C.

The foundation of this building was laid in 1793. British troops burned the structure in their invasion of 1814. Rebuilding of the Capitol was undertaken in 1827.

called the Whiskey Rebellion. The rebels were resisting the collection of the excise tax. Hamilton himself led 15,000 militia against the "Whiskey Boys," and the rebellion broke up.

Hamilton dominated Washington's cabinet to such an extent that he was sometimes called "prime minister." By his political as well as economic moves, he did a great deal to create a healthy respect for the authority of the new government at home. Now attention had to be turned to the same problem with regard to other nations.

FOR YOUR REVIEW

These Should Be Easy for You Now

1. When was the "critical period" in American history? Why was it so called? Make a list of the problems the new country faced at the close of the Revolution.
2. Explain the government created by the Articles of Confederation. Why were the Articles called "a rope of sand"? What was their greatest weakness?
3. What were the provisions of the Northwest Ordinance?
4. What attitude did the new nation adopt toward land it owned that was not included in the thirteen original states?
5. Why did the states object to the idea of a strong central government?
6. Why was the meeting at Annapolis called? At Philadelphia?
7. Distinguish between the Virginia plan and the New Jersey plan for a new government. Point out advantages and disadvantages of each. What compromise was reached?

8. How did the delegates at the Constitutional Convention dispose of the slavery question?
9. What three departments compose our government? Explain what is meant by a system of "checks and balances."
10. What does compose the American Bill of Rights? Why was it added all at one time?
11. Enumerate the personal liberties guaranteed by the Bill of Rights.
12. Where did the new Congress meet? Who was elected President? Vice-President?
13. Who was appointed Secretary of State? Of the Treasury? Of War? Attorney General? Chief Justice of the Supreme Court?
14. What arrangement did Hamilton propose in order to maintain the nation's good credit standing?
15. How did the Tariff Act of 1792 demonstrate the power of the central government over farmers?

Associated Dates

1777—Articles of Confederation adopted by the Continental Congress, November 17
1781—Articles of Confederation go into effect
1786—Annapolis Conference, September 11
1787—Constitutional Convention, May 25 to September 17
    Northwest Ordinance adopted
1788—Constitution goes into effect June 21
1789—Washington inaugurated as President April 30
1791—Bill of Rights added to the Constitution
    Bank of the United States created

Why Are These To Be Remembered?

Articles of Confederation	Anti-Federalists	Henry Knox
Shays' Rebellion	Bill of Rights	Edmund Randolph
Northwest Ordinance	Thomas Jefferson	John Jay
Federalists	Alexander Hamilton	Whiskey Rebellion

Suggested Readings

BACHELLER, IRVING, *In the Days of Poor Richard*
    Benjamin Franklin
BOYD, JAMES, *Drums*
    The Revolutionary War; John Paul Jones
CHURCHILL, WINSTON, *Richard Carvel*
    Maryland at the time of the Revolution
COOPER, JAMES FENIMORE, *The Spy*
    George Washington is one of the characters
EDMONDS, W. D., *Drums Along the Mohawk*
    The Dutch in New York during the Revolution
EGGLESTON, G. C., *Long Knives*
    George Rogers Clark's expedition to Illinois

ELLSBERG, EDWARD, *I Have Just Begun To Fight*
    John Paul Jones
KJELGAARD, JAMES, *Rebel Siege*
    Southern colonies during the war
ROBERTS, KENNETH L., *Arundel*
    The struggle for Quebec
ROBERTS, KENNETH L., *Rabble in Arms*
    Sequel to *Arundel;* more about Benedict Arnold
MILLER, J. C., *Origins of the American Revolution*
VAN DOREN, CARL, *Secret History of the American Revolution*
RODELL, FRED, *Fifty-Five Men*
    The men who established our Constitution
BOWEN, CATHERINE DRINKER, *John Adams and the American Revolution*

BOWERS, CLAUDE G., *Jefferson and Hamilton*
The originators of our two major political parties

ADAMS, HENRY, *The Life of Albert Gallatin*
Story of the Swiss immigrant lad who became Jefferson's Secretary of Treasury

HART, W. S., *A Lighter of Flames*
Life of Patrick Henry

BEVERIDGE, A. J., *Life of John Marshall*
Our great Chief Justice who did much to establish the supremacy of the Federal government

BRANT, IRVING, *James Madison* (2 vols.)
The "Father of the Constitution"

RICHARDS, L. E., *Abigail Adams and Her Times*
Our first feminist leader and wife of our second President

SEYMOUR, FLORA W., *Meriwether Lewis, Trail Blazer*
An account of the leading explorer of the great Northwest

THOMAS, LOWELL J., *Hero of Vincennes*
George Rogers Clark, frontier explorer

VAN DOREN, CARL, *Benjamin Franklin*
Biography of the "First American" and his great contributions

WILSON, WILLIAM E., *Shooting Star: The Story of Tecumseh*
Story of a great native American

The Nation Expands and Survives Internal Conflict

INTRODUCTION

The Revolutionary War had given the English colonies in America their political freedom from the British Empire. But they were still very much under England's domination commercially. The United States had been created, but the new government commanded very little respect abroad. It took a second struggle, the War of 1812, to make the break with Britain's commercial empire complete and to establish the United States as a nation to be respected.

The basis of United States foreign policy during most of the nineteenth century was the Monroe Doctrine. President Monroe's statement set up a policy not only for the United States but, in a sense, for all the Western Hemisphere. Already the United States was making itself felt in world affairs.

During the course of the nineteenth century, the new nation expanded its control until it reached from the Atlantic to the Pacific, from Mexico to Canada. But within this vast expanse dissension arose, due largely to the fact that the South had become an agricultural area which found the use of slaves beneficial, while the North was industrial and frowned upon the idea of slavery. When the ensuing problems were not solved, southern states tried to withdraw from the Union, and a great war followed. Those forces that favored a continuation of the Union won, and the decision was finally made that this should be one nation, indivisible. To make the idea of liberty and justice for all effective, slavery had to be eliminated.

Chapter 8

The New Nation Charts Its Course in International Relations

THE UNITED STATES ATTEMPTS TO WIN RESPECT FOR ITSELF AMONG
THE NATIONS OF THE WORLD

Problems of Foreign Affairs. As stated previously, the young United States was treated with considerable disrespect by other nations—especially by Great Britain, and by France and Spain who had fought with the Americans in the Revolution. They did their best to take advantage of the new nation, for their own benefit.

Outposts Held by British. Although England had recognized the Mississippi River as the western boundary of the United States, the British still held outposts in the land north of the Ohio. British Canada had enlisted the aid of the Indians in the area with promises that they would get their land back. It became dangerous for settlers to move into the Great Lakes territory, and many people wanted to go there because of the rich fur trade. Finally it became necessary to send troops to put down the Indian threat. The victory (1794, Treaty of Greenville) encouraged settlement in the Ohio territory. But the basic problems with Great Britain remained unsettled.

New Orleans Held by Spain. Spain held Louisiana,[1] a vast region west of

the Mississippi stretching from the Gulf of Mexico to the Canadian border. She held New Orleans, the outlet for trade on the Mississippi. Settlers in the western lands south of the Ohio became discontented; they thought the federal government cared little about their problems. Spanish agents tried to capitalize on their discontent and get the western settlements to pull away from the United States and put themselves under Spain's protection. But the ties across the mountains to the east were too great to permit that. In 1789 Kentucky secured permission from Virginia to form a state out of her western land. In 1791 Vermont was admitted as a state, and the next year Kentucky came in. Tennessee became a state in 1796, carved out of land formerly held by North Carolina.

The Pinckney Treaty. About this time Spain became involved in war with France, and the latter planned expeditions against Florida and New Orleans. Spain's attitude softened at once, and we were able to reach agreement with her on several matters. The treaty arranged by Thomas Pinckney in 1795 cleared up the location of the Florida boundary, and gave western settlers the right to the free navigation of the Mississippi River and to ship goods from

---

[1] Spain had acquired Louisiana from France by treaty at the end of the Seven Years' War (the French and Indian War in America).

84

New Orleans. So the immediate difficulty with Spain was ended.

A Proclamation of Neutrality. We have already pointed out that the American Revolution was an indirect cause of the French Revolution, which started in 1789. Soon Austria and Prussia came to the aid of the French monarchy. In 1793 King Louis XVI and Queen Marie Antoinette were beheaded, and almost at once England and Spain joined Austria and Prussia against France. The treaties of 1778, which had brought France into the American Revolution, were still in effect. In them both we and France had promised to make war on the enemies of the other. But instead of joining France, Washington issued a Proclamation of Neutrality (1793).

The Jay Treaty. Immediately two factions formed: those who favored neutrality and those who opposed it. Both France and England were seizing neutral ships, some of them ours, carrying supplies to the other country. It looked as if war might come. But Washington counseled moderation and sent John Jay to London to try to make a treaty. In the Jay Treaty, England agreed to withdraw her troops from posts on our northern frontier, and we agreed to pay debts owed British subjects, but no mention was made about seizure of our ships and seamen. It was humiliating, but the Senate finally accepted it, and war was averted.

Farewell Address of Washington. Washington had made it known in his Farewell Address that he would not accept a third term as President, thereby establishing a precedent that was not broken until nearly one hundred fifty years later. John Adams was elected as his successor (1797), and Thomas Jefferson as Vice-President. In the Farewell Address, Washington urged the people of the nation to work hard for unity. In it he also sounded the keynote of foreign policy which the nation has tried to follow in the main ever since. Said Washington: "The great rule of conduct for us, in regard to foreign Nations, is, in extending our commercial

Chicago Historical Society

STEPHEN DECATUR

His exploits on the sea have enrolled him among the immortals who have achieved great things for liberty.

relations, to have with them as little *political* connection as possible. So far as we have already formed engagements, let them be fulfilled with perfect good faith. Here let us stop.

"Europe has a set of primary interests, which to us have none, or a very remote relation. Hence she must be engaged in frequent controversies, the causes of which are essentially foreign to our concerns. Hence, therefore, it must be unwise in us to implicate ourselves, by artificial ties, in the ordinary

THE BARBARY PIRATES LOSE THEIR PRIZE

On February 16, 1804, a group of American seamen under Lieutenant Stephen Decatur, raided Tripoli Harbor at midnight, set fire to the "Philadelphia," which had previously been captured by the Barbary pirates. Decatur's band escaped through a storm of shot and shell without a single loss. Admiral Nelson of the British Navy hailed the deed as "the most bold and daring act of our age."

vicissitudes of her politics, or the ordinary combinations and collisions of her friendships or enmities." But the invention of the steamship, the airplane, and radio have brought Europe and all the rest of the world much closer to us— so near as to make the policy Washington advocated far less realistic today than it was when he stated it.

At the time, it was the only policy the United States could safely follow. Our position had not improved very much in the eyes of the world. The war continued in Europe, and France and England went on interfering with our trade, so much so that at various times we were near to war. Shortly after the

new century began we were forced to take naval action against the pirates along the Barbary Coast (south shore of the Mediterranean) to put an end to the old practice of forcing our ships to pay tribute for the right to trade in the Mediterranean.

The Predicament of the United States. Napoleon had put an end to the infamous French Revolution by seizing the power and making himself dictator. The war in Europe narrowed down to a struggle for empire between Napoleon and Great Britain. Each tried to starve the other out. Certain British Orders in Council (1806–7) set up a blockade of the French coast and specified

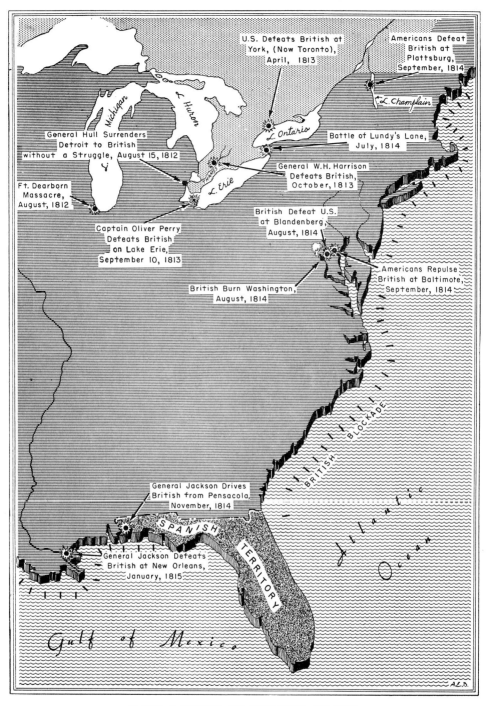

LAND BATTLES OF THE WAR OF 1812

Except for the engagements on the high seas, the principal actions of the war between the United States and Great Britain are shown on this map.

"OLD IRONSIDES" SINKS THE "GUERRIERE"

In one of the first actions of the War of 1812, the United States frigate "Constitution," dubbed "Old Ironsides," engaged and completely wrecked the British brig "Guerriere" in a brief but furious battle on the Atlantic. Isaac Hull commanded the victorious American ship.

CAPTAIN OLIVER PERRY AT THE BATTLE OF LAKE ERIE

When his flagship "Lawrence" was put out of action, Perry ordered several crew members to row him through raging gunfire to the "Niagara," another vessel of the American fleet. From the "Niagara" he continued the attack on the British squadron until the enemy surrendered.

THE BRITISH CAPTURE THE CITY OF WASHINGTON

British troops occupied Washington in 1814. They put to fire the original Capitol building that was begun in 1793. The interior of both wings was destroyed, and the executive mansion of the President was gutted, with only the walls left standing. A new presidential residence was built around the original walls which were painted white to hide the fire marks. Thus was the name "White House" derived.

MacDONOUGH TURNS BACK THE BRITISH INVASION OF THE HUDSON VALLEY

In September, 1814, an invading British force moved from Canada toward the Hudson Valley. A small flotilla of American ships under Thomas MacDonough defeated a superior enemy fleet on Lake Champlain. American control of the lake deprived the British of naval support for their land assault.

that ships bound for France must first stop at English ports and pay duty. Napoleon came right back with his French Decrees (1806–7) for a blockade of England. Here was a fine state of affairs. If we obeyed the British Orders, the French seized our ships; if we obeyed the French Decrees, the British took them.

Before long England was seizing our sailors, too. Many British seamen were deserting and escaping to American boats. The British navy would stop our ships and search them for British sailors, often taking some of ours as well.

SECOND WAR FOR INDEPENDENCE

The United States Tries to Prevent a War. Jefferson and Congress tried to meet the situation by peaceful means. Congress passed the Non-Importation Act (1806), which cut off imports of certain British goods. When this didn't work, the Embargo Act of 1807 was passed. This law cut off almost all trade with the outside world. The loss of American goods did not change the British or French attitude, but in a year American trade was practically ruined. Congress then repealed the Embargo Act and passed the Non-Intercourse Act (1809), which was aimed against only England and France. Before it expired, Congress passed the Macon Act (1810). This provided that if either England or France should repeal its regulations against our shipping, the Non-Intercourse Act would then be applied against the other country.

The crafty Napoleon saw his chance. He sent word that the French laws were no longer in operation (1810). James Madison was now President (elected 1809), and he promptly notified England that the Non-Intercourse Act was being applied to her. Napoleon had no intention of abiding by his word, and the French, like the British, went right on interfering with our shipping as before. Only now we were in the position of favoring France. Conditions became worse; there was increased clamor for war, and public sentiment favored France. On June 18, 1812, Congress declared war against England, her "second war for independence." George III was still King of England.

Just two days earlier the British government had directed that the British Orders be withdrawn. Had modern means of communication been available, there probably would have been no war. As it was, when the news reached America, things had gone too far. The war went on.

Victory of Captain Perry. We were fortunate in the War of 1812 as we had been in the Revolution. England was fighting Napoleon in Europe, and she could not turn her full strength against the United States. Some tempestuous young Congressmen,[2] known as "War-Hawks," had been crying for the conquest of Canada. The first move in the war was in that direction, but repeated attempts were unsuccessful. Our most notable victory was that of Captain Oliver H. Perry (September 10, 1813) on Lake Erie, whose report is famous for its brevity: "We have met the enemy and they are ours. Two ships, two brigs, one schooner, and one sloop." The victory did not let the British advance in the northwest.

Burning of Washington. In the course of the war a British force at-

---

[2] Among them Henry Clay of Kentucky and John C. Calhoun of South Carolina.

FORT McHENRY REPULSES BRITISH BOMBARDMENT

Fort McHenry guarded the water approach to the city of Baltimore. The British scrapped their plans to capture the city when the Fort's guns repulsed the warships committed to support the attacking land forces.

tacked Washington, D.C. (summer of 1814). The defending militiamen, although outnumbering the attackers, were untrained and no match for them. The President and government officials fled and, at the British commander's order, the Capitol building, the President's home, and other government offices were burned. The British said this was to even the score for the burning of government buildings at York (now Toronto) the year before. There was a difference, however. The burning at Toronto had been the work of individual soldiers, acting on their own. The burning at Washington was done at the direction of the officer in charge.

Battle at Baltimore. From Washington the British moved on to Baltimore. There Fort McHenry put up a valiant defense and saved the city. It was during the attack on the fort that a young attorney, Francis Scott Key, wrote the "Star-Spangled Banner." He was detained overnight on a British ship in the harbor, where he had gone to secure the release of a friend. In the excitement of seeing the American flag still flying over the fort after the all-night battle, he wrote down, on the back of an envelope, the verses that more than a hundred years later (1931) were to be officially named as our national anthem.

New Orleans and Andrew Jackson. In 1800 the vast Louisiana Territory passed from Spain back into the hands of the French. Napoleon hoped to use it to build a great overseas empire to compete with the British Empire. But his plans went awry, and in 1803 he sold the whole territory to the United States. (The story is told in the next chapter.) The British now moved against New Orleans. General Andrew Jackson, with a little army of frontiers-

ANDREW JACKSON SCORES VICTORY AT NEW ORLEANS

Frontier lawyer and soldier from Tennessee, Andrew Jackson became a national hero after his raw and rough militiamen won a brilliant victory over trained British regulars who outnumbered them two to one. New Orleans marked with dismal failure the final British attempt to successfully invade the United States during the War of 1812.

men from the West, had just brought to terms the strong Creek Indians, the most hostile of the Indians between Florida and the Ohio River. Now he hurried to the defense of New Orleans.

On December 23, 1814, the British landed on a narrow peninsula eight miles below the city. Jackson attacked at once, stopped the British advance, and then dug in. The British looked with contempt upon the rough frontiersmen who made up Jackson's force. On January 8, 1815, they attempted to break the American lines by direct attack. Jackson's men waited until the British, many of them crack troops who had been fighting Napoleon, were close to their breastworks and then let loose with a withering blast of fire. Each attack received the same treatment, and

the "backwoodsmen" with their squirrel-rifles didn't miss very often. Losses in the British army totaled 1,971; Jackson lost only 13. The victory ranks among the great events in American history. It kept the mouth of the Mississippi open as an outlet for western trade, and it brought to the forefront one of the most picturesque characters in our country's public life.

The Treaty of Ghent. Modern communications might have prevented the war. Modern communications would have prevented the Battle of New Orleans. Efforts at peace had been made, somewhat halfheartedly, shortly after the war began. They were renewed in earnest in 1814. Agreement was finally reached, and the Treaty of Ghent was signed on December 24, 1814. The Battle of New Orleans was fought after the war was officially over. Neither side gained anything. The situation remained as it had been before the war. But Napoleon had been defeated in Europe, and the United States knew it would have no more trouble with Great Britain on the seas.

The War of 1812 finished the job that was started back in 1775. The American Revolution gave the English colonies their political independence. The War of 1812 brought the United States its commercial independence. The new nation now commanded more respect from other governments. It did not worry much about foreign relations. Americans were confident they could lick anyone.

THE MONROE DOCTRINE

The United States Establishes a New Foreign Policy. When Napoleon controlled Europe, he removed the Spanish King Ferdinand VII from his throne (1808) and put his own brother, Joseph Bonaparte, on it. This was a signal for the Spanish colonies in South and Central America to revolt and declare their independence. Then Napoleon was defeated and driven into exile. A conference was held at Vienna, Austria (attended by Russia, Austria, Prussia, and France, and called the Congress of Vienna), which tried to restore political Europe just as it had been before Napoleon appeared on the scene. The so-called Holy Alliance (Austria, Prussia, and Russia) was formed and was used principally to hold down liberal and democratic moves in Europe. The King of Spain wanted back his South American colonies and called upon the rest of Europe to help him get them. England

viewed this move with alarm. After the loss of the American colonies, she had looked to South America for trade to replace what she had lost in North America. After the Spanish colonies cut themselves loose from the mother country (actually with British assistance), England did gain most of their trade. Now, if they went back to Spain, their trade would go with them. England refused to join with other European countries to help Spain. When it looked as if Europe would go ahead without England, that country asked the United States to join with her in opposing the return of the Spanish colonies.

The United States was not unaware of the situation. The government, because of our own experience, was sympathetic toward what had happened in South America. We did not want to see Spain move back in again. But Secretary of State John Quincy Adams didn't like the idea of following England's leadership. He knew England had her eye on Cuba. Russia owned Alaska and was moving down the west coast; no one knew how far she might try to go. Washington had urged this country to stay out of foreign entanglements. We were perfectly willing to stay out of affairs in the rest of the world, but when other nations came over here, it was an entirely different matter.

With the full knowledge of President Monroe and the cabinet, Secretary Adams prepared a statement of this government's position. England agreed to go along with us and lend her support. President Monroe included this statement in his annual message to Congress on December 2, 1823. It is commonly called the Monroe Doctrine.

The Monroe Doctrine left no question as to where this government stood on several questions. This government would let Europe alone, so long as our rights were not threatened. European nations must not interfere with established governments in this hemisphere nor make any attempt to gain control of any territory in this hemisphere. Said President Monroe: "In the wars of the European powers in matters relating to themselves, we have never taken any part, nor does it comport with our policy so to do. It is only when our rights are invaded or seriously menaced that we resent injuries or make preparation for our defense. With the movements in this hemisphere we are, of necessity, more intimately connected, and by causes which must be obvious to all enlightened and impartial observers. The political system of the allied powers is essentially different in this respect from that of America . . . We owe it, therefore, to candor, and to the amicable relations existing between the United States and those powers, to declare that we should consider any attempt on their part to extend their system to any portion of this hemisphere as danger-ous to our peace and safety. With the existing colonies or dependencies of any European power we have not interfered and shall not interfere. But with the governments who have declared their independence and maintained it, and whose independence we have, on great consideration and on just principles, acknowledged, we could not view any inter-position for the purpose of oppressing them, or controlling in any other manner their destiny, by any European power, in any other light than as the manifestation of an unfriendly disposition toward the United States."

So the United States set itself up as the champion and defender of all the Western Hemisphere. It was the new nation's first big voluntary step in foreign policy. The Monroe Doctrine was to serve as the basis of the nation's foreign policy down through the remainder of the nineteenth century. The stop sign was turned against outside empire-builders. In the meantime, the United States went about building an empire of its own.

FOR YOUR REVIEW

These Should Be Easy for You Now

1. What incidents led to the Pinckney Treaty of 1795? What did the treaty accomplish for the United States?
2. What events in Europe got us into difficulty with both France and England near the end of the eighteenth century? Why was the Jay Treaty humiliating?
3. Who became the second President of the United States? Vice-President?
4. What policy did Washington recommend the United States follow when he retired from office? How have changing times forced the country to alter this policy?
5. What did the British Orders in Council do? The French Decrees? How did these orders affect the United States?
6. What was the Non-Importation Act supposed to do? The Embargo Act? The Non-Intercourse Act? The Macon Act?
7. Why did the United States declare war on England? What British territory did the United States try but fail to take?
8. What famous buildings did the British burn during the war? Why do we remember the attack on Fort McHenry?

9. How might better communications have prevented the Battle of New Orleans?
10. What did the War of 1812 accomplish for the United States?
11. What events caused the United States to issue the Monroe Doctrine? What policy did the Monroe Doctrine set up for the United States?

Associated Dates

1795—Jay Treaty signed, August 14
       Pinckney Treaty concluded, October 27
1797—Inauguration of John Adams, March 4
1800—Capital moved to Washington from Philadelphia
1801—Thomas Jefferson becomes President, March 4
1807—Non-Importation Act in effect, December 14
       Embargo Act, December 22
1809—Non-Intercourse Act, March 1
       James Madison inaugurated, March 4
1810—Macon Bill in effect, April 27
1812—War declared on Great Britain, June 18
1813—Perry's victory on Lake Erie, September 10
1814—British take Washington, August 24
       Treaty of Ghent, December 24
1815—Battle of New Orleans, January 8
1817—James Monroe becomes President, March 4
1823—Monroe Doctrine contained in the President's message to Congress, December 2

Why Are These To Be Remembered?

Thomas Pinckney	Non-Importation Act	Francis Scott Key
John Jay	Embargo Act	Andrew Jackson
Barbary Coast	Non-Intercourse Act	Ferdinand VII
Order in Council	Macon Act	Joseph Bonaparte
French Decrees	Captain Oliver H. Perry	Congress of Vienna

Chapter 9

The New Nation Pushes Its Control to the Pacific

THE UNITED STATES EXPANDS, BY VARIOUS MEANS, UNTIL IT EXTENDS
FROM THE ATLANTIC OCEAN TO THE PACIFIC

Expansion by Diplomacy. It was obviously out of the question to expect the United States to remain just the thirteen original states. With all the land to the west of them into which they could expand, it was inevitable that they should add to the Atlantic coast territory they already occupied and the land to the Mississippi to which they held claim. From colonial days the more adventurous people had been making their slow way over the Appalachian Mountains onto the fertile plains along the Ohio River and the Great Lakes. The Northwest Ordinance of 1787, providing for the future government of this area, had encouraged further migration westward.

The people of the western settlements found themselves, of necessity, facing west still, instead of east. There were no facilities—no canals or railroads—for shipping their produce to the eastern states or seaports. Rather, they had to use the natural waterways of the West to carry their goods down the Mississippi to New Orleans and from there to foreign markets or around to the eastern states. International problems involved in this trade were solved by the purchase of the Louisiana Territory from France in 1803.

Louisiana Purchase. Napoleon had got Louisiana back from Spain in 1800. France also owned the island of Haiti (Santo Domingo), and Napoleon thought he could build the two territories into a colonial empire. Before this could be done, however, he had to put down a rebellion of the black-skinned natives of Haiti that was being led by their emperor, Toussaint L'Ouverture. Toussaint was finally induced to surrender, but then Napoleon gave orders to restore slavery in the

RIVER FERRY

The picture shows a primitive ferry of the type used to carry goods and passengers across waterways before bridges were built. More than a few such ferries are still in use in out-of-the-way localities.

island, and the natives rose up once more. Fierce fighting and an outbreak of yellow fever convinced Napoleon it would require many men to reconquer

Haiti—men he couldn't spare because war with England was again approaching.

President Jefferson had sent James Monroe to Paris to confer with our ambassador, Robert Livingston, and try to buy New Orleans and West Florida from France. The idea was to prevent the closing of the port at New Orleans to our goods, an act which had been threatened. When the discussions were under way, Talleyrand, French foreign minister, suddenly offered to sell the whole of Louisiana. The price was set at $15,000,000 for a territory that more than doubled the size of the United States. All or part of fifteen states have since been carved from it.

Florida Purchase. Although the boundaries of the Louisiana Purchase were indistinct, Jefferson interpreted them to include West Florida. In 1812 the state of Louisiana was made from this area. Florida itself was owned by Spain. It was clear that as long as she held it, the United States would have trouble. England had used it as a base of operations during the War of 1812. Spain had promised to protect our southern settlers against Indian attacks but either couldn't or wouldn't make good. In 1818 Andrew Jackson pursued some Indians into Florida and took the Spanish forts at St. Marks and Pensacola. Jackson claimed he had been given the authority to do this. President Monroe denied that he had. Anyway the deed was done.

Secretary of State John Quincy Adams sent bold messages to Spain. He claimed that Jackson was simply doing what Spain had said she would do but hadn't done. Spain knew she couldn't fight the United States over Florida, so when the United States made an offer of $5,000,000 for the territory, she decided to accept (1819). Florida was gone anyway; she might as well have the money. Andrew Jackson became the first American governor of the territory. In 1845 Florida came into the Union as a state.

Webster-Ashburton Treaty. The treaty that closed the American Revolution did not clearly establish the boundary between Maine and Canada. The line was supposed to begin at the mouth of the St. Croix River, but it developed that several rivers in northern Maine were called the St. Croix, and England and the United States couldn't agree which one was the right one. Settlers in the area nearly came to blows from time to time over its disputed ownership.

In 1841 Daniel Webster became Secretary of State. Under his direction a treaty was arranged with England to fix the boundary. An early map, discovered later, shows that the Webster-Ashburton Treaty (1842) gave to England some 5,000 square miles more than she had claimed under the treaty of 1783 at the end of the Revolution. Previous agreements had established the boundary through the Great Lakes and as far as Oregon in general along the forty-ninth parallel.

Oregon Territory. The United States wanted to extend the forty-ninth parallel boundary on to the Pacific Ocean. England refused, because she wanted the Columbia River as the southern boundary of Canada there. England based her claims upon Captain Cook's explorations along the Pacific Coast in 1778 and the later development of fur interests there by the Hudson Bay Company. American claims were based upon several incidents. Captain Gray had discovered the Columbia River in 1792. In 1804 President Jefferson had sent Captain Meriwether Lewis and Lieutenant William Clark up the Missouri River to explore the newly acquired Louisiana Territory. The following year they reached the Pacific by way of the Columbia River and claimed the Oregon Territory for the United States. In 1811 the fur trader John Jacob Astor had built Fort Astoria.

By 1844 enough settlers were in Oregon to bring matters to a head. We were not disposed to accept the Columbia River boundary England wanted. The Oregon question became an issue in the presidential campaign that year, and "Fifty-Four Forty or Fight" was one of the slogans. We wanted Oregon as far north as fifty-four degrees and forty minutes. England, not wanting to fight over so little, reopened negotiations, and a treaty was signed (1846) fixing the boundary at the forty-ninth parallel.

Back in 1817 England and the United States had agreed to keep on the Great Lakes only such ships as were required to police the lakes. The same idea was extended to the entire boundary between the United States and Canada. For more than 130 years now, in a world in which border wars have been frequent, the 3,000 mile boundary has stood without any defenses whatever as an example of what can be accomplished when nations are determined to settle all differences peacefully and each is trusted not to take sudden advantage of the other.

WAR WITH MEXICO

Texas and "Remember the Alamo!"
In the treaty of 1819 by which Spain agreed to sell Florida, the United States gave up its claims to Texas as a part of the Louisiana Purchase. Shortly after that Mexico won its independence from Spain, and Texas was included in the new nation. American settlers had been crossing the border to take up land in Texas.[1] The understanding was that they were to become Mexican citizens and accept the Catholic religion.

Many American frontiersmen had moved into Texas before Mexico became independent; after that the settlers had to deal with Mexico instead of Spain. They weren't anxious to abide by their promises; they wanted to rule themselves. In addition, Mexico was trying to do away with slavery, and the Texans were afraid they would be ruined. The United States tried unsuccessfully to buy the area. Revolution just had to come.

The revolt began in 1836. Immediately Mexican President Santa Anna led an army north to put down the uprising. He caught 183 Texans in the Alamo, a mission-fortress at San Antonio, and either killed them during the siege or executed them after the surrender. From then on "Remember the Alamo!" was the battlecry of the Texan army under Sam Houston, an old friend of Andrew Jackson. Finally Houston caught Santa Anna in a bad position on the San Jacinto River and forced the Mexican army to flee. Santa Anna was captured. The Texans drew up a constitution, made Sam Houston president, and asked the United States to annex the new republic.

Mexico was inclined to hold the United States responsible for what had happened in Texas, although our government was in no way involved. Presi-

---

[1] Stephen F. Austin led the first group.

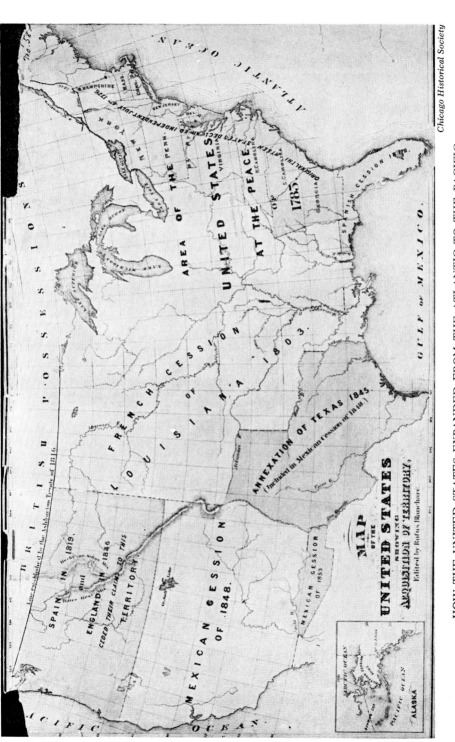

HOW THE UNITED STATES EXPANDED FROM THE ATLANTIC TO THE PACIFIC

Seven distinct phases mark the historical growth of the nation from the original thirteen states: to the Mississippi, the Louisiana Purchase, the purchase of Florida from Spain, the annexation of Texas, acquisition of the Pacific Northwest by treaties with Spain and England, the Mexican Cession, and the Gadsden Purchase (shown on map as Mexican cession of 1853).

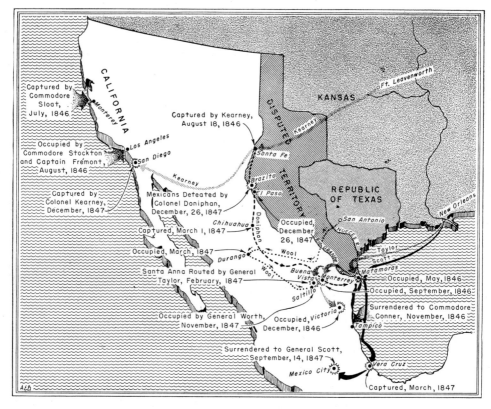

MEXICAN WAR ACTIONS

Superior generalship and marksmanship gave the American forces a succession of victories in the War with Mexico. United States troops were outnumbered in each of the major battles of the conflict.

dent Jackson wanted to keep the issue out of the coming presidential campaign, and Congress feared annexation would be looked upon as an act of imperialism. Annexation of Texas was refused, but just before the end of his term, in 1837, Jackson did recognize the independence of Texas.

Before it was decided, the question of the annexation of Texas became a political football. All attempts to add Texas failed until President John Tyler (Tyler finished W. H. Harrison's term, who died after a month in office, 1841) hurried to push annexation through just before he went out of office in order to get credit for it himself. Congress was more willing to take action now because it had been discovered that England, very much interested in Texas cotton, was moving to make Texas a part of her great commercial empire. As soon as Congress annexed Texas, Mexico broke off diplomatic relations and stated that the admission of Texas into the Union[2] would be the same as a declaration of war.

War Declared. President James Polk had now taken office (1845). He had his eye on California. He sent an envoy

—————

[2] Texas came in on December 29, 1845.

GENERAL WINFIELD SCOTT'S ENTRANCE INTO MEXICO

Scott was a resourceful military commander. His successful campaign to capture the Mexican capital wound up hostilities of a war that lasted less than two years.

to Mexico to try to buy California and New Mexico and some land along the Rio Grande in dispute between Mexico and Texas. To back up his offer, Polk sent General Zachary Taylor with an army to occupy the disputed territory along the Rio Grande.

Mexico refused to receive the envoy. Then on April 25, 1846, some Mexican soldiers came across the Rio Grande and engaged an American force. The President immediately asked Congress to declare war on the ground that our territory had been invaded, a point not very convincing since Mexico had at least as good a claim to it as we did. In fact, it could well be argued that we had been guilty of aggression when Taylor's men moved into the Rio Grande area. But Congress agreed with Polk and declared war.

Campaigns of the War. Polk at once sent Colonel Stephen Kearny to seize

and hold New Mexico and California for fear England would beat us to it. General Taylor engaged Santa Anna in northern Mexico. General Winfield Scott landed in March, 1847, and took Vera Cruz. Then he began the march which was to end in Mexico City on September 17.

In the meantime, Kearny had taken Santa Fe in New Mexico without a struggle and had gone on to California with only 100 men because word had reached him (by Kit Carson, the famous frontiersman) that California had already staged a successful revolt. It was true. Led by John C. Frémont, an explorer, the Americans had raised their flag over the territory, with the assistance of some American ships which had been lying offshore for just such a break. Kearny took over when he arrived. Frémont was disappointed because he was not made governor.

THE AMERICAN INDIAN IN THE SOUTHWEST

The territory which now forms the states of New Mexico and Arizona has been the home of the largest surviving Indian population in the country. The Sky City of Acoma, New Mexico, shown here, traces its history back centuries before the Spaniards first heard of it in 1539.

Treaty of Guadalupe-Hidalgo. The Treaty of Guadalupe-Hidalgo (February, 1848) was written on our own terms. We received clear title to Texas, and got all of New Mexico and California. True, we already held all this land, but to make matters look better we paid $15,000,000 for it and agreed to pay also any claims of American citizens against Mexico. These amounted to a little more than $3,000,000. From New Mexico and California were later carved the states of California, Nevada, Utah, most of Arizona, and part of New Mexico and Colorado.

Gadsden Purchase. Five years later we wanted some additional land below New Mexico as a route for a new railroad to southern California. James Gadsden was sent to buy the land. It cost $10,000,000 and is known as the Gadsden Purchase. Our southwestern boundary was now established.

TESTS OF THE MONROE DOCTRINE

England and Texas. We have previously said that the Monroe Doctrine served as the foreign policy of the United States until the close of the nineteenth century. The country fancied itself secure behind this statement, apparently not realizing that it was the support of the British navy that had made it effective in the beginning. It is doubtful if the United States could have enforced the doctrine if she had been called upon to do so. Fortunately, she was not. A series of opportune events took place at the right time to prevent a real showdown.

The first situation in which our foreign policy came near to a showdown was in connection with our trouble with Mexico. England was well on the way to establishing a sort of protectorate over Texas. Had she done this, the only way to get her out would have been by war. Happily, Congress annexed Texas before England had moved in. We got a war with Mexico as a result, but fighting Mexico was much easier than fighting England would have been. It is interesting to note that England, who was threatening our Monroe Doctrine in Texas, was supposed to be backing up our anti-imperialistic foreign policy with her navy.

France in Mexico. A second test of the Monroe Doctrine came at the time of our War between the States. Napoleon III of France, wanting to follow in the footsteps of his famous ancestor, was looking for land to include in an overseas empire. He thought he saw his chance in Mexico. That country owed money to several European nations, and they were having trouble collecting. To force payment, England, France, and Spain sent troops to occupy Mexico. The financial matter was promptly settled, and England and Spain withdrew. France stayed on. Archduke Maximilian of Austria was placed in command as France's emperor of Mexico.

The United States knew what was going on but was hardly in a position to do anything about it. She had her hands full. But when the war was over, we immediately demanded that France get out and sent troops to the Rio Grande to back up our demands. And France got out, leaving Maximilian to his fate at the hands of the Mexicans. But it was not fear of the United States, weakened by the War between the States, that caused France to leave. Rather, Napoleon III was finding his

position threatened at home. War with Prince Otto von Bismarck, the "Iron Chancellor" of Prussia, was approaching, and Napoleon needed all his troops to protect France. So another serious showdown on American foreign policy was avoided.

Alaska and Russia. The third challenge to our Monroe Doctrine was eased away when we were able to buy Alaska from Russia in 1867. Russia had been expanding down the west coast from Alaska and was causing us considerable anxiety. But the czar was having trouble ruling Alaska so far from his own capital, and he feared that, if he got into a war with England, he would lose it anyway. He let it be known that he would sell, and Secretary of State Seward jumped at the chance. The Senate ratified the treaty at once, but it took a year for the House to vote the money—$7,200,000. The members couldn't see the point in spending that much money for "Seward's ice-box," as it was called. But Alaska has paid for itself many times over, both in products and in strategic value in time of war.

With the adding of Alaska, United States' expansion on the North American continent was complete. The country now stretched from the Atlantic to the Pacific, from the Gulf of Mexico to Canada without a single break. The United States had acquired—sometimes by diplomacy, sometimes by purchase, sometimes by force—a great empire in which she proposed to see to it that every part should have the same rights and privileges as any other part. While the methods used to build the empire were not much different from those employed by European empire-builders, the purpose to which the co-

Bettmann Archive

THE UNITED STATES BUYS A TERRITORY

Signing the treaty for the purchase of Alaska are Secretary of State Seward (sitting at desk at left), and Russian Chargé d'Affaires Bodisco (standing in center background).

lonial territory was to be put was altogether different. But a good end does not ever justify imperial means. There are a few pages of American history of which we cannot be very proud.

While the United States was growing from coast to coast, she had to take time out to decide, once and for all, that the Union she was building should not be broken up. We must stop here to consider the attempt to divide the United States into two nations.

FOR YOUR REVIEW

These Should Be Easy for You Now

1. What was Napoleon's plan for empire in the Western World? Why did he give up the idea?
2. Why was the United States interested in buying French territory along the lower Mississippi River?
3. How did the United States acquire Florida? From whom?
4. What boundary did the Webster-Ashburton Treaty fix?
5. What was the basis of the British claim to Oregon? Of the United States' claim?
6. Why did American settlers in Texas revolt against Mexico? What events led to war between the United States and Mexico? What were the terms of the Treaty of Guadalupe-Hidalgo?
7. What land was added to the United States by the Gadsden Purchase?
8. Cite three instances in which related circumstances prevented our Monroe Doctrine from being seriously threatened.
9. From whom did we acquire Alaska?
10. How did the American Empire differ from the empires of European nations?

Associated Dates

1803—Louisiana Purchase, April 30
1804–1806—Lewis and Clark explorations
1809—James Madison inaugurated President, March 4
1810—annexation of West Florida
1817—James Monroe becomes President, March 4
1819—Florida purchased, February 23
1825—John Quincy Adams inaugurated, March 4
1829—Andrew Jackson inaugurated, March 4
1836—Texas wins independence
1837—Martin Van Buren becomes President, March 4
1841—William Henry Harrison inaugurated, March 4
      John Tyler becomes President, April 6
1842—Webster-Ashburton Treaty, August 9
1845—James K. Polk inaugurated, March 4
      Annexation of Texas
1846—War with Mexico declared, May 13
      United States gets Oregon, June 15
1848—Treaty of Guadalupe-Hidalgo, February 2
1849—Zachary Taylor becomes President, March 4
1850—Millard Fillmore inaugurated, July 10
1853—Inauguration of Franklin Pierce, March 4
      Gadsden Purchase, December 30
1857—Inauguration of James Buchanan, March 4
1861—Inauguration of Abraham Lincoln, March 4
1865—Andrew Johnson becomes President, April 15
1867—Purchase of Alaska

Why Are These To Be Remembered?

James Monroe
Robert Livingston
Talleyrand
Captain Cook
Captain Gray
The Alamo

Captain Meriwether
   Lewis
Lieutenant William
   Clark
John Jacob Astor
Stephen F. Austin

Santa Anna
Sam Houston
General Zachary
   Taylor
Colonel Stephen
   Kearny

General Winfield
   Scott
John C. Frémont
Maximilian
Otto von Bismarck
Secretary Seward

Chapter 10

The New Nation Fights To Preserve Its Unity

PERPLEXING INTERNAL PROBLEMS THREATEN TO DIVIDE THE UNITED STATES INTO TWO NATIONS

Events Leading to War between the States. The English colonies in America had won their freedom from the British Empire. They had converted themselves into the United States. The United States had expanded until it reached the Pacific, building a great empire of its own. But the United States was not united. There were some people who felt that this country should have one government over all, with the people of all the states deciding the nature of that federal government. Others believed our government should be a federation of sovereign states, free to do about as they pleased. Only a great war between the states (the Civil War) was finally to decide that issue.

It was only natural that, in a land this size, not all parts would be alike. From the start there was a recognized North and a South. Later there developed a West. Slavery passed out of existence in the North at an early date. In the South it decreased for a time and then flourished again after the invention of the cotton gin. As new lands were added, the question of whether slavery would be permitted kept coming up. As the North became industrialized, it desired protective tariffs, which the South didn't like. Around 1850, with the extension of railroads westward, the West, no longer dependent upon the Mississippi waterway for an outlet for its products, gradually turned away from the South and toward the North.

All of these things were factors in creating a gradual but definite division among the states. As time went on, it became more and more pronounced and bitter, and only an armed conflict between the two sections could bring about a decision. We shall have to consider these problems carefully in order to understand the background of the War between the States.

Slavery. Selling human beings became a profitable business for the early empire-building nations. Certain people, Arabs in particular, would capture African natives and sell them to European merchants. These merchants, in turn, would sell them to Europeans who were going to live in the new colonies. In 1619 about twenty African Negroes were brought into Virginia. As other English colonies were settled, more slaves were brought in. The Southern colonies in particular liked slave labor. The Negroes could stand the heat better than the white settlers. Slaves meant cheap production of tobacco, rice, sugar, and indigo, and wealth for the plantation owner, permitting him to live a life of ease and luxury.

During the Revolution a great deal

of public sentiment was created against slavery. Many of the men who wrote the Constitution would have liked to include in it a provision for doing away with slavery. However, no provision was included, for the Southern states would never have ratified the Constitution; and right then the adoption of the Constitution was the more important problem. But when the Northwest Ordinance was passed (1787), it provided that there should be no slavery in the Northwest Territory. Washington and Jefferson arranged in their wills for their slaves to be freed. More and more the North was becoming opposed to slavery. Vermont, New Hampshire, and Massachusetts had abolished slavery by 1783; other Northern states were moving in that direction. But in the South slavery was increasing: Eli Whitney's invention of the cotton gin in 1793 had made it easier and quicker to separate the seed from cotton, and the raising of cotton was given a new impetus.

In the same year (1793) Samuel Slater built the first power-driven factory in the United States. It was located at Pawtucket, Rhode Island, and produced cotton cloth. Rapidly new factories were built. Soon the North was turning its full attention to industry, just as the South turned to agriculture. As the South increased production until it was raising seven-eighths of the world's supply of cotton, the North was shipping that cotton for the South to the world markets. Cotton meant wealth, and the South was not interested in industry. Cotton, for Southerners, was "King."

Increased cotton production meant more slaves. By the middle of the century about three-fourths of all the slaves were tied up with the growing of cotton. It should be pointed out,

however, that only about one-fourth of the white people of the South were slave owners. It was the large plantation owners who were interested in keeping slavery as an institution; here was an example of how minority interests often control the policies of the majority.

Protective Tariff. When the War of 1812 began, the tax on imported goods was doubled (from 12½ per cent to 25 per cent) to raise money for the war. It was understood that one year after the war was over, the tax would drop again to where it had been. But after the war the "infant industries" of the North were fearful they could not stand the competition of European-produced goods, which cost less to make than American-produced goods. The idea of the "protective tariff" was born and incorporated in the Tariff Act of 1816. It levied a duty on imports high enough to give the advantage to goods produced here, thereby protecting them from outside competition. There was also the idea that American industry should be encouraged so that we should not be dependent upon foreign nations, especially in time of war.

In the beginning the South went along with the idea of the protective tariff, even though it did not benefit the agricultural interests of the country. But later, when Northern manufacturers demanded higher and still higher protective tariffs, the South turned against the idea. As more and more cotton was raised in the South, the price went down, and the Southerners blamed it on the tariff. The tariff did appear unfair: it meant higher prices in all areas of the country, but only the industrial North benefited from it. Here was another point of division between the North and the South.

Still another fundamental difference in thinking between the North and the South was brought out by the argument over the tariff. In 1828 Congress passed a new tariff law which the South disliked very much—so much that people called it the "Tariff of Abominations." Southerners decided it was time something was done. They had found a champion in John C. Calhoun, who

Chicago Historical Society

JOHN C. CALHOUN

This renowned political leader from South Carolina was, in the course of his career, Secretary of War, Vice-President, Secretary of State, and United States Senator. He became the nation's leading exponent of states' rights.

was then Vice-President under Andrew Jackson. Calhoun now wrote what came to be known as "The South Carolina Exposition," which was in the form of a report to the South Carolina legislature of the committee on relations with the federal government.

The paper set forth the fundamental idea of states' rights, the South's conception of the national government. It held that the Union was simply a compact of equal states and that the federal government was just the agent of the states, created by them to do whatever they wanted done, according to the instructions contained in the Constitution. It went further to declare that an act of the federal government was null and void when it violated or went beyond the instructions of the states, and that it was the right of each state to decide when its instructions had been violated. Then the threat was made that South Carolina might legally declare the protective tariff null and void, since it was not authorized by the Constitution.

Webster-Hayne Debates. The opposing stands of the North and the South on the interpretation of the federal government was brought clearly before the people by the Webster-Hayne debates (1830). Starting on an entirely different subject, this series of speeches in the Senate soon swung to the most vital question of the moment. Speaking for the South was Robert Y. Hayne, Senator from South Carolina. He called the protective tariff unconstitutional and reaffirmed his belief in the right of any state to declare the law null.

The cause of the Union was taken up by Senator Daniel Webster of Massachusetts. Tall and dignified, with a rich voice, he was perhaps the best orator ever to speak in the Senate. He argued that the power to declare laws of the federal government unconstitutional must rest with the Supreme Court, not with the state. What would happen if some of the states declared a law null and void and the remainder did not? He attacked the idea that the national government was created by the states and was their agent. Rather, he said, it had been created by the people

Chicago Historical Society

DANIEL WEBSTER

The great statesman from New England employed his genius as an orator to defend the Constitution and to strengthen the bond of our Federal Union.

and must answer only to them. If the people did not like what their government did, they had the power to change things by electing other men to serve them or by amending the Constitution. Webster closed with his now famous words: "Liberty *and* Union, now and forever, one and inseparable!"

President Jackson and States' Rights. Although President Jackson had never stated his position on states' rights, the South was counting on his support. When he continued to remain silent, the Southerners determined to smoke him out. The annual Jefferson Day dinner was to be held soon, and the South Carolinians were in charge of arrangements. They planned the speeches to give voice to their idea of states' rights. The President was invited, and it was expected that he would propose a toast. Under the circumstances, the Southerners thought he certainly would make his position clear on the subject of the evening. Jackson did. When the time came, he rose and raised his glass. "Gentlemen," he said, "our Federal Union: it must and shall be preserved!"

Southerners were amazed. Theirs was clearly a lost cause so far as the President was concerned. They could look for no help from that source. Then in 1832 Congress passed another tariff law; it lowered rates as a gesture to the South, but made protection a permanent consideration of all tariff laws. The South had lost in Congress, too.

Ordinance of Nullification. South Carolina acted at once. A special convention by an overwhelming vote adopted the Ordinance of Nullification. It declared the Tariff Acts of 1828 and 1832 null and void in South Carolina.

Compromise Tariff Act of 1833. Jackson was mad through and through. He made ready to enforce the laws of the nation, by force if necessary. Things looked bad. But South Carolina didn't get as much backing from the rest of the South as she had expected. Calhoun, who had resigned as Vice-President to take a seat in the Senate, was in a bad spot: he didn't want to be guilty of treason. Henry Clay, who had engineered other compromises, was urged to try again. With the co-operation of Calhoun and Webster, Clay introduced into Congress a Compromise Tariff Act (1833). It provided for a reduction of the tariff over a period of ten years until it was at the same level as after the War of 1812. South Carolina agreed to the compromise and repealed her Nullification Ordinance. Peace was restored. Both sides claimed victory, as can always be done in the case of a compromise. But the problem was not solved; it was merely shelved for the time, to be brought out again nearly thirty years later.

Balance of the States. As we have said, shortly after the Revolution the Northern states did away with slavery. The Northwest Ordinance of 1787 extended the North-South division to the Mississippi by prohibiting slavery north of the Ohio River. But nothing was said about the matter in the great Louisiana Territory west of the Mississippi when we purchased it in 1803.

The rivalry of sectionalism was already growing up. The North and the South eyed each other closely in the Senate, where each tried to keep the balance of power in its favor. When Missouri asked to be admitted as a state in 1818, the question of slavery in the Louisiana Territory was raised. Alabama came into the Union in 1819 as a slave state, and that made the number of slave and free states[1] equal,

---

[1] Slave states—Delaware, Maryland, Virginia, North Carolina, South Carolina, Georgia, Alabama, Mississippi, Louisiana, Tennessee, and Kentucky; free states—Maine, New Hampshire, Massachusetts, Rhode Island, Connecticut, New Jersey, New York, Pennsylvania, Ohio, Indiana, and Illinois.

eleven of each. Slaveholders dominated Missouri; she would be a slave state and that would throw the balance in favor of the South. Then Maine applied for admission as a free state. This permitted a compromise. Maine came in as a free state, Missouri as a slave state. The Missouri Compromise of 1820 also provided that in the remainder of the Louisiana Territory slavery was to be prohibited north of the parallel of thirty-six degrees and thirty minutes. This division of the territory obviously favored the North; there was more land north of the dividing line than south of it. It is possible that the South agreed to the compromise because it was generally thought then that much of the northwest was no good for settlement, could not be cultivated.

In the South, in the main, slavery was looked upon as an economic necessity. The North didn't use slaves, either on farms or in factories, because hired help was cheap. This help could be laid off and didn't have to be supported in slack times. Slaves must be provided for the year 'round. To the North, slavery was becoming more and more a moral issue. The most outspoken Northerner on the subject was a radical newspaper publisher of Boston, William Lloyd Garrison. He even went so far as to burn a copy of the Constitution because it recognized slavery. He advocated the immediate abolition of all slavery. Soon people who felt as he did were called *abolitionists*. As Boston became the center of abolitionism in the North, so Oberlin, Ohio, with its coeducational college that admitted Negroes, became the center in the West.

The admission of Arkansas as a slave state in 1836 and Michigan as a free state the following year kept the power in the Senate evenly divided at thirteen states on each side. Then in 1845 both Texas and Florida came in as slave states and this gave the South the balance of power, fifteen to thirteen. The following year the Oregon Territory was added, giving the North a chance to even things up, but no states were created in the territory at that time. But Iowa was admitted in 1846 and Wisconsin in 1848 to restore the balance at fifteen slave and fifteen free states.

Now the struggle shifted to a new field—the land obtained from Mexico. A decision had been made about slavery in the Northwest Territory, in Louisiana, and in Oregon. But not in New Mexico and California. In 1848 gold was discovered in California. The following year enough people flocked to the west coast in the famous gold rush to give California a large enough population to ask to be admitted as a free state. The South was alarmed. If California came in as a free state, the North would gain the balance of power in the Senate. And furthermore, what about the rest of the land purchased from Mexico? Was it to be free or slave?

Various ideas were advanced. The debate in the Senate brought forth famous speeches from the three great orators whose voices had spoken out so often on this and other matters. All three had seen the nation formed and had watched it grow until now it was on the verge of being torn apart. Henry Clay offered the basis for a compromise and pleaded for harmony but refused to support the idea of secession. John C. Calhoun was old and sick; he listened while another Senator read his speech. He admitted the South could no longer hold its own against the North in the Union. But he held that the South had

a perfect right to slavery. Therefore, he said, the South had but one choice: to submit to abolition which the North wanted to force upon it, or withdraw from the Union. The North, and the North only, said Calhoun, had it in its power to save the Union. If it loved the Union, then the North would cease interfering with slavery in the South. If the North was not willing to do this, then let her permit the South to leave the Union peacefully. If the North would not do this either, then resistance would be all there was left.

Daniel Webster spoke for compromise. He believed it was better to keep slavery than to divide the Union. He spoke against the radical abolitionists of the North and in favor of a fugitive slave law. He was widely condemned by the antislavery people for his stand, but he did help to achieve a compromise.

Compromise of 1850. The Compromise of 1850 favored the North just a bit. It provided for six things: (1) California was admitted as a free state. (2) The rest of the Mexican Cession was divided into the territories of New Mexico and Utah. States formed from these territories would decide for themselves whether they were to be slave or free. This was called the doctrine of "popular sovereignty." (3) New Mexico was enlarged by land procured from Texas for $10,000,000. (4) Trading in slaves was prohibited in the District of Columbia. (5) A strict law was passed governing the return of runaway slaves to their masters. (6) Congress went on record that it did not have the power to stop the sale of slaves across state borders.

The Compromise of 1850 avoided a showdown at the time. Leaders hoped it had prevented it for all time. The

HENRY CLAY ADDRESSING THE SENATE ON THE COMPROMISE OF 1850

Clay, like Calhoun and Webster, was a gifted orator and conspicuous public figure during the years of mounting tension between the North and South. He became known as the "Great Pacificator" because of his frequent efforts to conciliate differences and effect compromises in legislative affairs. He aspired to become President, but political fortunes denied him that high office.

slave question had now been decided in all the territories. If everyone would observe the terms of the Compromise strictly, perhaps a serious split could be prevented.

But it was not to be. The Compromise broke down on the fugitive slave law. Many people of the North refused to return runaway slaves. In fact, they did just the opposite; they helped them get away. The so-called "Underground Railroad" had been established earlier; now traffic on it increased. The "railroad" consisted of a series of secret

"stations," properly spaced to permit slaves to flee from one to the next by night, there to hide until they could be on their way to freedom again. In many cases the "railroad" operated more or less openly, for public sentiment was in its favor, law or no law.

Antislavery feeling in the North increased after the publishing (1852) of *Uncle Tom's Cabin,* by Harriet Beecher Stowe. Its purpose was to urge people to violate the fugitive slave law. It was sincerely written, but it was not a fair picture of slavery in the South. The story of Old Uncle Tom and Little Eva did much to bring people to feel that slavery must be done away with, once and for all.

As sentiment for abolition increased in the North, oppression of the Negro increased in the South. Since slaves were sure of help in the free states, more and more of them tried to escape. This brought harsher regulations; slaves were even forbidden to learn to read and write.

Kansas-Nebraska Act. No compromise is likely to last when the men who made it are no longer around to keep it. Calhoun had died in 1850, Clay and Webster two years later. New men had taken over—men like William H. Seward of New York, Jefferson Davis of Mississippi, and Stephen A. Douglas of Illinois. Douglas wanted to be President; he needed the support of the South. Also, he was interested in seeing a railroad built from the Pacific coast to Illinois. Before this could be done, a government had to be provided for the land just west of Missouri and Iowa, called Nebraska. Attempts were made to make Nebraska a territory, but the South prevented that. They would agree, however, Southerners said, if the people of Nebraska were allowed to decide the slave question for themselves. According to the Missouri Compromise of 1820 the land was to be free. But Douglas caught the idea and proposed a bill which was finally passed. It provided, in its final form, for two territories instead of one: Nebraska, and below it, Kansas. In states made from these territories the people were to decide whether slavery would or would not exist. The Kansas-Nebraska Act of 1854 repealed the Compromise of 1820. The South had a new

chance to win control of the Senate. The act touched off a series of events which led right into war.

Douglas gained the support of the South all right, but he was soundly hated in the North, where he was frequently burned in effigy. The doctrine of popular sovereignty he had applied to Kansas and Nebraska was called "squatter sovereignty." North vied with South to see which could send the greater number of settlers into the area to decide the issue, especially in Kansas, where the South had the better chance. For two years a regular war was waged for control of Kansas—a miniature of what was to come. Things did not straighten out enough to permit Kansas to become a state until after the War between the States had begun (1861). When she did come in, it was as a free state.

Dred Scott Case. From time to time there had been considerable insistence to have the Supreme Court rule upon the status of slavery in the territories. Now a case came before it which gave it that opportunity. Dred Scott had been a slave in Missouri. He was taken by his master into Illinois, a free state, and into Minnesota, made a free territory by the Missouri Compromise. Then he was returned to Missouri. There he brought suit in the courts for his freedom, claiming that his residence in free territory entitled him to it. The lower courts ruled against him, and the case, financed by the antislavery group, was taken to the Supreme Court. Five of the nine judges were from the South. In a decision rendered March 6, 1857, the court decided that Dred Scott was still a slave, just as any other personal property would still belong to its owner, even though he had taken it with him into Illinois, Minnesota, and then back to Missouri. The decision then went on to declare the Missouri Compromise unconstitutional—that is, that Congress did not have the power to prohibit slavery in the territories. The minority opinion, taking the opposite view, was well written, but it was clear that the Su-

Meserve Collection

JOHN BROWN

A fanatical foe of slavery, he neither wanted nor gave any quarter in his fight against it.

preme Court only reflected the divided opinion already existing in the country. From then on it was also clear that the courts could not settle the matter; it was an issue the people would have to decide for themselves.

Lincoln-Douglas Debates. In Illinois, history was being made. Stephen A. Douglas was a Democratic candidate

to succeed himself in the Senate. The Republican party had been formed[2] in 1854 by men who openly opposed the extension of slavery in the territories. The Republicans now put up Abraham Lincoln to oppose Douglas. Lincoln had served one term in Congress ten years earlier and had retired from politics, but his dislike of Douglas' Kansas-Nebraska Act had brought him back into politics again.

Lincoln was definitely the underdog in the campaign. He decided to pin his hopes on showing up the contradictions and inconsistencies in Douglas' position on slavery. He challenged "the Little Giant," as Douglas was called, to a series of debates. Douglas was a self-made man, an accomplished orator and debator. Lincoln, too, was a self-made man, and he wasn't impressed with the job he had done. He was tall and awkward, and a slow speaker. However, he had the ability to put words together in a simple but powerful way. For example, when he accepted his party's nomination, he had said "A house divided against itself cannot stand. I believe this government cannot endure permanently half slave and half free. I do not expect the Union to be dissolved—I do not expect the house to fall—but I do expect it will cease to be divided. It will become all one thing, or all the other." This statement was ahead of the thinking of most people and it showed the farsightedness of the man.

There were seven debates in all.[3]

---

[2] It was not a new party, as you will see in Chapter 22. The Southerners called its members "Black Republicans" because of their stand on behalf of the slaves.

[3] The first was held in Ottawa, where this book was written.

They were the most important series of debates in our history. Lincoln, in his shrewdness, put Douglas consistently on the spot and forced him to so compromise himself in his statements that he lost the support of the South. Douglas won the seat in the Senate from Illinois, but he lost all chance of becoming President at the next election. Clear-cut division was now evident in the political parties: the Democratic party became the party of the South, the Republican the party of the industrial North. In the election of 1858 the Republicans gained control of the House of Representatives. The Democrats still held the Senate, but they could see the handwriting on the wall for the presidential election to come two years later.

John Brown's Raid. Before that election took place, however, an incident occurred which greatly increased the tension between the North and the South. John Brown was a firm believer in abolition, but he thought there was too much talk about it and not enough action. He interested some of the antislavery men in the North in his plan to free the slaves in the South by force. He proposed to establish a mountain stronghold somewhere in Virginia or Maryland and send out raiders to seize and carry off slaves. He rented a farm near Harper's Ferry, Virginia, and on October 16, 1859, he and his men overran the arsenal at Harper's Ferry. This was an armed insurrection, and Colonel Robert E. Lee and the marines were sent to put it down. Brown himself was tried, convicted, and hanged. In the North he was hailed by many as a martyr to the cause of abolition. The South was aroused for fear more attempts of a like nature would be made. Talk of leaving the Union increased.

Election of 1860. The presidential election was approaching. Two factions existed in the Democratic nominating convention held at Charleston, South Carolina (spring of 1860). The Southern Democrats demanded a platform

Meserve Collection, Chicago Historical Society

ABRAHAM LINCOLN

This likeness of the Civil War President was copied from an actual photograph taken by Alexander Gardner in Washington, four days before Lincoln was assassinated.

that sanctioned slavery. The Northern Democrats refused. The vote of the delegates on the platform supported the North's position, and Alabama, followed by seven[4] other states, walked out of the convention. Later these states held a convention of their own. The

------

[4] South Carolina, Mississippi, Louisiana, Florida, Texas, Arkansas, and Georgia. Compare this action with what happened in the Democratic convention at Philadelphia in 1948, to be discussed later.

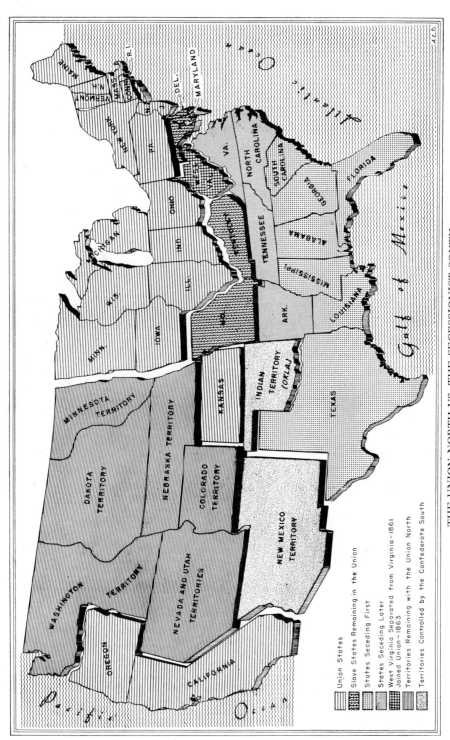

THE UNION NORTH VS. THE SECESSIONIST SOUTH

After more than three-quarters of a century of growth, the country was threatened with partition because of internal strife,

Union States

Slave States Remaining in the Union

States Seceding First

States Seceding Later

West Virginia Separated from Virginia—1861
Joined Union—1863

Territories Remaining with the Union North

Territories Controlled by the Confederate South

Northern Democrats nominated Stephen A. Douglas of Illinois for President; the Southern Democrats nominated J. C. Breckinridge, of Kentucky.

On the third ballot the Republican party selected Abraham Lincoln of Il-

Chicago Historical Society

JEFFERSON DAVIS

The man who became President of the Confederate States of America was a West Point graduate and a veteran of the Mexican War who had distinguished himself in the desperate battle of Buena Vista. After the fall of Richmond in 1865, Davis was captured and imprisoned, but he was released not long afterward. Charges of treason against him were withdrawn following the general amnesty of 1868.

linois as its candidate for President. A fourth candidate, presented by minor parties, was John Bell, of Tennessee. The other three candidates all warned that the election of the Republican candidate would mean disruption for the

Union. The people either didn't believe this or didn't care. Abraham Lincoln was elected.

The "Confederate States of America." Reaction in the South came at once. On December 20, 1860, South Carolina, in a convention, broke off the union between herself and the United States. Georgia, Alabama, Mississippi, Louisiana, Florida, and Texas followed. On February 4, 1861, the "Confederate States of America" was born at Montgomery, Alabama. Jefferson Davis became its President.

Lincoln had not yet taken office. President James Buchanan (president from 1857 to 1861) clearly favored the South. Both sides marked time. Attempts were made at a compromise, but the slavery and antislavery groups held fast to their positions. They did not realize that a new problem—one nation or two—had really displaced in importance the old problem of extension of slavery.

Another question came up. Did a state have the right to secede from the Union? The Constitution had nothing to say on this point. The Declaration of Independence supported the right of any people to revolt against their government whenever that government abuses their rights. Southerners thought they had been abused. But Lincoln made clear his position. On March 4, 1861, he took the oath of office. In his Inaugural Address he pointed out that only the people could bring on war. The government would not attack them. On the other hand, the President had taken an oath to "preserve, protect, and defend" the government, and he intended to do just that, to the best of his ability.

Chicago Historical Society

OUTBREAK OF THE WAR BETWEEN THE STATES

This view of the bombardment of Fort Sumter shows the guns of Fort Moultrie firing upon the Union stronghold in Charleston Harbor.

THE WAR BETWEEN THE STATES

The Fall of Fort Sumter. The United States still held two forts in Southern territory, Fort Pickens at Pensacola, Florida, and Fort Sumter, at Charleston, South Carolina. Certain of Lincoln's advisers wanted to withdraw the garrisons, but Lincoln determined to hold the forts if possible; he dispatched ships with aid for Fort Sumter. Before they arrived, the Confederate forces at Charleston had opened fire on April 12, 1861. The fort could not possibly hold out; Major Anderson and his men finally surrendered. Not a man was killed on either side, but the fort was wrecked.[5] The war had begun.

President Lincoln immediately

[5] Fort Pickens was reinforced and held throughout the war.

called for 75,000 volunteers; by July 1, 1861, he had 310,000 men. He declared a blockade of the Southern ports and called in the ships of the navy to make it effective.

The slave states along the border between the North and the South had to make their choice. Arkansas, Virginia, North Carolina, and Tennessee joined the Confederacy. Maryland, Kentucky, and Missouri remained in the Union.

The Opponents. Let's look at the two opponents. The South was united in a common cause which its people felt keenly. But the North had more people—22,000,000 as against 9,000,000 in the South, 3,500,000 of whom were Negroes. The slaves were valuable to the South, though, for they raised food, thereby releasing the white men to

Chicago Historical Society

BATTLE BETWEEN THE "MONITOR" AND THE "MERRIMAC"

The South's "Merrimac," rechristened the "Virginia," carried ten guns, the North's "Monitor" but two. Neither vessel, however, could put the other out of action.

fight. Not all the white Southerners had supported the cotton-growing slave-owning plantation owners up to this time, but the war united all of them against the North. The Confederate army was fighting a defensive war on its own soil, which the soldiers knew well. And Southerners considered their soldiers to be better fighters than Northern soldiers.[6] The North had the money and the factories to produce the supplies of war and the means to transport them. The South had much less transportation, no factories to speak of, and its ports were blockaded so supplies could not be brought in from the outside. In addition, and perhaps as important as all the other factors favoring it, the North had Abraham Lincoln, a leader of rare natural ability.

The Confederacy hoped to get aid from foreign countries, especially Eng-

land. The South was shipping her cotton to England and buying manufactured goods in return. Various incidents brought strained relationships between the United States and England, but war was avoided, and England did not recognize or help the Confederacy. The same, in general, was true of France. At one time, Czar Alexander of Russia sent fleets to both New York and San Francisco to show he favored the United States and to help prevent British and French recognition of the Confederacy.[7] This loss of anticipated outside aid was a bitter blow to the South.

The Blockade. Northern strategy was simple. Besides blockading the Southern coast, the Mississippi River was to be seized, thereby dividing the Confederate states. Then Northern armies would push down and capture all the seceded area.

---

[6] A Southern arithmetic textbook put it this way: "If one Confederate soldier can whip seven Federal soldiers, how many Federal soldiers can nine Confederate soldiers whip?"

[7] Czar Alexander made it clear he did this not for love of the United States, but for Russia.

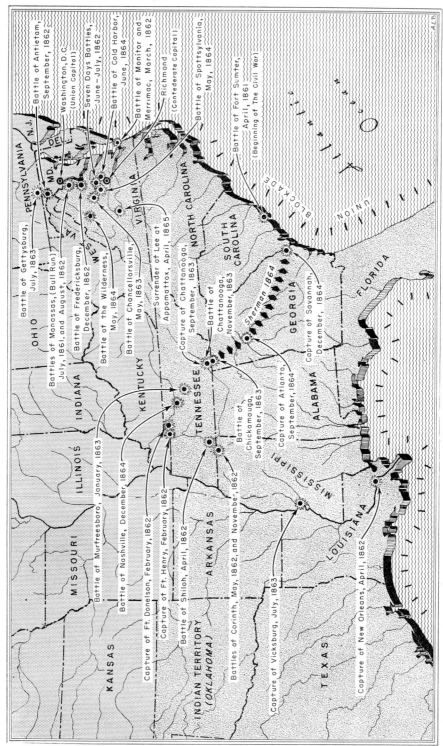

Battle of Antietam, September, 1862

Washington, D.C. (Union Capital)

Seven Days Battles, June–July, 1862

Battle of Cold Harbor, June, 1864

Battle of Monitor and Merrimac, March, 1862

Richmond (Confederate Capital)

Battle of Spottsylvania, May, 1864

Battle of Fort Sumter, April, 1861 (Beginning of The Civil War)

Battle of Gettysburg, July, 1863

Battles of Manassas, (Bull Run) July, 1861, and August, 1862

Battle of Fredericksburg, December, 1862

Battle of the Wilderness, May, 1864

Battle of Chancellorsville, May, 1863

Surrender of Lee at Appomattox, April, 1865

Battle of Chattanooga, September, 1863

Battle of Chattanooga, November, 1863

Capture of Savannah, December, 1864

Battle of Murfreesboro, January, 1863

Battle of Nashville, December, 1864

Capture of Ft. Donelson, February, 1862

Capture of Ft. Henry, February 1862

Battle of Shiloh, April, 1862

Battle of Chickamauga, September, 1863

Capture of Atlanta, September, 1864

Battles of Corinth, May, 1862, and November, 1862

Capture of Vicksburg, July, 1863

Capture of New Orleans, April, 1862

N.J.

DEL.

PENNSYLVANIA

MD.

VIRGINIA

WEST VA.

OHIO

INDIANA

ILLINOIS

KENTUCKY

NORTH CAROLINA

SOUTH CAROLINA

TENNESSEE

GEORGIA

ALABAMA

Sherman 1864

FLORIDA

MISSOURI

KANSAS

ARKANSAS

INDIAN TERRITORY (OKLAHOMA)

MISSISSIPPI

LOUISIANA

TEXAS

BLOCKADE

UNION

BATTLES OF THE CIVIL WAR

The Civil War was fought mainly on the soil of the South. Union ships blockaded Southern coasts. Yet, the Confederacy, with fewer troops and smaller industrial resources, mustered enough manpower and morale to contest the North for four full years.

The blockade was largely successful. The South tried blockade-running, but that didn't help very much. There was much suffering, as the South tried to produce for itself the goods it couldn't import. The war off the coast was marked by one important skirmish between the Northern ship "Monitor" and the Confederate "Merrimac" (early in 1862). They were both wooden vessels with iron plates bolted on their sides. The battle was a draw, but it spelled the end of wooden naval vessels.

Battle of Bull Run. In the East there was a great hue and cry for an "On to Richmond" campaign. Richmond was the Confederate capital. The Union army started out but met sudden defeat at Manassas (the first battle of Bull Run, July, 1861).[8] Union soldiers needed more training, so the campaign was called off for the time, and General George B. McClellan was given the job of getting the Army of the Potomac ready.

War in the West. Meanwhile, in the West the campaign on the Mississippi progressed. Under the leadership of General Ulysses S. ("Unconditional Surrender") Grant, control of the river as far south as Vicksburg was achieved. At the same time (April 25, 1862) Admiral David G. Farragut captured New Orleans and moved up the river. On July 4, 1863, Vicksburg surrendered to Grant, and shortly after that he and Farragut joined forces to divide the Confederate states into two parts.

War in the East. The war in the East was going badly. Repeated Union attempts to take Richmond failed, and the Army of the Potomac suffered numerous defeats at the hands of the smaller Confederate army under General Robert E. Lee. At one of these (Chancellorsville, May, 1863) Stonewall Jackson was shot by mistake in the darkness by his own men.

Gettysburg and Vicksburg. It was a question whether the Confederacy

ROBERT EDWARD LEE

The commanding general of the Confederate armies.

could be defeated. Lee now invaded the North, marching into Pennsylvania. The Army of the Potomac, now under General George G. Meade, gave battle at Gettysburg.[9] After three days of fierce fighting, Lee was forced to retreat. He had lost 23,000 men, and

---

[8] It was in this battle that Confederate General Thomas J. Jackson got the name of "Stonewall."

[9] On November 19 of the same year (1863) a part of the battlefield was dedicated as a national cemetery. On that occasion Lincoln gave his famous Gettysburg Address.

Chicago Historical Society

GETTYSBURG (left panel)

The great expanse of the Gettysburg battlefield (25,000 acres) is shown in two panoramic paintings in which the artist depicts one of the few great battles of the Civil War fought on Northern soil. This struggle, which took place in lower Pennsylvania, was a crucial one, not only because of its magnitude, but also because of its power to affect general morale in

Meade, 18,000. The battle ended just the day before Grant's victory at Vicksburg. The North had some good news for a change.

Sherman's "March to the Sea." General Grant was now placed in command of all Union armies. His job was to go after Lee, while General William T. Sherman, Commander of Union forces in the West, went deep into the South and tried for Atlanta. Grant fought his way south and laid siege to Petersburg, the southern defense of Richmond. Sherman took Atlanta and then began his famous "march to the sea." Ordering his men to live off the land, he cut a swath of destruction through Georgia 60 miles wide and 360 miles long from Atlanta to Savannah. In his report Sherman said: "I estimate the damage done to the state of Georgia and its military resources at $100,000,-000, at least $20,000,000 of which had inured to our advantage and the remainder is simply waste and destruction." It was one of those unfortunate and unnecessary things that often hap-

pen in time of war. But it had its effect; it broke the heart of the South.

The Surrender of Lee. Lee, at Richmond, was afraid Grant might catch him there, so he withdrew and let the Army of the Potomac take the Confederate capital city. Then Grant pursued Lee and caught him at Appomattox Court House, southwest of Richmond. There, on April 9, 1865, Lee surrendered. In a striking new Gray uniform, with a bejeweled sword, the dignified Lee presented a sharp contrast to Grant, who wore the straps of a lieutenant-general on a private's Blue uniform.[10] Grant was generous. He refused Lee's sword and allowed the men in Gray to keep their horses "for the spring plowing." The South's struggle for independence was over.[11]

---

[10] It was a meeting of two great leaders. Lee praised Grant highly, saying he did not know in all history his superior as a general. Lee is considered by many to be America's greatest soldier.

[11] Lee's surrender meant the end, although the last Confederate army held out until April 26.

GETTYSBURG (*right panel*)

the North. By midyear of 1863, many civilians in the North and not a few Union soldiers in the ranks were wavering in their will to prosecute the war. Northern enthusiasm was at low ebb. The Federal victory that materialized on the third day of the battle turned back the invasion from the South, and put new life and hope in the Union cause.

The Assassination of Lincoln. With almost the precision of a Hollywood production, the assassination of President Lincoln five days later rang down the curtain on one of the most unfortunate and destructive wars in history —a war that found not only the nation divided but families as well: brother fought against brother and father against son. On the evening of April 14, 1865, the President and Mrs. Lincoln attended Ford's Theater in Washington. During the performance John Wilkes Booth stepped into the President's box and shot him. It was part of a plot to kill several high government officials. That same evening Secretary of State Seward was stabbed, but not fatally.

The following morning the President died. In the North the joy of victory was turned to sadness. Even in the South the loss was felt deeply, for people there knew of his kindness, his patience, and his generosity. General Johnston spoke for many of them when he called Lincoln "the best friend the South had." His simple view of the war

as a task he had to do won the admiration of friend and foe alike. His best

ULYSSES SIMPSON GRANT

An earlier photo before he was appointed to command the Union armies.

expression of that task is in the well-known words of his Second Inaugural

U.S. *Department of the Interior*

MANEUVER AT VICKSBURG

In a daring passage, the Union fleet of gunboats and transports ran past the Confederate batteries at Vicksburg in the grand campaign to reduce the Mississippi fortress.

Address: "With malice toward none, with charity for all, with firmness in the right, as God gives us to see the right, let us strive on to finish the work we are in, to bind up the nation's wounds, to care for him who shall have borne the battle and for his widow and his orphan, to do all which may achieve and cherish a just and lasting peace among ourselves and with all nations."

RECONSTRUCTION FOLLOWING THE WAR

Emancipation Proclamation. The war was over. The Union had been preserved. The right of any state to secede had been denied by force of arms. The Union was more powerful than any of the states. But what about slavery?

President Lincoln had stated that the war was being fought to preserve the Union and not to free the slaves. If freeing any or all slaves would save the Union, he would gladly do it. If freeing none of them would keep the states together, he would do that, too. In the early months of the war, when things were going badly for the Union, Mr. Lincoln realized that the slave question would have to be met. The slaves were of too much help to the Confederacy. On September 23, 1862, the President issued his Emancipation Proclamation, declaring that on January 1, 1863, all slaves in states still in rebellion would be free. It was a war measure intended to induce some of the Confederate states to give up. It failed to cause any state to quit; the only way it could be enforced was by conquest.

GRANT AND LEE AT APPOMATTOX

The courageous leader of the Southern forces felt that further resistance would be futile. The Federal blockade had deprived the South of needed supplies, and large pools of trained manpower were swelling Union armies. Putting an end to hostilities would avert useless sacrifice. Lee surrendered—Grant wrote an honorable peace.

Within a short time, however, the loyal slave states of Missouri, Maryland, and West Virginia set their slaves free, as did Tennessee after she was conquered.

Thirteenth Amendment. As the end of the war approached, Congress wasn't sure that the Emancipation Proclamation would stand up in the courts and it prepared an amendment to the Constitution. By the end of the year (1865) it had been ratified by enough states to put it into effect. The Thirteenth Amendment says "Neither slavery nor involuntary servitude, except as punishment for crime whereof the party shall have been duly convicted, shall exist within the United States, or any place subject to their jurisdiction." So slavery was abolished in the United States and its territories.

Fourteenth and Fifteenth Amendments. Three years later (June, 1866), to clarify the status of freed Negro slaves, the Fourteenth Amendment was added. It defines citizens of the United States as "all persons born or naturalized in the United States and subject to the jurisdiction thereof." It denies to any state the power to limit the rights of any citizen. The amendment recognizes, however, the right of a state to deny the right of vote to male citizens for reasons it may set up. This obviously

FIRST READING OF THE EMANCIPATION PROCLAMATION

The original painting by F. B. Carpenter portrays Lincoln reading the first draft of the Proclamation to his Cabinet on July 22, 1862. Preliminary announcement of the order was made on September 22, 1862, and the Proclamation was officially issued on January 1, 1863.

gave the South the means for keeping Negro citizens from voting, so in 1870 the Fifteenth Amendment was added. It states pointedly that "the right of citizens of the United States to vote shall not be denied or abridged by the United States or by any State on account of race, color, or previous condition of servitude."

The Republican Congress was anxious to make up for lost time on the slave question. As we look back over it now, apparently a better policy would have been a slow preparation of the Negro for citizenship with a gradual extension of rights and privileges to him as he became able to handle them. Much that was unfortunate in the reconstruction period in the South fol-

lowing the war might have been prevented.

Conditions in the South. Reconstruction—patching the war-torn Union together again—wasn't simple. The South was in bad condition. Most of her trade was gone. Since she could not import goods, she had found it necessary to learn to produce many new things. Plantation mansions were turned into factories where the women and slaves made, by hand, the clothing and supplies the soldiers needed. Food was very scarce in some parts and abundant in others because there was little or no transportation. "Hard" money, too, was scarce, and quantities of paper money were printed. Prices were high: flour cost $1,000 a barrel and shoes

FACSIMILE OF THE EMANCIPATION PROCLAMATION

Most of the text of the original draft of the Proclamation was hand-written by Lincoln. The original instrument was destroyed in the Great Chicago Fire of 1871.

$200 a pair. By the end of the war the Confederate paper money was worthless. Cities were burned out, plantation buildings destroyed. And in the midst of all this the slaves had gone right on working to help the South—the very slaves the North was fighting to set free.

SCENE OF LINCOLN'S ASSASSINATION

An artist's sketch depicts John Wilkes Booth invading the presidential box in Ford's Theater, Washington, D.C., on the night of April 14, 1865, during a performance of *Our American Cousin*. As Mr. and Mrs. Lincoln, together with Major Henry Rathbone and his fiancée, faced the stage, Booth approached unnoticed and fatally shot the President with a derringer, and then slashed Major Rathbone with a dagger.

Conditions in the North. It was a different story in the North. There was a great demand for everything that could be produced. Agriculture flourished and industry expanded. As usual in time of war, there was considerable "profiteering." Many people became wealthy. Over against this, though, was the heavy loss of life of the men in Blue.

The Share-Cropper. The South's one hope was to get cotton to growing again. Soon planters had worked out an arrangement with their former slaves by which the slave rented land from the plantation owner. The Negro got equipment and supplies from the owner and paid the rent with a share of his crop—often as much as two-thirds. Before long the share-cropper had become a fixture in the South, not only among Negroes but among the poor white population as well.

Plans for Reconstruction. What was to be done about the Confederate states? Northerners went to opposite extremes in their answers. Some felt the Southern states should be considered conquered territory and treated as such. Others, like Lincoln, took the position that the states had been unsuccessful in trying to leave the Union and must only prove their loyalty to it now to come back into good standing.

President Lincoln had a plan for reconstruction. He would pardon all Confederates who would take an oath to be loyal to the Union, and return their property to them, except their former slaves. Excluded from this were the leaders in the Confederate government or the Confederate army during the war; the old leadership was not to regain control. When one-tenth as many men as voted in the election of 1860 had taken this oath, a state government could be organized. In due time it was expected Congress would permit such a state to send representatives to Washington again. In addition, every such state must ratify the Thirteenth Amendment. It was the kind of liberal program befitting a great President.

But Mr. Lincoln never had the chance to put it into operation. After his death, Vice-President Andrew Johnson became President. He hated slavery, although a Southerner himself, and might have been harsh with the South had he not been persuaded to follow a program much like Lincoln's. Most of the Southern states met the plan, but when Congress convened, it refused to accept what the President had done. Apparently it wanted to exert its power over the President and to deal more harshly with the South. The Republicans had been Abolitionists, and now they wanted to see the Negro given full rights. They felt sure most of them would join the Republican party.

Congress now set up its own plan for reconstruction. It divided the South into five military districts to be ruled by a military government. Negro men were to be permitted to vote, but not Confederate leaders. The voters were to create the new state governments. In most states the result was bad. Many of the Northerners who came down to help in reconstruction were crafty swindlers who came to be called "carpetbaggers" because they carried all their possessions with them in a bag made of carpet. Even worse were the unscrupulous white Southerners who joined them, called "scalawags." The new governments were dominated by Negroes who could neither read nor write, "carpetbaggers," and "scala-wags." Corruption was common; law was disregarded; the public debt mounted; and general chaos reigned. But the sensible Southerners could do nothing; the new governments were backed up by United States troops.

President Johnson's opposition to what Congress had done was open and violent. The struggle between the two became more and more bitter. Finally the House of Representatives impeached Johnson, and from March to May, 1868, he was on trial before the Senate. That body lacked just one vote of convicting the President. Johnson has been our only President to be impeached, and certainly the action taken against him was unjustified.

Secret Societies. By 1870 all the Southern states had been restored to the Union. In an attempt to hold down the Negro's power, men organized secret societies whose members went around at night in white robes to scare the Negroes and keep them from voting. The best known of these organizations was the Ku Klux Klan. As could be expected, what had started out as a harmless means of playing upon the Negro's superstition soon became an instrument of violence. Eventually, under federal leadership, such organizations were suppressed.

Southern Whites in Control. In 1877 the last United States troops were withdrawn from the South, and the carpetbag governments soon fell. Before long Southern whites were back in control again. Restrictions were set up to prevent Negroes from voting. They were required to pay a poll tax (a tax at the polls before voting, which most of them couldn't pay), to be able to read and write (most of them couldn't), and to be able to explain the Constitution (Could you?). Ways were found to permit uneducated whites to get around these limitations. You get more about this in Chapter 21.

In general, Southerners despised the reconstruction period more than they did the war. They thought the North was trying to humiliate them at the hands of their former slaves. To have their land, after surrender, occupied by Northern troops was a bitter pill to swallow. The Republican Congress was responsible for most of this; practically all the Southerners joined the Democratic party. Since then the Southern states have been known as the "solid South."

So the struggle was over. The states remained united in one Union. The power of the states had been made secondary to a union of free people. The United States was a single unit, not just a loose federation of independent states. The Negro was free. He had the Constitutional right to vote but found it denied to him throughout most of the South. The Union was preserved, but the racial problem was not yet completely solved. In fact, it is not completely solved today.

FOR YOUR REVIEW

These Should Be Easy for You Now

1. Why did the Southern colonist like to use slaves? Why was slavery not mentioned in the original Constitution? Why did the North have less use for slaves than the South?
2. How widespread was slave ownership in the South?

3. Distinguish between tariff for revenue and protective tariff. Why did the South dislike protective tariffs?
4. Explain the Southern conception of states' rights.
5. What was the doctrine of nullification? What stand did President Jackson take on it?
6. What did the Ordinance of Nullification do? How was the matter disposed of temporarily?
7. What conditions led to the Compromise of 1820? What did it provide for?
8. Who were the Abolitionists?
9. Why was California settled so quickly?
10. What events led to the Compromise of 1850? What were its terms? On what point did it break down?
11. How did the Kansas-Nebraska Act repeal the Compromise of 1820?
12. What was the Dred Scott case? What was the general effect of the decision?
13. What is the significance of the Lincoln-Douglas debates?
14. What did John Brown try to do? What effect did he have upon the North-South difficulty?
15. Who was elected President in 1860? What party did he represent?
16. With what incident did the War between the States actually begin?
17. Make lists of the states that remained in the Union and those that joined the Confederacy.
18. Compare the advantages and disadvantages of the North and South at the outbreak of the war.
19. From what other countries did the South hope to get help? Was she successful?
20. What was the Union strategy for the war?
21. Why is the battle between the "Monitor" and the "Merrimac" important?
22. Why did the North want to take Richmond? How did the campaign turn out?
23. What two leaders co-operated to cut the Confederate states into two parts?
24. What was the effect of the Battle of Gettysburg? Of Sherman's march to the sea?
25. When and how did the War between the States end? What did the Union victory decide?
26. What was the purpose of the Emancipation Proclamation? Was it successful?
27. What does the Thirteenth Amendment to the United States Constitution do? The Fourteenth? The Fifteenth?
28. How had the war affected the South? The North?
29. What plan had President Lincoln had for reconstruction? What plan did Congress adopt? What kinds of government were set up in the Southern states? How was this changed after Union troops were withdrawn?
30. How did the war affect the politics of the South?

Associated Dates

1619—first Negroes brought to the New World (Virginia)
1793—invention of the cotton gin (Eli Whitney)
1793—first successful cotton mill in the United States (Pawtucket, R.I.)
1828—Tariff of Abominations
1830—Webster-Hayne debates
1852—*Uncle Tom's Cabin* published
1854—Kansas-Nebraska Act, May 30
      Republican party formed
1857—Dred Scott decision, March 6
1858—Lincoln-Douglas debates

1860—Lincoln elected President
 South Carolina secedes from the Union, December 20
1861—Confederate States of America formed, February 4
 Fort Sumter fired on, April 12
 Battle of Bull Run, July 21
1862—Battle of the "Monitor" and the "Merrimac," March 9
 Admiral Farragut takes New Orleans, April 25
 Second Battle of Bull Run, August 30
1863—Emancipation Proclamation issued, January 1
 Battle of Gettysburg, July 1–3
 Vicksburg taken by Grant, July 4
 Lincoln's Gettysburg Address delivered, November 19
1864—Sherman takes Atlanta, September 2
 Sherman takes Savannah, December 21
1865—Fall of Richmond, April 3
 Lee surrenders at Appomattox, April 9
 President Lincoln assassinated, April 14; Andrew Jackson becomes President
 Thirteenth Amendment ratified, December 18
1868—Fourteenth Amendment ratified, July 28
1869—Ulysses S. Grant becomes President, March 4
1870—Fifteenth Amendment ratified, March 30

Why Are These To Be Remembered?

Eli Whitney
Samuel Slater
John C. Calhoun
Robert Y. Hayne
Daniel Webster
Henry Clay
William Lloyd Garrison
Stephen A. Douglas
Dred Scott
John Brown
Jefferson Davis
Stonewall Jackson
General George B.
 McClellan
General Ulysses S. Grant
Admiral David G. Farragut

General Robert E. Lee
General George G. Meade
John Wilkes Booth
Abraham Lincoln
Harper's Ferry
Fort Pickens
Fort Sumter
Richmond
Protective tariff
Tariff of Abominations
"South Carolina Exposi-
 tion"
Ordinance of Nullification
Compromise of 1820
Abolitionists
Popular sovereignty

Underground railroad
General William T.
 Sherman
Manassas
Vicksburg
Gettysburg
Appomattox
Confederacy
"Monitor" and "Merrimac"
Emancipation Proclama-
 tion
Share-cropper
Carpetbagger
Scalawags
Ku Klux Klan
Poll tax

Suggested Readings

EMMONS, DELLA F. G., *Sacajawea of the Shoshones*
 One of the key figures of the Lewis & Clark expedition
FINGER, C. J., *Cape Horn Snorter*
 The war of 1812
NICHOLSON, MEREDITH, *The Cavalier of Tennessee*
 Andrew Jackson
PIDGIN, C. F., *Blennerhasset*
 Story of Aaron Burr

PEATTIE, DONALD C., *Forward the Nation*
 Lewis & Clark expedition
HOLLAND, R. S., *Freedom's Flag*
 Francis Scott Key and "The Star Spangled Banner"
ALDRICH, BESS STREETER, *Song of Years*
 The settlers come to Iowa
BINNS, ARCHIE, *The Land Is Bright*
 The Westward movement along the Oregon Trail

DAVIS, J. F., *The Road to San Jacinto*
Independence in Texas
EHRLICH, LEONARD, *God's Angry Man*
The story of John Brown
QUINN, VERNON, *War-Paint and Powder-horn*
Story of the Santa Fe Trail
COLE, A. C., *The Irrepressible Conflict, 1850–1865*
Conditions that brought on the War between the States
KANTOR, MACKINLAY, *Long Remember*
The Battle of Gettysburg

WILLIAMS, BEN AMES, *House Divided*
The War between the States
YOUNG, STARK, *So Red the Rose*
The South before and during the war
SANDBURG, CARL, *Abraham Lincoln, the Prairie Years*
SANDBURG, CARL, *Storm Over the Land*
The War between the States
WASHINGTON, BOOKER T., *Up from Slavery*
A famous Negro's story of his people after the war

The United States Reaches the Stature of a World Power

INTRODUCTION

In the second half of the nineteenth century the United States expanded its control beyond the continental limits of the North American continent. In various ways we acquired territory in different parts of the Atlantic and Pacific Oceans, notably the Philippine Islands, where we were on the very shores of Asia and were projected definitely into Asiatic affairs. Our "open door" policy for China greatly enhanced our position in Asia. Shortly after the beginning of the new century we played mediator to end the Russo-Japanese War.

Various Latin American countries have at times looked with considerable question upon the avowed friendliness of the United States, accusing us of economic imperialism. The "good neighbor" policy of Franklin D. Roosevelt was designed to overcome this feeling among our sister republics to the south.

For a long time Great Britain's balance-of-power policy had kept her the world's greatest power. But early in the twentieth century Germany built up her military power to the point that she was ready to challenge Britain's position. World War I resulted, and the United States was drawn into it in 1917.

When the war was over, the United States attempted to withdraw from world affairs. Our people were disillusioned because the war had not brought the results we had hoped for. But as the years passed, it became clear that a nation cannot stay out of world affairs simply by deciding that she will not be involved. Sometimes world developments reach out and engulf her anyway. So, in spite of our desires, we were forcibly projected into World War II.

Chapter 11

The United States Expands Beyond Its Continental Limits

THE UNITED STATES BECOMES A WORLD POWER BUT DOESN'T REALIZE
THE FULL SIGNIFICANCE OF THE DEVELOPMENT

American Foreign Trade. We have already seen (in Chapter 9) how the United States had grown as much as it naturally could on the North American continent. But it didn't stop there. Today American possessions include many territories outside North America, some of them thousands of miles away. The continued growth was due chiefly to two things: our expanding trade and our sticking to the Monroe Doctrine as a major part of our foreign policy.

Before the Revolution the colonists had enjoyed a prosperous trade in the British Empire. The Revolution changed all that; trade and shipbuilding virtually died out, but commerce recovered quickly after the war was over, and new areas of trade were opened up. Two years after the treaty of peace was signed, the "Empress of China" completed a round trip from New York City to Canton, China, and back again. It brought silk and tea from China. But what to trade for these Oriental goods?

The answer was soon found. Some sea captains from the eastern coast were trying to establish fur trade with the Indians of the Northwest. One of them, Captain Gray, who discovered the Columbia River, sailed on to China with a cargo of furs and came back

with a ship full of tea. Soon a flourishing trade with China was going on.

American foreign trade suffered another setback during the War of 1812, when both England and France interfered with our shipping. The Embargo and Non-Intercourse Acts of our own government, intended to hurt England and France, almost ruined our commerce.

After the war was over, business picked up again. Soon came the period of the famous clipper ships—those streamlined sailing vessels that carried a maximum of canvas in sails and attained unheard-of speeds. One of them covered 436 miles in a single day. Time after time these famous ships "rounded the Horn" (Cape Horn, at the southern tip of South America) on their way from New York or Boston to San Francisco, Canton (China), or Singapore (Malaya). The best known of these clipper ships was the "Flying Cloud."

The Opening of China. The British were already firmly established in India. From there, British merchants smuggled opium, made from Indian poppies, around the Malay peninsula, up the east coast of Asia, and into China. Chinese leaders didn't want the drug in their country; they knew the undesirable effects its use had on peo-

136

ple. But all appeals to England to stop the trade were useless. Finally, in 1839, China took up arms against Britain to try to stop the traffic in opium. Of course, the Chinese lost. England got Hong Kong, and five Chinese ports were opened to foreign trade.[1] China tried again a few years later (1856–1860); this second Opium War opened more ports and legalized the trade of opium in China.

The United States, as well as England and other European countries, profited from the opening of China. Of all of the nations that moved into China, bent on carving out their own spheres of influence, the United States was looked upon more favorably than the others because she appeared least inclined to take land for herself. People who settled in China were granted *extraterritoriality*—that is, if they committed any crime, they were privileged to be tried in their own courts and not in Chinese courts.[2] American relationship with China has been especially friendly and profitable during most of the years since China was reopened to trade.

Japan Is Westernized. There had been no corresponding trade with Japan. From the days of Marco Polo[3] and Francis Xavier,[4] Europeans had been helping themselves to the re-

sources of both China and Japan. Christianity gained a strong foothold in Japan. Then a new leader[5] came to power. He was fearful of the power of the priests and rebellious at the exploitation of foreign traders. The new religion was banned and all foreigners driven out. Decrees were issued to prevent any Japanese from leaving the country and any foreigner from coming to Japan.[6] The isolation of Japan was completed by 1638.

Japan remained closed to the outside world for more than two centuries. American sailors, unfortunate enough to be shipwrecked on Japanese islands, were badly mistreated. Finally the United States decided something should be done about it. In 1853 Commodore Matthew C. Perry was sent with a fleet of ships and a letter for the Emperor of Japan. Perry took along with him several new inventions—such as a sewing machine, a complete telegraph system, and a small scale railroad that actually worked. Western ingenuity and American guns turned the trick. Japan opened her ports to foreign trade once more.[7]

---

[1] China had been closed to most of the outside world since 1724. Her self-imposed isolation was set up because foreigners were engaging in wholesale exploitation of China's resources.

[2] The United States voluntarily gave up this special privilege during the war of 1941–1945.

[3] Early explorer whose tales of Cathay (China) greatly increased Europeans' interest in the Far East.

[4] Founder of the Jesuits, who introduced Christianity into Japan.

[5] A member of the Tokugawa family.

[6] The only exception was one Dutch trading ship a year, which was permitted to dock at an island in Nagasaki harbor. This was a reward for the assistance of Dutch merchantmen that had shelled Nagasaki castle where the last of the persecuted Christians had fled. They were Roman Catholics, and the Dutch had just revolted successfully against the domination of Roman Catholic Philip II of Spain.

[7] "Coming events cast their shadows before." In addressing the Emperor at the time of Perry's visit, Lord Hatta said: "The present condition of the world shows that it is lacking in a ruler sufficiently powerful and virtuous, under whom all countries could be united. Among the rulers of the world at present, there is none so noble and illustrious as to command universal vassalage, or who can make his virtuous influence felt throughout

But Japan's experience with the outside world was no better this time than it had been before 1638. Again Japan tried to drive the foreigners out (1863). That was when we joined with the British to send some warships up the coast of the islands and to literally blow some towns off the map to let the Japanese know we were there to stay. Immediately Japanese strategy changed. Clearly Japan couldn't accomplish her purpose with the ancient methods she was using. She must modernize, must adopt the ways of the Westerner so she would be able to meet him on his own level of development. Accordingly, Japan set out upon a great period of change. She began to westernize herself, particularly her military and industrial systems. We were glad to help her, not realizing that eventually she would use her new skills against us. Japan's relations with the United States were very friendly until the middle 1930's.

AMERICA ACQUIRES NEW POSSESSIONS

Pan-Americanism. After the Monroe Doctrine was issued, the United States

---

the length and breadth of the whole world. To have such a ruler over the whole world is doubtless in conformity with the Will of Heaven. Before the countries of the world can be unified under a great ruler, international conditions show the necessity of establishing relations among the nations . . . in establishing relations with foreign countries, the object should always be kept in view of laying a foundation for securing the hegemony over all nations . . . .

"Our national prestige and position thus secured, the nations of the world will come to look up to our Emperor as the Great Ruler of all the nations, and they will come to follow our policy and submit themselves to our judgment. This ideal realized, the Ruler of Japan will have accomplished a deed commensurate with the great responsibilities he owes to Heaven and Earth."

more or less lost interest in South America. Although the doctrine opened the way for closer co-operation among the nations of the Americas, nothing much was done about it until 1889, when the first Pan-American conference was held in Washington. Nothing very important was accomplished, but the International Union of American Republics was formed (April 14, 1890); this was the forerunner of our present day Pan-American Union, housed in a fine marble building in Washington, the gift of Andrew Carnegie. The ministers of the Latin-American nations represent their countries in the Union.

Later meetings of the new organization were largely unproductive, too, until the administration of Franklin Roosevelt began in 1933. The principal reason for this was the fact that the Latin American countries came to feel they could not trust the United States. Their fears were not wholly unfounded, as we shall see.

The Venezuelan Boundary Dispute. Trouble had been brewing between Venezuela and Great Britain over territory. Britain owned a part of Guiana on the north coast of South America. The boundary between the colony and Venezuela was under dispute; England kept pushing the border over to take in more and more of Venezuelan territory. When England refused to arbitrate the matter, it looked as if her intention was to keep on seizing land in violation of our Monroe Doctrine. In 1895 President Grover Cleveland, in a stern note to Britain, demanded that she submit the boundary question to arbitration. Again England refused, and it appeared we might have to use force to uphold the Monroe Doctrine. But other circumstances caused England to change her attitude, and the boundary dispute was successfully arbitrated. The circumstances that caused England to alter her position were those which were leading Britain into a war in South Africa with the Boers, Dutch farmers who had settled there and from whom England had taken Cape Colony. Again, as several times before (see Chapter 9), a showdown on our foreign policy had been avoided.

The people of Venezuela were grateful for the assistance of the United States, but Latin Americans in general wondered about a statement in the United States' message to England which said that "today the United States is practically sovereign on this continent." Latin Americans became suspicious as to what that meant for them.

The Cuban Revolt. Our attitude toward Cuba increased this distrust. Before the War between the States the South had looked longingly at Cuba as a possible addition to the Southern slave bloc. After the war our interest in Cuba grew for two reasons. First, a great deal of American capital was invested in Cuban sugar plantations, and the investors didn't want to lose their money. Second, Cuba was agitating for independence from Spain, a European empire-builder. We remembered our ancestors' experiences in a like situation and were extremely sympathetic.

The revolution for independence broke out in Cuba in 1868 and continued intermittently for thirty years. It was given added impetus in 1894 when a new American tariff law placed a duty on sugar imports to favor home production. The new tariff brought hardships to the Cuban sugar plantations and more unrest to the people. Both sides were guilty of cruelty and destruction, but the Spanish received more publicity in this country. There was already considerable sentiment against Spain. Some people felt that Cuba naturally belonged with the United States and that we ought to take it. We had tried unsuccessfully to buy the island. Others believed that the Monroe Doctrine should be used not only to prevent outside nations from expanding their holdings in the Western Hemisphere but also to dispossess them of colonies they already held. Spain had only two colonies left in this hemisphere: Cuba and Puerto Rico. By seizure, usually followed by payment, the United States had taken all Spanish territory in the Americas that had not won its freedom.

Sinking of the "Maine." Private individuals in the United States aided the Cuban rebels. This didn't help matters. Spain seized some of the people engaged in this business and executed a number of them. These Americans had not been acting under the authority of their government, but feeling in the United States reached a high pitch. Early in 1898 the battleship "Maine" was sent to the harbor at Havana to protect American interests. On February 15 the ship was mysteriously blown up with the loss of 260 men. The cause of the explosion was never learned nor the responsibility for it fixed. It only served to increase the tension between the United States and Spain. From then on "Remember the 'Maine'!" became the war cry in the United States.

War with Spain. President William McKinley now demanded that the Spanish stop their practice of putting Cubans into concentration camps and that an armistice be arranged with the Cuban rebels. Spanish diplomats maneuvered for a time, and McKinley prepared a war message for Congress. The people were anxious for war with Spain. On April 5, 1898, the Spanish Queen promised that her troops would stop fighting if the Cubans would. On April 10 word came that an armistice had been declared. The President was informed by our representative that Spain did not want war with the United States and would agree to anything we wanted to do about Cuba.

Although we had everything we had asked for, and more, President McKinley sent his war message to Congress on April 11. War officially began on April 21.[8]

It wasn't much of a war. Assistant Secretary of the Navy Theodore Roosevelt had alerted Commodore George Dewey and the Pacific fleet at Hong Kong, China, to be ready to proceed against Spain in the Philippines. Dewey went immediately when war started and destroyed the Spanish fleet at Manila (not an American was killed). Then he blockaded the port until American troops arrived. Manila surrendered on August 13.

In Cuba, a Spanish fleet was bottled up in Santiago harbor. A hastily organized army[9] landed and began the land attack on the city. When the outcome became evident, the Spanish fleet tried to run the blockade and was destroyed. Two weeks later the city surrendered. Shortly after the fall of Santiago (July 17), American troops landed in Puerto Rico (July 21), where they met with almost no opposition.

Spain was beaten; she asked for an armistice (signed August 12, 1898, and ratified February 6, 1899). The terms McKinley laid down were harsh, but they were the terms upon which the peace was made. Spain granted Cuba its independence. The United States got Puerto Rico and Guam in the far Pacific. Manila had not surrendered until the day after the armistice was signed, but President McKinley demanded that Spain sell the Philippine Islands to us. That was what the American people wanted. Spain didn't like it, but there was nothing she could do about it. She gave up the Philippines for $20,000,000. The transaction marked the end of the once great Spanish empire.

Much as we disliked the way the Spanish were treating the Cubans, there was no excuse for war. A wide gulf of misunderstanding, however, brought conflict. We promised to withdraw our forces from Cuba when her independence was achieved. Before we took them out in 1902, we made many improvements in government, sanitation, and education, but we forced the Cubans to place certain provisions in their constitution which virtually made the island a protectorate of the United States. We reserved the right to send troops in at any time to keep order or to preserve Cuban independence. Also, Cuba agreed to sell or lease to us ports we might want for coaling stations.

The Philippines. Most of the people of the United States did not realize the significance of what had happened.

---

[8] It was necessary to get word to the Cuban rebels that the United States was at war with Spain. There was no radio; the message had to be taken personally. It was entrusted to a Lieutenant Rowan. The story of how he delivered the message to the rebel leader prompted Elbert Hubbard to write his famous essay, "A Message To Garcia." It was more widely translated during the lifetime of the author than anything else ever written.

[9] In it were the famous "Rough Riders," under Theodore Roosevelt and Leonard Wood. Roosevelt had resigned from the Navy Department to join the regiment.

Bettmann Archive

TEDDY ROOSEVELT LEADS HIS ROUGH RIDERS AT SAN JUAN HILL

At the outbreak of the Spanish-American War, Roosevelt and his friend Leonard Wood, a young army surgeon, organized the 1st U.S. Volunteer Cavalry. In command of the regiment, Roosevelt personally led the assault at San Juan which resulted in a spectacular American victory.

When we got the Philippines, the United States became so involved in world affairs that we could not possibly withdraw. No longer were we a continental power. We had literally "stuck our neck out" all the way across the big Pacific Ocean. And we were in no way ready or capable to live up to the job we had taken on. We were not equipped to defend the Philippines against a major power in 1899. In fact, we weren't ready even in 1941, when the test did come.

Defeating the Spanish didn't end our trouble in the Philippines. The Filipinos did not want to be ruled by the Americans any more than by the Spaniards. It took us three years to subdue the islanders. Then a government was gradually set up, with a governor appointed by the President, and a two-house legislature, the lower one to be made up of Filipinos. But the general feeling was that independence could not come for a long time. We thought the Filipinos were not nearly as far advanced as the Cubans. The United States began a program of education, sanitation, and preparation of the people for self-government. As time went on, the natives were given greater political privileges. With these improvements came greater prosperity. In 1934 Congress passed a law promising to grant independence to the islands in about ten years. Then, as a war meas-

Chicago Historical Society

THE UNITED STATES EMERGES AS A GROWING NAVAL POWER

Shown here is an artist's conception of the U.S.S. "Indiana," a front-line battleship of our Navy at the turn of the century.

ure to strengthen resistance to the Japanese in the islands, Congress recognized the independence of the Philippine Islands late in 1943, although actual freedom did not come to the islands until July 4, 1946.

Puerto Rico. Puerto Rico has not fared so well. Although her people are citizens of the United States, she has not yet been given complete home rule, much less independence. The economic condition in the island is bad. Few natives own any land of their own; instead, they work on large sugar or tobacco plantations owned by American capital. A poor sugar or tobacco market means hard times in Puerto Rico, and the population is so large, its support is difficult even in good times.

Hawaiian Islands. Between the Philippines and the United States lay

the Hawaiian Islands. Hawaii's history was in some ways similar to that of Texas. American traders and missionaries had operated in Hawaii for years, and in 1884 the United States was granted the use of Pearl Harbor as a naval base. American capital was invested in the sugar and pineapple plantations. American interests really ran the islands. A native princess tried to change this; she wanted to rule the islands herself. The Americans revolted (1893), while the marines looked on, and overthrew the native government. Then they asked to be annexed to the United States. But President Cleveland felt such action was too imperialistic, so the Americans set up a republic in Hawaii. Next came the action against Spain in the Philippines in the war of 1898, and the value of Hawaii to our fleet became apparent. Congress hastened to annex Hawaii before the war was ended.

Samoan Islands. The United States was not the only nation interested in Pacific islands. Other empire-building nations were busy there, too, particularly Great Britain and Germany. The interests of all three first came into direct conflict in the Samoan Islands. By the middle of the nineteenth century the United States, Great Britain, and Germany had established trading posts there. There was usually considerable turmoil among the natives, and in 1877 they offered the islands to the United States. The government still remembered our traditional anti-imperialistic policy and refused. But the next year we made a treaty with the natives by which we got the use of the harbor of Pago Pago (pronounced Pango Pango) for a coaling station and agreed to protect the islands to the best of our ability. Then the natives made similar treaties with England and Germany.

Germany tried to seize the advantage by promoting a revolution to put in power a chieftain favorable to her. The situation became tense, and for a time it looked as if war was coming. In March of 1889 there were in the harbor at Apia three American warships, three German, and one British. Then on March 16 a hurricane swept in and beached all the ships except the British man-of-war. With the equipment for fighting gone, the three nations had to go back to negotiations again, and an agreement was reached for the joint protection of the islands. This didn't work very well, though. In 1899 England withdrew, and the United States and Germany divided the islands between them. The United States took Manua and Tutuila, with its harbor at Pago Pago; Germany took the rest. The German islands came under British rule as mandates after World War I.

Other Pacific Islands. From time to time the United States has obtained other islands in the Pacific. Their chief value has been as coaling and cable stations and, in more recent years, as bases on the transpacific air lanes. Among these island possessions are Baker, Jarvis, Howland, Midway, Johnston, Palmyra, Wake, and the Aleutian Islands that stretch out from Alaska toward Asia.[10] The United States has rather extensive holdings in the Pacific.

Two More States? Alaska and Hawaii are, at present, self-governing territories of the United States. According to that status, each has a locally elected legislature, and each sends a delegate to the House of Representatives in Washington. Sentiment for admitting Alaska and Hawaii as states has been mounting in recent years—both in Washington and in the territories themselves. Legislative proposals to create the forty-ninth and fiftieth states have been prepared for several recent sessions of Congress. Upon attaining statehood, Alaska and Hawaii will have the distinction of being extensions of our Federal Union beyond and entirely separate from the continental mainland of the United States.

China and the Open Door Policy. On the other side of the Pacific, European nations had been strengthening their holds on China since the Opium War of 1839–42 had reopened Chinese

---

[10] Several of these Pacific islands figured prominently in World War II. You can find them on the map on page 189.

Alaska Is Bigger Than You Think

Few People, Lots of Resources

POPULATION: 100,000   **AREA:** 585,000 square miles, one fifth the size of the U.S.   **TRANSPORTATION:** 471 miles of railroads • 3,000 miles of highways and roads • 7 million air miles flown per year   **CLIMATE:** Ranges from that of the North Pole to that of Philadelphia   **FARM LAND UNDER CULTIVATION:** 12,000 acres   **UNDEVELOPED FARM LAND:** 2 million acres suitable for cultivation • 4 million acres suitable for grazing   **CHIEF INDUSTRIES:** fishing, mining (chiefly gold), furs, lumber   **UNDEVELOPED RESOURCES:** Minerals—coal, oil, zinc, nickel, tungsten, tin, chromite, iron, mercury, graphite, limestone, antimony, platinum • Timber—on a vast scale • Hydroelectric power —A potential 50 billion kilowatt hours a year is almost untouched

U.S. News & World Report (11–18–49). © *U.S. News Pub. Corp.*

ports to their trade. They had extended their influence—particularly England, France, Germany, and Russia—and by the end of the century were on the verge of dividing up China among themselves. In addition, when Japan began to modernize and to read what other nations had been doing while she was isolated for 200 years, she discovered how the people of a little group of islands on the other side of the world had reached out gradually until they had gained control of one-fifth of the earth's surface and one-fourth of the earth's population. The Japanese reasoned that if the British could do it, so could they. As they looked about for land to seize, their eye fell naturally on the great bulk of China so close to them on the mainland, weak and apparently theirs for the taking. So they prepared

to take it. In 1894–95 Japan fought her first war with China and got the island of Taiwan, which she renamed Formosa. Then she turned her attention to the mainland.

England was disturbed because other nations were threatening her position and trade in China. She turned to the United States for help. This country, too, did not want to lose Chinese trade. Also, we didn't want to see China lose its independence and be divided up among outside nations. Accordingly, in 1899, Secretary of State John Hay, prompted by Great Britain, sent notes to the foreign powers in China suggesting that all agree to an "open door" policy there. By that he meant that China would be open equally to all outside nations, that there would be no "spheres of influence" for particular nations. England, as was to be expected, sent a favorable reply. Russia refused. Other nations were indefinite in their answers.

The Chinese people were well aware of what was happening to their country. It was the same old story. Foreigners were not as interested in helping the Chinese as they were in helping themselves. It was the same question that has plagued colonies in all empire systems: should the wealth of China be used for the Chinese or for just anyone who was strong enough to take it?

Boxer Rebellion. Antiforeign sentiment was pretty high in China. The most outspoken of the Chinese who disliked all foreigners were the members of a secret society called the Order of Literary Patriotic Harmonious Fists. They were popularly known as the Boxers, because athletic training was part of their program. Their purpose was to drive all foreigners out of China.

The Boxers became very strong. By June of 1900 they controlled all the land between Peking (the name has since been changed to Peiping) and the seacoast. The imperial government was forced to place their leader in charge of foreign affairs. Then all the ministers of foreign powers were ordered out of the country. The German ambassador was killed in the streets of Peking, and the rest were afraid to leave the city. Instead, they withdrew to the British embassy and fortified the place as best they could. Here they held out until an army made up of troops from the nations involved marched into China and took Peking.

There never was a better excuse or opportunity for empire-builders to divide up a country. But Secretary of State Hay announced that the United States would take no territory, and Britain, France, and Germany agreed to go along with us. There was nothing for the remaining powers to do but agree also. Instead of land, the foreign powers got from China money payments for damages done. The United States won a more friendly attitude from China by giving back more than half our damages to be used to send Chinese students to this country to study in our colleges and universities.[11] The Boxers had failed to rid China of foreign influence, but our "open door" policy for China had been maintained.

War between Japan and Russia. The United States soon found another opportunity to assert itself in Asiatic affairs. The Russian empire was growing eastward across northern Asia. Russia wanted land farther south; she needed a warm-water port—one that was not ice-blocked part of each year. She turned her attention to Manchuria and Korea, parts of China. But there her ambitions clashed with those of Japan, who wanted to add the same territory to her growing empire. In 1904 Japan, with British backing, started a war against Russia with a sneak attack on Port Arthur. Most of the world settled back to enjoy this "side show." Imagine little Japan taking on the big Russian bear![12] But as the war went on, the world was astonished. Little Japan was pushing big Russia all over that part of the map. To put a stop to the massacre, President Theodore Roosevelt invited Japan and Russia to send peace representatives to a conference at Portsmouth, New Hampshire (1905).

---

[11] $13,000,000 out of $24,000,000.

[12] Cartoonists usually picture Russia as a big bear because of a reference of Shakespeare in *Macbeth*, Act III, Scene 2.

By the treaty Japan got the southern half of Sakhalin Island. She extended her influence in Manchuria and to such an extent in Korea that she was able to go ahead and annex the peninsula outright in 1910. The Asiatic picture was changing. Our "open door" policy might save China from non-Asiatic countries. But how to save China from Japan?

Venezuela and Her Debts. In 1902 trouble came up again in Venezuela. Investors from England, Germany, and Italy couldn't collect what Venezuela owed them. Finally the three nations sent warships to blockade the coast and seized some Venezuelan gunboats. President Theodore Roosevelt was afraid the powers might take land to satisfy the debts, and this would be a violation of the Monroe Doctrine. However, he recognized the right of nations to collect just debts and urged arbitration. The President of Venezuela asked that all nations having claims against his government include them in the arbitration. The tendency of great powers to make money at the expense of weaker nations was clearly demonstrated in this incident. The amount demanded of Venezuela was about $38,000,000. The arbitration commission allowed claims amounting to only about $8,000,000. Claims of citizens of the United States were scaled down from about $16,000,000 to about one-half million.

Does the Constitution Follow the Flag? In our expansion, both political and economic, several important questions were raised. One was, "Does the Constitution follow the flag?" That is, do the rights and privileges guaranteed to American citizens by our Constitution apply to people in our colonies as well? This will remind you of the pre-Revolution argument. But Congress decided that the people of the possessions are to have only those rights which Congress grants them. It made a difference in our thinking when we were the mother country rather than the colony. People in the possessions have not always been too pleased.

A second question was, "Does trade follow the flag?" There really seemed to be no question about it. In empires trade had always followed the flag, and it was no different with us. In fact, in various instances, such as Cuba and Hawaii, trade got there first and virtually turned the land over to us politically as well.

This raised a third question, "Will the flag always follow trade?" It looked as if this might become a practice of the United States, especially in Latin America. Our stand on the Venezuelan debt matter in 1902 prompted Foreign Minister Drago of Argentina to state that his country would not agree to the right of any nation to interfere in a Latin American country to collect a debt. He took the stand that private investors who put their money into weak nations to make private profit must run the risks involved and that the investor's government does not have the right to use military power to force the payment of private debts. This appears to be a reasonable position, but the United States government has frequently disregarded it.

The Panama Canal. For a long time the United States had been interested in a shorter water route from the Atlantic coast of the country to the Pacific coast. The distance around South America was almost half the distance around the world. The adding of Oregon and California, and the gold rush to California in 1849, called more attention to this need. In 1850 a treaty was made with England[13] which provided for the joint guarantee of any canal the two countries might build across the Isthmus of Panama.

The Suez Canal was completed in 1869, and Ferdinand de Lesseps, its builder, began plans at once for a similar canal through Panama. In 1883 work was begun, but six years later the company was bankrupt and the canal was not finished. Many people thought the United States should take over, but our treaty with England called for joint action. By this time we were sure we wanted the canal all to ourselves. In 1901 a new treaty[14] was made with England giving us sole right to build a canal.

Some people favored a canal through Nicaragua; others thought we should buy the French diggings in Panama. After much discussion, the Panama site was decided upon and Congress authorized the government to procure from Colombia, the South American country that owned Panama, the right of way for the canal.

The United States offered $10,000,-000 outright and $250,000 a year for the rental of a strip six miles wide across the Isthmus of Panama. Colombia refused. Panama was a sort of colony of Colombia's that was paying well. And Colombia undoubtedly thought that by holding out she could get a better deal. Panama felt it had been "milked" for a long time by Colombia; now the people were sure of it. Talk of revolution

spread. The idea received the quiet moral support of the United States and the French company that wanted to sell its partially completed canal.

The revolution was planned for November 4, 1903. On November 2 an American gunboat arrived at Colon, on the Atlantic coast, "to protect American interests." The following day Colombia landed 450 soldiers and four generals. The officers went at once to Panama, on the Pacific side, the center of the revolutionary activity, where they were promptly seized by the rebels. The soldiers wanted to go to their aid, but they had no money to buy transportation on the American owned railroad. When they threatened to seize the railroad, fifty marines landed from the American gunboat "to protect the railroad," as a treaty with Colombia required us to do. Not ready to start a war with the United States, the Colombian soldiers boarded a mail ship and sailed away. At Panama three Colombian gunboats were anchored in the harbor. Two of them joined the rebels, and the third fired three shots and sailed away. One shot killed a Chinaman; not another person was killed or injured in the revolution.

On November 4 the new government was organized, and two days later the United States recognized it. On November 18 a treaty was made with the Republic of Panama by which we got a ten-mile-wide right-of-way for the canal on the terms originally proposed to Colombia.

There was little excuse for the United States to use force to get the canal it wanted. Undoubtedly it could have been obtained otherwise. Latin America became more alarmed. Later

---

[13] The Clayton-Bulwer Treaty.
[14] The Hay-Pauncefote Treaty.

HE SPLIT A MOUNTAIN TO LET PROGRESS THROUGH

George Washington Goethals was the son of immigrants who had named him for the father of their chosen country. He was a soldier and builder who was called upon to link the Atlantic and Pacific by digging a canal through the slime and jungle of the Isthmus of Panama. Men had failed before him, but Goethals directed 65,000 workers to split a mountain, dam a river, build great water gates, and let the oceans flow together through the great Panama Canal.

Theodore Roosevelt said, "I took the Canal Zone and let Congress debate, and while the debate goes on the canal does also." This disregard for democratic processes caused the nations to the south of us to wonder just how much more we might take. Any price we might have had to pay to get the Canal Zone peacefully would have been better for us in the long run than to create the impression that we were ready to take whatever we wanted by force.

Work on the canal was started the following year. The construction was carried on under the direction of Colonel George W. Goethals. The biggest handicap in building the canal was the tropical diseases that made life difficult in Panama. The hero of the story was Dr. William C. Gorgas. Under his direction the mosquito was discovered to be the carrier of yellow fever, and a war was waged to exterminate all mosquitoes and breeding places for mosquitoes. With sanitation improved and disease wiped out, the canal was pushed on to completion. In August, 1914, it was opened to traffic.

America, the Debt Collector. Trouble continued to pile up for us in the Caribbean. Several of the little countries were troubled with frequent revolutions,[15] which made it difficult for them to pay their debts to foreign investors. When these debts weren't paid, European countries threatened to use force to collect them. We were building the Panama Canal, and we didn't want the Monroe Doctrine violated; in several cases we beat the European countries to it and intervened ourselves in the internal affairs of some of the little countries. President Theodore Roosevelt took the position that if a country in this hemisphere is too weak to protect itself or meet its obligations, then in carrying out the Monroe Doctrine it might be necessary for the United States to move in and set affairs in order, for the country's own good. The Latin American countries didn't see it that way. It looked to them as if we had set up the Monroe Doctrine to keep European powers out so we could have a free hand ourselves. We were going to protect them from European empire-builders, but who would save them from the United States? Clearly it wasn't a very good way to make friends.

Santo Domingo. In 1905 President Roosevelt put Americans in all ports of Santo Domingo to collect import duties and distribute them to the Dominican government and foreign creditors. This plan was followed for several years.

Then in 1916, the Dominican government attempted to stop this procedure. American marines landed and took over, and the country operated under our military dictatorship for eight years. Then it was agreed that Americans should again collect the taxes, for a period of twenty years, and the marines were withdrawn.

Nicaragua and Haiti. Practically the same story can be told of Nicaragua and Haiti. Our marines were in Nicaragua from 1912 until 1933 (with exception of a brief period in 1925), and in Haiti from 1914 until 1934. Such action has been referred to critically as "Yankee imperialism." It should be pointed out, however, that the United States had no intention of seizing land. Our government felt this action was necessary to keep other nations out and to protect the Panama Canal.

Acquisition of the Virgin Islands. Attempts had been made since as far back as 1867 to purchase the Virgin Islands (Danish West Indies) from Denmark. These islands lie just east of Puerto Rico, and we were afraid some big European power might get them. Finally a deal was put through in 1917 whereby we bought them for $25,000,000. Conditions have not been too good there. The principal product in the islands was rum, and prohibition in the United States brought depression from which the islands have never fully recovered.

Mexican Revolutions. Trouble developed with Mexico, too. For a long time we had enjoyed friendly relations with our neighbor on the south. Mexico was ruled by a dictator, Porfirio Diaz, from 1877 to 1911. Diaz favored the wealthy group in Mexico and permitted foreign capital to be invested in the

[15] An attempt was made in 1907 to stabilize political conditions in Latin America. Several countries formed a peace league. A court was created to act in any disputes. Andrew Carnegie provided the funds for an elaborate "temple of peace" at Cartago, Costa Rica. But the peace league was not equal to the quick Latin temperament, and the agreement was soon forgotten. In 1917 an earthquake destroyed the "temple of peace."

John Hancock Mutual Life Insurance Co., Aero Digest

AMERICAN EXPLORERS OF THE TWENTIETH CENTURY

Acquisition of new territorial possessions by the United States added to the nation's traditional interest in discovery and exploration. The two least explored regions of the world at the turn of the century—the Arctic and Antarctic—challenged daring men of several nations to penetrate their frozen wastes. In meeting that challenge, a number of Americans distinguished themselves in leading expeditions to the top and bottom of the globe. Robert E. Peary (in the top picture) discovered the North Pole in 1909. Richard E. Byrd is shown in the lower picture at the left as he appeared with a companion on one of his Polar trips. In 1929 Byrd made the first plane flight over the South Pole and, in more recent years, has mapped and gathered scientific information about a large area of the Antarctic continent.

mines, oil fields, and ranches of his country. Much of that capital came from the United States.

The Mexican people naturally resented this. They felt that the natural resources of their land should be used for their benefit. Conditions for the poor peon (serf) were getting no better. In an agricultural country, 85 per cent of the people working the soil owned no land.

The Diaz government was overthrown by revolution in 1911. Other revolutions and more dictators followed, and our relations with Mexico were strained for several years. Twice American troops moved in. At one time we held Vera Cruz for more than six months. On another occasion President Woodrow Wilson sent General John J. Pershing after a Mexican bandit, Pancho Villa, who had been making forays across the border into New Mexico (1916). When the Mexican government appeared to be protecting Villa, sentiment rose in the United States in favor of armed intervention. But war was avoided. One reason was that the United States feared she would be drawn into the war going on in Europe (World War I) and dared not risk a war over here, too.

A new constitution in 1917 prevented anyone but Mexicans from owning the land and natural resources of the country. Holdings of foreign companies or individuals were not disturbed at that time, but native-owned large estates were divided among the poor farmers. Mexico was entirely within her rights in doing this, but foreign investors were alarmed. However, as they were reassured their rights would not be violated, better relations were created. We felt so much more kindly toward Mexico that in 1938, when the government did force all foreigners to sell their oil lands in Mexico, the incident was passed over without much trouble.

MONROE DOCTRINE BECOMES MODERN

American Republics Unite. The policy of armed intervention in Latin American affairs was becoming more and more troublesome, and trade with Latin America was not growing as we wanted. We came to realize that as long as the people of those countries felt as they did about us, the situation wouldn't change. Under President Herbert Hoover our government began to relax its military hold on the little countries south of us. When Franklin D. Roosevelt became President, he promptly announced his "good neighbor" policy. He said this government was opposed to armed intervention in the internal affairs of any state in the Americas. In 1934 we gave up the right to intervene in Cuba. In 1933 our marines were taken out of Nicaragua, in 1934 out of Haiti, and in 1941 out of Santo Domingo. In 1939 we surrendered our right to intervene in affairs of Panama. Thus Franklin Roosevelt repudiated the policies toward Latin America put into practice by Theodore Roosevelt.

Our stand at various Pan-American conferences since then has verified our new attitude toward our neighbors to the south. Gradually in these conferences a new kind of interpretation of the Monroe Doctrine was being developed. Instead of the doctrine being used for the benefit of the United States only, it was now to be used for the benefit of all the American republics.

Instead of the United States protecting all the Western Hemisphere, the American republics were to join together for this purpose. This new interpretation was openly stated at the Inter-American Conference at Mexico City in 1945 in the Act of Chapultepec, which says "that every attack of a state against the . . . sovereignty or the political independence of an American state shall . . . be considered as an act of aggression against the other states which sign this Declaration." The Monroe Doctrine had at last caught up with the times. Instead of one sponsor, the Doctrine came to have many sponsors.

FOR YOUR REVIEW

These Should Be Easy for You Now

1. What articles formed the basis of early trade with China?
2. Why did China fight two wars with Great Britain between 1839 and 1860? What were the results?
3. Explain what is meant by extraterritoriality.
4. Why was Japan closed to the outside world? When? Who was responsible for reopening the country? When was this done? How?
5. Why did Japan begin an extensive program of modernization?
6. What circumstances prevented difficulty with Great Britain over the Venezuelan boundary issue?
7. What events led to war with Spain in 1898? What territory did the United States gain by the war?
8. What was the real significance of our acquisition of the Philippines?
9. What has been the story of our relationship to the Philippines?
10. How did the United States get control of the Hawaiian Islands? Of part of the Samoan Islands?
11. Make a list of the United States' possessions.
12. What was the "open door" policy intended to accomplish? What were the Boxers trying to do? Results?
13. Why did Japan fight Russia in 1904–1905? How was the United States instrumental in bringing about the end of the war? What were the terms of the peace treaty?
14. What difficulty arose in 1902 over Venezuela? How was it settled?
15. How has the United States answered the question: Does the Constitution follow the flag? Does trade follow the flag? Does the flag follow trade?
16. How did the United States get control of the Panama Canal Zone?
17. Why has there been considerable dislike in Latin America for the United States? What incidents can you cite that seem to support this Latin American feeling?
18. What was President Franklin D. Roosevelt's "good neighbor" policy? How has this policy improved our relations with Latin America?
19. What important change in the interpretation of the Monroe Doctrine has been made in recent years?

Associated Dates

1785—Voyage of the "Empress of China" from New York City to Canton, China
1839–1842—First Opium War in China
1850—Clayton-Bulwer Treaty
1853–1854—Commodore Perry reopens Japan
1856–1860—Second Opium War

1885—work started on a canal across Panama
1889—first Pan-American conference (Washington)
1893—Republic of Hawaii created
1894–1895—Japan seizes Formosa from China
1898—Loss of the battleship "Maine" in Havana harbor, February 15
    war declared against Spain, April 21
    annexation of Hawaii, July 7
    surrender of Santiago, July 17
    surrender of Manila, August 13
    treaty with Spain, December 10
1899—acquisition of part of Samoa
    American "open door" policy advanced toward China
1900—Boxer Rebellion
1901—Hay-Pauncefote Treaty
1903—United States gets control of the Panama Canal Zone, November 18
1904–1905—Russo-Japanese War
1910—Japanese annexation of Korea
1914—Panama Canal opened
1917—United States purchase of the Virgin Islands from Denmark
1945—Act of Chapultepec
1946—the Philippines become independent, July 4

Why Are These To Be Remembered?

"Flying Cloud"
Extraterritoriality
Marco Polo
Francis Xavier
Commodore Perry
Pan-American Union
The "Maine"
Commodore Dewey
Rough Riders
Pago-Pago
Taiwan
Port Arthur

Sakhalin
Boxers
John Hay
Clayton-Bulwer Treaty
Hay-Pauncefote Treaty
Ferdinand de Lesseps
Colonel George W. Goethals
Dr. William C. Gorgas
Diaz
Pancho Villa
General John J. Pershing
Robert E. Peary

Chapter 12

The United States Becomes Involved in World Conflict

TRY AS IT WILL, THE UNITED STATES CANNOT STAY OUT OF WORLD
WAR I

Events Leading to World War I. This has been a familiar pattern in history: people having the same general ancestry, customs, language, and religion have banded themselves together to form a national state or nation; as a nation became powerful, it often wanted to conquer other people and their lands to build an empire. We have mentioned European empire-builders several times in earlier chapters.

For a long time the great Roman Empire ruled Europe. When it fell, there was no strong central government to take its place. Feudalism grew up as a substitute for government. Feudalism was a system of land holding: people gave land they owned to powerful lords and then rented it from them; in return they were protected against the bandits and marauders that had free run of Europe. To protect his subjects (called vassals) the lord built big fort-like castles and kept his own private army of knights.

As time went by, a few lords became more powerful than the rest; they became the kings of the new national states that developed in Europe in the later Middle Ages. Practically all the nations of modern Europe had their beginning at that time. There were two notable exceptions: Germany and Italy.

The people of those lands were unable to build national states under kings because the power of the Roman Catholic Church and the medieval city-states[1] was too great to be broken at that time. While nations appeared all around them, Italy and Germany continued to be lands of little duchies and principalities.

The first crop of empire-builders consisted of Portugal, Spain, Holland, and France. Portugal and Holland were too small to hold big empires. Spain's empire gradually diminished: we have seen how the United States took the last of it in 1898. Then England began to build her empire and fought France all over the globe for territory. The colonial wars in America and the American Revolution were parts of that struggle. France was beaten until Napoleon appeared on the scene and tried again. The War of 1812 was a part of that conflict. The threat from France was put down, and the British Empire remained supreme.

Having built the world's largest empire, England wanted to keep it. With the coming of the Industrial Revolution and the mechanization of industry,

[1] Such as powerful Genoa and Venice, that Shakespeare wrote about in his *Merchant of Venice.*

154

England built a great merchant marine to bring to her factories raw materials from all over the world and to carry out to world markets her manufactured goods. To protect her merchant fleet, she built the world's largest navy. And she adopted her "balance of power" policy. Whenever some nation became strong and set out to build an empire that threatened the British Empire, England would join with the weaker nations against that power and put down its threat. It was the rule of force of the old Roman Empire, but on a world-wide scale.

After Napoleon was disposed of, the next threat to England's position came from Russia. Russia needed a warm-water port. She tried to get it at Constantinople, then in the Indian Ocean, and later in China. In each case England was able to stop her, the last time by aiding Japan. Then a new threat appeared.

About 1870 three new nations appeared in the world. All the little German states were united under the leadership of Prussia by the Prussian Chancellor (prime minister) Otto von Bismarck. The unification was completed by the Franco-Prussian War (1870), which broke France's hold on the last of the German states.[2] The same war completed the unification of Italy. All of Italy except Rome had been brought under the rule of the King of Sardinia-Piedmont, one of the little Italian states. Rome was all that was left of the land that the Pope had ruled (the Papal States), and French troops were holding it for him. When the Franco-Prussian War started, these French troops were called home. When they marched out of Rome, Italian troops marched in and made the city the capital of united Italy. On the other side of the world, at about the same time, Japan was throwing off its old feudal system and setting out to modernize herself on the pattern of Western nations.

As other nations before her, new Germany wanted colonies.[3] So did Italy. So did Japan. But getting them wasn't as easy as it had been two or three hundred years earlier. Now practically all the land of weak peoples had been gobbled up. All parts of North and South America were free or already included in existing empires. Anyway, the Monroe Doctrine made the Americas "out of bounds" to empire-builders. Africa had already been divided up. Asia was partly gone, and only our "open door" policy for China had kept her free. From here on, with a very few exceptions, any nation that wanted territory had to try to take it from some other empire-builder.

A conflict of ambitions developed in Europe. The German emperor (kaiser) had a dream like that of Napoleon before him. He wanted to build an economic empire in Europe in which Germany would have the factories and the rest of the empire would supply the raw materials. He had visions of an empire stretching through southeast Europe into southwestern Asia, to be tied together by a Berlin-to-Bagdad railroad. France was looking for a chance to get back Alsace-Lorraine, which Germany had taken from her in the Franco-Prussian War. Italy wanted land to the north and east. Russia still

---

[2] William I of Prussia was crowned Emperor of Germany in the Hall of Mirrors in Louis XIV's palace at Versailles, outside Paris.

[3] The Kaiser said Germany wanted "a place in the sun."

wanted Constantinople. Austria wanted to enlarge her central European empire.

In the empire of Austria-Hungary there were several nationalities of people. Among them were the Serbs, the Croats, and the Slovenes—all of them Slavs. They wanted to be free. Just south of Austria in the Balkans was the little country of Serbia, whose people also were Slavs. Serbia wanted to help the Slavs in Austria to win their free-

Bettmann Archive

THE KAISER AND HIS CHIEFS IN COMMAND

The German government committed the resources of its empire to a war effort that ended in defeat and the loss of all colonies. The above picture shows Emperor Wilhelm II conferring with Field Marshal Von Hindenburg and Major General Ludendorff over a phase of World War I strategy.

dom. Austria, therefore, was looking for a chance to conquer Serbia before she caused Austria any more trouble.

The increasing friction in Europe caused the nations to line up in two armed camps. In 1882 Germany, Austria, and Italy had formed the Triple Alliance. Then France and Russia joined in an alliance, and a little later England joined them to form the Triple Entente (understanding). Italy, to be

in a position to go either way, allied herself with France while remaining in the Triple Alliance. Russia, whose people were Slavs, too, lent moral support to Serbia and the Slavs in Austria. Things were pretty badly mixed up. Europe of that time has been compared to a powder keg just waiting for someone to apply the match.

THE WORLD AT WAR

Start of the War. The explosion came in July, 1914. The match was the assassination by a Slav of the Archduke Francis Ferdinand, heir to the Austrian throne, in southern Austria late in June. A month later Austria had her war with Serbia, and Germany supported Austria. Russia mobilized to help Serbia, and Germany declared war on Russia. Then France indicated she would honor her alliance with Russia, and Germany declared war on her, too. When Germany marched into Belgium and violated her neutrality, England came in against Germany. Soon almost all of Europe was at war; before it was over all the countries were involved except Norway, Sweden, Denmark, Holland, Switzerland, and Spain. Italy went back on the Triple Alliance and came into the war on the side of France when the Allies promised her colonies. Austria, Germany, Bulgaria, and Turkey were called the Central Powers. The nations on the other side were called the Allies. Eventually nations all over the world came into the war until there were twenty-eight Allies fighting the four Central Powers. It was truly a world war.

Early Years of the War. Germany hoped that she could strike at Paris, defeat France quickly, and then turn on Russia. But the French lines held along the Marne River, and the war settled down for a long run. Germany and Austria were prepared, and throughout 1915 and 1916 they were more successful than the Allies. Then their opponents began to recover, and Germany would have liked to end the war, if it could be on her terms. But peace efforts accomplished nothing, and then the United States came in.

America Tries Neutrality. At the outbreak of the war President Wilson had declared us to be neutral. That was easier said than done. Our people all were of European ancestry, and they naturally favored one side or the other. Although we intended not to favor either side, we continued selling supplies to both. The country became prosperous. Both prices and wages rose. European nations first spent their gold reserves. Then they used the money people in this country owed them. When that was gone, they began to borrow heavily here in order to continue buying. When the war began, the United States was in debt to Europe. When it was over, Europe was in debt to us. In a few years the United States had changed from a debtor to a creditor nation.

Neither the Central Powers nor the Allies respected our neutrality. Each side seized our ships; it was the same thing that had happened to us before the War of 1812. We were angry at both sides. It looked as if we might go to war, but we weren't at all certain whom we wanted to fight.

Germany had developed the submarine as an effective weapon and was using it in trying to break England's blockade of the European coast and to prevent supplies from reaching the Allies. England was taking our goods, but German submarines were sinking our ships and killing our people. After the British ship, the *Lusitania,* was sunk off the coast of Ireland (May 1, 1915) with the loss of 128 Americans among the 1,198 killed, this country sent Germany a strong note, and she eventually promised not to sink ships without warning. She broke her promise about a year later, and in January, 1917, Germany announced any and all ships would be sunk on sight.

Sentiment had been swinging to England's side because of Germany's actions. There was no radio, but England controlled the cables and other means of communication which brought us news from Europe. She saw to it that the propaganda we received was favorable to the Allies. When a German note was made public asking Mexico to join in the war against the United States to get back former Mexican land now in our southwest, there was no longer any question about what we would do.

President Wilson had been re-elected partly because "he kept us out of war." In December, 1916, he sent notes to all the nations at war asking that they state their specific aims. His hope was that a basis for compromise could be found and the war ended. But the replies showed clearly that the war would have to go on. The situation changed rapidly thereafter. Private concerns here had loaned a lot of money to European countries,[4] and it looked as if the Allies were going to be beaten. If they were, the debts would never be paid, and our prosperity would be ended. We were being told that this was a war of autocracy against

---

[4] Two and one-half billion to the Allies; about one-quarter billion to Germany.

SINKING OF THE "LUSITANIA"

It was the unrestricted submarine warfare of Germany that, in great measure, provoked the United States to enter World War I on the side of the Allies. The torpedoing of the great, 760-foot-long "Lusitania" was the most outrageous act of that warfare.

democracy, and the Germans were nicknamed Huns to compare them to the ferocious Asiatic barbarians who overran much of Europe in the early Middle Ages. Tales of German atrocities were spread—tales that never were verified. When the Germans announced unrestricted submarine warfare in January, 1917, we broke off diplomatic relations at once. Germany knew her action would bring us into the war, but she was not very worried. She had watched our troops chasing Pancho Villa in Mexico and was not impressed with their fighting ability. She thought we couldn't send any more supplies than we were already sending. And she thought her submarine campaign would win the war for her before we could do anything.

America Goes to War. On April 2, 1917, President Wilson asked Congress to declare war on Germany "to make the world safe for democracy." Two days later the Senate obliged, and on April 6 the House joined in. War against Austria was not declared until December and never against Bulgaria or Turkey.

We had been sending our supplies to Europe. Now we needed to send our men. A Selective Service (draft) bill was passed, and an army of four million men was called up and trained. Half of them were eventually sent overseas.

The stream of supplies had to be continued, also. Production was increased. The government was given power to control the distribution of food, fuel, machinery, and equipment. People submitted voluntarily to meatless days and wheatless days. The government took over and operated the railroads to speed up transportation.

"Liberty Loan" drives were oversubscribed. Generous contributions were made to the Red Cross and other similar organizations. Financing the war was now the job of the American people, and they responded nobly. They were fighting a crusade to "make the world safe for democracy," a "war to end war."

General Pershing and his troops were taken from the Mexican border and sent to France. Pershing and his staff arrived June 13, 1917. But not enough troops got over that year to be of much help.

The situation in Europe was critical. Revolution in Russia had forced her to surrender and get out of the war (December, 1917). That meant Germany was freed from war on the Eastern front and could turn her full attention to the west. She began another drive toward Paris, hoping to end the war quickly.

American soldiers proved themselves in stopping the drive. General Pershing was in charge of all American troops, and all Allied forces, including the American, were under Marshal Foch of France. The second German advance on Paris was stopped, like the first, at the Marne River. Paris was saved.

The Second Battle of the Marne was the beginning of the end for the Central Powers. The tide turned completely. Where events had been favoring Germany, now they began to go against her. One by one the Central Powers dropped out until only Germany was left.

The Armistice. On October 4, 1918, Germany asked for an armistice. On November 5 the Allies made known their terms, which included occupation

Bettmann Archive

"LAFAYETTE, WE ARE HERE!"

This picture, which shows General Pershing arriving in France to lead American forces in Europe during World War I, appropriately suggests the words of the title. Pershing, however, disclaimed authorship of the famous salute, saying that another American, Colonel C. E. Stanton, voiced it during an address at Lafayette's grave in 1917.

of all of Germany west of the Rhine River. On November 8 a revolution that had overthrown the monarchy in Austria swept into Berlin. Two days later

AMERICAN TROOPS MAN FRENCH RENAULT TANKS

Mechanized armored units were used extensively for the first time in World War I. The mobile hitting power of tanks and similar gun carriers materially changed strategic and tactical concepts of ground warfare.

the kaiser fled to Holland. On November 11 at 5 o'clock in the morning the armistice was signed, and at eleven o'clock the cease-fire order was given. Germany was beaten. The war was over.

Cost of the War. The cost of the war was tremendous. It was a more mechanized war than any other up to that time. The dead and missing in the armed forces of all countries at war totaled almost 16,000,000. The number of civilians killed was even larger. For the United States, 126,000 men in uniform were killed in battle or died from disease and other causes; 235,000 were wounded; 4,500 were held as prisoners or were listed as missing. If you could stand on a street corner and watch the soldiers who died in the war march past in military formation, ten men in a row, with a row passing you every two seconds, you would have to stand on that street corner for forty-six days

before all of them had marched by.[5]

The total cost of the war, in dollars and cents, to all the nations in it has been estimated at 400 billion dollars. It is difficult to comprehend such an amount. Let's put it another way. It is "enough to furnish every family in the United States, Canada, Russia, England, France, Germany, and Australia with a $2,500 house on a $500 five-acre lot furnished with $1,000 worth of furniture, and a $5,000,000 library for every community of 20,000 or more in these countries, and a $10,000,000 university for every such community. And that's only part of it! Another part set aside at 5 per cent interest would yield enough to pay for all time, every year, $1,000 each to an army of 125,000 teachers and an army of 125,000 nurses, and still there would be enough left to buy every single bit of property and all

[5] From World Peaceways, Inc., New York City.

wealth in France and Belgium, including every cathedral and church, all public buildings, every railroad, every factory, and every farm and home."[6] The cost of operating all the hospitals in the United States for a year went up in smoke in the war every ninety-six hours. All that 2,150 men, each earning $2,500 a year, would earn over a period of forty years would equal the cost of the war for just one day. The total cost of the war equaled $20,000 an hour since the birth of Jesus.

The American part of this was about one hundred billion. Your children and grandchildren and their children and grandchildren will still be paying for World War I. In addition, the debts we fought to protect have never been paid to the American people, and after the war we loaned European nations more money for reconstruction. The amount of the World War I debt still owed the United States is over $15,000,000,000.

"A War to End War." The years from 1914 to 1917 made the United States the world's banker. Loans were made for private profit. Then the people of the United States were called upon to safeguard those loans. Our shipping was menaced, and Americans were killed. Many of our people had relatives still in Europe; our emotions were tied up in European affairs. The British navy had backed up our foreign policy throughout most of the nineteenth century, or at least we assumed that it had. We could not sit idly by and see England defeated because of the danger that would mean for us. Germany was pictured as an autocratic power and a threat to the world. The fact is, the old empire game had become so dangerous that the world

would not countenance it any longer, at least not in its violent form. As long as building an empire meant killing or dominating "heathen" people in far parts of the world, the Western nations were not too disturbed. But when it came to a Western nation trying to extend its power over another Western nation, that was an entirely different matter. Bringing Chinese, Indians, or Africans into an empire was simply accepting the "white man's burden"—the burden of carrying our civilization to the "backward" peoples of the world, even though they often preferred their own. But Germany's attempt to bring Europeans into her empire and dominate their lives was a threat to all Western people that was not to go unchallenged.

The American people were sincere in believing this was a "war to end war," a war "to make the world safe for democracy." They did not know until later that the war was prolonged by the munitions makers of the world who made private fortunes from the death of others. On the commons in a little English village today stands a cannon captured from the Germans. It is a memorial to the men of that village who lost their lives in the war. Close inspection reveals the plate which shows the cannon was made in England. French steel was shipped during the war to neutral Switzerland and then to Germany, there to be made into guns and tanks to be used against the French. Profit to be made talked louder than the call of loyalty to one's own country or to humanity.

The Americans didn't know these things. In the Revolution they had separated themselves from the empire system. Then, unconsciously, they had set about building one of their own. In 1917, as in 1812, they were drawn re-

[6] *Ibid.*

luctantly back into the empire struggle. They believed they had attained their objectives in World War I. President Wilson said, "Everything for which America fought has been accomplished." Events were to show the President and the American people how badly fooled they were.

FOR YOUR REVIEW

These Should Be Easy for You Now

1. Why were the Germans and Italians unable to build national states in the later Middle Ages?
2. What European nations were early empire-builders? Which one was most successful?
3. Why did England build a huge merchant fleet? A great navy?
4. Explain how England's "balance of power" policy operated. What nations have, at one time or another, threatened Britain's position?
5. When and how did Germany and Italy become national states? What Asiatic country became a nation at about the same time?
6. Why has empire-building been more difficult in recent years than it was earlier?
7. What was the German emperor's dream of empire?
8. Why did trouble develop between Austria and Serbia?
9. What nations made up the Triple Alliance? The Triple Entente? How was Italy allied with both sides? Why?
10. What incident marked the outbreak of World War I? What nations were called the Central Powers? What were their opponents called?
11. How did the war change the United States from a debtor to a creditor nation?
12. What events led the United States into World War I?
13. Who led the American Expeditionary Forces (AEF)? Who was placed in charge of all Allied forces?
14. Why had Russia been forced out of the war? How did this help Germany?
15. What was the total cost of the war? What did it cost the United States?

Associated Dates

1870–1871—Franco-Prussian War
1882—Triple Alliance formed
1907—Triple Entente formed
1914—World War I begins, July 28
1917—Germany announces unrestricted submarine warfare, February 1
    United States declares war on Germany, April 6
    United States declares war on Austria-Hungary, December 7
1918—Battle of Chateau-Thierry, May 27 to June 1
    Battle of Belleau Wood, June 11
    Battle of St. Mihiel, September 12 to 15
    Battle of the Argonne Forest, September 26
    Armistice signed, November 11

Why Are These To Be Remembered?

National state	Triple Alliance	"Lusitania"
Otto von Bismarck	Triple Entente	Huns
Papal States	Archduke Francis Ferdinand	Liberty Loan
Kaiser	Central Powers	General John J. Pershing
Alsace-Lorraine	Allies	Marshal Foch
Serbia	Marne River	

Chapter 13

The United States Is Disillusioned

WORLD WAR I LEAVES THE UNITED STATES DISILLUSIONED AND
DETERMINED TO STAY OUT OF FUTURE WORLD CONFLICT

Striving To Obtain and Preserve Peace. On January 8, 1918, President Wilson, in a message to Congress, outlined what he thought the United States and the Allied powers were fighting for. It sounded good. It was quite a list of things, such as no secret treaties, freedom of the seas, removal of economic barriers, disarmament, fair distribution of colonies, the rebuilding of France and Belgium, rearrangement of territorial claims in Europe, the right of any people to decide their own government, and "a general association of nations" to provide "mutual guarantees of political independence and territorial integrity to great and small states alike." These items are usually called the Fourteen Points.

President Wilson felt it necessary to make his statement in defense and justification of American participation in the war. In his war message to Congress he had said, "We have no quarrel with the German people. We have no feeling toward them but one of sympathy and friendship. It was not upon their impulse that their government acted in entering this war. . . . We have no selfish ends to serve. We desire no conquests, no dominion. We seek no indemnities. . . . But the right is more precious than peace, and we shall fight for the things which we have always carried nearest our hearts. . . .

The day has come when America is privileged to spend her blood and her might for the principles that gave her birth and happiness and the peace which she has treasured. God helping her, she can do no other."

But after the Bolshevik Revolution took place in Russia in November, 1917, certain treaties made among the Allied nations came to light. They didn't sound like the high ideals we said we were fighting for. Each of the big European Allies was fighting for specific territory. President Wilson said we didn't expect or want any land. But treaties already made promised many of the German colonies to England, others to Japan. France was to have territory in Germany as far as the Rhine River; Italy was to get part of the Austrian empire; Poland and Constantinople were to go to Russia.

Clearly, so far as Europe was concerned, this was just another war for empire. We thought we were fighting for the principles we had fought for in the Revolution. When we discovered that the other Allies didn't have the same aims we had, we were already in the war; we actually were fighting to extend the territorial possessions of the European empire-builders.

In stating his Fourteen Points, President Wilson tried to win the support of the other Allies for our high princi-

163

Bettmann Archive

ARCHITECTS OF THE PEACE—WORLD WAR I

Italy's Orlando, Britain's Lloyd George, France's Clemenceau, and America's Wilson are shown (seated) in this picture taken when the "Big Four" met at the opening sessions of the Peace Conference. The Treaty of Versailles, which provided for the establishment of the League of Nations, was written on the basis of terms formulated by the Conference.

ples instead of their own selfish aims. The Allies were perfectly willing to let Wilson speak for them, but they did not give up their intentions to take land when the war was over.

The Peace Conference. Germany had signed the armistice with the understanding that the peace would be made on the basis of Wilson's Fourteen Points. The peace conference was to open in January, 1919. President Wilson decided to attend it himself, although such a thing had never been done before. He wanted to be on hand to fight for his Fourteen Points. But his position was weakened at home before he left. Almost as if in repudiation of the President's policies, the people had elected a Republican Congress to serve under Wilson, who was a Democrat.

President Wilson was hailed by the people of Europe as the man who was going to give them a new chance and a better life. It was soon apparent, how-ever, that this was not to be. The President's hands were tied. The conference met, but four men—later three—made the decisions. The Big Four were David Lloyd George, Prime Minister of England; Georges Clemenceau, Premier of France; Vittorio Orlando, Premier of Italy; and President Wilson. Everyone knew Italy had held off entering the war until she found which side would make her the better offer. Now, when Italy demanded the colonies she had been promised, Wilson opposed her, and Lloyd George and Clemenceau were glad to back him on this point. Angered, Orlando withdrew from the conference, and the Big Four became the Big Three.

President Wilson wanted a "peace of justice." Lloyd George and Clemenceau were demanding revenge against Germany that would strip her of possessions and so ruin her that never again could she regain her former position in Europe. Wilson was outnum-bered. As the weeks went by, he fought desperately, but one by one his Four-teen Points were discarded until only the last one was left. He felt justified in giving in on some points to get the others to agree to the establishment of a League of Nations to prevent future wars. He was not satisfied with the terms of the peace, but he hoped the League of Nations would be able to ad-just the unfair provisions.

The treaty was a harsh one. All of Germany's colonies were taken from her and divided among some of the victors, principally Great Britain, France, and Japan. Part of her home-land was taken from her and given to Belgium, Poland, and Denmark; Alsace-Lorraine was returned to France, who held it earlier. Germany's navy and merchant fleet were taken from her, and her army was reduced to 100,000 men. Heavy reparations (damages), the exact amount to be determined later, were assessed against her. Austria and Hungary were made into separate nations. Later, treaties with the other Central Powers were signed. Land was taken from both Bulgaria and Turkey and added to Rumania, Greece, Serbia, and Italy. Land from both Germany and Austria-Hungary was made into the new country of Czechoslovakia. Un-der the guise of satisfying Wilson's de-mand for "self-determination" for all European people, land taken from Rus-sia was made into four new countries: Finland, Latvia, Lithuania, and Estho-nia. The real purpose in forming these countries was to shut Russia off from the Baltic Sea. Poland became a nation again,[1] to serve as a wall between Germany and Russia. Czechoslovakia

served about the same purpose. Serbia was enlarged to take in more Slavs and became Yugoslavia. This new country stretched all the way to the Adriatic Sea, to check any possible German or Austrian expansion in that direction. The United States had asked for no territory; she took none. The formation of a League of Nations was one of the terms of the treaty.

On June 28, 1919, Germany signed the treaty in the Palace of Versailles near Paris.[2] She had agreed to the ar-mistice because she had been promised the treaty would incorporate Wilson's liberal Fourteen Points, and she pro-tested that the treaty had not been drawn up that way. But she had no choice other than to sign.

The co-operation that had existed during the war among the Allies was gone. President Wilson was still fight-ing for high principles, but the other powers were bent on satisfying selfish ambitions. At home, the co-operation between the two major political parties during the war was ended. As we have said, Wilson now had to deal with a Republican Congress. The Senate was opposed to the League of Nations; the Senate indicated it would accept the treaty if the League were taken out of it. Wilson refused to consider this pos-sibility, and on July 10 he sent the treaty to the Senate for consideration.

League of Nations. The League of Nations was similar to the United Na-tions organized after World War II. An Assembly was composed of repre-sentatives from all member nations. There was a Council that served as a

---

[1] She had been gobbled up by Russia, Prussia, and Austria in 1795.

[2] France insisted it be signed there to wipe out the dishonor heaped on her when the German Emperor had been crowned there dur-ing the Franco-Prussian War almost fifty years before. For obvious reasons, the treaty with Germany is called the Treaty of Versailles.

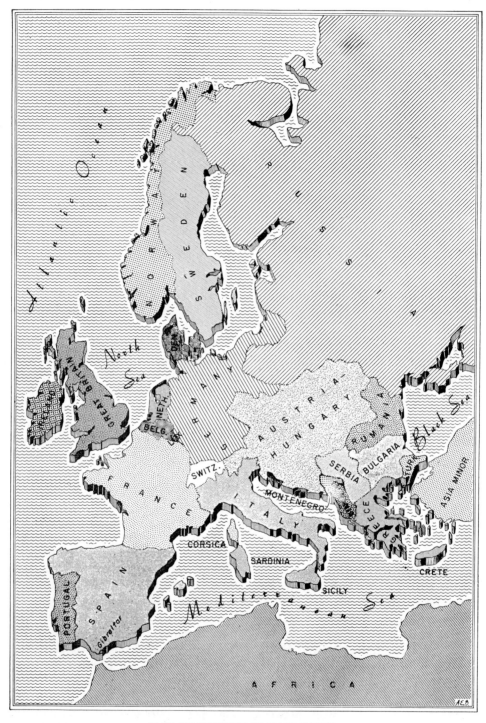

MAP OF EUROPE IN EARLY 1914

Before World War I, Europe included the states of Montenegro, Serbia, and the Austro-Hungarian Empire. The war and its aftermath caused these states to disappear and otherwise changed the political face of Europe.

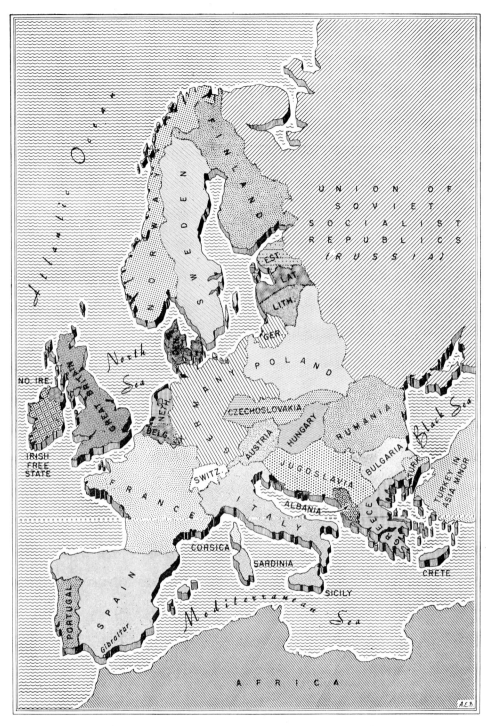

MAP OF EUROPE AFTER THE TREATY OF VERSAILLES

The Treaty of Versailles resulted in the creation of a number of new European states. Czechoslovakia, Jugoslavia, Finland, Estonia, Latvia, Lithuania, a restored Poland, and the separate countries of Austria and Hungary appeared on the European scene.

sort of executive committee, similar to the United Nations Security Council. The headquarters were located at Geneva, Switzerland, where the permanent Secretariat operated. A Permanent Court of International Justice was created to hear any cases member nations wanted to bring before it. Besides attempting to prevent war, the League was empowered to deal with such world matters as health, social improvement, and labor problems.

Opposition in the Senate to the League was led by Henry Cabot Lodge of Massachusetts who was Chairman of the Senate Committee on Foreign Relations, William E. Borah of Idaho, and Hiram Johnson of California. There were three particular things about the League that the Senators didn't like. India and four of the self-governing dominions in the British Empire[3] had a vote along with England in the Assembly. It was thought that this gave England an advantage, that she could control at least six votes to our one. In the second place, the Covenant of the League provided that "the members of the League undertake to respect and preserve as against external aggression the territorial integrity and existing political independence of all members of the League." Senators feared this would involve the United States in war anywhere in the world. Thirdly, the League was given the responsibility of enforcing the Treaty of Versailles, which was recognized as a most unjust treaty.

When the President could get nowhere with the Senate, he appealed directly to the people. He did not have the advantage of radio; he had to travel across the country, speaking as often

[3] Canada, Australia, New Zealand, and South Africa.

as he could. He had been working hard all through the war; his speaking tour was too much for him. Before it was over, he suffered a stroke from which he never fully recovered.

The treaty with Germany became a major issue of the political campaign of 1920. The Democrats favored its ratification; the Republicans opposed it. The Republicans won, and the treaty was defeated. Later, the United States made separate peace treaties with Germany, Austria, and Hungary (ratified October 18, 1921).

In January, 1920, the League of Nations held its first meeting. The United States was not represented; it never did become a member. The man who conceived the idea of the League and fought for its adoption had been repudiated by his own country. In spite of this, the League began its business of considering world political, economic, and social problems. During its existence it did a great deal of good. But it was not able to prevent another war. Twenty years later the world was at it again. The inevitable question has been asked many times: would the League have been successful if the United States had been a member? Most people have their own opinions, but no one can know the answer. The League did not have the benefit of the help of the United States. We had given military victory to the Allies, but we refused to help Europe try to solve the problems that had brought on the war in the first place.

The Hague Court. In 1899, at the suggestion of Russia, a meeting was held at The Hague in the Netherlands, and The Hague Court was formed to serve in the arbitration of disputes between nations. The American steel magnate Andrew Carnegie[4] gave the money to build the great "Peace Palace" in which the court was housed. The United States has used the services of the court on various occasions.

The World Court. Along with the League of Nations, provision was made for the Permanent Court of International Justice. This Court was located at The Hague, also; it was created to deal with legal problems between nations. Its actions gave us the basis for international law. Its services were available to all nations who wished to join it. In the United States it was called the World Court. Several attempts were made to get the United States to join the Court. In 1926 we offered to join if we were permitted to keep the power to veto the court's consideration of any case in which we had an interest. The member nations of the Court were slow in accepting, and President Coolidge announced we would not press the matter at that time. The last attempt to get the United States in was made in 1935, but the Senate again voted down the proposal.

Washington Arms Conference. Although the United States had turned its back on the League and the World Court, our people were very interested in aiding other movements for peace. In 1921 President Warren G. Harding, prompted from London, called a conference to be held in Washington to discuss armament limitation and the Asiatic situation. During the war Japan had presented her Twenty-One Demands to China (1915), and only Pres-

---

[4] In 1910 Mr. Carnegie had founded in this country the Carnegie Endowment for International Peace. The Endowment is still functioning, with headquarters in Washington, D.C.

ident Wilson's firm stand had prevented Japan from taking China over. As it was, Japan had seized German interests in the Shantung peninsula in China, and had occupied Vladivostok and Eastern Siberia, land that belonged to Russia. Japan was threatening our "open door" policy.

Great Britain, France, Italy, Japan, China, Portugal, Belgium, and the Netherlands sent representatives to the Washington Arms Conference. They were the nations who either had large navies or were especially interested in China.

The conference agreed that the number and size of big warships should be limited. It was decided that England and the United States should have the same tonnage, and Japan three-fifths as much. France and Italy were to have each about one-half as much as Japan. This limitation was expressed in a 5:5:3:1⅔:1⅔ ratio. To conform to this ratio, the powers agreed not only to restrain from building more big ships for ten years but also to scrap some of the vessels they already had. This agreement was to last for ten years unless renewed. Naval experts were not disturbed, for they believed that future naval warfare would be carried on with smaller ships than those affected by the limitation program.

Great Britain had made a treaty with Japan in 1902 to stop Russia in her search for a warm-water port on the Pacific. England had accomplished her desires by the Russo-Japanese War of 1904–5, but the treaty still stood and was a source of anxiety to other nations interested in Asia. This treaty was now replaced by one signed by the United States, Great Britain, France, and Japan in which each agreed to respect the rights of the others in the Orient and to confer as to measures to be taken if an outside power ever threatened. A Nine-Power Treaty was signed guaranteeing the independence of China and the "open door" for trade there. A similar treaty left the control of Chinese tariffs to the Chinese. Finally, Japan agreed to turn back to China the former German interests she was holding in Shantung. Japan also withdrew her forces from Siberia in 1922.

The Washington Conference was hailed as a great success. It had accomplished far more than careful observers had expected. One important result, however, was generally overlooked. At the end of World War I the United States was almost convinced it should have a two-ocean navy—one big enough to defend the country in both the Atlantic and the Pacific Oceans. The attempt to build so great a navy, however, was almost certain to provoke a race with both Great Britain and Japan. That would be both costly and useless. So the 5:5:3 ratio was agreed upon. This meant the United States would keep a navy only large enough for defense in the Pacific and would continue to be dependent upon the British navy for protection in the Atlantic, as we had depended upon it for the support of our Monroe Doctrine for the last century. This meant, too, then, that at any time in the future that England was threatened, we were bound, for our own sake, to go to her aid. The American people were committed to participation in the next war from then on. But we didn't realize it.

At the London Naval Conference in 1930 the big powers agreed not to build any more big warships until 1936. The whole program to limit naval arma-ments ended, however, with Japan's announcement (1934) that she would not renew the naval limitation agreement after 1936. Her intention was clear; she was going to build huge warships. The naval armament race that the Washington agreement of 1921 had been designed to prevent had simply been postponed for fifteen years.

Kellogg-Briand Pact. The world was thinking seriously about peace. In 1927 Aristide Briand, Foreign Minister of France, suggested that his country and the United States join in a treaty to outlaw war. Frank B. Kellogg, United States Secretary of State, proposed that other nations be invited to join France and the United States in such a treaty.

The Kellogg-Briand Pact (sometimes called the Paris Pact) may well lay claim to being the shortest of all treaties; it contains but two short paragraphs. Nations that signed it did two things: they denounced war as a means of settling disputes, and they renounced war—that is, they agreed they would never resort to war to settle arguments with other nations.

The United States State Department submitted a treaty, and on August 27, 1928, France, the United States, and thirteen other nations signed the pact in Paris. Eventually more than sixty nations signed. But the Kellogg-Briand Pact made no provision for enforcing the agreement. It depended upon the good faith of each signer. And even as they signed, some nations were already planning moves that would most surely lead to war. Other nations, who would have sincerely kept their pledge if they could, soon found themselves so involved in the new struggle for empire that the choice for or against war finally was not theirs to make.

The War Debt Problem. The United States government was much concerned over the payment—or more accurately, nonpayment—of war debts. As we have already noted, when World War I was over, the European countries owed us a large sum of money. Then we loaned them more to help them get back onto their feet again. As time passed, it became evident that the European countries were in no condition to pay. In 1922 a commission was created to take up with each country the matter of funding its debt so it could be paid over a period of years. At the same time the debts were funded, they were also substantially reduced.

But the nations that owed us were depending upon the reparations (damages) Germany was to pay them as a source of money to pay us. And Germany couldn't pay. The original reparations figure was high for a defeated nation—thirty-three billion dollars. When Germany couldn't pay, we sent General Charles G. Dawes to see what could be done. The Dawes Plan (1924) scaled down German reparations and provided for changes in Germany's financial structure to assist her in geting back to normal. But Germany was in trouble again a few years later, and in 1929 Owen D. Young headed a commission which further reduced reparations. In 1931 Germany was on the verge of bankruptcy again. The world was in the midst of a great depression, and President Herbert Hoover declared a moratorium (recess) for one year in debt payments.

The next year the European countries cancelled the reparations Germany still owed them, expecting that the United States would in turn cancel their debts to us. We didn't. Several countries made no payment that year and only "token" payments the following year. From 1934 on, only Finland kept up payments regularly. Although they are still on the books, we know that these debts never will be paid.

There has been much discussion over this debt matter. Many people contend that they were honest debts and should be paid. Others point out that we had none of the destruction Europe suffered in the war and should therefore be glad to consider the amount of the debts as our contribution toward the winning of the war. Feeling over these war debts has made many people bitter and increased their determination never to have anything more to do with the affairs of other parts of the world. Congress passed the Johnson Act in 1934 preventing the loaning of money to any country that had not made regular payments on its debt to our government or any person or organization in this country. In the next chapter we shall see how we got around this law in World War II.

PEACE SUCCUMBS TO WAR

Communism and Fascism Reign. As we pointed out earlier, a revolution took place in Russia in 1917. Actually there were two revolutions, one in March and the other in November. In March the Romanov czar was overthrown, and a government controlled by the middle class was set up. The revolution in November ousted the middle class government[5] and put the

---

[5] The Prime Minister under this government was Alexander Kerensky, who later came to the United States to live. Leaders of the Bolshevik Revolution were Nikolai Lenin and Leon Trotsky. The body of the former is enshrined in Moscow. The latter was later exiled and fled finally to Mexico, where he was mysteriously murdered.

Bolsheviks (Bolshevik means majority party) in power. Theirs was a communist government; the working class was supposed to rule through workers' committees called soviets. The country was divided into several parts; each was to be a republic, and all were joined in the Union of Soviet Socialist Republics

Bettmann Archive

STALIN AND THE MASSES

The Bolshevik leader is shown here as he was frequently pictured during the early years of the Soviet regime—against a background scene of demonstrating proletarians.

(U.S.S.R.). After 1927 Joseph Stalin made himself dictator, and the government became totalitarian. Instead of being operated by and for the working people, it was operated by Stalin for the leaders of the Communist Party, the only political party permitted to exist in the country.

After World War I was over, the new government in Russia caused quite a stir in other parts of Europe. The workers were dissatisfied in various other countries, and what had hap-

pened in Russia encouraged them. It was feared that communism would spread, with Russian assistance; leaders in Russia were appealing to the workers of the world to unite. European leaders began looking for ways to stop communism, ways to keep it from spreading to their countries.

England was the first to find what she thought was a way. She began to pour capital into Germany to make that nation strong again. This move served two purposes for England. She reasoned that, first, a strong Germany would prevent communism from spreading westward to England. In the second place, she believed that a strong Germany would serve as a constant threat to France and would keep France from becoming too powerful and a threat to England's dominant position in Europe—that is, she thought it would keep France too weak to disturb the balance of power. England followed this policy for several years. Then she discovered that she had helped Germany to become the very danger she had been intent on preventing France from becoming. This disruption in the balance of power was to bring another great war.

Italy countered communism in a different way. After the war Italy was on the verge of anarchy. The country had been counting on getting some colonies as her prize for being on the winning side. As we have said, President Wilson, with the hearty support of England and France, had thwarted this. Italy, always a poor country, went from bad to worse. It looked as if the communists might take over. Then Benito Mussolini, the son of a blacksmith, left the Socialist Party and organized a new party of his own (March, 1919). The kind of government his new party stood for he called Fascism.

It was a new kind of government. It was intended to be a compromise between capitalism and communism. Capitalism has always stood for private ownership and operation of the means of production—factories, farms, etc. Communism, at the opposite extreme, in theory stands for government ownership and operation of those means of production. Fascism was in between; it adopted something from both capitalism and communism. It stood for private ownership but government control of the means of production. Mussolini hoped that his new theory of government would attract enough support to keep communism out of Italy.

By 1922 Mussolini was ready. With a little band of followers he started from Milan and, like Julius Caesar long before, marched on Rome. The king was forced to make him premier (he called himself Il Duce). Mussolini restored order to Italy and made certain needed improvements. The theory was that the government would be operated by the various economic groups in the country. But, as was true of communism in Russia, the theory soon broke down, and Mussolini made himself absolute dictator as had Stalin in Russia. Factory owners, for example, soon found it meant little to keep title to factories when the government made all the decisions about their operation.

The fascist form of government was adopted in Germany by the National Socialist (Nazi) party, led by Adolf Hitler, formerly an Austrian paper hanger. As in Italy, the original theory of fascism gave way to a complete totalitarian dictatorship. Germany, after the war, had been stripped of colonies and merchant ships; part of her homeland was gone; much of her resources was taken by the victors—minerals and even livestock; her money became valueless; she was given a republican form of government—that is, her people were supposed to govern themselves when they didn't know the first thing about it; and she had 60,000,000 people to feed. Faced with such difficulties as these conditions provoked, the German people readily listened to Hitler when he promised to solve their problems for them if they would but surrender their political liberties to him—give him absolute power. In 1933 he was so strong President Paul von Hindenburg had to appoint him chancellor (prime minister), and when the president died the following year, Hitler combined the offices of chancellor and president and called himself Der Fuhrer—the Leader. What happened in Germany after that is common knowledge.

Events Leading to World War II. World War II actually began in Asia in 1931, but the world didn't recognize the fact at the time. The Japanese pulled a sneak attack on Manchuria, the northern part of China, and then sat back to see what the League of Nations would do about it. The League sent a commission to investigate. On the basis of its report, made a year later, the League asked Japan to withdraw from Manchuria. Instead, Japan withdrew from the League of Nations. Then she proceeded to take more of north China in outright defiance of the League. And the League was powerless to stop her.

Although the United States was not a member of the League, we thought something ought to be done to make Japan honor the treaties concerning

China which she, as well as we, had signed. We protested her action directly, and Secretary of State Henry Stimson called British Foreign Minister Sir John Simon by long-distance telephone to suggest joint action of some kind against Japan. But Sir John was unwilling to take any action; in fact, he had already spoken favorably of what Japan had done. So neither the United States nor Britain did anything. Japan got away completely with her seizure of Manchuria.

Italy became the second nation to expose the weakness of the League of Nations. In 1896 Italian soldiers had tried to take Abyssinia (Ethiopia) but had failed—because England helped the Abyssinians. In 1935 Mussolini sent his forces into the little country again. This time England helped Italy, and Abyssinia was conquered. Again the League was powerless to stop aggression. It had no forces to use against an invader save those made available to it by the member nations. And the stronger member nations were more concerned with their own selfish interests than they were with stopping aggression.

In 1936 a revolution broke out in Spain. The uprising was headed by General Francisco Franco of the army, who had the open support of Germany and Italy and the less open backing of certain interests in England and France and of the Roman Catholic Church. Hitler and Mussolini used the revolution to test their new weapons of blitz (lightning) warfare that were designed to defeat an enemy nation almost overnight. The weapons obviously were not yet perfected. The war in Spain dragged on for three years, although the Loyalists clearly did not have the

advantages the revolutionists did. Finally Franco won out and established a Fascist government in Spain, with himself as dictator.

In 1938, while Italy was very occupied in Abyssinia and could do nothing to prevent it, Hitler sent German troops into Austria and overthrew the

Acme

HITLER AND MUSSOLINI

The dictators who created the Rome-Berlin Axis are shown on the occasion of a jubilant meeting when they predicted that Nazi Germany and Fascist Italy would become the two greatest powers in Europe.

government of Chancellor Kurt von Schuschnigg. Soon Hitler was demanding the western part of Czechoslovakia (the Sudetenland, so named because of the Sudeten Mountains), where he claimed Germans were being mistreated by the Czech government. United States President Franklin D. Roosevelt and Prime Minister Neville Chamberlain of England asked Mussolini to arrange a conference of European powers to try to avert war. The four-power conference was held at Munich, in southern Germany (September, 1938). Hitler and Mussolini were there; Prime Minister Chamberlain represented England, and Premier Daladier, France. England and France refused to make good on their treaties to defend Czechoslovakia and gave Hitler the go-ahead sign. Without help, the Czechs could not fight; Hitler moved in unmolested. Before long he took the remainder of Czechoslovakia, although he had specifically promised not to do so.

The greater significance of the Munich Conference was not, however, in what it did to Czechoslovakia. Rather, it lay in what it did to Russia. England, still following her balance-of-power policy, was disturbed by the two rising camps in Europe—the communist nations and the Fascist nations. Sooner or later she had to choose between them; she must decide which was the bigger threat to her. At Munich she made that choice. Russia was not invited, although clearly she was involved in any European settlement. From then on England would co-operate with the fascist powers against Russia. And from then on Russia, who had been advocating collective security, followed a "lone wolf" policy in international affairs.

The next important step toward war was the signing of a nonaggression treaty by Germany and Russia in 1939. It practically assured war. It relieved both Germany and Russia of the danger of war on two fronts at the same time. It gave Russia time to get her war machine ready for use against Japan, her old enemy. It gave Germany free reign to go ahead with her expansion pro-gram in Europe, which was almost certain to bring war with England.

Soon Hitler was demanding the return of the free city of Danzig and a motor road through Poland to East Prussia.[6] Poland refused, and tension mounted. On September 1, 1939, Hitler sent his troops into Poland from the west, and two weeks later Stalin's troops moved in from the east. They divided Poland between them. England and France declared war on Germany on September 3. Europe was at war once again.

United States Attempts Neutrality. From this steady march of events leading to war, the United States had tried to remain separate and apart. We were greatly disillusioned as the result of our experiences in World War I. In the wake of the war "to make the world safe for democracy" came a big crop of dictatorships. A Senate investigating committee headed by Senator Gerald P. Nye exposed the huge profits made by financiers and munitions makers in the war. We learned how large money interests in the United States had first extended credit to the Allies to finance the purchase of war supplies here. When all their credit was used up, private concerns loaned money to the Allies so they could go on buying. Then in 1917 it looked as if the Allies would lose, and if they did, their debts would never be paid. These private companies exerted considerable pressure upon our government, and we went to war. The private companies unloaded their debts onto the American people, who, even though the Allies won, are still holding

---

[6] After World War I East Prussia was cut off from the rest of Germany to give Poland an outlet to the sea. Danzig had formerly been a city in Germany.

MILITARY DEMOLITION

The destruction of anything—human life or property—that could hinder the attainment of a military objective is an expedient of war and aggression. The war prisoner from whom this picture was taken reported it to be a photograph of German troops burning a Polish village in 1939.

the bag. The more our people learned about the real causes of our participation in the war of 1914–1918, the more determined they became not to be drawn into another. Let the nations of the world cut each other's throats if they liked, we said, but we wanted no part of it. And most of our people believed the big oceans on both sides of us would serve as huge insulators to protect us from conflicts that might rage elsewhere in the world.

So we did our best to keep out of trouble. The Johnson Act (1934) was supposed to prevent us from becoming economically interested in the future of nations that still owed us debts from the last war. When the war broke out between Italy and Ethiopia (1935), Congress passed the Neutrality Act. This law provided that whenever the President declared a state of war to exist anywhere in the world, no one in this country could export any war material to any of the warring nations or to any neutral nation to be sent on to a nation at war. American citizens traveled on ships of nations at war at their own risk. Nor could anyone lend money or extend credit to any belligerent power. The Neutrality Act was renewed and strengthened in 1937.

The idea was to keep anyone in this country from making money out of war. Take the profit out of war, many said, and there will be no war. But it didn't work; the wars went on in spite of our refusal to help either side. Other nations had no scruples about selling war supplies to anyone who would buy them, and so the fires were fed. But as they grew larger, we refused to do anything about putting them out.

Government leaders were ahead of the people in their thinking on this subject. President Roosevelt and Secretary of State Hull began to prepare for anything that might come. Conferences were held to promote co-operation among the American republics and Canada. The United States recognized the revolution-born government of Russia because Russia was the old enemy of both Germany and Japan, two of the new crop of would-be empire-builders. To strengthen our moral position in the Pacific, we promised independence to the Philippines on a definite date.

On October 5, 1937, President Roosevelt made a significant speech in dedicating the Outer Drive Bridge in Chicago. In it he attempted to arouse the people of the country to the peril of a do-nothing policy in the face of aggression in the world. "Let no one imagine," he warned, "that America will escape, that America may expect mercy, that this Western Hemisphere will not be attacked, and that it will continue tranquilly and peacefully to carry on the ethics and the arts of civilization."

The President put into his address a veiled suggestion of what he thought should be done. "When an epidemic of physical disease starts to spread," he said, "the community approves and joins in a quarantine of the patients." But he apparently felt public opinion was not yet far enough advanced to permit him to suggest specific ways for "quarantining" the aggressor nations in the world community of nations.

He did, however, express his belief in collective action as the means for preserving peace. In the speech he stated, "If we are to have a world in which we can breathe freely and live in amity without fear, the peace-loving nations must make a concerted effort to uphold laws and principles on which alone peace can rest secure. The peace-loving nations must make a concerted effort in opposition to those violations of treaties and those ignoring of humane instincts which today are creating a state of international anarchy and instability from which there is no escape through mere isolation or neutrality. . . . The peace, the freedom, and the security of 90 per cent of the population of the world are being jeopardized by the remaining 10 per cent who are threatening a breakdown of all international law and order. . . . The will for peace on the part of peace-loving nations must express itself to the end that nations that may be tempted to violate their agreements and the rights of others will desist from such a course. There must be positive endeavors to preserve peace."

The Chicago quarantine speech was a trial balloon to see just what the American people would stand for in the way of foreign policy. The President probably had his answer before he got back to Washington. Led by certain powerful and influential newspapers, a great wave of protest swept over the country. Why, it was said, such a policy as the President proposed might lead us into war again. And we didn't want another war, for any reason.

In 1937 Japan, flushed with success in Manchuria and North China, began her all-out war for the rest of China. She expected that six months would do the job, but Chinese resistance was far greater than she had thought it could be, and the war dragged on and on. People in this country sympathized with the people of China, whom we considered the victims of unprovoked aggression. Our government loaned large sums of money to the Chinese

THE OVERBURDENED LABORER

This laden figure might well symbolize the Orient's poverty-ridden and war-distressed common people.

government for defense. But while this was going on, American merchants were selling to Japan the oil and steel and scrap-iron and leather and chemicals to make her war against China possible. We wanted China to win, but we couldn't resist the profit to be made from the sale of war supplies to Japan. As we look back upon it, we realize that such a policy didn't make sense, but right then it made dollars, and that was the controlling factor at the time.

Sir John Simon had never told the British cabinet of the Stimson proposal

of joint action against Japan in 1931. Only later did the facts become known, and then Sir John was promptly transferred to the Home Office. In 1937, when Japan began her total war against China, a second opportunity presented itself. This time Britain was ready to act. Winston Churchill, speaking unofficially for the British government, said, "There is one simple rule: we must act in support of the United States. If they are prepared to act, you are quite safe working with that great branch of the English-speaking countries. If our two countries go together, I doubt whether any great harm could come to either of us. Alone we cannot intervene effectively. It is too far off and we are not strong enough. Our rule must be to give more support to the United States. As far as they will go, we will go."

The League of Nations was dying, but President Roosevelt felt collective action should be taken anyway, by direct action among the nations. A conference was called at Brussels, Belgium (November, 1937), of the signers of the Nine-Power Treaty (to guarantee China's independence) to consider what was to be done about Japan's aggression. The President chose Norman Davis to represent this country and outlined to him what apparently was a specific proposal for united action by the nations concerned. If other countries were reluctant to move, the United States and Britain would go ahead anyway.

But the Roosevelt proposal was never made to the Brussels Conference. By the time Norman Davis reached Europe, his instructions had been cancelled. The stock market had broken sharply just before he left, and the country seemed headed for a business recession, which is a nice term for a mild depression. President Roosevelt realized that this economic change would command first attention from the American people. In addition, they were decidedly opposed to his "quarantine" proposal. The step he intended taking at Brussels could not succeed without the support of the people, and obviously he couldn't get that at this time. Mr. Davis was told to forget the whole thing.

For years Russia had been advocating a policy of collective action to insure peace. At Brussels Maxim Litvinov, Russian Commissar of Foreign Affairs, made it clear to Mr. Davis that that was the last opportunity to get Russian co-operation in such a policy. If nothing was done at Brussels, said Litvinov, Russia would have to turn to some other course of action to secure peace for herself. Mr. Davis had to tell Mr. Litvinov that nothing would be done. Litvinov left before the conference was over and not long after was removed as head of the Russian department of foreign affairs.

At Brussels and at Munich apparently the last opportunities faded for the nations of the world to join in a common plan of action to stop aggression. The world was looking to the United States for leadership, but our people were then determined to play no part in world affairs. We wanted to stay neutral. Our traditional belief in fair play was temporarily pushed into the background. We insisted on being neutral in the Ethiopian affair, while England helped Italy conquer the country. We declared our neutrality in the Spanish revolution, while Italy and Germany helped Franco win. In each case our sympathies were with the people who were finally defeated. Some of our boys even enlisted and fought in the defeated forces. Gradually more and more people came to realize that there is no such thing as neutrality. In refusing to help either side, almost certainly that decision is bound to help one side or the other. As one American put it, "Only the stars are neutral." [7]

President Roosevelt and Secretary of State Hull were more aware than the American people of the futility of attempts at neutrality for a big power like the United States. While the people continued to cling to isolation, Mr. Roosevelt and Mr. Hull went ahead with plans for our defense and for the aid of our friends. In January, 1938, the President asked Congress to build our navy beyond the limits set by the Washington and London treaties. He arranged for the sale of arms and planes to England and France. King George VI and Queen Elizabeth of Great Britain were invited to visit the United States to increase the bond of sentiment already existing between the two great English-speaking peoples. Such was the state of affairs in this country when war broke out in Europe in 1939.

---

[7] These words became the title of a book by Quentin Reynolds.

FOR YOUR REVIEW

These Should Be Easy for You Now

1. What was the nature of President Wilson's Fourteen Points? Why were they issued?
2. Why was Italy angered to the point of withdrawing from the peace conference?
3. What happened to Wilson's Fourteen Points at the peace conference?

4. Describe in general the terms of the peace settlement in Europe.
5. What purpose did the new countries in Europe serve? Name them.
6. What was the over-all purpose of the League of Nations? Where was its head-quarters located?
7. What were the Senate's chief objections to the League of Nations? Did the United States join? How successful was the League?
8. Distinguish between the Hague Court and the Permanent Court of International Justice. Under what provision did the United States offer to join the latter?
9. What world situation prompted the Washington Arms Conference? What nations were represented? What did the conference accomplish? What was its real significance for the United States? What country was responsible for ending the naval limitation agreement?
10. What was the purpose of the Nine Power Treaty?
11. Who were the men who engineered the Paris Pact? What was its purpose? Why was it unsuccessful?
12. How were German reparations the key to the war debt problem? What was the purpose of the Dawes Plan and the Young Plan?
13. What changes did the two revolutions in 1917 bring about in Russia?
14. What did England do to prevent the western spread of communism? How did the British policy disrupt the balance of power in Europe?
15. How does fascism differ from both capitalism and communism? In what European countries was fascism established?
16. What conditions made it easy for Mussolini and Hitler to seize power?
17. Trace the events that led to World War II, beginning with the Japanese invasion of Manchuria in 1931.
18. For what purpose did Germany and Italy use the Spanish Revolution?
19. What men met at the Munich Conference? What did they do? What was the greatest significance of the conference?
20. Why did the Russo-German nonaggression pact practically guarantee war in Europe?
21. How was the Neutrality Act intended to keep us out of war? Why didn't it work?
22. What was the attitude of the American people to the spread of aggression in the world? What was our position toward the war between Japan and China?
23. What were Norman Davis' first instructions for the Brussels Conference? Why were they changed? With what effect?

Associated Dates

1917—Communist government established in Russia, November 7
1918—President Wilson's Fourteen Points issued, January 8
1919—Treaty of Versailles signed in Paris, June 28
1920—first meeting of the League of Nations, January 10
1921—United States peace treaties with Germany, Austria, and Hungary ratified, October 18
1922—Fascist government established in Italy, October 28
1931—Japanese invasion of Manchuria
1934—offices of Reich President and Reich Chancellor combined under Hitler in Germany, August 2
1935—United States Neutrality Act passed in August
       Italian invasion of Ethiopia begins, October 3
1936—Revolution in Spain

1937—beginning of Japan's war for the remainder of China, in July
1938—German troops invade Austria, March 11
       Munich Pact signed, September 30
1939—Russia and Germany sign a nonaggression pact, August 24
       World War II begins in Europe, September 3

Why Are These To Be Remembered?

David Lloyd George
Georges Clemenceau
Vittorio Orlando
Woodrow Wilson
Henry Cabot Lodge
William E. Borah
Hiram Johnson
Andrew Carnegie
Aristide Briand
Frank B. Kellogg
Charles G. Dawes
Owen D. Young
Nikolai Lenin
Leon Trotsky
Joseph Stalin
Alexander Kerensky
Benito Mussolini
Adolf Hitler

Paul von Hindenburg
Henry L. Stimson
Sir John Simon
Francisco Franco
Kurt von Schuschnigg
Gerald P. Nye
Norman Davis
Maxim Litvinov
Fourteen Points
Versailles
Permanent Court of International Justice
Hague Court
Washington Arms Conference
Twenty-One Demands
Nine Power Treaty
Moratorium

Johnson Act
Bolshevik
Soviet
U.S.S.R.
Communism
Fascism
Nazi
Totalitarianism
Il Duce
Der Fuhrer
Chancellor
Manchuria
Abyssinia (Ethiopia)
Sudetenland
East Prussia
Danzig
Neutrality Act
Quarantine Speech

Chapter 14

Global War Envelops the United States

IN SPITE OF ITS INTENTIONS, THE UNITED STATES IS UNABLE TO STAY
OUT OF A SECOND GREAT WORLD CONFLICT

From Isolation to Intervention. The United States moved, slowly and without knowing it, from isolation to intervention. The problem of our government was a delicate one. It had to try to protect the United States from war in Europe and Asia when the American people didn't think they needed protecting. The actions of the government were anything but neutral. We got around the Johnson Act (see Chapter 13) by modifying our Neutrality Act to permit the sale of munitions on a "cash and carry" basis. This gave England and France the advantage, for they could pay cash for their purchases. We sent more and more aid to England until we were actually in an undeclared war with Germany. Later, when the war increased in intensity, we used our navy to insure delivery of munitions. We continued our expressions of sympathy for China while we went on supplying Japan with war materials.

The War in Europe. Although a state of war existed in Europe, for months nothing much happened, except that Russia attacked Finland when the latter refused to give in to Russian demands as had Latvia, Lithuania, and Esthonia. Then in the spring of 1940 it became a real war. In rapid succession Germany overran Denmark, Norway, Holland, Belgium, and France. In June Italy joined Germany and that fall at-

tacked Greece. In the spring of 1941 Germany gave Italy aid by crushing Bulgaria, Yugoslavia, and then Greece. In June of 1941 Germany turned on her ally Russia and declared war.

The Selective Service Act. After the fall of France Germany began an air "blitz" of England as an obvious prelude to attempted invasion. In September, 1940, Japan joined Germany and Italy and pledged herself to attack the United States if we became involved in the European war. Events in Europe waked up the American people somewhat, but they still put their hope in neutrality. President Roosevelt was reluctant to take full advantage of the new sentiment at just that time, however, for an election was coming up, and he had decided to run for a third term. He asked Congress to adjourn, but Congress stayed in session and passed the Selective Service Act (1940). For the first time the United States had agreed to compulsory military training during peacetime. In the beginning men between the ages of twenty-one and thirty-six were called for twelve months' service; they could be sent anywhere in the Western Hemisphere or to any of our possessions. Later the age limits were broadened to twenty to forty-four and finally, after war was declared, from eighteen to forty-four years.

182

Election of 1940. The Republicans nominated Wendell Willkie, a former Democrat. In the campaign both candidates expressed sympathy for the people attacked by Germany, Italy, and Japan, and asserted their determination to keep this country out of war. President Roosevelt assured American mothers with the statement: "Your boys are not going to be sent into any foreign wars. . . . The purpose of our defense is defense." President Roosevelt was re-elected; he became the first President to serve more than two terms.

In his annual message to Congress in January, 1941, the President envisioned the defeat of aggression in the world and a new world order based upon "four essential freedoms"—freedom of speech, freedom of religion, freedom from want, and freedom from fear. These were ideas to which all Americans could subscribe.

America's Defense Program. In the name of defense, we had been pushing our security bases farther and farther toward Europe and Asia. The Declaration of Panama, October 3, 1939, set up a zone around the American continents in which we said we would disapprove of operations by war vessels of belligerent nations. In 1940 President Roosevelt traded with England fifty destroyers for bases in Newfoundland and British islands in the Caribbean. Later we obtained other bases in Greenland, Iceland, and Northern Ireland.

Also in the interest of defense, we took certain moves to increase the solidarity of the Americas. The Act of Havana, July, 1940, authorized American nations, jointly, to administer the government of areas in the Americas owned by non-American states which had or might become conquered countries. The Ogdensburg Agreement, August 17, 1940, established a joint United States–Canada Board of Defense. The Hyde Park Declaration of April 20, 1941, provided for the coordination of United States and Canadian defense and war production.

As the war went on in Europe, our participation became greater, all in the name of defense. The President sent Admiral Leahy as his personal representative to Vichy, the capital of the Nazi puppet government of France, to try to keep the French fleet from falling into the hands of the Germans. In January, 1941, President Roosevelt sent to Congress a bill asking authority to sell, exchange, lease, or lend to the countries at war with the Axis Powers (Germany, Italy, Japan) munitions and other war supplies. The President called it a bill "to promote the defense of the United States" and argued that the best way to keep out of war was to help other countries defeat the Axis by making this country an "arsenal of democracy." After much discussion, Congress passed the bill on March 11 and appropriated seven billion dollars for its operation.

When Russia was attacked by Hitler in June, 1941, the Lend-Lease Act, as it was called, was extended to that country, too, although we did not like what Russia had done in Poland and the Baltic countries nor did we like the government of Russia. However, the fact that she had been forced onto our side made us feel more kindly toward Stalin and his government.

Before the war was over, the United States had invested more than fifty billion dollars in lend-lease and had obtained seven billion in reverse lend-lease, principally in food and quarters for our troops abroad. All in all, more

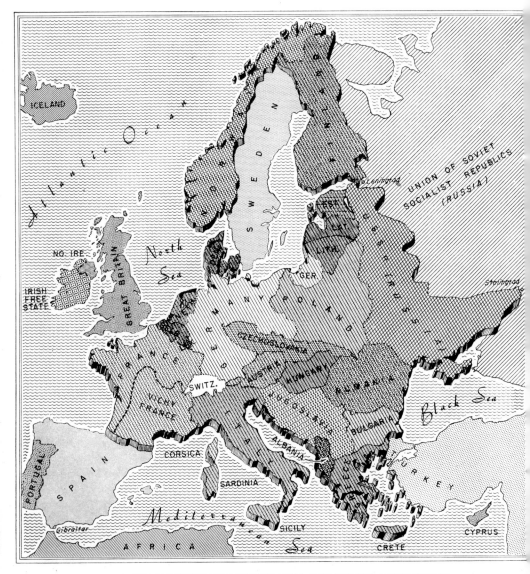

THE AXIS POWERS DOMINATE THE EUROPEAN CONTINENT

The shaded portions of this map (with lines running downward from left to right) show the full extent of the Axis military conquest of neighboring countries at the crest of the Nazi-Fascist power in 1941.

than 60 per cent of our lend-lease went to England and the British Commonwealth of Nations and 22 per cent to Russia.

The Atlantic Charter. In August, 1941, President Roosevelt and Prime Minister Winston Churchill of England met on shipboard off the coast of Newfoundland to discuss steps to be taken. Out of this meeting came the famous Atlantic Charter. It was a restatement of some of Mr. Wilson's Fourteen

Acme

ROOSEVELT AND CHURCHILL FORMULATE THE ATLANTIC CHARTER

At their historic meeting aboard the British battleship "Prince of Wales" off the Newfoundland coast in August, 1941, the two chiefs of state pledged the destruction of Nazi tyranny and a peace that would guarantee security against aggression.

Points. It recognized the right of any people to choose their own government. It promised that England and the United States "will endeavor, with due respect for their existing obligations, to further the enjoyment by all States, great or small, victor or vanquished, of access, on equal terms, to the trade and to the raw materials of the world which are needed for their economic prosperity." It expressed the hope that, after the "destruction of the Nazi tyranny," a peace could be established that would guarantee security against aggression to all nations. In the Four Freedoms and the Atlantic Charter the American people felt they had something they could fight for, if necessary.[1]

The Shooting Begins. All this time we were becoming more involved in a shooting war. American destroyers were

[1] Later, when Mr. Churchill was asked if the Atlantic Charter applied to Britain's possessions, he replied with a now famous statement. With his eye on the phrase "with due respect for their existing obligations," he said, "I did not become the King's Chief Minister to preside over the liquidation of the British Empire."

convoying lend-lease material abroad. In September, 1941, the President ordered the navy to sink on sight any German or Italian submarines or warships in waters "the protection of which is necessary for American defense." On October 27 the President reported that some of our merchant ships had been sunk and our destroyers attacked. Several sailors were killed. We openly abandoned neutrality and armed our merchant vessels. The shooting had started.

AMERICAN PEOPLE UNITE FOR WAR

Japan Becomes an Enemy. Affairs in the Pacific were becoming more tense, too. Japan was not winning, and the war was becoming more and more of a threat to us. On July 26, 1939, our government announced that our 1911 commercial treaty with Japan would be terminated six months later. Two years after that (July 22, 1941) the President froze Japanese assets in the United States after Japan had seized control of Indo-China. In a similar manner he froze assets in this country of the war-involved European nations. In the spring of 1941 we embargoed the shipment of war materials to Japan. In the fall of 1941 we made it clear to Japan that the prerequisite to the resumption of Japanese-American relations was the withdrawal of Japanese troops from China. This Japan refused to do. ·

A special agent of the Japanese government, Saburo Kurusu, arrived in Washington on November 17. He and Ambassador Kichisaburo Nomura held lengthy conversations with our State Department to try to find a peaceful settlement of the Far Eastern situation. These talks made it clear that the United States could not agree to

Japan's policy in Asia and that Japan would not abandon that policy.

While these discussions were still going on, Japan staged a sudden attack on our naval base at Pearl Harbor, Hawaii, on December 7, 1941. Eight ships were destroyed or damaged badly; virtually all the aircraft were destroyed before they could get into the air; 4,500 men were killed or wounded. The base was caught completely by surprise, and the result gave Japan a great advantage in the Pacific for some months.

War Declared. The next day President Roosevelt went before Congress and asked it to declare that a state of war existed between this country and Japan. On December 11 Germany and Italy declared war on the United States, and we on them. We also declared war on Bulgaria, Hungary, and Rumania, German satellite nations, on June 5, 1942. Great Britain followed us into the war against Japan, and soon most of the nations of the world were drawn into the war in either Europe or Asia. In Europe only four countries were able to cling to neutrality and keep out of active warfare: Sweden, Switzerland, Spain, and Portugal. It was clear this was possible not because of the strength of these four nations or their ability to protect themselves but simply because no warring nation saw any particular advantage in conquering them.

War Organizations. When war came, our government set up new agencies to cope with new problems. This was mechanized war, and it called for greatly expanded production. To deal with production problems the War Production Board was created. To distribute war supplies to our armed forces all over the world, the government created the Office of Defense

JAPAN LAUNCHES ATTACK ON OUR FLEET AT PEARL HARBOR

Like an electric shock, the surprise bombing of Pearl Harbor by Japanese planes on December 7, 1941, plunged the United States into World War II. Three American battleships that were targets during the attack are shown here: the U.S.S. "West Virginia," "Tennessee," and "Arizona."

Transportation and the War Shipping Administration. To deal with labor problems we had the National War Labor Board and the War Manpower Commission. The job of rationing goods and controlling prices was given to the Office of Price Administration. We had a Board of Economic Stabilization and an Office of War Mobilization. The Office of War Information put out news about the war for the government, and the Office of Censorship controlled all communication between the United States and other countries and the release of information within the United States.

War Production. American industry soon showed its ability to produce in a volume never before imagined. Facto-ries were expanded rapidly and countless new ones were built, some by private concerns and others directly by the government. Factories that had turned out automobiles, locomotives, refrigerators, and other consumer goods now began to produce a steady stream of guns, tanks, planes, and other war supplies. Ocean-going war vessels began to spring up even on the prairies of the Midwest.

The number of people employed in war production grew from about seven million in late 1941 to around twenty million in 1943. In 1939 not 2 per cent of our production went for war; in 1944, it was 40 per cent. Women worked side by side with men on war jobs, even at such rigorous work as outdoor welding.

Higgins Industries, Inc.

OUR SHIPBUILDING SET ALL-TIME RECORDS IN WORLD WAR II

These are cargo ships built for the Army during wartime. Thousands of such vessels, turned out on a mass-production basis, gave the Allies overwhelming superiority in sea transport that made possible the successful landings in Africa, Europe, and in the Pacific.

Wages were high, and prices increased accordingly. The OPA (Office of Price Administration) took steps to control somewhat both wages and prices, but still they were higher than ever before. The government was forced to bid against private industry for more workers, and that forced wages higher and higher. Farm workers were frequently exempt from military service to help produce more foodstuffs. More people had more money to spend than ever before.

Office of Civilian Defense. Civilians not engaged directly in war production found ways to help the war effort, too. The Office of Civilian Defense helped point out things people could do. They were urged to save and to put money regularly into war bonds and war savings stamps. Boys and girls and professional people helped on farms during the summer. Everyone was urged to consume less and waste less of everything. Air-raid shelters were designated, and black-outs and dim-outs were practiced to prepare for possible attack. People watched for and reported passing planes, did Red Cross work, substituted as nurses in hospitals, operated nurseries for the children of mothers working in war plants, and helped in any and all ways to keep the life of every community going in spite of the heavy drain of men and women into war industry and the armed forces.

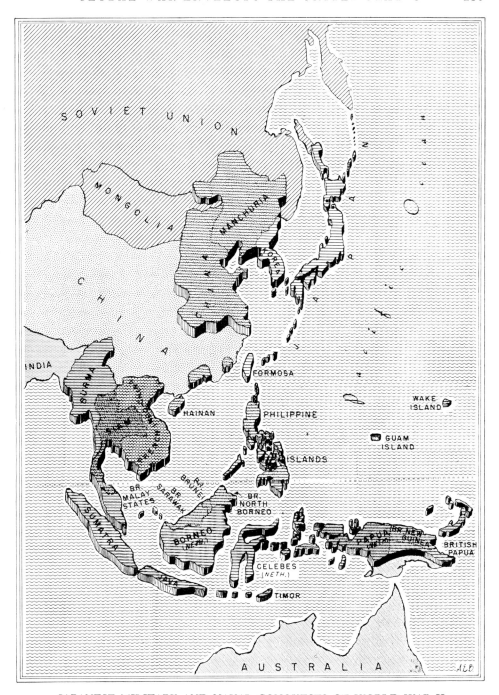

JAPANESE MILITARY AND NAVAL CONQUESTS OF WORLD WAR II

Like her Axis partners in Europe, Japan reached the crest of her power through armed aggression early in the war. This map shows the extent of her acquisitions within twelve months after Pearl Harbor.

Women Join Armed Forces. Even in the armed forces women helped. Auxiliary organizations were created. We had the Women's Army Auxiliary Corps (WAAC), the Women's Naval Reserve Corps (the WAVES), the Women's Reserve of the Coast Guard Reserve (the SPARS), and the Auxiliary Marine Corps. Women in these organizations were sent overseas just the same as men were. In addition, we had the United Service Organization (USO), made up of men and women entertainers who followed the fighting units into all parts of the world.

Critical Months. After the attack on Pearl Harbor the Japanese took Guam, Wake, Hong Kong, and landed in the Philippines. American and Philippine troops were pushed back steadily until all they held was the island of Corregidor in Manila Bay. General Douglas MacArthur escaped from the islands to Australia, and in May, 1942, Corregidor fell. Soon Japan controlled most of the Dutch East Indies, Malaya, Burma, and many smaller islands in the West Pacific.

The United States was not prepared for war. The best we could do was try to keep the Japanese out of Australia and strike crippling blows at them whenever and wherever possible. Some of these encounters were heroic successes. There was the battle of the Coral Sea, off the Bismarck Archipelago, in May, 1942. A month later a Japanese advance toward Hawaii was stopped near the Midway Islands. American and Japanese troops engaged in jungle combat in Guadalcanal and other southern Pacific islands. They fought all along Pacific Asia, even in the Aleutian Islands, off Alaska.

We could not do much to help in Europe, either, at the beginning. Hitler had been unable to take England, and now we sent bomber and fighter planes, in ever-increasing numbers, to help in the attack upon German industrial centers. Germany was pushing Russian forces back steadily in her march toward Moscow. The cry for help came from Stalin, and soon there was a general demand for a "second front" in Europe.

The Tide Turns. Late in 1942 British and American forces had landed in Morocco and Algeria in North Africa. There, with the co-operation of Free French forces, they were able to defeat the Germans and Italians who were already there. The Axis forces surrendered on May 12, 1943. This move was designed to prevent an attack upon South America by way of Africa.

On July 10 the invasion of the "soft under-belly" of Europe began. Americans and British conquered Sicily and moved on across to Italy. German forces were sent to the aid of the Italians, and the invasion was slow and costly. Rome was not occupied until in June, 1944. The struggle continued until German and Italian troops had been driven into the mountains of northern Italy. A large German army was kept occupied for a long time, and Mussolini's forces were put out of business. The Italian campaign was an important factor in the war in Europe.

The time was ripe for the invasion of western Europe. D-Day came on June 6, 1944. The Anglo-American invasion forces were directed by Supreme Commander General Dwight D. Eisenhower of the United States. With a blanket of planes overhead and a screen of fire from the warships in the Channel, a bridge of boats carried Allied troops

OUR TECHNICAL ADVANCES SPEEDED VICTORY AT SEA

Scientific developments in naval weapons kept us ahead of the Axis. Our radar proved itself in the great battles of the Pacific. The picture above shows one of our warships launching rockets.

U.S. ASSAULT TROOPS RECAPTURE A PACIFIC ISLAND

Bloody fighting on the coral reefs and beaches of Pacific islands marked the road from Pearl Harbor to Tokyo Bay for American forces.

ALLIED TROOPS AND EQUIPMENT LAND AT ALGERIA

The successful landing of combined American and British forces in North Africa in 1942 gave the Allies a toehold in the drive to strike at Europe from the south.

across from England to establish a beachhead in Normandy. By August 25 they were in Paris. By that time troops had landed on the southern coast of France. Allied troops withstood a final German attack in Belgium in the Battle of the Bulge (December 16, 1944). Axis forces were driven from France and Belgium. Germany came next.

Russian lines had held finally, and their troops, with American aid brought in through Iran (Persia), had turned the German advance into a retreat. Russia had knocked Rumania and Bulgaria out of the war and was attacking the Germans in Hungary and Poland. The British and Americans broke through the German "West Wall" in February, 1945. Soon they were across the Rhine and on their way to Berlin from the west. The Russians were moving toward Berlin from the east.

V-E Day. At this point the British and American advance was halted to permit the Russians to reach Berlin first. On May 2 the Germans in Italy and Austria surrendered. Mussolini was captured and killed by his own people.

Hitler, according to the best of evidence (his body was never found), was dead, and Grand Admiral Karl von Doenitz was in charge of the German government. On May 7 that government surrendered to American General Dwight D. Eisenhower, Commander-in-Chief of the Allied forces in western Europe. May 7, 1945, is popularly called V-E

THEY PLANNED STRATEGY

General of the Army Dwight Eisenhower (center) confers with British Field Marshal Montgomery and U.S. General Omar Bradley.

THIS WAS THE PRELUDE TO MUSSOLINI'S DOWNFALL

The Allied victory in the Battle of Anzio Beach in 1944 paved the way for the invasion of Italy and the destruction of Hitler's Fascist partner. Anti-aircraft crews like the one shown here helped turn back the Axis air attack.

THE MAJOR ASSAULT ON HITLER'S EUROPE BEGAN AT NORMANDY

Allied troops that went ashore behind the tanks at Omaha Beach in 1944 spearheaded the invasion of France. The drive ended with the occupation of Berlin and the end of the European phase of World War II.

GENERAL MACARTHUR ACCEPTS THE SURRENDER OF JAPAN

At formal ceremonies aboard the U.S.S. "Missouri" anchored in Tokyo Bay, General of the Army Douglas MacArthur, as Supreme Commander of Allied Powers, signed the document that officially ended hostilities with Japan.

Day (Victory in Europe Day). The victorious powers—United States, Britain, France, and Russia—divided Germany into four zones, with each nation occupying a zone.

V-J Day. By 1943 American war production and training had reached the point where an offensive against Japan could be started. American troops began to fight their way northward from their bases in the South Pacific. Names long to be remembered began to appear in the headlines of news reports: Tarawa, Makin, Kwajalein, Guam, Iwo Jima, Okinawa. The Philippines were recaptured. On August 6, 1945, American airmen dropped an atomic bomb on Hiroshima, with ter-rifying loss of life and destruction. Two days later another bomb was dropped on Nagasaki with similar results. On August 8 Russia declared war on Japan and moved into Manchuria. Japan surrendered on August 14. The papers were signed on the American battleship "Missouri" on September 2, 1945 (V-J Day). The war was over.

Victory through American Production. As in 1918, participation of the United States had meant the difference between victory and defeat. That does not mean that the United States won the war singlehanded. But during the last three years of the war we were supplying our Allies with most of their war needs through lend-lease. Our boys bore the greater part of the burden of attack in Italy and in western Europe. We defeated Japan with almost no other help except from China, who had held the Japanese war machine at bay for more than four years before we became involved in the Pacific.

It was American production that won the war. This was mechanized war, and we could manufacture the machines of destruction faster than anyone else. Our production record is an awesome thing. As the number of people employed in our war plants rose, speed of production increased. For example, in 1940, twenty million man hours were required to build a bombing plane. In 1941 this had shrunk to two million; in 1942, to 200,000; and by 1944, to 13,800. That is, in 1944 we were turning out 1,450 bombers where we had produced one in 1940. The world had never seen such a display of industrial strength and ability.

The Cost of Victory. The direct cost of the war to the American people was well over the 300 billion mark—nearly half the cost to all the United Nations. The total cost—past, present, and future—may never be calculated, for many, many generations from now people will still be paying the bill.

Our armed forces suffered more than a million casualties—killed, wounded, missing, and imprisoned. About 300,000 of our men in uniform were killed. But even with this vast cost in lives and fortune, the United States was more fortunate than the other great powers involved in the war. Our cities were not destroyed; our civilian population was not subjected to indiscriminate bombing raids. And our actual number of lives lost was less than that of any of the other big nations.

The total casualties in Russia alone are estimated at perhaps as many as fifteen million.

THE UNITED NATIONS

Early Plans for UN. Throughout the war frequent meetings were held by

The American Weekly

ATOMIC ERA OPENS

World War II ended with man facing the problem of controlling the destructive power of the atom bomb shown exploding here.

officials of the big powers to co-ordinate their fighting efforts. There was a genuine desire for co-operation to win the war. Shortly after the Japanese attack on Pearl Harbor, President Roosevelt coined the name "United Nations" to stand for all those countries who were at war with Germany, Italy, and Japan. On January 1, 1942, twenty-six nations signed the United Nations Declaration in Washington. They pledged themselves to stand together until victory

THE GUY WHO RELAXES IS HELPING THE AXIS!

Higgins Industries, Inc.

THESE BOATS LANDED OUR MEN ON ENEMY SHORES

The ramp landing boats shown here were the most widely used type of small craft that carried beach assault troops ashore in amphibious operations of World War II.

was won. Thus the United Nations as a co-operative fighting unit was born.

A year later, in January, 1943, President Roosevelt and Prime Minister Churchill met at Casablanca, in North Africa, for a conference. Also present were representatives of the French government in exile. Out of this meeting came the joint statement that the war would go on until the "unconditional surrender" of the enemies had been attained.

In October of that year (1943) an important meeting was held in Moscow, attended by the foreign ministers of the Big Three. Secretary of State Hull was there for the United States, Anthony Eden for Great Britain, and Molotov for Russia. The conference went on record as recognizing "the necessity of establishing at the earliest practicable date a general international organization based upon the principle of the sovereign equality of all peace-loving states, large and small, for the maintenance of international peace and security."

The next month (November, 1943) Roosevelt, Churchill, and Chiang Kai-shek of China met in Cairo, Egypt. There they made plans for the defeat of Japan. They also decided that Japan's colonies should be taken from her when the war was over and that the lands she had seized should be returned to the powers that had ruled them before the war started. Thus the old empires were assured of their continuance, but the decision disregarded one of the basic trends of modern world history—the desire of all people to be free.

Immediately following the Cairo Conference another was held at Teheran, Persia, attended by Roosevelt, Churchill, and Stalin. Here plans were made for the defeat of Germany and Italy, and an invitation was issued to all nations to join the "world family of democratic nations." The idea of a world organization to keep peace was growing.

The Dumbarton Oaks Proposals. The way had been paved; the time was ripe for action. From August 21 to October 7, 1944, representatives of the United States, Great Britain, Russia, and China met at Dumbarton Oaks, a famous old mansion near Washington, D.C. Together they worked out a suggested framework for a world organization that was designed to hold together in peacetime the nations that had been co-operating in war. Their suggestions were known as the Dumbarton Oaks Proposals. A later meeting of lawyers from forty-four countries drew up a plan for an International Court of Justice.

The United Nations Charter. The final big conference of the war was held at Yalta in the Crimea in February, 1945. Roosevelt, Churchill, and Stalin were there. They made final plans for the defeat and division of Germany and scheduled a conference for San Francisco to meet on April 25, 1945, to draw up a charter for "a general international organization to maintain peace and security."

The basis for discussion at San Francisco was the Dumbarton Oaks Proposals. On June 26, 1945, representatives from fifty nations signed the United Nations Charter. It could not go into effect until signed by the United States, Great Britain, France, China, and the Soviet Union. This was accomplished in October when Russia ratified. Provision was made for other nations to become members when recommended by the Security Council and approved by the General Assembly.

The purposes of the United Nations, as stated in the charter, are:

1. To maintain international peace and security, and to that end: to take effective collective measures for the prevention and removal of threats to the peace, and for the suppression of acts of aggression or other breaches of the peace, and to bring about by peaceful means, and in conformity with the principles of justice and international law, adjustment or settlement of international disputes or situations which might lead to a breach of the peace.

2. To develop friendly relations among nations based on respect for the principle of equal rights and self-determination of peoples, and to take other appropriate measures to strengthen universal peace.

3. To achieve international co-operation in solving international problems of an economic, social, cultural, or humanitarian character, and in promoting and encouraging respect for human rights and for fundamental freedoms for all without distinction as to race, sex, language, or religion.

4. To be a center for harmonizing the actions of nations in the attainment of these common ends.

As set up, the United Nations was divided into six main branches: the General Assembly, the Security Council, the International Court of Justice, the Economic and Social Council, the

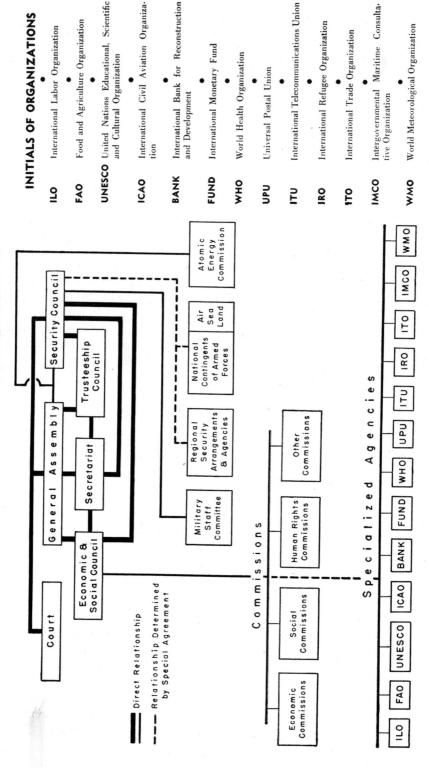

INITIALS OF ORGANIZATIONS

ILO	International Labor Organization
FAO	Food and Agriculture Organization
UNESCO	United Nations Educational, Scientific and Cultural Organization
ICAO	International Civil Aviation Organization
BANK	International Bank for Reconstruction and Development
FUND	International Monetary Fund
WHO	World Health Organization
UPU	Universal Postal Union
ITU	International Telecommunications Union
IRO	International Refugee Organization
ITO	International Trade Organization
IMCO	Intergovernmental Maritime Consultative Organization
WMO	World Meteorological Organization

DIAGRAM OF U.N. ORGANIZATION

Court

Economic & Social Council

General Assembly

Security Council

Trusteeship Council

Secretariat

Atomic Energy Commission

National Contingents of Armed Forces — Air Sea Land

Regional Security Arrangements & Agencies

Military Staff Committee

— Direct Relationship

--- Relationship Determined by Special Agreement

Commissions

Economic Commissions

Social Commissions

Human Rights Commissions

Other Commissions

Specialized Agencies

ILO FAO UNESCO ICAO BANK FUND WHO UPU ITU IRO ITO IMCO WMO

GREAT HOPES FOR PEACE ATTEND BIRTH OF UNITED NATIONS

A war-weary world shared momentary optimism in 1946 for an effective peace organization. Hopes grew less bright as world tension grew. This view shows the General Assembly delegates standing in silent prayer at the opening session of September, 1950, at Flushing Meadow, New York.

Trusteeship Council, and the Secretariat. The following brief outline will give an over-all view of the purposes, duties, and methods of operation of these branches.

I. General Assembly:

  A. Purpose: to serve as a "sounding-board of international public opinion," a "town meeting of the world."

  B. Membership: representatives of all member nations.

  C. Operation:

    1. Each nation has but one vote; no member nation may have more than five representatives.

    2. The Assembly elects its own president.

    3. On simple matters only a majority vote is needed; on important questions, a two-thirds vote is needed for passage.

  D. Duties:

    1. It is the duty of the Assembly to discuss and make recommendations concerning all problems of world affairs, especially those that might lead to a disturbance of relations among nations.

    2. The Assembly elects the nonpermanent members of

the Security Council and the members of the other councils.

3. The Assembly considers and approves the budget of the organization.

II. Security Council:

A. Purpose: to maintain international peace and security.

B. Membership: the Security Council has five permanent members—China, France, Russia, Britain, and the United States; the six other members are elected by the Assembly for two-year terms.

C. Operation:

1. Matters are settled by a majority vote. But in voting military action against a member, all five of the permanent members must vote in favor of it.

2. How the Security Council works:

   a) A complaint is made to the Council by a member nation.

   b) The Council by a majority vote decides to discuss the case.

   c) A majority, including the Big Five, vote to investigate.

   d) The Council suggests a settlement, exhausting all peaceful means.

   e) The Council proceeds with economic or military action if all other means fail, using the UN military force which can be drawn from all member nations.

III. International Court of Justice:

A. Purpose: to resolve legal disputes among nations

B. Membership: fifteen judges elected by the Assembly and the Security Council for terms of nine years; they may be re-elected.

C. Jurisdiction:

1. The Court has the right to interpret a treaty.

2. The Court can consider any question based upon international law.

3. The Court can investigate the existence of any fact which, if established, would constitute a breach of an international obligation.

4. The Court can determine the nature or extent of the reparation to be made for the breach of an international obligation.

D. Operation:

1. The Court is to be located at The Hague, Netherlands.

2. The use of the Court by member nations is voluntary.

3. Any member may appeal to the Security Council to have the Court's decisions enforced.

IV. Economic and Social Council:

A. Purpose: to promote—

1. Higher standards of living, full employment, and conditions of economic and social progress and development.

2. Solutions of international economic, social, health, and related problems, and international cultural and educational co-operation.

VETO POWER'S USE DIVIDES THE SECURITY COUNCIL

The alignment of opposing interests between the Western Powers led by the United States and the Soviet bloc led by Russia developed a wide breach in the Security Council of the United Nations.

THE INTERNATIONAL COURT OF JUSTICE CONVENES

In this photo the justices are hearing a case concerning the interpretation of the peace treaties with Bulgaria, Hungary, and Romania. The proceedings took place at the Peace Palace, The Hague, Netherlands, on February 28, 1950.

3. Universal respect for, and observance of, human rights and freedoms for all without distinction as to race, sex, language, or religion.

B. Membership: eighteen nations elected by the Assembly: six each year for three-year terms; members may be re-elected.

C. Commissions:

1. Economic and Employment Commission to deal with international trade, raw materials, and unemployment.

2. Social Commission to deal with such problems as slavery and drug traffic.

3. Commission on Human Rights to work on a "bill of rights" for the world.

4. Statistical Commission to make statistical studies for the UN.

5. Demographic Commission to study population problems.

6. Transport Commission to tackle international problems of transportation.

D. Specialized Agencies:

1. International Monetary Fund; the plans for this were drafted at Bretton Woods, New Hampshire, in 1944 to stabilize the monetary systems of the world.

2. The International Bank for Reconstruction and Development was also provided for at Bretton Woods.

3. The Food and Agriculture Organization was planned at Hot Springs, Arkansas, in 1943 to raise food and nutrition standards over the world.
4. The International Civil Aviation Organization to encourage free use of the world's air.
5. The International Labor Organization to raise world labor standards.
6. The Educational and Cultural Organization to encourage cultural development.
7. The Health Organization to control disease and to improve health.

V. Trusteeship Council:
  A. Purpose: to help subject peoples to move toward self-government or independence.
  B. Membership: the five permanent members of the Security Council, plus an equal number of representatives from Trustee nations and non-Trustee nations, but including all Trustee nations.
  C. Operation:
    1. Who may be trust territories:
      a) Territories now held under mandate for the League of Nations.
      b) Territories taken from defeated nations at the end of World War II.
      c) Territories voluntarily placed under the Council by nations now responsible for their administration.

    2. The placement of any territory under the jurisdiction of the Council is purely voluntary.
    3. Each Trustee nation must make a yearly report to the Assembly.

VI. The Secretariat:
  A. Purpose: to act as secretary for all departments, prepare the agenda of meetings, collect information, take care of correspondence, register treaties, publish documents and reports, make an annual report on the UN to the Assembly, call to the attention of the Security Council any matter that may threaten world peace.
  B. Membership: a Secretary-General and as much help as may be necessary.

The Potsdam Conference. A conference of representatives of the principal victor nations was held in Potsdam, Germany, beginning July 17, 1945. In attendance were President Harry S. Truman of the United States, Generalissimo Joseph Stalin of the U.S.S.R., and Prime Minister Winston Churchill of Great Britain. During the conference an election was held in England, and Mr. Churchill was replaced by Mr. Clement Attlee as Prime Minister and as Britain's representative at Potsdam.

The conference reaffirmed the plan for military occupation of Germany by Britain, France, Russia, and the United States and military government in the four sections of the country already established. The purpose of the occupation was to be "the complete disarmament and demilitarization of Germany and the elimination or control of all

United Nations Achievements in Four Years

Where UN Stopped Wars or Settled Disputes

In four years the United Nations has put into operation the most heartening international mobilization efforts for peaceful, progressive purposes that the world has yet seen. Mediation and conciliation have stopped fighting that might have developed into World War III. Nations have been brought together in co-operative efforts against poverty, hunger, disease and ignorance. The record is not perfect but it is impressive.

Berlin — UN negotiations led to the lifting of the Russian blockade.

Syria and Lebanon — UN action brought withdrawal of British and French troops and eventual independence of two countries.

Iran — UN action led to withdrawal of Russian troops from Iranian territory.

Greece — UN commissions helped to prevent Greek civil war from spreading.

Korea — UN supervised elections in South Korea resulting in independent Korean government.

Palestine — UN cease-fire ended fighting between Israel and Arab states.

Indonesia — UN cease-fire ended fighting and brought agreements between Dutch and Indonesians on independence of Indonesia.

Kashmir — UN cease-fire ended fighting between India and Pakistan over possession of Kashmir.

Economic and Social Achievements of UN and Specialized Agencies

Food
World food problem is being attacked by better distribution of essential foods among nations and programs to increase food production in areas where there are scarcities.

(Food and Agriculture Organization FAO)

Health
World-wide campaign is under way to wipe out malaria, tuberculosis and other diseases. A cholera epidemic has been stopped in Egypt, malaria is under control in Greece, and TB is being attacked in India.

(World Health Organization WHO)

Children's Aid
Emergency fund provides food and essential supplies to aid millions of children and expectant mothers in Europe and Asia. At present, supplementary meals are being provided to 4.5 million children.

(United Nations International Children's Emergency Fund UNICEF)

Human Rights
The Universal Declaration of Human Rights has inspired nations to think of fundamental human rights and freedoms as a common achievement. UN seeks also to protect minorities and prevent discrimination. (Commission on Human Rights, Mrs. F. D. Roosevelt, chairman)

Genocide
Convention on genocide declares it to be a crime under international law to persecute or exterminate groups of people because of race, color or creed. It urges punishment of guilty individuals.

(Convention on genocide passed by General Assembly in 1948)

Refugees
Care has been given to about 875,000 refugees and displaced persons. Efforts are being made to find a permanent solution by means of a resettlement program expiring in June, 1950.

(International Refugee Organization IRO)

Economic Aid
UN economic commissions in Europe, Asia, Far East and Latin America are helping nations in economic reconstruction and solution of urgent postwar problems.

Education
Educational program is aiding many countries to develop better school systems. It encourages international understanding, spreads scientific knowledge.

(United Nations Educational, Scientific and Cultural Organization UNESCO)

Loans
The International Bank for Reconstruction and Development has loaned about $731 million for reconstruction purposes. The International Monetary Fund has extended credits of $725 million.

Other specialized agencies and various commissions have programs too numerous to mention. These include a 1950 world census, economic surveys, world statistical practices, women's rights, child welfare, and labor surveys. For further information: United Nations Association of Chicago, 116 S. Michigan Av.

UN Trusteeship Areas

Libya (UN) Independence by 1952
Eritrea (UN)
AFRICA
Br. Togoland, Br. Cameroons (Britain)
Ital. Somaliland 10-year trusteeship (Italy)
Fr. Togoland, Fr. Cameroons (France)
Tanganyika (Britain)
Ruanda-Urundi (Belgium)

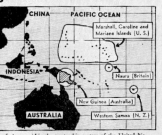

CHINA — PACIFIC OCEAN
Marshall, Caroline and Mariana Islands (U. S.)
INDONESIA
Nauru (Britain)
New Guinea (Australia)
AUSTRALIA
Western Samoa (N. Z.)

Map shows thirteen non-self-governing territories of the world, with approximately 15 million people, that are within the trusteeship system of the United Nations. Source: United Nations, Lake Success, N. Y.

Increasing Costs (UN annual budgets)

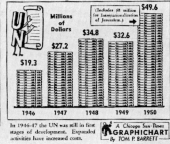

Year	Millions of Dollars
1946	$19.3
1947	$27.2
1948	$34.8
1949	$32.6
1950	$49.6 (Includes $8 million for Internationalization of Jerusalem.)

In 1946-47 the UN was still in first stages of development. Expanded activities have increased costs.

A Chicago Sun-Times GRAPHICHART — By TOM P. BARRETT

Chicago Sun-Times, Tom P. Barrett

HOW THE UN HAS PROMOTED PEACEFUL ACTION AMONG NATIONS

Before the outbreak of the Korean War on June 25, 1950, this summary review of the United Nations' achievements indicated that the hopes of its founders had in some measure been realized. Whether the UN would be able to prevent another world war was the question still to be answered.

German industry that could be used for military production." It was agreed that local self-government should be restored on democratic principles as rapidly as possible. In spite of the four sections into which Germany was divided, the conference decreed that "during the period of occupation Germany shall be treated as a single economic unit."

When it came to reparations, Russia got the lion's share in recognition of the wholesale destruction she had suffered during the war. She was to be permitted to remove wealth from her section and was to be given also a share of the production of the other sections. Reparations for the other powers were to be taken from their own zones of occupation.

It was further agreed that the men chiefly responsible for the war and its atrocities were to be brought to trial speedily as criminals. The conference made plans toward concluding peace treaties with the defeated nations and created a Council of Foreign Ministers to consider matters that might come up from time to time regarding the relationships of the winners with the losers.

First Session of General Assembly. The first session of the United Nations General Assembly opened in London, England, in January, 1946. The members chose Paul-Henri Spaak of Belgium as their first president, and Trygve Lie of Norway was selected to be Secretary-General. In another meeting of the General Assembly which began in New York City in October it was voted to accept the offer of John D. Rockefeller, Jr., of an $8,500,000 site in New York City for a permanent home for the United Nations. Until this home was built, activities were to be carried

United Nations

HOME OF THE UNITED NATIONS

This towering 39-story skyscraper of steel and glass is the Secretariat Building of the UN permanent headquarters in New York.

on largely in temporary quarters in New York City and at Lake Success, New York.

With the war ended and the United Nations organized to keep the peace, the people of the United States looked with pleasure at the prospect of getting back to "normal" again. But there were many surprises ahead. The war, instead of solving problems, had merely created

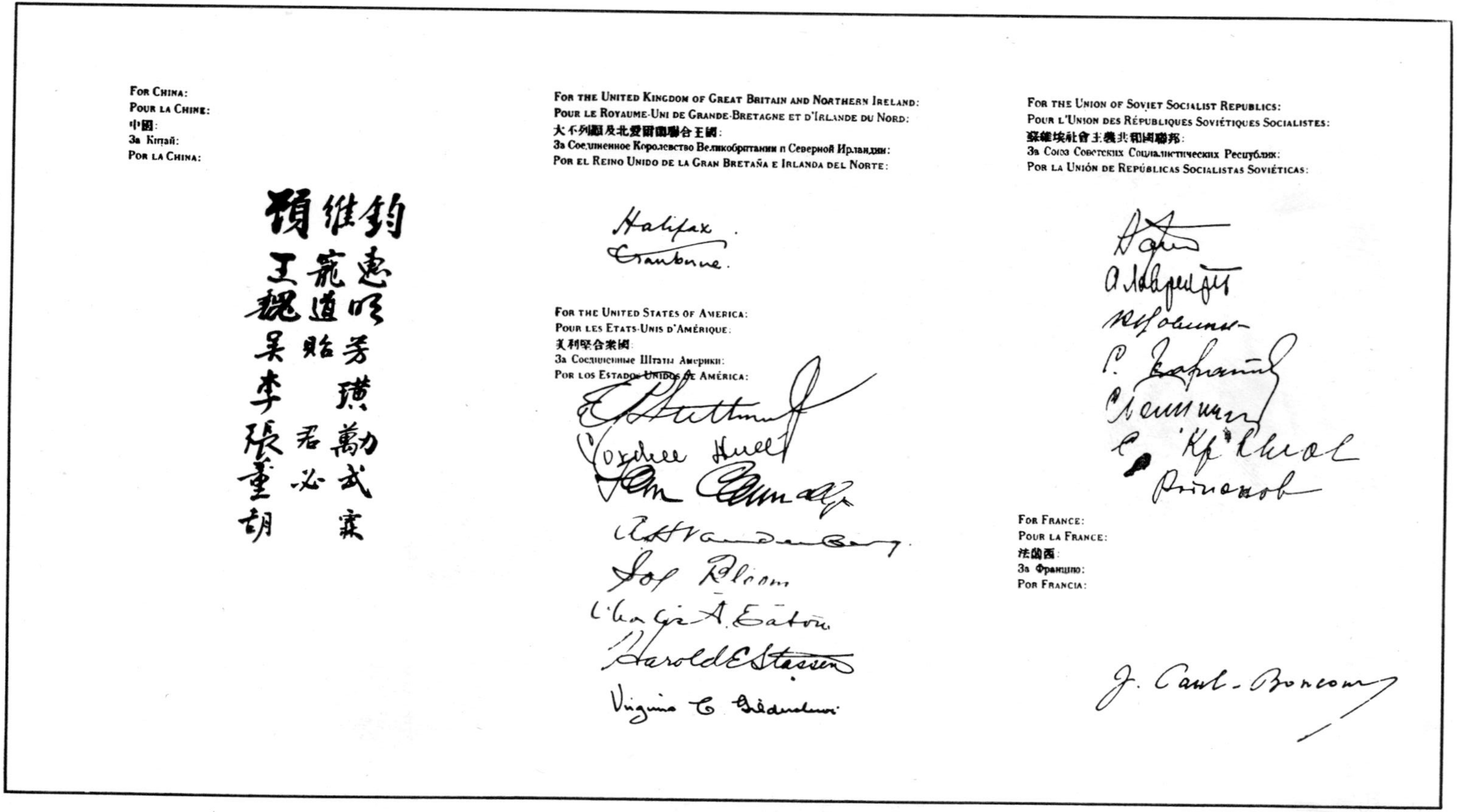

FOR CHINA:
POUR LA CHINE:
中国
За Китай:
POR LA CHINA:

FOR THE UNITED KINGDOM OF GREAT BRITAIN AND NORTHERN IRELAND:
POUR LE ROYAUME-UNI DE GRANDE-BRETAGNE ET D'IRLANDE DU NORD:
大不列顛及北愛爾蘭聯合王國
За Соединенное Королевство Великобритании и Северной Ирландии:
POR EL REINO UNIDO DE LA GRAN BRETAÑA E IRLANDA DEL NORTE:

FOR THE UNITED STATES OF AMERICA:
POUR LES ÉTATS-UNIS D'AMÉRIQUE:
美利堅合眾國
За Соединенные Штаты Америки:
POR LOS ESTADOS UNIDOS DE AMÉRICA:

FOR THE UNION OF SOVIET SOCIALIST REPUBLICS:
POUR L'UNION DES RÉPUBLIQUES SOVIÉTIQUES SOCIALISTES:
蘇維埃社會主義共和國聯邦:
За Союз Советских Социалистических Республик:
POR LA UNIÓN DE REPÚBLICAS SOCIALISTAS SOVIÉTICAS:

FOR FRANCE:
POUR LA FRANCE:
法蘭西
За Францию:
POR FRANCIA:

THE HANDWRITING OF THE UN CHARTER'S SIGNERS

The signatures of the "Big Five" delegates are here reproduced as they appear on the United Nations Charter. The Charter itself is printed in five official languages—Chinese, English, French, Russian, and Spanish. Note that the signature designations shown above are in each of these languages.

many new ones. It was a case of "out of the frying-pan into the fire." The world soon found that what it had was neither war nor peace. The dominant feeling was not that of security; it was fear. Our victory began to look like an empty one. We shall discuss this post-war world in the last unit of this book.

FOR YOUR REVIEW

These Should Be Easy for You Now

1. What did the Johnson Act provide? How did our government avoid the limitation of the act? How did we become more involved in spite of our declared neutrality?
2. What territory did Germany conquer in Europe? What former ally did she attack? What other two nations joined Germany in the war?
3. In what ways did the election of Franklin D. Roosevelt in 1940 parallel the election of Woodrow Wilson in 1916?
4. List the four freedoms President Roosevelt talked about. Do you believe them necessary to the elimination of war?
5. What actions were taken by the United States and neighbor nations for the defense of the American continents?
6. What did the Lend-Lease Act provide for? What nations received the bulk of the assistance?
7. When and how did the United States become openly involved in World War II?
8. How was American defense production increased? How did the war force prices higher? In what ways did people not engaged directly in war production help in the war effort?
9. What part did women have in our armed forces?
10. What territory did Japan conquer?
11. What was the American plan for the war? What part did Russia play in the defeat of Germany? What countries shared in the occupation?
12. When and how was the war ended in the Pacific?
13. How can it be said that American production won the war?
14. What was the cost of the war?
15. What important decision was reached at the Casablanca Conference? What was accomplished at the Moscow Conference? The Cairo Conference? The Teheran Conference?
16. What were the Dumbarton Oaks Proposals?
17. What is the importance of the San Francisco Conference?
18. What are the purposes of the United Nations other than preventing war?
19. What are the six main branches of the United Nations? What are the purposes and duties of each?
20. Make a list of the important decisions reached at the Potsdam Conference.
21. Where is the temporary home of the United Nations located? Where is the permanent home to be?

Associated Dates

1939—Declaration of Panama, October 3
1940—Trade treaty with Japan ended, January 26
    Italy joins Germany in the war, June 10
    Inter-American Conference, Havana, Cuba, July 21 to 30
    Ogdensburg Agreement, August 17
    United States Selective Service Act passed, September 16
    Japan signs agreement with Germany and Italy, September 27
    President Roosevelt re-elected to third term

1941—Lend-Lease Act passed, March 11
    Hyde Park Declaration, April 20
    Germany attacks Russia, June 22
    Atlantic Charter drawn up, August 9 and 10
    Japanese attack Pearl Harbor, December 7
    United States declares war on Japan, December 8
    Germany and Italy declare war on the United States, December 11
1942—United Nations Declaration signed, January 1
    Battle of the Coral Sea, May 7 and 8
    United States declares war on Bulgaria, Hungary, and Rumania, June 5
    Battle of Midway Island, June 6
    United States forces land in North Africa, November 7
    Battle of Guadalcanal, November 13 to 15
1943—Casablanca Conference, January 14 to 24
    Surrender of Axis forces in Africa, May 12
    invasion of Southern Europe begins, July 10
    Moscow Conference, October 19–30
    Cairo Conference, November 20–25
    Teheran Conference opens, December 1
1944—invasion of Western Europe begins, June 6
    Dumbarton Oaks Conference, August 21 to October 7
1945—Philippine Islands retaken, January to May
    Yalta Conference, February 3 to 11
    Iwo Jima taken, February 19 to March 16
    Death of President Roosevelt, April 12
    San Francisco Conference, April 25 to June 26
    Execution of Mussolini by Italian partisans, April 28
    Germany surrenders, May 7
    United Nations Charter signed by representatives of fifty nations at San Francisco, June 26
    Potsdam Conference, July 17 to August 2
    atom bomb dropped on Hiroshima, Japan, August 6
    Nagasaki, Japan, atom-bombed, August 8
    Russia declares war on Japan, August 8
    Japan surrenders, August 14
    Japan signs surrender terms, September 2
    trials of Nazi leaders begin in Nuremberg, Germany, November 20
1946—first meeting of the United Nations General Assembly begins, January 10 (London)
    first meeting of the United Nations Security Council begins, January 17 (London)

Why Are These To Be Remembered?

Wendell Willkie	Pearl Harbor	WAAC
Admiral Leahy	War Production Board	WAVES
Saburo Kurusu	War Shipping Administration	SPARS
Kichisaburo Nomura	War Labor Board	USO
Douglas MacArthur	War Manpower Commission	Corregidor
Cordell Hull	Office of Defense Transpor-	Guadalcanal
Anthony Eden	tation	Tarawa
V. M. Molotov	Office of Price Administra-	Kwajalein
Winston Churchill	tion	Iwo Jima
Dwight D. Eisenhower	Office of War Mobilization	Okinawa
Paul-Henri Spaak	Office of War Information	D-Day
Trygve Lie	Office of Censorship	V-E Day
Vichy	Office of Civilian Defense	V-J Day

Suggested Readings

MARSHALL, EDISON, *Seward's Folly*
Alaska purchase
HOBART, ALICE T., *Oil for the Lamps of China*
American business goes to China
HENDERSON, D. MacI., *Yankee Ships in China Seas*
American trade in Asia
KANTOR, MacKINLAY, *Cuba Libra*
Cuba after the Spanish-American War
BOYCE, W. D., *United States Colonies and Dependencies*
COBB, IRVIN S., *Paths of Glory*
World War I as I saw it from the Front
THOMAS, LOWELL, *Raiders of the Deep*
Submarine warfare
COOLIDGE, A. C., *The United States as a World Power*
Our relations with Europe and Latin America to 1923
MILLIS, WALTER, *Road to War*
How we got into World War I
ALLEN, F. L., *Since Yesterday*
The United States in the 1930's
GOLLOMB, JOSEPH, *Armies of Spies*
Propaganda in North and South America

GREW, JOSEPH C., *Ten Years in Japan*
Pre-Pearl Harbor Japanese-American relations by the American Ambassador to Japan during those years
KIRK, G. L., *Philippine Independence*
Analysis of the problems
HUNT, FRAZIER, *MacArthur and the War against Japan*
HERSEY, JOHN, *Hiroshima*
Results of dropping the first atom bomb against an enemy
PYLE, ERNIE, *Brave Men*
Stories of the GI by the famous correspondent who lost his life in the war
ROMULO, CARLOS P., *I Saw the Fall of the Philippines*
ROMULO, CARLOS P., *I Saw the Philippines Rise*
STETTINIUS, E. R., *Lend-Lease, Weapon of Victory*
HAINES, C. G. and HOFFMAN, R. J. S., *Origins and Background of the Second World War*
LOW, DAVID, and HOWE, QUINCY, *Years of Wrath; a Cartoon History, 1931-1945*

How Ideals of Freedom Have Flourished in America

INTRODUCTION

It may be said correctly and with great pride that American greatness has been built upon three splendid cornerstones. These are those cornerstones: (1) The idea that any government should operate by the consent of the governed. This does not necessarily mean that the government should have been selected by the people, as we hold in this country, but that it at least should be acceptable to the majority of the people. (2) The idea that every person should have complete freedom of expression. That means not only the right to say what he thinks about his government and the men who operate it, but the same freedom to express himself as he sees fit in the fields of science, literature, painting, sculpture, architecture, and all the other areas of human life and endeavor. (3) The idea that all people should have equal opportunity under their government. To us, in theory at least, this means that every person should have not only the right to an equal part in his government with every other person, but the opportunity also to develop himself as an individual to the full extent of his potential capabilities. It includes the belief that no limitation should be placed upon any person because of his color, religious beliefs, financial status, or anything else—that the only barrier to further development should be whatever natural limitations he may possess or his own unwillingness to work for further advancement.

You will note that each of these cornerstones of American greatness is an idea. Ideas have been responsible for the development of America to its present position in the world, both domestically and internationally. In fact, behind every important advancement is first a noble idea. Ideas are the most powerful things in the world; they can promote greater changes than any atom or hydrogen bomb. The important thing is that all ideas given widespread circulation should be as fine and noble as the ideas which have formed the cornerstones upon which has been built the structure we know as the United States of America.

211

Chapter 15

Americans Believe in Government by the Consent of the Governed

THE IDEA THAT AMERICAN CITIZENS HAVE THE RIGHT TO DO AS THEY
PLEASE SO LONG AS THEY DO NOT INTERFERE WITH THE RIGHTS OF
OTHERS IS A CORNERSTONE OF AMERICAN GREATNESS

Early Beginnings of Government.
The government of the United States
has been looked upon as an example in
the modern world—an example of
something new and different in the way
of government. Actually, the idea was
far from new; but the concrete expression of that idea as set up here was an
experiment of greater magnitude than
had ever been tried anywhere else.

The problem of who is to have the
authority has existed from the time man
first began to live in groups. In the period in man's history when people lived
in clans and tribes and roamed about
to find food and shelter, authority usually rested with the oldest member of
the clan, the patriarch. As early man
learned how to make animals and
plants grow where he wanted them, it
was no longer necessary to search for
food. He could settle down and live in
permanent locations. Thus the first
communities were established along
great river systems in China, India,
Egypt, and Mesopotamia. Civilization
began in those early communities.

In each of these communities some
strong warrior probably came to be
accepted as ruler, or perhaps assumed
such leadership by force. He became a

king. Perhaps he conquered near-by
kingdoms and became ruler of an empire—an emperor. History records the
names of several of these—Genghis
Khan in China, Baber the Mongol in
India, Cyrus the Great of Persia, and
Alexander the Great of Greece.

Democracy Begins in Greece. Before Alexander's father, Philip of Mac-
edon, conquered the Greek city-states
and deprived them of their freedom,
the people of Greece had worked out a
new idea about government. We call it
democracy, from the Greek words
meaning "people rule." It was based
upon a wholly new concept of authority: that the people being ruled should
have the right to decide what kind of
government they wanted. Of course,
the Greeks didn't look upon everyone
as "people." In the beginning only
wealthy land-owners had a part in the
government. Even this was something
new. Up to that time rulers had done
as they pleased, showing little or no
consideration for the people they governed. The little city-states that sprang
up in the mountain villages of Greece
were relatively small, and direct government by the people was often possible. But the city-states could not

unite. They were conquered and their new idea of government more or less forgotten for centuries.

Roman Idea of a Republic. Soon Rome became the dominant world power. As Rome's empire grew, citizenship was extended to all free men who came under her rule. Rome was too large to be governed as a direct democracy. Instead, she developed the idea of the republic—a sort of representative democracy.

Probably the greatest period of peace the world has ever known came under Rome's rule. The large empire was controlled by a rather wise combination of force and justice. Perhaps Rome left us a practical example we may have to follow in working out our problem of peace for the world.

Rome did, however, leave us an example we want to avoid duplicating, if possible. She showed us what can happen to government by the people when those people become indifferent to the quality and integrity of their government. When this happened in Rome, things went from bad to worse. Soon all a man needed in order to be emperor was the support of the army, and that support went to the man who could pay the most for it. It wasn't long before Rome fell to the conquering barbarians from outside the empire.

Feudalism Substitutes for Government. The fall of Rome in the fifth century left a great void in western Europe. There was no strong central government. The basic function of government became very clear. There was no organization with authority or power to protect the people and none in prospect. So the people met the situation themselves; they created the feudal system. They turned their land over to some noble and then rented it from him. In return, he built a castle and hired an army of professional soldiers called *knights* to protect those people under his care.

The National State. But feudalism was at best only a substitute for government. Its sole purpose was to provide protection, and it did that on a small scale only. Feudal units dotted the countryside of western Europe, and fighting was almost constant among them. Gradually a few superpowerful lords appeared—men who brought other nobles under their rule. Soon people of the same general ancestry, religion, language, and customs were banded together under the same ruler. This new political unit was the *national state,* and its ruler was a king.

The kings that established their power in western Europe in the later Middle Ages were absolute monarchs who ruled with little if any consideration for their people. But the national state was a better means for protecting the people than the feudal system had been. The kings had large armies supplied with the newer weapons—the crossbow and later the rifle—for which the knight in armor with his swords and lances was no match.

THE AWAKENING OF EUROPE

Effects of the Renaissance. The Renaissance—the awakening of western Europe from the "Dark Ages"—was a result of the crusades (which occurred in the eleventh, twelfth, and thirteenth centuries). The barbarian rule of western Europe after the fall of Rome meant little progress. But life moved ahead in the Eastern Empire, with its capital at Constantinople, and in the Arab Empire in the Near East. Then

LEONARDO DA VINCI—GENIUS OF THE RENAISSANCE

Few men in history have matched the versatility of this great Italian master (1452–1519). His distinguished work in the arts and sciences made contributions to the advance of Western civilization. He was a painter, sculptor, architect, inventor, and natural philosopher. It was inevitable that even the New World should fall heir to his influence.

the crusades came—that series of religious-military expeditions from western Europe into the Near East to take the Holy Land from the Turks and open it to Christians once more. The crusades brought people of western Europe into contact with more advanced civilizations, and they came home determined to make some changes. They brought back many new ideas.

In southwestern Europe—Italy in particular—the Renaissance (which began early in the fourteenth century) meant a flowering of culture, fine new cathedrals, a new interest in painting,

sculpture, and things of this earthly life. But Renaissance scholars of Italy did not question the teachings of the Church. That institution was still their supreme authority for all knowledge.

It was different in northwestern Europe. When the new ideas of the Renaissance crossed the Alps, they had an altogether different effect upon the thinking of people there. Many scholars of northwestern Europe began to think in terms of experience. They refused, finally, to accept anything that they could not tangibly prove. They turned to their material environment for their authority, rating it ahead of both the

Church and the classics of ancient Greece and Rome, which were being widely read.

This refusal to accept any authority but their own judgment was bound to lead to changes. In government it meant a revival of the Greek philosopher Plato's idea that government should exist "by the consent of the governed." In England, in the fifteenth century, John Locke in his writings asserted that the legislature, as the voice of the people, should be supreme in government; that the king should be responsible to the people; and that the people have the right to resist when their ruler fails to govern in the manner they desire. In France, in the next century, Jean Jacques Rousseau echoed the same ideas in his book *The Social Contract*.

These and other men of similar thinking paved the way for the period of political revolution that followed. They planted the ideas that grew into open rebellion and violence which overthrew absolute rule and established, in various areas, government "by the consent of the governed."

Dutch Win Freedom. The Dutch had long chafed under the domination of Spain. Philip II was trying to force them to give up their new Protestant religion and become Catholics again. Led by William the Silent they fought Spain and won their freedom.

England Revolts. The revolution against the English king affords us an excellent example of the persistence of a people in trying to get the kind of government they wanted. In 1603 Queen Elizabeth died. The new king was James I; he had been ruling in Scotland as James VI. Ironically, he was the son of Mary Stuart, Queen of Scots, whom Elizabeth had ordered executed while under her protection because she feared Mary was trying to get the throne of England. James was a firm believer in "the divine right of kings"—that is, that kings ruled by divine right and as God willed and, therefore, could do no wrong. James came to the throne of England determined that the people should do as he wanted, whether they liked it or not.

The English people were not used to this. Under Elizabeth they had enjoyed a comparatively liberal government. But the English are peace-loving people; they put up with James I, hoping that the next king would be better. He wasn't. Charles I, who succeeded James I in 1625, was just as headstrong and determined as his father had been.

In 1628 the English tried to limit the power of their king by getting him to sign the Petition of Right. This document stated various rights the people wanted assured to them, and in particular it attempted more or less to outline the powers of Parliament. Charles signed against his will and probably with no intention of observing the terms. At any rate, he refused to call Parliament back into session and ruled as he pleased by direct decree.

Eventually his duplicity caught up with him. He needed more money, and he couldn't get it unless Parliament voted the taxes. In desperation he called the members back into session again after eleven years. They met in an angry mood. Before long they were in armed rebellion against King Charles. Charles was captured, held prisoner for several years, and finally executed in 1649.

Parliament was in power. A republic was set up in England called the Commonwealth and Protectorate. Oliver Cromwell became Lord Protector. But the English people soon discovered that their problem was not solved. They had simply replaced autocratic rule by Charles I with autocratic rule by Cromwell, and they didn't like it. Cromwell tried to pass his power on to his son Richard when he died, but Richard soon gave up the job. The army tried to rule for a time, but things went from bad to worse, and Parliament asked Charles Stuart, son of executed Charles I, to come back from France (where he had fled on the death of his father) and become England's king. So the monarchy was restored with Charles II as ruler (1660).

The people expected Charles II to be a better king than Charles I had been. They thought he certainly would have had his attitude changed by the treatment given his father. They were disappointed. Charles II was in many respects as autocratic a ruler as Charles I had been. But the English people had had enough bloodshed; they decided to wait and see what the next king was like.

Charles II died in 1685 and was succeeded by his brother James II. The new king was no improvement, but the patient people continued to hope for better rulers to come. Then something happened which told them that the next in line for the throne could not be acceptable to them. A son was born to James II and his second wife, a Roman Catholic. The people knew that normally the boy would succeed his father, and they didn't want a Roman Catholic king. Until the boy was born, they had expected their next ruler to be James' Protestant daughter Mary. They rose up against James II and forced him to abdicate. Then they invited Mary, a daughter of James I and his first wife, who was a Protestant, and her husband, William of Orange, to come from Holland and become the new rulers of England (1688). Before they would turn the throne over to William and Mary, however, they got from them the promise to accept the Bill of Rights, which was subsequently adopted in 1689. The Bill of Rights permanently gave Parliament more power than the king in England. The people had finally triumphed over their king.

Other Countries Follow England's Example. The English colonists who came to America brought this heritage of freedom with them. It was a primary cause of their revolution against the English king, a revolution that ended in complete separation from the British Empire. In quick succession followed the revolt of the common people of France against the nobles and the king, and the revolt of the Spanish colonies of Central and South America against unjust Spanish rule.

But the people of France simply replaced a stupid and autocratic king with the stupid and vengeful mob. Conditions were worse than before. Out of the upheaval came the dictatorship of Napoleon Bonaparte. France had started with an autocratic ruler and ended with one.

In Latin America the rule of Spain was thrown off and republics established. But the government of most of our neighbors to the south has not been very democratic.

A Distinctly American Government. The government set up in the new United States was a distinct departure from other governments already in existence. Thomas Jefferson sounded the keynote for the new government when he wrote into the Declaration of Independence these words: "We hold these truths to be self-evident, that all men are created equal, that they are endowed by their Creator with certain unalienable Rights, that among these are Life, Liberty, and the pursuit of Happiness. That to secure these rights, Governments are instituted among Men, deriving their just powers from the consent of the governed." But even then these ideas were not new to America; their counterparts can be found in various early agreements, colonial charters, and state constitutions. They are ideas that are fundamentally and basically American—ideas that form one of the cornerstones of American greatness.

FOR YOUR REVIEW

These Should Be Easy for You Now

1. What is the basic problem of government in any society?
2. In what four countries did civilization get its start?
3. Why did the Greek city-states lose their independence? What lesson may there be for our modern world in their experience?
4. Distinguish between a direct or pure democracy and a republic.
5. How did Rome maintain peace in her vast empire? What warning for us is found in Rome's history?
6. Why was the feudal system created?
7. How did the first national states develop?
8. What events led to the Renaissance? What was the Renaissance? How did it differ in northwestern Europe from southwestern Europe?
9. What Greek idea of government was revived in western Europe during the Renaissance? What political revolutions did it lead to?
10. What was meant by "the divine right of kings"?
11. Show that the story of the English Revolution illustrates well the fact that the will of the people is not to be denied. What did the English Bill of Rights do?
12. Although the ideas embodied in American government were not new, in what ways did the new government differ from all others?

Associated Dates

753 B.C.—legendary date of the founding of Rome
600–100 B.C.—period of Greek domination of world history
550 B.C.—approximate time of Cyrus the Great
356–323 B.C.—Alexander the Great
476 A.D.—date usually given for the fall of Rome
1095—beginning of the Crusades
1162–1227—Genghis Khan
1648—Dutch independence recognized
1649—Charles I of England executed; monarchy abolished
1649–1660—Commonwealth and Protectorate in England
1660—Stuart kings restored in England (Charles II)
1689—English Bill of Rights accepted by William and Mary
1775—beginning of the American Revolution
1776—American Declaration of Independence signed
1789—beginning of the French Revolution
1810–1824—revolutions in Latin America

Why Are These To Be Remembered?

Genghis Khan	Republic	Charles I
Baber	National state	Petition of Rights
Cyrus the Great	Feudalism	Oliver Cromwell
Philip II	Renaissance	Charles II
William the Silent	Plato	James II
Queen Elizabeth	John Locke	William and Mary
Alexander the Great	Rousseau	Bill of Rights
Philip of Macedon	James I	Declaration of Independence
Democracy	"Divine right of kings"	

Chapter 16
Americans Believe in Freedom of Expression

THE IDEA THAT EVERY AMERICAN CITIZEN HAS THE SAME RIGHT TO
SELF-DEVELOPMENT AS EVERY OTHER AMERICAN CITIZEN IS A SECOND
CORNERSTONE OF AMERICAN GREATNESS

Struggle for Religious Freedom. Like government "by the consent of the governed," the American idea of free expression of one's beliefs, thoughts, and talents was not entirely new in the world. But the fervor with which early American colonists insisted upon these rights gave promise of greater realization along such lines than had been attained elsewhere up to that time.

Power of the Church. Many of the settlers of the New World came because they wanted to escape religious persecution. Now, the persecution of people because their religious beliefs did not correspond to those of their rulers was not peculiar to England in the seventeenth century. It had been common all down through history. In ancient times all religious activity was controlled by the government. Rites conducted in accordance with the animistic religion of primitive man were under the direction of the political leaders.

The gods of the Greek people possessed more human characteristics than divine. The Olympic Games, which are held somewhere in the world every four years, began with the Greeks. They were religious festivals, held under political as well as religious sponsorship, and so named because the Greeks thought their gods lived on Mt. Olympus.

Rome, after her conquest of Greece, adopted the gods of the Greeks and gave them new names. In Rome the connection between religious and political authority became complete. When Octavian changed the government from a republic to an empire and made himself emperor, he also took the title of Pontifex Maximus—High Priest. For some time after that, Roman citizens were required to worship their Caesar as a god. The refusal of the Christians to do this made them guilty of treason against the emperor and brought on the infamous period of persecution marked by violence in many forms.

After the fall of the Roman Empire, there was no strong central government in western Europe. The Church became the most powerful single organization in that part of the world during the early Middle Ages. This was possible because of the tremendous hold the Church exerted on the minds of the people. Life in these times was dark and unpleasant. Life in Heaven was pictured as being the complete opposite. Because the Church was the agency that would get people to

219

CLASSIC ARCHITECTURE WAS AN EXPRESSION OF GREEK RELIGION

The most magnificent classic Greek buildings were the temples—the Parthenon at Athens, shown restored in the above picture, was one of them. The growth of ancient Greek architecture was inspired by religious worship.

Heaven, it was able to control almost their every act. Powerful lords were brought under this over-all control because the Pope held that all the world belonged to God and that he, as God's earthly representative, therefore controlled everything in the world.

This tremendous power of the Church continued until the time of the Renaissance. Then, as people became more interested in this world, which they had looked upon as something to be endured before one could get to Heaven, they became less inclined to permit the Church to control their lives so rigidly. Kings were able to sell the people on the idea that they received political power direct from God, just as the Pope received religious power. The new idea—that kings ruled by God's commission—was called "the divine right of kings." Armed with this new weapon, the kings extended their authority and built the first national states in western Europe—the forerunners of modern European nations.

Revolution in the Church. The new ideas brought into western Europe by the Renaissance resulted in the period of revolution, most of it political, that we mentioned in Chapter 15. There was also a revolution in the Church. Some people who had learned to read felt they should have the right to interpret the Bible for themselves instead of having to accept the teachings of the Church. Many of the clergy thought certain practices of the Church were wrong, that it needed reforming. When Martin Luther, a professor-priest in Germany, dared express his beliefs and criticisms publicly, he was excommunicated, and his congregation with him. But excommunication did not force Luther to change his position. Instead, he and his followers stayed out of the Roman Catholic Church and established a new branch of Christianity—Protestantism, so named because its followers protested against many of the practices of the Roman Church.

But the founding of Protestantism did not bring freedom of individual choice in matters of religion. Rather, it was expected that a person's religion would still be that of his political ruler.

THE COLOSSEUM—GREAT STADIUM OF THE ROMAN ERA

Many Christians suffered martyrdom within the walls of this vast gathering place in the days of the Roman Empire. Early Christians were put to death here on the charge of treason against the emperor.

If the ruler was Catholic, his people were Catholic too. If he turned Protestant, his people became Protestant also. The attempt of Philip II of Spain to force the people of Holland to become Catholic again was the most immediate cause of their successful revolt, which made them politically free of Spanish rule. Philip sent the famous Spanish Armada against England in 1588 to try to force that country to become Catholic again.

The change from Catholicism to Protestantism in England had not been made for reasons of a religious nature. That change had made the king head of the church as well as the state in England. The revolution of the Puritan Parliament against Charles I was fought primarily to limit his political power but partly to limit his religious authority as well. The monarchy was overthrown and a republic set up under Oliver Cromwell. But Cromwell's government turned out to be just as dictatorial about both political and religious matters as the Stuart monarchy had been.

Beginnings of Religious Freedom. The religious situation in England was a primary reason for the colonization of America, as we have seen. In many of the early colonies the Anglican Church (Church of England) became the established church. In the north, where the Puritans settled, especially in Massachusetts, Connecticut, and New Hampshire, the Congregational Church was the state-supported church. In 1689 the Bill of Rights in England had granted freedom of religion to all Protestant denominations. But it seems to be human nature not to realize that we cannot enjoy freedom ourselves unless we are willing to grant it to others. In most of the colonies freedom to worship as one pleased was unknown. One church was designated by law as *the* church for the colony, and all the people were taxed to support it.

The break from such a rigid pattern came in Rhode Island, Maryland, and

Pennsylvania. We have already seen that Rhode Island was founded by Roger Williams on the very principle that every person should have the right to determine for himself his own religious beliefs. In Maryland, Catholic Lord Baltimore welcomed Protestant settlers, and the legislature guaranteed freedom of worship to all who believed in Jesus Christ, thereby barring only Jews and Unitarians among the immigrants. In Pennsylvania the Quakers granted freedom of worship to all who believed in God.

Religion was a powerful influence in early America. The clergy were often the only people in a community who could read and write. They became the molders of public opinion. The Sabbath was strictly observed, and anyone failing to follow the rigid rules regarding it was liable to severe punishment. Occasionally, religious fanaticism was whipped up against people accused of being witches, and unfortunate things were done in the name of religion. But the idea of religious toleration spread as the colonies grew.

Perhaps it can be said that freedom of expression in religious matters encouraged freedom of thinking in matters of politics, too. The fact that many colonists felt free to decide for themselves about their religion, may have contributed to their feeling that they ought not to look to England for decisions about their government.

The revolt against England tended to increase religious freedom in the colonies. A natural result was the complete break with the Anglican Church. If the colonies were not to be ruled politically from England, their religious activity was not to be controlled from there either. From then on the Anglican Church in America was just one Prot-

estant church among the various denominations already established here. It became known as the Episcopal Church.

In 1786 Virginia adopted a Statute for Religious Freedom proposed by Thomas Jefferson. For the people of Virginia the new act provided that every person was to have the right to decide all religious matters for himself, that he could not be taxed to support or required to attend any church. It was a long step forward in the movement toward religious freedom for all.

The writers of the Constitution recognized this movement. They provided that no religious restrictions at all were to be placed upon any official of the United States Government. And so far as the federal government was concerned, the First Amendment in the Bill of Rights permanently took care of the question of religious freedom in the United States. It provided that "Congress shall make no law respecting an establishment of religion, or prohibiting the free exercise thereof."

So all connection between the federal government and religion was broken. But in various states restrictions upon religious freedom remained for many years. In some cases religious qualifications were placed upon the right to vote, particularly to keep Jews and Catholics out of office. The Congregational Church remained the official church in New Hampshire until 1817, in Connecticut until 1818, and in Massachusetts until 1833. But gradually, through all the states, the movement toward complete freedom of expression in religious matters pushed steadily ahead.

The Church Today. A natural result of increased freedom in religion was the establishment of new sects or denominations of Protestantism. Wherever differences of opinion developed, a new branch often resulted. In recent years, a tendency to unite has appeared, and several denominations have been combined, in the belief that greater service can be rendered by a larger group. In spite of this, there are more than 250 religious groups operating in the United States today.

In 1790 the Roman Catholic Church in the United States was given a bishop of its own. Since then the Catholic hierarchy in this country has grown until it now includes four members of the College of Cardinals.

A significant upsurge of church membership was noted during the years of World War II. The United States Bureau of the Census listed a membership in all churches in the United States in 1936 as 55,807,366. By the end of the war in 1945 this had grown to 72,492,669. This would seem to bear out the contention that people are more religiously inclined in time of trouble.

As the United States moved through the nineteenth century and into the twentieth, it became more liberal in many ways. In religion, the strict requirements of the early churches were gradually relaxed, and even mild forms of amusement were permitted on Sunday, after church services were over. When the automobile, the moving picture, and the radio became firmly established in American life, church attendance dropped off noticeably. From a position of dominance in early American life, the church has been pushed back by modern inventions and commercialized amusement, with all of which it must compete for the time of busy people, living more and still more complex lives.

RISE OF FREE EDUCATION

Contributions of the Church. The church had a great deal to do with education in the English colonies in America. Frequently, the men who occupied the pulpits on Sunday were behind the teachers' desks during the week. Rivalry was keen among the Protestant denominations in the colonies. Members of each sect desired that their children should be instructed in the beliefs of that particular church. Schools of different types sprang up to fill this need. Mostly they were volunteer schools, and often they were kept by the pastors of the churches. The Bible was supplemented by a book of questions and answers on religious subjects, called a catechism. Children, and adults as well, were taught to read the Bible. If no schools were available, parents who could read and write taught their own children. The illiteracy that marked the early population was soon on its way out.

The first colleges and universities were founded as religious institutions. Their chief purpose was to train young men for the ministry. Harvard, founded in 1636, led off the list of early schools of higher education. In New England, next came Yale, in 1701, and Dartmouth, in 1769.

The Anglican Church of England was not without representation in the colleges of the New World. William and Mary was established in Virginia in 1693, and King's College, which later became Columbia University, in New York in 1754. Near by, Princeton began as the College of New Jersey in 1746. It started as a Presbyterian school.

Before long, a trend away from the operation of colleges principally for religious training became evident. This was noticeable especially in Brown, founded in Rhode Island in 1764, and in the University of Pennsylvania, established as the Philadelphia Academy by Benjamin Franklin, where training for business and public affairs was emphasized.

Higher learning in colonial times, however, was not for the masses. For most people, if the meager elementary training was to be followed by more advanced learning, it had to be at the initiative of the individual. Some tutors were available, but many people continued their education by sheer hard work on their own part. They read as widely as they could on diverse subjects to improve their knowledge. This method of self-education has always been an important factor in the intellectual development of America.

When the Constitution was written, nothing was said in it about education. However, the leaders of the federal government recognized its importance, and provisions were made to grant areas of public land for the support of schools. Many states followed suit. In this manner the first state universities got their start. The University of Virginia was founded by Thomas Jefferson in 1825.

But popular education did not grow very rapidly. The public land set aside for the support of schools did not yield very much income, and people were unwilling to tax themselves for education. The church schools were still the most important. The Sunday school, originated by John Wesley in England, was brought over and put into use in the United States. It included more than just religious training. It utilized the "day of rest" for a basic attack upon ignorance. People who had learned the fundamentals of reading and writing were urged to teach what they knew to others. So the meager learning was spread.

Education Free to All. The demand for greater educational opportunity was an insistent one. The type of government established in the United States required it. Government by the people couldn't be very effective if the people were unable to read or write. Such leaders as Horace Mann led the movement to secure tax-supported schools that would be available to all, free of charge. The idea of taxing all people, whether they had children or not, for the operation of schools was not popular to start with. But by the middle of the nineteenth century all of the northern and some of the southern states had accepted the principle of universal taxation for the maintenance of schools.

The American people were not satisfied with free elementary education alone. In 1821 the first public high school was established in Boston. The first teacher-training school opened its doors in 1839. The idea of state operated universities spread as new states came into the Union. And, here and there, technical schools began to appear.

Gradually, women have won the right to educational advantages on a par with men. In the beginning, women were not allowed to attend colleges and universities. This led to the founding of some of the famous girls' seminaries, such as Mount Holyoke and Vassar. Oberlin College, founded in Ohio in 1833, led the way toward co-education by accepting girls as well as boys.

The two great wars of the twentieth century have been eyeopeners to the

John Hancock Mutual Life Insurance Co.

HORACE MANN—HE FOUGHT FOR OUR RIGHT TO LEARN

The poor farmer boy who nibbled at a few borrowed books and went a-hungering for all the world's learning performed a service that has become a bright saga in American education. He rose to become President of the Massachusetts Senate, then resigned to devote his tireless energy to give America better public schools.

American people about the status of education in this country. The illiteracy rate of people over ten years old had been lowered from 17 per cent in 1880 to about 6 per cent in 1920. But the tests given our boys who entered the service in World War I showed a lack of education that made us ashamed. The American people demanded better educational facilities, and in ten years increased the expenditures for public education from about 750 million dollars to more than 2 billion dollars a year.

Attendance in the schools of the nation increased greatly after World War I. Just before World War II started, there were about 23 million boys and girls enrolled in our elementary schools, nearly 7 million in our high schools, about 1½ million in our colleges and universities, and another 1½ million engaged in adult education through evening and home-study schools. In World War I only about 20 per cent of the men in uniform had an elementary school education; in World War II the figure was 65 per cent.

Following World War II, more people were enrolled in the educational institutions of the United States than

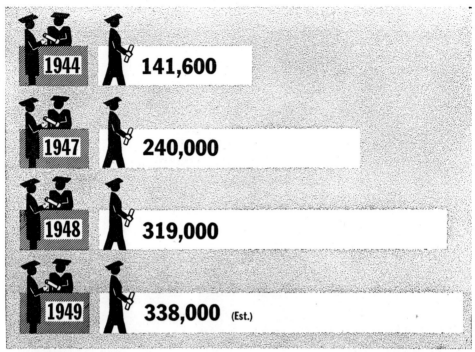

U.S. News & World Report (5–6–49) © U.S. News Pub. Corp.

STEADY INCREASE IN COLLEGE GRADUATES AFTER WORLD WAR II

An all-time high in the number of young men and women receiving diplomas from schools of higher learning was reached in 1949.

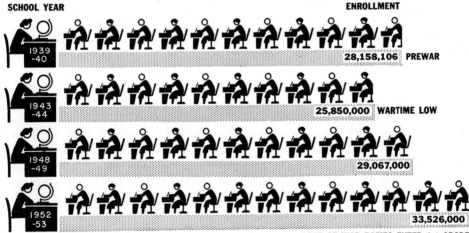

U.S. News & World Report (9–3–48) © U.S. News Pub. Corp.

THE CROWDED SCHOOLROOM BECOMES A NATIONAL PROBLEM

The tremendous jump of school enrollment, from 28,156,106 in 1939–40 to an expected 33,526,-000 in 1952–53, provides an idea of why school facilities are being burdened with the largest load in American history.

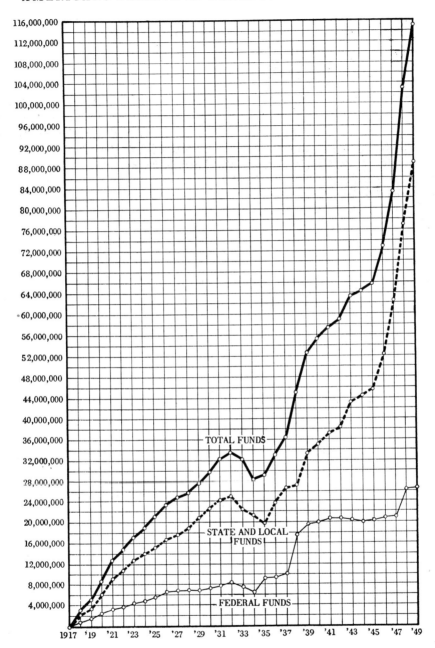

TRENDS IN EXPENDITURES FOR VOCATIONAL EDUCATION

The steady upward climb of expenditures for vocational education in the United States was interrupted but once—during the depression years.

at any previous time in our history. This was partly due to the provision for further schooling made available to men and women who had served in the armed forces of the nation during the war.

The New Philosophy of Education. The philosophy of education in the United States has changed greatly over the years, too. In the beginning, as has been shown, the purpose was to train young men for the ministry or at least train them in the teachings of their church. Then another purpose of education was added: to reduce the illiteracy of the nation. The purpose of secondary education first was to prepare for college entrance. Today, our high schools are endeavoring to train many young people who never expect to go to college. Technical and vocational training is now a confirmed part of secondary education, along with courses in homemaking. The tendency is to broaden the curriculum to include many courses in the arts, in physical, social, and practical science, and in business.

Teacher Shortage. During World War II many teachers were attracted into war industries by the high wages that were paid. A shortage of teachers developed that continued after the war was over. Salaries have generally been raised, both because they have been too low in the past and because it is hoped this will attract more young people to the teaching profession.

Self-education on the Increase. While formal schooling has been extended greatly in the United States, opportunities for self-education have been increasing also. Almost every community has its public library. The larger communities have museums and zoos. Universities and high schools offer night classes and extension courses. Correspondence schools serve a real need for many Americans. Our newspapers and magazines and books bring us up-to-date information upon every subject imaginable. Lyceum courses and the Chautauqua have been largely replaced by the radio as a means of bringing firsthand personal knowledge, experience, and opinion to interested listeners all over the country.

The people of the United States have long recognized that extensive free education must be made available to all our people as a necessary requisite for a successful democracy. We know that only educated people can govern themselves wisely.

THE PUBLIC PRESS

Freedom of Expression. A public press, free from government censorship, has been as important in the development of America as has our free educational system. And, like education, its growth has been slow, but sure.

Although the first printing press was brought over to the colonies within twenty years after the Pilgrims landed at Plymouth Rock, it was used for religious publications only. During this period many dissertations on theology were produced by such famous colonial preachers as Cotton Mather and Jonathan Edwards. Before the end of the century the first newspaper had appeared in Massachusetts, but it had been forced to stop publication by the government of the colony because of an article on politics.

Early Publications. The *Boston News-Letter* printed its first issue in 1704. It was more careful about what it said, so it continued. Others followed. By 1771 the colonies had twenty-five

Intertype Corporation

THROUGH EDUCATION WE FEED THE TREE OF DEMOCRACY

Thomas Jefferson said: "I know of no safe depository of the ultimate powers of society but the people themselves; and if we think them not enlightened enough to exercise their control with a wholesome discretion, the remedy is not to take it from them, but to inform their discretion by education."

newspapers. They weren't much, compared to today's papers, but they were in considerable demand by a news-hungry public.

Free Press Triumphs over Censorship. The English colonies in America inherited their censorship of all publications from the mother country. From the time the printing press was invented in Europe by John Gutenberg, the church had controlled its use. In England, that privilege was taken over by the ruler during the time of Queen Elizabeth and remained an exclusive right of the crown until abolished by Parliament in 1695.

In the American colonies, the pub-lisher of a newspaper was liable to arrest and prosecution if he printed something any of the colonial officials didn't like. Out of such a situation came the circumstances that established the precedent for a free press in this country.

In New York a newspaper publisher named Peter Zenger was arrested and jailed in 1735 for printing articles which criticized the government of the colony. The things he had printed were true, but the colonial officers controlled all justice in the colony, and conviction appeared certain. Lawyers who tried to defend him suddenly found their licenses to practice law in New York had

AMERICANS REGARD CENSORSHIP AS A FORM OF TYRANNY

The tradition of a free press unhampered by government censorship was written into our Constitution as a safeguard against despotic rule. In such measure as censorship exists, democracy ceases to exist.

been revoked. But one such disbarred lawyer rode all the way to Philadelphia and brought back with him a wise old attorney who appeared in court in Zenger's defense. He astonished everyone by admitting to the jury that his client was guilty—guilty of printing the truth. Then he went on to point out that it was not only Peter Zenger who was on trial. It was everyone, and the right of everyone to speak the truth as he sees it. Liberty itself, he said, was being threatened. The jurors caught the idea quickly, and Peter Zenger was acquitted. Freedom of speech and of the press had been established in America.

Newspapers and Magazines Flourish. With the shackles of control removed, newspaper publishing became more attractive. By 1810 there were nearly four hundred newspapers issued regularly. At least twenty-five of them were daily papers. Interest in politics and in newspapers became inseparable; as one increased, so did the other. Many papers identified themselves with one or another political party as organized politics became a firmly established part of American life.

In the nineteenth century new inventions helped to speed the production and circulation of newspapers. First came the telegraph, in 1832, which greatly facilitated the collection of news. In 1846 the first rotary printing press was produced in the United

HIS TRIAL CONFIRMED OUR FREEDOM OF THE PRESS

New York publisher John Peter Zenger's defense was ably handled by Attorney Andrew Hamilton, who told the court that all men have the right "publicly to remonstrate against the abuses of power . . . and to assert with courage the sense they have at the blessing of liberty . . . and their resolution at all hazards to preserve it." Zenger was acquitted.

States; this meant quicker printing. The sulfite process of making paper from wood pulp, perfected in 1866, resulted in cheaper paper. After 1868 newsrooms resounded to the clatter of the typewriter, and in 1885 the first mechanical typesetter, called the linotype, made its appearance. The rapidly growing network of railroads, extending from coast to coast, brought quick distribution for papers, permitting editors to reach ever-increasing numbers of people. These developments, plus the printing of paid advertising, soon brought the price of newspapers down so the poorest people could afford to buy them. The newspaper rapidly became the principal instrument for shaping public opinion in America.

Next came magazines. Weekly and monthly periodicals appeared, many of them to support or oppose some particular movement, such as temperance or antislavery. Some of our current magazines can boast steady publication for about a century. Among these are the *North American Review*, *Harper's Magazine*, and the *Atlantic Monthly*. But soon, in addition to the heavy reading of these magazines, less expensive monthly and weekly publications were put on the market, containing light stories, pictures, and the type of things that appealed to the mass of the people.

The invention of photographic film to take the place of the sensitized plate, and of chemical engraving processes to replace hand engraving, meant that photographs could be taken and quickly and easily converted into

Intertype Corporation

TYPESETTING MACHINE

Lines of type for our printed publications are set on machines such as these, making possible the tremendous volume of newspapers, books, and periodicals today.

"cuts" for printing. Pictures became a standard part of all newspapers. Soon the cartoon came in to supplement photographs. In 1918 the first picture newspaper, called the *tabloid,* made its appearance in New York. Add to these developments news and pictures speedily sent by radio from all over the world, color printing, the syndicated columns and critical commentaries of

such men as Walter Lippmann, and, of course, the "comic" strips, and you have today's newspaper.

Influence of Radio and Television. In this brief discussion of the dissemination of news as a factor in the development of America, we must give radio more than a mere mention. A recent invention, it has grown by leaps and bounds. Today five huge networks of stations serve the people nation-wide—the National Broadcasting Company, the Columbia Broadcasting System, the American Broadcasting Company, the Mutual Broadcasting System, and the Liberty Broadcasting System. In addition, there are thousands of small community stations that present a more local aspect of news and entertainment. The American public has come to count on radio just as much as on newspapers for news coverage, for radio can bring us the latest developments just as soon as they have occurred. Regular AM (amplitude modulation) radio has now been supplemented by FM (frequency modulation) radio, which reproduces music with more naturalness and less interference. And, of course, television is moving into the homes of America very rapidly. Soon we shall have television coverage of news events as they happen, carried to us at once so we can see as well as hear history as it is made. Another modern invention that may gain wider use is facsimile—the transmission of newspapers by radio. A device attached to an ordinary radio would receive and print news in much the same manner as the teletype does now.

Beware of Propaganda. With all these methods of spreading news, we have become the best informed people in the world. But with all our informa-

The Town Hall, Inc.

HOW THE RADIO INFORMS PUBLIC OPINION

Both radio and television have provided the means by which mass communication of ideas can be achieved within a matter of seconds. Nationwide forums of the air, such as "America's Town Meeting," offer dramatic evidence of this great development of the twentieth century. "America's Town Meeting" programs are cast in the form of debates.

tion, we have to beware of propaganda. Propaganda is anything which is said or printed with the intent of getting the listener or the reader to accept the ideas of the speaker or the writer. Propaganda may be good, or it may be harmful. Whether it is one or the other depends upon the ideas being advocated. If the propagandist wants you to do something that will benefit only him or a small group of people and at the same time harm a great many more, we shall want to view that propaganda with disfavor. If, on the other hand, the ideas being urged upon us will stir us to action that will benefit the majority of people and us in the long run, we can probably look upon such propaganda as healthy. As we read our newspapers and magazines and listen to our radios, we must remember that frequently what we read and hear will be colored and slanted according to the interests of the owners of the newspapers and radio stations or the sponsors of the programs. The best safeguard against being misled by selfish propaganda is to get information on all sides of a question first, and then weigh the evidence and logically decide what we honestly believe to be the best opinion to hold to or the best course of action to follow. Debates, whether spoken or written, are particularly valuable as a means of providing the public with a great deal of pertinent information on both sides of a question.

DEVELOPMENT OF SCIENCE

A Guide to Scientific Investigation. Just a few years before the Pilgrims landed at Plymouth Rock, a very important development in the field of science had taken place in England. Prior to that time people had gained their scientific knowledge chiefly from two sources: the teachings of the Church, and the writings of early Greek and Roman scholars. At the beginning of the seventeenth century Francis Bacon, an Englishman who had been doing some experimenting, broke with tradition. He asserted that there was only one sure way of arriving at scientific truth, and that was by studying nature itself. Said Bacon, first one should observe nature and from these observations formulate a theory about the answer to a scientific problem. The next step, according to Bacon, is to experiment to either prove or disprove the theory. In such a manner, Bacon believed, and only in such a manner, could correct scientific information be obtained.

Practical Scientific Discoveries. Americans have always been more interested in practical scientific discoveries than in abstract science. Probably this was partly due to the type of life the early settlers led, which invited practical developments that served to make that life easier and more pleasant. Benjamin Franklin, for example, won quite a name for himself as an inventor. One of his early inventions was an improved stove, which gave more heat with less fuel. And, of course, his curiosity about electricity resulted in the kite experiment for which he is famous. He sent up a kite in a thunderstorm and discovered that lightning, or electricity, would travel down the string and jump from a key at its end. That discovery resulted directly in the invention of the lightning rod.

From a small beginning, the scientific development of the United States has been rapid and extensive. In the field of practical science no other nation has shown such great progress in so short a time. In pure scientific research our development has not been so great, although more and more at-

PRACTICAL SCIENTIFIC DEVELOPMENTS

Invention	Inventor	Date
Lightning rod	Franklin	1752
Submarine	Bushnell	1776
Steamboat	Fitch	1787
Cotton gin	Whitney	1793
Steamboat (first practical)	Fulton	1793
Electromagnet	Henry	1828
Telegraph	Morse	1832
Reaper	McCormick	1833
Revolver	Colt	1835
Process for vulcanizing rubber	Goodyear	1839
Use of ether as an anesthetic	Long	1842
Pneumatic tire	Thompson	1845
Rotary printing press	Hoe	1846
Sewing machine	Howe	1846
Elevator	Otis	1852
Machine gun	Gatling	1861
Process for making paper from wood pulp	Tilghman	1866
Typewriter	Sholes and Glidden	1868
Telephone	Bell	1876
Talking machine	Edison	1877
Incandescent lamp	Edison	1878
Fountain pen	Waterman	1884
Linotype	Mergenthaler	1885
Motion pictures	Edison	1893
Airplane (experimental)	Langley	1896
First motor-driven practical airplane	Orville and Wilbur Wright	1903
Radio vacuum tube	DeForest	1907

THE "CLERMONT" PROVED THE WORTH OF THE STEAMBOAT

Inventor Robert Fulton's early attempts were received with derision. But the successful trip of his steamboat on the Hudson River made transportation history.

tention is being paid to such research work. The wartime discovery of the method of releasing the energy contained in the atom is a notable achievement of American scientific research, but even here we were dependent upon earlier findings of European scientists.

There is no point in attempting to set down a list of all the practical scientific developments that have aided in the advance of this country. However, it does seem right that a few of them should be mentioned. The list on page 234 is a very short one. It could easily be increased to many times its length.

America, Land of Inventors. Even though our scientific and industrial development has been rapid, new inventions do not always catch on quickly. New ideas are often met with considerable skepticism. After he operated successfully a steam ferryboat near Philadelphia in 1790, John Fitch was called crazy when he tried to interest people in investing money to help him build boats to operate on the Ohio and Mississippi rivers. Not until Robert Ful-

ton's "Clermont" made its now famous run from New York City to Albany and back on the Hudson River in 1807, was the steamboat accepted as practical.

The last seventy-five years have been marked by one memorable "first" after another. Alexander Graham Bell first transmitted the human voice over a wire in 1876. In 1893 Henry Ford brought out his first automobile. The first wireless message was flashed across the Atlantic in 1901. The Wright Brothers gave the first public exhibition of their airplane in 1908. In 1919 Alcock and Brown flew nonstop across the Atlantic. The next year saw the first radio broadcast, from station KDKA, in Pittsburgh, and in 1927 came the first transatlantic broadcast, the same year that Charles Lindbergh flew across the Atlantic, alone, in his little plane, the "Spirit of St. Louis." Five years later Amelia Earhart Putnam became the first woman to accomplish the same feat. And so on, almost without end.

The story of these achievements can be seen in one location in the United

HENRY FORD—HE PUT AMERICA ON WHEELS

From his modest shop on Bagley Avenue in Detroit, Ford launched a manufacturing enterprise that made automobile transportation available to millions.

CYRUS FIELD—HE WIRED AN OCEAN AND BROUGHT MEN CLOSER

He pursued the idea that a cable of copper could be stretched across the ocean to establish quick communication between the Old World and the New. In 1866 he saw his efforts result in the first successful laying of a transatlantic cable that reached from Newfoundland to Ireland.

THOMAS EDISON—HE MADE WELL ENOUGH BETTER

Thomas Edison coaxed electricity to glow inside glass, taught pictures to move on a screen, and made wax rolls that could talk and sing.

LUTHER BURBANK—HE FOUND A SECRET IN THE FLOWERING EARTH

This great naturalist sought mixtures for enriching soil and patiently tried ways of cross-breeding plant species until he could grow bigger potatoes, pit-free plums, and an array of plants that were more useful and beautiful than any before them.

States today. Back in 1846, partly with funds donated by an Englishman, James Smithson, the federal government established in Washington, D.C., the Smithsonian Institution, a national museum of science. Here one can trace in actual equipment the splendid story

ALEXANDER GRAHAM BELL

The great system of telephone networks that bind the nation bears his name.

of the advance of American scientific achievement.

The increased mechanization of warfare stepped-up scientific research and activity in the United States during the two great wars of the twentieth century. Scientific progress was pushed in order to gain and hold the military supremacy necessary to win those wars. After World War II our civilian popu-

lation has been benefiting somewhat from the wartime discoveries. A variety of new medicines have become available, notably the sulfa drugs and others of a similar nature. We now know how to rid whole areas of objectionable insects for days and even weeks at a time. And the Atomic Energy Commission is at work trying to channel the power of the atom to peace-time uses. If all our scientific intelligence and capacity could be directed exclusively to non-war production, what lives we would all live!

For the protection of American inventors, the United States Government has established the Patent Office in the Department of Commerce. Here a person may register an invention and thereby assure himself of whatever benefits may come from the use or the sale of the invention. The number of applications for patents varies from 50,000 to 90,000 a year, and the patents granted from 45,000 to 55,000. So freedom of expression in invention is encouraged.

AMERICAN LITERATURE

Colonial Writers. Although there was no great amount of it, the American colonies were not without their own literature. Most early writing dealt with religious subjects, and we have already mentioned the long sermons of Cotton Mather and Jonathan Edwards. But the colonies produced some early historians, too. Notable among these was Captain John Smith, of Pocahontas fame, who published in England in 1608 a record of early events in Virginia. In later books he told more of his adventures in the New World, and at times his imagination got the best of

FIRST AIRPLANE TO FLY OVER THE ATLANTIC

This strut-laden two-wing airplane, known as the NC–4, was the first heavier-than-air machine to negotiate a successful flight across the Atlantic (1919). The crew was in command of Lieutenant-Commander Albert C. Read.

his truthfulness, so that his accounts were not entirely reliable. The historian of Plymouth Colony was Governor William Bradford, and of Massachusetts, Governor John Winthrop. Numerous others wrote accounts of their travels from colony to colony, and some kept very interesting diaries. Anne Bradstreet was probably the best of the early poets.

A very popular type of early writing was essays and almanacs, such as Benjamin Franklin's *Poor Richard's Almanac*. In these writings the virtues of the good life were extolled in a simple manner that had a wide appeal among people who could scarcely read and write. Quotations from *Poor Richard* spread throughout the colonies. Said Franklin, "Dost thou love life, then do not squander time, for that's the stuff life is made of." And "experience keeps a dear school but fools will learn in no other and scarce in that."

The basic ideals of our American government were firmly fixed in the minds of some of these early writers, even though they were not practiced in the colonies. For example, a Massachusetts preacher, John Wise, in 1717, put some of them into words—statements that were probably far ahead of his time. Notice how familiar they sound to us today. Said John Wise, nature had "set all men upon a level and made them equals," and "the end of all good government is to cultivate humanity and to promote the happiness of all."

Until well into the nineteenth cen-

Museum of Science & Industry, Chicago

WHERE TRIBUTE IS PAID TO AMERICAN INVENTIVE GENIUS

The beautiful Museum of Science and Industry in Chicago, gift of Julius Rosenwald, houses a treasure house of models and historic originals of the great industrial and scientific developments that have marked American history.

tury, however, the United States produced little literature that was great. There were some early novelists, dramatists, and poets, but none whose work is very popular today. The Revolutionary period brought forth several historians of the war and, of course, the heroes soon had their biographers. Mason L. Weems, called "Parson Weems," wrote a life of Washington in which he told the somewhat doubtful story of young George and the cherry tree.

Great Names in American Literature. Beginning about 1820, America did produce a literature that was all her own. Merely the mention of the great writers of the period and their works which gained world-wide fame is sufficient proof that American letters were finally coming of age. The subjects were entirely American. James Fenimore Cooper wrote of many things in the new land—the Revolutionary War, spies, pirates, but mostly of the American Indian and life on the westward-moving frontier. Washington Irving wrote of New York in a humorous vein, and Nathaniel Hawthorne of New England in such well-known tales as *The House of Seven Gables* and *The Scarlet Letter.* Herman Melville told tales of the sea, and his *Moby Dick* is undoubtedly one of the most famous American books ever written. Harriet Beecher Stowe's *Uncle Tom's Cabin* is acknowledged as having had a great effect upon public opinion in the North in the years just before the War between the States.

RALPH WALDO EMERSON

His pen left a great impact upon the nineteenth century American scene.

In the field of poetry, James Russell Lowell, too, wrote about slavery from the Northern viewpoint. Henry Wadsworth Longfellow was a splendid storyteller in verse, and John Greenleaf Whittier, also an ardent antislavery poet, wrote about nature. William Cullen Bryant is best remembered for the philosophy of his *Thanatopsis*. Walt Whitman wrote of his great faith in the people and the future of America in his free verse. And Edgar Allan Poe left weird and somber poems, such as *The Raven*, as well as the reputation of being "the father of the American short story."

Americans since the colonial period have generally stood staunchly for freedom of thought and expression. In the nineteenth century the champion of intellectual freedom was Ralph Waldo Emerson. A Bostonian, Emerson started out in the ministry but gave it up soon to devote his time to lecturing and writing. Although he wrote some poetry,

most of his work was in the form of essays. He dealt with the current problems of his time, and his philosophy emphasized the idealistic approach to their solutions rather than the materialistic. He was the William Ernest Henley of American literature, maintaining always that every person is "the master of his fate, . . . the captain of his soul." With Emerson should be mentioned also Henry David Thoreau, another idealist, who lived close to nature and wrote charmingly of it.

Two nineteenth century historians deserve mention, too. Between 1834 and 1882, George Bancroft produced a long account of the early period of American history. It was a somewhat impassioned story, but well documented. At about the same time, Rich-

HENRY DAVID THOREAU

His famous work, *Walden*, has become an American classic.

ard Hildreth produced a history that was more honest in its approach and in the evaluation of the men responsible for founding the nation and charting its early course.

As the country moved from the nineteenth into the twentieth century,

Great American Group of Insurance Companies

GREAT FIGURES OF AMERICAN LITERATURE

This painting by Christian Schussele shows, from left to right, Henry T. Tuckerman, Oliver Wendell Holmes, William Gilmore Simms, Fitz-Greene Halleck, Nathaniel Hawthorne, Henry Wadsworth Longfellow, Nathaniel Parker Willis, William H. Prescott, Washington Irving, James K. Paulding, Ralph Waldo Emerson, William Cullen Bryant, John P. Kennedy, James Fenimore Cooper, and George Bancroft.

new names appeared in American writing. Samuel Langhorne Clemens, better known by his pen name taken from his Mississippi River steamboat days, Mark Twain, won the right to be called the greatest American humorist. We still enjoy the adventures of Tom Sawyer and Huckleberry Finn. There was much "local color" in Mark Twain's stories, as there was in the works of Hamlin Garland about the Midwest, of Bret Harte about the Far West, and of Joel Chandler Harris, who wrote his famous Negro stories at this time.

Also into the literature of this period was creeping the struggle between the materialism of our growing industry and the idealism upon which the country was founded. The first signs of it appear in such works as *The Octopus* and *The Pit,* by Frank Norris, which dealt with the growing of wheat in the

Far West and the Chicago grain market. In 1907 Jack London wrote *The Iron Heel,* in which he attacked our whole economic system. And Sinclair Lewis, Sherwood Anderson, and Theodore Dreiser were picturing the struggle of people against the ever-more-complex conditions of living. American literature was becoming less romantic and more realistic.

No account of our prose, however brief, could pass over the names of three voluminous writers of light fiction, Harold Bell Wright and Gene Stratton Porter, who told simple stories of people and nature, and Zane Grey, who wrote of the old "Wild West."

After the days of Longfellow and Bryant, American poetry declined somewhat, until the 1920's and 30's produced a new group of poets who pictured life of their time. In this group

MARK TWAIN'S FAMOUS PORTRAYAL OF AMERICAN BOYHOOD

Tom Sawyer and "Huck" Finn have become permanent fixtures in America's literary heritage. Their creator was one of the most famous humorists of his time.

were such big names as Robert Frost, Edwin Arlington Robinson, Edna St. Vincent Millay, Archibald MacLeish, and Carl Sandburg, who is known for his prose as well as his poetry.

About this time the American short story was coming into its own. More and more writers of this form of fiction appeared, and more magazines began publication to serve as outlets for their work. Best sellers included the *Saturday Evening Post,* the *Ladies' Home Journal,* and the *American Magazine.* This period brought the "pulp" magazines, the leader of which became *True*

Story Magazine, published by Bernarr McFadden, who was also an enthusiastic exponent of physical culture. The 1930's saw the rise in popularity of such magazines as the *Reader's Digest,* which was distinguished by the fact that it ran no advertising; *Time,* a weekly news magazine; and *Life,* a pictorial weekly about current events.

The 1930's were the years of the big depression, and some of the literature reflected the strained times. One such book that attracted a lot of attention was *The Grapes of Wrath,* by John Steinbeck. A best seller of the period

John Hancock Mutual Life Insurance Co.

HE BUILT A COUNTRY WITH A WOODSMAN'S AXE

The raw strength and productive energies of expanding America were well personified by the fabled giant of the North Woods, Paul Bunyan. The Bunyan legend is part of the humorous folklore that has fed our literary tradition.

was Pearl Buck's *The Good Earth,* a story of China. Others were *Anthony Adverse* by Hervey Allen, and *Gone with the Wind,* a Civil War story of the South, by Margaret Mitchell.

The first half of the 1940's was taken up with World War II, and war is not conducive to the production of great literature. In the post-war period, the big names in prose include Sinclair Lewis, Carl Sandburg, Hervey Allen, Lloyd Douglas, who is known for his religious stories, such as *The Robe,* Christopher Morley, John P. Marquand, Walter Edmonds, and MacKinlay Kan-

tor. If there is a new trend in prose, it is to be found in the writing of William Saroyan, who uses no plot but presents merely a series of incidents in a matter-of-fact manner. Robert Frost and Archibald MacLeish (former Librarian of Congress) remain the leading poets of this decade. Paul Engle seems to be pointing toward a new trend in his desertion of free verse for the traditional poetic forms of the past.

Of the twentieth century historians, none stand out as do Charles and Mary Beard, whose exhaustive research and intelligent interpretation probably are unequaled in American historical writing. Deserving mention also is Will Durant, who has done much to popularize reading along historical lines.

AMERICAN FINE ARTS

American Drama. As was true of literature, there was very little early American drama. Most plays that were presented were of English origin. There were few theaters, for the church looked upon them as sinful, and not entirely without reason. But toward the middle of the eighteenth century the theater became very popular, in spite of the criticism of religious leaders. Famous actors frequently toured the country and put on plays with local casts in which they played the leading parts. The foremost actor of the time was Edwin Forrest, who distinguished himself in Shakespearean roles.

In the period following the Civil War, religious prejudice against the theater declined. In conventional drama, English productions still dominated, and Edwin Booth and John Drew became famous as Shakespearean actors. Joseph Jefferson won a name for himself portraying the American character Rip Van Winkle.

American writers were expressing themselves in new forms of drama, however. The western play, with such heroes as Buffalo Bill, became a favorite. A good many melodramas were produced, notably *East Lynne*. The period saw the rise of variety shows in the form of vaudeville, with its many kinds of acts, and burlesque, which featured scantily-clad girls.

The early years of the twentieth century saw the theater growing and producing all kinds of drama. The great names of the period are still well known: Maude Adams, Otis Skinner, and the Barrymore family. Vaudeville, too, was going strong with such performers as Fred Stone, Marie Dressler, Weber and Fields, and Al Jolson. Drama was combined with music to make a new kind of show called the

Acme

VICTOR HERBERT

His light operas have delighted the hearts of countless millions.

operetta. The popularity of this form in the theater was undoubtedly at least partly due to the tuneful compositions of Victor Herbert, who turned out many operettas, among them *The Red Mill, Babes in Toyland,* and *Naughty Marietta.*

During these years another form of dramatic production put in its appearance. The moving picture camera and projector had been invented, and com-

SCENE FROM ONE OF THE FIRST BIG MOVIE PRODUCTIONS

A Civil War engagement is depicted in this scene from D. W. Griffth's motion picture, *The Birth of a Nation,* which was shown throughout the country.

panies began to make motion pictures. Most of the early ones were melodramas, westerns, or slapstick comedies. They were shown in special theaters called "Nickelodeons," to the accompaniment of piano music which the pianist tried to suit to the scene appearing on the screen. The pictures were of poor quality and, of course, silent. One of the first big productions was *The Birth of a Nation,* filmed in 1915.

Another form of variety attraction that became a favorite about this time was the Chautauqua, named for a New York lake where the first meetings of this sort were held. A circuit of towns was arranged and talent hired. Usually a big tent was erected on a vacant lot, and the schedule ran for a week or two. The series included plays, musical programs, and lectures. The Chautauqua provided a great opportunity for people in smaller communities. Another type of tent show, the circus, came to town almost every year; Barnum and Bailey started together in 1881. The "road show" made the rounds, too, with its melodramatic productions of *Uncle Tom's Cabin* and *East Lynne.* Along the great river systems, like the Ohio and the Mississippi, these companies traveled and played on the river "show boats." The period also saw increased popularity for minstrel shows, variety productions featuring black-faced comedians.

Then there was the medicine show. It usually traveled from town to town in a sort of wagon. One man often handled the whole performance. He would entertain people with variety acts—juggling, magic, dancing—until a crowd had gathered, and then he would sell some kind of patent medicine that he declared would cure almost anything and was "good for man or beast."

The 1920's gave us one of the most famous plays ever to appear on the American stage, *Abie's Irish Rose*. It had a long run in drama form, and the radio serial version has continued to the present. Doubtless it will be presented again and again on television.

About this time Eugene O'Neill began to write plays. Some of them were extremely long. *Strange Interlude* would open in the afternoon and run through the evening, with time out for dinner. Many critics think O'Neill is the greatest playwright this country has ever produced.

In recent years probably the best liked stage productions have been the musical comedies, such as *Oklahoma*, *Annie Get Your Gun*, and *South Pacific*. Although vaudeville died out, many of its performers caught on in radio. Among them were Al Jolson, Jack Benny, and Edgar Bergen. Now, with the growth of television, interest in drama is again on the upsurge in America.

American Music. Along with literature and drama, there was little early music that was truly American. About the only songs we know today from that period are those that were associated with the Revolutionary War, like "Yankee Doodle" and "The Star Spangled Banner," written during the War of 1812. "America" wasn't written until 1830.

For a long time America didn't have enough trained musicians to produce much music of its own. But people enjoyed concerts, and famous European artists like the Norwegian violinist, Ole Bull, and the Swedish soprano, Jenny Lind, came to tour the larger cities of this country. A big step toward giving our people some musical training came in 1834 when Lowell Mason introduced music into the public schools of Boston.

Toward the end of the nineteenth century symphony orchestras were organized in a few of the large cities— New York, Boston, Chicago. The Metropolitan Opera House opened in New York in 1883. But little music was as yet produced in this country. The light operas of the English composers Gilbert and Sullivan were popular, and Victor Herbert was beginning to turn out similar work here.

In the early years of the twentieth century, interest in music boomed. More symphony orchestras and choral societies appeared, and operas drew large crowds. Some evidence of truly American music was showing. Edward MacDowell was writing pieces like *To a Wild Rose*, and Irving Berlin gave great impetus to a new type of music called "jazz" with his *Alexander's Ragtime Band*. The period after World War I brought such well-known composers as Jerome Kern and George Gershwin. Famous dance bands were playing in large cities—those of Paul Whiteman, Benny Goodman, Tommy Dorsey, and Wayne King, "the waltz king."

The growth of radio has done much

HE GAVE AMERICANS THE MUSIC THEY MADE THEMSELVES

Stephen Foster captured the spirit and folk music of growing America and composed tuneful ballads that swept the nation.

to enhance the appreciation of music in America. Not only does radio bring us the big name dance bands of the land, but it also makes available the music of the great symphony orchestras as well. Today, in many homes, the radio has replaced the piano as the principal musical instrument. The hit tunes from the latest Broadway shows are carried at once all over the country by the big radio networks. Famous soloists and orchestras present concerts in almost every home through radio or television. The recording business has become a big industry, as has the sheet music business. Schools everywhere offer music courses, and private instruction of all kinds is available. Walt Whitman would be pleased if he could today "hear America singing."

American Painting. Of the painters of the Colonial period, the one best known today is Gilbert Stuart, for his portraits of George Washington and other colonial leaders. Although Charles Willson Peale and his son, Rembrandt Peale, did work comparable to that of Stuart, they are not so well remembered. Others, such as John Trumbull, left us paintings of historic events of the Revolutionary War, among them the signing of the Declaration of Independence and the surrender of Cornwallis.

In the first half of the nineteenth century Americans turned from portraits to out-of-door scenes. There was so much wild beauty in the new nation just being carved out of the ruggedness of the continent that many painters were inspired to put it on canvas. It was an encouraging trend. This period saw also the beginning of the newspaper cartoon, with which the name of Thomas Nast is most closely associated.

In the early 1900's, along with libraries, art schools were established in the large cities and students began to take up painting seriously. John Singer Sargent and James A. M. Whistler did their best work—Sargent in portraits and Whistler in conveying moods, as in his *Mother*. Maxfield Parrish became famous for his use of shades of blue in his fantasies. And James Montgomery Flagg, Charles Dana Gibson, and Howard Chandler Christy made the American girl the subject of their work.

Modern painting in America has been somewhat interested in modernistic and futuristic designs, but people in general are still most pleased by the local color work of artists like Grant Wood and Grandma Moses.

American Sculpture. Sculpture got a very late start in the United States. After the Civil War and on into the twentieth century almost every home had its plaster figures on the marble-topped tables and the piano or organ in the "parlor," that room which was kept closed most of the time and opened only on special occasions. The

1893 World's Fair in Chicago, called the Columbian Exposition, gave considerable impetus to sculpture, for the buildings erected were ornamented with all kinds of work. Sculpture probably was at its height in the early part of this century. The big names then were Augustus Saint-Gaudens, Lorado Taft, Jo Davidson, and Gutzon Borglum. The most outstanding recent work in sculpture has been the carving

A PEALE PORTRAIT

This painting of General George Washington is the work of the nineteenth century artist, Rembrandt Peale.

of the faces of Washington, Jefferson, Lincoln, and Theodore Roosevelt on the side of Mount Rushmore in the Black Hills of South Dakota. The work was begun in 1927 by Gutzon Borglum. Since his death in 1941, it has been carried on by his son.

American Architecture. Our first houses were log huts, built for service only and with no thought of beauty. As time went by and some people became

Acme

THE MOUNT RUSHMORE MEMORIAL—SHRINE OF DEMOCRACY

George Washington, Thomas Jefferson, Theodore Roosevelt, and Abraham Lincoln surmount the granite peak of this South Dakota hill. The dimensions of these stone carvings are impressive—sixty feet from top of the head to bottom of the chin.

wealthy, they wanted massive and ornate homes. Builders copied the styles of the countries from which they came, so colonial homes followed the English, Dutch, or Spanish traditional designs.

Later, there was quite a swing to classical architecture—styled after that of Greece and Rome, probably because they, too, had been self-governing. Jefferson had his home at Monticello built in this style, with many columns, and the new capital city of Washington reflected the influence of this trend.

SKYLINE OF THE NATION'S SECOND LARGEST CITY

This photograph shows an eastward view of Chicago's skyscrapers from the site of old Fort Dearborn. The conspicuous white structure to the left is the famous Wrigley Building.

For a long time, wood, stone, and brick were the only construction materials available. Then, as the country became industrialized, iron and later steel came into use, particularly in business and public buildings. The Home Insurance Building, in Chicago, put up in 1885, is often called the first skyscraper, although it was only ten stories high. As cities grew larger and became more congested, skyscrapers were pushed up farther and farther. Today the New York skyline is marked by the towers of the Woolworth Building, the Chrysler

A FRANK LLOYD WRIGHT BUILDING

The famous architect, whose ideas about functional construction have been a storm center among more conventional builders, has exercised a unique influence on twentieth century styles. "Robie House," shown above, is a residence in Chicago that was designed by Wright and built in 1909. The horizontal lines of this house bespeak Wright's genius for designing with an awareness for the landscape.

Portland Cement Association

MODERN AMERICAN ARCHITECTURE

The clean lines, lack of heavy decorative ornaments, and sleek appearance characterize contemporary architecture in the United States, as exemplified by the Research and Development Building of the Portland Cement Association. Considerable accent on the admittance of light and air can be detected in the design of this building's front landscape.

Building, and the Empire State Building.

In the nineteenth century houses had been decorated with cupolas and carvings. In the twentieth century these gradually disappeared, and houses became more functional in their design. The leader of this movement was the Midwesterner, Frank Lloyd Wright. Wright produced some very radical designs in trying to plan homes that would be chiefly useful. He's the man who planned the Imperial Hotel in Tokyo, Japan, so that it would withstand the frequent earthquakes. Modern homes are using more glass, and some are designed so as to catch more of the sun's rays to aid in heating. The trend at present is toward smaller houses, built low and rambling in the "ranch" style.

The industrialization of the United States has brought big cities and their accompanying slums. Most of these cities have just grown, following no plan. Today, more attention is being paid to slum clearance and better housing, with the federal government lending a hand. And cities are becoming beauty conscious, with the result that zoning ordinances have been adopted restricting the types of buildings that may be erected in any section, and boards have been appointed to plan for future development and changes. All of this promises well for our cities of the future.

Throughout the history of the United States, its people have enjoyed almost complete freedom of expression of their beliefs, their thoughts, and their talents. The results have not always been good, but this personal freedom has had a great deal to do with the growth and development of America and has made it attractive to people all over the world.

FOR YOUR REVIEW
These Should Be Easy for You Now

1. How was the religion of the people determined in early times?
2. Why were Christians persecuted in the Roman Empire?
3. How was the Church able to exert so much influence in the early Middle Ages? How was this power broken?
4. What situation led to the establishment of Protestantism?
5. What was the status of religious freedom in the early American colonies? What effect may religious thinking in the colonies have had upon political thinking? What effect did the American Revolution have upon the religious situation?
6. What does the Constitution say about religion?
7. What is the history of religion in modern America?
8. What connection did religious interests have with early education in America?
9. Why is the education of all the people especially important to the welfare of the United States?
10. Trace the development of free public education in the United States. Cite evidence to show that educational opportunity has been greatly increased. How has the purpose of education in the United States changed over the years?
11. What incident established freedom of the press in the United States?
12. What inventions aided the development of newspapers? What other means of disseminating news do we have in modern America?
13. What is propaganda? What is the best safeguard against harmful propaganda?

14. What important new idea about scientific truth did Francis Bacon advance?
15. What is meant by the statement that "Americans have been more interested in practical scientific discoveries than in abstract science"? Give evidence to prove or disprove the statement.
16. What was the nature of early American literature?
17. List various types of dramatic performances Americans have enjoyed during one period or another.

Associated Dates

1821—first public high school established in the United States
1833—first coeducational college opened (Oberlin)
1893—Henry Ford built his first car
1901—first wireless message sent across the Atlantic
1903—first airplane flight by the Wright brothers
1918—first tabloid newspaper
1919—first nonstop flight across the Atlantic
1920—first radio broadcasting station (KDKA, Pittsburgh)
1927—first transatlantic broadcast
      first solo flight across the Atlantic (Charles A. Lindbergh)

Why Are These To Be Remembered?

Olympic Games	Roger Williams	Facsimile
Octavian	Catechism	James Smithson
Martin Luther	John Wesley	Patent Office
Armada	Horace Mann	Nickelodeon
Anglican Church	Chautauqua	Stephen Foster

People Associated with the Cultural Development of America

Maude Adams	Will Durant	Henry Wadsworth Long-
Hervey Allen	Jonathan Edwards	fellow
Sherwood Anderson	Ralph Waldo Emerson	James Russell Lowell
Barnum and Bailey	James Montgomery Flagg	Edward MacDowell
Ethel, Lionel, and John	Edwin Forrest	Archibald MacLeish
Barrymore	Robert Frost	John P. Marquand
Charles and Mary Beard	Hamlin Garland	Lowell Mason
Jack Benny	George Gershwin	Cotton Mather
Edgar Bergen	Charles Dana Gibson	Edna St. Vincent Millay
Irving Berlin	Benny Goodman	Margaret Mitchell
Edwin Booth	Zane Grey	Christopher Morley
Gutzon Borglum	Joel Chandler Harris	Grandma Moses
William Cullen Bryant	Bret Harte	Thomas Nast
Pearl Buck	Nathaniel Hawthorne	Frank Norris
Ole Bull	Victor Herbert	Eugene O'Neill
Howard Chandler Christy	Washington Irving	Maxfield Parrish
Samuel Langhorne Clemens	Joseph Jefferson	Edgar Allan Poe
James Fenimore Cooper	Al Jolson	Gene Stratton Porter
Jo Davidson	MacKinlay Kantor	Edwin Arlington Robinson
Tommy Dorsey	Jerome Kern	Augustus St. Gaudens
Lloyd Douglas	Wayne King	Carl Sandburg
Theodore Dreiser	Sinclair Lewis	John Singer Sargent
Marie Dressler	Jenny Lind	William Saroyan
John Drew	Jack London	Otis Skinner

John Steinbeck

Fred Stone

Harriet Beecher Stowe

Gilbert Stuart

Lorado Taft

Henry David Thoreau

John Trumbull

Weber and Fields

James A. M. Whistler

Paul Whiteman

Walt Whitman

John Greenleaf Whittier

Grant Wood

Frank Lloyd Wright

Harold Bell Wright

Chapter 17

Americans Believe in Equal Opportunity for All

THE IDEA THAT AMERICAN CITIZENS HAVE THE RIGHT TO DETERMINE THE KIND OF GOVERNMENT UNDER WHICH THEY LIVE IS A THIRD CORNERSTONE OF AMERICAN GREATNESS

"All Men Are Created Equal." When Thomas Jefferson set into words the Declaration of American Independence, he included in it this statement: "We hold these truths to be self-evident —That all men are created equal, that they are endowed by their Creator with certain unalienable rights . . ." Now, of course, everyone knows that people aren't born equal, that there are many characteristics and abilities that are inherited and that actually no two people are exactly the same. What Jefferson meant, and what the citizens of this country recognize as being the true meaning of his statement, is that in the United States all persons should have equal treatment by their government and equal opportunity under it—that is, the opportunity to develop and advance themselves just as much as their natural abilities permit. To this interpretation most of our citizens are willing to subscribe today.

This idea was not entirely new in the world. But it was new to have a nation dedicated to the observance of this principle.

Throughout most of man's history an aristocracy of religious and political leaders have ruled the great majority of the people, politically and economically, almost entirely for the good of the rulers. Wherever governments have existed, there have been few exceptions.

As has been pointed out earlier, in ancient times religion and politics were usually closely co-ordinated in government. Perhaps the earliest instance of a division of the two came when the Pharaohs and priests of Egypt struggled for sole control of the government, with the Pharaohs finally winning out.

Rome, with its idea of citizenship, was apparently making a big step forward, but the fact is that citizenship was extended only to the "free men" under Roman rule. This meant that a great many people had almost no rights at all, for slavery was common. It was the practice to enslave prisoners of war. Soon a rule of wealth developed in Rome. The senators became rich and sold slaves to themselves, although that was against the law. They used these slaves on their farms to produce grain for less than the legitimate farmer could. To compete, the farmers were forced to mortgage their land, and soon, of course, they lost it. When this happened, two courses were open to them. They could join the army, or they could go to Rome and become "clients"

WITH THESE SIGNATURES MEN PLEDGED THEIR LIVES, FORTUNES, AND
SACRED HONOR

A facsimile scroll commemorates the illustrious signatures of the men who attached their names
to the Declaration of Independence—the birth certificate of our nation.

or "partisans." A client sold the only thing he had left, his vote, to some political boss in Rome. In return, he received his living—food, clothing, and shelter. To house these clients, the political bosses built up in Rome what were probably the world's first tenements, many of them made of concrete. But clearly there was no equality of opportunity here.

When the national states appeared in western Europe in the later Middle Ages, they were ruled by kings who established ruling families or dynasties that, in some cases, lasted for hundreds of years. The names of some of these ruling families are very familiar to you. We associate the Stuart family with Britain, the Bourbon family with France, the Romanovs with Russia, the Hohenzollerns with Germany, and the Hapsburg family with the central European empire of Austria-Hungary. These families were absolute monarchs who ruled with little thought for the welfare of the mass of their people but saw to it that the nobility lived in wealth and luxury.

You have already read the story of the Renaissance in Chapter 15. The Renaissance brought into the world a new idea: that the "common" man had rights of his own. That *was* a new idea. Up to that time all the people, nobles and peasants alike, had believed that all but the nobles and clergy existed merely to work for and to support the upper classes. The new and rebellious spirit created by the Renaissance was not to be denied. It brought widespread changes. It promoted an era of revolution during which numerous governments were overthrown and new ones established—governments that were in the main more acceptable to all the people than the previous autocratic ones had been.

But the revolutions that limited the power of the absolute monarchs did not extend greater rights to the common man. The attainment of equality of opportunity is a slow process. The political struggle began in England with the Magna Carta, which the nobles forced headstrong King John to sign in 1215. It continued through the Franchise Act of 1918, which granted the right of vote to women.

Although the Declaration of Independence, the birth certificate of our nation, clearly stated the principle, the struggle for political equality in the United States has not as yet reached the point of achievement where all people are satisfied. There is still ground to be gained, as we shall see in the next unit.

From the American Revolution to the early years of the twentieth century, the emphasis in the struggle for equality has been upon political opportunity. People everywhere have moved or have tried to move toward political democracy. Since the Russian Revolution of 1917, world attention has been focused more on the economic side— the struggle for economic democracy.

We turn now to a consideration of these two major trends in modern history, as they have been and are working themselves out in the United States of America.

FOR YOUR REVIEW

These Should Be Easy for You Now

1. What does the idea "that all men are created equal" mean as applied in the United States?
2. Show that, even though citizenship was extended throughout the Roman Empire, freedom of opportunity was unknown to many people.
3. What situation prevented opportunity for most people in the new national states?
4. What new idea concerning the common people was introduced by the Renaissance? How has that idea changed the history of many parts of the world?
5. What two lanes have been and are being followed in the struggle of the world's people for equality of opportunity?

To Identify

Client	Bourbon
Partisan	Romanov
Dynasty	Hohenzollern
Stuart	Hapsburg

Suggested Readings

EATON, JEANETTE, *Lone Journey*
Story of Roger Williams
READ, HARLAN EUGENE, *Fighters for Freedom*
Liberty through the ages

STONE, EUGENIA, *Free Men Shall Stand*
The story of Peter Zenger
STOKES, ANSON PHELPS, *Church and State in the United States*
Relations of the last 160 years

The United States Moves
toward Political Democracy

INTRODUCTION

The United States was founded on the belief that the government of the people should be established and operated by the people themselves. Yet in the beginning of our history as an independent nation, this was not the case. Gradually, over the years, extensions of democracy have come until today the opportunity for every citizen to have a part in his government has almost been realized. The principal problem now is to get people to accept that responsibility.

The story of the growth of political parties has been an interesting one. You will note as you read it that many switches have been made since our country began before the present two major party systems became firmly established.

As the country became more industrialized, business came to play an important part in government. Other segments of our economy have increased in importance, also, and all have felt they wanted specific things from government. Accordingly, numerous pressure groups have developed which have been able to influence government in their own behalf, and not always for the welfare of the people as a whole.

The greatest increase of power for the central government was brought about during the administrations of Franklin D. Roosevelt, largely because of the emergencies presented by the great depression and World War II. The size, cost, and power of the federal government today poses many problems with which you must deal in your lifetime. Failure to recognize these problems and to be willing and ready to work on them can mean that they will be solved for you by someone or some agency, but not necessarily in the manner you would prefer. Government by the people can continue efficiently only if the people are interested in doing the job that must be theirs in a democracy.

Chapter 18

The Common People Win a Greater Part in Their Government

THE ORIGINAL CONCEPT OF AMERICAN DEMOCRACY IS CONSIDERABLY
MODIFIED BY THE FARMERS FROM THE WESTERN PLAINS

The Federalists in Control. The Constitution made no provision for political parties nor did it recognize the certainty that organized groups with conflicting political philosophies would vie with one another for control of the federal government. But actually, the makings of our first two political parties were already in existence when the Constitution was adopted. In the struggle to get it ratified by the states, two groups had appeared: the Federalists, who favored adoption, and the Anti-Federalists, who opposed it. In between the two were the mass of the American people. The Federalists were the wealthy merchants and the landed gentry, while the Anti-Federalists group contained mostly small farmers and workers who possessed no property. They were afraid of domination by the educated wealthy group and thought their own interests would be endangered.

Washington Favors the Federalists. When Washington organized his Cabinet, he placed in it men who he knew favored the Constitution, for he felt that only in co-operation with such men could he succeed in getting the new nation off to a good start. The only man whose opinions were not too well known was Thomas Jefferson, Secretary of State, who had been in France.

It has already been pointed out that Alexander Hamilton, Secretary of the Treasury, dominated the new Cabinet. His financial policies have been described in Chapter 7. They were aimed at strengthening the federal government, for the Federalists believed sincerely in a strong central ruling body.

Hamilton's program, by its very nature, seemed to operate for the benefit of the wealthy merchants and manufacturers more than the poorer people, who complained that they paid the bulk of the taxes, while the rich reaped the profits from government protection and operation. Gradually opposing thinking became more definite, with leading men lining up with both sides. The old names of Federalist and Anti-Federalist stuck.

Frequent clashes between Hamilton and Jefferson soon brought out the differences of opinion of these two men. Naturally Jefferson became the leader of the Anti-Federalists. Washington tried to keep peace between the men, but because of his background he was forced to side with Hamilton more than with Jefferson. If Washington had not decided to run for re-election in 1792, there would have developed an open fight for votes between the two new political parties. As it was, out of respect for Washington, he was elected

262

without opposition. Jefferson soon found that he was overruled on all matters of policy in the Cabinet, and in 1793 he resigned his position.

Republicans Begin To Organize. But Jefferson was not inactive. Privately he wrote many letters to men who felt as he did and thus began to draw into a tighter organization the opposition to the Federalists. These men disliked Hamilton and his followers, for they felt this group represented an administration of privilege and the aristocracy of wealth and smacked too much of monarchy. Because of their stand, they soon came to be known as Republicans. Hamilton's party retained the name Federalist.

Chicago Historical Society
GEORGE WASHINGTON

Perhaps it would be wise to stop here and clarify a confusion that might easily result in misunderstanding. Federalists, in derision, soon were applying the name *Democrat* to Jefferson's followers. It's hard for us to understand,

but the use of the name *Democrat* at that time was an attempt to belittle; that is, it was not at all a complimentary title. For a time the Jefferson group

Chicago Historical Society
ALEXANDER HAMILTON

were called Democratic-Republicans, but the first part of the name was not used widely until the time of Andrew Jackson. Today the Republican part has been dropped, and the principles Jefferson championed are essentially those of our Democratic party, while the Federalist party has evolved into our present-day Republican party. It will be necessary to keep this switch in names straight in order not to be confused.

Differences between the Two Parties. There were three major differences between these two early political parties. In the first place, the Republicans stood for a strict application of the Constitution with regard to the powers of Congress, while the Federalists favored the liberal use of the "elastic clause" which states that Congress shall have the power to make such laws as shall be necessary and proper to carry into execution the powers enumerated for it in the Constitution.

In the second place, as has already been stated, the Federalists favored a strong central government. The Republicans, on the other hand, were anxious to protect the rights of the states and of the individual and feared that too strong a federal government would endanger those rights.

Thirdly, the financial policies of the two parties soon lined the Federalists up with the industrial North, while the Republicans leaned more toward the agricultural South and rapidly growing West.

The Federalists and the Republicans acted very much like the members of political parties today. Members of each attacked members of the other, often to the extent of "mud-slinging." Washington himself, who had now gone over definitely to the Federalist side, was not spared. Undoubtedly this fact had much to do with his refusal to consider a third term. Before he left the government, he delivered his famous Farewell Address. In it he voiced three warnings. One of these, about foreign alliances, has been discussed on page 85. In a second, he decried the obvious growth of sectionalism and pleaded for a union of the entire country in spirit and action. Thirdly, he warned of the effect of division into political parties.

The Administration of Adams. Washington's warnings were forgotten in the heat of the campaign to elect his successor. The Federalists, fearing Hamilton would not be popular, nominated John Adams for President and Thomas Pinckney for Vice-President. The Republicans put up Thomas Jefferson and Aaron Burr. All kinds of influence were brought to bear on the people before the election. The French minister even threatened war if Jefferson was not elected, and Hamilton, disliking Adams, worked to get the Presidency for Pinckney. When the electoral votes were counted, Adams had seventy-one, Jefferson sixty-eight, and Pinckney fifty-nine. Under the Constitution, that meant that Adams was elected President, while Jefferson, of the opposing party, became Vice-President. To correct this obvious error the Twelfth Amendment was added to the Constitution in 1804.

Although he left the government under not too happy circumstances, the value to the new nation of Washington's two administrations should not be underestimated. Their chief importance lay in the fact that his prestige and popularity had held the new government together and had minimized party strife during the first eight critical years. By the time he retired, the nation was firmly enough established to permit the wrangling and criticism of opposing parties which is absolutely essential to the free expression of democratic principles in any government.

The new administration was not a happy one. Adams was extremely patriotic, but at the same time vain and hotheaded. He was a Federalist, while his Vice-President was a Republican. The chances for close co-operation seemed remote.

Federalists Lose Their Popularity. The Federalists were frightened by their loss of popularity. They were inclined to blame much of their trouble on the foreign-born in this country. To strike at them, the government resorted to some very un-American legislation. Certain laws were passed, the most notorious being the Alien and Sedition Acts. The Alien Act gave the President power to deport any aliens who, in his judgment, were "dangerous to the peace and safety of the United States." The Sedition Act provided that anyone who, in his speech or writing, attacked the government, Congress, or the President should be fined and imprisoned.

Actually the laws, instead of strengthening the position of the Federalists, worked to the advantage of the Republicans because the laws obviously were contrary to the personal liberties guaranteed in the Constitution. Kentucky and Virginia passed resolutions against them which set forth the Republican viewpoint: that the federal government was created by the states and was the instrument of the states, to do their will; that any act of the federal government contrary to the desires of the states could be declared null and void by the states. This basic concept of the function of the central government was to persist and grow until it led directly into the War between the States. The acts themselves later either expired or were repealed.

The candidates in the election of 1800 were the same as in 1796. This time, however, Jefferson and Burr received seventy-three votes each; Adams had sixty-five and Pinckney sixty-four. Since Jefferson and Burr were tied, neither was elected President, and the decision was thrown into the House of Representatives. There, after thirty-six ballots, Jefferson was chosen. The Twelfth Amendment prevents such a tie between Presidential and Vice-Presidential candidates from happening

again. Hamilton had thrown his influence onto Jefferson's side because he disliked Burr more than he did Jefferson. This private political war grew in intensity until Burr challenged Hamilton to a duel in 1804 and killed him.

The Federalists had lost out because they refused to trust the majority of the

Chicago Historical Society

THOMAS JEFFERSON

people. They wanted to keep control of the government in the hands of a few. The country had been founded on the ideal of "government by the consent of the governed," and the people rebelled. The Republicans under Jefferson now took over.

The twelve years of Federalist control had accomplished much, however. It had put the country on a firm financial basis. An organized government had been established. Peace had been kept with other nations, and the Northwest Ordinance had established a policy toward the rest of the land to the west. Perhaps most important is the fact that many domestic political struggles since that time have been fought on the same principles that marked the struggle between the two original parties, so great was the impression the Federalists had left upon the country.

REPUBLICANS RULE

Jeffersonian Republicanism. Thomas Jefferson as President proposed to make no great changes in the administration of the country. He did hold a very sincere belief that the government should be in the hands of the mass of the people, and that the federal branch should confine its activities to those affairs that had to do with foreign relations, leaving domestic matters to the states. He was committed to the encouragement of agriculture and commerce, rather than industry.

The new President soon found, as have Presidents ever since, that circumstances often prevent one from following the principles in which he believes. Take the Louisiana Purchase for instance. (See page 96 for the story.) Remember that Jefferson stood for a strict application of the Constitution. When the opportunity came to buy Louisiana, he hardly knew what to do, for the Constitution gave Congress no power at all to buy land. The President wanted to submit an amendment to the people, but he knew that by the time they had ratified it, Napoleon probably would have changed his mind. So, he took authority into his own hands and authorized the purchase. This was not strict application of the Constitution; it was the most liberal construction possible.

But Jefferson defended his act, while the Federalists, the original loose constructionists, condemned him for doing the very type of thing they had long advocated. So goes politics.

This switch in policies became more evident in the years that followed. When war broke out between England and France during Jefferson's second term, the United States became involved in the European argument. War, however, did not come until after the election of James Madison, who became President when Jefferson refused to seek a third term. The Federalists, who now came mostly from the New England states, opposed the war because they feared that war with England would ruin their commerce, and they felt it was already threatened at home by the rising power of the agricultural South and West. When commerce almost reached a standstill in 1814, a meeting was called in Hartford, Connecticut, and there in secret convention the Federalists condemned many actions of Congress and proposed seven selfish amendments to the Constitution. The convention upheld the doctrine of states' rights that had formerly been one of the chief tenets of the Republicans. The war ended before anything further could be done, and the Federalist party was ridiculed out of existence. On the wave of war victory James Monroe was swept into the White House to succeed Madison.

Era of Good Feeling. The two terms of James Monroe (1817–1825) are often referred to as the "era of good feeling." The new President had the almost undivided support of the people. The westward movement was now in full swing, and six new states were added to the Union. The period was marked by the adoption of high tariffs to protect our industries, the Missouri Compromise and the Monroe Doctrine. The country, more sure of itself than it had ever been, was turning its back on the rest of the world and devoting its attention to its own internal development. The Republicans were thinking more in terms of the nation than of the rights of the states, as they had been earlier.

Our Greatest Chief Justice. Probably the greatest boost given to the growing power of the central government during the administrations of the three Presidents from Virginia—Jefferson, Madison, and Monroe—came from John Marshall, Chief Justice of the Supreme Court. He had been appointed to the position by John Adams in 1801, in one of Adams' last acts in the hope that a Federalist Chief Justice would check the Republicans. Marshall is generally regarded as the greatest Chief Justice in the history of our court system. During his period of service (1801–1835), he consistently handed down decisions that followed the Federalist loose construction viewpoint. It probably was not too hard to convert the Republicans who were appointed to the court to his way of thinking, for the Republican concept of the Constitution was becoming more liberal all the time.

Marshall left firmly fixed in American law several attitudes that have persisted to the present and have undoubtedly had much to do with the progress and development of the country. Marshall early claimed for the Supreme Court the authority to decide whether or not Congress had exceeded its reasonable right in applying the "elastic clause" to meet the changes that were bound to come with progress. Thus, by

practice, the Judicial Department became the strongest branch of the government because of its assumed power to declare any act of Congress unconstitutional. Marshall also established the right of the court to declare any act of a state legislature unconstitutional and to reverse a decision of any state court.

Chicago Historical Society

JAMES MONROE

Important Democratic Changes. At this point in the story of democracy in the United States it is necessary that we go back a bit and trace another side of the struggle, the extension of the right to vote, because it brought about the next big step toward real democratic government.

The Constitution did not attempt to tell the states what people should be given the right to vote. The ideal of government by the consent of the governed, mentioned in the Declaration of Independence, remained just an ideal so far as most of the people in the states were concerned. The first state constitutions set up requirements for the privilege of voting that prevented many people from exercising that right. In general those requirements were designed to give the vote only to people who paid taxes. In some states a man— and of course, at this time, only men voted—had to own land before he could vote. In others he could vote if he owned any kind of property.

There were limitations of another kind, too. Only men who owned property were permitted to hold public office in many states. The amount of property a candidate had to possess varied from ten thousand pounds (£ 10,- 000) down, depending upon the state and the office for which he was a candidate. And, as has been noted in Chapter 16, some states established restrictions that prevented people of certain religious beliefs from voting or from holding office.

These restrictions were not established without real reasons behind them, at least in the thinking of the people of that time. The chief argument for them was that a man who owned property was more likely to be a permanent citizen of a community and therefore more interested in its welfare than a man who owned no property. The general feeling was that property owners were more stable and virtuous than "vagrants" or "the hordes of our large cities."

Naturally these required qualifications for voting were bound to create a great deal of dissatisfaction. There were many wealthy men—bankers, lawyers, doctors, etc.—who had no part in their government simply because they owned no property. They saw poorly educated, sometimes illiterate, small farmers who possessed a few acres of land going to the polls to vote when they could not. It was only a matter of time until their protests had to be heard.

Gradually, state by state, the laws that allowed only property owners to vote were repealed. As early as 1792, when Vermont was admitted to the Union, its constitution contained no such laws. In 1820, when the matter came up for consideration in Massachusetts, complete manhood suffrage was opposed by both John Adams and Daniel Webster, but to no avail. In some states the property requirement was eliminated and the payment of a small tax established in its place. In others, no restrictions at all were set up. Also, in most cases, all limitations on the holders of public office were removed at the same time as limitations upon voting. So democracy was extended in the United States.

During this same period another important change was brought about. The Constitution provided that the President should be elected by electors chosen by the state legislatures in any way they saw fit. From the beginning members of these legislatures, rather naturally, had made their own selection of electors. Now pressure was applied by the people to give them the right to select these men who in turn voted for the man to occupy the country's highest office. And, state by state, oftentimes not at all graciously, the legislatures yielded.

Another established practice of the time was thrown into the discard also. Again in a most natural fashion, the selection of candidates for President and Vice-President had been taken over by the members of the parties in Congress. They would meet in a caucus and choose the men they wanted for candidates. This procedure of course kept many deserving men from ever being considered for these high offices. Democracy was on the rise. The people objected. And in 1831 the party caucus gave way to the new national nominating convention. Delegates were elected by the voters in the parties; these delegates then met and selected the party candidates. The change was an improvement but not by any means a complete solution of the problem, for most of the delegates were office seekers themselves, and the convention method did not guarantee the selection of the best men available for the positions.

Era of Political and Economic Unrest. The election of John Quincy Adams, son of former President John Adams, marked the end of an era in American political history. It was the era of the "afterglow" of the Revolution and the founding of the nation. The Presidents of the period were the men who had played large and significant parts in establishing the United States. Their election was more or less the result of recognition of their leadership and the desire to reward them for their valuable services. But now death was taking them from the picture. They had represented the wealthy property owners who controlled the government during those early years. As the influence of the masses rose, that of the wealthy aristocracy waned in proportion. By 1824 the personal prestige of Revolutionary leaders was about gone. With the election of John Quincy Ad-

ams the "era of good feeling" came to an end and a real struggle for control of the government began.

The post-Revolution period had been one of growing nationalism. During Monroe's two administrations there had been great pride in the new nation.

Parker-Allston Associates, U.S. Fire Insurance Co.

WHEN BALLOTING BEAT BULLYING

New York City's Mayor Wood strenuously campaigned for re-election in 1855. When he was accused of hiring ruffians and corrupt policemen to intimidate voters at the polls, he was put out of office. Such was the public protest against interference with the voter's right to cast a secret ballot of free choice.

This was to quite an extent a natural result of the second victory over Great Britain. But as the country grew, varying political, social, and economic interests were fixing their hold upon different parts. Sectionalism was appearing.

In fact, the pattern was quite definite. The states along the northeastern seaboard, from New York, New Jersey, and eastern Pennsylvania on up, had developed an industrial economy. They were interested in a high protective tariff, good prices for manufactured goods, and a strong system of banks. The Southern states wanted no protective tariffs, low prices for manufactured goods, but high prices for cotton; they were interested in acquiring more land

JOHN QUINCY ADAMS

to the west where their system might spread. The invention of the cotton gin by Eli Whitney in 1793 had made cotton "King" in the South; the result was an economy based upon cotton and slavery. The growing West was agricultural. It wanted better transportation, cheap land, cheap money, and a protective tariff only if the money raised thereby was used to improve conditions in their part of the country. There was a sharp conflict of interests here that was destined to bring a clash between North and South, with the West divided.

Each section put up candidates for the election of 1824. The North presented the name of John Quincy Adams, apparently because it couldn't find anyone else, for although he was an able man, he did not have a pleasing personality. The South nominated William H. Crawford of Georgia. The West had two candidates. Kentucky put up Henry Clay, Speaker of the House of Representatives, and Tennessee nominated Andrew Jackson, hero of the Battle of New Orleans in the War of 1812.

When the election was over, Jackson and Adams had the most votes, but no one had a majority, so the decision was up to the House of Representatives again. Clay threw his support to Adams, who was elected. Clay was rewarded with the position of Secretary of State. John C. Calhoun of South Carolina had been elected Vice-President.

Adams soon discovered he didn't have the people behind him. Even in his own official family things were not at all rosy. Adams and Clay and their followers made up one clique; Vice-President Calhoun threw in with defeated Jackson to form the leadership of the opposition. So the Republican party was split. The Adams-Clay group soon attracted the name of National Republicans because of their nationalistic tendencies. The Jackson-Calhoun group took the name Democratic-Republicans, hoping that the resurrection of the name that had been applied to Jefferson and his followers would identify them with the doctrine of states' rights and win them support.

The changes that had been made in the selection of electors and in extending the right to vote to more people took effect in the election of 1828. Andrew Jackson defeated John Quincy

Adams by a big majority. The farmers of the West, the planters of the South, and the mechanics and professional people of the North joined to defeat the industrial wealthy aristocracy of the North. Jackson won all the electoral votes of the South and the West, and even some in the North. Calhoun became Vice-President again.

JACKSONIAN DEMOCRACY

Andrew Jackson as President. The election of Andrew Jackson, Indian fighter, backwoodsman, and hero of New Orleans, marked a big change in the political development of the United States. Jefferson had talked about the "revolution" that took place when he became President. But Jefferson's brand of democracy was very different from that of "Old Hickory." Jefferson was one of the upper class who believed in a sort of paternal democracy for the "common-man," so long as it didn't go too far. Jackson was one of the "common" men; he had been elected by a lot more of the same type who were voting for one of their own men and against the "high-toned" aristocracy of wealth, birth, and privilege that had controlled the country up to that time. There were a great many people who regretted the basic changes that came with Jackson's election, but those who thought clearly recognized that such changes had to come if the ideals of democracy were to be followed to their logical conclusions. Jefferson's democracy was of and for the people; Jackson's was *by* the people as well.

Events at the inauguration on March 4, 1829, demonstrated the difference between the new administration and those that had preceded it. At earlier inaugurations there had been little fuss and few changes in government officials. Not so with Jackson. He invited the people to his inauguration and to a reception in the Executive Mansion afterward. Ten thousand came. Most of them got to the Mansion before Jackson did, and when he arrived, he found them milling about like a mob. What followed was really a free-for-all. To

Chicago Historical Society
ANDREW JACKSON

get a view of "Andy," people climbed all over the chairs and tables and left the muddy imprints of their boots wherever they went. To get at the food, they pushed and shoved, with the result that trays were overturned, punch bowls were broken, furniture was ruined, and finally Jackson had to leave for his own safety. Clearly, "the people" had taken over.

And Jackson was determined that "the people" should rule. He sensed the dislike and contempt with which most of the employees of the government in Washington looked upon him. He wanted only people he could trust around him. To this end, he adopted the slogan, "To the victor belong the spoils," discharged officials who were not his supporters, and replaced them with men "fresh from the people." If anyone questioned his tactics, he answered that under a democracy any man should be able to handle the work of any government office or could learn to do it in a short time. The Spoils System, as it came to be called, did not make for good government, but it persisted until conditions forced a change more than fifty years later. Actually, we are not completely rid of it even today.

Jackson approached the job of President as he had the job of frontier fighting. He had no preconceived plan; he met circumstances and situations as they arose. If he had one continuing principle, it was to defend and advance the rights of the common people. This lined him up in every case on the side of the little man against the privilege and power of industry and business. He was convinced that he had a "mandate from the people," and he intended to conduct himself in a manner he deemed worthy of their trust.

Before long Jackson was in the middle of a struggle with the South over the question of nullification—the right of the states to declare an act of the federal Congress unconstitutional. It was raised over the tariff by the "South Carolina Exposition" (see Chapter 10). Although a states' rights man, Jackson's position favored the Union. A compromise was finally worked out that did not actually solve the problem but simply postponed the decision on it for about thirty years.

A second source of trouble was the extension of the charter of the Bank of the United States, which had been established in 1816. Jackson was opposed to it, and not without some reason. It had been proved that the bank used its financial power to control the attitudes of newspapers and individuals and thereby influence political decisions. Jackson held that the bank was unconstitutional because it was a private business granted special powers by Congress rather than a public bank, owned and operated by the government. Worried by the President's views, the bank asked for a renewal of its charter in 1832, four years before the charter expired. Congress voted renewal, but Jackson promptly vetoed the bill. Then he proceeded to make sure that the bank would not continue by slowly withdrawing the funds of the United States from its custody.

Election of 1832. Henry Clay made the matter of the bank the chief issue in the election of 1832. The National Republicans had nominated Clay, and Jackson was put up again by the Democratic-Republicans, who now called themselves just Democrats. Jackson was re-elected, with Martin Van Buren of New York as his Vice-President.

Jackson's ready use of power brought a decided change in the government of the United States. Through the administrations of several Presidents, Congress had been increasing its power at the expense of the Executive Department. Jackson reversed the trend. He ordered Congress about, openly flouted decisions of the Supreme Court, disregarded his Cabinet, and listened mostly to a small group of friends, who came to be called popularly the "kitchen cabinet" because they came into the Executive Mansion more or less by the back door. He used the veto more than any other President had, and frequently because of personal and not constitutional reasons. He was usually defiant, riding roughshod over opposition of any kind and from any source. But the people still liked him, and in 1833 even staid Harvard University conferred upon him an honorary degree.

Jackson's determination to do as he pleased, however, was causing his opposition to grow. Soon his enemies were referring to "the reign of King Andrew." In 1834 they organized a new political party and called themselves Whigs. They took the name from a party in England that had earlier opposed the tyrannical use of power by the king. The party included those men who had been members of the National Republican group and any others who were dissatisfied with the administration. Because of the strange mixture, the party never became very strong, for the members couldn't agree on a unified program. Their interests were too widely separated.

Van Buren and Financial Panic. In 1836 Jackson refused to run for a third term and named Martin Van Buren as his choice for the nomination. The Whigs put up three candidates, one each from the North, the South, and the West, hoping to split the vote and throw the election into the House of Representatives. The popularity of Jackson won the election for Van Buren by an overwhelming majority.

Van Buren was immediately in hot water. A great financial panic hit the country in 1837. This was at least partly due to the termination of the Bank of the United States in 1836. The states then founded banks of their own and began issuing paper money, although this was contrary to the Constitution. There were almost as many kinds as there were states, and the value of the money was indefinite. Because of this uncertain value, the government issued the "Specie Circular" in 1836, requiring that purchases of public lands be paid for in gold or silver rather than in the paper money of the state banks. In the panic banks closed, business tightened up, and unemployment increased. Van Buren seemed not to know what to do about conditions, so did nothing. As is customary, the people blamed the current administration for their troubles.

The End of Jacksonian Democracy. In spite of his unpopularity, Van Buren was nominated for a second term, simply because he was Jackson's choice. This time the Whigs passed up twice-defeated Henry Clay for one of the candidates in the 1836 race, General William Henry Harrison. Harrison, like Jackson, was a military hero, although not so great a one. The son of a Virginian who had signed the Declaration of Independence, Harrison was remembered chiefly for a skirmish with Indians in Indiana, the Battle of Tippecanoe. John Tyler of Virginia was nominated as Vice-President, and soon the slogan of "Tippecanoe and Tyler too" caught on. Against New Yorker Van Buren, the people turned to military hero Harrison, and he was elected.

Within a month Harrison died as a result of a cold, and Tyler became the first Vice-President ever to be elevated to the Presidency. He was a Democrat whom the Whigs had put on the ticket simply to get votes. Now the Democrats would have nothing to do with him, and the Whigs wished they didn't have him. It was a most unfortunate situation.

The period of Jacksonian democracy was over. It had been marked by a great extension of democratic privileges to more and more people and by Jackson's highhanded domination of the government. A new era was opening, one in which the rights and privileges of people were again prime factors. But the problems were different. They were national in scope and threatened the very existence of the Union. The principal problem was that of slavery and its extension as the nation expanded, a problem that led finally into the great War between the States.

Slavery Becomes a National Problem. In 1844 the Democratic party again came to power through the election of James K. Polk, a friend of Andrew Jackson. During his administration occurred the unwarranted Mexican War (see Chapter 9). As a result of that war, another Whig moved into the White House in 1849, military hero General Zachary Taylor. In just a little more than a year he died, and Vice-President Millard Fillmore became President.

In 1852 the Whigs put up another Mexican War hero, General Winfield Scott, but he lost the election to the Democratic candidate, Franklin Pierce. The people hoped that the Compromise of 1850 (page 111) would solve the slavery problem and felt that the Democrats could best administer the compromise since the Whigs were hopelessly split over the slavery issue.

But it didn't work out that way. Instead, the country became more definitely split than ever, principally over the Fugitive Slave Law. In 1854 a new party was organized in the Middle West, made up of those men who ardently opposed slavery in the North. Party leaders took the name of Jefferson's political group, Republican, although the principles they adhered to were altogether different from those Jefferson held. The Republican candidate lost out to James Buchanan in 1856, but in 1860 the Republican candidate, Abraham Lincoln, was elected. He remained in office until his assassination in his second term. Then Andrew Johnson was elevated to the Presidency just as the Civil War came to an end.

At the conclusion of the war the Thirteenth Amendment was added to the Constitution. It contained a simple statement that there was to be no slavery in the United States. Actually, the amendment did away with slavery only in Kentucky and Delaware, the remaining states in which it had not been abolished prior to that time.

In 1868 the Fourteenth Amendment was added. The most important of its five sections was the first which granted citizenship and civil rights to Negroes. It states: "All persons born or naturalized in the United States, and subject to the jurisdiction thereof, are citizens of the United States and of the State wherein they reside. No State shall make or enforce any law which shall abridge the privileges or immunities of citizens of the United States; nor shall any State deprive any person of life, liberty, or property, without due process of law, nor deny to any person within its jurisdiction the equal protection of the laws."

The Fourteenth Amendment, in granting citizenship to Negroes, clearly recognized two kinds of citizenship: first, in the nation, and second, in a state. Then it stated definitely that no state law will be permitted to "abridge the privileges or immunities of citizens of the United States." This meant that the federal government could legally declare unconstitutional an act of a state legislature. Similar government action could be taken if any state tried to "deprive any person of life, liberty, or property without due process of law . . ." The Fourteenth Amendment meant the end of states' rights. From then on the federal government has remained supreme.

The "due process of law" clause was written into the amendment to protect the rights of Negroes in the South. It has not been used very much for that purpose. But many corporations have brought suit under the amendment and have succeeded in getting certain state and local laws declared unconstitutional. For, under the law, a corporation is "a person," and many laws therefore were interpreted as violating the provisions of the amendment and annulled.

Two years later (1870) the Fifteenth Amendment was ratified. It attempts to assure the right of vote to Negroes. It says: "The right of citizens of the United States to vote shall not be denied or abridged by the United States or by any State on account of race, color, or previous condition of servitude." But the amendment takes a negative approach. It lists three conditions which may not be used as basis for denying the vote. It does not prevent states from setting up other conditions, such as the payment of a special poll tax, which can and does operate to deprive some poor people, many of them Negroes, of the right to a voting part in their government.

Immediately after the war, the "carpetbaggers" and "scalawags" ran the South. The new state constitutions put them and the Negroes in control; it was a period of turmoil, and violence developed. Intimidation, through such organizations as the Ku Klux Klan, held the Negroes somewhat in check. Gradually, especially after the Union troops were withdrawn, the Southern whites worked themselves back into power and dominance. The radical state constitutions were replaced by new ones that, in violation of the spirit if not the actual wording of the Fifteenth Amendment, set up requirements of the payment of a tax or proof of literacy or ability to interpret the Constitution to keep the Negroes from voting. Ordinarily the restrictions were applied only to Negroes, although they might have been just as operative against certain classes of whites. The war had guaranteed the preservation of the Union and the supremacy of the federal government over the states, but it had not brought political and civil liberty to all the Negroes. There was still work— much work—to be done in the extension of political democracy in the United States.

FOR YOUR REVIEW

These Should Be Easy for You Now

1. How did our first two political parties get their start? Who, in general, composed the two groups? Who became the leaders?
2. Explain the evolution of the names of our principal political parties of today.
3. What were basic differences of opinion between the Federalists and the Republicans? What is meant by the "elastic clause"?
4. What situation caused the Twelfth Amendment to be added to the Constitution? What does it provide for?

5. Why were the Alien and Sedition Acts passed? What was their nature?
6. Why did the Federalists lose control of the government? What had been accomplished under their leadership?
7. In the story of the Federalists and the Louisiana Purchase and the War of 1812, show that the policies of a political party are often dictated by the personal interests of the members rather than the welfare of the country as a whole.
8. What major developments of the growth of the United States came during the administration of James Monroe?
9. How did John Marshall increase the power of the central government?
10. What early limitations were placed upon the right to vote or hold office in the United States? Why was this done? Why was it a cause for dissatisfaction?
11. What change was brought about in the method of electing the President of the United States? In the method of selecting candidates for President and Vice-President?
12. How did the administration of John Quincy Adams mark the end of an era?
13. Into what three sections was the country gradually dividing? What were the characteristics of each?
14. Who became the leaders of the National Republicans? Of the Democratic-Republicans?
15. What was the significance to the government of the country of the election of Andrew Jackson?
16. What is the Spoils System? How did Jackson justify it? Does it make for good government? Why?
17. How did Jackson put an end to the Bank of the United States? Why?
18. Why was Jackson sometimes referred to as "King Andrew"? Who were the Whigs?
19. Why was the "Specie Circular" issued? What was its effect?
20. Who was the first Vice-President in our history to become Chief Executive?
21. What was the central problem that commanded governmental attention for the quarter century after 1840?
22. How did the Thirteenth Amendment extend democracy in the United States? The Fourteenth Amendment? The Fifteenth Amendment?
23. How does the Fourteenth Amendment assure the supremacy of the federal government?
24. How has the Fourteenth Amendment proved of advantage to corporations?
25. Why is a poll tax not illegal and not contrary to the Fifteenth Amendment? How does it, and other similar state laws, violate the spirit of the amendment?

Associated Dates

1792—Washington re-elected for second term
1797–1801—administration of John Adams
1798—Eleventh Amendment adopted
1801–1809—administrations of Thomas Jefferson
1803—Louisiana Purchase
1804—Alexander Hamilton killed in a duel by Aaron Burr
      Twelfth Amendment adopted
1809–1817—administrations of James Madison
1817–1825—administrations of James Monroe
1820—Missouri Compromise
1823—Monroe Doctrine stated
1825–1829—administration of John Quincy Adams
1829–1837—administrations of Andrew Jackson
1837–1841—administration of Martin Van Buren
1841—administration of William Henry Harrison, March 4–April 6

1841–1845—administration of John Tyler
1845–1849—administration of James K. Polk
1846–1848—War with Mexico
1849–1850—administration of Zachary Taylor
1850–1853—administration of Millard Fillmore
1853–1857—administration of Franklin Pierce
1854—organization of the new Republican party
1857–1861—administration of James Buchanan
1861–1865—administrations of Abraham Lincoln
1865—assassination of President Lincoln, April 14
      Thirteenth Amendment adopted
1865–1869—administration of Andrew Johnson
1868—Fourteenth Amendment adopted
1870—Fifteenth Amendment adopted

Why Are These To Be Remembered?

Federalists	Aaron Burr	Kitchen cabinet
Anti-Federalists	John Marshall	Specie Circular
Elastic clause	Spoils System	Whigs
Alexander Hamilton		

Chapter 19

Politics Becomes a Profession

POLITICAL PARTIES AND CAREER POLITICIANS COME TO PLAY A MAJOR
PART IN AMERICAN GOVERNMENT

Republicans in Power. When the War between the States was over, the Republican party was firmly in power. Its hold on national politics was made stronger by the fact that Union troops occupied the South and controlled political activity there. This situation was responsible for the decided shift in Southern political tendencies after the troops were removed and white supremacy restored. Since that time the South has been almost always Democratic; hence the term, "the Solid South."

The war also removed the brake the Southern plantation system had long applied which prevented growing industry from controlling government completely. Most industrial leaders were members of the Republican party, and party policies were fixed in accordance with their desires. The Republicans supported a high protective tariff, a sound money system, the extension of industry and transportation to the West, with government aid usually in the form of free or cheap land to assist in this program. Add to this the moral glow that came from freeing the slaves and preserving the Union (the Republicans claimed full credit, although many Democrats had stood by the Union, too), and you have the reasons for the great strength of the party in the years following the close of the war. Republican Presidents occupied the

White House without break until 1885. After Andrew Johnson's unfortunate experiences with Congress, the Republicans put up and elected Ulysses S. Grant, another war hero like Andrew Jackson and William Henry Harrison before him.

Graft and Corruption Reign. Grant's two administrations were an unfortunate blot upon the story of democracy in the United States. Grant himself was inefficient and certainly unqualified for the position he held. Up to this time there had been many wrangles among officials of the federal government, and some had resorted to "horse-trading" to secure their ends. Others had used their power to get what they wanted. But seldom had the charges of graft and corruption been leveled at men in high places.

During Grant's administrations things sunk to a new low. Scandals involving theft of public funds and bribery reached out, as the evidence became known, to take in many members of Congress, judges, and even some of the men in the President's Cabinet. The opportunity for graft was large because of the extension of railroads to the Pacific Coast and the general development of the West. While no one actually thought Grant dishonest, his support of his friends who were in on the deals brought him much criticism.

Corruption was not limited to the

federal government by any means. The same conditions existed in virtually all the states and in many city governments as well. The best known example was the Tweed Ring in New York City. Since the beginning of the century Tammany Hall had been a Democratic political machine in New York, and in 1869 "Boss" Tweed became its leader. His operations reached clear into the state capitol at Albany, and his gang made off with perhaps as much as $200,-000,000. Eventually public opinion was aroused sufficiently to send Tweed to jail.

There were reasons for this sudden growth in corrupt government. In the period following the Civil War the country turned to the job of developing its own interior, and the operations involved made large-scale graft possible. Industry was growing, and business was learning how to "play politics." The development of a class of professional politicians, many of whom looked upon public office as an opportunity to fatten their own purses rather than serve the people, made bribery to gain privilege easy. Also, the Spoils System had fastened itself upon the nation, a system that promoted dishonesty. Government was controlled now by political parties, and these parties maintained large organizations. Such organizations were necessary to secure voters for the party and to keep it in power or try to get it back into power. The awarding of jobs to those who helped the party most was the means used to build and keep an active machine. For the next two or three decades after Jackson adopted the idea on a national scale, virtually all government offices were swept clean when a new party came into power and filled with faithful party followers. (The

practice is still followed to a large extent.) This was a vicious thing that certainly didn't operate for the welfare of the country. And, above all, there was a marked indifference on the part of the people to what went on in politics, so that corruption held sway with little, if any, check upon it.

Hayes Attempts Reform. Another Republican, Rutherford B. Hayes, followed Grant in the White House, although only by a strange turn of affairs. When the electoral votes were counted, Hayes had 165 to 184 for his Democratic opponent, Samuel J. Tilden of New York. Tilden lacked but one vote of having enough to be elected. The remaining 20 votes were disputed by three southern states—that is, two sets of votes were sent in from each state. The Constitution made no provision for such a situation, so a commission was appointed to reach a decision. Although the attempt was made to keep it impartial, it turned out to have eight Republicans and seven Democrats, so all the disputed votes were given to Hayes and he was declared elected. There were many who thought the decision flouted the obvious desire of the majority of the people, but in the interest of democracy and harmony they accepted the result.

President Hayes knew the need for reform and tried to do something about it. One of his first acts was to withdraw the last of the federal troops from the South, because he felt that the sooner differences between the North and South could be forgotten, the better it would be for the country. He tried to stop the practice of collecting money from men in office for use by the party in the next election. He did prevent federal officials from leading political organizations. And, after quite a struggle, he was able to remove the top officials in the New York Customs House, where graft had been open and flagrant. But in so doing, he stepped upon the toes of several influential Republicans, and he was not renominated.

Garfield Assassinated. Another Republican, however, was elected in 1880,

Chicago Historical Society

CHESTER A. ARTHUR

James A. Garfield. It was hoped by some that he would improve political conditions, but he had been involved in some shady dealings and didn't dare strike out too hard. The fact is he had little opportunity to do anything. Shortly after he was inaugurated, he was shot (July 2, 1881) in a railway station in Washington by a man who had been passed over when the jobs were handed out after Garfield's election. The President lived until September 19.

Arthur, the Changed Man. Garfield's assassination set the stage for one

of those queer quirks of fate that from time to time seem to step in and alter the course events appear to be taking. The Vice-President was Chester A. Arthur, one of the men Hayes had removed from a New York Customs job when he was President. In the 1880 election Arthur had been put on the ticket as Vice-Presidential candidate in order to make the New York Republicans feel better about what had happened. Now a man who had been guilty of wholesale graft, by accident became President of the United States.

The circumstances under which he became President must have had a profound affect upon Chester Arthur, for his conduct in the office indicated a greatly changed man. He broke with his old friends and carried out his new duties with a high purpose and very nearly the understanding of a statesman.

President Arthur's greatest contribution to the advancement of democracy in the United States had to do with reform in the civil service. Probably this was due to the fact that the man who shot President Garfield was a disappointed office-seeker. The incident served to emphasize strongly the arguments for reform that had been advanced by a few people for some time. Chester Arthur now announced that he was in favor of reform and that he would support practically any legislation along that line.

Undoubtedly the most important reform act passed during Arthur's administration was the Pendleton Civil Service Act. Adopted in 1883, it provided for a Civil Service Commission and a procedure for making available men for government offices. Competitive examinations were to be given to all applicants and the names listed in the order of the scores made on the examinations, the highest at the head of the list. Then political appointments were to be made from these lists, from the top down. Another provision struck at the Spoils System and professional politics from the other side: no one could be removed from office for political reasons. So the United States adopted the merit system, a system England had had for some thirty years and China for centuries.

In the beginning the list of public offices that came under the new Civil Service Act was small, numbering only about 10 per cent. Since 1883, however, the list has been extended from time to time, both by act of Congress and by Presidential order. At present well over three-fourths of all federal government officials are selected in accordance with the provisions of the Civil Service Act. Of course, this still leaves room for a very considerable amount of Spoils System activity, for the number of people employed by the national government has grown greatly since 1883. Particularly has this been true in the last decade. Today our government employs more than two million people, with a daily turnover of about five hundred.

STRUGGLE FOR REFORM

Campaign of 1884. Although one of the areas ticketed for reform had been bettered by adoption of the merit system, there still remained plenty of others. The campaign of 1884 revolved about the cry for more changes that continued to be heard all over the country. The workers in the East felt they were being exploited by industry. The farmers in the West objected to domination and control by the "capitalists of Wall Street," who, the farmers claimed, were amassing great wealth from the production of western farms, while the men who did the work remained poor.

The Republicans passed over Chester Arthur, who had by then made a good name for himself, and selected as their candidate James G. Blaine from Maine, a professional politician who had been trying for some time to get the nomination. He was a smooth-voiced orator who could talk charmingly to people without committing himself on questions of importance. The Democrats chose Grover Cleveland, a lawyer who had risen to the position of governor of New York chiefly because of the record he made as mayor of Buffalo. He had none of Blaine's sparkle, but he was as honest as the day is long and equally intent upon doing whatever he thought to be the right thing always, regardless of whether the people supported him or not.

The campaign was marked more by attacks upon the characteristics, abilities, and associations of the candidates than upon national issues. Anything that might cast a reflection in any way upon the good name of either man was thrown into the breach. It was a disgraceful exhibition, but in the end Cleveland won by a small number of popular votes, although his electoral advantage was greater. The people had expressed themselves. Apparently, although it was the Republican party that had "saved the Union," the people felt the country needed a change. Cleveland's victory was clearly that of a reform candidate over a professional politician.

The Reforms of Cleveland. The new President approached his work with the same determination that had marked his previous political activity. He added to the list of offices under civil service. He curtailed the granting of pensions, where he suspected considerable graft was taking place. He used the veto against bills of Congress more than all previous Presidents together. He was able to get the Tenure

Chicago Historical Society

GROVER CLEVELAND

of Office Act repealed, a law, passed when Congress was feuding with Andrew Johnson, that prevented the firing of any government official without the consent of the Senate. His constant desire to do whatever he thought was best for the country, even to the extent of refusing to follow his own party, cost him a lot of support, not only in the Democratic party but outside it as well.

Harrison Not a Great Reformer. As a result, a Republican went back into the White House in 1889. He was Benjamin Harrison, grandson of former President William Henry Harrison. Cleveland received 100,000 more pop-

ular votes than Harrison, but a majority of the electoral votes went to the Republican candidate. This is possible under our present electoral system. Each party presents a list of electors, but the entire electoral vote of the state goes to the party whose list receives the majority of the popular votes in that state. There is growing dissatisfaction with this system. Many people claim it does not really reflect the will of the people and that some changes ought to be made. Various proposals have been made from time to time, but no reform has yet been adopted.

Harrison was by no means as strong a personality as Cleveland had been, and as a result, Congress regained some of the ground it had lost during the previous administration. It proceeded to authorize greatly increased pensions. It passed huge appropriations for river and harbor improvement. It put through the McKinley Tariff Act that boosted rates drastically. But while it was doing these things, it was also changing some of the rules and regulations for its own operation, rules that had needed changing for some time. For instance, previously it had been possible for House members to prevent action by simply refusing to be considered present and eligible to vote by not answering roll call.

The tendency, particularly during the last three-quarters of a century of our history, has been for the annual expenditures of the national government to rise constantly. Of course, this is to be expected in time of war. At other times, however, there appear to be three reasons for this increased cost. First, as the country has grown larger, naturally it has cost more to handle government affairs. Secondly, the people have demanded more and still more in services from their government, all the way from free garden seeds up. In the third place, frequently the party in control, whichever one it was, has been rather free in its use of public funds, hoping to win favor and support at the polls and thereby to stay in power. Not always, by any means, has the growing national budget reflected increased benefits to the people in proportion to its growth.

The Populist Party. Failure to get the reforms they wanted had angered the farmers of the West more and more. Even so, it was not easy to secure any kind of organization to push their desires. Most of the men, by this time, were identified with either the Republican or the Democratic party, and they were slow to leave "the party" and organize a separate political group, a "third party." However, events and conditions finally drove them to it, and the People's or Populist party was created in Cincinnati, Ohio, in 1891. The following year it held its first convention in Omaha, Nebraska, and nominated General James B. Weaver for President.

The platform adopted at that convention sounds very much like a great deal of writing during the depression years of the 1930's. Just listen to a part of it. "The people are demoralized. . . . The newspapers are largely subsidized or muzzled; public opinion silenced; business prostrated; our homes covered with mortgages; labor impoverished; and the land concentrating in the hands of the capitalists. . . . We have witnessed . . . the struggles of the two great political parties for power and plunder, while grievous wrongs have

been inflicted upon the suffering people. We charge that the controlling influences dominating both these parties have permitted the existing condition to develop without serious effort to prevent or restrain them. Neither do they now promise us any substantial reform. . . ."

The new party then proceeded to go on record as favoring a specific program. Its terms were indeed radical for the time, although many of them have been adopted since then. The most decided change the Populists favored was the free and unrestricted coinage of silver, prompted by the opening of several new silver mines in the West. The value of silver was going down as the supply increased. Coinage of silver had stopped earlier because of its scarcity. Now Westerners reasoned that to start making silver coins again would cause people to hoard gold, because it was more valuable, and use silver money. Thus the market for silver ore would be increased. The platform smacked of socialism when it advocated that the national government take over and operate the railroads and the telephone and telegraph systems. The Populists wanted a secret ballot, and the right to start laws themselves (the initiative) and to have the final say on them by means of a referendum. They wanted the senators in Washington elected directly by the people instead of by the state legislatures, and they thought every President should be allowed only one term in the office. They even went on record as favoring an income tax.

The new Populist party immediately rallied much support in the West. Here was the old struggle between the East, dominated by industrial motives, and the West, principally agricultural in its economy and its thinking. The South no longer figured in the rivalry because "King Cotton" had been rendered impotent by the War between the States. The farmers were angry because they were getting very low prices for their products, while they had to pay high prices for the manufactured goods that came from the East; the high tariff hindered rather than helped them. Low prices had forced many farmers to mortgage their land, and the interest rates were out of reason. Taxes were high, and the new railroads, enjoying a monopoly in transportation, got big fees for hauling farm produce east. The farmers wanted the government to own or control the railroads; they wanted free land and cheap money. And to get these things, they wanted to elect their men to Congress and thereby get control of the government. The country was growing, interests were varied, problems were more complex, and it was becoming increasingly difficult to create a government that would fairly represent and consider all parts and interests of the country—a major problem to this day.

Cleveland Back in Office. In the election of 1892 the Republicans nominated Benjamin Harrison again, and the Democrats stuck by Grover Cleveland. Cleveland, out of office for one term, now went back in. The interesting part of the election was the strength shown by the Populist party. It carried four states: Kansas, Colorado, Idaho, and Nevada. Out of a total popular vote of nearly twelve million, it won more than one million, a surprising show of strength.

Cleveland's second administration was not nearly as happy as his first. The problems facing the country, aggravated by the panic of 1893, were more severe, and feeling was more intense. His conservative approach to all the problems and his opposition to free silver lost Cleveland the support of the West and also of his own party.

Free Silver the Issue. The question of free silver was destined to become the big issue of the 1896 election. The Republicans nominated Major William McKinley and adopted a platform which was not favorable to silver. The Democrats were quick to seize their opportunity; their platform declared for free coinage of both gold and silver "at the present legal ratio of sixteen to one. . . ."

The chief feature of the Democratic convention, however, was the sudden rise of one of the greatest orators this country has ever known. A young Midwestern lawyer (he was thirty-six years old), William Jennings Bryan, captured the convention in Chicago with his now famous "cross of gold" speech. The differences between the agricultural West and the industrial East he turned into a direct challenge. "Burn down your cities and leave our farms," he said, "and your cities will spring up again as if by magic; but destroy our farms and the grass will grow in the streets of every city in the country." He ended his speech with the crowd cheering wildly, saying, "Having behind us the producing masses of this nation and the world, supported by the commercial interests, the laboring interests, and the toilers everywhere, we will answer their demand for a gold standard by saying to them: You shall not press down upon the brow of labor this crown of thorns, you shall not crucify mankind upon a cross of gold." The

Democrats promptly nominated Bryan, and the Populists swung their support to him rather than present a candidate of their own.

McKinley conducted a "front porch" campaign, sitting at home in Canton, Ohio, and letting the congratulations and good wishes of all who favored the gold standard pour in. Bryan took his campaign to the people. He traveled from state to state, speaking several times each day, carrying his doctrine of free silver to the people everywhere he went.

The moneyed interests of the country naturally opposed Bryan. If he were elected and could put through the unlimited coinage of silver on a par with gold, they were ruined. For the amount of silver in a dollar was at that time worth about 52 cents. If debts could be paid off in 52-cent silver dollars instead of in 100-or-more-cent gold dollars, the debtors of the West would certainly bring about the rapid decline of their creditors in the East. Everywhere big business brought pressure to defeat Bryan. Industrialists even told their employees that their factories would be closed if McKinley was not elected.

McKinley received only a half mil-

Meserve Collection, Chicago Historical Society

WILLIAM JENNINGS BRYAN

lion more popular votes than Bryan, but his electoral vote majority was decisive. Most of the people of the country had decided they wanted a sound money based on gold. The election meant the end of the Populist party as such. The Republican party and big business interests were returned to power in the country.

FOR YOUR REVIEW
These Should Be Easy for You Now

1. Give reasons for the great strength of the Republican party in the years following the War between the States.
2. Why is Grant's administration so open to criticism? What conditions made large-scale graft easy? Why does the Spoils System promote corruption and inefficient government?
3. Cite the circumstances under which Rutherford B. Hayes was elected. Why was he not renominated?
4. How did Chester A. Arthur make a better President than had been expected? What was his greatest contribution toward the extension of democracy?
5. How does the civil service system operate? To what extent is it used today?
6. Why were the workers of the East and the farmers of the West dissatisfied with their lot?

7. What was the significance of the election of Grover Cleveland? What reforms did he bring about?
8. How was it possible for Benjamin Harrison to be elected President although Cleveland received more popular votes in the election? What happened to the power of Congress under President Harrison?
9. What three reasons does your text list for the growing cost of government?
10. What was the platform of the new Populist party? It was a radical program for the time, but many parts of it have since been adopted. Point out which ones.
11. Into what two sections was the country now divided? What were the principal points of difference?
12. What was the important problem of "free silver"? Why did the people decide they wanted a money based principally on gold?

Associated Dates

1869–1877—administrations of Ulysses S. Grant
1871—Tweed Ring overthrown in New York City
1877–1881—administration of Rutherford B. Hayes
1877—Federal troops withdrawn from the South
1881—administration of James A. Garfield
       assassination of President Garfield; shot July 2; died September 19
1881–1885—administration of Chester A. Arthur
1883—Pendleton Civil Service Act
1885–1889—first administration of Grover Cleveland
1889–1893—administration of Benjamin Harrison
1890—McKinley Tariff Act
1891—formation of the People's or Populist party
1893–1897—second administration of Grover Cleveland
1897–1901—administration of William McKinley

Why Are These To Be Remembered?

The Solid South	Tammany Hall	Populist party
Boss Tweed	Civil Service	William Jennings Bryan

Chapter 20

The United States Is Governed by Minority Pressure Groups

THROUGH THE USE OF CAREFULLY APPLIED PRESSURE, VARIOUS
GROUPS IN AMERICAN LIFE HAVE OFTEN BEEN ABLE TO CHANNEL
GOVERNMENT ACTION

Business in Politics. The period following the Civil War had produced a class of professional politicians. The result was that the struggle between the two major parties, the Republicans and the Democrats, became more intense. The party in power wanted to stay there, and the other wanted to get in. Campaigns became more bitter, and more expensive. As the cost rose, it soon got to the place where many candidates could not afford to make the race at their own expense, so contributions were accepted, first from party members and then from outsiders.

This was also the period that saw business greatly expanded. Railroads became a power in the country. Big investment banks were established. Many of the enormous trust companies developed at this time. Big business was interested in seeing that certain policies were followed by the national government, such as a high tariff and a sound monetary system. Therefore, so business reasoned, it was to the advantage of the country that whichever party was in power, either locally or nationally, should conduct governmental affairs in such a way that would be most advantageous to business. To this end industry began to contribute heavily to the campaign funds of the parties. In general, business tried to help the party it thought would win. There was nothing illegal about this procedure, but there was an implied obligation that went with the acceptance of such contributions. So business became a tremendous force in politics.

Under President McKinley business thrived. A new high tariff bill was passed, and the Gold Standard Act was put through in 1900. The Sherman Anti-Trust Act had recently been passed, but it was not enforced. The railroads continued to operate with little regulation. Big business became bigger.

The war with Spain that came during McKinley's first administration has been discussed in Chapter 11. There were probably several factors that led the nation into war, but certainly one of them was the fact that financial interests in this country had large investments in Cuba, and our industrialists were enjoying an annual trade with the island of about $100,000,000. It was to the advantage of big business that Cuba should be free, although the Democrats promptly dubbed the war an act of imperialism.

The question of imperialism became

the central argument in the election of 1900. But times were getting better after the slump of a few years before, and the party in power naturally got the credit. McKinley was elected again over Bryan, and Theodore Roosevelt, Governor of New York, became Vice-

Chicago Historical Society

THEODORE ROOSEVELT

President. In September, 1901, McKinley fell before an assassin at Buffalo and died a week later. Theodore Roosevelt was now President.

THEODORE ROOSEVELT IN POLITICS

"Square Deal" Roosevelt. Roosevelt was not at all like McKinley. He had a forceful personality, tireless energy, and a sincere desire for reform in the best interests of the people. The politicians

had not wanted him as a vice-presidential candidate, and business interests didn't want him as President. He had already held several political offices, among them Police Commissioner of New York City, and Assistant Secretary of the Navy, as well as Governor of the Empire State. Also, he was a Colonel in the Spanish-American War. He had written several books, and he was widely known for his big game hunts in various parts of the world.

Whatever we may think of Theodore Roosevelt's actions as President, we must recognize his sincerity of purpose. He obviously believed that the Chief Executive should be a real leader. He himself was an independent thinker, and he was quick to put his thoughts into action. He did not favor government by privilege of business interests with the masses of the people left out of consideration. He was direct in his attempted solutions to any problem and absolutely fearless in carrying them out. He believed the Constitution to be "the greatest document ever devised by the wit of man to aid a people in exercising every power necessary for its own betterment, and not as a straitjacket cunningly fashioned to strangle growth." He stood, he said, for a "square deal" for all. Everyone was to receive just treatment, and the President proposed to carry a "big stick" to see there was no violation of this high principle.

Roosevelt went to work at once. He clamped down on the trusts. He applied new regulations to the railroads. He brought pressure to bear and settled a troublesome Pennsylvania coal strike. He pushed civil service reform. An outdoor man himself, he started a movement for the conservation of natural resources. He had Congress pass a Pure Food and Drug Act for the protection of the people. In foreign affairs, especially with regard to Santo Domingo and the Panama Canal Zone (see Chapter 11), his actions smacked of imperialism. In doing these things he naturally stepped on a lot of toes and was severely attacked by those affected. We weren't bothered by Communism then, so those who were hurt called Roosevelt a Socialist, a pretty severe charge for the time. But in the face of all opposition, Roosevelt went right ahead doing those things he thought fair and in the best interests of the country.

Theodore Roosevelt finished McKinley's term and then was elected President on his own right. At the end of his full term he refused to be a candidate for another and recommended to his party the nomination of his Secretary of War, William Howard Taft of Ohio. The Democrats put up William Jennings Bryan for the third time. Taft won handily.

Taft—Revolt in Republican Party. Taft was not a Theodore Roosevelt. He didn't have the personality and drive that his predecessor had. To an extent he was a reformer, but he did not favor a loose construction of the Constitution; he would take for the President only that authority specifically granted to the Chief Executive. And, of course, he lacked much of the glamor that always surrounded Teddy, the "Rough Rider."

Nevertheless, Taft continued many of the things Roosevelt had started. He kept up the suits against trusts and further extended the civil service. He applied more regulations to the railroads and established postal savings

banks and the parcel post system. During his administration, the Sixteenth Amendment, which provides for the income tax, was added to the Constitution, and the Seventeenth Amendment, giving the people the right to elect United States Senators directly, was sent to the states for ratification. It became a part of the Constitution after Taft was out of office.

On other scores Taft did not do so well by those who wanted to see this country continue to grow progressively more liberal. This was particularly true with regard to the tariff. Taft supported a raise in the rates, although he was more or less committed to a general reduction. Taft soon found himself with a revolt in the Republican party on his hands. Moreover, in many of the states the general dissatisfaction with the Republicans had caused a swing to the Democrats.

A wide-open split soon developed in the Republican party. In 1911 the more liberal wing organized itself, under the leadership of Senator Robert M. La Follette, formerly governor of Wisconsin. Senator La Follette was known popularly as "Fighting Bob" for his determined stand on many issues. Theodore Roosevelt, also, let it be known that he did not approve of what President Taft had been doing, but he refused to join the new National Progressive Republican League of Bob La Follette. Instead, he allowed himself to be pushed to the front as a candidate for the Republican nomination by the party convention of 1912. It is even reported that he himself drafted the letter which several Republican governors then wrote him asking that he consent to run.

The strategy didn't work. Roosevelt didn't have enough support, and La Follette was disliked by too many members of the party to even be considered. Taft won the nomination on the first ballot when the convention met in Chicago in June, 1912.

Roosevelt and the Progressive Party. But Roosevelt wasn't through. He and his followers met in Chicago two months later and organized a third party—the Progressive party. Theodore Roosevelt, of course, was nominated for President. With Hiram Johnson of California as the Vice-Presidential candidate, he went out to campaign with almost a religious fervor.

The Democrats finally nominated Governor Woodrow Wilson of New Jersey, a former President of Princeton University, after forty-six ballots. In the election the thing happened that often occurs when a third party enters the field. Enough Republican votes were drawn to the Progressive party (or "Bull Moose," as it was called, because of the symbol it adopted) to give the Democrats the election. For the first time since Grover Cleveland's second term ended in 1897, the Democrats were back in power. The refusal of the Republicans to bring about reform within their own party had brought the rise of a third party from their ranks and had cost them the election.

WILSON, HARDING, COOLIDGE, AND HOOVER

Wilson, the Man of Peace. Wilson was not a good mixer, so he never became a popular President. He was, however, a good Democrat in that he had the best interests of the people at heart. He was completely opposed to government by special interests and to

business monopoly that tended to stifle the little fellow. He struck out in the campaign repeatedly against lobbying, a practice that had gradually grown up in Washington, and of course, in several states as well. A lobbyist is a person, often a former member of Congress, who is sent to Washington by some group to exert as best he can any influence possible on the Congressmen to get them to support legislation that is favorable to the group the lobbyist represents. The system has had telling effect because the lobbyist is right there to contact a Congressman personally, while the people who elected that Congressman are far away and ofttimes unaware of what is going on. So successful has the system been that it is often a question of who runs the country, the people or the lobbies. All kinds of people are guilty of this attempt to govern the country by minority pressure groups—big industries, labor organizations, utilities, farmers, veterans, etc. Each has its own particular axe to grind and puts a lobbyist in Washington to see that the grinding gets done. And frequently what is good for one of these pressure groups is not good for the country in general.

With a clarity of vision not often found in public officials, Woodrow Wilson sounded what perhaps is to be the keynote of the entire twentieth century in the history of the United States. He recognized that this country had had a remarkable development industrially, but that both our economic and social systems have not kept pace. That is, while we had been creating a great industrial empire, the welfare of the masses of the people had been largely forgotten. Furthermore, he knew that the United States cannot become the great democratic nation which both its political heritage and its natural resources permit it to be, until the economic and social status of the people as a whole has been brought to the same stage of development as our industry. Put another way, it is simply the question of whether man is to be a servant of the machine, or the machine the servant of man. The readjustment to place man once again in his proper position as the most important single thing in the universe, with everything else—industry, government, and all—gaining importance only as it serves to help him develop himself to the fullest extent of which he is capable—this readjustment may well turn out to be the most important characteristic of this century.

Wilson went right to work. He got Congress to pass a new tariff bill which brought the rates down to a lower level than they had reached at any time since the Civil War. He struck at monopolies and trusts with other legislation. He revised our banking system with the Federal Reserve Act, which established the Federal Reserve Banks. And he extended the scope of the civil service system to take in more government officials.

It was the international situation that was Wilson's undoing as a President. Although war had broken out in Europe in 1914, we had managed to remain out of it, and the President won the re-election over the Republican candidate Charles Evans Hughes on the slogan "He kept us out of war." But soon we were in anyway.

Woodrow Wilson was a farsighted leader. He realized that there is no hope for real peace in the world so long as we have a rule of gun law. He had visions of the nations of the world uniting voluntarily into a great organization to maintain peace through the media of discussion and arbitration rather than through attempts to settle disturbing questions on the battlefield. As the last of his Fourteen Points (see Chapter 12) he proposed a League of Nations. By this time the Senate was

Acme

WOODROW WILSON

dominated by Republicans and would not go along with the Democratic President. So Wilson took his case to the people. He traveled all over the country pleading for support of his plan. In the end he was discredited by his own Congress, who refused to permit the United States to enter the League, and his health was ruined by his long and arduous efforts in its behalf. He died a broken man, but still believing he was right and that eventually the world would have to do the very thing he had been advocating. Only time can give him his proper place among the Presidents we have had. Many historians rank him high, along with Jefferson, Jackson, and Lincoln.

Women Become Voters. Another big extension of democracy came during Wilson's second administration. For years, as has been noted, there had been growing agitation for woman suffrage. Women, who were playing an increasingly important part in the business world, felt they should have an equal place with men in the world of politics. This could not be so long as they were denied the right to vote. In the long struggle the names of several women appear prominently, among them Susan B. Anthony and Carrie Chapman Catt. Finally, in 1918, the President asked Congress to take action on the question. By that time fifteen of the states had already granted complete suffrage to women. The Amendment (Nineteenth) was ratified and became a part of our Constitution in 1920.

Another question of suffrage rights has been raised in recent years, particularly during World War II. Many people have claimed that a young man or woman old enough to fight for his or her country is also old enough to vote. The age limit, however, throughout the nation has stood at twenty-one. In the current agitation only one state so far, Georgia, has lowered the limit to eighteen for both men and women.

Election of 1920. The reaction from World War I and the fight over the League of Nations put a Republican back in the White House. The cam-

paign in 1920 was between two men from Ohio, Warren G. Harding, the Republican, and James M. Cox, the Democrat. Harding won by a big majority. His short period in office was marked by a boost in tariff rates again and by scandal that involved even some Cabinet members, notably the "Teapot Dome" affair over some government oil lands.

Harding died in 1923 and was succeeded by his Vice-President, former Governor Calvin Coolidge of Massachusetts. The new President continued Harding's efforts to get the country back to normal after the war, and in addition he stressed economy. Normal, to both Harding and Coolidge, apparently meant giving business a free hand.

Coolidge Re-elected. In 1924 the Republicans put up Coolidge again, with General Charles G. Dawes of Illinois for Vice-President. After a record 103 ballots, the Democratic national convention nominated John W. Davis of West Virginia and Charles W. Bryan of Nebraska, brother of crusading William Jennings Bryan. Again a third party entered the picture. The Progressives selected Republican Robert M. La Follette of Wisconsin for President and Democrat Burton K. Wheeler of Montana as his running-mate. Coolidge was easily re-elected.

The country continued on a wave of prosperity, but not all classes of people were happy. The farmers, in particular, were uneasy. The President seemed content to let things run their course rather than to set up any kind of constructive program. People were becoming more and more dissatisfied.

Hoover and Hard Times. In spite of this, Coolidge might have had the nomination again (he had been elected President only once) but he "did not choose to run." The Republicans then selected Herbert C. Hoover from California, the Secretary of Commerce. Hoover was well known as an engineer and for the relief work he had

Acme

HERBERT C. HOOVER

done in Europe after World War I. He promised to continue the policies of the Coolidge administrations but took no stand on any issues.

The Democrats nominated Governor Alfred E. Smith of New York. Smith was a product of the Tammany Hall machine and a Catholic. On one issue alone he took a stand that perhaps cost him the election. In 1919 the Eight-

eenth Amendment had been added to the Constitution. It is the famous Prohibition Amendment, which banned the sale of intoxicating liquor in the country. (It was later repealed in 1933 by the Twenty-First Amendment.) Smith came out strong against prohibition, and many Democrats who were "drys" voted against him. The result was a landslide for Hoover, who carried forty of the forty-eight states, including four of the traditionally Solid South. Unfortunately, also, the religious affiliation of the Democratic candidate had considerable influence on the vote.

As a result of his popular acceptance, President Hoover came to the White House under extremely favorable conditions. In a few months, however, came the stock market crash of 1929 and business in general took a nose dive. Thus the stage was set for some of the most far-reaching changes ever brought about in the history of American democracy—changes that came under Democratic leadership during the following decade. This story is told in the next chapter.

DEMOCRACY IN THE UNITED STATES

The Political Party. Let's take a look at the status of democracy in the United States. Political parties had started out by representing very different policies of government. This had remained true through the War between the States. In the later years of the nineteenth century, however, and in the early part of the twentieth, industry had grown large and business began to take a close interest in politics, even to the extent of influencing policies and action wherever possible. This was done partly by contributions to party campaign funds and partly by

SYMBOL OF SELF-GOVERNING PEOPLE

The ballot box has come to stand for self-government—when the people have a free choice at the polls. Through it they give direction to government that derives power from them.

lobbying. The tendency was, then, for the principal parties to lose any identity because of what they stood for and to become traditional organizations with traditional names. Their chief aim seemed to be, not the support of certain policies but rather either the maintenance of the party in power or the winning of power again. In other words, it appears rather clear that the success of the party was now of greater importance than the best interests of the country. So the word "politics" took on a rather disreputable meaning. It denoted almost anything from selfishness to outright corruption. And as campaigns became more and more expensive, the parties looked increasingly to those agencies that could contribute on a large scale, with the natural result that those agencies assumed even greater importance in determining the course of the party when it controlled the government.

Little has been done to relieve this situation on the national scale. In the states and in some city and local governments, however, steps have been taken to secure a type of government more responsive to the will and the welfare of the people. Most states have now adopted the direct primary to replace the convention or caucus as the means of selecting candidates. Nearly half the states now have the initiative and the referendum. By the initiative the people can themselves initiate legislation in the state, and the referendum gives them a chance to vote on legislation passed by the state lawmaking body if they so desire. A few states have the right of recall, by which the people can vote a man out of public office. In many cities the mayor-council type of government has given way to the commission type. In the latter a mayor and a few commissioners, often five, are elected by the people. The big advantage in the system is that there are fewer people charged with the job of running the city, and it is therefore easier to fix responsibility. It is still easier to establish responsibility in the city-manager type of government. In this the commissioners hire a man to take executive charge, and all the responsibility is directly his. Each of these newer systems tends to produce better government by making it harder for graft and mismanagement to be covered up.

Government by minority pressure groups for their own interests has been made possible at least partly by the indifference of the voters of the country to what kind of government exists so long as they personally are enjoying at least a reasonable degree of prosperity. Government by these groups has, in turn, promoted a lack of interest on the part of the citizens, for, they say, there is little they can do to throw the political machines out of control. At the close of the eighteenth century about 80 per cent of the voters usually went to the polls to express themselves. Now, ofttimes, not even 50 per cent go. The situation raises a troublesome question: how can good democratic government be attained when so large a percentage of the American people refuse to take part in their own government?

FOR YOUR REVIEW

These Should Be Easy for You Now

1. How did business become a force in politics? Why?
2. How was business financially interested in the freedom of Cuba?
3. How did Theodore Roosevelt view the office of Chief Executive? Cite evidence to show how he carried his views into action.
4. What attitude did Taft take toward the powers of the President?
5. What does the Sixteenth Amendment provide for? The Seventeenth?
6. What cost the Republican party the election of 1912?
7. How are lobbies able to exert great influence in government?
8. Name various minority pressure groups that make their influence felt in government from time to time.
9. What does your text say may prove to be the keynote of the twentieth century in American history?
10. What development ruined President Wilson's health during his second administration?
11. How does the Nineteenth Amendment represent a further extension of democracy?
12. What was the dominant note of the Coolidge administrations?
13. What situations conspired to defeat Alfred E. Smith?
14. Summarize the conditions that gave the word *politics* a rather disreputable meaning.
15. What is the direct primary? The initiative? Referendum? Recall? How do they promote better government?

16. What is the big advantage of the commission and city-manager types over other kinds of city government?

17. What basic attitude of the American people makes possible government by minority pressure groups?

Associated Dates

1897–1901—administration of William McKinley

1901—assassination of President McKinley; shot September 6; died September 14

1901–1909—administrations of Theodore Roosevelt

1906—Pure Food Act

1909–1913—administration of William Howard Taft

1913–1921—administrations of Woodrow Wilson

1913—Federal Reserve Banking Act

1914—beginning of World War I

1917—the United States enters the war

1919—Eighteenth Amendment adopted
   Senate refuses to ratify the Treaty of Versailles

1920—League of Nations organized without the United States
   Nineteenth Amendment adopted

1921–1923—administration of Warren G. Harding

1923–1929—administrations of Calvin Coolidge

1929–1933—administration of Herbert Hoover

1929—stock market crash, October 24

Why Are These To Be Remembered?

Robert M. La Follette	League of Nations	Teapot Dome
Progressive party	Susan B. Anthony	John W. Davis
Hiram Johnson	Carrie Chapman Catt	Alfred E. Smith
Lobbyist		

Chapter 21

President Franklin Roosevelt Inaugurates the New Deal

THE GREAT DEPRESSION OPENS THE DOOR TO WIDESPREAD CHANGES IN THE UNITED STATES

Roosevelt in the White House. In the face of very bad economic conditions, President Hoover continued to express the belief that prosperity was "just around the corner." It was like whistling in a graveyard. Banks were failing right and left. Others were closing to protect themselves against "runs" by depositors who had lost faith and wanted to withdraw all their funds. Farm prices had dropped below the cost of production, and almost everybody was in debt. Factories were closed or operating only part time. Millions of people—probably at least 12,-000,000—were unemployed. With all the things they had believed in and had relied upon gone, people turned to their government for help. But there was no plan to deal with such an emergency, and President Hoover didn't appear able to find one at the time. The Democrats now had a majority in the House of Representatives, and this ended the President's control of Congress. In addition, people were losing faith in his leadership.

When election time came, the Republicans nominated Hoover and Vice-President Charles E. Curtis again. The Democrats turned to Governor Franklin D. Roosevelt of New York and John N. Garner of Texas. There wasn't much difference between the platforms the two parties presented, but the feeling abroad in the country that a change in government was needed gave Roosevelt the electoral votes of forty-two states, 472, to 59 for Hoover. Although Franklin Roosevelt was a cousin of Theodore, the overwhelming vote was a protest against the leadership of Hoover rather than one for Roosevelt. The people just wanted a change—any change.

Roosevelt Tackles Financial Problems. The new President got to work as soon as he took office. His first move was to close all the banks in the country. Telegrams containing the executive order were sent out one day, and the banks simply didn't open the next morning. It was a new experience for the American people. Regardless of how much money anyone had on deposit in a bank, he couldn't get a dime of it. People were caught flat, or with very little cash on hand. Stores extended credit where absolutely necessary, pending the reopening of the banks. Congress gave the President more control over banking, and gradually individual banks were permitted to open their doors again, after an investigation of their affairs showed they were in sound financial condition. If the au-

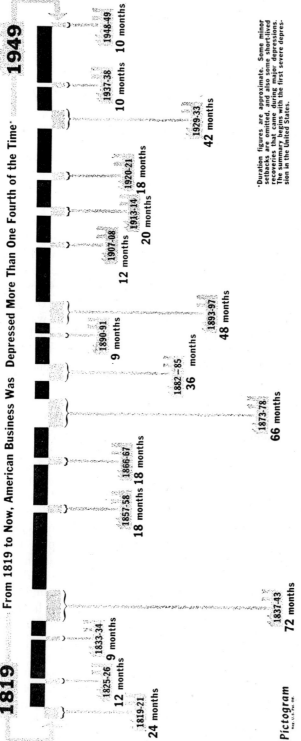

ECONOMIC DEPRESSIONS AND RECESSIONS

Some periods of "bad times" existed for only a few months, but one lasted for six years.

U.S. News & World Report (9–2–49). © U.S. News Pub. Corp.

dit showed them to be on shaky foundations, they never did open, but their assets were liquidated and the depositors paid off to as great an extent as possible. Soon the government came out with a plan to insure deposits up to $5,000 in banks that had been permitted to reopen; it was hoped that this would

Acme

FRANKLIN DELANO ROOSEVELT

increase confidence in the banks and prevent further "runs."

The uncertain financial setup reached clear into the United States Treasury. When the country had gone on the gold standard exclusively, all the paper money in circulation was backed by gold in the treasury and could be exchanged for gold coins. That is, it could in theory. Actually, there wasn't enough gold in the country to redeem all the paper money. To safeguard our gold supply the President did several things. The weight of gold in a gold dollar was reduced to but 59 per cent of its previous weight. This, then, meant our supply of gold would go farther. To prevent people from hoarding, the President called in all the gold in circulation, both from banks and from individuals. The metal was paid for in paper money, which put more of it into use. Silver certificates, backed by the silver in the treasury, were issued to replace the gold certificates which could no longer be redeemed. In addition, the government began to buy quantities of gold from other countries at a price higher than could be obtained anywhere else. The result was that this country gradually built up a huge supply of the valuable metal until it possessed more than all the rest of the world together. A depository for our gold was built at Fort Knox, Kentucky. By these moves President Roosevelt hoped to create a cheaper money and to stimulate business for both agriculture and industry.

The Alphabetical Agencies. The President also moved directly against the problems that hampered industry and agriculture. In June of 1933 the National Industrial Recovery Act went into effect. It was referred to as NIRA. In fact, so many new governmental agencies and bureaus were created during these years that together they were commonly called the alphabetical agencies. NIRA was intended to bring all industry under government supervision and, through planning on a wide scale, to increase production, employment, buying power, and to improve conditions in general. To do this the major industries were asked to draw up codes for their operation, to be approved by the government. In the codes each industry agreed to hire more people, but

THE DARK DAYS WHEN MILLIONS WERE IDLE AND BROKE

Duplicated time and again, during the great depression, was the spectacle of jobless men and women seeking help from private and public relief agencies. This photo shows unemployed men in a "breadline" outside the Central Union Mission, Washington, D.C., in 1930.

not children, to establish minimum wages and hours, and to hold prices down. Industry responded quickly, under the leadership of General Hugh Johnson, head of the National Recovery Administration (NRA). The plan remained in effect for about two years. Then in 1935 the Supreme Court declared it unconstitutional, holding that the act virtually gave the President power to make laws, a right reserved for Congress, and that the federal gov-

ernment had no authority to fix wages or hours in the states except in the case of interstate commerce.

To help agriculture, the Agricultural Adjustment Act (AAA) was passed in 1933. It was intended to bring forcibly into play the old economic law of supply and demand. Since farm prices were so low, it was reasoned, the cause must be that there was too much farm produce. The law provided that the Secretary of Agriculture, Henry A.

THE GOLD DEPOSITORY AT FORT KNOX, KENTUCKY

Literally billions of dollars worth of the gold bullion that serves as a basis of value for our money is stored at Fort Knox in underground vaults.

Wallace, should make agreements with farmers to raise less and to receive payments from the government in proportion to the amount they reduced their production. In addition, the government bought great quantities of farm products and gave them to the people who could not find work and were on relief. Later this program was applied to cotton as well. The bill was paid by means of a processing tax levied upon the industries that used farm produce in manufacturing.

Railroads were finding the going tough, also. Many of them were already heavily in debt, and some had passed into receivership because they were bankrupt. Their troubles rose from excessive duplication of services in trying to compete with one another, and from the competition given them by busses, trucks, and airplanes. The President appointed Joseph B. Eastman as Co-ordi-

nator to work out a co-operative plan of operation that would reduce costly competition. In addition, provision was made for loans to the railroads by the Reconstruction Finance Corporation.

Of course, the effects of these agricultural and industrial programs were not to be felt immediately. And millions of people were unemployed and in need of help. So the Federal Emergency Relief Administration (FERA) was created to help these people indirectly through the agencies set up by state, county, and city governments. To help people threatened with the loss of their farms or homes, the government made money available through the Federal Land Banks, the Home Owners' Loan Corporation (HOLC), and other similar agencies.

The President recognized that outright relief is usually embarrassing to people who must, because of circum-

Acme

MORALE-BUILDING EMPLOYMENT SPURRED YOUNG MEN TO REPLANT
AND REBUILD

Many worth-while work projects were undertaken in the nation's forests and elsewhere through-out the country by the Civilian Conservation Corps. Here, CCC boys are shown clearing driftwood from the shore of a lake in Grand Teton National Park, Wyoming, in 1933.

stances, accept it. Accordingly, he at-tempted to devise means of creating employment through the construction of public works and buildings. At one time as many as 600,000 young men of the country were enrolled in the Civil-ian Conservation Corps (CCC). Under the control of army officers, these young men were placed in camps over the country and put to work in various con-servation projects, such as stopping soil erosion, and the improvement of public parks, playgrounds, and the like. They lived an army life, with all expenses paid by the government, and were given a small salary each month, part of which they had to send home to their families. The boys thrived under the program, and the country profited.

In an attempt to stimulate business activity, the Public Works Administra-tion (PWA) was created to take over much of the work of FERA. PWA was operated by Harold Ickes, Secretary of the Interior. The idea was to engage in construction that did not compete with private industry, if possible. Roads were built, water systems and sewers laid, sewage disposal plants con-structed, and all similar projects un-dertaken. Local governments appealed to the federal government for help in a project, and received up to nearly half of the cost from the national treas-ury.

Later the PWA was overshadowed by the WPA, the Works Progress Ad-ministration, under Harry Hopkins. It did the same kind of work as PWA, but all the labor employed on a WPA proj-ect had to be taken from the relief lists. For this reason production under WPA was often neither rapid nor efficient. This was not hard to understand. Many people were working at a kind of job entirely unfamiliar to them and to

Acme

THEY RAKED LEAVES AND BUILT SOLID ROADS

Despite many instances of misdirected effort and "boondoggling," the federal make-work programs accomplished their primary aim of providing subsistence income opportunities for the jobless on a pay rather than a dole basis. In addition, they partially accomplished their secondary aim of having projects result in tangible public improvements. This picture shows drought-victim farmers at work on a WPA road project in North Dakota.

which they were unaccustomed. To conserve special skills various types of projects were developed. Actors on relief were used to write and put on plays, often dealing with the lore of the community in which they lived. Authors and schoolteachers were put to work doing research and writing histories of communities or areas of the country. The basic purpose was to help a man keep his self-respect and at the same time earn a living, but many people who didn't understand poked fun at the "shovel-leaners."

Of the many new bureaus and agencies created, a few more of them deserve mention here. The Federal Hous-ing Administration (FHA) would lend money to home owners who wanted to improve their property or make necessary repairs. The National Youth Administration (NYA) helped young people stay in school by making funds available to schools to employ students for part-time work. It also helped young people who were out of school to find work or set up special projects to provide work for them. The Tennessee Valley Administration (TVA) was created to develop water power and produce electrical power for that area. The Resettlement Administration (RA) helped farmers who had been trying to make a living on poor land to find a new location on land that would be more productive.

The great proportion of the acts passed by Congress under President Roosevelt's "New Deal" (as he called it) were intended to meet the immediate situations of the national emergency. However, some of them were more far-reaching in scope. The Social Security Act (1935) was one of these. It operates to help people in three ways. First, the federal government will aid a state in providing payments to people during such time as they may be unable to find work. Our industrialized economy has made this necessary. When most of our people made their living through agriculture, they were at least assured of a living at all times even though prices were low. But now that most people work in factories or in offices, a stop in their work and their income leaves them with no means of support except whatever they have been able to lay away for a "rainy day." In the second place, the national government will help a state in payments to old people who are unable to work and earn a living for themselves. This applies to people who are now so advanced in age that they have been unable to store up any benefits under the Social Security plan. In the third place, both the worker and the employer make regular payments into a fund, the amount based upon the salary earned. When the worker reaches sixty-five, he can begin to draw payments, the size of which is determined by the amount and the length of time he has paid in.

It is not our purpose here to go into these Social Security plans in detail. This you can get more properly in some other social studies course. The actual plans vary from state to state, and undoubtedly will be changed as the years go by. Various reforms are needed. For example, at the present Social Security applies to only about half of our people. Farmers, professional people, self-employed workers, and others are not covered. The United States has been slow in adopting legislation of this type; many European countries had it long before we did. Since it is rather new with us, it is bound to be subjected to frequent changes and modifications.

Opposition to the New Deal. Much of the legislation passed in the early years of President Roosevelt's first administration was put through in a hurry and usually just about as the President asked for it. It is true these laws tended to give the Executive Department a great deal of power. Soon those people who opposed the President were charging that he wanted to make himself a dictator. They also accused Congress of being simply a "rubber stamp" that placed its approval automatically upon anything Mr. Roosevelt asked.

As time permitted and opposition moved to challenge some of the laws that had been passed, the Supreme Court heard several cases and declared some of the New Deal legislation to be unconstitutional. Among the laws thrown out were those that created the NRA and the AAA. President Roosevelt apparently looked upon this action as an attempt to interfere with what he considered to be a necessary program for the welfare of the people. Of course, he was bound to draw considerable criticism from big business because almost his entire program was designed to lift the incomes and improve the living conditions of the people with lowest incomes; that is, to narrow the chasm between those at the top and those at the bottom of our economic scale. Improving conditions at the bottom usually meant higher taxes and restrictions at the top.

Mr. Roosevelt felt that several of the Justices on the Supreme Court were so advanced in age that their views and attitudes were excessively conservative and that therefore they would continue to be a stumbling block to progressive legislation. He wanted to alter this situation. Accordingly, he proposed to Congress that a law be passed permitting the President to appoint a new Justice to the Court whenever a member reached the age of seventy and didn't resign. At that time there were six men on the Court who were over seventy, and if Congress had agreed, the President could have appointed six new Justices, thus increasing the number from nine to fifteen.

Immediately great opposition was aroused. Part of it was because the President referred to the Supreme Court Justices as "the nine old men." Part of it was because a lot of people, many of them Democrats, thought Mr. Roosevelt was trying to "pack the Court"—that is, to enlarge it with men of his own choice who would vote as he wanted on the constitutionality of legislation he was able to get through Congress. Because of the widespread opposition, the proposal never came to a vote in Congress. The President soon got a Court to his liking anyway, for within a few years all but two members had died and had been replaced by Roosevelt appointees.

"Lame Duck" Amendment. During the President's first term the Twentieth Amendment was added to the Consti-

tution. It is frequently called the "lame duck" amendment. Up to that time congressmen were delayed a long time in taking office, and in the meantime the defeated Senators and Representatives (the "lame ducks") continued to hold office. The delay was about a year —from election in November of one year until December of the following year, unless a special session was called. The President wasn't sworn in until March 4 after the election. Under the new law congressmen take their seats on January 3 after their election, and the President's inauguration was moved up to January 20. Thus the expressed will of the people in the election of their officials was to be carried out more quickly.

Roosevelt's Second Term. For the 1936 election the Democrats unanimously nominated Roosevelt and Garner again. The Republicans selected Governor Alfred M. Landon of Kansas for their Presidential candidate and publisher Frank Knox of Chicago for Vice-President.

Again the platforms were very similar. In the campaign the Republicans failed to present any constructive program but relied wholly on attacking Roosevelt and the New Deal. In return, the President based his campaign on the promise to continue what he had been doing.

The contest then boiled itself down to this. The Democrats believed in and were putting into operation a planned economy, with the federal government providing the planning and the restrictions necessary to make the New Deal program work. Clearly the Democratic program benefited the lower income people most. And there are more low income people than there are those with big incomes. Those people apparently preferred to have their way of living planned for them by a benevolent government than to be left to the uncertainty of their prosperity under the American industrial system with few or no controls applied. At any rate, Roosevelt was re-elected in the greatest landslide in our history, getting all but eight of the electoral votes and carrying all the states except Maine and Vermont.

In Roosevelt's second term the New Deal lost some of its popularity. The measures it had taken to solve the problems facing the country had not done all that had been expected or promised. There was still a lot of unemployment, and farm prices were too low to permit the farmer any degree of prosperity. The Republicans were gaining ground in the states and in Congress. In 1940 they nominated Wendell L. Willkie, who had been a Democrat but was one of the chief opponents of the TVA because of his own connection with a public utility company. For his running mate they chose Charles L. McNary of Oregon.

Roosevelt Breaks Tradition. The big question in everybody's mind was: Would Roosevelt run for a third term? Not until the Democratic convention was under way did he make his own feelings known. Then he sent the convention a statement saying simply that he had no desire to be nominated. The delegates interpreted this correctly as meaning that he would not refuse the nomination if it were given to him. It was, on the first ballot. Henry Wallace was selected as his running mate.

Again the platforms were almost identical. The fact that they have differed so little in recent years indicates one thing: both parties know that votes win elections; they know also that a program like the New Deal appeals to the masses of people and therefore wins votes. There has been little the Republicans could do except adopt a platform very like the Democrats' and offer to do the same things, only better. This has frequently been referred to as the "me, too" attitude of the Republicans. In the 1940 election Roosevelt won again, getting the electoral votes of thirty-eight states this time. The tradition of only two terms for any President was broken.

Roosevelt Begins Fourth Term. Four years later it was Roosevelt again. The Republicans put up Governor Thomas E. Dewey of New York and Governor John W. Bricker of Ohio. The Democrats nominated Senator Harry S. Truman of Missouri as Roosevelt's running mate.

The Republicans knew they had no chance if they offered a reactionary platform. They had to go along with most of the reforms brought about by the New Deal. World War II was not yet over, and the big job was to finish it and then to write a peace. The best the Republicans could do was to insist it was time for a change. To this President Roosevelt replied that his experience would be a valuable asset in the months ahead. The people apparently thought so, too, for they gave him the electoral votes of thirty-six states and sent him back to the White House for his fourth term.

The strain of his long period of service, with the heavy problems of the depression years and the war, had undoubtedly taxed the President's strength greatly. The nation was not prepared, however, for the startling news of his sudden death at Warm Springs, Georgia, on April 12, 1945. Immediately Harry Truman was sworn in as the new President of the United States.

It is difficult to evaluate the greatness of a contemporary. The qualities of greatness cannot be certainly identified until they have been tested by time. Franklin Delano Roosevelt came to the highest office in the land when the affairs of the nation were at a low ebb. The prospect was challenging; the opportunity was great. FDR, as people came to know him, was of a wealthy family; he did not need to seek public office for the income it brought. And he had another very good reason for refusing whenever committees came calling, asking permission to propose his name. He had gone through a siege with infantile paralysis which left his body weak and in part useless. But he could rise above such handicaps. Here was a man who reaffirmed belief in the old American tradition of equal opportunity for all, one who believed that the "common man" did not yet occupy his full place in American life. And so came the New Deal with all its accompanying efforts to improve living conditions for the little fellow who did the nation's work. Not everybody, by any means, agreed wholly with the program the President followed, in both domestic and foreign affairs. Many objected greatly to basic policies he adopted. Probably no President has been so criticized and so caricatured. People laughed and scoffed and condemned, but all the time they must have known that many of the changes were here to stay.

Mr. Roosevelt wrote a speech the night before he died. He expected to deliver it three days later by radio, the medium he liked so much to use. In it he said this: "Today as we move against the terrible scourge of war—as we go forward toward the greatest contribution that any generation of human beings can make in this world—the contribution of lasting peace, I ask you to keep up your faith. I measure the sound, solid achievement that can be made at this time by the straight-edge of your own confidence and your resolve. And to you, and to all Americans who dedicate themselves with us to the making of an abiding peace, I say: The only limit to our realization of tomorrow will be our doubts of today. Let us move forward with strong and active faith."

TRUMAN TAKES CHARGE

Truman Also a New Dealer. The American people accepted Harry S. Truman on faith. They knew little about him, and they knew it would be very difficult for any man to fill Mr. Roosevelt's shoes. He had been a strong executive whose influence was felt in all departments of government. Mr. Truman pledged himself to carry on the program of the New Deal, and he had the good will of the entire country as he took up the job that had been thrust so suddenly upon him.

But soon, as some correspondents put it, "the honeymoon was over." The Republicans gained control of Congress after the war ended and were unwilling to go along with the New Deal type of program that the new President proposed. Truman lost rapidly in popularity.

Campaign of 1948. As the election year of 1948 rolled around, there was great speculation as to what might happen. The Republicans thought they saw an excellent chance to get back into power. They nominated again Governor Thomas E. Dewey of New York and Governor Earl Warren of California as his running mate. The Democrats hardly knew what to do. They felt Truman would not be a strong vote-getter, but couldn't seem to think of anyone who might do better. Then someone remembered General Dwight D. Eisenhower, Commander-in-Chief of all the Allied forces in Europe during World War II. He would be a sure thing. A movement was started in his behalf. But General Eisenhower refused to accept if he were nominated by the party convention, so the Democrats were right back where they had started.

When the convention met, there were three groups of Democrats who didn't want to see Truman nominated. The Southern Democrats disliked him because he had already gone on record as favoring a civil rights program which would extend greater democratic rights in actual practice to the Negroes. The staunch New Dealers didn't like him because, they said, he had ditched the New Deal and had gone conservative on them. The politicians of the big city Democratic machines opposed him because they thought he didn't have a chance of getting himself elected, and if he didn't, then they, too, would lose out because of the likelihood that many people would vote a straight Republican ticket.

The question of the civil rights plank in the platform became the central issue of the convention. Truman's nomination was almost a sure thing from the start, simply because there wasn't anyone else to whom the Democrats could turn. But on civil rights they fought it out.

Northern Democrats felt that an end should be put for all time to the restrictions the Southerners had been placing on the rights of the Negro. Men of the South were just as opposed to doing anything of the sort. In all fairness it should be pointed out that many Southerners are sympathetic to the advancement of the Negroes, but they believe that interference by people who don't understand the problem would lead to trouble. They know what happened after the Civil War, when outside interference led to strife between the races. Enlightened Southerners were afraid that any civil rights program dictated by the North would simply intensify friction and would actually hold back the advancement of the Negroes. But President Truman had gone on record in favor of a dictated policy. He wanted the government to handle civil rights problems directly from Washington. His answer to the Southerners was that they had had enough time to put a program of their own into operation.

The civil rights fight was carried to the floor of the convention, and there the President's supporters were able to get the program he wanted written into the platform. Some of the Southern delegates walked out of the convention and met in a few days in Birmingham, Alabama, to select candidates of their own. There was no doubt but that Truman's insistence on the civil rights plank would cost him votes in the South, but people generally had to admire him for the courage of his stand for something in which he believed.

As usual, there was little difference between the platforms of the two major parties. So Truman based his campaign on an attack on the record of the Republican Eightieth Congress, which he called the "do nothing" Congress. He pointed out that the very things the Republicans said they stood for in their platforms were things he had been unable to get the Republican Congress to adopt—a new housing bill, health insurance and more adequate social security and old-age pensions, price control to get the cost of living down, federal aid to education, and a fair employment practices law. Republican candidate Dewey studiously avoided committing himself on any major issue, apparently believing that such a campaign was unnecessary to win.

Before election day it seemed almost no one thought Mr. Truman had a chance. Practically every public opinion poll in the country reported a big majority favored Dewey. The Dixiecrats, as the Southerners who had bolted the Democratic party were popularly called, didn't gather as much strength as had been expected. A third party (Progressive) organized and nominated Henry A. Wallace, but the charge that its members were pro-Communists kept it from becoming very strong. Both these parties, however, were expected to pull votes from the Democrats and make Dewey a sure winner.

Truman's Victory. But it didn't work out that way. When the votes were all in and counted, Truman had 23,500,000 popular votes and 304 in the electoral college; Dewey had 21,600,000 popular votes and 189 electoral; J. Strom Thurmond, the Dixiecrat candidate, had

910,000 popular votes and 38 electoral votes; and Henry A. Wallace had 1,100,-000 popular votes and none in the electoral college.

The election was almost completely a personal victory for Harry S. Truman. In the face of the fact that almost the entire country believed he was licked, Mr. Truman came out swinging and got the knockout he was after. Faced with the choice between a man who openly stood against Congress and one who refused to make his position clear on the record of that Congress, the people voted for Truman and changed the Congress while they were at it.

The Truman victory in 1948 assured the Democrats of twenty years of unbroken control of the national government. The Democrats under the New Deal had identified themselves as the party which promised to give most to the common people of the nation. In the 1948 election the people voted for the party whose program appealed most to the economic self-interest of the rank-and-file of the American people.

The trend today definitely is toward a stronger vote by the masses of the people to give power to that party which by its record will make living better among the lower income group. The trend was evident in England after World War II, where not even the popularity of Winston Churchill, who had led the country to victory in the war, could stop the election of the party which promised greater economic advantage to the mass of the people. Actually, the movement is world wide. In the English-speaking world it is working itself out within the framework of political democracy. Elsewhere there is little political democracy. In many countries dictators stay in power by promising the people whatever they want.

If our kind of democracy, which is now political and becoming economic, is to survive, our political parties must both move with the trend of history, a trend that no party can stop. The attempt to do that presents many problems, which we shall consider in the next chapter.

FOR YOUR REVIEW

These Should Be Easy for You Now

1. What were conditions like in the early 1930's? How were they responsible for the election of Franklin D. Roosevelt?
2. What changes were made to stabilize the country's financial condition?
3. What did the National Industrial Recovery Act provide for? What was its purpose? Why was the Act declared unconstitutional?
4. What was the purpose of the Agricultural Adjustment Act? How did it operate?
5. What was the task of the Federal Emergency Relief Administration?
6. Why were the Federal Land Banks and the Home Owners' Loan Corporation established?
7. Show how such agencies as the CCC, PWA, and WPA were designed to bring relief to people without subjecting them to the embarrassment of having to accept direct charity. Why was work done by these agencies often inefficient?
8. How did the FHA, NYA, and RA aid in the emergency?
9. Point out the three ways in which the Social Security Act is intended to aid people.
10. What were some of the reasons for which people criticized President Roosevelt?
11. What change did President Roosevelt propose be made regarding the Supreme Court? Why did he think this should be done?
12. What changes did the Twentieth Amendment bring?
13. What were the basic issues involved in the election of 1936?
14. What is meant by a "me, too" Republican attitude?
15. Why did Southern Democrats oppose the nomination of Truman in 1948? The New Dealers? The big city Democratic machines?
16. What was the civil rights matter that became the central issue of the Democratic National Convention? What break in the party did this cause?
17. Why did Truman call the Eightieth Congress a "do nothing" Congress?
18. What were the four major parties represented in the 1948 election?
19. How did the Truman victory in 1948 represent a phase of a world-wide trend?

Associated Dates

1933–1945—administrations of Franklin D. Roosevelt
1933—Emergency Banking Act, March 9
      Civilian Conservation Corps created, March 31
      Agricultural Adjustment Act, May 12
      Federal Emergency Relief Act, May 12
      Tennessee Valley Authority created, May 18
      Home Owners' Loan Act, June 13
      National Industrial Recovery Act approved, June 16
      Twentieth Amendment adopted, October 15

1935—NIRA declared unconstitutional, May 27
    Social Security Act, August 14
1936—AAA declared unconstitutional, January 6
    Soil Conservation and Domestic Allotment Act, March 1
    Flood Control Act, June 22
1937—Farm Tenancy and Rural Rehabilitation Act, July 22
    United States Housing Authority created, September 1
1938—new Agricultural Adjustment Act, February 16
1945—death of President Roosevelt, April 12
1945—administrations of Harry S. Truman begin

Why Are These To Be Remembered?

Charles E. Curtis	John W. Bricker	AAA
John N. Garner	Harry S. Truman	FERA
Hugh Johnson	Earl Warren	HOLC
Henry A. Wallace	Fort Knox	CCC
Joseph B. Eastman	Reconstruction Finance Cor-	PWA
Alfred M. Landon	poration	WPA
Frank Knox	New Deal	FHA
Wendell L. Willkie	Lame duck	NYA
Charles L. McNary	Dixiecrats	TVA
Thomas L. Dewey	NIRA	RA

Chapter 22

American Democracy Faces a Serious Test

AMERICAN DEMOCRACY CAN BE PRESERVED AND EXTENDED ONLY
THROUGH THE ENTHUSIASTIC INTEREST AND ACTION OF OUR CITIZENS

[The author feels that no consideration of American democracy would be complete without a survey of the status of democracy at the mid-point of the century and some analysis of the problems we face in the second half. Obviously, this is not all history in the strict sense of the word. Therefore, the reader must look upon this chapter as expressing the editorial opinions of the author, with which you may be free to agree or not as you yourself may honestly believe.]

Federal Government—a Big Business. The future of democracy in the United States does not appear to be exactly rosy. It is to be hoped that the country will continue its unprecedented growth and development in order that it may truly merit and hold its position as the greatest nation in the world, but it is far from a foregone conclusion that this will happen. In a government by the people too much depends upon the people themselves, every one of them, to make any future course certain.

The attitude of the American people all too often is one of believing that somehow, no matter how dark the prospect may be, everything will turn out all right. We seem to feel, with the English poet Robert Browning, that "God's in his Heaven; all's right with the world." Frequently, then, both as individuals and in our national policy, we have closed our eyes to facts and hoped for the best. Usually this act of playing the ostrich and hiding our collective heads in the sand has left us undesirably exposed and has brought us trouble in the end.

If the United States is to continue on a sound basis as a government by the people, the citizens will have to develop a vital and unbiased interest in public affairs. Not only must there be intelligent public opinion about matters of government, but those opinions must be transformed into action. The people of Rome lost control of their government because they lost interest in it. It could happen here. It is important, then, that we consider some of the big problems of American democracy at the mid-point in the twentieth century.

Our federal government is the biggest business in the United States today. It employs more people than any other business. Its yearly operating cost is the largest in the nation. And the scope of its activity is more far-reaching. This has become true because of two things: (1) the country is bigger and its problems are more complex than ever before, and (2) the people of the nation expect more in the way of services from their government than at any time in the past.

Proof of the extended activity of our

national government lies in the number of people it employs. From a figure that was almost nothing in Washington's time, the number of people on the government pay rolls grew, until in 1939, just before World War II, it had almost reached the million mark. During the war, at the height of employment, the figure stood at more than 3,700,000. Even in 1949, four years after the end of the war, the number of government employees was still above two million. It has been estimated that one person in every ten, perhaps even one in every eight, works for the government, be it national, state, or local.

The great enlargement of the public employee lists came during the administrations of Franklin Roosevelt. New Deal activity to cope with the depression and later with the war meant the creation of many new bureaus and agencies to handle the new work taken on by the government. In 1945 there were some 1,100 of these bureaus operating within the national government. Out of this situation has come the word "bureaucracy," meaning carrying on the business of government by means of appointive offices, by people who are not subject to election by the people.

There are a great many people who feel that our bureaucratic type of government has become top-heavy; that too many people are involved for the work done; that bureaus are too expensive and inefficient; that they actually slow up the processes of government instead of hastening them; that "bureaucrats" are inclined often to prolong their work needlessly just to stay on the pay roll.

OUR NATIONAL DEBT

Study These Figures. This brings us to a companion problem—that of ex-

pense. Let's get some comparative figures. The average yearly cost of the federal government 150 years ago was less than $6,000,000. A century later, in 1900, government expenditures had risen to about $500,000,000, and most of it was covered by the revenue taken in. The year 1929 is often used as an example of a prosperous year; that was just before the stock market crash. That year our government spent a little less than four billion dollars and took in more than it spent. Then came the depression and government efforts to counteract it. New Deal economists entered upon what they called "deficit spending," which simply meant extending the nation's activities and their cost beyond the amount of money realized in revenue. Frequently in the depression years government expenditures ran well over twice the amount received in taxes. The theory was that in bad times the government, better than any private agency, could afford to go into debt to see to the welfare of the people, and then in good times the scales could swing to the other extreme, and the excess of revenue over expense would wipe out the debt.

But it didn't work out that way. Just as we were making some headway on the depression, along came World War II, with its enormous expense. We had no chance to reduce our debt very much before we were again borrowing from the people to defray the cost of the war. In 1945 our yearly expenditure ran over 100 billion dollars, 90 billion for war alone, and our income was a little over 46 billion. Since the war we have been able to balance our national budget in a few years, but the big debt we piled up has not yet been reduced very much.

Let's get the figures on that debt

WORKING FOR THE GOVERNMENT
UNITED STATES; 1900-1949

IN 1949...
I OUT OF 8 WORKERS
WORKED FOR THE GOVERNMENT

IN 1900...
I OUT OF 23 WORKERS
WORKED FOR THE GOVERNMENT

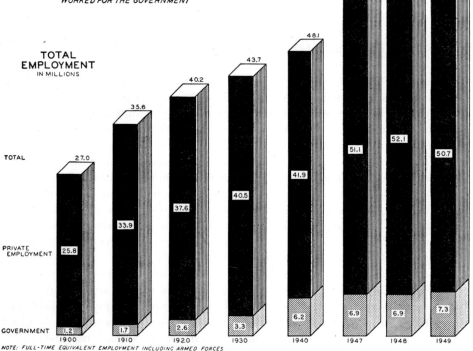

TOTAL
EMPLOYMENT
IN MILLIONS

NOTE: FULL-TIME EQUIVALENT EMPLOYMENT INCLUDING ARMED FORCES

More than 7 million persons, or one out of every eight persons working, held jobs under federal, state and local government in 1949. In 1900 slightly over one million persons worked for government, or one out of twenty-three workers. While total employment also expanded greatly, it fell short of the growth in government. From 1900 to 1949, total employment increased 115 per cent; government employment, over 525 per cent.

SOURCES: Department of Commerce, National Bureau of Economic Research, The Conference Board.

National Industrial Conference Board, Inc.

CENSUS OF EMPLOYEES IN ALL LEVELS OF GOVERNMENT

This chart indicates the total number of persons on federal, state, and local government payrolls for selected years from 1910 to and including 1949. It is to be noted that the total number for each year includes soldiers, sailors, and all other personnel of our national armed forces, as well as policemen, firemen, transit workers, and other employees of state and local governments. The number of nonmilitary employees of the federal government in 1949 was about two million —roughly, one out of every twenty-nine workers.

now. In this century it was at its lowest in 1915—just over one billion. That amounted to $11.83 for every person in the country. The debt mounted, because of World War I, to a high of 25½ billion in 1919—$240 per person. It was reduced steadily until the depression came. Then, as we have pointed out, it rose sharply. In 1939, just before World War II, it stood over 40 billion, a per capita debt of $308. The war, of course, sent it skyrocketing. At one time it reached almost 280 billion dollars. In 1946 it had dropped to about 270 billion—a debt of $1,911 dollars for every man, woman, and child in the country. In 1948 it was down to about 252 billion.

Two Schools of Thought. Now, there are two schools of thought about the national debt. Our country was founded on the idea of thrift, and many of our people today are firm believers in the theory that happiness comes to the person who spends less than he earns. They believe that our government ought to operate that way. They recognize that at times it may be absolutely necessary to borrow money for emergencies, but they believe that the debt ought to be paid off as rapidly as possible through frugal operation and economy.

But the task of raising more money than the government costs today is not at all an easy one. The original tax, the property tax, has been strained about to the breaking point. It is doubtful if it can be raised much higher than it is now. All kinds of new taxes have been devised, on incomes, on gasoline, direct and indirect taxes on almost everything. But the increasing cost of government demands more and still more income. As the income tax rose, a "pay as you earn" plan was devised. Employers were instructed to estimate each employee's income tax for the year from tables prepared by the government, divide the tax by the number of pay checks in the year, and then withhold the proportionate amount from each check to be paid directly to the government. It was easier for people to pay their income tax this way, and the government was sure of getting it. The problem is still there, however. How can we pay the current cost of government and at the same time keep reducing our national debt?

There are other people in the country who feel that a big national debt is no cause for alarm. They point out that it is very different from a private debt. The people are the government, they say, and the people simply owe the money to themselves. As long as we raise enough money to operate from year to year and pay the interest on the debt, we have nothing to worry about. The debt is in the form of government bonds, held by millions of people all over the country. Whenever any bonds mature, the government can borrow more money by selling more bonds and then redeem those that are due. So the debt just keeps on revolving. The debt, these people point out, has been enlarged only in the interest of the country as a whole. When a depression comes, it is much easier for the nation to borrow from the reserves of individuals and use this stored wealth to carry us over than it is for individuals to take the chance in investing those reserves in bad times with the greater risks involved. Financial experts who hold with this school of thought believe there is no danger to the country from a big national debt so long as the national income remains at least half as large as the debt. Since our yearly income has varied between 175 and 225

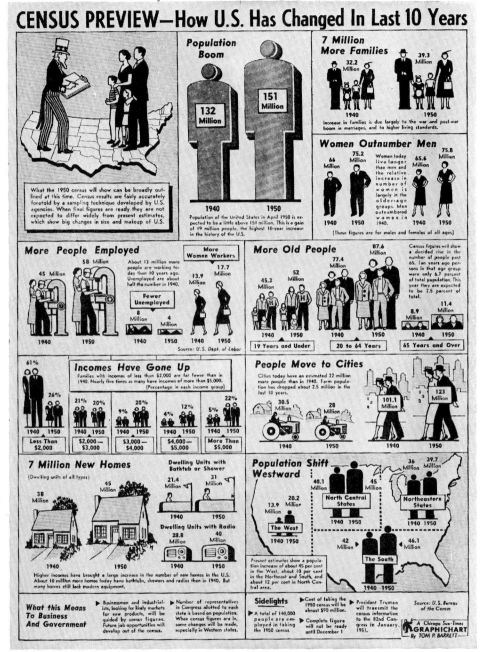

Chicago Sun-Times, Tom P. Barrett

PROFILE OF THE NATION AT THE MIDCENTURY MARK

Population trends, changes in income and employment conditions, and developments in housing in the United States during the ten-year period from 1940 to 1950 are pictured in this forecast of midcentury census findings. The *graphichart* details are based on results obtained by the Census Bureau through sampling techniques.

billions during the past five years, they insist our debt need cause us no concern.

Economy Is Needed. The danger, however, lies in the fact that it seems to be most difficult, in fact nearly impossible, to maintain a balanced budget —that is, to spend no more than we take in. Each year of deficit spending adds just that much more to our debt, and the day may come when the debt will actually be more than we can carry, unless we can keep boosting our national income, too. The alternative seems to be a lowering of the cost of government.

That this can be done no one doubts. Economy is clearly possible in a federal government that costs 100 million dollars a day. Many bureaus could be eliminated entirely because of considerable duplication of work. Take, for instance, housing. The United States government has forty-five separate agencies dealing with housing alone. Better over-all planning of government work would reduce cost, too. In a recent year one agency spent $100,000,000 trying to keep prices down, and another agency spent $80,000,000 trying to keep prices up. This sort of waste adds up rapidly. Clearly, a general overhauling of our government is needed badly, but getting Congress to do it seems an almost impossible task. Proposals for reorganization of the government have been presented several times since Theodore Roosevelt was President. A commission under former President Hoover, after lengthy investigation, made a detailed report dealing with the various departments in the late months of 1948 and early 1949. It specifically pointed out how reorganization could save the American people perhaps as much as four billion dollars a year. As this is written Congress has done little toward adopting the suggestions of the commission. President Truman, by executive order, did combine all the branches of the armed services under one head, to be called the Secretary of Defense. But a wholesale reorganization is necessary if much is to be accomplished.

Expansion of Government Services. There are always at least two sides to every question. So it is with the expansion of government services and the corresponding added expense. On one side Senator Styles Bridges of New Hampshire, Chairman of the Senate Appropriations Committee, said late in 1948: "I am a firm believer in adequate government service. . . . But I say that at present we are building up to an extremely dangerous situation, both economically and morally. We are inviting higher taxes and more socialization. But, more ominous, we are undermining the self-reliance of the individual citizen. The spirit of do-it-yourself is gradually being crushed in America by an omnipotent, monolithic Federal Government."

On the other side, many people maintain that increased government action, both in the way of control and services, is necessary if we are to realize the true democracy expressed by Thomas Jefferson in our Declaration of Independence—equal opportunity for all. They say that in a complex industrial civilization it is impossible for many of the citizens at the lower end of the economic scale ever to enjoy equality of opportunity with other citizens, unless some kind of over-all control is established to hold big business in check and to permit the worker to enjoy a greater amount of the profit from his labor. The only organization

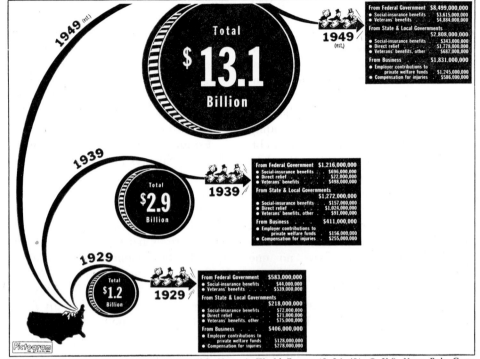

From Federal Government	$8,499,000,000
● Social-insurance benefits	$3,615,000,000
● Veterans' benefits	$4,884,000,000
From State & Local Governments	$2,808,000,000
● Social-insurance benefits	$343,000,000
● Direct relief	$1,778,000,000
● Veterans' benefits, other	$687,000,000
From Business	$1,831,000,000
● Employer contributions to private welfare funds	$1,245,000,000
● Compensation for injuries	$586,000,000

From Federal Government	$1,216,000,000
● Social-insurance benefits	$696,000,000
● Direct relief	$22,000,000
● Veterans' benefits	$498,000,000
From State & Local Governments	$1,272,000,000
● Social-insurance benefits	$157,000,000
● Direct relief	$1,024,000,000
● Veterans' benefits, other	$91,000,000
From Business	$411,000,000
● Employer contributions to private welfare funds	$156,000,000
● Compensation for injuries	$255,000,000

From Federal Government	$583,000,000
● Social-insurance benefits	$44,000,000
● Veterans' benefits	$539,000,000
From State & Local Governments	$218,000,000
● Social-insurance benefits	$72,000,000
● Direct relief	$71,000,000
● Veterans' benefits, other	$75,000,000
From Business	$406,000,000
● Employer contributions to private welfare funds	$128,000,000
● Compensation for injuries	$278,000,000

U.S. News & World Report (6–24–49). © U.S. News Pub. Corp.

GROWTH OF THE WELFARE STATE

The increasing total of money benefits rendered to the aged, to widows and other dependents, to the disabled and unemployed, and to veterans by the federal and state governments and by business is shown in this *pictogram* which charts the trend in ten-year jumps.

in the country able to do this, they say, is the federal government.

This struggle toward economic equality of opportunity will be discussed more fully in the next unit. In considering the political aspect of it, however, these are your problems: (1) How can the cost of government be lowered? (2) How can government be made more efficient? (3) What is to be done about the national debt? (4) The average person wants lower taxes and more government services at the same time. How can citizens in a democracy be educated to understand that whatever they get from government is not free; that they themselves as taxpayers

must bear its expense? (5) How can citizens in our American democracy be brought to understand that we must operate on the basis that whatever is best for the majority of the people in the country is best, in the long run, for each of us individually? How can we get the expression of this basic view of democracy carried into all phases of government and public affairs?

PROBLEM OF CRIME

Cost of Crime. Crime is another problem with which we all have to deal. As the nation has grown in size and population, crime, too, has increased. It is estimated that today the cost of crime in the United States to the American taxpayer may run as high as eighteen billion dollars each year.

Spread of Crime. Organized crime increased sharply during the period of attempted enforcement of the Eighteenth or Prohibition Amendment. It was not a popular law and was widely violated. Bootleggers soon learned that they could operate more easily if they were organized—that is, if they worked together. Out of this experience came the "gangs" for which some of our cities became notorious, such as the Al Capone gang in Chicago. All kinds of "rackets" developed. One of the principal types provided "protection" in return for regular payments from the business being protected. Actually, it was a sort of blackmail demanded to buy off the gang from causing the destruction from which it was supposed to be protecting the businessman.

The repeal of the Eighteenth Amendment, along with better methods of law enforcement, brought a drop in crime in the 1930's. With the coming of World War II, however, the people of the nation had another cause for worry. With women working alongside men in the war plants, children were often left without supervision at home, and juvenile delinquency became a source of national concern. The average age of criminals dropped steadily. Many communities took action to meet the situation through organized recreation projects and facilities for young people. Other communities recognized that the problem was often as much a question of parental delinquency and neglect as of juvenile delinquency, and began hailing fathers and mothers into court whenever their children got into trouble.

Eliminate the Causes of Crime. Our methods of dealing with criminals were brought under close scrutiny, also, and some startling situations were revealed in our prisons and reform schools. More consideration was given to the scientific study of the causes of crime in order that we might better fit the cure to the cause. The belief was more widely accepted that society as a whole was often just as responsible as the criminal himself and that criminal institutions should be operated along lines that would tend to rehabilitate miscreants and make them good members of society again, if at all possible. People came to believe more and more that the best way to reduce crime is to prevent it from happening in the first place by eliminating those factors that tend to cause crime—undesirable environment, broken homes, insecure financial conditions, and the like.

Correct Attitude Toward Laws. Another phase of the crime problem demands attention from all of us. We have the reputation of being the most lawless country in the world. Whether we deserve this estimate or not can be argued, but there are plenty of facts to support the accusation. A great many of our people seem to feel that they do not have to observe any law they don't like. The early American colonists held this attitude, as evidenced by the Boston Tea Party and other such deliberate violations of the regulations laid down by the British government. We still seem to feel the same way about our modern laws. There is no question but that we have on our statute books many laws that do not belong there. They are outmoded, and they do not reflect the will of the majority of our people. However, if we are really interested in making our democratic system work, we shall all have to take this stand regarding such laws: that as long as they are on the books, they are to be obeyed; that if we don't like them, we then should work to have them repealed by the proper legislative means. And we need also to recognize that laws are adopted for the protection of the majority of the people. They are not intended to act as infringements on the rights of people but simply to protect their rights against those few individuals who have not yet acquired the true concept of democracy—that in order to be assured of my own personal rights and privileges, I must be absolutely sure that I at no time trespass upon the rights and privileges of others. Such an attitude toward our laws could go a long way toward reducing the amount of crime and its accompanying cost in the United States.

Changes in Family Life. Two important changes in the status of the American home have been sharply reflected in the life of our people. Time was when the business of making a living for the family was tied up closely with the home; ofttimes the actual work was done there. Then when the country became industrialized, the wage earner of the family was forced to spend his time in the factories, and the economic importance of the home declined. Later, as women came to enjoy greater freedom, they became wage earners, too. They went into offices and factories and held down jobs just as men did. But working in industry and keeping house, too, was often more than a woman could handle, and it was usually the work at home that suffered. Today homes are looked upon by many people as just filling stations, where the members stop in when they are either hungry or sleepy. The close-knit family life of the past is gone. With mother and father both working, and the children at school during the day, there is little opportunity for family activity. And in the evening, modern organized and commercialized amusement attracts the various members away from home. Father goes to lodge or his club, mother to play bridge, and the children to the movies or some other form of entertainment. The absence of working together as a unit for a common cause has undoubtedly aided our rising divorce rate and has contributed considerably to the increase in the number of broken homes. And always, when a home is divided, it is the children who suffer most.

Importance of Church and School. The loss of influence of the home has shifted a great responsibility upon the school and the church. Instead of teaching just readin', 'ritin', and 'rithmetic, and in some cases preparing young people for college, schools today are supposed to train children for all phases of life—health, morals, recreation, vocation, manners, social responsibilities, and all. This is indeed a big task, and schools are only gradually altering their curricula and their physical setup to enable them to provide all this training. But in general schools have done an excellent job of trying to meet the situation, although they have frequently been hampered by lack of adequate funds. After World War II people became more concerned about the general quality of American education and voted more money for schools, especially for teachers' salaries.

During World War II schools in many communities were called upon to enlarge their services to provide training of specific types for men and women who were going into defense jobs. The schools rose nobly to the occasion, many of them operating some departments twenty-four hours every day to meet the emergency.

In 1944 Congress passed an act which provides, among other things, that returning servicemen may continue their education at government expense. The length of this college course or on-the-job vocational training depended upon the length of time the veteran had been in the service. When the war was over literally hundreds of thousands of G.I.'s flocked to our colleges and universities to take advantage of this opportunity.

Housing a Factor in Crime. Poor housing has contributed its share toward crime in the United States. The shift from home production to factory production meant the rapid growth of cities, with their undesirable slum areas. It has been estimated that one-third of the people of our country are inadequately housed. And poor housing conditions are recognized as a major factor in producing criminals.

The housing situation became acute in the years following World War II. During the war construction of houses almost stopped, except for war workers and the army. When the war was over, millions of returning servicemen wanted to build houses and establish homes of their own. But materials were scarce and the cost was high. The government made funds available to G.I.'s at low interest rates, and local agencies helped, but the task of providing adequate housing for everyone at a price people could afford remained one of the country's major problems.

HEALTH INSURANCE

The Health of the Nation. Another situation of national concern is the health of our people. It is true that science has done a great deal in recent years to conquer disease. In the last twenty-five years the average life-span

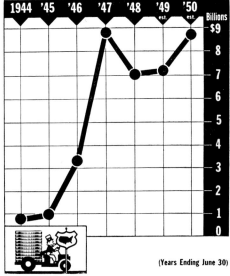

(Years Ending June 30)

U.S. News & World Report (8–12–49). © U.S. News Pub. Corp.

VETERANS' AID

This chart shows the upswing in the cost of veterans' benefits following World War II. Popularly approved veterans' claims are debts of honor which the nation will continue to pay as one of the aftermath expenses of war.

in the United States has been increased fifteen years. But the problem lies in the fact that the cost of medical and dental care is still so great that it is beyond the reach of many of our people. Many communities have established free clinics, and some hospitals accept a certain number of free or reduced-rate patients; but the fact remains that there are a lot of men and women, boys and girls who receive no medical care until

44 FEDERAL AGENCIES NOW DEAL WITH HEALTH AND MEDICINE

ONE OUT OF EVERY SIX PERSONS IN THE U.S. RECEIVED MEDICAL AID FROM THE GOVERNMENT IN 1948

U.S. News & World Report (1–7–49). © U.S. News Pub. Corp.

MEDICAL CARE—GOVERNMENT'S GROWING ROLE

The Hoover Commission's Task Force Report revealed the two sets of statistics shown in this chart. The Report gave impetus to the movement for government reorganization.

a serious situation has developed, and often then the attention they can procure is not adequate to their condition.

In recent years various types of health insurance have been offered to the public by insurance companies. The policies provide for hospitalization and in some cases surgery; they have helped to bring health services within the financial reach of many more people. Some, however, cannot buy this insurance because poor health makes them uninsurable.

In his administration President Truman proposed that a national system of health insurance be set up. Several of the states were thinking along this line, too. In Washington, Oscar Ewing prepared a report on the state of the health of the nation. He stated that half of the people of the country live in families whose income is not more than $3,000 a year and that these families cannot afford adequate medical care. With such care purveyed as it is at the present, Mr. Ewing claimed that only about 20 per cent of our population can afford it. He outlined a plan for national insurance to be operated through the Social Security Agency. This would reach about 85,000,000 people at the outset and could be enlarged later to reach almost all of our population.

The plan for national health insurance was immediately attacked on a wide front by many of the doctors of the country, and the American Medical Association in particular. It was called "socialized medicine." Perhaps this was partly due to the fact that the Socialist Government of England had adopted such a plan. There it was costing the government about one billion dollars a year, but far more people were receiving medical care than ever before. The chief fears expressed by the medical profession in this country were that doctors would be working for the government and would lose their independence, that they could be sent anywhere the government felt they were needed, that they must accept any patients that came to them, and that their incomes would be reduced.

It is not our purpose here to argue either for or against a program of national health insurance. The problem, however, is a national one. For the welfare of our people we as a nation need to make available adequate medical facilities for all at a cost that anyone can afford. If this can be done through private agencies, it should be done. If it cannot or is not, almost certainly we can expect government to enter the picture and see that it is done.

EXTENSION OF SOCIAL SECURITY

All Groups Are Not Covered. The extension of Social Security is another problem that will demand your attention. At the present not nearly all of our people come under its provisions. The tendency will be to enlarge the scope of its coverage until everyone is protected against penniless old age.

Social Security has been attacked as undermining the moral fiber of people by encouraging their dependence upon government and making them less likely to save for independence in the years after they quit working. The facts do not seem to support this contention. Social Security recognizes two situations that most people now accept as true: (1) While it is certainly desirable, many people cannot or will not save

sufficiently, during the years they are earning, to care for themselves when their earning years are past; therefore, a program by which small amounts are regularly withheld from their pay checks and held for future use is a service to them. (2) The provision under the present law that requires employers also to contribute along with employees is a recognition of the moral obligation of an employer to assist with the welfare of his employees after they have ceased working for him because they have given to his business the productive years of their lives. This humanitarian concept of working and earning, if extended to the rest of our population, can bring us to the day when charity homes for aged are a thing of the past and when people can enjoy the later years of their lives in financial security and independence. And the Social Security program need not in any way prevent a person from saving on his own initiative. In an increasing number of cases, this problem is being met through industrial and professional pension systems set up by the co-operative effort of both employer and employee. Each contributes to a fund while the employee is working, and a pension is paid from the fund to the employee when he retires. As American free enterprise expands this program, the need for Social Security naturally declines. Greater acceptance of this responsibility by private business reduces the need for government participation.

THE ELECTORAL COLLEGE

Reforms in Election of President. Another matter that will require your attention is the reform of our system of electing the President of the United

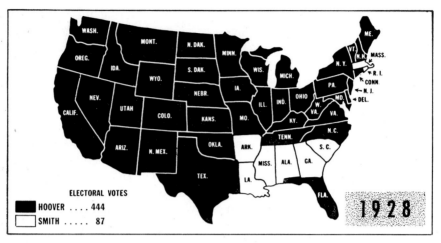

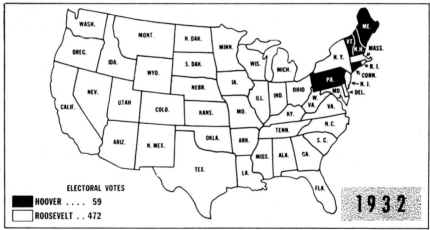

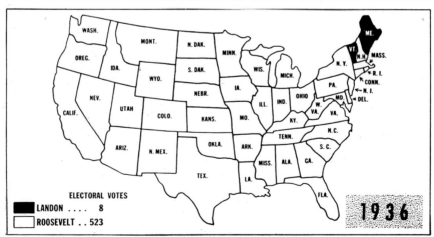

U.S. News & World Report (11–12–48). © *U.S. News Pub. Corp.*

THE ELECTORAL VOTE—STATE BY STATE, 1928–1936

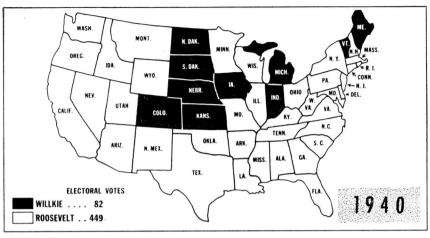

ELECTORAL VOTES
WILLKIE 82
ROOSEVELT .. 449

1940

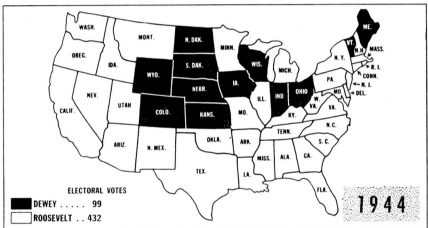

ELECTORAL VOTES
DEWEY 99
ROOSEVELT .. 432

1944

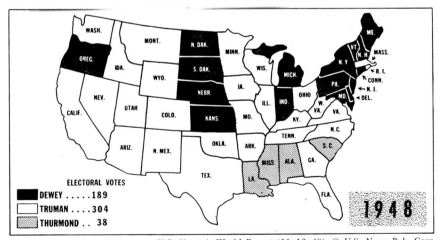

ELECTORAL VOTES
DEWEY 189
TRUMAN 304
THURMOND .. 38

1948

U S. News & World Report (11–12–48). © U.S. News Pub. Corp.

THE ELECTORAL VOTE—STATE BY STATE, 1940–1948

States. At the present, under the system set up by our Constitution, our people vote for electors, who, in turn, elect the President and the Vice-President. There is a historical reason for the establishment of this system.

When our country was founded, political democracy was not very far advanced. People generally were not well educated and certainly were not familiar with the problems of operating a national government. The Founding Fathers of the American Constitution knew these facts well, so they did not believe that the people could exercise good judgment in selecting their President. Also, transportation and communication were such that it was practically impossible for the people every place in the country to know the men who were candidates for high public office. There were no radios, no newsreels, no airplanes, no television, no cross-country transportation of any kind, and very few newspapers.

Under these circumstances, it was sensible to have people vote for men they knew and trusted. These men, then, were in a position to select a good President and Vice-President because they were usually leaders who knew men of high integrity who would serve the nation well.

In early days no names of Presidential candidates appeared on the ballots. Instead, a slate of electors was voted upon. Today, in general, that procedure is reversed. When a voter puts a cross beside the name of a Presidential candidate, he actually is not voting for that candidate but for the group of state electors who are supposed, in turn, to vote for the man to whom they are pledged. There is considerable feeling that this system should be changed and that every voter should be permitted to vote directly for the candidate of his choice.

Many people feel that other changes should be made also. Each state has as many electoral votes as it has members in both houses of Congress. At the present, under the unit rule, a state's total electoral vote goes to the candidate whose electors get more votes than any other party's electors. That means that the winning candidate does not need a majority of the people's votes. For example, in a state where three parties are fairly equal in strength, it would be possible for a candidate to get all the electoral votes of that state if his party received as few as 34 per cent of the popular vote cast.

This has happened on a national scale. Abraham Lincoln had far less than a majority of the popular vote, but he piled up a big electoral college majority. Rutherford B. Hayes won only 48.5 per cent of the popular vote in 1876, but he became President. In the 1944 election the Democrats had only about a 3½ million plurality in the popular vote, but Franklin Roosevelt got 432 electoral votes to Thomas Dewey's 99.

Digging deeper into the facts of that 1944 Presidential election reveals some very interesting information. A 1.7 per cent plurality in the popular vote in Illinois gave the state's 28 electoral votes to the Democrats. In Michigan the Democrats won by only 11,000 votes, which is only one-half of one per cent. In Ohio the Republicans got 25 electoral votes on the basis of a plurality of just 5,000 votes. That means that in 1944, of the 47½ million people who voted, a few more than 5,000 controlled one-tenth of the electoral votes needed to elect a President. And that 5,000 could just as easily have been 1,000 or 100, or even one vote—any-

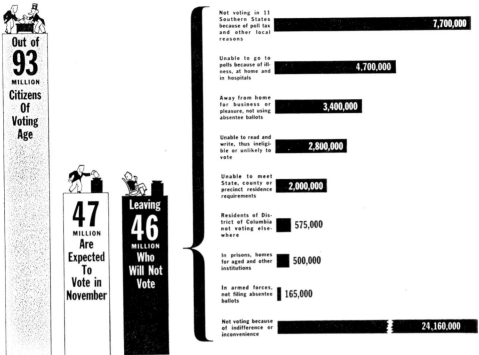

Out of
93
MILLION
Citizens
Of
Voting
Age

47 MILLION Are Expected To Vote in November

Leaving **46** MILLION Who Will Not Vote

Not voting in 11 Southern States because of poll tax and other local reasons	7,700,000
Unable to go to polls because of illness, at home and in hospitals	4,700,000
Away from home for business or pleasure, not using absentee ballots	3,400,000
Unable to read and write, thus ineligible or unlikely to vote	2,800,000
Unable to meet State, county or precinct residence requirements	2,000,000
Residents of District of Columbia not voting elsewhere	575,000
In prisons, homes for aged and other institutions	500,000
In armed forces, not filing absentee ballots	165,000
Not voting because of indifference or inconvenience	24,160,000

U.S. News & World Report (10–15–48). © U.S. News Pub. Corp.

WHY PEOPLE DON'T GO TO THE POLLS

This drawing was a pre-election forecast in 1948. It was published before the Presidential election, and it proved quite accurate in its estimate of the number of people who actually failed to vote. Nonvoting is recognized as a grave threat to government by democratic process.

body's. Perhaps the system needs to be changed, but until it is, the fellow who says, "Why should I vote? My vote won't count" just doesn't know the facts. Yet there is a marked apathy on the part of citizens when it comes to going to the polls on election day. Look in the above chart at the figures for the 1948 election.

In the United States there are more than 90 million citizens of voting age. Only half of them voted in 1948.

HOW TO PRESERVE DEMOCRACY

Co-operative Effort Is Necessary. In the United States today, if our democracy is in danger, the biggest enemy it has is this indifference of our people to the problems of governing ourselves.

Sometimes it appears that the dollar sign is about to replace the eagle as the symbol of America. We have become such a wealthy nation that many of our people have acquired the idea, unconsciously perhaps, that money is the solution to all problems. We seem to think that we can buy our way out of every difficulty.

But paying our taxes and making contributions to the Community Chest and the Red Cross are not all there is to democratic citizenship. We can neither buy nor inherit freedom. Freedom is the reward of hard and persistent work.

Nor is freedom the license to infringe upon the rights of others. General Omar N. Bradley says, "It is im-

THE CONSTITUTION GUARANTEES A FREE PRESS

The unhampered right to print the truth is an American tradition. It grew from a firm belief by the early founders of our nation that a universally free press is indispensable to a self-governing people—that a press that is muzzled or controlled denies the people a chance to make intelligent decisions.

moral for us to claim freedom of the ballot unless we are ready to share that freedom with every other American. It is ungodly for us to claim freedom of religion, unless we are prepared to be tolerant of all beliefs that differ from ours. It is hypocritical to insist upon freedom of opinion unless we grant equal freedom to those who oppose us. And it is fraudulent to insist upon freedom of the press if we deny that right to others. Democratic institutions will continue to prosper and flourish only so long as they are fed on freedom for all, not on abridgment for some."

Life under a democratic system is much harder than under a dictatorship or any other kind of system. It requires

co-operation and generosity. If we don't want a "leader" telling us what to do, we must work together to solve our own problems. And it is much harder to live for democracy than to die for it. It requires more courage to think for oneself and to stand bravely by his own convictions before criticism than to face enemy guns in the heat of battle. Much is said and done in the name of "Americanism" and "patriotism" that does not represent our best thinking or our most honest judgment. Good democratic citizenship calls for adequate background information, plus straight thinking in terms of the greatest welfare for the greatest number.

A democracy cannot be defeated. It

can only defeat itself. Your land and mine will never fall because of the weight of attack from without. Its failure can result only from indifference within. This is the "fifth column" against which we must always be on guard.

You know many examples of lack of interest in governmental affairs. Here's just one. In a small town in Texas an election was held to decide whether or not the school tax rate should be raised from $1.00 to $1.50. If the new rate were not approved, the school district would suffer a loss in state aid. Possibly the length of the school term would have to be shortened. There are 774 people in the town. Only 15 persons voted. Seven were for the raise; eight were against it. Parents discovered the next morning that their children would pay directly the price for their fathers' and mothers' indifference. Lack of interest is always expensive.

As a nation of people, we seem inclined to judge everything on the basis of its dollars and cents value. On every hand you hear the question, "What's in it for me?" An eminent psychologist has described a young person of the present generation this way: "He is healthier, better schooled, and more adept at learning than his brother of the previous generation. He is also undisciplined, jealously aware of his rights but not of his responsibilities. Moreover, he is mercenary and antagonistic to authority in almost any form." Right or wrong, this obviously is a charge that deserves serious consideration on the part of all young people.

Unfortunately, the same kind of indictment can be levied against far too many of our older citizens. This condition is a symptom that can develop into something serious. When we are more interested in what government can do for us (what there is in it for us) than we are concerned about our responsibilities under the democratic system, we have set the stage for the seizure of government by that person or group that will promise us the most. Such dictatorship can be very efficient in getting things done, but only at the sacrifice of personal rights and freedom. If we want to preserve democracy, we shall all have to work together to make it as efficient as dictatorship, so that we shall be impervious to the suggestion of would-be rulers that they will provide all the things we cannot provide for ourselves in return for our giving up the rights we do enjoy.

"Democracy," to quote General Bradley again, "is a two-way street; with its benefits comes the necessity for also giving service . . . A nation's strength is not to be found in its treasury statements. It lies instead in the national character of its people, in their willingness to sacrifice leisure, comfort, and a share of their talents for the welfare of the nation of which they are part.

"Self-government is not a luxury on which men may grow fat and indulgent. Rather it is an instrument by which men can—if they have the wisdom—safeguard their individual freedom and employ that freedom in pursuit of happiness and fair reward for their ingenuity, labor, and intellect. Because self-government is weighted as heavily with obligation as it is with privilege.

"Our democracy is much like a tall stand of timber. We cannot cut from it more than we plant in it without periling its survival. And forests—like gardens—cannot be bought. They must be cultivated by toil and nourished by the sweat of those who would keep them."

Actually, when it's all boiled down, there are only two kinds of government in the world. In one, the people exist to support and do the bidding of an all-powerful ruling group. In the other, an organization has been created by the people to do their bidding. The role of government in a democracy should be clear. It must provide enough political control, and only enough, to guarantee to the people the right to rule themselves—that is, to protect them from government by pressure groups who might be inclined to operate the country for their own selfish interests instead of for the welfare of all. Government under a democracy must also provide enough economic control to guarantee equality of opportunity for all our people.

Democracy can never become static. It must move either forward or backward. American democracy will continue as long as it produces more and still more democracy—more and more freedom and happiness for more and more people. Keeping our democracy progressive is not a simple task. It calls for the best knowledge, wisdom, and judgment we individually and collectively can muster. We must be well informed, unbiased in our thinking, always fair in our opinions. This is our job—yours and mine—if we are to be good democratic citizens.

FOR YOUR REVIEW

These Should Be Easy For You Now

1. Why has the federal government become the biggest business in the United States today?
2. What is bureaucracy?
3. What is meant by deficit spending? What is the theory behind it? Why did the United States adopt a program of deficit spending? Why have we been unable to stop?
4. Explain the two opposing viewpoints concerning the national debt.
5. What is the "pay as you earn" income tax plan?
6. How much does our federal government cost?
7. Point out the opposing viewpoints regarding the constant expansion of government services.
8. State in your own words the five big problems of government listed in this chapter.
9. How large is our national crime bill each year?
10. What factors do you think are involved in juvenile delinquency? In crime in general?
11. What do you think is the proper attitude one should have toward laws and regulations?
12. How has the position of the home changed in American life? With what effects?
13. What is the status of housing in the United States today?
14. Investigate on your own and find out the facts regarding the need for better medical attention and care in the United States. Report your findings to your class. Then discuss as a class how you think this need might best be met. What

arguments can you advance against a program of national health insurance? For such a program?
15. Why do we have our present electoral system? What is it? How do you think it might be bettered?
16. What do you think are dangers to democracy? What can you do to further political democracy in this country of ours?

Associated Dates

1919—Eighteenth Amendment adopted
1933—Twenty-First Amendment adopted (repealing the Eighteenth)

Why Are These To Be Remembered?

Bureaucracy	Juvenile delinquency	Al Capone
Deficit spending	"Socialized medicine"	Oscar Ewing

Suggested Readings

PAGE, ELIZABETH, *The Tree of Liberty*
  Study of American democracy
ADAMS, J. T., *The Living Jefferson*
  Jefferson's concept of democracy
MOSES, BELLE, *John Marshall*
  His interpretation of the United States Constitution

KERSEY, V., and WALKER, E. E., *Our National Constitution*
SCHLESINGER, ARTHUR M., *Age of Jackson*
  Industrial and economic forces of Jackson's time
SCHLESINGER, ARTHUR M., *New Deal in Action*

The United States Moves toward Economic Democracy

INTRODUCTION

In the beginning, naturally the livelihood of the people of the United States stemmed from agriculture, and the desire for more and better land had a great deal to do with the settlement of the West. In the course of this expansion, America became a land of small farms and large cattle ranches, privately owned, but there was no continuation of the big estates and the feudal system that long prevailed in Europe.

While the country was still quite young, the Industrial Revolution spread to its shores. The growth of an industrial system has been faster in the United States than anywhere else in the world. The country was early divided into sections by the change from home to factory production, and this division helped to bring on the War between the States. Today, the United States is the greatest industrial nation in the world. Our ability to produce manufactured goods has brought us many benefits and, at the same time, some very perplexing problems.

With the growth of industrial production, big business has become a power in the United States, both economically and politically. More recently, big business has been joined by big labor as a force in American life. In the beginning, business was dominant, with labor looked upon as a necessary raw material of production. Gradually, the scale was tipped the other way, and labor came to exert great power. Now, at mid-century, it looks as if a way has been found to permit the two to work together for the common good of the American people.

Just as American democracy must produce more and more democracy if it is to survive, so American capitalism must produce more and more capitalists—sharers in American business—if it is to survive. Some of the most important, yet troublesome, problems you will be called upon to deal with are those that grow out of our attempt to find the proper relationship that should exist among big business, big labor, and big government. But deal with them you must—or give up the right to a part in your own government and permit someone else to solve your problems for you, with the loss of at least a part of your freedom.

Chapter 23
The Land Builds the United States

THE SEARCH FOR MORE AND BETTER LAND HELPS TO EXPAND THE
UNITED STATES ACROSS THE CONTINENT

Who Should Own the Land? Colonial America was, of course, an agricultural America. There was as yet no mechanized industry, and agriculture was the most direct means of providing a living. So life in early America was tied up closely with the soil.

Very early the question of who should own the land presented itself. Behind the colonists who came to the New World from Europe was the tradition of large estates, a carry-over from the days of feudalism, when great tracts of land belonged to feudal lords, whose sole duty was to protect the vassals and serfs who tilled the land for them. This system meant widely separated classes —the land or estate owners at one extreme, and the farmers, who owned nothing and had no opportunity to buy since there were no small farms, at the other.

So the question arose: What plan of land-holding should prevail in America? In most of the colonies the land was granted by the king to some company or person, so there was an excellent opportunity for a continuation of the European system. In those colonies, operated under a proprietor, this feudal system was set up. In the North the large estates were called manors, just as they had been in Europe in the early Middle Ages. In the South they were called plantations, and Negro slaves

were imported from Africa to do the work done by the serfs on the feudal estates of Europe a thousand years earlier. In true feudal fashion, the rent collected on these manors and plantations went to the owners, who in the beginning, as we have said, were the proprietors of the colonies. In the crown colonies, this rent went to the king of England. Even when land was sold, either by the proprietors or the king's agents, it was still subject to an annual payment also, which was called "quit-rent." This practice was another source of dissatisfaction with the mother country.

The plan the settlers liked most permitted each to own outright a piece of land. This was natural, too, since almost all phases of the settlement of America carried some form of opposition to conditions in Europe. And in America there was plenty of land and a scarcity of settlers. Little by little, this plan of making it possible for every person who wanted it to own a farm of his own came to be the accepted procedure in America. Many settlers even refused to come unless they were guaranteed ownership of land. Thus private ownership of individual farms became the basis of our present great agricultural system.

It is interesting to note in passing that at both Jamestown and the Plym-

334

outh settlement, and in a few others, communism was tried. There the settlers were supposed to work for the welfare of the colony. No one owned any land, but all were to share alike in the crop they produced. The plan didn't work. There were too many lazy people who insisted upon sharing equally in the produce but who were unwilling to do their share of the work necessary to raise the crops. Finally things became so bad in Jamestown that Captain John Smith was forced to issue his famous "no work, no food" edict.

Before long most of the big estates of the North were broken up into small farms, but the plantations of the South continued. In fact, this plantation system was partly responsible for the North becoming industrialized while the South remained an agricultural area. The South sold directly to England, and in large quantities, at first chiefly tobacco and later cotton. Many of the manufactured articles the people needed were produced by hand right on the plantations. But since farming in the North was more of an individual matter rather than a collective project, trading cities grew up there to supply the people with goods they were unable to make for themselves. This lack of self-sufficiency made for greater trading in the North than in the South, and the cities of the North provided ready-made locations for the new factories when the Industrial Revolution spread to this country.

THE WESTWARD MOVEMENT

Motives for Westward Movement. The next phase of the building of America after the Revolution had won our freedom from England was the westward movement that carried settlers

from the Atlantic seaboard all the way across the continent to the Pacific Ocean. One of the big motives behind this westward movement was the desire for more and better land. Along with this driving force went the love of adventure and the desire to get away from the growing complexity of life in the East—to be free to do as one pleased in the great spaces of the West. That this westward movement is still continuing is shown by the location of the center of our population.[1]

1790—23 miles east of Baltimore
1800—about 40 miles to the west
1850—nearly 250 miles farther west
1900—6 miles southeast of Columbus, Indiana
1940—2 miles southeast by east of Carlisle, Indiana
1950—at Illinois-Indiana boundary near bottom of Wabash River

Land for Sale. The treaty with Great Britain in 1783 at the close of the American Revolution gave the new United States full rights to all land west to the Mississippi River. But this land could not be occupied until the claims of the various states had been settled and the land was surveyed and mapped. One by one the states gave up their long-standing claims to this land, and the Northwest Ordinance of 1787 provided for the government of part of the region. Eventually all British troops were withdrawn and United States troops sent in.

Here again the wealthy person and the adventurer had an advantage. Congress, anxious to sell land to pay off the national debt, set the price at $2 per acre, but put no limit on the amount of land one could buy. Furthermore, purchase was permitted on the install-

[1] *World Almanac.*

CONESTOGA WAGON—FREIGHT CARRIER OF THE NINETEENTH CENTURY

For many years during the nineteenth century, shippers used rugged "Conestogas" to haul freight between eastern cities—the trip from Philadelphia to Pittsburgh was made in twenty days—and hardy pioneers drove them across plains and mountains to new settlements in the West. The sway-back design of the Conestoga wagon's body was intended to reduce shifting of cargo while the vehicle was in motion. The broad wheels were made to travel in soft soils and across prairies.

ment plan. Speculators could buy huge areas of land for a few thousand dollars down and pay the installments out of their receipts from sales. Later (1821) installment buying of land was stopped and the price lowered to $1.25 an acre, which still permitted moderately wealthy people to get control of lots of land. But even a small farmer could buy 160 acres for $200, and many did. Also, it was difficult to get settlers for the large areas individually held, and they gradually were broken up. The United States was to be a land of relatively small farms.

And so the settlers came. From the New England states they came, happy to exchange the rocky farms they had tried to cultivate for the rich soil of the West. From the South they came, and even from the countries of Europe. The hunter, trapper, and adventurer came first, then the farmer and his hardy wife, to cut the trees and build their own home with the logs, to clear the land for crops, and to convert a wild country into the fertile farms of our Midwest. Over the eastern mountain ranges and into the West crept the long queues of Conestoga wagons; down the Ohio

River floated the boats and rafts that carried the pioneers to new frontiers of growing America. And into the history of America the well-known names of trail-blazers found their way: men like Daniel Boone, Kit Carson, and George Rogers Clark.

The purchase of Louisiana in 1803 opened to settlement all the land between the Mississippi River and the Rocky Mountains. The settlers who later became known as Mormons were the first big group to migrate into this area. They were a religious group who had first organized in New York as the Church of Jesus Christ of Latter Day Saints, but persecution there had forced them to move westward to Missouri and Illinois. Persecution followed them, and again they were driven from their homes. At the death of their founder, Joseph Smith, many of them accepted the leadership of Brigham Young and set out across the great stretches of the West, finally arriving in Utah in 1847, where they founded Salt Lake City. The gold discovered in California the following year provided a powerful magnet that drew settlers in droves to the Pacific coast. But gold was not the only valuable resource of the West. Soon the earth was yielding silver, copper, iron, coal, and timber in Montana, Colorado, Nevada, Utah, Wyoming, Arizona, Idaho, and other parts of the West.

There, in the West, the real foundation of American democracy was laid. Among the settlers the people were equal, with the exception of the slaves in the South. Pioneer life had a great leveling influence. People learned unselfish co-operation because their livelihood, and sometimes their lives, depended upon it. They were rough and

DANIEL BOONE

The intrepid frontiersman who opened Kentucky's wilderness to settlement is shown here as he appeared in his later years, when an artist painted his portrait.

sometimes crude, simple and unreserved, but they learned how to get along with one another and to work together, which is probably the most important lesson anyone can learn to become a real democratic citizen. These people were not going to stand by for long and see the East elect the nation's leaders. In 1828 they sent one of their own number—Andrew Jackson —to the White House.

The War between the States brought a pause in the westward movement, but after that unfortunate war was over, the migration to the Pacific began anew. Railroad companies had been given large tracts of land by the government to encourage them to ex-

BRIGHAM YOUNG AND HIS FOLLOWERS REACH THE GREAT SALT LAKE

Led by the resolute Brigham Young, the Mormons migrated three-quarters of the way across the continent, and found their "promised land" in the Utah desert. There, beside a lake of salt water, they built a community that grew into a great city—the capital of the forty-fifth state to enter the Union.

Woodward Governor Company

THE IRON HORSE

More than any other means of transportation, the railroads promoted the growth of commerce and industry, and helped to knit the nation into closer union. Sketched above is a locomotive of the type common during the Civil War period—an early version of the "Iron Horse" that played a key role in developing the West.

tend the trails of the "iron horse" to the new settlements of the West. The companies then sold land cheap in order to get settlers to move into the right-of-way of a projected railroad line. The Homestead Act of 1862 gave 160 acres of land to anyone who paid a small fee and lived on the farm for five years. Even the five-year rule was waived for veterans of the war to help them get a new start. Settlement was rapid. As an area acquired a large enough population and established a satisfactory government, it usually applied for admission to the Union as a new state. The story of the settlement of the West can be rather easily traced in a list of the states and the dates they were admitted to the Union.

The original 13 states:
    Delaware—1787
    Pennsylvania—1787
    New Jersey—1787
    Georgia—1788
    Connecticut—1788
    Massachusetts—1788
    Maryland—1788
    South Carolina—1788
    New Hampshire—1788
    Virginia—1788
    New York—1788
    North Carolina—1789
    Rhode Island—1790
Entry of the remaining states:
    Vermont—1791
    Kentucky—1792
    Tennessee—1796
    Ohio—1803
    Louisiana—1812
    Indiana—1816
    Mississippi—1817
    Illinois—1818
    Alabama—1819
    Maine—1820

Missouri—1821
Arkansas—1836
Michigan—1837
Florida—1845
Texas—1845
Iowa—1846
Wisconsin—1848
California—1850
Minnesota—1858
Oregon—1859
Kansas—1861
West Virginia—1863
Nevada—1864
Nebraska—1867
Colorado—1876
North Dakota—1889
South Dakota—1889
Montana—1889
Washington—1889
Idaho—1890
Wyoming—1890
Utah—1896
Oklahoma—1907
New Mexico—1912
Arizona—1912

Bettmann Archive

THE INDIANS FOUGHT TO RETAIN THEIR ANCESTRAL LANDS

When white pioneers began to stream into the West in ever-increasing numbers, the Indians saw their last great land domain being invaded, and gave fierce resistance. The westward-bound emigrants, in order to better defend themselves, often formed large wagon trains for long journeys overland. Before the bloody struggle for territory was over, the Indians had attacked many such expeditions. The red men, in turn, suffered counterattacks, and were finally crowded back into remote sections of the country.

BEEF ON THE HOOF HEADED FOR THE MARKET

Cattle raising became a major industry in the West as settlers moved west to the lands beyond the Mississippi. Longhorns were branded and turned loose to roam the open country. After round-ups, stockmen had to organize and run long cattle drives in order to get their animals to market, because the railroads were far distant from the western ranches and ranges. The above reproduction of a painting by Norman Price shows cowboys driving a huge herd across a river en route to a railhead in Kansas where buyers paid cash for livestock.

White Man Takes Over. In the process of carving states out of the West, gradually the Indians were pushed aside, but not without some violence. Finally, as the "white" man moved in and took over completely, the "red" men were grouped on reservations. Actually, the passing of the buffalo caused them to accept this new life rather willingly. In 1924 Congress granted full American citizenship to all American Indians, but our treatment of the original inhabitants of what we now call our country has often been a source of shame. Frequently we have found ourselves spending more for the welfare of people in other parts of the world than we have, even in proportion, for those whose land we took over as we built America from coast to coast.

Days of "Wild and Woolly West." As the railroads pushed westward across the great plains, cattle and sheep raising became the big business, for the railroads provided access to markets in the East. American legend and literature contain many stories of the cowboys who drove the cattle from the ranches across the plains to the nearest railroad, as from the great ranches of Texas up to the railroad in Kansas. These men were a law unto themselves, enforcing it with the six-guns they wore. Those were the days of the "wild and woolly West," with its open ranges, its cattle rustlers, its hard-riding bandits, and occasionally a champion of law and order like the Lone Ranger. But gradually the open ranges were fenced, and farmers moved in and began irrigation projects to turn the dry prairies and desert lands into fertile fields. The huge herds of cattle became greatly reduced in size, and the picturesque cowboy was soon on his way out.

New Problems Arise. By 1890 almost all of the free land was gone. The extension of America to its con-

tinental limits had brought new problems. Factory workers in the East who were dissatisfied could no longer leave the factories and move to free land in the West. This meant new attention had to be given to the problems of industry and the organization of labor. And as free land became a thing of the past, our government was faced with the undeniable need for practicing conservation. The Reclamation Act of 1902 made available federal funds for the building of irrigation canals and dams to store up water, such as the Roosevelt and Hoover Dam. In recent years we have made great progress, too, in reforestation and in the protection of our other natural resources. Farmers have become more and more conscious of the great cost of erosion and have,

Chicago Historical Society

WESTWARD THE COURSE OF EMPIRE TOOK ITS WAY

By ship and river boat, on horseback, riding stage coaches and wagons, via railroad—by one means of transportation or another—American pioneers spread across the continent and settled the land from ocean to ocean.

with government help, begun a concerted attack on it.

So the land was responsible for the great westward movement that carried settlers from the East all the way across the continent to the Pacific Coast. And wherever he went, the American farmer carved out of the wilderness a little niche that was all his own, his home and the source of his livelihood and independence. And wherever large areas of land were held by a few people, both the national and state governments took steps to break up these big estates and make the land available to the people who still wanted it. Thus, so far as ownership of land was concerned, economic democracy followed the American farmer as he built America westward across the continent.

FOR YOUR REVIEW

These Should Be Easy for You Now

1. What system of land holding was used in the proprietary colonies in Colonial America? What system appealed most to the colonists?
2. What experience did the early colonists have with Communism? Why?
3. How was the early agricultural development of the North and South partly responsible for the North later becoming chiefly an industrial area and the South remaining agricultural?
4. What were the reasons for the westward movement across North America?
5. What did the Northwest Ordinance provide for?
6. What inducement did the government offer to get settlers to go west? How did they travel?
7. Who were the Mormons? Where did they first organize? Where did they finally settle?
8. For what new reason did settlers suddenly move in large numbers to California?
9. How was the frontier a good training ground for democratic living?
10. What new impetus to the westward movement came after the War between the States?
11. When was your state admitted to the Union? If you are not familiar with the history of your state, it would be worth your while to get some books on the subject and inform yourself on it.
12. What is the status of the American Indian today?
13. What became the chief occupations of the West?
14. What new problems were created for the nation when the frontier had been pushed to the Pacific Coast?
15. How did the development of agricultural America represent true economic democracy?

Associated Dates

1787—Ordinance creating the Northwest Territory passed
1803—Louisiana purchased from France
1804–1806—exploration of the Northwest by Lewis and Clark
1846—the Mormons migrate to Utah
1849—gold rush to California
1862—Homestead Act
1902—Reclamation Act
1924—citizenship granted to American Indians

Why Are These To Be Remembered?

Daniel Boone	Feudal system	Quitrent
Kit Carson	Serf	Erosion
George Rogers Clark	Manor	Conservation
Mormons	Plantations	Conestoga wagon
Brigham Young		

Chapter 24

The Industrial Revolution Transforms the United States

THE SHIFT FROM HOME PRODUCTION TO FACTORY PRODUCTION
BRINGS GREAT CHANGES IN AMERICAN LIFE

Colonial Trade and Manufacturing.
Even though agriculture was the principal business in Colonial America, trade and manufacturing were increasing. Here we are using the term "manufacture" in its original meaning, which was "to make by hand." For the people of Colonial days had none of the machines that play such large parts in our lives today. Most goods were made in the home. As life became more settled, more goods were produced, and soon there was enough to permit exports from colony to colony. New England sent wool and linen cloth to the southern colonies and even to the West Indies. New England also produced many iron utensils and articles for the home, for building, and for ships. Shipbuilding became an important industry in New England, as did fishing.

Soon the colonies were exporting their products to other countries, and their trade came to rival that of the countries of Europe. From New England went flour, fish, furs, and iron products. The central colonies sent flour, grain, lumber, and furs. The South exported tobacco, rice, lumber, and tar. In exchange for these articles the colonies imported manufactured articles from Europe and tea and other goods from "the Indies" by way of England. From the near-by West Indies came sugar and molasses, and from Africa, slaves. In this foreign trade, and also in trade within the colonies, certain towns became important as marketing centers. Among them were Philadelphia, Boston, New York, and Charleston, South Carolina.

Little advance had been made in manufacturing or transportation for thousands of years before the founding of America. Man's biggest development in transportation had been made when he tamed animals and trained them to carry him upon their backs. But Paul Revere had no better means of transportation at his command than had the knights of the Middle Ages. The same condition existed in manufacturing.

It was true that in home manufacture, some people proved more adept at making certain articles than others. Take shoes, for example. Some man found by experience that he had a "knack" for making shoes, and soon he was taking orders to make them for his neighbors, accepting in payment goods that he himself didn't have time to make because he was too busy making shoes. Perhaps he even set up a shop as a cobbler. Others who became especially skilled at making other articles did the same in the trading

344

centers that were already developing. But it was a slow process, at best.

INDUSTRIALIZATION

Era of Inventions. Then, shortly after the middle of the eighteenth century, something happened in England that was to change the course of history, perhaps more than any other single event ever has. An Englishman by the name of James Hargreaves was helping his wife with her spinning. Accidentally, he knocked over her spinning wheel. As it lay on its side on the floor, the wheel still turning, an idea was born in the mind of James Hargreaves. He went to his workshop and, in time, turned out a new kind of spinning wheel—one that he improved until it would spin not one but eight threads at the same time and with the same effort that had previously produced only one. He called it the "spinning jenny" in honor of his wife. The Industrial Revolution had begun.

One invention always leads to another. Soon Edmund Cartwright had applied water power to a loom in order to weave faster and keep up with the increased production of thread from the spinning jenny. This helped some, but the big advance came when the steam engine, made practical by James Watt, was used to supply power for the new machines.

In America, Robert Fulton put

Titusville Herald, Kaywoodie Company

THE WORLD'S FIRST OIL WELL WAS DRILLED IN PENNSYLVANIA

The development of petroleum resources has spurred scientific and industrial progress in the United States. It was Titusville, Pennsylvania, in 1859, that two Americans brought in the world's first oil well. E. L. Drake and William Smith had been drilling for water when they hit oil at a depth of sixty-nine feet—the shallowest strike ever made. Once it became known how to get oil, practical men lost little time in devising ways to use it.

John Hancock Mutual Life Insurance Co.

ELI WHITNEY—HE MADE INDEPENDENCE ON AN ASSEMBLY LINE

Eli Whitney saw American boys marching off to fight for their independence . . . with foreign guns. He watched his neighbors going to church in their Sunday best . . . made of foreign cloth. And he decided such things wouldn't do. So he tinkered. He tinkered with a little wooden box and a spool of brass wire—and they became the cotton gin. He arranged gears and levers and rolls of drawing paper—and he manufactured American guns with standard parts that could be interchanged at any time. He thus established the basic pattern for mass production in American industry. With a few tools and a wealth of ideas, he contributed his great share to the economic independence of his country.

Watt's steam engine into a boat called the "Clermont" and traveled from New York to Albany, a distance of 150 miles, in 32 hours in 1807. In 1838 the "Great Western" made the first trip across the Atlantic by steam power.

In England, George Stephenson applied Watt's engine to a railroad by making the first practical locomotive. An American, Eli Whitney, invented the cotton gin, a machine for pulling the seeds from cotton bolls, and so boomed the production of cotton in the South. Later, in manufacturing guns, Whitney developed the principle of interchangeable parts that make possible our present-day mass production. Elias Howe brought out his sewing machine in 1846. And so it went. For a longer list of these men who contributed much to the industrial development of the United States (see Chapter 16).

The Industrial Revolution started in England, as we have noted. England was quick to recognize the importance of the new inventions. At the beginning she had a monopoly on them, and she wanted to keep it, for reasons we'll delve into more a little later in this chapter. To keep her monopoly, she passed laws against taking machines or plans for machines out of the country. But Samuel Slater worked for several years in mills in England and then came to America and built this country's first cotton thread spinning mill at Pawtucket, Rhode Island, entirely from memory, in 1793. In 1814 Francis Cabot Lowell was responsible for building at Waltham, Massachusetts, a factory housing all the machinery for spinning thread and weaving it into cloth. It was the first such complete factory in the United States, perhaps in the world. This factory was a direct result of the War of 1812. During that war, Congress passed the Non-Intercourse and Embargo Acts which almost completely stopped all foreign trade and drove the people of New England from the sea as a means of their livelihood. It was then that they became interested in the textile industry. More factories were built, and New England became an industrial center.

Improvements in Transportation and Communication. The Industrial Revolution spread westward across the continent, as had agriculture. Although

Bettmann Archive

THE GENERAL STORE CAME TO THE CUSTOMER

Merchandising enterprise prompted the traveling peddler to bring manufactured wares to rural homes and frontier farms before the days of shopping in town.

WHEN TRAVELING AFLOAT BEAT TRAVELING ON WHEELS

Inland waterways became the first arteries of commerce in the United States. During the early years of the Republic, passengers and goods, especially heavy cargoes, could be moved more cheaply and conveniently by ship or barge than by any other available means of transportation. Canals were built to connect natural waterways, and shipowners increased regular schedules of service along rivers and on the Great Lakes. Not until extensive railroad lines had been built and could offer speedier transportation did water-borne carriers face competition to be reckoned with. The scene above depicts a flatboat traveling along the Erie Canal a century ago. This famous canal stretches a distance of some 350 miles in New York state, between Albany and Buffalo.

the West could be settled by people who made their slow way over the mountains and through a wilderness, it could not be industrialized until better means of transportation were developed. Transportation in the East was greatly improved by the building of a new type of rock-covered road called a turnpike. Such all-weather roads were a great boon to farmers and merchants who wanted to get goods to markets. Then Congress authorized the construction of the National, or Cumberland, Road. The starting point was Cumberland, Maryland, and the first section was completed in 1818. Eventually 834 miles of this road were built, stretching all the way to Vandalia, an early capital of Illinois, in 1852.

As the West was settled, too much of its produce was being carried down the Ohio and the Mississippi rivers by steamboat to New Orleans to suit the industrialists of the East. So a new means of transportation came into vogue. Many canals were built. Among the best known was the Erie Canal (1825), between Albany and Buffalo, New York, connecting the Atlantic Ocean and the Great Lakes. The Pennsylvania Canal tied the Atlantic and the Ohio River together. For several years canals were built in various parts of the East and the Northwest, greatly facilitating trade and the settlement of new areas.

But before many years, the railroads had almost put the canals out of business. Railroads were cheaper to build than canals, and transportation on them was faster. The added speed compensated for the higher cost. Already the tempo of American life was beginning to pick up speed. By 1860 the railroads had reached from New York all the way to Chicago and

STAGE COACHES LINK THE COMMUNITIES OF A SPRAWLING WEST

Before the railroads stretched across the western plains, pony express and stage coaches provided "fast" transportation for mail, freight, and passengers. The picture shows one of the "Concord Coaches" used by Wells, Fargo & Company—the pioneer express and banking firm which, beginning in 1852, maintained stage lines throughout the West. At intervals, or "stages," along the routes of travel, fresh horses were provided to pull the tough, free-rolling coaches.

THE LAST SPIKE CONNECTS RAIL TRAVEL ACROSS THE CONTINENT

At Promontory Point, near Ogden, Utah, a final section of track was completed which linked America by rail across the continent for the first time. There, on May 10, 1869, public dignitaries and railroad officials gathered to see the Governor of California, Leland Stanford, drive a golden spike beside new rails that extended 1,850 miles from Omaha to San Francisco. A reproduction of Thomas Hill's painting depicts the scene.

St. Louis. The big lines in the East were the New York Central and the Pennsylvania Road.

The freeing of slaves as a result of the War between the States forced the South to turn to industry, too. For the first time valuable natural resources were tapped: iron, coal, oil, lumber. Factories were built to manufacture into finished products the cotton the South raised. Slowly the railroads crept into the South, too.

After the War between the States, the railroads were pushed all the way to the Pacific Coast. The first transcontinental railroad was finished when the Union Pacific, building west from Nebraska, and the Central Pacific, building east from California, were joined with a golden spike in 1869. The Northern Pacific was completed in 1883 and the Atchison, Topeka & Santa Fe the following year. Soon the Southern Pacific and Great Northern were added.

With better transportation came better communication, also. In 1844 Samuel F. B. Morse invented the telegraph, and in 1876 Alexander Graham Bell introduced the telephone. And, of course, preceding the railroad across the western plains went the Pony Express and the stagecoach lines.

The extension of the railroads across the continent aided greatly in the development of industry in the West. While the principal business was still agriculture, in many places industries were established. Included were lumbering, mining, packing houses for the beef and mutton of the ranges, and canneries for fish, such as the salmon of the Northwest, and for vegetables.

At the end of the century, men were experimenting with a new mode of transportation—the "horseless carriage." There was no single inventor for the automobile, but it was Henry Ford who made it available to people with moderate incomes. The coming of the automobile opened up a whole new era of transportation. Today the United States leads the world in the number of passenger cars, busses, and trucks in operation.

One development always calls for another. The increasing number of automobiles created a real demand for better roads. The result has been the excellent network of improved roads of concrete, macadam, gravel, and brick that stretch to all parts of the nation.

Next, man took to the air. Samuel P. Langley, Wilbur and Orville Wright, and Glenn Curtiss were the pioneers in this field. The first flight was made by Orville Wright at Kittyhawk, North Carolina, on December 12, 1903. It lasted only twelve seconds, but it made history. The story of the development of air transport is generally too well known to warrant retelling here. The extent of that development is clearly shown in the name of one of the big present-day companies—Trans-World Airlines. Not only are hundreds of thousands of passengers carried every year, but now the airlines have gone into the freight business, too.

The growth of industry and transportation was bound to bring increased trade. As we have pointed out, the United States has always been a trading nation and from the first has been involved in world affairs. Our foreign trade was first interrupted by the American Revolution. A decade or two later it picked up sharply because of the Napoleonic Wars in Europe. We found it profitable to sell supplies to

Aero Digest, New York

FIRST HEAVIER-THAN-AIR ASCENT

The above picture is copied from an actual photograph of the first successful flight by man in a heavier-than-air machine. The event took place at Kittyhawk, North Carolina, in 1903. Orville Wright was at the controls of the historic craft.

Smithsonian Institution

FIRST AIRPLANE TAKE-OFF AT SEA

An actual photograph records the feat of an American aviator who first took an airplane aloft from the deck of a ship at sea.

Eastern Air Lines

A SKY LINER OF THE MODERN AIR AGE

In half a century, aeronautical progress has raced from the pioneer flying machines of the Wright Brothers to huge cabin aircraft that can fly nonstop for thousands of miles.

both sides in that series of wars, until both France and England tried to do something about it by preventing our ships from getting through. The outcome of that was war with England in 1812, and that war cut into our trade again, largely because of the Non-Intercourse and Embargo Acts. After 1815 and continuing through the first half of the century, our shipping kept on increasing. There were several reasons for this. We found new markets in the Pacific. The Opium Wars in China opened that country to foreign trade, and our own Commodore Perry pried open the door of Japan in 1854. The California gold rush also helped. Those were the days of the clipper ships, like the famous "Flying Cloud" that made the trip from New York to San Francisco in eighty-nine days. They were the fastest ships carrying sails that were ever built, but they couldn't compete with the new iron steamships that were just coming into use. The steamship and the new interest in the

development of the West after the War between the States brought the decline of our merchant marine. That decline continued until World War I. The chief reason for it was that more money could be made in other ways. World War I and World War II saw spurts in building up our merchant marine again, but neither lasted. This time the big reason has been that our high standard of living meant we could neither build nor operate ships as cheaply as other countries. The result is a rather definite lag for our American merchant marine.

Industrial Revolution Spreads to the Farm. While transportation was improving and industries were being built up in the West, the Industrial Revolution was spreading to the farm, also. Here there was a real need for labor-saving devices, for there was an abundance of land and a scarcity of labor. From the time Cyrus McCormick patented his reaper in 1834, the improvement of conditions of farm life

Smithsonian Institution

BOTH SAILS AND ENGINES PROPELLED THE EARLY STEAMSHIPS

An original drawing by C. P. Hudson shows the "Phoenix"—the first American-built steamship used for ocean travel. Like many of the early, engine-equipped vessels, the "Phoenix" carried sails, evidence of a lack of complete faith in steam power.

has continued, but the greatest advance has been made during and since World War I. The war created a great need for food abroad, for fighting nations were too busy to raise much of their own. Prices skyrocketed in the United States. In the rush to raise as much high-priced wheat as possible, farmers of the western states broke and planted the great plains. They produced a lot of wheat, but the removal of the prairie grass that broke the sweep of the wind across the plains later turned that area into the famous "dust bowl" in which the valuable topsoil was blown off the fields and piled up like snowdrifts against the buildings and the few other obstacles that remained on the man-made desert.

The shortage of man-power in the war years was met by turning the new gasoline motor to farm use. Tractors became standard pieces of equipment

Woodward Governor Company

BOILER ON WHEELS

Movable steam engines of the type sketched above were introduced on American farms in the late nineteenth century. They furnished power to operate threshers and other mechanical equipment. With them came the mechanization of our agricultural industry.

on American farms. They made it possible for one man to do the work of several, thereby increasing greatly his productive ability. As more and more machinery has found its way onto American farms, more and more farm boys have been released for work in the cities, so that urban populations have grown, while rural populations have decreased steadily.

The building of a new system of roads all over the country in the 1920's and 1930's brought the markets closer to the farm, and likewise, the farm closer to the marketing centers. They made it easier for the farmer to get his produce to town, thus making it easier for town people to have fresh foods direct from the farm. Also, it brought the farmer more frequently into contact with the stores of the towns and cities, thereby making it easier for him to purchase the products of the city factories.

Since World War II the activities of some private companies and the government's rural electrification program (REA) have brought electric power to many of the farms of the nation. This, as much as any one thing, has helped to remove the one-time great difference between life in town and life on the farm. Today, on many of the farms of this country, people have the same conveniences that people in our cities enjoy, and the many labor-saving devices—from combines that harvest the grain to electric milking machines—have made farming a mechanized and, therefore, a comparatively simple and easy type of work. Farmers have learned a great deal about science, too, and know how to rotate crops and fertilize their land to put back into it

Underwood & Underwood

AMERICAN FARM PRODUCTION HAS HELPED TO FEED THE WORLD

The enormous total yield obtained from American farms made it possible for the United States to supply many nations of the world with food during and after two great wars—in addition to providing for home needs. Modern farm equipment, such as the tractor-drawn combine shown above, has contributed greatly to America's capacity to produce bountiful crops.

WATER-DRIVEN DYNAMOS HAVE HELPED TO SPREAD LIGHT AND POWER
ACROSS AMERICA

Great dams, such as the Grand Coulee on the Columbia River in the state of Washington, harness
the floodwaters of many streams and generate some of the electricity used on American farms.

the minerals that are used naturally in producing crops. Today the farmer's big aim is to be able to sell his produce at prices high enough to permit him to buy manufactured goods in the city in ever-increasing quantities to make farm life still easier and more pleasant.

Over-All Effects of Industrialization.
Now, let's take a little time to look at the over-all effects of industrialization upon the United States. Many of the results have been beneficial in a splendid way, but with all the benefits have come numerous difficult problems which we are still trying to solve. With increased production came reduced unit cost of goods, for wages did not rise anywhere nearly in proportion to the increased productivity of each worker. Because goods cost less, more people could afford to buy, and the

general standard of living of the country became more comfortable and convenient than anywhere else in the world. Industrialization meant a greatly changed mode of living, too, for now we have machines to do most of our work for us, leaving us more time for other things.

As the Industrial Revolution spread over the country, cities grew rapidly. In 1790 most of our people lived in rural areas; today, more than half our population live in urban districts. City life has offered many advantages not to be found on the farm, but large cities have their disadvantages, too. They grew up originally so that factory workers could live near to their work, but today many cities are so large that workers often must travel, sometimes uncomfortably, for many miles before

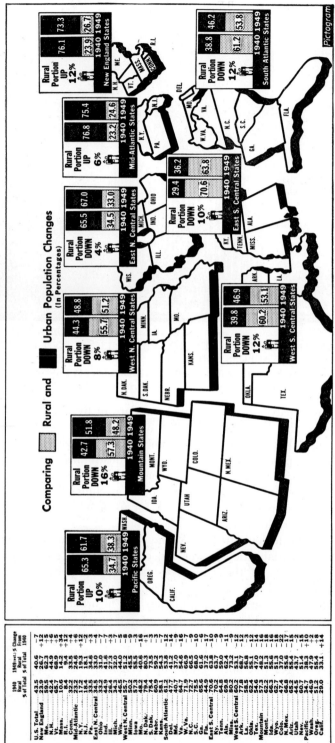

Comparing ▨ Rural and ■ Urban Population Changes
(In Percentages)

New England States — Rural Portion UP 12% — 1940: 76.1 / 23.9 — 1949: 73.3 / 26.7

Mid-Atlantic States — Rural Portion UP 6% — 1940: 76.8 / 23.2 — 1949: 75.4 / 24.6

South Atlantic States — Rural Portion DOWN 12% — 1940: 38.8 / 61.2 — 1949: 46.2 / 53.8

East N. Central States — Rural Portion DOWN 4% — 1940: 65.5 / 34.5 — 1949: 67.0 / 33.0

East S. Central States — Rural Portion DOWN 10% — 1940: 29.4 / 70.6 — 1949: 36.2 / 63.8

West N. Central States — Rural Portion DOWN 8% — 1940: 44.3 / 55.7 — 1949: 48.8 / 51.2

West S. Central States — Rural Portion DOWN 12% — 1940: 39.8 / 60.2 — 1949: 46.9 / 53.1

Mountain States — Rural Portion DOWN 16% — 1940: 42.7 / 57.3 — 1949: 51.8 / 48.2

Pacific States — Rural Portion UP 10% — 1940: 65.3 / 34.7 — 1949: 61.7 / 38.3

	1940 Rural % of Total	1949 (est.) Rural % of Total	% Change Rural from 1940
U.S. Total	43.5	40.6	−7
New England	23.9	26.7	+12
Me.	59.5	62.3	+5
Vt.	65.7	68.9	+5
Mass.	10.6	14.2	+34
R.I.	8.4	9.4	+12
Conn.	23.2	24.6	+6
Mid-Atlantic	23.2	24.6	+6
N.Y.	17.2	19.3	+12
N.J.	33.5	34.6	+3
Pa.	33.2	34.6	+4
East N. Central	34.5	33.0	−4
Ohio	33.0	31.6	−4
Ind.	26.4	27.3	+3
Ill.	24.3	22.0	−7
Mich.	34.3	32.0	−7
Wis.	46.3		−8
West N. Central	55.7	50.2	−9
Minn.	50.2	45.5	−9
Ia.	58.3	53.0	−9
Mo.	48.3	40.6	−16
N. Dak.	79.4	80.3	+1
S. Dak.	75.4	73.5	−3
Nebr.	58.1	54.3	−7
Kans.	61.2	53.8	−12
South Atlantic	47.7	41.2	−14
Md.	47.7	41.2	−14
Va.	64.7	54.6	−16
W.Va.	71.9	66.9	−7
S.C.	75.5	68.0	−10
Ga.	65.6	61.6	−6
Fla.	44.9	37.2	−17
East S. Central	70.2	63.7	−9
Ky.	64.8	59.0	−9
Tenn.	65.2	58.8	−1
Miss.	80.2	73.2	−9
West S. Central	60.2	53.1	−12
Ark.	57.8	58.7	−12
La.	62.4	55.1	−12
Okla.	54.6	47.0	−14
Tex.	62.2	51.3	−16
Mountain	66.3	55.6	−16
Mont.	65.2	51.3	−18
Ida.	62.7	51.3	−18
Wyo.	66.8	55.6	−17
Colo.	65.2	55.4	−15
N.Mex.	60.7	51.4	−15
Ariz.	34.7	38.3	+10
Utah	46.9	47.9	+2
Nev.	29.0	33.1	+14

Pictogram

U.S. News & World Report (2-25-49). © *U.S. News Pub. Corp.*

THE POPULATION MOVEMENT IN THE FORTIES WAS FROM FARM TO CITY

The predominantly rural-to-urban change in the complexion of the American population during the nine years elapsing between 1940 and 1949 is shown in the above chart. Although the shift to cities was larger in total measure than the shift to farms, note that the Pacific states, the middle Atlantic states, and the New England states experienced sizable increases in their rural populations at the expense of their cities.

reaching the factories or offices. And with the growth of cities came the growth of slum areas, partly because wages paid in early factories were too low to permit any but the poorest housing conditions. In modern America the elimination of slums from our cities is one of our biggest problems.

As industry has grown, so have big business and labor organizations, both of which we shall consider in the next chapter. Each presents its problems, and the unsettled relationship that all too often has existed between the two has frequently disrupted the economy and welfare of the nation greatly.

The industrialization of farming has made it possible for fewer people to raise more food than ever. In spite of this fact, we still have people in this country who simply do not have enough to eat, proving that the solution to the problem is not one of production only.

The progress of industrialization brought with it an ever-increasing demand for better transportation. So we have moved rapidly out of the "horse and buggy" days into the age of the jet plane. Improved transportation has made all the nation a market for factories and has carried raw materials from anywhere in the country to factories thousands of miles away. This has tended in many ways to standardize America and has made all of our cities basically alike—New York or San Francisco, Portland, Oregon, or Portland, Maine.

We have not been unaffected by the results of the Industrial Revolution on a world scale. The general effect of industrialization has been to set off a new wave of empire building. With the building of factories, colonies be-

came desirable for two new reasons: (1) they were needed to supply raw materials for the factories; and (2) they were needed to furnish markets for the finished products of the factories. Various nations, notably Great Britain, have acquired and used colonies for these purposes. The theory has been that their only purpose was to provide greater wealth for the mother country. This has been called the "mercantile" theory of trade. The mother country controlled trade in the colonies and limited work there to agriculture and the production of raw materials. It was in pursuit of this policy that Great Britain did her best to prevent the American colonies from becoming industrialized.

But there were many nations that were simply not big enough to build empires as Great Britain did. They were forced to be content with acquiring a sort of economic empire by staking out "spheres of influence" in backward countries—areas in which they were privileged to have exclusive control of trade, even though they did not control the territory politically. A good example of this arrangement is China from about 1840 to the present. In our own case, we made "protectorates" of some areas to get their business, as in certain parts of Central America, and for this we have often been accused of "economic imperialism."

Whether political empire, spheres of influence, or protectorates, the tendency has been to keep the lands from becoming industrialized; for each newly industrialized country ceases to be a market and becomes, instead, a competitor for markets. Hence, in today's world, the struggle for empire has been severe, resulting in frequent

FROM THE FUNNEL-TOP TO THE SLEEK, DIESEL-ELECTRIC STREAMLINER

These locomotive models typify three stages of progress in American rail transportation. Advances in comfort, speed, and operating efficiency of train travel have kept pace with the improvements in design of the motive-power units.

and destructive wars. And, try as we have, we have been unable to keep ourselves unaffected by those wars, and several times have been a party to them. Political developments frequently result from economic causes.

Proud as we all are of the great industrial development of our country, cold analysis reveals that our economic and social systems have not kept pace with our industrial system. The speed with which the Industrial Revolution has come in this country has tended to make us servants of the machine, rather than the machine our servant to make it easy for us to supply the necessities, even the luxuries, of life, thereby giving us time to develop our personalities and abilities, and to make living really worth while. We shall consider this phase of the Industrial Revolution at greater length in a later chapter.

FOR YOUR REVIEW

These Should Be Easy for You Now

1. What products did Colonial America have to export?
2. What is the Industrial Revolution? How did it begin?
3. How did the War of 1812 help make New England an industrial area?
4. Show that improved transportation had much to do with the settlement of the West and the development of industry there.
5. Trace the growth of American trade from Colonial days to the present. Why does the United States not have a big merchant fleet today?
6. Show how the Industrial Revolution has changed farm life.
7. What was responsible for creating the "dust bowl"?
8. Make a list of the effects of industrialization upon the United States.
9. Why have certain nations attempted to prevent the industrialization of other parts of the world? How has this affected the history of our country?

Associated Dates

1793—first complete cotton spinning mill built in the United States (Pawtucket, Rhode Island)
1807—Fulton's "Clermont" made the trip from New York City to Albany
1811—Cumberland Road started
1814—first factory to weave cloth in the United States (Waltham, Massachusetts)
1818—first section of the Cumberland Road completed
1825—Erie Canal opened
       Baltimore & Ohio Railroad chartered
1834—invention of the reaper
1838—"Great Western" crosses the Atlantic by steam power
1844—invention of the telegraph
1852—Cumberland Road completed
1869—first coast-to-coast railroad completed
1876—invention of the telephone

Why Are These To Be Remembered?

James Hargreaves	Samuel Slater	Spinning jenny
Edmund Cartwright	Francis Cabot Lowell	"Clermont"
James Watt	Samuel F. B. Morse	"Great Western"
Robert Fulton	Alexander Graham Bell	Turnpike
George Stephenson	Henry Ford	Cumberland Road
Eli Whitney	Wright Brothers	Dust bowl
Elias Howe	Cyrus McCormick	REA

Chapter 25

Labor Organizes and Makes Important Gains

THE LABOR UNION BECOMES AN IMPORTANT FACTOR IN AMERICAN LIFE

Growth of Big Business. A characteristic of the Industrial Revolution in the United States was the growth of big business, followed by the organization of labor on a national scale. The ensuing struggle between big business and big labor is the source of much of the domestic unrest with which the country is still afflicted.

Formation of Trusts and Corporations. In the early days of the industrialization of the United States, owners and operators of factories were beset with many problems. As factory after factory sprang up like mushrooms, the matter of selling the products of those factories became a serious one. Soon producers were cutting prices in order to undersell their competitors. Then the competitors cut still lower, and the race was on. As might well be expected, many companies were forced out of business.

To put an end to this disastrous price cutting and to control prices and keep them high, trusts or corporations were formed. A board of trustees or directors would be selected to operate several factories, thereby securing a sort of monopoly in production of a certain article. Thus competition was eliminated and, of course, business conditions from the standpoint of the operator were vastly improved. The forma-

tion of trusts and corporations became very popular, and by 1900 three-fourths of the national output of industry was handled by such corporations in oil, steel, iron, copper, and the like. The same device worked equally well for the rapidly expanding railroads and light and power companies.

Such huge organizations needed great sums to finance their growth. For, as transportation improved and goods could be moved about more readily to markets in all parts of the country, the monopoly of a corporation could be maintained only if it enlarged itself to take in more and more factories over an ever-increasing area. The money needed for this expansion could no longer be obtained from individuals, for the amounts were too large. Gradually a new system of financing industry developed. Certain banking houses became powerful through selling the stocks and bonds issued by a corporation and by supplying the corporation with the funds it needed. One result was the creation of great banking families, such as that of John Pierpont Morgan. Again, through the purchase of stocks and bonds, the people of this country became the owners of most of its big industries. Thus America became a land of capitalists, large and small, for capital is simply any wealth

Industry	Per Cent of Output Provided by Four Largest Companies
Telephone & telegraph equipment	95.7%
Electric lamps	91.8%
Cigarettes	90.4%
Glass, flat	88.1%
Rubber footwear	80.7%
Typewriters	79.4%
Soap & glycerin	79.0%
Phonograph records	78.8%
Synthetic fibers (nylon, rayon, etc.)	78.4%
Tin cans, other tinware	77.8%
Sewing machines	77.1%
Tires & inner tubes	76.6%
Cereals	74.9%
Distilled liquors	74.6%
Photographic equipment	61.2%
Automobiles, trucks, and parts	55.7%
Petroleum refining	37.3%
Magazines, other periodicals	34.3%
Bread & other bakery products	16.4%
Cotton fabrics, broad woven	13.1%

U.S. News & World Report (12–16–49). © U.S. News Pub. Corp.

AMERICAN BIG BUSINESS AFTER WORLD WAR II

The extent to which the largest companies dominated their fields in 1949 is shown by figures for percentage of output.

that is put to work to make more wealth, and any person who possesses such wealth, be it a whole factory or just a share of stock in a factory, is a capitalist.

Advantages and Disadvantages of Big Business. Big business is frequently under attack these days. There are those who would have us believe that such concentration of economic power is a bad thing for the country. Perhaps it is. But we should see both sides.

First, let's look at the advantages the American people have enjoyed because of the formation of great corporations. It would seem to be a generally accepted truth that, up to a certain point, the larger the concern, the greater its efficiency of operation. And the greater the efficiency, the lower the

Underwood & Underwood

PETROLEUM PRODUCTION AND COAL MINING

Oil and coal are two of the principal kinds of fuel used in our industrial life. The working of oil and coal deposits demands large capital investments. Both of these extractive industries are organized largely on a corporate basis.

cost of the manufactured product. Thus more people could afford to buy more things. This meant greater income for the corporations, who could then afford to put more money into improved machines, higher wages for employees, and research on a large scale to make a better product. It is highly doubtful, to say the least, if small factories and businesses could have produced on the scale and at the prices that have raised the standard of living of the American people to its present unequaled level.

On the other hand, there are some disadvantages which have resulted from the formation of big corporations. In some cases they have become so large as to be virtual monopolies in their fields. This means such corporations are able to control prices of their products and to stamp out most if not all of their competition. Thus the product the consumer has to buy may have a price and quality decided upon by the whim of the manufacturer rather than determined by open competition with other similar products in a free market. And all too often it is the consumer who suffers. Again, it has been the practice of big corporations to operate lobbies in the state capitals and in Washington for the purpose of influencing legislators to pass laws favorable to their businesses and to refuse to pass bills that would in any way hamper them, even though such a law might actually operate for the welfare of the country as a whole. And big business concerns have frequently been heavy contributors to political campaigns to help elect men favorable to their cause. These facts have led directly to the claim that the government of the United States is operated chiefly by and for "big business." You,

yourself, from your own knowledge and experience will have to judge the accuracy of this charge.

New Relationship between Owner and Worker. One thing is certain. The building of large corporations has brought a changed relationship between the owner and the worker in business. In early industry the owner had often been a worker, too, and had taken his turn each day alongside the other workers in the plant. As business grew, and factories came to be owned by many people instead of just one, this was no longer possible. The usual practice of stockholders was to employ a manager for the factory, and naturally his first interest was to make money for the people who employed him. Because of the mutual desire of both the stockholder-owners and the manager to show as big a profit as possible, often neither was concerned about how labor fared. In fact, the tendency was to look upon labor as another of the raw materials of production, to be bought as cheaply as possible. To this end immigration was encouraged, because the new arrivals had lower standards of living than our own citizens and therefore would work for less. The big growing period of business saw a considerable influx of immigrants from southern and eastern Europe, from Italy, Austria, Hungary, Poland, and Russia.

Attitude of Business toward Government. In general, this has been the attitude of business toward government: (1) that government should provide protective tariffs (i.e., tariffs high enough to make imported goods sell at a price higher than home-manufactured goods), encourage immigration of cheap labor, and give grants of land to railroads and to men who would

United States Steel Corporation

FROM IRON ORE IN THE EARTH TO FINISHED PRODUCT

The iron and steel industry in the United States, like coal and iron, is big business, requiring tremendous outlays of money and large-scale organization.

develop the natural resources of the country; and (2) that government should leave all the details of the operation of business to business itself. This is the "laissez-faire," or "hands off," policy first set forth by Adam Smith in his book, *The Wealth of Nations*. At first it was chiefly evident in the East, while the agricultural West plumped for free trade. Later, however, as industry spread westward, the West, too, turned to protective tariffs.

THE ORGANIZATION OF LABOR

Need for Organization. The growth of big business, which brought the changed relationship between owner and worker mentioned above, came at a time when free land was rapidly becoming a thing of the past. Previously, if an employee had not liked the conditions under which he had to work, he could quit his job, go west, and take up a piece of land for himself. There he could be his own boss. This was no longer possible. Therefore, the only hope an individual worker had of improving conditions for himself lay in his helping to improve conditions for all laborers. Naturally this led to more tightly knit organizations of workers. Sometimes business has opposed all labor organizations, forgetting that in this country we cannot have democracy in government and autocracy in industry.

Company Unions. A statement that business in general has been unmindful of the welfare of its employees simply would not be true. Many industries early assisted in the organization of company unions and gave them a considerable voice in the operation of the plant. Through such a union the company would listen to grievances, offer

bonuses, and sometimes a share in the profits or the opportunity to buy shares of stock in the corporation. The company often employed personnel directors to aid employees in solving problems connected with their work. Many concerns quickly learned that the greater the buying power of the people, the greater the market for manufactured articles, and raised wages accordingly.

Craft Unions and National Unions. From the early local company unions, the next step in labor organization was the formation of craft unions that took in several cities. So the organization of people doing the same kind of work was enlarged to take in a wider area. Eventually this led to national organizations. Efforts along this line first appeared in 1834 but were not effective until a half century later. In 1881 the American Federation of Labor (A.F. of L.) was created, made up of various trade and craft unions on a nation-wide basis. The Congress of Industrial Organizations (C.I.O.), formed in 1935, is set up on a different basis. It brings together into a nation-wide organization unions made up of all the men in a particular industry, regardless of the kind of work they do. In 1949 the A.F. of L. claimed about seven and one-half million members and the C.I.O. claimed six and one-half million.

Early national unions had failed largely because they were political as well as industrial in nature. The A.F. of L. did its best to stay away from politics. Even when the Socialist Labor party, formed in 1892, tried to get the A.F. of L. to adopt its stand for socialism—that is, government ownership of the means of production—the A.F. of L., led by Samuel Gompers, refused.

Covergram   *U.S. News & World Report (9–2–49). © U.S. News Pub. Corp.*

THE LABOR FORCE IN THE UNITED STATES

The great growth of organized labor has been one of the significant developments of the first half of the twentieth century. By 1949, membership in unions totaled some fifteen million; non-union workers still outnumbered them by a ratio of over three to one.

But labor has, from time to time, swung its weight to one side or another in political campaigns, especially to obtain laws abolishing imprisonment for debt and limiting the use of the injunction against unions. Political parties soon learned that labor's support would be given or denied on the basis of a party's actions regarding labor when in power.

Mediation Board for Railroad Disputes. National unions meant national strikes and more consumers affected.

To minimize this inconvenience to the public, Congress, by two acts in 1888 and the famous Railway Labor Act of 1926, set up a mediation board to work out solutions to labor disputes concerning the railroads. All in all, the plan has worked very well. Some people have thought that the success of this plan should be extended by making such mediation compulsory in all union disputes. But such a law in Kansas (1920) was declared unconstitu-

UNION MEMBERSHIP AND AFFILIATION
UNITED STATES*, 1949-1950

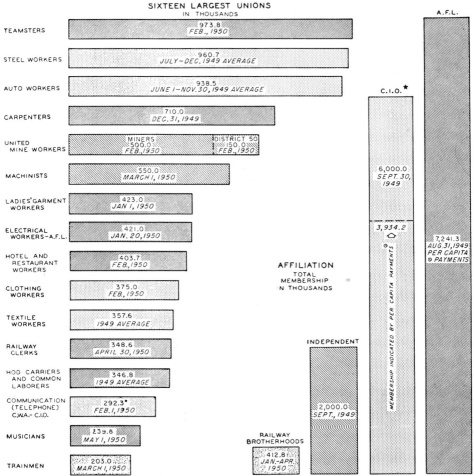

SIXTEEN LARGEST UNIONS
IN THOUSANDS

Union		
TEAMSTERS	973.8 FEB., 1950	
STEEL WORKERS	960.7 JULY-DEC. 1949 AVERAGE	
AUTO WORKERS	938.5 JUNE 1-NOV. 30, 1949 AVERAGE	
CARPENTERS	710.0 DEC. 31, 1949	
UNITED MINE WORKERS	MINERS 500.0 FEB., 1950	DISTRICT 50 150.0 FEB., 1950
MACHINISTS	550.0 MARCH 1, 1950	
LADIES' GARMENT WORKERS	423.0 JAN 1, 1950	
ELECTRICAL WORKERS-A.F.L.	421.0 JAN. 20, 1950	
HOTEL AND RESTAURANT WORKERS	403.7 FEB., 1950	
CLOTHING WORKERS	375.0 FEB, 1950	
TEXTILE WORKERS	357.6 1949 AVERAGE	
RAILWAY CLERKS	348.6 APRIL 30, 1950	
HOD CARRIERS AND COMMON LABORERS	346.8 1949 AVERAGE	
COMMUNICATION (TELEPHONE) C.W.A.- C.I.O.	292.3* FEB. 1, 1950	
MUSICIANS	239.8 MAY 1, 1950	
TRAINMEN	203.0 MARCH 1, 1950	

A.F.L.

C.I.O. *

6,000.0
SEPT. 30,
1949

3,934.2

7,241.3
AUG. 31, 1949
PER CAPITA
PAYMENTS

AFFILIATION
TOTAL
MEMBERSHIP
IN THOUSANDS

MEMBERSHIP INDICATED BY PER CAPITA PAYMENTS

INDEPENDENT

2,000.0
SEPT., 1949

RAILWAY
BROTHERHOODS

412.8
JAN.-APR.
1950

▲ INCLUDES CANADIAN MEMBERSHIPS ESTIMATED BY CANADIAN DEPARTMENT OF LABOR AT 675,044 IN 1948   ● WORKERS UNDER CONTRACT

★ C.I.O. FIGURES PREDATE EXPULSION OF SIX UNIONS   ⊙ PER CAPITA PAYMENTS UNDERESTIMATE MEMBERSHIP

Unions with headquarters in the United States have between 14 and 16 million members. This range of about 2 million is the difference between CIO-claimed membership and CIO membership computed from per capita payments. Totals include Canadian membership of 675,000, leaving United States membership at 13.3 to 15.3 million. The sixteen largest unions account for 8,193,859 members, or more than half the total union strength.

Six unions reported membership losses since 1948 and seven reported gains. Both the CIO-expelled UE and the newly chartered IUE-CIO, each claiming over 250,000 members, are excluded from the sixteen largest, pending NLRB elections. (All figures were supplied by unions to The Conference Board.)

SOURCE: "Union Membership in the United States," The Conference Board Management Record, June, 1950

National Industrial Conference Board, Inc.

UNIONISM IN THE U.S.A.

This chart presents figures and scale projections representing the 1949–50 size of sixteen American unions. The shading of each bar opposite the name of a union group indicates whether or not that group is affiliated with the American Federation of Labor, the Congress of Industrial Organizations, the Railway Brotherhoods, or is an independent body.

tional by the United States Supreme Court, and enforced arbitration has not been tried seriously since.

Problem of Immigration. One of the biggest problems faced by national organizations of workers was caused by the wide-open policy our government followed in immigration. Transportation to America was cheap, and even women and children could secure jobs in factories. Low cost immigrant laborers were preferred to slaves. They were more adept at machine tending, and in slack periods they could be laid off and were not a continuous financial obligation to the employer.

A potato famine in Ireland (1845–46) was responsible for an influx of nearly a million Irish immigrants in the next fifteen years. Because of poor food and political conditions, about a million and one-half Germans came between 1840 and 1860. But although America has called itself a "melting pot," actually it has been more of a "mixing bowl." Though immigrants came in large numbers to the "land of opportunity," many of them made no attempt to become citizens, and frequently their purpose in coming was to make money which they could take home with them to their native land. Often they found homes in sections of our large cities that were like little transplanted parts of the countries from which they came. All in all, while there were many notable exceptions, a sizeable percentage of these people contributed little to the advancement of this country. They created a real problem for American labor, for they would work for less than any American laborer could. You must remember that in this paragraph we are talking about immigration prior to 1882.

An immigration wave of laborers from China finally brought matters to a head. Thousands of them were attracted here by the discovery of gold in California and the railroad building program following the War between the States. Because they provided so much cheap competition for American labor, Congress in 1882 banned any more Chinese workers. At first it was to be a temporary measure, but later the exclusion was made permanent. Not until China became our ally against Japan in World War II was the Exclusion Act repealed (1943).

Also in 1882 Congress took steps to keep out of the country criminals, insane persons, and those who were destitute. Since then our immigration laws have been made even more rigid. In 1917 a law was passed keeping out anyone who cannot read. While this was certainly no infallible test of a person's desirability, it was an easy way to limit immigration. In 1924 Congress adopted the quota system, to go into effect in 1929. This act limited the total number of immigrants to be admitted in any year to 150,000. The quota from each country was determined by dividing the number of people from that country in the United States in 1920 by the population of the United States in 1920. This per cent of 150,000 was the number to be allowed to enter from that country per year. The quota system was not applied to Canada and the free countries of Latin America. At the same time, however, the Exclusion Act was extended to cover Japanese as well as Chinese.

Year by year, the labor unions have won concessions from industry and favorable laws from Congress. At times labor has resorted to strikes, boycotts, and similar devices to gain these advantages. The general effect has been to make the lot of the American laborer better than that of anyone in a comparable position anywhere else in the world. At that, there is still much room for improvement.

Labor and War. American labor stood by the government in World War I. At the end of the war, along with the League of Nations, an international labor office was set up to work for improved labor conditions throughout the world. Again in World War II labor went all-out for victory and agreed not to strike for the duration. Although the promise was not kept entirely, strikes were few and short-lived.

Two Important Labor Laws. Two laws since 1935 have had considerable influence upon American labor. The National Labor Relations Act (Wagner Act, 1935) has been called "Labor's Magna Carta." It specifically forbids employers' interference in any way with the organization of laborers in their places of business and requires employers to bargain collectively with their employees if the employees so desire. There is no question but that the act represented a great gain for labor. Many people feel it is one-sided because it does not provide corresponding restrictions upon labor in behalf of the employer.

The other law is the Taft-Hartley Act (1947). The feeling of Congress when the law was passed was that the laws of the land gave labor a distinct advantage over management, and the new act attempted to correct this lack of balance. There were several important provisions. (1) The act outlawed the closed shop—the provision that made union membership a condition to

employment. It does, however, permit the union shop, which requires workers to join the union after they are employed, if the majority of the workers already employed in the plant are union members. (2) It requires a cooling-off period before a contract can be terminated or changed by either party. (3) Both employers and unions are allowed to file damage suits against each other. (4) It prohibits contributions in any form to political campaigns for federal offices. (5) It provides that unions must file financial statements yearly with the government. (6) The act further provides that officers of local, national, and international unions must file affidavits with the government stating that they are not Communists and do not advocate the overthrow of the government by any unconstitutional means.

The Taft-Hartley Act was passed over President Truman's veto. He did not like the terms of the law because he thought they were too severe upon laboring men, and at times he managed to avoid using the law in labor disputes. This brought him a great deal of criticism, particularly in the drawn out on-again off-again coal strike during the winter of 1949–1950. He repeatedly asked Congress to repeal the law and won considerable support from labor as a result, but at the time this book goes to press, the act is still a part of the law of the land.

Labor and Inflation. After World War II labor made great gains in the generally inflationary conditions that prevailed. The change-over from war production to peace production could not be rapid, and it took several years for industry to catch up with the backlog of demand that could not be satis-

HOW THE CONSUMER SPENT HIS DOLLAR
UNITED STATES, 1901-1949

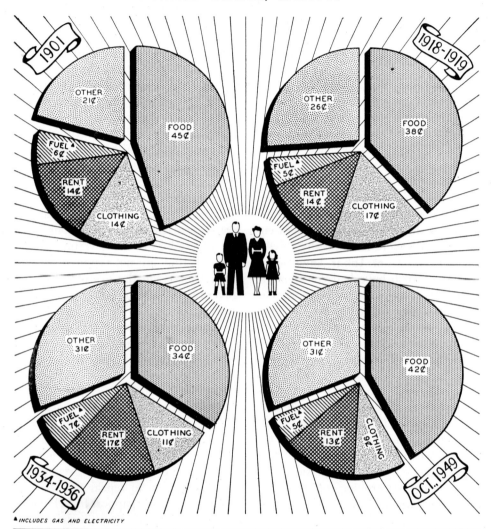

1901

OTHER
21¢

FOOD
45¢

FUEL▲
6¢

RENT
14¢

CLOTHING
14¢

1918-1919

OTHER
26¢

FOOD
38¢

FUEL▲
5¢

RENT
14¢

CLOTHING
17¢

1934-1936

OTHER
31¢

FOOD
34¢

FUEL▲
7¢

RENT
17¢

CLOTHING
11¢

OCT. 1949

OTHER
31¢

FOOD
42¢

FUEL▲
5¢

RENT
13¢

CLOTHING
9¢

▲ INCLUDES GAS AND ELECTRICITY

The share of the moderate-income family's dollar spent for necessities, such as food and clothing, declined appreciably from 1901 to 1934-1936. At the same time, there was an increase in the portion of each dollar spent for optional or "Other" items, such as recreation, housefurnishings, automobiles, etc. These trends have been halted for the time being. High food prices are taking a larger part of the dollar, but the proportion is still below the 1901 level.

For 1901, 1918-19, and 1934-36, the pies are based on actual surveys of family buying habits; for 1949 the budget of 1934-36 has been used, but at October, 1949, prices.

SOURCES: The Conference Board; Bur. of Labor Statistics

National Industrial Conference Board, Inc.

CONSUMER SPENDING ADJUSTMENTS

During the first half of the twentieth century, consumers adjusted their budgets and spending habits considerably as prices varied and as buying desires changed through the years. The above chart gives a picture of how "moderate-income" families split each of the dollars they spent during four selected periods extending from 1901 to 1949.

fied during the war. People wanted cars, refrigerators, stoves, clothes—almost everything, and they had the money saved up to pay for what they wanted. Congress removed virtually all war-time price controls soon after the war was over, and the big market and limited production forced prices up almost at once. Soon the spiral of inflation was going full swing. Higher prices prompted labor to ask for higher wages, and then the higher wages they were paying caused manufacturers to raise prices even more. Then workers asked for another wage raise because of the increased cost of living, and so it went, first one and then the other, up and up. But in the later months of 1949 a buyer's market began to return in some commodities. A buyer's market exists when the consumer can walk into a place of business and have a choice of articles. He can "shop around" for what he wants; no longer must he accept whatever the seller can supply, whether it is just what he wants or not, and he does not have to wait for delivery. This condition, coupled with the general expectation that prices would drop considerably, curtailed buying and forced prices down somewhat in a sort of leveling-off process after the constant rise that had prevailed during the months immediately after the war. It began to look as if the top of the spiral might have been reached, but 1950 opened with the A.F. of L. stating that a big goal for the year would be a wage increase of from seven to fifteen cents an hour, which A.F. of L. leaders claimed industry could pay without any increase in prices to the consuming public. Prices and wages continued to rise, and no one expected them ever to drop again to the level of 1939.

In May, 1950, General Motors Corporation and the United Automobile Workers signed what was hailed as the

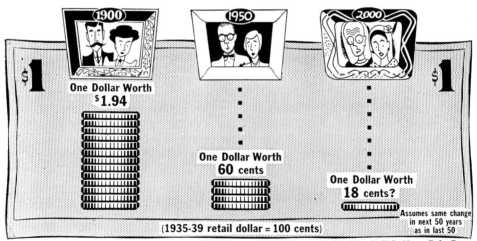

U.S. News & World Report (1–20–50). © U.S. News Pub. Corp.

WHAT WILL THE DOLLAR BE WORTH IN 2000 A.D.?

Whether or not the dollar will shrink in value during the last half of the century as much, less, or more than it did during the five decades from 1900 to 1950, is the question that inspired this speculative drawing. Assuming that the rate of change will remain the same, a 2000 A.D. dollar will be worth considerably less than a 1935–39 quarter.

harbinger of an entirely new era in labor-management relations. Some of the provisions were real innovations.

For the employees, gains included a 4¢ an hour pay raise from the current average of $1.65, effective at once, with a guaranteed raise of 4¢ an hour in each of the next four years. In addition, workers are to get more per hour as living costs go up, the rate to be adjusted if necessary every three months. But if living costs go down, the cost-of-living bonus will drop also, although it cannot drop more than the 3¢ which had been added at the time the contract was adopted under a previous agreement, plus any more that may be added before the drop might occur. Thus a base pay is guaranteed. Any worker who has been employed by General Motors for twenty-five years or more will be paid a $100 a month pension if he retires at age 65 or more. This figure includes all Social Security payments; but if the government should increase these, General Motors will raise the pension to a maximum of $117.50 a month. In addition to these, definite payments for disability were provided: life insurance, averaging $4,000, is available to workers; sickness and accident benefits, averaging $38.50 a week, and hospital and medical care can be had for an average of 70¢ a week; and vacation pay was doubled for workers with longer service.

The union gained by the agreement, too. The contract provided for a "union shop." That means that a man does not have to belong to the union to get a GM job, but he does have to join after he is employed. He may, however, drop out after a year if he so desires. Men who were in the union must remain in for the duration of contract—five years. But men employed by GM when the contract went into effect, and not in the union, cannot be forced to join. Also, the union is to decide jointly with GM management what workers are eligible for pensions. Thus the union was assured an excellent income through dues for the next five years.

Under the new contract General Motors gained greatly along with the employees and the union. It is assured of industrial peace for the next five years, barring major changes in the nation's economy. GM officials believe this alone will increase production enough to offset the increased labor costs. The big handicap to industry in the years after World War II has been the frequent reopening of contracts to discuss adjustment of wage scales. Because of this, a company could not plan more than a few months ahead, for it could never be sure what its costs would be very far in the future. The result was a natural hesitancy about venturing much capital in expansion; this put a definite ceiling on production. The new contract removed that handicap and permits GM management to plan for the future without fear of labor upheaval. Strikes and lockouts are barred by the contract, and, if wildcat strikes should occur, GM has the right to lay off or discharge the strikers. The company has not guaranteed an annual wage, and the union cannot demand it in the next five years, although UAW leader Walter Reuther has made it plain that that is now his principal objective for the future.

In still another way of GM-UAW contract heralds a new era in labor relations. The union has promised that it will make no objection to the introduction of new machinery and new pro-

General Motors Corporation

A PRODUCTION UNIT OF THE WORLD'S LARGEST AUTO MANUFACTURER

These are buildings of the Oldsmobile Division of General Motors Corporation, greatest automobile firm in the world in volume output of motor cars. Its 1950 contract with organized labor was hailed as a milestone in labor-management relations.

duction methods, even though this may mean fewer jobs. This is a decided change of attitude on the part of the union. Too often union organizations have been used to hold back progress rather than to promote it. Too often jobs have been created in name only by the union rather than by the needs of industry. Take, for example, the union order that required plumbers be permitted to install drain pipes under every electric refrigerator that was placed in Chicago apartment houses. Such attempts to make work for union members have only served to win the disfavor of the public who must pay the bills; the union cause has not been served by such attitudes. Now, in the GM-UAW contract both sides have recognized the rightness of the principle

that—to quote the contract—"to produce more with the same amount of human effort is a sound economic and social objective." If this principle can now be accepted by labor unions generally, a great deal of public favor and support can be gained.

At the time the contract was signed, both sides maintained that it would not result in increased prices of automobiles. Both sides claimed this as a moral victory. The union said that it proved wage increases can be granted without resulting in higher prices of products. Management said that prices could be held down because of labor's changed attitude toward greater technological efficiency.

Following the signing of the GM-UAW contract, other corporations began to adopt the same general formula for agreements with labor unions. It seemed very possible, as the months passed, that a new era in labor-management relations may have arrived. For a long time labor had felt it was fighting for its life, always on the defensive. The worker was torn by a sort of dual allegiance. On one hand, he was bound to his union, for it provided security in his job. On the other hand, he owed considerable allegiance to the company, for its investment of capital made that job possible. The resulting pull in opposite directions created difficulty that sometimes ran all the way from confusion to violence. Now it appears that management has accepted the union as a partner in business and has backed this acceptance with a long-term contract. The workers, in turn, have promised not to stand in the way of industrial progress. For the first time in several years it looks as if both management and labor are going to pull in the same direction, together. The result can well be increased production, a greater national income, and a higher standard of living for more people throughout the nation.

FOR YOUR REVIEW

These Should Be Easy for You Now

1. Why were trusts and corporations formed in the United States? How were they financed? What advantages have they brought to the American people? Disadvantages?
2. What effect has the formation of big corporations had upon the relationship between owner and employee?
3. What has American business usually felt the function of government should be? What is the "laissez-faire" theory?
4. Trace the development of labor organizations in the United States.
5. Explain the difference in organization between the A.F. of L. and C.I.O.
6. Why have immigrants come to America? Why has American business wanted immigrants in the past?
7. Why is it not very accurate to call the United States a "melting pot"?
8. Why did many Chinese laborers come to the United States? What action did Congress take?
9. What limitations has Congress placed upon immigration? Explain how the quota system operates.
10. How did the National Labor Relations Act represent a great gain for labor organizations in the United States?
11. Explain provisions of the Taft-Hartley Act.
12. Why did prices rise generally after World War II? What is meant by a "spiral of inflation"?
13. What is a buyer's market?
14. What is the probable significance of the GM-UAW agreement reached in May, 1950?

Associated Dates

1881—American Federation of Labor organized
1882—all Chinese immigration banned
1890—Sherman Antitrust Act; attempt to prevent restraint of trade by trusts
1913—Department of Labor established

1914—Clayton Antitrust Act; to strengthen Sherman Act
    Federal Trade Commission created
1924—quota system adopted to control immigration; in effect in 1929
1926—Railway Labor Act
1935—Congress of Industrial Organizations formed
    National Labor Relations Act
1943—Chinese Exclusion Act repealed
1947—Taft-Hartley Act

Why Are These To Be Remembered?

J. P. Morgan	Wagner Act	Laissez-faire	Buyer's market
Adam Smith	Taft-Hartley Act	A.F. of L.	Union shop
Samuel Gompers	Immigration	C.I.O.	Wildcat strike
Walter Reuther	Protective tariff	Inflation	Annual wage

Chapter 26

American Capitalism Faces a Serious Test

THE AMERICAN ECONOMIC SYSTEM IS CALLED UPON TO PROVE ITSELF
CAPABLE OF CREATING GREATER ECONOMIC DEMOCRACY

[*Again, at this point, as in the previous unit, the author believes that some treatment of present problems concerning our capitalistic system must be undertaken, or he would not be fulfilling his obligation to you, the reader. You are not asked to agree with the opinions he expresses; but he hopes that when you disagree, it will be with the spirit of the French philosopher Voltaire, who said, "I do not agree with what you say, but I would defend to the death your right to say it."*]

Government Control. A source of great concern to people of the United States at the middle of the twentieth century has been the amount of control exerted over their everyday lives by our federal government. Not only have people objected to widespread control, but they have feared also that federal regulation would be extended to more and more fields and increased in those areas where it already existed. Since the relationship that exists between government and business is always important to us, we turn now to a specific consideration of this matter.

Reasons for Government Control. A marked growth in government control occurred between 1932 and 1945. There were perhaps three reasons for this: (1) When Franklin Roosevelt became President, the country was in the throes of the Great Depression. Emergency, and sometimes drastic, measures were called for. To meet situations quickly, it was necessary for the federal government to have extraordinary powers, and Congress was willing to grant them to the Executive Department to meet the emergency. Considerable government control of industry and business resulted. (2) As the country was moving out of the depression period, it was plunged into another great war. The task of fighting on several fronts at the same time, in Europe and Africa and Asia, again meant that the people of the United States had to surrender some of their personal liberty so that the federal government might have the authority to deal with the problems of winning the war. The scope of the struggle meant a very considerable increase of control of people's lives by government. (3) The third factor entering into this whole problem of government control is not the result of some emergency situation. The fact is that government regulation always tends to breed more regulation. Once controls are set up, it's difficult to remove them. For regulations must be administered by branches of government created for that purpose, usually called *bureaus*. When bureaus are once established, they are not easily abolished, for they naturally tend to per-

376

THE CAPITOL BUILDING AT WASHINGTON, D.C.

Legislative seat of our national government, this building is occupied by both the Senate and House of Representatives. Construction on the present Capitol was started in 1827. The wings and dome were added during the Civil War years.

petuate themselves. People employed in the work of bureaus see their jobs disappearing if the bureau is abolished and will, therefore, work for the continuation of the regulations and controls that make the bureau necessary.

Such have been the major reasons for the establishment of most present-day government control over industry and business. The creation of that control to meet the emergencies of depression and war was not overly protested by the American people, who recognized the need for centralized authority in solving problems quickly. The question that has disturbed people is: When the national emergency is over will government control be removed?

Political Democracy and Economic Democracy. The whole matter, to be seen in its proper light, must be viewed from various angles. There are two kinds of democracy for which the American people have been striving: political democracy and economic democracy—that is, a part in their own government, and the opportunity to earn a reasonably high standard of living. For practical purposes, we may consider that the country has attained a fairly high degree of political democracy, although we know certain segments of our population are still prevented from voting in some parts of the country. In the field of economic democracy, the trend is definitely toward a better standard of living for more people, with the ultimate goal of reasonable prosperity for everyone.

Certainly, no one will object to this goal. Regardless of how wealthy a person may be, he realizes that his economic position is more nearly secure if people around about him also enjoy the prosperity of a comfortable life. The American people are not opposed to "two chickens in every pot, two cars in every garage." The problem is: How to get them?

Capitalistic System. In this country we have felt that the capitalistic system offers the best opportunity for the improvement of any person's economic status. Capitalism has done an amazing job of providing our people with the conveniences to make life easier than ever before. We have more automobiles, more refrigerators, more bathtubs, more telephones than all the rest of the world. But we also have a big segment of our population still unable to purchase the type of standard of living that has made our country famous. So long as such a condition exists, there is still much to be done.

Communism as a Solution. Some Americans, disgruntled because they have not done better in this country, have turned to other types of government. Some feel that communism is the answer. Under communism, the existing government would be overthrown by violent revolution, and the new government would take over both the ownership and the operation of the means of production. The result, with everyone working for the government, would be a tendency to level off all incomes so that there would be little difference between the high and the low. These people would trade the freedom of individual initiative for the security of guaranteed income. Others would achieve the same end through socialism, where the shift to government ownership and operation would be made by peaceful, legislative means.

Fascism as a Solution. Still others in America would solve the problem by converting the country into a fascist state. Fascism is a type of government developed in Italy and Germany after World War I. It was intended to solve the problems of the Italian and the German people and, at the same time, to keep those people from turning to communism. Fascism represents a compromise between capitalism and communism. From capitalism it takes the idea of private ownership, and from communism, that of total government operation. But the people of Italy and Germany soon found it meant little to own a factory if the government was going to dictate to you just how it must be operated. With the growth in power of organized labor in the United States (see Chapter 25), there has been some feeling, even among capitalist leaders of industry, that a fascist setup would be a good way to hold labor in check and permit management to continue to enjoy good profits.

DEMOCRACY AND THE CAPITALISTIC SYSTEM

An Ever-Increasing Standard of Living. Almost all Americans, however, look with disfavor upon any other type of government than democracy. We know our democracy is not perfect. But rather than throw it out in favor of some other type, most of us believe we can do better by improving upon the system that has worked so well for us thus far. And, even though we may take longer to get the job done, we prefer to make the changes democratically.

The approach to the solution of the economic ills of the world made by theories of government other than democracy seems to assume that the total

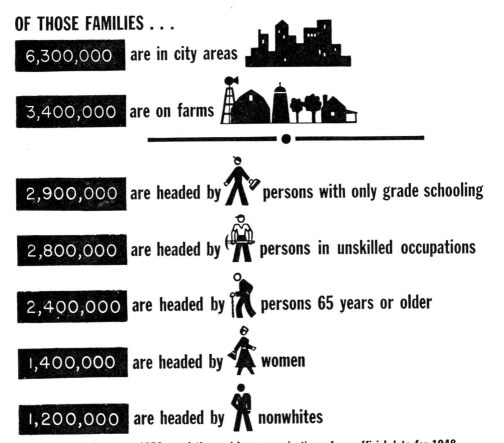

Out of 39,200,000 families in the U. S. there are 9,700,000 with incomes of less than $2,000 a year

OF THOSE FAMILIES . . .

6,300,000 are in city areas

3,400,000 are on farms

2,900,000 are headed by persons with only grade schooling

2,800,000 are headed by persons in unskilled occupations

2,400,000 are headed by persons 65 years or older

1,400,000 are headed by women

1,200,000 are headed by nonwhites

Estimates based on 1950 population and income projections, from official data for 1948.

U.S. News & World Report (1–20–50). © U.S. News Pub. Corp.

LOW-INCOME FAMILIES IN THE UNITED STATES

Nearly one-fourth of all families in the nation had incomes of less than $2,000 during the years of prosperity after World War II. This picture has a bright side, of course, for a converse statement of the finding would emphasize that an income of $2,000 or higher was had by more than 75 per cent of the nation's families.

amount of production and wealth in any given area is a static, fixed thing; that is, that the amount of the world's goods available to the people as a whole is limited. Therefore, to follow the apparent reasoning of such "isms," the only way to improve conditions for people of the lower income group is to take wealth from the rich and give it to the poor, either by outright revolution and violence or by legislation.

But democracy and the capitalistic system offer us another way. Whether we as individuals stand near the top or the bottom of our economic scale, we oppose any theory of government that calls for the seizure of private property. What we have acquired as our own we believe no government should have the power to take from us. The surest way to maintain our present system is to so modify it as to produce the results desired, without an enforced division of existing wealth. A virile, active capitalism will attain those goals through increased production. Greater production is, in the final analysis, the only satisfactory way of increasing the world's wealth and increasing the prosperity of all its people. Just how to obtain greater production and more equitable distribution are the problems American capitalism must solve if it is to survive.

Importance of the Individual. In the United States, big government, big business, and big labor have come in for considerable criticism. Most of that criticism has grown out of the feeling by our people that government, business, and labor have often lost sight of their fundamental purpose in the United States. Under our American democracy, the individual is all-important. The chief objective of our government, our business, and our organized workers must be service to our people. Whenever government, business, or labor loses sight of this fundamental purpose, the American people have an inherent right to be critical. Too often in our economic dispute it is the consumer who is the forgotten man. When business puts profit above service, when labor puts wages above service, and when government puts the influencing of votes above the welfare of the American people, then we have the cart before the horse, and some changes need to be made. The citizens of this country will not permit themselves to be

exploited by either capital, labor, or government.

Control and Planning. At this point it might be well to distinguish between two terms that ofttimes cause confusion: *control* and *planning*. The word control often carries with it a suggestion of limitations imposed against the will of the person or persons who are affected. Planning, on the other hand, suggests a co-operative movement in which most people concerned join to try to find solutions for common problems. Traditionally, the American people shy from controls. The days of the American Revolution are not so far past for us to have forgotten the things for which we fought.

But, while our people dislike controls, most of us recognize the need for planning. We realize that the results we desire are not likely to come if we just sit and wish for them. Whether we are trying to guard against depression or war, we have to lay careful plans if we expect to attain our goal. Such planning must be a co-operative move. Time was when, if things did not go according to our liking, we could pack up and move on to new frontiers and start over again. Thus, in a sense, we could dodge perplexing problems; run away from them. Today, we can't do that any more. We have to stay where we are and either lick our problems or be licked by them.

But planning doesn't necessarily mean government control. There seems to be no real reason why government must do the planning. Why shouldn't we people do it? Surely the American people have the collective intelligence to solve their problems. Surely capital and labor can plan together to provide steady employment, and at a reasonable wage that will keep the standard of living high. Surely citizens can do a capable job of selecting informed, unbiased statesmen to represent them in Washington and carry out their desires. But if we the people are not willing to accept the responsibility of solving our problems ourselves, fairly and for the welfare of all, then we cannot object if government is forced to undertake to do the job for us. For certainly it must be done. If the future of America is worth fighting for, surely it's worth thinking about and planning for.

It is generally recognized that in this country our industrial system has developed and advanced so rapidly that our social and economic systems have not been able to keep pace. Now, with the high productive capacity of our factories, it is only natural that workers the country over should want to see specific efforts made to bring both our social and economic systems to a state of development on a par with that of our industrial system. If the majority of the people of the country want such steps taken, they will be taken. The only choice is: Will these objectives be attained through co-operative planning on the part of business management, organized labor, farmers, and the whole of our citizenry, or will they be gained through regulations and laws formulated by the elected representatives of the people at large—that is, government?

Already, in numerous cases, business and industry have seen the handwriting on the wall. Many concerns have taken steps to make it possible for employees to become part owners of the business. To cite just one such instance—in proposing a stock-purchase plan for employees, a spokesman for General Mills, Inc., said: "Our contemplated employee stock purchase plan is only one facet of the general problem before us—the problem of securing more partners in American industry. To obtain more partners, business should find ways of interesting more small investors in its securities, especially stocks."

This is the answer to communism. If capitalism provides the opportunity for workers to satisfy their normal desires for food, clothing, and shelter, and at the same time enables them to buy shares in industry (that is, to become capitalists themselves), the American people cannot be interested in communism or any theory of government other than our own democratic-capitalistic system. Capitalism will succeed so long as it continues to produce more and more capitalists. Obviously, that means we must have ever-increasing production.

Problem of Our National Debt. The triangular relationship that exists in this country among the American people, American industry and business, and American government gives rise at this

THE TREASURY BUILDING

The nation's fiscal policies are directed from headquarters in Washington, D.C.

TAXES AND NATIONAL INCOME
SELECTED YEARS, 1902-1949

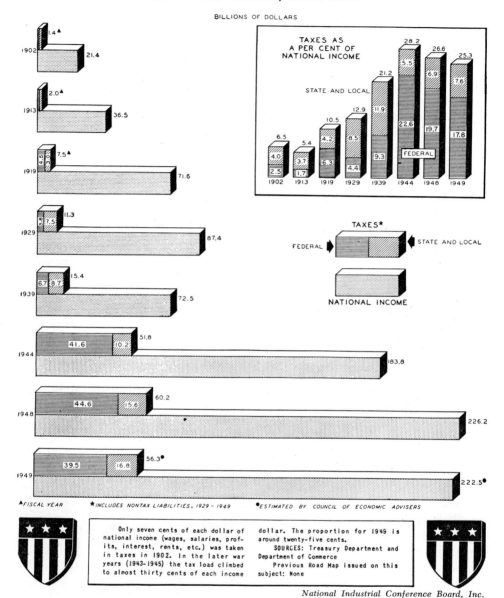

BILLIONS OF DOLLARS

TAXES AS A PER CENT OF NATIONAL INCOME

Year	1902	1913	1919	1929	1939	1944	1948	1949
Total	6.5	5.4	10.5	12.9	21.2	28.2	26.6	25.3
State and Local	4.0	3.7	4.2	8.5	11.9	5.5	6.9	7.6
Federal	2.5	1.7	6.3	4.4	9.3	22.6	19.7	17.8

TAXES*
FEDERAL ◄ ► STATE AND LOCAL

NATIONAL INCOME

Horizontal bars:
- 1902: 1.4▲ / 21.4
- 1913: 2.0▲ / 36.5
- 1919: 4.5 / 3.0 / 7.5▲ / 71.6
- 1929: 3.8 / 7.5 / 11.3 / 87.4
- 1939: 6.7 / 8.7 / 15.4 / 72.5
- 1944: 41.6 / 10.2 / 51.8 / 183.8
- 1948: 44.6 / 15.6 / 60.2 / 226.2
- 1949: 39.5 / 16.8 / 56.3● / 222.5●

▲FISCAL YEAR   ★INCLUDES NONTAX LIABILITIES, 1929 - 1949   ●ESTIMATED BY COUNCIL OF ECONOMIC ADVISERS

Only seven cents of each dollar of national income (wages, salaries, profits, interest, rents, etc.) was taken in taxes in 1902. In the later war years (1943-1945) the tax load climbed to almost thirty cents of each income dollar. The proportion for 1949 is around twenty-five cents.

SOURCES: Treasury Department and Department of Commerce

Previous Road Map issued on this subject: None

National Industrial Conference Board, Inc.

GOVERNMENT REVENUES MEASURED AGAINST NATIONAL INCOME

In order to function and render the public services that it is called upon to perform, government —federal, state, and local—raises money in the form of taxes to meet expenses. This tax money must come from earnings and other forms of private income and wealth. In the above chart, the differently shaded portions of the horizontal bars show (1) taxes by the federal government, (2) taxes by the state and local governments, and (3) total national income for each of eight selected years. In the box at the upper right corner of the chart, taxes are shown in percentages of the national income.

mid-point of the twentieth century to two very basic questions with which the future of our democracy and our capitalism are closely tied up. The first question is simply: How expensive can government get? In 1950 Americans paid to the federal government nineteen cents out of every dollar they earned. In addition to this, we have a national debt that amounted in 1950 to about 250 billion dollars and aren't doing anything about it except paying the interest. The cost of national government has been rising steadily. Twenty years ago it required but four cents of every dollar you earned. During the war, government spending shot up, naturally, until Washington was spending fifty-five cents for every dollar of your income. Of course, it didn't collect that much in taxes. It borrowed, instead. That's how we got most of our national debt. After the war, the rate of spending declined. In 1948 it was sixteen cents for every dollar of national income, but in 1949 it started up again. No one knows just how expensive government can become before the national economy can no longer bear the burden. But certainly we do know that it cannot continue to mount at its present rate in relation to the total earnings of all the people of the country.

We know why the cost of government has mounted so rapidly. We have spent great sums of money to meet national crises. First, there was World War I, when we joined with most of the world to put down the threat from Germany under Kaiser Wilhelm II. When that was over, it wasn't long before we faced another emergency—the depression. Mass unemployment and the general crumbling of our economic system called for emergency measures—meas-

ures which the federal government had to go into debt to undertake. Most people have felt such moves are the duty of government in time of great need, provided the account is balanced during good years when they come again. But before we had a chance to repay our depression debts, we had to take on Hitler, Mussolini, and the Japanese war-lords, again at great expense. And now it's Stalin who is causing us the expense of a "cold war," plus preparation for a possible shooting war some day. So the merry-go-round keeps on turning, faster and faster, and we get dizzier and dizzier.

Now, all of us would like to see the yearly expenditures of our federal government reduced. But when we realize that approximately seventy cents out of every dollar our government spends goes to pay for wars we have already fought and for preparation for wars we may have to fight, it's fairly easy to see that the opportunity for cutting the budget greatly is most remote. Savings can be made all along the line, of course, but it appears we shall have to resign ourselves to a yearly expenditure that is high by all standards. Apparently our brightest hope is that somehow we can keep it from going higher.

But here we are, faced with another crisis: The spread of Russian imperialism, which is now just as much of a threat to our security as was German imperialism which already led to two wars in this century. With our present high cost of government and our big national debt, we run smack into the second big question: Can the people of the United States meet the growing responsibilities of governing themselves, or must we eventually adopt a

HOW THE GOVERNMENT SPENDS YOUR MONEY
SELECTED NONWAR FISCAL YEARS 1902-1951

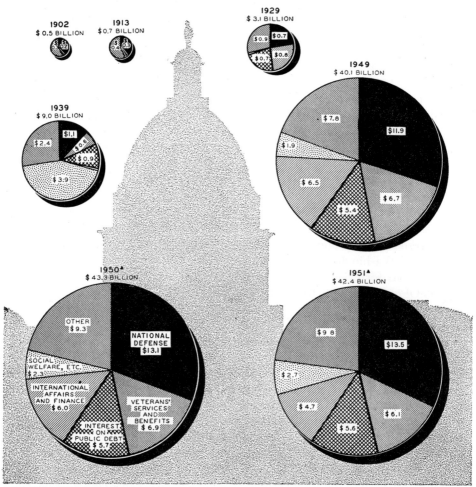

1902
$ 0.5 BILLION

1913
$0.7 BILLION

1929
$ 3.1 BILLION
$0.9 | $0.7
$0.7 | $0.8

1949
$ 40.1 BILLION
$ 7.8 | $ 11.9
$ 1.9
$ 6.5
$ 5.4 | $ 6.7

1939
$ 9.0 BILLION
$1.1
$2.4 | $0.6
$0.9
$ 3.9

1950★
$ 43.3 BILLION
OTHER $ 9.3
NATIONAL DEFENSE $13.1
SOCIAL WELFARE, ETC. $ 2.3
INTERNATIONAL AFFAIRS AND FINANCE $ 6.0
VETERANS' SERVICES AND BENEFITS $ 6.9
INTEREST ON PUBLIC DEBT $ 5.7

1951★
$ 42.4 BILLION
$ 9.8 | $13.5
$ 2.7
$ 4.7 | $ 6.1
$ 5.6

NOTE: DATA EXCLUDE DEBT RETIREMENT; ALSO REFUNDS OF RECEIPTS FOR 1929 AND SUBSEQUENT YEARS ★ESTIMATED

More than seventy cents out of every dollar the Federal Government is spending in fiscal 1950 and 1951 is taken by defense and outlays arising from past wars. Expenditures for defense, veterans, debt service, and international affairs far surpass what was spent for all functions of government in any year prior to World War II. Functional breakdown for 1929 and prior years is not strictly comparable with later years; where no breakdown is shown, data are unavailable. "Other" includes maintenance of the general government and many departments and independent agencies.

SOURCES: Treasury Department; Bureau of the Budget
Previous Road Map issued on this subject: No. 657

National Industrial Conference Board, Inc.

APPORTIONMENT OF FUNDS SPENT BY THE FEDERAL GOVERNMENT

In pies drawn for each of five selected years, the upper part of the above illustration shows just how much of a money outlay the national government made for various purposes in 1902, 1913, 1929, 1939, and 1949. The two pies in the lower part of the illustration were estimates of expenditures for the years 1950 and 1951—estimates which had to be revised in the face of sharply mounting defense needs after the outbreak of hostilities in Korea. Note that foreign aid and defense costs, including veterans' services and benefits plus interest on the public debt, have come to consume major portions, approaching 75 per cent, of our total national expenditures in recent years.

form of totalitarianism to solve our complex problems?

Four Decisions Americans Must Make. Obviously, there are no quick and easy answers to these questions. But to find the answer, the American people, with whom the final decisions must rest, must first think through and resolve for themselves an intelligent philosophy regarding the relationships of industry, government, and themselves. As the author writes this, it seems to him there are four such matters that must be decided.

(1) What tasks do we the people want our federal government to undertake? Probably the basic things we want government to take care of are our protection among the nations of the world and the guaranteeing of our freedom within our own country. We want our government always to be the servant of the people, not the people the servants of the government. We want always to keep the power to control that government and to decide what it is to do for us.

(2) Having defined the duties of our federal government, are we then ready to accept the remainder of our objectives as our own to work out, either individually or collectively in relatively small groups. We must understand that the key to the question of what to do about big federal government begins at home. The more efficient we can make local government, the less need there will be for federal action. Those things which we cannot possibly do for ourselves through local government, we obviously must be ready to turn over to our federal government to handle. But we had better be absolutely certain the problem must be handled nationally or internationally

THE SUPREME COURT BUILDING

The stately columns at its entrance symbolize the dignity and integrity of the nation's highest tribunal.

before we relinquish our control of it.

(3) As former President Hoover recently said, if we are going to have government by the people, then the people are going to have to govern. To do this intelligently, we shall have to avoid snap judgments and decisions. We shall have to make ourselves as intelligent as possible on public affairs. But, also, we shall have to trust and respect the judgment of scientific and economic experts on those matters we do turn over to our federal government to handle. Can we make ourselves sufficiently informed on complex national and world problems to deal with them intelligently in a democratic way?

(4) Are we willing to pay for what we want, to pay our way as we go? Any one of us would like, personally, to have a great many things for his home if we could buy them, charge them, and never have to pay for them. But no one of us could get away with it personally. If such a procedure is not sound busi-

FARMS, CITIES, AND INDUSTRIES REFLECT AMERICA'S GROWTH

America can look with confidence to a future built upon private ownership and distributive equity. Private ownership offers an incentive to production that is without equal. An equitable dis-

tribution of the things produced increases the order and well-being of society. An economic way of life based on these two principles and functioning within the framework of democratic government offers the nation a sure promise of expanding progress and whole-

some stability. The free American economic system has produced within a relatively short period of time the world's highest standard of living.

JUSTICES OF THE UNITED STATES SUPREME COURT

The nine Supreme Court Justices are appointed by the President with approval of the Senate, and hold life tenure. Shown in the photo above are, from left to right, *seated:* Associate Justices Felix Frankfurter, Hugo Black, Chief Justice Fred Vinson, Associate Justices Stanley Reed, William Douglas. *Standing:* Associate Justices Wiley Rutledge, Frank Murphy, Robert Jackson, Harold Burton. Rutledge and Murphy were succeeded upon their deaths by Associate Justices Sherman Minton and Tom Clark.

ness for us individually, is it sound for our nation? We must eliminate graft, waste, and duplication of effort. What we cannot eliminate, we shall have to pay for, sooner or later. We can ask our government to do anything in the world for us that we want, provided we're willing to pay the bill for it right then. And, if we are a businesslike people, we shall need to set up a specific formula for the payment of our national debt so that we can pay off the mortgage on our nation.

These are problems for all of us, for they concern our freedom to govern ourselves and to earn and improve our standard of living. If we want to preserve democracy, we must make it as efficient as dictatorship so that we shall

be impervious to the suggestion of would-be rulers that they will provide all the things we cannot provide for ourselves in return for our giving up the rights we do enjoy. If we want to preserve capitalism, we must make private ownership and control as serviceful as government ownership and control could possibly be. We must make it serve all the people better than any government could.

The trend today is toward greater economic democracy for all people. The danger lies in the means it finds to work itself out. American capitalism has brought us a higher standard of living than can be found anywhere else in the world. American capitalism can bring all of us a great deal more than we have

Growth In
National Output

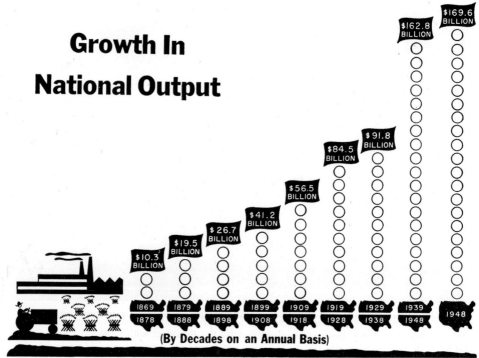

(By Decades on an Annual Basis)

U.S. News & World Report (4–22–49). © U.S. News Pub. Corp.

HOW AMERICAN PRODUCTIVE CAPACITY HAS GROWN

This chart shows the great strides made in the expansion of our ability to produce goods as our technology found new and better ways of doing work.

even now, if we can keep it as our economic system and make it work for all of us better than it has ever worked up to this time. It can do the same for other peoples as well. The question is: Have we the intelligence and determination to work with the trend of history and harness the world's energy to realize order, liberty, and the abundant life for all?

FOR YOUR REVIEW

These Should Be Easy for You Now

1. What three reasons for greatly increased government control in the last two decades does your text list? How do bureaus tend to perpetuate themselves?
2. What two kinds of democracy do the American people want?
3. How would you evaluate the job done by American capitalism?
4. Distinguish between communism and socialism. What is fascism? What is the basic assumption behind these theories of government? What is capitalism's answer to these theories?
5. What are the two big problems American capitalism must solve?
6. What do you believe should be the chief objective of government, business, and labor in the United States?

7. If the American people fail to solve their problems for themselves, who is most likely to do it for them?
8. What is meant by the statement that our social and economic systems have not kept pace with our industrial system?
9. What does your text say can be capitalism's answer to the appeal of communism? Do you agree? Give reasons for your answer.
10. How has the cost of our federal government grown? How large is the national debt?
11. Approximately what part of the cost of government goes for war? What threat seems likely now to boost the cost of government still more?
12. How would you answer the four questions the author says he believes repreent basic matters the American people must decide about?

Why Are These To Be Remembered?

Capitalism	Communism	Fascism
Bureaucracy	Socialism	

Suggested Readings

RAWSON, MARION W., *Of the Earth Earthly*
  The beginnings of American democracy

DAVIE, M. R., *World Immigration, with Special Reference to the United States*

BINNS, ARCHIE, *You Rolling River*
  Settlement of the Columbia River country

FERBER, EDNA, *Cimarron*
  Opening of Oklahoma for settlement

ROLVAAG, O., *Giants in the Earth*
  Frontier life in South Dakota

HOLBROOK, S. H., *Iron Brew*
  Iron and steel in American development

NORRIS, FRANK, *The Pit*
  The stock exchange

ALLEN, F. L., *The Lords of Creation*
  Industry in America

BAER, MARIAN E., *Pandora's Box*
  The need for conservation

CHASE, STUART, *Men and Machines*
  The Machine Age in America

YATES, R. F., *Machines over Men*
  Effects of the Machine Age on American labor

GREEN, WILLIAM, *Labor and Democracy*
  Modern labor problems

BARBASH, JACK, *Labor Unions in Action*

HUGHES, RUPERT, *The Giant Awakes*
  Life of Samuel Gompers

The United States Faces Today's World

INTRODUCTION

It seems fitting that we should close this brief review of the history of our land with a survey of the place of the United States in the world today. The United States led the nations fighting Germany and Italy and Japan through World War II. Then the United States took the lead in organizing and establishing the United Nations, a world organization designed to prevent further war. The United States was the most powerful nation in the world, and it seemed willing to assume the great responsibility that goes with such power. But it was not at all certain that the United States recognized the full extent of that responsibility. It seemed probable that this country would have to learn through experience the full scope of activity it must undertake if it were to discharge the obligations of its world position.

In this unit we trace the history of the United States as a world power in its relations with the nations of the postwar world. Then the last chapter of the book is an attempt by the author to set you thinking about the future of our land. The value to you in knowing the story of our nation in the past is that you may do a better job of shaping its future. The United States of tomorrow can be whatever we want it to be. But if it is, we shall all have to work hard at the job. To work together to attain the results we want, is your task and mine in this land of ours.

Chapter 27

The United States Tries To Help the Postwar World

WORLD LEADERSHIP BRINGS THE UNITED STATES A TREMENDOUS AMOUNT OF WORLD RESPONSIBILITY

Conditions of the World After the War. In this last unit of a brief look at the history of our land, it seems fitting that we should consider the status of the United States in the world today. In this chapter we shall confine ourselves to the most important developments that concern our relationship to the rest of the world in the years that have passed since the end of World War II.

Let's begin with a look at the world in which we found ourselves at the conclusion of the war. Actually, it was a postwar world only in the sense that there was no military action going on in a large scale; there were plenty of international crises and even minor wars, some of which threatened to become serious challenges to the peace that had so recently been established, if we may use the word *peace* here in a very loose sense.

Responsibility of the United States. As the months passed, it became increasingly clear that what had happened in World War II could well be summed up in this fashion. Most of the nations of the world had co-operated to destroy the Fascist Powers. That didn't mean we liked the so-called Communist Powers; joining the anti-Fascists was a marriage of necessity, not of love, although we hadn't always recognized it as such. Now that the war was over, the world was returning to its historic struggle for power. It appeared we had fought a war to keep Germany, Italy, and Japan from building empires, but in the process we had assisted the Soviet Union to get a start on building one of its own. This was due largely to the fact that our wartime policy was the negative policy of defeat for the three Axis Powers; there was no positive, constructive policy to hold the victors together after the negative, destructive policy had been realized.

Someone has said that the only thing the United States won by World War II was permanent possession of the crisis. This is just another way of saying that when the war was over, the United States was recognized the world over as the most powerful of all nations and the natural one to assume the leadership in a world-wide move to prevent another war. That is, most of the world held this opinion except, notably, the Soviet Union and, perhaps, the United States itself. It is not at all evident that the American people, while they liked to think of themselves as the greatest nation in the world, realized the tremendous responsibility that must go with such a position.

England Fights for Life. Great Britain, long the dominant power in world affairs, was obviously no longer able to continue in that role. Britain's power had begun to wane when the United States became the world's number one industrial nation prior to World War I and the world's banker following that war. The tremendous bombing attacks that England had undergone during World War II, plus the fact that the prosecution of the war had forced her to use up her money reserves, both of cash and credits, over the world, left her in a weaker condition than she had known for centuries. Britain's problem after the war was not how to maintain her empire; that she could not do. Her biggest problem was how to maintain life for her own people.

The English people chose to try to meet this problem by voting a socialist Labor Government into power. Regardless of the merit or lack of merit of socialism as a form of government, it would appear that this was not a wise time to try it in England. There was the huge cost of paying for the nationalization of industry at the same time that the bill had to be paid for reconstruction, and the attempt to regain the world market for British goods that had been lost during the war, and without which Britain could not possibly pay her own way in the world. With regard to Great Britain, the United States was forced to decide two things: (1) that we have no right to attempt to determine the kind of government the people of any other nation put into power, and (2) that we must assist Britain in its reconstruction because, in our new position of world leader, we need a strong Britain as our ally.

Russia Advances as a World Power. On the European scene also, the Union of Soviet Socialist Republics, unlike Great Britain, was advancing as a world power, a power with goals yet to be realized. Russian territory is consolidated, more like that of the United States than the far-flung empire Britain was trying to hold on to or, failing to hold on, to release gracefully. Russia is in an ideal position, geographically, to dominate all Europe and Asia, and possibly most of the world. Vast natural resources and manpower make her a threat to the balance of power that has been favorable to the English-speaking peoples so long. Russia was damaged greatly during the war, perhaps more than any other country, but her comeback was rapid, for dictator-disciplined people respond well to government planning.

During the war, while the United States and our allies were driving Germany, Italy, and Japan from land they had seized, the Soviet Union was busy adding territory to its own growing empire. During the war it succeeded in acquiring Latvia, Lithuania, Esthonia, and part of Finland in the Baltic region, as well as East Prussia, Poland, and Bessarabia in central Europe, and the Kurile Islands, the rest of Sakhalin, part control of the ports of Dairen and Port Arthur, and railway rights through Manchuria in Asia. Since the war she has added spheres of influence that extend from the Baltic Sea through the Balkans to the Mediterranean in Europe, through Manchuria into Korea and China in the Far East, and include oil rights in the Middle East.

The Soviet policy has been to move into any vacuum that appeared, rather than forceful aggression. The ravages of the war left many weak areas in the world, into which Russia has been quick to extend her influence to the point of setting up friendly governments, often with the assistance of her willing tool, communism. Russia clamed she was doing this for her own security. As the United States faced this situation, we were confronted with three big questions: (1) Where does security stop and imperialism begin? (2) How can Russian expansion be stopped? (3) Is war with Russia inevitable?

France and Her Need for Help. France had been one of our principal allies in both world wars of the twentieth century. World War I left her the strongest power on the European continent. At the end of World War II she was weak and virtually defenseless. This was due in large part to her lack of coal, most of which she had to get from the Ruhr Valley. This explains France's continuing desire to annex the Ruhr.

France stood between the two giants of the postwar world, and her position was fraught with considerable danger. Her chief fear was that she should have to choose between the United States and Great Britain on one hand and the the Soviet Union on the other. By her culture, her government, and her economic dependence, she was tied to the West, but after the war there was a noticeable leaning toward Russia (1) because of her anti-fascist attitude, (2) because she chose to place considerable limitation upon her capitalism, and (3) because Russia is geographically much closer to her than the United States is.

No political party was strong enough to control a majority in the French Assembly, so a coalition government was inevitable. This meant a great deal of wrangling among the parties and an instability of government that did not bode well for France. All the parties did have at least one thing in common; they favored the nationalization of many French industries, so all were socialistic to some degree. Much of this desire for government seizure of industry resulted from the fact that many Frenchmen who controlled industry had collaborated with the Nazis during the war.

French production was low; her transportation facilities were sadly disrupted; she needed more raw materials and food and fuel. Clearly she would have to have economic aid if she were to get back onto her feet again. The Communists were quick to seize upon her weakness as their opportunity. It seemed clear that a United States policy that only opposed communism would not be enough, that a policy which would help France fill her needs would be best in the long run for this country to follow.

What Should We Do about Germany? Another big problem for the United States was what to do about Germany. Immediately at the end of the war we were upon both horns of the dilemma. We wanted to so control the country that it would be impossible for her to start another war. At the same time, we recognized the need to rebuild German industry as a prime requisite to German recovery and the self-sufficiency of western Europe. But Germany had been divided among Great Britain, France, the Soviet Union, and the United States, and the danger was that the four occupying powers could not agree on policies for Germany and would turn the country into a theater where the power-politics drama might play itself out.

What Should Be America's Policy? All in all, the problem was about the same for most of western Europe: how to deal with hunger, economic exhaustion, inflated prices, lack of jobs, and a reaction against Hitlerism that seemed likely to impel the various nations toward either the democracies of the West or the totalitarian imperialism of the East. In this situation several selfish interests in Europe were clamoring for American support, claiming in each case that they had the best solution to the problem. Among these interests was the Fascist Franco Government of Spain, which had been frankly pro-Nazi but had remained out of the war; the various governments in exile of nations that fell to an enemy power during the war; the imperialists of France and Holland; and the wealthy landowners in central Europe and the Balkans.

But the trend of history is toward greater economic democracy. A purely anti-Russian policy adopted by the United States, one which refused to work with any of the Leftist movements, would alienate most of the people and would only serve to give Russia a clear field with all the popular movements in the various countries and would thus abandon Europe to her. It appeared that the most realistic policy for the United States to follow would be one that would permit European nations to establish governments which provided opportunity for national planning for reconstruction and at the same time preserved freedom of individual initiative.

The New State of Israel. In the Middle East the turmoil was heightened by the establishment of the new state of Israel, a national home for Jews. Certainly they needed it, having been driven from most of the countries of Europe during the war, those who were not murdered. The creation of Israel touched off again the old struggle between Jews and Arabs for control of Palestine and surrounding territory. The lurking fear was that the Arabs would appeal to Russia for help and that Russia would be glad to fish in such troubled waters. And behind it all lay the fact that the Middle East possesses a great deal of oil, and many nations wanted to get control of it, including the United States.

Struggle for Control in the Far East. The situation in the Far East was an unhappy one, too. There the defeat of Japan had left a void which invited a struggle for control by outside powers. During the war basic support for the Kuomintang, or Nationalist Party in China, had shifted from the wealthy industrialists to the wealthy landowners. At the same time, the Chinese Communist group had enlarged its reform program to take in industry as well as agriculture. But both were resorting to totalitarian methods to gain or hold any advantage.

The big problem the United States faced in China was how to keep the Communists from gaining greater power, for a Communist-controlled China might easily fall under the influence of the Soviet Union. The soundest approach to this problem seemed to indicate continued support for Nationalist leader Chiang Kai-shek, coupled with a firm insistence that his program be enlarged to include greater reform—that is, to steal the thunder of the Chinese Reds and render them impotent.

To the south of China, in India, great changes were in the making. The new Labor Government of Great Britain had decided to grant India her long-sought independence. When the actual separation was to be made, religious differences forced the creation of not one but two new nations in the Indian peninsula—the Union of India, where Hinduism is the dominant religion, and Pakistan, in which Mohammedanism is the principal religion. On August 15, 1947, India and Pakistan became free dominions in the Commonwealth of Nations. But although independence had been gained, the future was not all rosy, for there were still many differences between the two to be resolved. And the danger was that these differences might not be worked out peacefully. War in the Indian peninsula would be an invitation for Russia to seek warm-water ports there. Great Britain would try to come to the defense of India and Pakistan, and the United States would probably feel obliged to do the same. Trouble in India could easily become trouble for all the world.

A similar danger existed in other parts of southern Asia. In Indonesia and Indo-China in particular there was a growing desire to be free from outside control in order that the people might build independent nations of their own. In this they were simply following the pattern of history, although centuries behind the more advanced countries. It was not that these peoples wanted just to rid themselves of their present rulers; they wanted to be free entirely of Western rule and influence. The problem for the United States was how could we best aid these peoples in achieving their natural desire for freedom peaceably, without being guilty of imperialism ourselves.

The problem of defeated Japan was almost identical with that of Germany. Before the war, Japan had been the industrial center of Asia. To permit her to become self-supporting again, her industry would have to be rebuilt. But the prewar industrial leaders had had a great deal to do with promoting the war, and certainly we did not want to rebuild Japan only to see her try again to create an all-Asia empire under her control. Here again were both horns of that perplexing dilemma.

The military occupation of Japan was organized under General Douglas MacArthur. It was early decided that the emperor was to be left on the throne, was not to be tried as a war criminal. Shinto, the state religion of emperor worship, was abolished by MacArthur's decree, and the Tenno (emperor) appealed to the people to look upon him from that time on as just an ordinary human being and not a god. The Zaibatsu, the combination of five wealthy families who had controlled about 95 per cent of the wealth of Japan before the war, was ordered broken up. After five years of occupation, Japan had a new constitution guaranteeing trial by jury, universal suffrage, and American concepts of civil liberties. The population had increased to 83,000,000; the health standards were the highest in history, the birth rate at a record high of 1,500,000 increase yearly. New farming methods had been introduced, and the nation had gone a long way toward full economic recovery. Early in 1951, President Truman sent John Foster Dulles to discuss terms of a peace treaty with the Japanese Prime Minister Yoshida.

Kay Tateishi Photo, Scene Magazine

U.S. DEVELOPS POLICY ON JAPAN'S RECONSTRUCTION

After V-J Day, the devastating effectiveness of B-29 raids over Japan during World War II was measured by the U.S. Strategic Bombing Survey. It found that Japan's war-making potential had been greatly reduced by destruction of such key industrial centers as Nagoya, where this picture was taken. In the postwar period, U.S. policy at first stressed the need to dismantle the remaining Japanese industrial machine. By 1951 that policy had shifted to a decision to help rebuild Japanese industry with U.S. aid.

Kay Tateishi Photo, Scene Magazine

WHERE JAPAN'S PARLIAMENT LAUNCHED A NEW ERA

The Japanese legislature, referred to as the "Diet," convenes in the marble building shown here. Built before World War II, it escaped bomb damage. Although the counterpart of the United States Congress, the Japanese Diet before the war exercised virtually no significant power. In postwar Japan, its role in the governing of Japan has increased greatly.

United States and the Western Hemisphere. Even in the Western Hemisphere the United States was not without its problems. For a century the leadership of the United States in American affairs had been unchallenged. During and following the war new and nondemocratic leadership arose in Latin America to contest the position of the northern neighbor. The principal challenger was the regime of Juan Perón in Argentina.

From the time the Spanish and Portuguese colonies in Central and South America had declared and won their freedom in the early part of the nineteenth century, the new nations that called themselves republics had actually operated as feudal societies under military dictatorships. There were frequent revolutions, often violent, that brought with them changes in government. We protected the new republics with our Monroe Doctrine, but we found dealing with them was difficult because of the sudden changes of leaders and policies.

Toward the Latin American republics the United States has pursued two rather opposing courses. We have staunchly supported the idea of political democracy for these countries. But often we have engaged in economic imperialism, even to the point at times of military intervention. The charge that the United States has sometimes been guilty of "dollar diplomacy" has not always been unfounded.

The Perón regime was a carry-over from the war. It has been openly pro-Fascist. There seems to be good evidence that originally it was a part of the plan Hitler had for his eventual move against the United States, through Latin America. We have not liked it. At first we tried to appease it after a fashion, in order to render it ineffective. That didn't work. Then we turned to a policy of firmness and exposure of its pro-Fascist tendencies. That was largely unsuccessful, too, because we stood alone; both England and Russia profited too much from trade with Argentina to back us up. As the months went by, it became rather clear that at home in the Western Hemisphere we needed the same kind of policy that appeared indicated for the rest of the world—a policy of support for democratic forces in their struggle to overcome totalitarianism in any of its forms.

This, then, was our postwar world, a world dominated by fear, when all its people wanted security. Great Britain, bled of her financial resources, was afraid of our economic power. She feared the spread of Russian Communism and the rising nationalism of her colonial peoples. Russia was afraid of internal uprisings, of a united, unfriendly western Europe, of the natural opposition of capitalism, and of an envisioned attempt by the rest of the world to build a circle of unfriendly na-

tions around her. France was afraid of a reconstructed, powerful Germany, of her old rival Britain, and, like Britain, of American economic power. China was afraid of all Western Powers, at whose hands she has suffered much, and of prolonged internal strife. The United States feared British diplomacy and trade, Russian imperialism, and the spread of communism. And all the world was afraid of a war with atomic weapons. Such was our postwar world. And in the midst of it stood the United States—fearful, uncertain, hesitant.

Thus far in this chapter we have considered the situation in various areas of the world following World War II in relation to the United States. Now let us see what the developments have been in the past five years regarding those situations.

RECENT DEVELOPMENTS OF POSTWAR SITUATIONS

Stimulating International Trade. The United States recognized that the problem of getting war-torn nations to the point where they could support themselves would not be an easy one to solve. The big difficulty was this. Most of the goods other nations needed could be procured only from the United States. That, of course, would be good for us. But the catch was that we expected to be paid for them in dollars, and the rest of the world had no dollars with which to buy. So trade was at a standstill.

In order to get trade moving again, the United States recognized the necessity for "priming the pump." That is, in order for other nations to be able again to buy from us, we must first make dollars available to them, either by loans or outright gifts. In three years immedi-

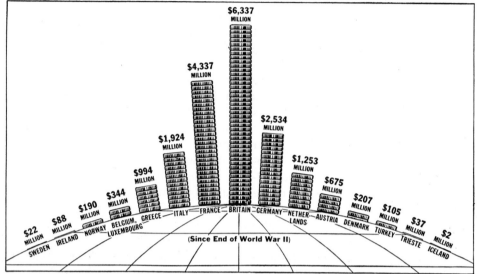

$6,337 MILLION

$4,337 MILLION

$2,534 MILLION

$1,924 MILLION

$1,253 MILLION

$994 MILLION

$675 MILLION

$344 MILLION

$207 MILLION

$190 MILLION

$105 MILLION

$88 MILLION

$37 MILLION

$22 MILLION

$2 MILLION

SWEDEN   IRELAND   NORWAY   BELGIUM, LUXEMBOURG   GREECE   ITALY   FRANCE   BRITAIN   GERMANY   NETHERLANDS   AUSTRIA   DENMARK   TURKEY   TRIESTE   ICELAND

(Since End of World War II)

U.S. News & World Report (5-27-49). © *U.S. News Pub. Corp.*

UNITED STATES LOANS AND GRANTS TO EUROPEAN COUNTRIES, 1945–1949

Some idea of the enormous amounts of money and goods made available by the United States to European countries, including Turkey and Iceland, after World War II can be gained from this graphic presentation of the record. The figures above the coin stacks measure, in millions of dollars, the amounts of assistance extended to the various countries represented. China, the occupied areas, and other non-European countries were also aided by the United States during this period, but such disbursements are not represented in the drawing.

ately following the war, the United States extended to other nations some twenty-two billion dollars in grants and credits.

The Marshall Plan. A major part of our assistance abroad has been accomplished under the European Recovery Program (ERP), popularly called the Marshall Plan because the idea for it was first advanced by then Secretary of State George C. Marshall in a speech delivered at Harvard University on June 5, 1947. Under ERP, American dollars were to be made available to those European countries who agreed to co-operate with us, with a high percentage of the dollars to be earmarked for the purchase of needed supplies in this country. In addition to the Marshall Plan, the United States has made

loans of money to countries in other parts of the world, among them notably China, Greece, and Turkey. Great Britain also has received extra credits, the first being a loan of $3,750,000,000.

In the beginning the Marshall Plan was seen entirely as an aid to reconstruction from the ravages of war. "Our policy," said General Marshall, "is not directed against any country or doctrine but against hunger, poverty, desperation, and chaos." The plan was intended to remain in operation, with decreasing amounts to be spent each year, until 1952. It was thought that by that time the countries of Europe should be able to go their way alone again.

Before long it became clear that the policy of aid to Europe would in all

POSTWAR FOREIGN ASSISTANCE
BY THE UNITED STATES GOVERNMENT

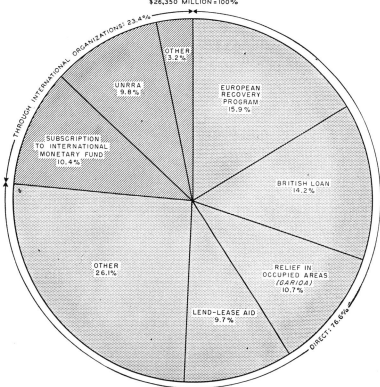

TOTAL, JULY 1, 1945 – JUNE 30, 1949
$26,350 MILLION = 100%

THROUGH INTERNATIONAL ORGANIZATIONS: 23.4%

OTHER 3.2%

UNRRA 9.8%

EUROPEAN RECOVERY PROGRAM 15.9%

SUBSCRIPTION TO INTERNATIONAL MONETARY FUND 10.4%

BRITISH LOAN 14.2%

OTHER 26.1%

RELIEF IN OCCUPIED AREAS (GARIOA) 10.7%

LEND-LEASE AID 9.7%

DIRECT: 76.6%

$123 MILLION

FISCAL YEAR 1949
$6,377 MILLION

$4,043 MILLION	$1,329 MILLION	$882 MILLION
EUROPEAN RECOVERY PROGRAM	RELIEF IN OCCUPIED AREAS (GARIOA)	OTHER

▲THROUGH INTERNATIONAL ORGANIZATIONS

The bulk of our foreign aid is now advanced through the European Recovery Program. Spending is handled by the Economic Cooperation Administration.

Total foreign aid, as shown in the chart, includes funds going directly to countries as business-type loans or in other forms. It also includes United States subscriptions to the capital of the International Bank and the Monetary Fund and other indirect aid.

Some direct aid is not identified. Examples are grants to Greece, Turkey and China, Export-Import Bank loans, property transfers through the Foreign Liquidation Commissioner.

Source: Bureau of the Budget

National Industrial Conference Board, Inc.

VARIOUS FORMS OF U.S. FOREIGN AID

A pie diagram in the above illustration shows in what manner the United States disbursed nearly 26.5 billion dollars worth of foreign assistance to countries all over the world during a four-year period from mid-1945 to mid-1949. This sum of almost 26.5 billion dollars represents a grand total of all aid given during the period—to non-European as well as European countries, as aid through international organizations as well as direct aid. The segments of the pie show the percentages of total aid that were extended as E.R.P. (European Recovery Program) funds—in the form of funds loaned to Britain, in the form of lend-lease funds, and so on.

probability have to be continued beyond 1952. And the European Recovery Program began to take on a new purpose. It was no longer concerned simply with improving the living conditions of the people. It now became a device for winning the friendship of European nations to our side and away from the Soviet Union.

The United States was experiencing a sad turn of affairs. We had just joined with most of the world to prevent Germany, Italy, and Japan from building empires, but now it became evident that in accomplishing that, we had also assisted another nation, the Soviet Union,

to get a start on building an empire of its own. We had joined with the so-called Communists during the war, but it had been a marriage of convenience rather than love. However, that fact was much more clear to the Communists than it was to citizens of the United States. We seemed to think that, somehow, when Hitler attacked Russia and forced Stalin over onto our side, that dictator's hands were suddenly cleansed of the blood of his many purges and mass exterminations. Later we were to realize that Russia's sole purpose in fighting on our side was self-preservation.

Acme

HARRY S. TRUMAN AND GEORGE C. MARSHALL

Pictured here are the two principals after whom the Truman Doctrine and the Marshall Plan were named.

As time went on, it was obvious that all the extension of Russian influence into country after country could not be written off simply as Stalin's desire to make his country secure from any future attack. Although the Soviet Union had signed as a charter member of the United Nations, clearly she was using the security excuse as an alibi to build an empire of her own. Soon the big question in the minds of people in this country was: Can the Soviet Union be stopped without our having to fight?

Truman Doctrine. Even before the Marshall Plan was proposed, President Truman had taken note of this situation. On March 12, 1947, he announced what has since been called the Truman Doctrine. At that time it was applied just to Greece and Turkey, to whom we agreed to grant loans and send equipment and men to assist the Greek and Turkish armies in a program of modernization. The basic idea of the Truman Doctrine seemed to be that this country would lend aid to any country that was interested in opposing the spread of communism. While the ideal may have been good, the prospect of the United States rushing here and there about the world trying to plug holes in every dike through which communism threatened to pour was not a happy one.

The "Cold War" and "Iron Curtain." As the months went by, the tension between the Soviet Union and the Western world became more and more intense. It was customary to refer to this tension as the "cold war," and to wonder just how soon, if at all, it might convert itself into a shooting war. The United States became gravely concerned less Russia should decide to engulf suddenly the war-weakened countries of western Europe before they were in a condition to defend themselves. As a warning to the Soviet Union and an attempt to bolster the courage of the nations of western Europe, the United States signed an alliance with several of those countries. The North Atlantic Alliance, or Atlantic Pact, went into effect on August 24, 1949. Counting the original signers and those who entered later, the Pact included Great Britain, France, Belgium, the Netherlands, Luxemburg, Italy, Norway, Denmark, and Portugal in Europe, Iceland in the North Atlantic, and Canada and the United States in North America. In the beginning the Pact was designed for its moral assistance principally, but later the United States decided to implement it with military help, and in 1950 began shipping military supplies to the other members. Of course, it was clear to everyone that the state of preparedness of the countries of western Europe could not possibly stop Russia if she should decide to move in, but it was hoped those countries would be encouraged to slow up the Russian advance long enough to permit the United States to get to their aid in an effective manner.

As is so often true of dictatorships, continued control of Russia by Stalin depends partly upon control of the people's thinking by the leaders of the Soviet Politburo, or ruling group. To this end, these men imposed a most rigid censorship upon all news of any kind coming into or going out of Russia. Freedom of the press was unknown. Any attempt at free speech was dangerous. Foreign newspaper correspondents were frequently expelled. It became customary to refer to the wall of silence thus erected between the Soviet Union

Acme

COLD-WAR PREPAREDNESS

British troops with armored cars stand ready for trouble in the Western zone of Berlin.

and the outside world as the "iron curtain."

As the "cold war" wore on, each side apparently hoped that some changes in the fortunes of the other would give it the advantage. The Soviet Union was counting on another economic depression in the United States to bring American withdrawal from world affairs. And the United States hoped that difficulty over who would succeed Stalin as leader in Russia would provoke a revolution there. On both sides it appeared to be wishful thinking. Although American business did experience a brief recession in 1949, business remained good and no depression of any size appeared imminent. No signs of any serious break could be seen in Russia, although serious defection did occur in Yugoslavia, one of the Soviet satellites.

Two Types of Communism. The break that did take place between Stalin and Marshal Tito (Josip Broz) of Yugoslavia served to distinguish for the world between the two types of communism that were developing. Stalin's communism allowed for no local rule; all the national leaders must be subservient to the will of the over-all leader, Stalin. But Tito, while staunchly communist, wanted his communism to be nationalistic. He wanted to operate it according to his desires and not those of Stalin. He himself wanted to be the top man and not have to take orders from Moscow. Stalin opposed Tito with all the means at his command, short of actual war, for if Tito were successful, it might mark the beginning of a series of revolts against the rule of the Kremlin. But in spite of all Stalin could do, Tito maintained his command of the situation in Yugoslavia.

A fundamental change was taking place in American foreign policy. Because this country needed friends badly, we let it be known that we might be willing to grant loans to Yugoslavia as a sort of reward for the attitude Tito was taking toward Stalin. This meant that the United States was now drawing a fine line of distinction between communism and Soviet imperialism. We were saying, in effect, that this country had no right to try to dictate the kind of government any other country should have and that we would accept on our side any country that opposed Russian imperialism, even if it were communistic. Later the United States did loan several million dollars to Yugoslavia. Our treatment of Tito raised the question of the possibility that similar treatment might be extended to the

Acme

AIR LIFT VERSUS BERLIN BLOCKADE

Berliners in the above picture stand amid the World War II ruins of their city as they watch an American plane fly in food and supplies to Tempelhof Airdrome, which lies within the Western sector of the German capital.

Fascist Franco Government of Spain.

Germany—a Big Sore Spot. Perhaps the biggest sore spot in Europe for the United States has been Germany. As has been pointed out, Germany was divided among the occupying troops of Great Britain, France, Soviet Russia, and the United States. Berlin, the former German capital, was likewise divided between Russia and the Western Powers. Here was a point of almost constant friction. Russia's obvious desire was to unite Germany again under her rule. She lost no opportunity to make things uncomfortable for the other occupying powers, in the hope, apparently, that they would become discouraged and get out. At one time Russia went so far as to close all train and truck routes into Berlin from the west,

thus making it extremely difficult to supply West Berlin with food and fuel. To meet the emergency, Britain and the United States inaugurated an air-lift— a steady stream of planes carrying into Berlin the goods needed. This air-lift operated from June 26, 1948, until September 30, 1949, and in those months carried into Berlin a total of 2,343,315 tons of food and coal on 277,264 flights. The lift was terminated only when Russia again opened the avenues of land transportation into the city.

On May 23, 1949, in Bonn, the Federal Republic of Germany was proclaimed. This new state was composed of the territory occupied by Great Britain, France, and the United States. It was the Western Powers' answer to

Russia's refusal to work toward a peace treaty for Germany that would permit the entire nation to be united again. The new state was received with mixed feeling. Looked at one way, it marked a defeat for Russia. But looked at another way, it seemed to presage further trouble, for the German people were not likely to accept willingly any move which would tend to keep them permanently divided.

Before long there was talk of inviting West Germany into the Atlantic Alliance. If this were done, it would probably mean that the new state would have to be permitted to rearm again, and this possibility was met with great objection by France, who viewed with alarm any chance that a powerful Germany might rise again.

In the early spring of 1950 there was considerable excitement in Germany for the rumor was abroad that a youth meeting was to be held in May in the Eastern or Russian zone and that this meeting would be used as an excuse to send armed youth and soldiers into the Western zone to seize control. Later information indicated that the invasion was to be for propaganda purposes only, but officials in the western part of Berlin made preparations for anything that might develop. Obviously, one of the main theaters of the "cold war" was in Germany, where both Western Powers and the Soviet Union vied with each other for the allegiance of the people all of them had so recently joined together to defeat. When the youth meeting was held, no serious difficulty resulted.

Conditions in the Middle East. In the Middle East a reasonable degree of peace seemed to have arrived. The credit for working out the details of arrangements between the Jews and the Arabs must go to United Nations' Representative Dr. Ralph Bunche, who in that dispute gave an excellent demonstration of the power of honest and fair-minded statesmanship.

Communists in Power in China. Another world area in which the United States has been caused a great deal of worry and no little chagrin is China. We had fought a war with Japan largely to protect the integrity of China. Then when the war was over, we continued to support the Kuomintang or Nationalist Government of Chiang Kai-shek in its civil war against the Chinese Communists. This was an old struggle, dating back before the war, which had been somewhat forgotten in the fight with Japan. When Japan surrendered, it broke out anew. The United States realized that Chiang's government had become corrupt and was not the liberal type of government the people wanted. We made repeated attempts to get Chiang to reform his government so that he could win the support of the Chinese people, but to no avail. Apparently the Nationalist leaders believed that they could continue to have American backing without reforming their government because of the mounting tension between the United States and the communist movement all over the world.

As the months went by, the Chinese Communists continued to gain ground against the Nationalists. General George C. Marshall was sent to China to try to get Chiang's government to put reforms into operation as the price of continued American assistance, but the aid kept right on coming, and the Marshall mission failed. Later, General Albert C. Wedemeyer went out to

China on a similar mission. On September 19, 1947, he presented his report to the State Department. It was not made public until 1951 when a Senate joint committee held hearings to investigate President Truman's dismissal of General MacArthur. The Wedemeyer report recommended in 1947 that Manchuria either be put under guardianship of the United States, Great Britain, China, France, and the Soviet Union, or that it be placed under a United Nations trusteeship. One of the reasons for not making the report public was that it contained an evaluation of the situation that would not have appealed to the American people. General Wedemeyer sized things up this way: He did not believe the Chinese Communists could be beaten by military moves only; Chiang Kai-shek was determined to use only military measures against them, refusing to reform his government to meet the needs of the people. Therefore, if the United States was to support Chiang, the obvious thing we must do was to go into China with enough men and equipment to win the war against the Communists for the Nationalists. The State Department knew the American people would not back such a policy, so said nothing about it.

General Wedemeyer himself must have realized that the American people would not want to see another war follow so close on the heels of the last one. He must have recognized even then that American influence was bound to wane in the Orient. Writing back from China, General Wedemeyer saw the situation this way:

With approximately 80 per cent of the population illiterate, it is in my opinion unsound to expect true democratic pro-

United Nations

DR. RALPH J. BUNCHE

As top-ranking director of the Division of Trusteeships for the United Nations, Dr. Bunche performed a notable service in mediating the Jewish-Arab disputes in Palestine in 1948–49. He was awarded the Nobel Peace Prize.

cedures. However, we Americans should support the aspirations of the Chinese to improve their cultural position and to participate intelligently and realistically in their government. I retain the conviction that the Generalissimo is sincere in his desire to accomplish these objectives. Contingent upon the assistance or the interference injected by outside countries, essentially the United States and the Soviet Union, the Generalissimo will make definite strides toward the attainment of these goals. Conditions in the Far East after the war were similar to those in Europe with disrupted economy, political dissensions and widespread disillusionment. The Soviet Union capitalized fully upon the disorganization and chaos in the area exactly as she has done in Europe. Soviet propa-

Acme

MAO TZE-TUNG

The communist boss of nearly a half-billion Chinese came from a farm home in Hunan Province. As a youth, he rebelled against his father's authority, skipped classes at the village school to read dialectical books, and persisted in his refusal to become an apprentice of a rice merchant. He left home to study in Changsha, took assorted courses, worked at odd jobs, and read Adam Smith, Spencer, Mill, Darwin, Rousseau, and Marx. China's revolution against the Manchu dynasty and Russia's Red revolution influenced his thoughts and actions and, beginning in the 1920's, Mao's name became more and more conspicuous in the affairs of China's Communist Party.

ganda and Soviet support of the Chinese Communist movement have increased the difficulties of establishing order in China. Also corruption and maladministration on the part of the Chinese National Government have greatly retarded stabilization and rehabilitation.

I am convinced that the bulk of the Chinese people do not want to become Communists. However, they are realists and accept passively any form of government that will provide food and shelter. They do not consider the implications of orienting themselves toward Moscow. The popularity of the National Government, and even of the Generalissimo, is waning and unless drastic reforms, particularly in the economic field, are implemented soon, China will be drawn into the Soviet orbit in spite of the assistance that we Americans might extend.

The United States did not send troops to Chiang's aid, and little by little the Communists took over. On September 21, 1949, the People's Republic of China was proclaimed with Peiping as the new capital. Communist leader Mao Tze-tung headed the new government, with Chou En-lai as Premier and Foreign Minister. The Nationalist Government fled from the mainland and set up new headquarters on the island of Formosa.

Great Britain and several other countries were quick to recognize the new government in China because they had large investments there and wished to continue to trade with China. The United States refused to take such a step at that time, although official recognition that a government controls a country does not necessarily carry with it approbation of the government. Several American officials in China were subjected to serious inconvenience and mistreatment, all of which only served to postpone indefinitely the day when American recognition might be granted. Instead, the United States continued to send supplies to Chiang Kai-shek, although we were careful to see that most of them were not of a military nature.

So, at the middle of the century, a Communist Government was in power in China, and it seemed likely to stay in power for a long time. The United States had fought a war with Japan to save China, and then through our untimely policy and the unalterable position of Chiang Kai-shek had lost the opportunity to assist in the modernization and development of China, with all the accompanying valuable trade that could have been ours. Even more significant, this country viewed with alarm the possibility that victorious communism in China would endeavor to continue its expansion into other parts of Asia. American prestige in the Orient had suffered a body-blow.

India and Pakistan Make an Agreement. In India things were not going too well. After India and Pakistan were granted their independence, the great Indian leader Mohandas Gandhi did much to help bring agreement on many of the points of conflict between the Hindu and Moslem nations. Then, on January 30, 1948, Gandhi fell before an assassin's bullet. The world was deeply shocked, and it would be difficult indeed to assess the loss to the people of the Indian peninsula. Jawaharlal Nehru, Prime Minister of India, succeeded to Gandhi's position in the hearts of the Indian people. Nehru later visited the United States, where he was given a royal welcome. Our government recognized the importance of winning the support of India as a maneuver in our "cold war" with Russia.

But as the months went by, tension rose between India and Pakistan, principally over trade matters and the relocation of people, and it looked as if war might easily result. The resulting weakness would be sure to provide a fertile bed for Communist propaganda. Then in the spring of 1950 an agreement was reached between India and Pakistan that greatly relieved the situation. It appeared there would be no war, for the time being at least.

The United States of Indonesia. At the mid-point of the twentieth century, the move for independent nationalism was strong throughout southeastern Asia. The Indian people had won their freedom and had set up two new nations. The people of the Dutch East Indies and of French Indo-China wanted to do the same. They had been conquered by the Japanese during the war and then had been freed, largely by the Americans and the British. But they did not want to be handed back to the Dutch and the French again.

For some time there was considerable fighting between Netherlands troops and the troops of the nationalist movement in Indonesia. Finally, late in 1949, an agreement was signed in The Hague providing for the creation of the United States of Indonesia, which was to have control of most of the territory of the Dutch East Indies. The United States of Indonesia were to be independent, but were to be bound together with the Netherlands in a union headed by Queen Juliana. Thus another empire was liquidated peacefully.

Indo-China and Its Two Governments. Things did not progress so well in Indo-China. A fairly strong Communist group had developed there, and the French were required to use considerable force to keep control. The

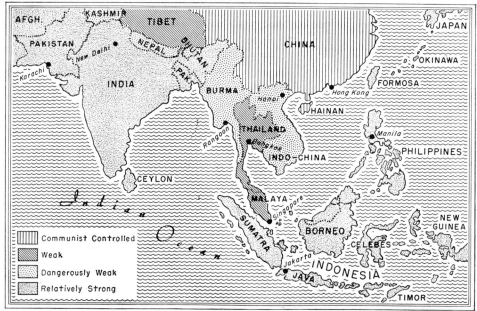

U.S. News & World Report (4-7-50) © U.S. News Pub. Corp.

STRENGTH AND WEAKNESS OF COUNTRIES IN SOUTHEAST ASIA

Many countries of southeast Asia find themselves in the difficult position of asserting their independence at a time when pressures are being applied on them by the communist and anti-communist world.

situation became more tense after the establishment of the Communist People's Government in China, for the Communists in Indo-China anticipated assistance from their friends across the border. The French had established a native government under its protection led by the Emperor Bao Dai, against the Communist Ho Chi Minh. Drawing the line more sharply, the United States gave recognition to the government of Bao Dai. There was the possibility that the Soviet Union might in turn recognize the Communist Government of Ho Chi Minh and thus create a situation in Indo-China comparable to the one that already existed in Germany. It was pretty clear that the regime of Bao Dai could exist only so long as either France or the United States supported it with troops and military supplies. The peo-

ple's desire to be free was not to be denied, even if they had to turn Communist to realize it. In the fall of 1950, Communist armies were highly successful against French troops in the northern part of the country, and it was generally feared that Indo-China might develop into another Korea.

American Control in Japan. In 1950 General Douglas MacArthur remained in control of Japan, but the Japanese people were asking more and more frequently when the American troops were to be withdrawn. There was some talk of proceeding with a peace treaty for Japan without Russia if that country refused to participate. The general tense situation throughout the world made it appear likely that in the terms of any peace treaty, Japan would be included in what came to be referred to as the American "perimeter of defense."

Organization of American States. The United States was losing no opportunity to promote the solidarity of the Americas. The mutual feeling that the states of North, Central, and South America should be bound together more tightly in a defensive pact, under the provision in the United Nations Charter for regional agreements, resulted in the establishment of the Organization of the American States at a meeting of twenty-one of the American republics at Bogota, Colombia, in 1948. The principal provision pledged the member nations to the defense of anyone that was attacked by a power from outside the American continents. In this manner, defense of the Western Hemisphere by the United States established by our Monroe Doctrine was replaced by the mutual protection of the American republics, working together. The conference at Bogota also approved a treaty calling for economic co-operation among the member states, and agreed upon united resistance to communism.

Most of the Latin American states showed a willingness to go along under the leadership of the United States, al-

U.S. Army Photo

U.S. OCCUPATION FORCES IN JAPAN

Duties performed by U.S. occupation personnel in such civilian affairs as directing traffic were soon turned over to the sole jurisdiction of the Japanese. In June, 1950, at the outbreak of the war in Korea, the U.S. armed forces stationed in Japan were virtually depleted as a result of the order to drive the North Korean invaders out of South Korea. General MacArthur then authorized the formation of a National Police Reserve Corps in Japan of 75,000 men to take over duties originally assigned to U.S. occupation forces.

though some of them made it plain that they would prefer economic assistance in the form of investment of private capital rather than government capital. Argentina continued to favor her European friends instead of the United States, but in 1950 this program threatened the breakdown of her economic system and forced her to reconsider her relationship with her neighbor in North America. The United States appeared willing to lend some economic assistance if Argentina were to adopt a more friendly attitude.

Search for Communists in Our Government. Beginning in 1947, and continuing into 1950, a series of charges from various sources that Communist spies were operating in high places in our government created considerable excitement in the United States. When the first charges were brought forth, government loyalty boards and the FBI undertook the investigation of many government employees. During the three-year period more than three million people were carefully screened. Some resigned; a few others are being investigated further; only one has been convicted of spying. That was Judith Coplon, an employee of the FBI. Suspicion was cast upon Alger Hiss, a former employee of the State Department, through charges made by Whittaker Chambers, a one-time member of the Communist party and admitted perjurer. Hiss was convicted in a second trial, not of spying, but of perjury in statements made before the Federal Grand Jury in New York. The Supreme Court refused to hear his appeal, and in March, 1951, he began serving a five-year sentence.

In the early months of 1950 newspaper headlines were filled with charges by Senator Joseph W. McCarthy of Wisconsin that there were at least fifty-seven Communists in the State Department. When pressed for names, he released a few, and those mentioned promptly denied the charges. Feeling in the country ran high on two scores. If there were Communists in our government, we certainly wanted them removed. On the other hand, fair-minded people objected to a procedure that tended to ruin a man's reputation and cause him loss of position without his having been proved guilty of anything. McCarthy was alternately called a great patriot and a "witch hunter." Finally he agreed to pin his entire case on one man, whom he claimed was the top Communist spy in the State Department. This man, said Senator McCarthy, was Owen D. Lattimore, a professor at Johns Hopkins University. Lattimore, on a mission to Afghanistan for the United Nations, denied all the charges by cable and then flew back to Washington to face his accuser. Senator McCarthy claimed that secret files possessed by the State Department would prove his charges, but President Truman refused to turn them over to the investigating committee. The FBI did make a summary of the file on Lattimore, and chairman of the committee Millard Tydings declared that Lattimore was completely cleared of all charges up to that time, at least. In spite of this, the investigation dragged on, with McCarthy promising to produce more evidence and witnesses to substantiate his charges, which had been reduced so that he was no longer claiming that Lattimore was a Communist but simply that he had had considerable influence in determining United States policy toward China.

Many Americans, who disliked Communists wholeheartedly, felt that a quiet investigation of any government officials, of the type that had been carried on by the loyalty committees and the FBI for three years, would have been better for the country and its position among the nations of the world than the type of investigation conducted by Senator McCarthy in Congress. During the war the country had operated under a bipartisan foreign policy—that is, one in which both major parties had a share. The principal Republican who had aided the State Department was Senator Arthur H. Vandenberg of Michigan. But he had become ill in 1949, and the bipartisan policy had been dropped, partly because one wing of the Republican party wanted it ended. The renewed agitation over Communists in our government seemed to stem from the gains made over the world by Russian imperialism and its willing tool, Communism, and the corresponding loss of prestige by the United States. An attempt was made to get back to a bipartisan—or more accurately, unpartisan—foreign policy with the appointment of Republican John Foster Dulles as consultant to Secretary of State Acheson. Dulles was slated to be Secretary of State, had Thomas E. Dewey been elected President in 1948.

The most unfortunate effect of the McCarthy spy disturbance was the idea it gave to other nations—that the United States was divided within itself, and was in a rather high state of hysteria. When all the noncommunist world was looking to the United States for active and positive leadership against Russian imperialism, our actions were creating among our friends abroad a big question as to what they could count on from us. The conservative English newspaper, *The Manchester Guardian,* put it thus in its issue of March 23, 1950:

After all the doubts that have been raised in the United States about the consistency of French, British, or West German foreign policy, it seems ridiculous as well as tragic that the whole Western world should hang on America's own uncertainties. But that is how things have stood ever since the New Year, and we still seem far from a solution. All of us know that Mr. Acheson has got a definite policy. Though this is itself a product of compromise, it has been expressed, and could be applied, with all the clarity and patient care that are the Secretary of State's virtues. Yet a majority of the Senate and a good part of the press have turned against him; the policy remains largely on paper; and its originator's main task for the moment is to defend both himself and it from none-too-scrupulous attacks.

In July, 1950, the Congressional investigating committee issued a Democratic majority report criticizing Senator McCarthy and finding his charges unsupported. Some Republicans on the committee refused to concur in the report. But in the minds of many Americans doubt about the loyalty of public figures remained. If the charges were untrue, injustice had been done.

In the face of these attacks Mr. Acheson was calling on the American people for "total diplomacy" to win the "cold war." The Secretary of State was appealing for the understanding that the winning of a "cold war" requires just as much the total effort of the American people as the winning of a shooting war. He seemed on the verge of laying before Americans a detailed plan that would call for greater unity and sacrifice than had been requested at any time since during the war with

Acme

FOREIGN POLICY CONFERENCE—1950

President Truman and Secretary of State Acheson confer with Warren R. Austin (center), chief of the United States delegation to the United Nations, about foreign policy matters.

Germany, Italy, and Japan. It seemed likely that at last the American people were to get a detailed blueprint of the price of peace. But as the weeks went by, that blueprint was not revealed.

In the spring of 1950, it appeared that the road ahead for the United States forked into three routes. One of those might have led to a sort of peace brought by a solution which the United States was powerful enough to force upon the Soviet Union, but the evidence seemed to indicate that Russian successes had put us definitely on the defensive and had lost us that opportunity. That road apparently was closed. The second fork in the road appeared to lead to an attempt by the Soviet Union to force a decision of its fashioning upon us. That route would certainly lead to another great war.

The third route, in the spring of 1950, seemed to offer the greatest hope for peace. It led toward a balance of power between the part of the world dominated by the Soviet Union and the part led by the western democracies, operating through the United Nations. If a stalemate could be created between these two world areas and maintained long enough, a clear realization of the futility of either trying to impose its will upon the other might lead to an eventual compromise of issues to the point that war might be prevented.

A matter of grave concern to people the world over in the spring of 1950 was the problem of the United Nations. Could it cope with the major world problem of Soviet expansion? Could it prevent another great war? The success of the United Nations had been predicated upon the willingness of all member nations to work together in a spirit of friendly co-operation to find workable and reasonable solutions to world problems. But such a spirit did not exist. The principal offender was the Soviet Union, which time after time used its veto power to prevent action from being taken. The seriousness of this situation was indicated by the remarks of Trygve Lie, Secretary-General of the UN, just before he left for a tour of European capitals to attempt to break the deadlock that was stifling the world organization. Mr. Lie pointed out that unless he was successful, there seemed little use in completing the fine new home of the UN under construction in New York City.

When Mr. Lie returned, his report on the trip seemed to indicate that further co-operation from Russia for peace depended upon further concessions being made to Russia. For several weeks the Soviet Union had refused to participate in deliberations by the UN because of its refusal to seat in the Security Council delegates from the new People's Government of China. This was the Soviet-sponsored Communist Government of China, and Russia said she wanted it recognized by the United Nations as China's official government. Certain nations, notably the United States, had refused recognition and opposed seating delegates of the regime headed by Communist Mao Tze-tung. Russia, angered, walked out on the UN, but made it plain that she was not withdrawing from the organization. For weeks UN activity was at a standstill. The organization's most important problem involved relations with Russia, and Russia was refusing to have any relations with the UN.

United Nations

TRYGVE LIE

Mr. Lie was elected the first Secretary-General of the United Nations on February 1, 1946, and was re-elected to that position in 1950.

Then it happened. On June 25 the Russian-backed Communist forces of North Korea moved across the 38th parallel in an open and unprovoked attack upon the Republic of South Korea. It had been known for some time that troops were massed along that border, but the attack came as a surprise. The United States immediately took the matter before the UN Security Council and ordered supplies and troops sent to Korea to beat back the aggressors. By a majority vote the Security Council supported the action of the United States and called upon all its members to join in whatever moves might be necessary to drive the invaders out of South Korea.

When World War II was over, the 38th parallel in Korea was designated as a dividing line for convenience in accepting the surrender of Japanese troops in the peninsula. The Russians were to accept the surrender of those troops above the 38th parallel, and our representatives were to do the same below that line. But from that time on the Russians took the order to mean that the country was thus to be divided for occupation purposes. Accordingly, they entrenched themselves in the northern part, and the United States, in self-defense, did the same in the south. The division was a bad one. The northern part had the coal, electricity, fertilizer, and factories; the southern

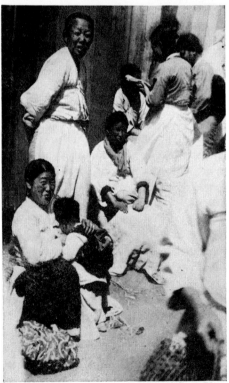

U.S. Signal Corps Photo

BEFORE WAR STRUCK

Korean farm women pass a moment's relaxation in the sun. Later, women like these had to flee their burning cities as war altered their lives.

is largely agricultural, in spite of the heavy mountain ranges. The North could get needed food from Manchuria, but the lack of fertilizer in the South cut agricultural production there by at least 30 per cent. For three years the United States and the United Nations tried to get the Russians to agree to some kind of over-all government for Korea, but the only kind they would accept was one that excluded all anti-Communist leaders and parties. Finally, rather than see South Korea absorbed for lack of any government, free elections were sponsored in May, 1948, the government of President Syngman Rhee was established in power, and United States forces were withdrawn. So the division became fixed. The northern part is somewhat larger than the southern, but South Korea has more than twice the population of the northern segment.

President Rhee is a long-time Korean patriot who has suffered much for the freedom of his country. But agitating for freedom and running a country are two very different things. Things did not go well in South Korea under Rhee. He was bothered by Communist guerrillas from the north and by fifth column activity. Graft and corruption soon crept into his government, and rapidly mounting inflation posed a serious problem. He became increasingly critical of American suggestions and moved more and more to make himself a dictator over his people. As a result, when new elections were held in May, 1950, the vote went decidedly against both Communism and President Rhee. Apparently the May elections helped determine the time of the invasion of South Korea by the Communists from North Korea. The United

THE 38TH PARALLEL

A Korean family migrates across the demarcation line between North and South Korea. The movement of civilians across the 38th parallel was unimpeded before the start of the Korean conflict.

States made it plain, however, that when it sent forces into South Korea to defend that area, it did this not to support the government of Syngman Rhee but to drive back Communist aggression.

It was not immediately clear just what the Soviet purpose behind the Korean invasion was. If the move was simply a feeler—a probe to see what the United States would do—then Russia had her answer at once. United States forces, under the authority of the United Nations, were moved back into Korea from Japan and later from the United States. Supplies were brought in by ship and by plane. But it seemed just as possible that Russia might have another motive. It was feared it might be her purpose to tie down a large number of American troops in a localized war in Korea and then, perhaps, do the same thing in such places as Indo-China, Malaya, Iran, Yugoslavia, and elsewhere. With American forces fighting Soviet satellite nations in various parts of the world, Russia herself would be left free to move wherever she might choose.

Whatever the Russian motive may have been, most of the people of the United States gave their approval to the action taken by our government in Korea. People remembered well how Japanese aggression in Manchuria in 1931 had gone unchecked and had turned out to be the opening move in a series that led the world into World

KOREANS WAIT FOR UNITED NATIONS FORCES

A banner of welcome was stretched across a small-town intersection when UN forces were expected to arrive. Sentiments on banners like these seemed out of place later, when UN forces were made to withdraw.

War II. Italy's attack on Ethiopia and Germany's aggression in Austria and Czechoslovakia had gone virtually unopposed by major world powers. This time it was different. When aggression occurred, the United States, supported by the United Nations, moved at once to beat it back. The UN appealed to its members, the majority of whom backed the United States, to send help of any kind possible to Korea, in order to make the struggle there a United Nations' undertaking. Several nations agreed to send aid, but it was not quickly available, for such things take time. The speed with which the United States could move was due to the location of our troops in near-by Japan.

The Soviet Union immediately claimed that the United Nations' action in Korea was illegal under the UN Charter. The Charter provides that action can be taken by the Security Council on a major issue only if a majority, including all five of the permanent members (United States, United Kingdom, Soviet Union, France, China), vote in favor of it. Although a majority voted in favor of action in Korea, Russia pointed out that she had no representative present to vote, and that the Nationalist delegates did not rightfully represent the government of China. Therefore, said Russia, according to the UN Charter, the action taken was illegal. Furthermore, Russian propaganda at once started spreading the claim that it was actually the South Koreans who had invaded North Korea, and that the North Koreans were merely fighting in self-defense. While this was obviously contrary to the facts, the danger was that a lot of people, particularly in Asia, would believe the Russian story, thereby imperiling the American position still more. If the idea could be spread widely that the United States was embarking upon an imperialistic course in Korea, there was a good chance this country would gain more criticism than assistance.

When the war started, in spite of all we could do with our very limited forces, the North Korean offensive rolled on southward. Seoul, the capital of the Republic of South Korea, was soon taken. General Douglas MacArthur was made Commander-in-Chief of the United Nations' forces in Korea, but it looked very much like he was fighting a losing battle. Equipped as they were with heavy Russian-made tanks and new weapons, the North Korean forces kept pushing our troops back toward the southern end of the peninsula, and it looked as if they might be pushed out entirely. But a staunch defense was made in the area around Pusan, seaport on the east coast, and as the weeks went by, it became ever clearer that we would be able to hang on.

The United States at once went on a sort of semi-wartime basis. Orders for war production were quickly placed, and the necessary priorities for scarce materials were established. A Korean "air lift," similar to the one used earlier in Berlin, was set up to get men and supplies to the Far East as quickly as possible. Soon it was evident that ultimate victory would depend only upon the massing of troops and equipment sufficient to make a big push possible. Eventually, the tide was turned, and UN forces, still mostly United States troops, began to move up the peninsula

and to win back territory previously lost.

Even then, it looked as if the war might go on for a long time, certainly through the winter. Then General MacArthur countered with a bold stroke. He landed forces on the west coast of Korea near Inchon and struck inland. Soon the capital city of Seoul was retaken and the government of Syngman Rhee re-established there. The back of North Korean resistance was broken, and Communist troops scurried north of the 38th parallel for protection.

Immediately, a new problem was raised. What was to be done when UN troops reached the 38th parallel? Should they consider that the aggressors had been driven out of the land they had invaded and stop at that point? Or should they pursue the invaders and force them to surrender? Although this question could have been anticipated, the UN had no answer ready. Accordingly, when our troops reached the dividing line, they were held, awaiting further directions. General MacArthur broadcast surrender orders to the North Korean troops, but no reply was forthcoming. Finally, after a delay of a week, the UN declared that the future of Korea must be decided on the basis of the country as a whole, and not again on the basis of a divided country—a north part and a south part. The aggressors must surrender or be conquered. Eventually, new elections to create a government for all of Korea would be held under UN sponsorship.

When the government of North Korea did not surrender, both South Korean and then American troops crossed the 38th parallel and continued north almost to the Manchurian border. North Korean troops scattered and began to operate as guerrilla bands. The war appeared to be really over, but the mopping-up process promised to take quite some time.

From the outset of the war, two possibilities bothered the United States and its allies greatly: that Russia might openly enter the war against us, and that Communist China might come in. The former possibility did not materialize; the latter did. Both Russia and China had been sending aid to North Korea, but the Soviet Union refrained carefully from becoming involved directly in the war. It seemed clear that United States and United Nations action had impressed the Communist world and that Russia, particularly, did not then want to go to war against the United States and its allies, who were fighting under the United Nations' flag.

But Communist China did come in. In late November of 1950, the United Nations' line, stretching across northern Korea close to the Manchurian border, was hit by masses of Chinese troops, including elements of reorganized North Koreans. Although United Nations' ground fire and air strafing took a heavy toll in enemy casualties, a seemingly endless stream of soldiers poured down from the region of the Yalu River and threatened the American, South Korean, and other United Nations' forces occupying the northern part of the peninsula above the 38th parallel. Encircling thrusts by the Red Chinese isolated several large sections of United Nations' troops, and it was only through expert generalship and desperate defensive fighting in sub-zero cold that most of these troops were finally able to make their way out of the traps without surrendering.

In the face of attacks by the numerically superior Chinese armies, the United Nations' forces conducted withdrawals to keep a moving line of defense as even as possible while inflicting maximum damage on the onrushing enemy. Large forces of United States marines and American and South Korean soldiers, which had been surrounded in the Changjin Reservoir area, battled their way to the Korean east coast where, with other United Nations' personnel, they were evacuated from the port of Hungnam in an operation that was reminiscent of the epic Dunkirk removal of World War II. Some 300,000 men and more than 300,000 tons of equipment were taken aboard ships at Hungnam and transported to landing points in South Korea, well below the main battle lines.

The general retreat continued south to and, then, below the 38th parallel where, for a second time, the South Korean capital of Seoul was relinquished to the Communists. But Red pressure lessened, and soon UN forces were back in Seoul and at the 38th parallel again. Late in March General MacArthur invited the Chinese to discuss peace with him, and the world awaited developments.

After Chinese forces had pushed south across the dividing parallel, a proposal to label Communist China an aggressor was advocated by the United States and was, in due order, voted as a formal declaration by the United Nations. Claims by the Peiping government that Chinese troops fighting in Korea were made up entirely of volunteers gained little acceptance in the United Nations or elsewhere.

Then, in the early hours of April 11, President Truman announced he had relieved General of the Army Douglas

MacArthur of all his commands. While the development was not entirely unexpected, it came with dramatic suddenness. The President said the action was taken because General MacArthur was not in accord with the policies of the Administration with regard to the war in Asia and because the General had publicly expressed his disagreement. General MacArthur flew back to the United States—it was the first time he had been in the country in fourteen years—and addressed a joint meeting of Congress. In his talk he outlined the policy he believed we should be following in Asia, thus bringing his disagreement with the Administration into sharp focus.

The policy of the President and the Joint Chiefs of Staff had been to fight a holding war in Korea in order to buy time for building up our war machine to the point where we could undertake wider operations, if they should become necessary. The Administration's hope was that a negotiated peace with the Chinese could be made. Maintaining that in war there is no substitute for victory, General MacArthur urged that we establish both an economic and a naval blockade of China, bomb Chinese bases in Manchuria, and use the troops Chiang Kai-shek had on Formosa against the Chinese on the mainland. It was the General's belief that this was the only way to end the war in Korea. The Administration said it dared not adopt General MacArthur's policy because of the danger that it might cause the Soviet Union to enter the war and thus provoke World War III. The government's point of view was that, if World War III must come, it should be because of Soviet acts, not ours.

The dismissal of General MacArthur touched off an investigation in Congress. With the General, members of the Joint Chiefs of Staff, and other government officials testifying, the American people were treated to a display entirely unique in the country's history. Transcripts of all the testimony, with the exception of small bits deleted by a censor because of their military significance, were made available to all who wanted them and were published widely. Thus the Soviet Union was given valuable information as to our state of preparedness, what we thought the USSR would do under certain circumstances, and what our most important military leaders thought we ought or could do to check the spread of Soviet imperialism and communism. As the investigation wore on, it became ever clearer that a great deal of opinion would be expressed but that comparatively little in the way of facts would be uncovered. At the same time, the United Nations voted economic sanctions against China, and the United States announced plans to send more aid to Chiang Kai-shek on Formosa. The Chinese Communists attempted another big push in Korea and were again stopped and forced into a disordered retreat. The world waited anxiously to see if the Chinese government would indicate any willingness to talk peace.

On October 24, 1950, the world celebrated the fifth birthday of the United Nations. In 1945, all five of the nations that became permanent members of the Security Council, plus a majority of the other nations whose representatives had signed the Charter at San Francisco, had ratified that Charter, and the UN became a reality.

The path of the United Nations in

those five years had not been an easy one. At the outset the people of the world held high hope that the new organization would be able to accomplish its primary purpose—the prevention of war. Perhaps our hopes were too high. Perhaps we thought the mere signing of the Charter would gain the end we desired. Probably we didn't realize that peace is something that must be attained a bit at a time, by giving a little here and taking a little there, that it is not something that can be grasped in its entirety all at once. Peace is something that must be fought for around the diplomatic conference tables and in the laboratories of science and on the testing grounds of industry. Peace is more than the absence of war. It is a condition that results from a serious cooperative effort to help all people everywhere to solve their problems, at the same time that it puts a check-rein on those who would use the people as pawns to satisfy their own selfish desires for power. Somehow we thought that affixing signatures to a document would do the job.

We soon found out it wouldn't. It might, if all nations were equally determined to make the document work in an atmosphere of friendly co-operation. But such co-operation was not forthcoming. Hardly was the ink dry on the Charter before the big powers began pulling in opposite directions. The veto, which we had insisted on for our own protection, rose up to plague UN action constantly—the Soviet Union used it with much more frequency than did any other permanent member of the Security Council. Then came Korea, and the other Security Council members discovered they could get something done because Russia had taken

another walk in January and didn't get back until August. Without Russia, ground could be gained. But the other nations were not ready to take the responsibility of reading Russia out of the UN. Instead, it was obvious that some way had to be found to get around the veto, some way to prevent a veto-brandishing power from blocking action.

United States Secretary of State Dean Acheson, in a speech before the UN, proposed that the General Assembly vote itself the power to act in cases where the Security Council might find itself incapable of action because of the veto. Specifically, the plan provided that, whenever a veto blocks action in the Security Council, any seven members of the Council could call a meeting of the General Assembly on twenty-four hours' notice, and the Assembly would be empowered to do what the Security Council could not—order the use of force to stop aggression. The UN Political Committee adopted the plan, and the General Assembly ratified it. It seems probable that the way has been found to prevent the Soviet Union from controlling the United Nations. It appears that means have been found to keep an imperialistic, aggressor nation from using the United Nations to further its own purposes and block the will of the majority of the nations of the world.

One thing seems almost certain. The action of the United Nations in Korea saved the UN from the same kind of death experienced by the League of Nations. On its fifth birthday, the UN appeared stronger than it had ever been. If it could grow as much in the next five years as it had in the past five, it might stand a fair chance of success in its principal task—the prevention of widespread, all-destructive war.

The United States learned from and profited by its experience in Korea, too. Although that war slackened at times, this country went right ahead with plans to rebuild its military might, so that we would not be caught short again. The United States was uncertain about what the future might bring, but it had learned that peace, while it cannot be obtained through force alone, cannot be gained without it. We were determined to meet the future with both moral *and* physical strength.

So, as we close this account of the United States as the most powerful nation in the postwar world, the big question in everyone's mind is: Has World War III begun?

FOR YOUR REVIEW

These Should Be Easy for You Now

1. From the standpoint of empire-building, what was the general result of World War II?
2. What was Great Britain's position after the war? What kind of government came to power in England?
3. Give reasons why the Soviet Union was a threat to other nations after the war. What territory did Russia add to her empire during the war? Where has she extended her influence since the war? Be sure to locate these areas on a map.
4. How has Russian expansion been accomplished?
5. What was France's condition after World War II? What was her position in the new alignment of nations? What was the nature of her government? What were her principal needs?
6. What was our dilemma concerning Germany after the war? Among what nations was the country divided for occupation purposes?
7. What big problems were involved in granting American assistance to the countries of Western Europe?
8. Why did various nations want to get control of the Middle East? What new nation was created there after the war?
9. What two groups were struggling for control of China?
10. What two new nations were created in the Indian peninsula?
11. What was the principal postwar problem in southeastern Asia?
12. How was the situation in Japan after the war like that in Germany?
13. How had the United States in the past followed conflicting courses with regard to Latin America?
14. Why did we dislike the Perón government in Argentina? What did we try to do about it? How successful were we?
15. Why was trade difficult in the postwar world? What did the United States do to improve the situation?
16. What was the original purpose of the Marshall Plan? To what other purpose was it later turned? Why?
17. What is the Truman Doctrine?
18. What is meant by the term "cold war"?
19. What is the purpose of the North Atlantic Alliance?
20. What does the term "iron curtain" refer to?
21. What did the Soviet Union count on to weaken America? The United States to weaken Russia?
22. Why did a rift occur between Stalin and Tito?
23. What important change was taking place in American foreign policy?

24. Why did Russia impose the Berlin blockade? How did the Western Powers meet it?
25. Why was the Federal Republic of Germany established?
26. What was the source of postwar difficulty in China? Why were Generals Marshall and Wedemeyer sent to China? Why was the Wedemeyer report not made public until much later? What was the nature of the new government that came to power in 1949?
27. Why was the United States concerned about developments in India?
28. Why was there fighting in the Dutch East Indies? What new nation was created there?
29. What was the situation in Indo-China?
30. In what way did the Organization of the American States supersede the Monroe Doctrine?
31. What conditions forced Argentina to change her attitude toward the United States?
32. How did United States Senator Joseph W. McCarthy win a great deal of publicity in 1950?
33. Why was Russia refusing to participate in United Nations deliberations in the summer of 1950?
34. Why was Korea divided along the 38th parallel?
35. Why did the United States fight in Korea in 1950? Why did the Soviet Union contend that the UN action in Korea was illegal?

Associated Dates

1946—first meeting of the UN General Assembly, January 10 (London)
      first meeting of the UN Security Council, January 17 (London)
1947—Truman Doctrine announced, March 12
      Marshall Plan announced, June 5
      India and Pakistan become independent, August 15
1948—assassination of Mohandas Gandhi, January 30
      Organization of the American States created in April
      Republic of South Korea established in May
1949—Federal Republic of Western Germany proclaimed, May 23
      North Atlantic Alliance in effect, August 24
      People's Republic proclaimed in China, September 21
1950—North Korea invades South Korea, June 25

Why Are These To Be Remembered?

General Douglas MacArthur	Owen D. Lattimore	Zaibatsu
Juan Perón	Arthur Vandenberg	Shinto
Tito	John Foster Dulles	Tenno
Ralph Bunche	Dean Acheson	ERP
Mao Tze-tung	Trygve Lie	Truman Doctrine
Chou En-lai	Syngman Rhee	"Cold war"
Gandhi	Coalition government	Politburo
Jawaharlal Nehru	Dilemma	"Iron curtain"
Bao Dai	Leftist movement	Bonn
Ho Chi Minh	Kuomintang	Bipartisan
Judith Coplon	Hinduism	38th parallel
Alger Hiss	Mohammedanism	Warren R. Austin

Chapter 28

The United States Is Apprehensive about the Future

[As in Chapters 22 and 26, this chapter does not deal strictly with history when the word is defined solely as the record of events that have already happened. But the author feels that he would not have discharged his full obligation to you the reader if he were to terminate this book at the end of Chapter 27. He feels definitely that there are some closing observations he would like to make that pertain vitally to the future of our country. Granted that they are personal viewpoints, no one can write any book and keep himself entirely out of it. You are not asked to agree—merely to do your best thinking that the future of our country may be the brightest all of us working together can possibly make it.]

Who Is Our Real Enemy? At the time of World War I a young soldier penned the lines of a little poem in which he spoke for the dead of that war who were buried beneath the crosses on Flanders fields. In the closing lines he stated a charge—almost a challenge—to those of us who were more fortunate than he. This is the charge:

Take up our quarrel with the foe;
To you from failing hands we throw
The torch; be yours to hold it high.
If ye break faith with us who die,
We shall not sleep, though poppies grow
    grow
In Flanders fields.

The foe in that war was, of course, the Central Powers—Germany, Austria, Turkey, and Bulgaria. But to most of us the foe was something bigger than that. It was war itself—all the forces that tend to disrupt our everyday life. We were fighting, we said, a war to

"make the world safe for democracy," a war "to end all wars." Then came the Armistice. We threw our hats into the air and celebrated. Our President succeeded in establishing a League of Nations, designed to keep the peace. Although we as a country refused to become a part of it, we hoped and counted on it to accomplish its purpose. But we soon discovered that other forces in the world with their own axes to grind had been grinding while we celebrated, and things had gone so far that no one could keep those axes from falling again. We had not, we discovered, made the world safe for democracy. Actually, we had a bigger crop of dictators after the war than we had had before. And soon we knew we had not fought our last war.

So, we were involved in another. The cast of characters was a little different. We had essentially the same

425

group on our side as in World War I, but we were fighting a new set of international bandits—Germany, Italy, and Japan. And the basic cause was the same: the attempt to build great empires when the empire-building game had gone out of style and was frowned upon by most nations, including some who had already passed through that stage of development.

Then that was over. And again our relief caused many of us to think that we had won something—that our problems were all solved. We didn't use the slogans of World War I, but during World War II we hoped that we were fighting for the freedoms that would insure democracy in our world, that we could fix things so we wouldn't have to go through it all again in a few years, perhaps never again at all. But we were no more realistic about it than we had been a quarter of a century earlier. We had only a negative policy that we followed. Our whole policy was designed to bring about the defeat of Germany, Italy, and Japan. And when that had been done, most of us thought we were through.

Since the end of World War II, the United States has lost a great deal of the prestige it had enjoyed over the world. We have lost the support of various peoples because our foreign policy has been negative—that is, it is directed *against* one power instead of being *for* people. The danger for us in regional agreements and pacts lies in the fact that we may spread ourselves too thin, and to no real advantage. Such pacts assume that the signers are as interested as we are in stopping the spread of communism. This is not always the case. Some nations are not nearly so anxious to oppose commu-

nism as we are or as we think they ought to be. In many cases communism actually offers them more than they have now. A communist government would seize the wealth now concentrated in the hands of a few and make it available for the use of more people. They wouldn't be losing the liberties we prize; they've never had them. We cannot expect these people to back our program unless we can show them the advantages of democracy, show them *how* they would be better off by keeping communism out. To them it's not a problem of the right to vote or worship as they please or say whatever they want about their government. It's purely and simply a problem of ham and eggs, of food. They will not oppose communism just to please us—and keep what they have.

Again, we shall have to watch our step on another score. Are we just against communism, or are we opposed to all forms of totalitarianism, to all forms of dictatorship? We've already slipped some. Portugal is in the Atlantic Pact, but Portugal is a dictatorship. Is Franco's Spain next? Or Tito's Yugoslavia? Are we organizing for freedom, or are we just gathering together any and all who will help us against Russia?

In an address in Boston in 1949, Winston Churchill, wartime Prime Minister of Great Britain, said: "Under the impact of communism, all the free nations are being welded together as they never have been before and never could be, but for the harsh external pressure to which they are being subjected." Welded together for what? We do not propose to huddle together like sheep before the fury of the storm. Neither do we propose to go out together on an atomic crusade against

Russian imperialism. Rather, with the strength of modern science to hold evil in check, we can march on together, not simply to root out communism, but to extend to all people who love liberty the democratic freedoms of economic opportunity and political decision. This is the challenge to the greatness of America: to lead the world out of the age of national rivalry into the age of personal freedom and individual well-being, and to save our own way of life in the process. The sixty-four dollar question is: Have we the intelligence and the determination necessary to do the job, and are we willing to pay the price?

War never really solves anything. Fighting alone does not bring peace; it only makes it a possibility. After World War II we began to wonder if we had prevented, at great cost of life and fortune, Germany and Italy and Japan from building empires only to help Russia to build one. We lost sight of the real foe we were fighting. We thought it was nations of people. It was an unfortunate mistake.

The real enemy we fight is not people but tyranny and oppression and hunger and unfair treatment. Our foe is aggression that runs roughshod over helpless people and forces them into molds and patterns they do not like. It is ruthless power that beats down resistance and forces submission to exploitation. It's anything that infringes upon personal freedom. This is our real enemy.

When we see our foe for what he really is, we realize that our fight is never done. When the shooting stops, the war really begins, or should begin. For a shooting war is but an insane interlude in the course of the whole struggle. Man resorts to physical force when reason fails. Then, exhausted, he sits down at the conference table to try again to solve the problems over which he lost his reason. For the problems are always still there when the armies have quit the battlefields. The war is over, but the struggle goes on—the struggle against aggression and oppression and hunger and mistreatment—the same old enemy.

But this kind of struggle isn't as easily understood as one with planes, tanks, and guns. It's always harder to fight an enemy with ideas than with bullets. The foe is much less tangible and the weapons less concrete. They're harder to use. And it's easy even to forget that the struggle is going on at all.

But the old enemy is still there. He's persistent, unrelenting. And unless he's conquered, sooner or later reason will again be pushed aside in favor of more tangible weapons—the weapons of destruction.

There is in the world today more power than ever before. The big question is—what are we going to do with it? All of us would like to see the world "beat its swords into plowshares and its spears into pruning-hooks," but obviously we aren't ready for that yet. We shall have to be satisfied now with the only kind of peace the world has ever known—a peace backed up by force. We must find a way to use our power to protect—to use it for constructive purposes rather than for destruction. But even then all force can do is hold evil in check long enough for moral ideas to take root. And moral ideas will not grow as weeds; they must be planted and cultivated and cared for constantly.

More than eighty years ago Abra-

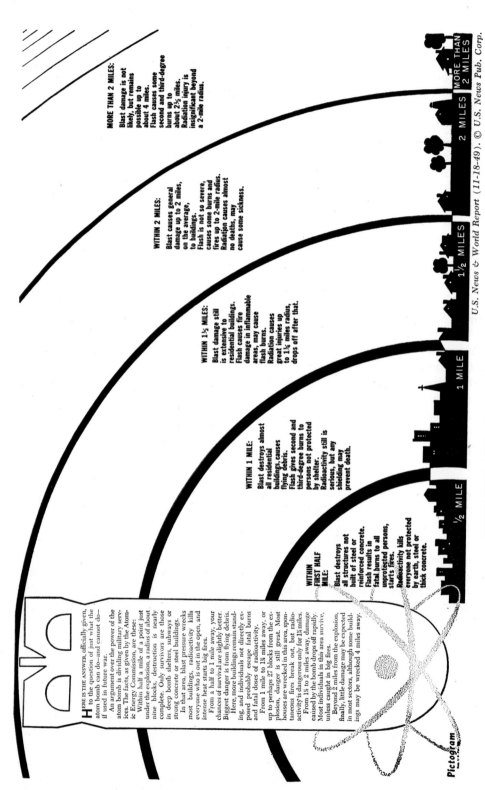

WHAT THE ATOM BOMB REALLY CAN DO

HERE IS THE ANSWER, officially given, to the question of just what the atom bomb can do—and cannot do—if used in future war.

An argument over the power of the atom bomb is dividing military services. The facts, as given by the Atomic Energy Commission, are these:

Within half a mile of a point just under the explosion, a radius of about nine blocks, destruction is nearly complete. Only survivors are those in deep bomb shelters, subways or strong concrete or steel buildings.

In that area, blast pressure wrecks most buildings, radioactivity kills everyone who is out in the open, and intense heat starts big fires.

From a half to 1 mile away, your chances of survival are slightly better. Biggest danger is from flying debris.

Here, more buildings remain standing, and individuals not directly exposed probably escape fatal burns and fatal doses of radioactivity.

From 1 mile to 1¼ miles away, or up to perhaps 27 blocks from the explosion, danger is still great. Most houses are wrecked in this area, spontaneous fires break out, but radioactivity is dangerous only for 1¼ miles.

From 1½ to 2 miles away, damage caused by the bomb drops off rapidly. Most individuals in this area survive, unless caught in big fires.

Beyond 2 miles from the explosion, finally, little damage may be expected in most sectors, although some buildings may be wrecked 4 miles away.

WITHIN FIRST HALF MILE:

Blast destroys all structures not built of steel or reinforced concrete. Flash burns to all unprotected persons, starts fires. Radioactivity kills everyone not protected by earth, steel or thick concrete.

WITHIN 1 MILE:

Blast destroys almost all residential buildings, causes flying debris. Flash gives second and third-degree burns to persons not protected by shelter. Radioactivity still is serious, but any shielding may prevent death.

WITHIN 1½ MILES:

Blast damage still is extensive to residential buildings. Flash causes fire damage in inflammable areas, may cause flash burns. Radiation causes great injuries up to 1¼ miles radius, drops off after that.

WITHIN 2 MILES:

Blast causes general damage up to 2 miles, on the average, to buildings. Flash is not so severe, causes some burns and fires up to 2-mile radius. Radiation causes almost no deaths, may cause some sickness.

MORE THAN 2 MILES:

Blast damage is not likely, but remains possible up to about 4 miles. Flash causes some second and third-degree burns up to about 2½ miles. Radiation injury is insignificant beyond a 2-mile radius.

½ MILE · 1 MILE · 1½ MILES · 2 MILES · MORE THAN 2 MILES

Pictogram

ham Lincoln uttered at Gettysburg those words you all know so well. "It is for us the living . . . to be dedicated here to the unfinished work which they who fought here have thus far so nobly advanced. It is rather for us to be here dedicated to the great task remaining before us, that from these honored dead we take increased devotion to that cause for which they gave the last full measure of devotion, that we here highly resolve that these dead shall not have died in vain."

This "unfinished work" Mr. Lincoln talked about is our never-ending struggle against the enemy that keeps real peace so far from us. "The great task remaining before us, . . . that cause for which they gave the last full measure of devotion" is the big battle to rid our world of the suffering and insecurity that drive men to desperation and the loss of reason that results in war.

From time to time, as we honor those who died in war, orators will repeat often the words "we here highly resolve that these dead shall not have died in vain." But how serious are we about that resolution? Those words were first spoken about the dead of the War between the States. To their graves we have since added countless more from several other wars. Are we really determined that they shall not have died in vain?

But, you say, what can I do about it? The problems of the world today are so complex, and I am so insignificant. True, each of us is. But peace, in the final analysis, is first of all an individual matter. Our democracy is weakened by every undemocratic citizen. No one has the right to criticize the tyranny of another if he himself is overbearing and inconsiderate, if he does not strive to see that others have the same rights he covets for himself. The struggle against the enemy—aggression, oppression, hunger, and mistreatment—is advanced as we individually resist that enemy in all our relations with those about us. For the question of peace and freedom and justice for the world is something each of us must attack on a personal basis. The position of any government on this question must reflect the thinking of the people it represents; in the final settlement, the people must be heard.

The World Cannot Exist "Half Slave and Half Free." Abraham Lincoln had the rare ability to put simple words together in a simple way to catch the fancy of people with his statements. Many of those statements are quoted again and again, and with each quoting they seem to gain in value and importance.

On the 16th of June in 1858, at the Republican State Convention held in Springfield, Illinois, Mr. Lincoln made the following statement concerning the troublesome difference between the North and the South. He said, "I believe this government cannot endure half slave and half free." The destructive War between the States determined that we were to remain one nation and that slavery was to be done away with throughout that nation.

Today we live in a world that is sometimes described as "half slave and half free," and we advance Lincoln's statement as proof that sooner or later we shall have to go to war to decide whether our world is to be democratic or communistic.

Actually, when we boil it all down, there are only two kinds of government, call them what you will. In one, the

THE LINCOLN MEMORIAL

This beautiful building in Washington, D.C., enshrines the nation's high esteem for its sixteenth President.

government exists to serve the people; in the other, the people exist solely to serve and support the government. This last concept is an old one. Throughout much of history it has been the accepted idea. For centuries the upper classes believed that the only purpose of the mass of the people was to support them, and the common people went through life, generation after generation, fulfilling this assigned task, accepting it as their necessary lot.

Then, not so long ago—500 years or so—a new idea began to get around. That idea was that there was nothing born into a person that made him a slave in a hut rather than a lord in a castle. The common people began to feel that perhaps education was denied them just so they would not object to this status in life. Soon there crept in the inevitable belief that they were being denied many things that were rightfully theirs. After that, changes had to come.

Someone read a statement that the Greek philosopher Plato had made cen-turies before. He said that any government should exist "by the consent of the governed"—that is, that any people should have the right to decide the kind of government under which they were to live. In France, Jean Jacques Rousseau advanced that idea, and Napoleon later said that, had there been no Rousseau, there would have been no French Revolution. But revolution did come, in Holland, in England, in the English colonies in America, in France, in Latin America, and elsewhere in the world. Old, established, tyrannical governments were overthrown, and governments that better recognized the will of the people were set up.

Over the years, this revolution has continued. In the beginning, the struggle was principally for political freedom, but now more and more emphasis is being placed on economic freedom as well. These are the freedoms the common people of the world are demanding for themselves today—the right to determine their own government, and the opportunity for any man, anywhere in the world, to earn for himself and his family a decent standard of living.

Considered from this viewpoint, the world cannot and will not permanently exist half slave and half free. Freedom will eventually come for all. The question is not—Will freedom come? but only—How?

In considering the difficult problems of his own time, Abraham Lincoln said this: "The dogmas of the quiet past are inadequate to the stormy present. The occasion is piled high with difficulty, and we must rise to the occasion. As our case is new, so we must think and act anew."

Intertype Corporation

THE BASIC LAW OF OUR LAND

"We the People," the opening words of the Constitution, strike a keynote of American freedom
—freedom founded in government of the people, by the people, and for the people.

That's what Lincoln said nearly a century ago. But his statement is just as true of the present as it was of Civil War days. As our case is new, so we must think and act anew. The solution of today's problems in today's little world calls for new concepts and attitudes to guide the thinking of people the world over.

What are those attitudes? Will you permit the author to suggest a few?

Today jet planes are crossing continents and oceans in a matter of a few hours. What better evidence could we ask of the smallness of our world? The day is gone when we can think of ourselves as citizens of Anytown, Whatever State, United States of America. Whether we want to be or not, we are now citizens of the world. Each of us

must learn to think of himself as one of the more than two billion people of the world—people who, in spite of the superficial differences of color, language, religion and the like, have the same basic desires—for freedom, for security, and for peace. An appreciation of the common cause of humanity everywhere will help us to advance that cause.

Sooner or later we shall have to recognize that the color of one's skin does not make him better—or worse—than someone of a different color. It's natural for us to think that so-called "white people" are better than the black or brown or red or yellow people of the world. But when we do permit that feeling to creep in, we're on pretty thin ice. Your author sat one afternoon in a garden in Peiping discussing this particular problem with a Chinese student. It had been covered quite thoroughly, pro and con, when finally the student pushed back his chair and, with that fine sense of humor the Chinese have, said, "Yes, I know you call yourselves white and you call us yellow, and we admit we're yellow. But you're not white. Do you know what you are? You're pink!" Put it to the test. Look at yourself in a mirror and see if you're not just as far from white as the Chinese are. We need to learn to evaluate a person not because of the color of his skin, or the language he speaks, or the food he eats, or the clothes he wears, or the house he lives in, or the religion he believes in, or the size of his bank account, but because of what, down under all these things, he really is.

Again, if we are sincere about doing away with war in the world, we must be willing to pay the price for peace. It cannot be had for the wishing. The winning of peace must be planned and worked out with the same care as the campaigns to win a war. For peace is more than just the absence of war. Peace involves the satisfying of basic desires and the solution of problems that lead to war, and that takes time. And it involves compromise and sacrifice. Sometimes it is necessary to give up something we value greatly in order to gain something more valuable. A century and one-half ago the original states in our new country were extremely jealous of their own sovereignty, but the problems created when they tried to operate as thirteen independent governments were overwhelming. Fortunately they had the leadership necessary to win approval for a plan whereby each state gave up some of its sovereignty and gained thereby security and stability. As we look back on it, we consider the adoption of our Federal Constitution an extremely wise move.

Today our world of states might be compared to our own country after the Revolutionary War. The winning of security and stability in our world is bound to involve compromise and sacrifice. If the result to be attained is obviously worth it, we must be ready and even eager to make those sacrifices.

The world will not endure permanently half slave and half free. Political and economic freedom will come. The only question is—How?

In meeting this question, we in the United States have a choice. It is a choice we cannot escape, for we are the most powerful nation in the world, and what we do—or don't do—is bound to be a determining factor. We can choose to follow the same course toward the rest of the world that has been traditional with the western empire-builders in the past. That is, we can dominate them by superior force and dictate to them. This they don't want. When you're on the receiving end of imperialism, you can't tell the difference between dictatorship and democracy. Give the weaker people of the world this kind of treatment, and some day they will band themselves together and rise up against us to overthrow our tyranny.

The other choice is to extend to all the world a policy of trying to help the people improve their living conditions, without domination, exploitation, or the kind of charity that kills initiative. It is this sincere assurance of help and a fair deal that will go furthest toward solv-

"KNOW-HOW" AT WORK

Helping people of underdeveloped regions to tap and more efficiently use their natural resources, as well as their native skills, has been advanced as a way of removing one important cause of war. A proposed program, under which the industrially prosperous nations of the world would share technological skills with their neighbors of lesser advantage, is held to be a realistic approach to the problem of fostering universal peace.

ing international problems. No power in the world can simply hand political and economic freedom to any people. We can only help them to earn it for themselves.

Freedom is more than just the absence of dictatorship. To have freedom we must have law and order in our world. If that rule of law is not to be imposed by others, then it must be created by all of us, voluntarily. Tied up closely with freedom is self-discipline, respect for mutually created authority, and consideration for others. Freedom grows from carrying the Golden Rule into every phase of human activity. Freedom begins in each of us. Someone has put it this way:

"They set the slave free, striking off his
    chains . . .
Then he was as much of a slave as
    ever.
He was still chained to servility,
He was still manacled to indolence
    and sloth,
He was still bound by fear and super-
    stition,

By ignorance, suspicion, and sav-
    agery . . .
His slavery was not in the chains,
But in himself. . . ."

To deal with the many problems of our complex world, we need to be armed with the most effective weapons available: correct and adequate information, plus unbiased, kindly attitudes toward all peoples. We need to realize that there can be no peace for us until there is peace for all, and that we can have no real freedom ourselves until all are free.

Each and every one of us needs these attitudes. We need them in our leaders. We need men with the knowledge and understanding to see, and the courage to do a job that must be done. If the future of America is worth fighting for, surely it's worth thinking about and planning for.

Are you doing all you can to equip yourself for efficient thinking and planning for America's future, so that fighting will not ever again be necessary for the preservation of our land?

Epilogue

And so we close our very brief review of the history of our land. But history never ends; it is a permanent, continuing thing. Today's events become tomorrow's record.

As we end our account for now, the following assessment of the present world situation appears warranted. (1) The United States enjoyed more than a century of relative freedom from serious involvement in international affairs because a friendly power, Great Britain, dominated the balance of power in the world. (2) At the end of World War II, Britain was no longer able to continue in that position, and the United States voluntarily wrecked its fine military machine. (3) This situation left the Soviet Union stronger than either Great Britain or the United States, a condition of which she proceeded to take full advantage. (4) It was expected that the United Nations would become the dominant factor in international relations, but it soon became apparent that, while the UN is a very valuable organization that can do a great deal of good in the world and merits our wholehearted support, it cannot, in its present form, prevent a powerful nation from going to war if that nation is determined to take up arms. There are several reasons for this: (a) the UN cannot prevent a great power from going to war unless the UN possesses greater military strength than any great power or any probable combination of powers; (b) the only way the UN can acquire such strength is through the disarmament of the nations of the world; (c) world disarmament cannot be accomplished except under a world government. And it is readily apparent that the world is not yet ready to take that step. (5) Because both Great Britain and the United Nations are too weak to take decisive action against Soviet imperialism, the United States has begun to arm itself again, to try to assume the role for which history has obviously cast it—the role of a nation strong enough to dominate the balance of power in the world.

In the Hall of Archives in Washington you will find an inscription that reads, "the past is prelude." History is a continuing thing. The record of our country's past is the prelude to its future. But prelude to what kind of future? Soon the United States will again be the most powerful nation in the world. And the world would like to know for what purpose we expect to use our power. Are we going to turn it to the same use

435

that empires have put their power in the past—to dominate and exploit peoples and keep things as they are? Or shall we employ it to help other people to help themselves? Shall we use our power as a barricade to progress, or shall we become the courageous leader of a world of people, all working with the trend of history to extend the American ideals of freedom and equality of opportunity to people everywhere?

Out past is simply prelude. Prelude to what? We Americans will supply the answer. Because so much depends upon it, it must be the result of careful, courageous, informed, and intelligent thinking on the part of every one of us. The future of the United States and perhaps of the world is your responsibility and mine. Together we shall have to do the best job we can, if our people are to remain free and our land is to continue to grow ever greater, in the fullest meaning of the word. Our country can be no more honest, no fairer, no wiser than its people are honest, fair, and wise. Are you doing your best to meet this responsibility?

Appendix

The Declaration of Independence[1]

When, in the course of human events, it becomes necessary for one people to dissolve the political bands which have connected them with another, and to assume among the powers of the earth, the separate and equal station to which the laws of nature and of nature's God entitle them, a decent respect to the opinions of mankind requires that they should declare the causes which impel them to the separation.

We hold these truths to be self-evident, that all men are created equal, that they are endowed by their Creator with certain unalienable rights, that among these are life, liberty and the pursuit of happiness. That to secure these rights, governments are instituted among men, deriving their just powers from the consent of the governed; that whenever any form of government becomes destructive of these ends, it is the right of the people to alter or to abolish it, and to institute new government, laying its foundation on such principles, and organizing its powers in such form as to them shall seem most likely to affect their safety and happiness. Prudence, indeed, will dictate that governments long established should not be changed for light and transient causes; and accordingly all experience hath shown that mankind are more disposed to suffer, while evils are sufferable, than to right themselves by abolishing the forms to which they are accustomed. But when a long train of abuses and usurpations, pursuing invariably the same object, evinces a design to reduce them under absolute despotism, it is their right, it is their duty, to throw off such government, and to provide new guards for their future security. Such has been the patient suffering of these Colonies, and such is now the necessity which constrains them to alter their former systems of government. The history of the present King of Great Britain is a history of repeated injuries and usurpations, all having in direct object the establishment of an absolute tyranny over these States. To prove this, let facts be submitted to a candid world.

He has refused his assent to laws, the most wholesome and necessary for the public good.

He has forbidden his governors to pass laws of immediate and pressing importance, unless suspended in their operation till his assent should be obtained; and when so suspended, he has utterly neglected to attend to them.

He has refused to pass other laws for the accommodation of large districts of people, unless those people would relinquish the right of representation in the legislature, a right inestimable to them and formidable to tyrants only.

He has called together legislative bodies, at places unusual, uncomfortable, and distant from the depository of their public records, for the sole purpose of fatiguing them into compliance with his measures.

He has dissolved representative houses repeatedly, for opposing with manly firmness his invasions on the rights of the people.

He has refused for a long time, after such dissolutions, to cause others to be

[1] The Declaration of Independence was adopted by the Continental Congress, in Philadelphia, on July 4, 1776. It was signed by John Hancock as President and by Charles Thomson as Secretary.

elected; whereby the legislative powers, incapable of annihilation, have returned to the people at large for their exercise; the State remaining, in the meantime, exposed to all the dangers of invasion from without, and convulsions within.

He has endeavored to prevent the population of these States; for that purpose obstructing the laws for naturalization of foreigners; refusing to pass others to encourage their migrations hither, and raising the conditions of new appropriations of lands.

He has obstructed the administration of justice by refusing his assent to laws for establishing judiciary powers.

He has made judges dependent on his will alone, for the tenure of their offices, and the amount and payment of their salaries.

He has erected a multitude of new offices, and sent hither swarms of officers to harass our people, and eat out their substance.

He has kept among us, in times of peace, standing armies, without the consent of our legislatures.

He has affected to render the military independent of and superior to the civil power.

He has combined with others to subject us to a jurisdiction foreign to our constitution and unacknowledged by our laws; giving his assent to their acts of pretended legislation:

For quartering large bodies of armed troops among us:

For protecting them by a mock trial from punishment for any murders which they should commit on the inhabitants of these States:

For cutting off our trade with all parts of the world:

For imposing taxes on us without our consent:

For depriving us in many cases of the benefits of trial by jury:

For transporting us beyond seas to be tried for pretended offenses:

For abolishing the free system of English laws in a neighbouring province, establishing therein an arbitrary government, and enlarging its boundaries so as to render it at once an example and fit

instrument for introducing the same absolute rule into these Colonies:

For taking away our charters, abolishing our most valuable laws and altering fundamentally the forms of our governments:

For suspending our own legislatures and declaring themselves invested with power to legislate for us in all cases whatsoever.

He has abdicated government here by declaring us out of his protection and waging war against us.

He has plundered our seas, ravished our coasts, burnt our towns, and destroyed the lives of our people.

He is at this time transporting large armies of foreign mercenaries to complete the works of death, desolation, and tyranny, already begun, with circumstances of cruelty and perfidy scarcely paralleled in the most barbarous ages, and totally unworthy the head of a civilized nation.

He has constrained our fellow citizens taken captive on the high seas to bear arms against their country, to become the executioners of their friends and brethren, or to fall themselves by their hands.

He has excited domestic insurrections amongst us, and has endeavoured to bring on the inhabitants of our frontiers, the merciless Indian savages, whose known rule of warfare is an undistinguished destruction of all ages, sexes, and conditions.

In every stage of these oppressions we have petitioned for redress in the most humble terms; our repeated petitions have been answered only by repeated injury. A prince whose character is thus marked by every act which may define a tyrant, is unfit to be the ruler of a free people.

Nor have we been wanting in attentions to our British brethren. We have warned them, from time to time, of attempts by their legislature to extend an unwarrantable jurisdiction over us. We have reminded them of the circumstances of our emigration and settlement here. We have appealed to their native justice and magnanimity, and we have conjured them by the ties of our common kindred to disavow these usurpations, which would inevitably interrupt our connections and correspondence. They too have been deaf to the voice of justice and of consanguinity. We must, therefore, acquiesce in the necessity which denounces our separation, and hold them, as we hold the rest of mankind, enemies in war, in peace friends.

We, therefore, the Representatives of the United States of America, in General Congress assembled, appealing to the Supreme Judge of the world for the rectitude of our intentions, do in the name, and by authority of the good people of these Colonies, solemnly publish and declare, That these United Colonies are, and of right ought to be, *free and independent States;* that they are absolved from all allegiance to the British crown, and that all political connection between them and the State of Great Britain is, and ought to be, totally dissolved; and that as *free and independent States,* they have full power to levy war, conclude peace, contract alliances, establish commerce, and to do all other acts and things which *independent States* may of right do. And for the support of this declaration, with a firm reliance on the protection of Divine Providence, we mutually pledge to each other our lives, our fortunes, and our sacred honor.

The Constitution of the United States

PREAMBLE

We, the people of the United States, in order to form a more perfect Union, establish justice, insure domestic tranquillity, provide for the common defence, promote the general welfare, and secure the blessings of liberty to ourselves and our posterity, do ordain and establish this Constitution for the United States of America.

ARTICLE I

Section 1—(Legislative powers vested in Congress.)

All legislative powers herein granted shall be vested in a Congress of the United States, which shall consist of a Senate and House of Representatives.

Section 2—(House of Representatives, how and by whom chosen. Qualifications of Representatives. Representatives and direct taxes, how apportioned. Filling of vacancies. Power of choosing officers, and of impeachment.)

1. The House of Representatives shall be composed of members chosen every second year by the people of the several States, and the electors in each State shall have the qualifications requisite for electors of the most numerous branch of the State legislature.

2. No person shall be a Representative who shall not have attained to the age of twenty-five years, and been seven years a citizen of the United States, and who shall not, when elected, be an inhabitant of that State in which he shall be chosen.

3. Representatives and direct taxes shall be apportioned among the several States which may be included within this Union, according to their respective numbers, which shall be determined by adding to the whole number of free persons, including those bound to service for a term of years, and excluding Indians not taxed, three-fifths of all other persons. The actual enumeration shall be made within three years after the first meeting of the Congress of the United States, and within every subsequent term of ten years, in such manner as they shall by law direct. The number of Representatives shall not exceed one for every thirty thousand, but each State shall have at least one Representative; and until such enumeration shall be made, the State of New Hampshire shall be entitled to choose 3; Massachusetts, 8; Rhode Island and Providence Plantations, 1; Connecticut, 5; New York, 6; New Jersey, 4; Pennsylvania, 8; Delaware, 1; Maryland, 6; Virginia, 10; North Carolina, 5; South Carolina, 5, and Georgia, 3.

4. When vacancies happen in the representation from any State, the Executive Authority thereof shall issue writs of election to fill such vacancies.

5. The House of Representatives shall choose their Speaker and other officers, and shall have the sole power of impeachment.

Section 3—(Senators, how and by whom chosen. Qualifications of a Senator. President of the Senate, his right to vote. President pro tempore, and selection of officers of the Senate. Senate to try impeachments. Judgment in cases of impeachment.)

1. The Senate of the United States shall be composed of two Senators from each State, chosen by the legislature thereof, for six years; and each Senator shall have one vote.

2. Immediately after they shall be assembled in consequence of the first election, they shall be divided as equally as may be into three classes. The seats of the Senators of the first class shall be vacated at the expiration of the second year, of the second class at the expiration of the fourth year, and of the third class at the expira-

tion of the sixth year, so that one-third may be chosen every second year; and if vacancies happen by resignation or otherwise, during the recess of the legislature of any State, the Executive thereof may make temporary appointments until the next meeting of the legislature, which shall then fill such vacancies.

3. No person shall be a Senator who shall not have attained to the age of thirty years, and been nine years a citizen of the United States, and who shall not, when elected, be an inhabitant of that State for which he shall be chosen.

4. The Vice-President of the United States shall be President of the Senate, but shall have no vote unless they be equally divided.

5. The Senate shall choose their other officers, and also a President pro tempore, in the absence of the Vice-President, or when he shall exercise the office of the President of the United States.

6. The Senate shall have the sole power to try all impeachments. When sitting for that purpose, they shall be on oath or affirmation. When the President of the United States is tried, the Chief Justice shall preside; and no person shall be convicted without the concurrence of two-thirds of the members present.

7. Judgment in cases of impeachment shall not extend further than to removal from office, and disqualification to hold and enjoy any office of honor, trust, or profit under the United States; but the party convicted shall nevertheless be liable and subject to indictment, trial, judgment, and punishment, according to law.

Section 4—(Times, etc., of holding elections. Congress must meet once in each year.)

1. The times, places, and manner of holding elections for Senators and Representatives shall be prescribed in each State by the Legislature thereof; but the Congress may at any time by law make or alter such regulations, except as to places of choosing Senators.

2. The Congress shall assemble at least once in every year, and such meeting shall be on the first Monday in December, unless they shall by law appoint a different day.

Section 5—(Membership, quorum, adjournments, and rules of the Houses. Power to punish or expel. Journal. Time of adjournments, how limited.)

1. Each House shall be the judge of the elections, returns, and qualifications of its own members, and a majority of each shall constitute a quorum to do business; but a smaller number may adjourn from day to day, and may be authorized to compel the attendance of absent members in such manner and under such penalties as each House may provide.

2. Each House may determine the rules of its proceedings, punish its members for disorderly behavior, and with the concurrence of two-thirds expel a member.

3. Each House shall keep a journal of its proceedings, and from time to time publish the same, excepting such parts as may in their judgment require secrecy; and the yeas and nays of the members of either House on any question shall, at the desire of one-fifth of those present, be entered on the journal.

4. Neither House, during the session of Congress, shall, without the consent of the other, adjourn for more than three days, nor to any other place than that in which the two Houses shall be sitting.

Section 6—(Compensation, privileges, and disqualifications of members of Congress.)

1. The Senators and Representatives shall receive a compensation for their services, to be ascertained by law, and paid out of the Treasury of the United States. They shall in all cases, except treason, felony, and breach of the peace, be privileged from arrest during their attendance at the session of their respective Houses, and in going to and returning from the same; and for any speech or debate in either House they shall not be questioned in any other place.

2. No Senator or Representative shall, during the time for which he was elected, be appointed to any civil office under the authority of the United States which shall have been created, or the emoluments whereof shall have been increased during such time; and no person holding any office under the United States shall be a

member of either House during his continuance in office.

Section 7—(House to originate all revenue bills. Manner of passing bills; veto power of President. Provisions as to orders, concurrent resolutions, etc.)

1. All bills for raising revenue shall originate in the House of Representatives, but the Senate may propose or concur with amendments, as on other bills.

2. Every bill which shall have passed the House of Representatives and the Senate shall, before it becomes a law, be presented to the President of the United States; if he approve he shall sign it, but if not, he shall return it, with his objections, to that House in which it shall have originated, who shall enter the objections at large on their journal, and proceed to reconsider it. If after such reconsideration two-thirds of that House shall agree to pass the bill, it shall be sent, together with the objections, to the other House, by which it shall likewise be reconsidered; and if approved by two-thirds of that House it shall become a law. But in all such cases the votes of both Houses shall be determined by yeas and nays, and the names of the persons voting for and against the bill shall be entered on the journal of each House respectively. If any bill shall not be returned by the President within ten days (Sundays excepted) after it shall have been presented to him, the same shall be a law, in like manner as if he had signed it, unless the Congress by their adjournment prevent its return; in which case it shall not be a law.

3. Every order, resolution, or vote to which the concurrence of the Senate and House of Representatives may be necessary (except on a question of adjournment) shall be presented to the President of the United States, and before the same shall take effect shall be approved by him, or being disapproved by him, shall be repassed by two-thirds of the Senate and the House of Representatives, according to the rules and limitations prescribed in the case of a bill.

Section 8—(Powers of Congress.)

The Congress shall have power:

1. To lay and collect taxes, duties, imposts, and excises, to pay the debts and provide for the common defence and general welfare of the United States; but all duties, imposts, and excises shall be uniform throughout the United States;

2. To borrow money on the credit of the United States;

3. To regulate commerce with foreign nations, and among the several States, and with the Indian tribes;

4. To establish a uniform rule of naturalization and uniform laws on the subject of bankruptcies throughout the United States;

5. To coin money, regulate the value thereof, and of foreign coin, and fix the standard of weights and measures;

6. To provide for the punishment of counterfeiting the securities and current coin of the United States;

7. To establish post offices and post roads;

8. To promote the progress of science and useful arts by securing for limited times to authors and inventors the exclusive right to their respective writings and discoveries;

9. To constitute tribunals inferior to the Supreme Court;

10. To define and punish piracies and felonies committed on the high seas, and offences against the law of nations;

11. To declare war, grant letters of marque and reprisal, and make rules concerning captures on land and water;

12. To raise and support armies, but no appropriation of money to that use shall be for a longer term than two years;

13. To provide and maintain a navy;

14. To make rules for the government and regulation of the land and naval forces;

15. To provide for calling forth the militia to execute the laws of the Union, suppress insurrections, and repel invasions;

16. To provide for organizing, arming, and disciplining the militia, and for governing such part of them as may be employed in the service of the United States, reserving to the States respectively the appointment of the officers, and the authority of training the militia according to the discipline prescribed by Congress;

17. To exercise exclusive legislation in all cases whatsoever over such district (not exceeding ten miles square) as may, by cession of particular States and the acceptance of Congress, become the seat of Government of the United States, and to exercise like authority over all places purchased by the consent of the legislature of the State in which the same shall be, for the erection of forts, magazines, arsenals, dock-yards, and other needful buildings; —And

18. To make all laws which shall be necessary and proper for carrying into execution the foregoing powers, and all other powers vested by this Constitution in the Government of the United States, or in any department or officer thereof.

Section 9—(Provision as to migration or importation of certain persons. Habeas corpus. Bills of attainder, etc. Taxes, how apportioned. No export duty. No commercial preference. Money, how drawn from Treasury, etc. No titles of nobility.)

1. The migration or importation of such persons as any of the States now existing shall think proper to admit shall not be prohibited by the Congress prior to the year one thousand eight hundred and eight, but a tax or duty may be imposed on such importation, not exceeding ten dollars for each person.

2. The privilege of the writ of habeas corpus shall not be suspended, unless when in cases of rebellion or invasion the public safety may require it.

3. No bill of attainder or ex post facto law shall be passed.

4. No capitation, or other direct, tax shall be laid, unless in proportion to the census or enumeration herein before directed to be taken.

5. No tax or duty shall be laid on articles exported from any State.

6. No preference shall be given by any regulation of commerce or revenue to the ports of one State over those of another; nor shall vessels bound to or from one State, be obliged to enter, clear, or pay duties in another.

7. No money shall be drawn from the Treasury but in consequence of appropriations made by law; and a regular statement and account of the receipts and expenditures of all public money shall be published from time to time.

8. No title of nobility shall be granted by the United States: And no person holding any office of profit or trust under them shall, without the consent of the Congress, accept of any present, emolument, office, or title of any kind whatever from any king, prince, or foreign state.

Section 10—(States denied certain powers.)

1. No State shall enter into any treaty, alliance or confederation; grant letters of marque and reprisal, coin money, emit bills of credit, make anything but gold and silver coin a tender in payment of debts, pass any bill of attainder, ex post facto law, or law impairing the obligation of contracts, or grant any title of nobility.

2. No State shall, without the consent of the Congress, lay any imposts or duties on imports or exports, except what may be absolutely necessary for executing its inspection laws, and the net produce of all duties and imposts, laid by any State on imports or exports, shall be for the use of the Treasury of the United States; and all such laws shall be subject to the revision and control of the Congress.

3. No State shall, without the consent of Congress, lay any duty of tonnage, keep troops or ships of war in time of peace, enter into agreement or compact with another State, or with a foreign power, or engage in war, unless actually invaded or in such imminent danger as will not admit of delay.

ARTICLE II

Section 1—(President and his term of office. Electors of President: number and how appointed. Electors to vote on same day. Qualifications of President. Filling vacancy in office of President. President's compensation and oath of office.)

1. The executive power shall be vested in a President of the United States of America. He shall hold his office during the term of four years, and, together with the Vice-President, chosen for the same term, be elected as follows:

2. Each State shall appoint, in such manner as the legislature thereof may direct, a number of electors, equal to the

whole number of Senators and Representatives to which the State may be entitled in the Congress: but no Senator or Representative, or person holding an office of trust or profit under the United States, shall be appointed an elector.

3. The electors shall meet in their respective States, and vote by ballot for two persons, of whom one at least shall not be an inhabitant of the same State with themselves. And they shall make a list of all the persons voted for, and of the number of votes for each; which list they shall sign and certify, and transmit sealed to the seat of the government of the United States, directed to the President of the Senate. The President of the Senate shall, in the presence of the Senate and House of Representatives, open all the certificates, and the votes shall then be counted. The person having the greatest number of votes shall be the President, if such number be a majority of the whole number of electors appointed; and if there be more than one who have such majority, and have an equal number of votes, then the House of Representatives shall immediately choose by ballot one of them for President; and if no person have a majority, then from the five highest on the list the said House shall in like manner choose the President. But in choosing the President, the vote shall be taken by States, the representation from each State having one vote; a quorum for this purpose shall consist of a member or members from two-thirds of the States, and a majority of all the States shall be necessary to a choice. In every case, after the choice of the President, the person having the greatest number of votes of the electors shall be the Vice-President. But if there should remain two or more who have equal votes, the Senate shall choose from them by ballot the Vice-President.[1]

4. The Congress may determine the time of choosing the electors, and the day on which they shall give their votes; which day shall be the same throughout the United States.

5. No person except a natural born

---

[1] This clause has been superseded by the 12th Amendment.

citizen, or a citizen of the United States at the time of the adoption of this Constitution, shall be eligible to the office of President; neither shall any person be eligible to that office who shall not have attained to the age of thirty-five years, and been fourteen years a resident within the United States.

6. In case of the removal of the President from office, or of his death, resignation, or inability to discharge the powers and duties of the said office, the same shall devolve on the Vice-President, and the Congress may by law provide for the case of removal, death, resignation, or inability, both of the President and Vice-President, declaring what officer shall then act as President, and such officer shall act accordingly, until the disability be removed or a President shall be elected.

7. The President shall, at stated times, receive for his services, a compensation, which shall neither be increased nor diminished during the period for which he shall have been elected, and he shall not receive within that period any other emolument from the United States, or any of them.

8. Before he enters on the execution of his office, he shall take the following oath or affirmation:—

"I do solemnly swear (or affirm) that I will faithfully execute the office of President of the United States, and will, to the best of my ability, preserve, protect, and defend the Constitution of the United States."

Section 2—(President to be commander-in-chief. He may pardon. Treaty-making power of President. Nomination of certain officers. When President may fill vacancies.)

1. The President shall be commander-in-chief of the army and navy of the United States, and of the militia of the several States, when called into the actual service of the United States; he may require the opinion, in writing, of the principal officer in each of the executive departments, upon any subject relating to the duties of their respective offices, and he shall have power to grant reprieves and pardons for offences against the United States, except in cases of impeachment.

2. He shall have power, by and with

the advice and consent of the Senate, to make treaties, provided two-thirds of the Senators present concur; and he shall nominate, and by and with the advice and consent of the Senate, shall appoint ambassadors, other public ministers and consuls, judges of the Supreme Court, and all other officers of the United States whose appointments are not herein otherwise provided for, and which shall be established by law: but the Congress may by law vest the appointment of such inferior officers as they think proper, in the President alone, in the courts of law, or in the heads of departments.

3. The President shall have power to fill up all vacancies that may happen during the recess of the Senate, by granting commissions which shall expire at the end of their next session.

Section 3—(President's duties.)

He shall from time to time give to the Congress information of the state of the Union, and recommend to their consideration such measures as he shall judge necessary and expedient; he may, on extraordinary occasions, convene both Houses, or either of them, and in case of disagreement between them, with respect to the time of adjournment, he may adjourn them to such time as he shall think proper; he shall receive ambassadors and other public ministers; he shall take care that the laws be faithfully executed, and shall commission all the officers of the United States.

Section 4—(All civil officers forfeited for certain crimes.)

The President, Vice-President, and all civil officers of the United States shall be removed from office on impeachment for, and conviction of, treason, bribery, or other high crimes and misdemeanors.

ARTICLE III

Section 1—(The federal courts of the United States.)

The judicial power of the United States shall be vested in one Supreme Court, and in such inferior courts as the Congress may from time to time ordain and establish. The judges, both of the Supreme and inferior courts, shall hold their offices during good behaviour, and shall, at stated times, receive for their services a compensation which shall not be diminished during their continuance in office.

Section 2—(Federal judiciary is supreme. Original jurisdiction and appellate jurisdiction of Supreme Court. Trial by jury.)

1. The judicial power shall extend to all cases in law and equity, arising under this Constitution, the laws of the United States, and treaties made, or which shall be made, under their authority;—to all cases affecting ambassadors, other public ministers and consuls;—to all cases of admiralty and maritime jurisdiction;—to controversies to which the United States shall be a party;—to controversies between two or more States;—between a State and citizens of another State;—between citizens of different States;—between citizens of the same State claiming lands under grants of different States, and between a State, or the citizens thereof, and foreign States, citizens or subjects.[1]

2. In all cases affecting ambassadors, other public ministers, and consuls, and those in which a State shall be party, the Supreme Court shall have original jurisdiction. In all the other cases before mentioned, the Supreme Court shall have appellate jurisdiction, both as to law and fact, with such exceptions and under such regulations as the Congress shall make.

3. The trial of all crimes, except in cases of impeachment, shall be by jury; and such trial shall be held in the State where the said crimes shall have been committed; but when not committed within any State, the trial shall be at such place or places as the Congress may by law have directed.

Section 3—(Treason defined: proof of; punishment of.)

1. Treason against the United States shall consist only in levying war against them, or in adhering to their enemies, giving them aid and comfort. No person shall be convicted of treason unless on the testimony of two witnesses to the same overt act, or on confession in open court.

2. The Congress shall have power to declare the punishment of treason, but no attainder of treason shall work corruption

---

[1] This section is abridged by Article XI of the amendments.

of blood, or forfeiture, except during the life of the person attainted.

ARTICLE IV

Section 1—(Each State must recognize the public acts and records of every other State.)

Full faith and credit shall be given in each State to the public acts, records, and judicial proceedings of every other State. And the Congress may by general laws prescribe the manner in which such acts, records, and proceedings shall be proved, and the effect thereof.

Section 2—(Privileges of citizens. Fugitives from justice to be delivered up. Fugitive slaves must also be returned.)

1. The citizens of each State shall be entitled to all privileges and immunities of citizens in the several States.

2. A person charged in any State with treason, felony, or other crime, who shall flee from justice, and be found in another State, shall on demand of the executive authority of the State from which he fled, be delivered up, to be removed to the State having jurisdiction of the crime.

3. No person held to service or labor in one State, under the laws thereof, escaping into another, shall, in consequence of any law or regulation therein, be discharged from such service or labor, but shall be delivered up on claim of the party to whom such service or labor may be due.[1]

Section 3—(Admission of new States. Regulations concerning territory.)

1. New States may be admitted by the Congress into this Union; but no new State shall be formed or erected within the jurisdiction of any other State, nor any State be formed by the junction of two or more States, or parts of States, without the consent of the legislatures of the States concerned as well as of the Congress.

2. The Congress shall have power to dispose of and make all needful rules and regulations respecting the territory or other property belonging to the United States; and nothing in this Constitution shall be so construed as to prejudice any claims of the United States, or of any particular State.

_____
[1] See 13th Amendment.

Section 4—(Republican form of government and protection guaranteed to the several States.)

The United States shall guarantee to every State in this Union a Republican form of government, and shall protect each of them against invasion; and, on application of the legislature, or of the executive (when the legislature cannot be convened) against domestic violence.

ARTICLE V

(How Constitution can be amended.)

The Congress, whenever two-thirds of both Houses shall deem it necessary, shall propose amendments to this Constitution, or, on the application of the legislatures of two-thirds of the several States, shall call a convention for proposing amendments, which, in either case, shall be valid to all intents and purposes, as part of this Constitution, when ratified by the legislatures of three-fourths of the several States, or by conventions in three-fourths thereof, as the one or the other mode of ratification may be proposed by the Congress; provided that no amendment which may be made prior to the year one thousand eight hundred and eight shall in any manner affect the first and fourth clauses in the ninth section of the first article; and that no State, without its consent, shall be deprived of its equal suffrage in the Senate.

ARTICLE VI

(Certain debts, etc., declared valid. Supremacy of Constitution, treaties, and laws of the United States. Who shall take oath to support Constitution. No religious test.)

1. All debts contracted and engagements entered into, before the adoption of this Constitution, shall be as valid against the United States under this Constitution, as under the Confederation.

2. This Constitution and the laws of the United States which shall be made in pursuance thereof; and all treaties made, or which shall be made, under the authority of the United States, shall be the supreme law of the land; and the judges in every State shall be bound thereby, anything in the Constitution or laws of any State to the contrary notwithstanding.

3. The Senators and Representatives

before mentioned, and the members of the several State legislatures, and all executive and judicial officers, both of the United States and of the several States, shall be bound by oath or affirmation to support this Constitution; but no religious test shall ever be required as a qualification to any office or public trust under the United States.

ARTICLE VII

(What ratification shall establish the Constitution.)

The ratification of the Conventions of nine States shall be sufficient for the establishment of this Constitution between the States so ratifying the same.

Ten Original Amendments (Bill of Rights)

ARTICLE I

(Freedom of religion, speech, of the press, and right of petition.)

Congress shall make no law respecting an establishment of religion, or prohibiting the free exercise thereof; or abridging the freedom of speech, or of the press; or the right of the people peaceably to assemble, and to petition the government for a redress of grievances.

ARTICLE II

(Right to keep and bear arms.)

A well-regulated militia being necessary to the security of a free State, the right of the people to keep and bear arms shall not be infringed.

ARTICLE III

(Quartering of troops.)

No soldier shall, in time of peace, be quartered in any house without the consent of the owner; nor in time of war but in a manner to be prescribed by law.

ARTICLE IV

(Right of search and seizure regulated.)

The right of the people to be secure in their persons, houses, papers and effects, against unreasonable searches and seizures, shall not be violated, and no warrants shall issue but upon probable cause, supported by oath or affirmation, and particularly describing the place to be searched, and the persons or things to be seized.

ARTICLE V

(Trials for crimes; compensation for private property taken for public use.)

No person shall be held to answer for a capital or otherwise infamous crime, unless on a presentment or indictment of a grand jury, except in cases arising in the land or naval forces, or in the militia, when in actual service in time of war or public danger; nor shall any person be subject for the same offence to be twice put in jeopardy of life or limb; nor shall be compelled in any criminal case to be a witness against himself, nor be deprived of life, liberty, or property, without due process of law; nor shall private property be taken for public use, without just compensation.

ARTICLE VI

(Right to speedy trial, witnesses, etc.)

In all criminal prosecutions the accused shall enjoy the right to a speedy and public trial, by an impartial jury of the State and district wherein the crime shall have been committed, which district shall have been previously ascertained by law, and to be informed of the nature and cause of the accusation; to be confronted with the witnesses against him; to have compulsory process for obtaining witnesses in his favor, and to have the assistance of counsel for his defense.

ARTICLE VII

(Right of trial by jury.)

In suits at common law, where the value in controversy shall exceed twenty dollars, the right of trial by jury shall be preserved, and no fact tried by a jury shall be otherwise re-examined in any court of the United States than according to the rules of the common law.

ARTICLE VIII

(Excessive bail, fines, and cruel punishment prohibited.)

Excessive bail shall not be required, nor excessive fines imposed, nor cruel and unusual punishments inflicted.

ARTICLE IX

(Federal government exercises no power over the unenumerated rights of the people.)

The enumeration in the Constitution of certain rights shall not be construed to deny or disparage others retained by the people.

ARTICLE X

(Rights of States under Constitution.)

The powers not delegated to the United States by the Constitution, nor prohibited by it to the States, are reserved to the States respectively, or to the people.

Amendments Since the Bill of Rights

ARTICLE XI [1]

(State cannot be sued by citizen of another state.)

The judicial power of the United States shall not be construed to extend to any suit in law or equity, commenced or prosecuted against one of the United States by citizens of another State, or by citizens or subjects of any foreign state.

ARTICLE XII [2]

(Manner of choosing President and Vice-President.)

The electors shall meet in their respective States, and vote by ballot for President and Vice-President, one of whom at least shall not be an inhabitant of the same State with themselves; they shall name in their ballots the person voted for as President, and in distinct ballots the person voted for as Vice-President; and they shall make distinct lists of all persons voted for as President, and of all persons voted for as Vice-President, and of the number of votes for each, which list they shall sign and certify, and transmit, sealed, to the seat of the Government of the United States, directed to the President of the Senate; the President of the Senate shall, in the presence of the Senate and House of Representatives, open all the certificates, and the votes shall then be counted; the person having the greatest number of votes for President shall be the President, if such number be a majority of the whole number of electors appointed; and if no person have such majority, then from the persons having the highest numbers, not exceeding three, on the list of those voted

for as President, the House of Representatives shall choose immediately, by ballot, the President. But in choosing the President, the votes shall be taken by States, the representation from each State having one vote; a quorum for this purpose shall consist of a member or members from two-thirds of the States, and a majority of all the States shall be necessary to a choice. And if the House of Representatives shall not choose a President, whenever the right of choice shall devolve upon them, before the fourth day of March next following, then the Vice-President shall act as President, as in case of the death or other constitutional disability of the President. The person having the greatest number of votes as Vice-President shall be the Vice-President if such number be a majority of the whole number of electors appointed, and if no person have a majority, then from the two highest numbers on the list the Senate shall choose the Vice-President; a quorum for the purpose shall consist of two-thirds of the whole number of Senators, and a majority of the whole number shall be necessary to a choice. But no person constitutionally ineligible to the office of President shall be eligible to that of Vice-President of the United States.

ARTICLE XIII [1]

(Slavery abolished.)

Section 1. Neither slavery nor involuntary servitude, except as a punishment for crime, whereof the party shall have been duly convicted, shall exist within the United States, or any place subject to their jurisdiction.

Section 2. Congress shall have power to enforce this article by appropriate legislation.

---

[1] Proposed September 5, 1794. Declared in force January 8, 1798.

[2] Proposed December 12, 1803; proclaimed as ratified September 25, 1804.

[1] Proposed February 1, 1865; proclaimed December 18, 1865.

ARTICLE XIV [1]

(Citizenship defined; privileges of citizens.)

Section 1. All persons born or naturalized in the United States, and subject to the jurisdiction thereof, are citizens of the United States and of the State wherein they reside. No State shall make or enforce any law which shall abridge the privileges or immunities of citizens of the United States; nor shall any State deprive any person of life, liberty, or property, without due process of law; nor deny to any person within its jurisdiction the equal protection of the laws.

Section 2. Representatives shall be apportioned among the several States according to their respective numbers, counting the whole number of persons in each State, excluding Indians not taxed. But when the right to vote at any election for the choice of electors for President and Vice-President of the United States, Representatives in Congress, the executive and judicial officers of a State, or the members of the legislature thereof, is denied to any of the male inhabitants of such State, being twenty-one years of age and citizens of the United States, or in any way abridged, except for participation in rebellion, or other crime, the basis of representation therein shall be reduced in the proportion which the number of such male citizens shall bear to the whole number of male citizens twenty-one years of age in such State.

Section 3. No person shall be a Senator, or Representative in Congress, or elector of President and Vice-President, or hold any office, civil or military, under the United States, or under any State, who, having previously taken an oath as a member of Congress, or as an officer of the United States, or as a member of any State legislature, or as an executive or judicial officer of any State, to support the Constitution of the United States, shall have engaged in insurrection or rebellion against the same, or given aid or comfort to the enemies thereof. But Congress may,

by a vote of two-thirds of each House, remove such disability.

Section 4. The validity of the public debt of the United States, authorized by law, including debts incurred for payment of pensions and bounties for services in suppressing insurrection and rebellion, shall not be questioned. But neither the United States nor any State shall assume or pay any debt or obligation incurred in aid of insurrection or rebellion against the United States, or any claim for the loss or emancipation of any slave; but all such debts, obligations and claims shall be held illegal and void.

Section 5. The Congress shall have power to enforce, by appropriate legislation, the provisions of this article.

ARTICLE XV [1]

(Equal rights for white and colored citizens.)

Section 1. The right of the citizens of the United States to vote shall not be denied or abridged by the United States, or by any State, on account of race, color, or previous condition of servitude.

Section 2. The Congress shall have power to enforce this article by appropriate legislation.

ARTICLE XVI [2]

(Income taxes authorized.)

The Congress shall have power to lay and collect taxes on incomes, from whatever sources derived, without apportionment among the several States, and without regard to any census or enumeration.

ARTICLE XVII [3]

(United States senators to be elected by direct popular vote.)

1. The Senate of the United States shall be composed of two Senators from each State, elected by the people thereof, for six years; and each Senator shall have one vote. The electors in each State shall have the qualifications requisite for elec-

---

[1] Proposed June 16, 1866; proclaimed July 28, 1868.

[1] Proposed February 27, 1869; proclaimed March 30, 1870.
[2] Proposed July 31, 1909; proclaimed February 25, 1913.
[3] Proposed May 15, 1912; proclaimed May 31, 1913.

452 UNITED STATES HISTORY—THE GROWTH OF OUR LAND

tors of the most numerous branch of the State legislature.

2. When vacancies happen in the representation of any State in the Senate, the executive authority of such State shall issue writs of election to fill such vacancies: Provided, That the legislature of any State may empower the executive thereof to make temporary appointments until the people fill the vacancies by election as the legislature may direct.

3. This amendment shall not be so construed as to affect the election or term of any Senator chosen before it becomes valid as part of the Constitution.

ARTICLE XVIII [1]

(Liquor Prohibition Amendment.)

Section 1. After one year from the ratification of this article, the manufacture, sale, or transportation of intoxicating liquors within, the importation thereof into, or the exportation thereof from the United States and all territory subject to the jurisdiction thereof for beverage purposes is hereby prohibited.

Section 2. The Congress and the several States shall have concurrent power to enforce this article by appropriate legislation.

Section 3. This article shall be inoperative unless it shall have been ratified as an amendment to the Constitution by the legislatures of the several States, as provided in the Constitution, within seven years from the date of the submission hereof to the States by the Congress.

ARTICLE XIX [2]

(Giving nation-wide suffrage to women.)

The right of citizens of the United States to vote shall not be denied or abridged by the United States or by any State on account of sex.

Congress shall have power to enforce this article by appropriate legislation.

ARTICLE XX [1]

(Terms of President, Vice-President, Senators, and Representatives.)

Section 1. The terms of the President and Vice-President shall end at noon on the 20th day of January, and the terms of Senators and Representatives at noon on the 3rd day of January, of the years in which such terms would have ended if this article had not been ratified; and the terms of their successors shall then begin.

Section 2. The Congress shall assemble at least once in every year, and such meeting shall begin at noon on the 3rd day of January, unless they shall by law appoint a different day.

Section 3. If, at the time fixed for the beginning of the term of the President, the President elect shall have died, the Vice-President elect shall become President. If a President shall not have been chosen before the time fixed for the beginning of his term, or if the President elect shall have failed to qualify, then the Vice-President elect shall act as President until a President shall have qualified; and the Congress may by law provide for the case wherein neither a President elect nor a Vice-President elect shall have qualified, declaring who shall then act as President, or the manner in which one who is to act shall be selected, and such person shall act accordingly until a President or Vice-President shall have qualified.

Section 4. The Congress may by law provide for the case of the death of any of the persons from whom the House of Representatives may choose a President whenever the right of choice shall have devolved upon them, and for the case of the death of any of the persons from whom the Senate may choose a Vice-President whenever the right of choice shall have devolved upon them.

Section 5. Sections 1 and 2 shall take effect on the 15th day of October following the ratification of this article.

Section 6. This article shall be inopera-

[1] Proposed December 19, 1917; proclaimed January 29, 1919. Repealed by Article XXI, effective December 5, 1933.

[2] Proposed June 4, 1919; proclaimed August 26, 1920.

[1] Proposed March 8, 1932; proclaimed January 23, 1933.

tive unless it shall have been ratified as an amendment to the Constitution by the legislatures of three-fourths of the several States within seven years from the date of its submission.

ARTICLE XXI [1]

(Repeal of the Prohibition Amendment.)

Section 1. The eighteenth article of amendment to the Constitution of the United States is hereby repealed.

Section 2. The transportation or importation into any State, Territory, or possession of the United States for delivery or use therein of intoxicating liquors, in violation of the laws thereof, is hereby prohibited.

Section 3. This article shall be inoperative unless it shall have been ratified as an amendment to the Constitution by conventions in the several States, as provided in the Constitution, within seven years from the date of the submission hereof to the States by the Congress.

---

[1] Proposed February 20, 1933; proclaimed December 5, 1933.

ARTICLE XXII [2]

(Presidential tenure limited to two terms.)

Section 1. No person shall be elected to the office of the President more than twice, and no person who has held the office of President, or acted as President, for more than two years of a term to which some other person was elected President shall be elected to the office of the President more than once.

But this article shall not apply to any person holding the office of President when this article was proposed by the Congress, and shall not prevent any person who may be holding the office of President, or acting as President, during the term within which this article becomes operative from holding the office of President or acting as President during the remainder of such term.

Section 2. This article shall be inoperative unless it shall have been ratified as an amendment to the Constitution by the legislatures of three fourths of the several states within seven years from the date of its submission to the states by the Congress.

---

[2] Proposed March, 1947; ratified February 26, 1951.

Northwest Ordinance of 1787

Be it ordained by the United States in Congress assembled, that the said territory, for the purposes of temporary government, be one district, subject, however, to be divided into two districts, as future circumstances may, in the opinion of Congress, make it expedient.

Be it ordained by the authority aforesaid, that the estates, both of resident and non-resident proprietors in the said territory, dying intestate, shall descend to, and be distributed among, their children, and the descendants of a deceased child, in equal parts; the descendants of a deceased child or grandchild to take the share of their deceased parent in equal parts among them: And where there shall be no children or descendants, then in equal parts to the next of kin in equal degree; and, among collaterals, the children of a deceased brother or sister of the intestate shall have, in equal parts among them, their deceased parents' share; and there shall, in no case, be a distinction between kindred of the whole and half blood; saving, in all cases, to the widow of the intestate her third part of the real estate for life, and one-third part of the personal estate; and this law, relative to descents and dower, shall remain in full force until altered by the legislature of the district. And, until the governor and judges shall adopt laws as hereinafter mentioned, estates in the said territory may be devised or bequeathed by wills in writing, signed and sealed by him or her, in whom the estate may be (being of full age), and attested by three witnesses; and real estates may be conveyed by lease and release, or bargain and sale, signed, sealed, and delivered by the person, being of full age, in whom the estate may be, and attested by two witnesses, provided such wills be duly proved, and such conveyances be acknowledged, or the execution thereof duly proved, and be recorded within one year after proper magistrates, courts, and registers shall be appointed for that purpose; and personal property may be transferred by delivery; saving, however, to the French and Canadian inhabitants, and other settlers of the Kaskaskias, St. Vincents, and the neighboring villages who have heretofore professed themselves citizens of Virginia, their laws and customs now in force among them, relative to the descent and conveyance of property.

Be it ordained by the authority aforesaid, that there shall be appointed, from time to time, by Congress, a governor, whose commission shall continue in force for the term of three years, unless sooner revoked by Congress; he shall reside in the district, and have a freehold estate therein in 1,000 acres of land, while in the exercise of his office.

There shall be appointed, from time to time, by Congress, a secretary, whose commission shall continue in force for four years unless sooner revoked; he shall reside in the district, and have a freehold estate therein in 500 acres of land, while in the exercise of his office; it shall be his duty to keep and preserve the acts and laws passed by the legislature, and the public records of the district, and the proceedings of the governor in his executive department; and transmit authentic copies of such acts and proceedings, every six months, to the secretary of Congress: There shall also be appointed a court to consist of three judges, any two of whom to form a court, who shall have a common-law jurisdiction, and reside in the district, and have each therein a freehold estate in 500 acres of land while in the exercise of their offices; and their commissions shall continue in force during good behavior.

The governor and judges, or a majority of them, shall adopt and publish in the district such laws of the original States, criminal and civil, as may be necessary and best suited to the circumstances of the district, and report them to Congress from time to time: which laws shall be in force in the district until the organization of the General Assembly therein, unless disapproved of by Congress; but, afterwards, the legislature shall have authority to alter them as they shall think fit.

The governor, for the time being, shall be commander-in-chief of the militia, appoint and commission all officers in the same below the rank of general officers; all general officers shall be appointed and commissioned by Congress.

Previous to the organization of the General Assembly, the governor shall appoint such magistrates and other civil officers, in each county or township, as he shall find necessary for the preservation of the peace and good order in the same: After the General Assembly shall be organized, the powers and duties of the magistrates and other civil officers shall be regulated and defined by the said Assembly; but all magistrates and other civil officers, not herein otherwise directed, shall, during the continuance of this temporary government, be appointed by the governor.

For the prevention of crimes and injuries, the laws to be adopted or made shall have force in all parts of the district, and for the execution of process, criminal and civil, the governor shall make proper divisions thereof; and he shall proceed, from time to time, as circumstances may require, to lay out the parts of the district in which the Indian titles shall have been extinguished, into counties and townships, subject, however, to such alterations as may thereafter be made by the legislature.

So soon as there shall be 5,000 free male inhabitants of full age in the district, upon giving proof thereof to the governor, they shall receive authority, with time and place, to elect representatives from their counties or townships to represent them in the General Assembly: Provided, that for every 500 free male inhabitants, there shall be one representative, and so on progressively with the number of free male inhabitants, shall the right of representa-

tion increase, until the number of representatives shall amount to twenty-five; after which the number and proportion of representatives shall be regulated by the legislature: Provided, that no person shall be eligible or qualified to act as a representative unless he shall have been a citizen of one of the United States three years, and be a resident in the district, or unless he shall have resided in the district three years; and, in either case, shall likewise hold in his own right, in fee-simple, 200 acres of land within the same: Provided, also, that a freehold in 50 acres of land in the district, having been a citizen of one of the States, and being resident in the district, or the like freehold and two years' residence in the district, shall be necessary to qualify a man as an elector of a representative.

The representatives thus elected shall serve for the term of two years; and, in case of the death of a representative, or removal from office, the governor shall issue a writ to the county or township for which he was a member, to elect another in his stead, to serve for the residue of the term.

The General Assembly, or legislature, shall consist of the governor, legislative council, and a House of Representatives. The legislative council shall consist of five members, to continue in office five years, unless sooner removed by Congress; any three of whom to be a quorum; and the members of the council shall be nominated and appointed in the following manner, to wit: As soon as representatives shall be elected, the governor shall appoint a time and place for them to meet together; and, when met, they shall nominate ten persons, residents in the district, and each possessed of a freehold in 500 acres of land, and return their names to Congress; five of whom Congress shall appoint and commission to serve as aforesaid; and, whenever a vacancy shall happen in the council, by death or removal from office, the House of Representatives shall nominate two persons, qualified as aforesaid, for each vacancy, and return their names to Congress; one of whom Congress shall appoint and commission for the residue of the term. And every five years, four months at least before the expiration of the time of service of the members of council, the said House shall nominate ten persons, qualified as aforesaid, and return their names to Congress; five of whom Congress shall appoint and commission to serve as members of the council five years, unless sooner removed. And the governor, legislative council, and House of Representatives shall have authority to make laws in all cases for the good government of the district, not repugnant to the principles and articles in this ordinance established and declared. And all bills, having passed by a majority in the House, and by a majority in the council, shall be referred to the governor for his assent; but no bill, or legislative act whatever, shall be of any force without his assent. The governor shall have power to convene, prorogue, and dissolve the General Assembly, when in his opinion, it shall be expedient.

The governor, judges, legislative council, secretary, and such other officers as Congress shall appoint in the district, shall take an oath or affirmation of fidelity and of office; the governor before the president of Congress, and all other officers before the governor. As soon as a legislature shall be formed in the district, the council and House, assembled in one room, shall have authority, by joint ballot, to elect a delegate to Congress, who shall have a seat in Congress, with a right of debating but not of voting during this temporary government.

And, for extending the fundamental principles of civil and religious liberty, which form the basis whereon these republics, their laws and constitutions, are erected; to fix and establish those principles as the basis of all laws, constitutions, and governments, which forever hereafter shall be formed in the said territory: to provide also for the establishment of States, and permanent government therein, and for their admission to a share in the federal councils on an equal footing with the original States, at as early periods as may be consistent with the general interest:

It is hereby ordained and declared by the authority aforesaid, that the following articles shall be considered as articles of compact between the original States and the people and States in the said territory, and forever remain unalterable, unless by common consent, to wit:

ARTICLE I

No person, demeaning himself in a peaceable and orderly manner, shall ever be molested on account of his mode of worship or religious sentiments, in the said territory.

ARTICLE II

The inhabitants of the said territory shall always be entitled to the benefits of the writ of *habeas corpus*, and of the trial by jury; of a proportionate representation of the people in the legislature; and of judicial proceedings according to the course of the common law. All persons shall be bailable, unless for capital offences, where the proof shall be evident or the presumption great. All fines shall be moderate; and no cruel or unusual punishments shall be inflicted. No man shall be deprived of his liberty or property but by the judgment of his peers or the law of the land; and, should the public exigencies make it necessary, for the common preservation, to take any person's property, or to demand his particular services, full compensation shall be made for the same. And, in the just preservation of rights and property, it is understood and declared that no law ought ever to be made, or have force in the said territory, that shall, in any manner whatever, interfere with or affect private contracts or engagements, *bona fide*, and without fraud, previously formed.

ARTICLE III

Religion, morality, and knowledge, being necessary to good government and the happiness of mankind, schools and the means of education shall forever be encouraged. The utmost good faith shall always be observed towards the Indians; their lands and property shall never be taken from them without their consent; and, in their property, rights, and liberty, they shall never be invaded or disturbed, unless in just and lawful wars authorized by Congress; but laws founded in justice and humanity shall, from time to time, be made for preventing wrongs being done to them, and for preserving peace and friendship with them.

ARTICLE IV

The said territory, and the States which may be formed therein, shall forever remain a part of this confederacy of the United States of America, subject to the Articles of Confederation, and to such alterations therein as shall be constitutionally made; and to all the acts and ordinances of the United States in Congress assembled, conformable thereto. The inhabitants and settlers in the said territory shall be subject to pay a part of the federal debts contracted or to be contracted, and a proportional part of the expenses of government, to be apportioned on them by Congress according to the same common rule and measure by which apportionments thereof shall be made on the other States; and the taxes, for paying their proportion, shall be laid and levied by the authority and direction of the legislatures of the district or districts, or new States, as in the original States, within the time agreed upon by the United States in Congress assembled. The legislatures of those districts or new States shall never interfere with the primary disposal of the soil by the United States in Congress assembled, nor with any regulations Congress may find necessary for securing the title in such soil to the *bona fide* purchasers. No tax shall be imposed on lands the property of the United States; and, in no case, shall non-resident proprietors be taxed higher than residents. The navigable waters leading into the Mississippi and St. Lawrence, and the carrying-places between the same, shall be common highways, and forever free, as well to the inhabitants of the said territory as to the citizens of the United States, and those of any other States that may be admitted into the confederacy, without any tax, impost, or duty therefor.

ARTICLE V

There shall be formed in the said territory not less than three nor more than five States; and the boundaries of the States, as soon as Virginia shall alter her act of cession, and consent to the same, shall become fixed and established as follows, to wit: The Western State in the said territory shall be bounded by the Mississippi, the Ohio, and Wabash rivers; a direct line drawn from the Wabash and Post St. Vincent's, due north, to the territorial line between the United States and Canada; and, by the said territorial line, to the Lake of the Woods and Mississippi. The middle State shall be bounded by the said direct line, the Wabash from Post Vincent's, to the Ohio; by the Ohio, by a direct line, drawn due north from the mouth of the Great Miami, to the said territorial line, and by the said territorial line. The Eastern State shall be bounded by the last-mentioned direct line, the Ohio, Pennsylvania, and the said territorial line: Provided, however, and it is further understood and declared, that the boundaries of these three States shall be subject so far to be altered, that, if Congress shall hereafter find it expedient, they shall have authority to form one or two States in that part of the said territory which lies north of an east and west line drawn through the southerly bend or extreme of Lake Michigan. And, whenever any of the said States shall have 60,000 free inhabitants therein, such State shall be admitted, by its delegates, into the Congress of the United States, on an equal footing with the original States in all respects whatever, and shall be at liberty to form a permanent constitution and State government: Provided, the constitution and government so to be formed, shall be republican, and in conformity to the principles contained in these articles; and, so far as it can be consistent with the general interest of the confederacy, such admission shall be allowed at an earlier period, and when there may be a less number of free inhabitants in the State than 60,000.

ARTICLE VI

There shall be neither slavery nor involuntary servitude in the said territory, otherwise than in the punishment of crimes, whereof the party shall have been duly convicted; Provided, always, that any person escaping into the same, from whom labor or service is lawfully claimed in any one of the original States, such fugitive may be lawfully reclaimed and conveyed to the person claiming his or her labor or service as aforesaid.

Be it ordained by the authority aforesaid, that the resolutions of the 23d of April, 1784, relative to the subject of this ordinance, be, and the same are hereby repealed, and declared null and void.

Done by the United States, in Congress assembled, the 13th day of July, in the year of our Lord 1787, and of their independence the twelfth.

Charter of the United Nations[1]

We, the peoples of the United Nations determined to save succeeding generations from the scourge of war, which twice in our lifetime has brought untold sorrow to mankind, and

To reaffirm faith in fundamental human rights, in the dignity and worth of the human person, in the equal right of men and women and of nations large and small, and

To establish conditions under which justice and respect for the obligations arising from treaties and other sources of international law can be maintained, and

To promote social progress and better standards of life in larger freedom, and for these ends

To practice tolerance and live together in peace with one another as good neighbors, and

To unite our strength to maintain international peace and security, and

To insure, by the acceptance of principles and the institution of methods, that armed force shall not be used, save in the common interest, and

To employ international machinery for the promotion of the economic and social advancement of all people, have resolved to combine our efforts to accomplish these aims.

Accordingly, our respective governments, through representatives assembled in the city of San Francisco, who have exhibited their full powers found to be in good and due form, have agreed to the present Charter of the United Nations and do hereby establish an international organization to be known as the United Nations.

---

[1] The Charter was drafted and adopted at the United Nations Conference on International Organization in San Francisco, California, April 25 to June 26, 1945.

CHAPTER I

PURPOSES

Article 1—The purposes of the United Nations are:

1. To maintain international peace and security, and to that end: to take effective collective measures for the prevention and removal of threats to the peace, and for the suppression of acts of aggression or other breaches of the peace, and to bring about by peaceful means, and in conformity with the principles of justice and international law, adjustment or settlement of international disputes or situations which might lead to a breach of the peace;

2. To develop friendly relations among nations based on respect for the principle of equal rights and self-determination of peoples, and to take other appropriate measures to strengthen universal peace;

3. To achieve international co-operation in solving international problems of an economic, social, cultural or humanitarian character, and in promoting and encouraging respect for human rights and for the fundamental freedoms for all without distinction as to race, sex, language or religion; and

4. To be a center for harmonizing the actions of nations in the attainment of these common ends.

PRINCIPLES

Article 2—The organization and its members, in pursuit of the purposes stated in Article 1, shall act in accordance with the following principles:

1. The organization is based on the principle of the sovereign equality of all its members.

2. All members, in order to ensure to all of them the rights and benefits resulting from membership, shall fulfill in good faith

the obligations assumed by them in accordance with the present Charter.

3. All members shall settle their international disputes by peaceful means in such a manner that international peace and security and justice are not endangered.

4. All members shall refrain in their international relations from the threat or use of force against the territorial integrity or political independence of any member or state, or in any other manner inconsistent with the purposes of the United Nations.

5. All members shall give the United Nations every assistance in any action it takes in accordance with the provisions of the present Charter, and shall refrain from giving assistance to any state against which the United Nations is taking preventive or enforcement action.

6. The organization shall ensure that states not members act in accordance with these principles so far as may be necessary for the maintenance of international peace and security.

7. Nothing contained in the present Charter shall authorize the United Nations to intervene in matters which are essentially within the domestic jurisdiction of any state or shall require the members to submit such matters to settlement under the present Charter; but this principle shall not prejudice the application of enforcement measures under Chapter VII.

CHAPTER II

MEMBERSHIP

Article 3—The original members of the United Nations shall be the states which, having participated in the United Nations Conference on International Organization at San Francisco, or have previously signed the declaration of the United Nations of Jan. 1, 1942, sign the present Charter and ratify it in accordance with Article 110.

Article 4—1. Membership in the United Nations is open to all other peace-loving states which accept the obligations contained in the present Charter and which, in the judgment of the organiza-

tion, are able and willing to carry out these obligations.

2. The admission of any such state to membership in the United Nations will be effected by a decision of the General Assembly upon the recommendation of the Security Council.

Article 5—A member of the United Nations against which preventive or enforcement action has been taken by the Security Council may be suspended from the exercise of the rights and privileges of membership by the General Assembly upon the recommendation of the Security Council. The exercise of these rights and privileges may be restored by the Security Council.

Article 6—A member of the United Nations which has persistently violated the principles contained in the present Charter may be expelled from the organization by the General Assembly upon the recommendation of the Security Council.

CHAPTER III

ORGANS

Article 7—1. There are established as the principal organs of the United Nations: A General Assembly, a Security Council, an Economic and Social Council, an International Court of Justice, a Trusteeship Council and a Secretariat.

2. Such subsidiary organs as may be found necessary may be established in accordance with the present Charter.

Article 8—The United Nations shall place no restrictions on the eligibility of men and women to participate in any capacity and under conditions of equality in the principal and subsidiary organs.

CHAPTER IV

THE GENERAL ASSEMBLY COMPOSITION

Article 9—The General Assembly shall consist of all the members of the United Nations.

Each member shall not have more than five representatives in the General Assembly.

FUNCTIONS AND POWERS

Article 10—The General Assembly may discuss any questions or any matters within the scope of the present Charter or relating to the powers and functions of any organs provided in the present Charter, and, except as provided in Article 12, may make recommendations to the members of the United Nations or to the Security Council, or both, on any such questions or matters.

Article 11—1. The General Assembly may consider the general principles of co-operation in the maintenance of international peace and security, including the principles governing disarmament and the regulations of armaments, and may make recommendations with regard to such principles to the members or to the Security Council or both.

2. The General Assembly may discuss any questions relating to the maintenance of international peace and security brought before it by any member of the United Nations, or by the Security Council, or by a State, which is not a member of the United Nations, in accordance with the provisions of Article 35, Paragraph 2, and, except as provided in Article 12, may make recommendations with regard to any such questions to the State or States concerned or to the Security Council, or both. A question on which action is necessary shall be referred to the Security Council by the General Assembly either before or after discussion.

3. The General Assembly may call the attention of the Security Council to situations which are likely to endanger international peace and security.

4. The powers of the General Assembly set out in this article shall not limit the general scope of Article 10.

Article 12—1. While the Security Council is exercising in respect of any dispute or situation the functions assigned to it in the present Charter, the General Assembly shall not make any recommendation with regard to that dispute or situation unless the Security Council so requests.

2. The Secretary General, with the consent of the Security Council, shall notify the General Assembly at each session of any matters relative to the maintenance of international peace and security which are being dealt with by the Security Council and shall similarly notify the General Assembly, or the members of the United Nations if the General Assembly is not in session, immediately the Security Council ceases to deal with such matters.

Article 13—1. The General Assembly shall initiate studies and make recommendations for the purpose of:

(a) Promoting international co-operation in the political field and encouraging the progressive development of international law and its codification;

(b) Promoting international co-operation in the economic, social, cultural, educational and health fields and assisting in the realization of human rights and basic freedoms for all without distinctions as to race, sex, language or religion.

2. The further responsibilities, functions and powers of the General Assembly with respect to matters mentioned in Paragraph (b) above are set forth in Chapters IX and X.

Article 14—Subject to the provisions of Article 12, the General Assembly may recommend measures for the peaceful adjustment of any situation, regardless of origin, which it deems likely to impair the general welfare or friendly relations among nations, including situations resulting from a violation of the provisions of the present Charter setting forth the purposes and principles of the United Nations.

Article 15—1. The General Assembly shall receive and consider annual and special reports from the Security Council; these reports shall include an account of the measures that the Security Council has adopted or applied to maintain international peace and security.

2. The General Assembly shall receive and consider reports from the other bodies of the organization.

Article 16—The General Assembly shall perform such functions with respect to the international trusteeship system as are assigned to it under Chapters XII and XIII, including the approval of the trusteeship agreements for areas not designated as strategic.

Article 17—1. The General Assembly shall consider and approve the budget of the organization.

2. The expenses of the organization

shall be borne by the members as apportioned by the General Assembly.

3. The General Assembly shall consider and approve any financial and budgetary arrangements with specialized agencies referred to in Article 57 and shall examine the administrative budgets of such specialized agencies with a view to making recommendations to the agencies concerned.

VOTING

Article 18—1. Each member of the United Nations shall have one vote in the General Assembly.

2. Decisions of the General Assembly on important questions shall be made by a two-thirds majority of those present and voting. These questions shall include: recommendations with respect to the maintenance of international peace and security, the election of the non-permanent members of the Security Council, and election of the members of the Economic and Social Council, the election of members of the Trusteeship Council in accordance with Paragraph 1(c) of Article 86, the admission of new members to the United Nations, the suspension of the rights and privileges of membership, the expulsion of members, questions relating to the operations of the trusteeship system, and budgetary questions.

3. Decisions on other questions—including the determination of additional categories of questions to be decided by a two-thirds majority—shall be made by a majority of those present and voting.

Article 19—A member which is in arrears in the payments of its financial contributions to the organization shall have no vote if the amount of its arrears equals or exceeds the amount of the contributions due from it for the preceding two full years. The General Assembly may, nevertheless, permit such a member to vote if it is satisfied that the failure to pay is due to conditions beyond the control of the member.

PROCEDURE

Article 20—The General Assembly shall meet in regular annual sessions and in such special sessions as occasion may require. Special sessions shall be convoked by the Secretary General at the request of the Security Council or of a majority of the members of the United Nations.

Article 21—The General Assembly shall adopt its own rules of procedure. It shall elect its president for each session.

Article 22—The General Assembly may establish such subsidiary organs as it deems necessary for the performance of its functions.

CHAPTER V

THE SECURITY COUNCIL COMPOSITION

Article 23—1. The Security Council shall consist of eleven members of the United Nations. The United States of America, the United Kingdom of Great Britain and Northern Ireland, the Union of Soviet Socialist Republics, the Republic of China, and France, shall be permanent members of the Security Council. The General Assembly shall elect six other members of the United Nations to be non-permanent members of the Security Council, due regard being specially paid, in the first instance to the contribution of members of the United Nations to the maintenance of international peace and security and to the other purposes of the organization, and also to equitable geographical distribution.

2. The non-permanent members of the Security Council shall be elected for a term of two years. In the first election of the non-permanent members, however, three shall be chosen for a term of one year. A retiring member shall not be eligible for immediate re-election.

3. Each member of the Security Council shall have one representative.

PRIMARY RESPONSIBILITY

Article 24.—1. In order to insure prompt and effective action by the United Nations, its members confer on the Security Council primary responsibility for the maintenance of international peace and security, and agree that in carrying out its duties under this responsibility the Security Council acts on their behalf.

2. In discharging these duties the Se-

curity Council shall act in accordance with the purposes and principles of the United Nations. The specific powers granted to the Security Council for the discharge of these duties are laid down in Chapters VI, VII, VIII and XII.

3. The Security Council shall submit annual and, when necessary, special reports to the General Assembly for its consideration.

Article 25—The members of the United Nations agree to accept and carry out the decisions of the Security Council in accordance with the provisions of the present Charter.

Article 26—In order to promote the establishment and maintenance of international peace and security with the least diversion for armaments of the world's human and economic resources, the Security Council shall be responsible for formulating with the assistance of the Military Staff Committee referred to in Article 47, plans to be submitted to the members of the United Nations for the establishment of a system for the regulation of armaments.

VOTING

Article 27—1. Each member of the Security Council shall have one vote.

2. Decisions of the Security Council on procedural matters shall be made by an affirmative vote of seven members.

3. Decisions of the Security Council on all other matters shall be made by an affirmative vote of seven members including the concurring votes of the permanent members; provided that, in decisions under Chapter VI and under Paragraph 3 of Article 52 a party to a dispute shall abstain from voting.

PROCEDURE

Article 28—1. The Security Council shall be so organized as to be able to function continuously. Each member of the Security Council shall for this purpose be represented at all times at the seat of the organization.

2. The Security Council shall hold periodic meetings at which each of its members may, if it so desires, be represented

by a member of the Government or by some other specially designated representative.

3. The Security Council may hold meetings at such places other than the seat of the organization as in its judgment may best facilitate its work.

Article 29—The Security Council may establish such subsidiary organs as it deems necessary for the performance of its functions.

Article 30—The Security Council shall adopt its own rules of procedure, including the method of selecting its president.

Article 31—Any member of the United Nations which is not a member of the Security Council may participate without a vote in the discussion of any question brought before the Security Council whenever the latter considers that the interests of that member are specially affected.

Article 32—Any member of the United Nations which is not a member of the Security Council or any State not a member of the United Nations, if it is a party to a dispute under consideration by the Security Council, shall be invited to participate in the discussion relating to the dispute. The Security Council shall lay down such conditions as it may deem just for the participation of a State which is not a member of the United Nations.

CHAPTER VI

PACIFIC SETTLEMENT OF DISPUTES

Article 33—1. The parties to any dispute, the continuance of which is likely to endanger the maintenance of international peace and security, shall, first of all, seek a solution by negotiation, inquiry, mediation, conciliation, arbitration, judicial settlement, resort to regional agencies or arrangements, or other peaceful means of their own choice.

2. The Security Council shall, when it deems necessary, call upon the parties to settle their dispute by such means.

Article 34—The Security Council may investigate any dispute, or any situation which might lead to international friction or give rise to a dispute, in order to determine whether its continuance is likely to endanger the maintenance of international peace and security.

Article 35—1. Any member of the United Nations may bring any dispute or any situation of the nature referred to in Article 34 to the attention of the Security Council, or of the General Assembly.

2. A state which is not a member of the United Nations may bring to the attention of the Security Council or of the General Assembly any dispute to which it is a party, if it accepts in advance, for the purposes of the dispute, the obligations of pacific settlement provided in the present Charter.

3. The proceedings of the General Assembly in respect of matters brought to its attention under this article will be subject to the provisions of Articles 11 and 12.

Article 36—1. The Security Council may, at any stage of a dispute of the nature referred to in Article 33 or of a situation of like nature, recommend appropriate procedures or methods of adjustment.

2. The Security Council should take into consideration any procedures for the settlement of the dispute which have already been adopted by the parties.

3. In making recommendations under this article the Security Council should take into consideration that legal disputes should as a general rule be referred by the parties to the International Court of Justice in accordance with the provisions of the statute of the court.

Article 37—1. Should the parties to a dispute of the nature referred to in Article 33 fail to settle it by the means indicated in that article, they shall refer it to the Security Council.

2. If the Security Council deems that the continuance of the dispute is in fact likely to endanger the maintenance of international peace and security, it shall decide whether to take action under Article 36 or to recommend such terms of settlement as it may consider appropriate.

Article 38—Without prejudice to the provisions of Articles 33–37 of this chapter, the Security Council may, if all the parties to any dispute so request, make recommendations to the parties with a view to a peaceful settlement of the dispute.

CHAPTER VII

ACTION WITH RESPECT TO THREATS TO THE PEACE, BREACHES OF THE PEACE AND ACTS OF AGGRESSION

Article 39—The Security Council shall determine the existence of any threat to the peace, breach of the peace, or act of aggression and shall make recommendations, or decide what measures shall be taken in accordance with the provisions of Articles 41 and 42, to maintain or restore international peace and security.

Article 40—In order to prevent an aggravation of the situation, the Security Council may, before making the recommendations or deciding upon the measures provided for in Article 39, call upon the parties concerned to comply with such provisional measures as it deems necessary or desirable. Such provisional measures shall be without prejudice to the rights, claims, or position of the parties concerned. The Security Council shall duly take account of failure to comply with such provisional measures.

Article 41—The Security Council may decide what measures not involving the use of armed force are to be employed to give effect to its decisions, and it may call upon members of the United Nations to apply such measures. These may include complete or partial interruptions of economic relations and of rail, sea, air, postal, telegraphic, radio, and other means of communication, and the severance of diplomatic relations.

Article 42—Should the Security Council consider that measures provided for in Article 41 would be inadequate, or have proved to be inadequate, it may take such action by air, sea or land forces as may be necessary to maintain or restore international peace and security. Such action may include demonstrations, blockade, and other operations by air, sea or land forces of members of the United Nations.

Article 43—1. All members of the United Nations, in order to contribute to the maintenance of international peace and security, undertake to make available to the Security Council, on its call and in accordance with a special agreement or agreements, armed forces, assistance, and facilities, including rights of passage, necessary for the purpose of maintaining international peace and security.

2. Such agreement or agreements shall govern the numbers and types of forces, their degree of readiness and general location, and the nature of the facilities and assistance to be provided.

3. The agreement or agreements shall be negotiated as soon as possible on the initiative of the Security Council. They shall be concluded between the Security Council and member States or between the Security Council and groups of member states and shall be subject to ratification by the signatory states in accordance with their constitutional processes.

Article 44—When the Security Council has decided to use force it shall, before calling upon a member not represented on it to provide armed forces in fulfillment of the obligations assumed under Article 43, invite that member, if the member so desires, to participate in the decisions of the Security Council concerning the employment of contingents of that member's armed forces.

Article 45—In order to enable the United Nations to take urgent military measures, members shall hold immediately available national air force contingents for combined international enforcement action. The strength and degree of readiness of these contingents and plans for their combined action shall be determined, within the limits laid down in the special agreement or agreements referred to in Article 43, by the Security Council with the assistance of the Military Staff Committee.

Article 46—Plans for the application of armed force shall be made by the Security Council with the assistance of the Military Staff Committee.

Article 47—1. There shall be established a Military Staff Committee to advise and assist the Security Council on all questions relating to the Security Council's military requirements for the maintenance of international peace and security, the employment and command of forces placed at its disposal, the regulation of armaments, and possible disarmament.

2. The Military Staff Committee shall consist of the Chiefs of Staff of the permanent members of the Security Council or their representatives. Any member of the United Nations not permanently represented on the committee shall be invited by the committee to be associated with it when the efficient discharge of the committee's responsibilities requires the participation of that member in its work.

3. The Military Staff Committee shall be responsible, under the Security Council, for the strategic direction of any armed forces placed at the disposal of the Security Council. Questions relating to the command of such forces shall be worked out subsequently.

4. The Military Staff Committee, with the authorization of the Security Council and after consultation with appropriate regional agencies, may establish regional subcommittees.

Article 48—1. The action required to carry out the decisions of the Security Council for the maintenance of international peace and security shall be taken by all the members of the United Nations, or by some of them, as the Security Council may determine.

2. Such decisions shall be carried out by the members of the United Nations directly and through their action in the appropriate international agencies of which they are members.

Article 49—The members of the United Nations shall join in affording mutual assistance in carrying out the measures decided upon by the Security Council.

Article 50—If preventive or enforcement measures against any state are taken by the Security Council, any other state, whether a member of the United Nations or not, which finds itself confronted with special economic problems arising from the carrying out of those measures shall have the right to consult the Security Council with regard to a solution of those problems.

Article 51—Nothing in the present Charter shall impair the inherent right of individual or collective self-defense, if an armed attack occurs against a member of the organization, until the Security Council has taken the measures necessary to maintain international peace and security.

Measures taken by members in the exercise of this right of self-defense shall be immediately reported to the Security Council and shall not in any way affect the authority and responsibility of the Security Council under the present Charter to take at any time such action as it may deem necessary in order to maintain or restore international peace and security.

CHAPTER VIII

REGIONAL ARRANGEMENTS

Article 52—1. Nothing in the present Charter precludes the existence of regional arrangements or agencies for dealing with such matters relating to the maintenance of international peace and security as are appropriate for regional action, provided that such arrangements or agencies and their activities are consistent with the purposes and principles of the organization.

2. The members of the United Nations entering into such arrangements or constituting such agencies shall make every effort to achieve peaceful settlement of local disputes through such regional arrangements or by such regional agencies before referring them to the Security Council.

3. The Security Council should encourage the development of peaceful settlement of local disputes through such regional agencies either on the initiative of the states concerned or by reference from the Security Council.

4. This article in no way impairs the application of Articles 34 and 35.

Article 53—1. The Security Council shall, where appropriate, utilize such arrangements or agencies for enforcement action under its authority. But no enforcement action shall be taken under regional arrangement or by regional agencies without the authorization of the Security Council, with the exception of measures against any enemy state, as described below, provided for pursuant to Article 107, or in regional arrangements directed against renewal of aggressive policy on the part of any such state, until such time as the organization may, on request of the governments concerned, be charged with the responsibility for preventing further aggression by such a state.

2. The term "enemy state" as used in Paragraph 1 of this article applies to any state which during the second World War has been an enemy of any signatory of the present Charter.

Article 54—The Security Council shall at all times be kept fully informed of activities undertaken, or in contemplation, under regional arrangements or by regional agencies for the maintenance of international peace and security.

CHAPTER IX

INTERNATIONAL ECONOMIC AND SOCIAL CO-OPERATION

Article 55—With a view to the creation of conditions of stability and well-being which are necessary for peaceful and friendly relations among nations based on respect for the principle of equal rights and self-determination of people, the United Nations shall promote:

(a) Higher standards of living, full employment, and conditions of economic and social progress and development;

(b) Solutions of international economic, social, health, and related problems and international cultural and educational co-operation; and

(c) Universal respect for, and observance of, human rights and fundamental freedoms for all without distinction as to race, sex, language, or religion.

Article 56—All members pledge themselves to take joint and separate action in co-operation with the organization for the achievement of the purposes set forth in Article 55.

Article 57—1. The various specialized agencies established by inter-governmental agreement, and having wide international responsibilities as defined in their basic instruments in economic, social, cultural, educational, health and related fields, shall be brought into relationship with the United Nations in accordance with the provisions of Article 63.

2. Specialized agencies thus brought into relationship with the organization are hereinafter referred to as "the specialized agencies."

Article 58—The organization shall make recommendations for the co-ordination of the policies and activities of the specialized agencies.

Article 59—The organization shall, where appropriate, initiate negotiations among the States concerned for the creation of any new specialized agency required for the accomplishment of the purposes set forth in Article 55.

Article 60—Responsibility for the discharge of the organization's functions set forth in this chapter shall be vested in the General Assembly and, under the authority of the General Assembly, in the Economic and Social Council, which shall have for this purpose the powers set forth in Chapter X.

CHAPTER X

ECONOMIC AND SOCIAL COUNCIL
COMPOSITION

Article 61—1. The Economic and Social Council shall consist of eighteen members of the United Nations elected by the General Assembly.

2. Subject to the provisions of Paragraph 3, six members of the Economic and Social Council shall be elected each year for a term of three years. A retiring member shall be eligible for immediate re-election.

3. At the first election, eighteen members of the Economic and Social Council shall be chosen. The term of office of six members so chosen shall expire at the end of one year, and of six other members at the end of two years, in accordance with arrangements made by the General Assembly.

4. Each member of the Economic and Social Council shall have one representative.

FUNCTIONS AND POWERS

Article 62—1. The Economic and Social Council may make or initiate studies and reports with respect to international economic, social, cultural, educational, health, and related matters and may make recommendations with respect to any such matters to the General Assembly, to the members of the United Nations, and to the specialized agencies concerned.

2. It may make recommendations for the purpose of promoting respect for, and observance of, human rights and fundamental freedoms for all.

3. It may prepare draft conventions for submission to the General Assembly, with respect to matters falling within its competence.

4. It may call, in accordance with the rules prescribed by the United Nations, international conferences on matters falling within its competence.

Article 63—1. The Economic and Social Council may enter into an agreement, approved by the General Assembly, with any of the agencies referred to in Article 57, defining the terms on which the agency concerned shall be brought into relationship with the United Nations.

2. It may co-ordinate the activities of the specialized agencies through consultation with and recommendations to such agencies and through recommendations to the General Assembly and to the members of the United Nations.

Article 64—1. The Economic and Social Council is authorized to take appropriate steps to obtain regular reports from the specialized agencies. It may make arrangements with the members of the United Nations and with the specialized agencies to obtain reports on the steps taken to give effect to its own recommendations and falling within its competence which are made by the General Assembly.

2. It may communicate its observance on these reports to the General Assembly.

Article 65—The Economic and Social Council may furnish information to the Security Council and shall assist the Security Council upon its request.

Article 66—1. The Economic and Social Council shall perform such functions as fall within its competence in connection with the carrying out of the recommendations of the General Assembly.

2. It may, with the approval of the General Assembly, perform services at the request of the members of the United Nations and at the request of the specialized agencies.

3. It may perform such other functions as are specified elsewhere in the present Charter and such functions as may be assigned to it by the General Assembly.

VOTING

Article 67—1. Each member of the Economic and Social Council shall have one vote.

2. Decisions of the Economic and Social Council shall be taken by a majority of the members present and voting.

PROCEDURE

Article 68—The Economic and Social Council shall set up commissions in economic and social fields and for the promotion of human rights, and such other commissions as may be required for the performance of its functions.

Article 69—The Economic and Social Council shall invite any member of the United Nations to participate, without vote, in its deliberations on any matter of particular concern to that member.

Article 70—The Economic and Social Council may make arrangements for representatives of the specialized agencies to participate, without vote, in its deliberations and in those of the commissions established by it, and for its representatives to participate in the deliberations of the specialized agencies.

Article 71—The Economic and Social Council may make suitable arrangements for consultation with non-governmental organizations which are concerned with matters within its competence. Such arrangements may be made with international organizations, and, where appropriate, with national organizations after consultation with the member of the United Nations concerned.

Article 72—1. The Economic and Social Council shall adopt its own rules of procedure, including the method of selecting its president.

2. The Economic and Social Council shall meet as required in accordance with its rules, which shall include provision for the convening of meetings on request of a majority of its members.

CHAPTER XI

DECLARATION REGARDING NON-SELF-GOVERNING TERRITORIES

Article 73—Members of the United Nations which have or assume responsibilities for the administration of territories whose peoples have not yet attained a full measure of self-government recognize the principle that the interests of the inhabitants of these territories are paramount, and accept as a sacred trust the obligation to promote to the utmost, within the system of international peace and security established by the present Charter, the well-being of the inhabitants of these territories, and, to this end:

(a) To insure, with due respect for the culture of the peoples concerned, their political, economic, social, and educational advancement, their just treatment, and their protection against abuses;

(b) To develop self-government, to take due account of the political aspirations of the peoples, and to assist them in the progressive development of their free political institutions, according to the particular circumstances of each territory and its peoples and their varying stages of advancement;

(c) To further international peace and security;

(d) To promote constructive measures of development, to encourage research, and to co-operate with one another and with appropriate international bodies with a view to the practical achievement of the social, economic, and scientific purposes set forth in this paragraph; and

(e) To transmit regularly to the Secretary General for information purposes, subject to such limitation as security and constitutional considerations may require, statistical and other information of a technical nature relating to economic, social, and educational conditions in the territories for which they are respectively responsible other than those territories to which Chapters XII and XIII apply.

Article 74—Members of the United Nations agree that their policy in respect to the territories, to which this chapter applies, no less than in respect of their metropolitan areas, must be based on the general principle of good-neighborliness, due account being taken of the interests and well-being of the rest of the world, in social, economic and commercial matters.

CHAPTER XII

INTERNATIONAL TRUSTEESHIP SYSTEM

Article 75—The United Nations shall establish under its authority an international trusteeship system for the administration and supervision of such territories as may be placed thereunder by subsequent individual agreements. These territories are hereafter referred to as trust territories.

Article 76—The basic objectives of the trusteeship system in accordance with the purposes of the United Nations laid down in Article I of the present Charter, shall be:

(a) To further international peace and security;

(b) To promote the political, economic, social and educational advancement of the inhabitants of the trust territories, and their progressive development toward self-government or independence as may be appropriate to the particular circumstances of each territory and its peoples and the freely expressed wishes of the peoples concerned, and as may be provided by the terms of each trusteeship agreement;

(c) To encourage respect for human rights and for fundamental freedoms for all without distinction as to race, sex, language or religion, and to encourage recognition of the interdependence of the peoples of the world; and

(d) To insure equal treatment in social, economic and commercial matters for all members of the United Nations and their nationals, and also equal treatment for the latter in the administration of justice, without prejudice to the attainment of the foregoing objectives, and subject to the provisions of Article 80.

Article 77—1. The trusteeship system shall apply to such territories in the following categories as may be placed thereunder by means of trusteeship agreements:

(a) Territories now held under mandate;

(b) Territories which may be detached from enemy states as a result of the second World War; and

(c) Territories voluntarily placed under the system by states responsible for their administration.

2. It will be a matter for subsequent agreement as to which territories in the foregoing categories will be brought under the trusteeship system and upon what terms.

Article 78—The trusteeship system shall not apply to territories which have become members of the United Nations, relationship among which should be based on respect for the principle of sovereign equality.

Article 79—The terms of trusteeship for each territory to be placed under the trusteeship system, including any alteration or amendment, shall be agreed upon by the states directly concerned including the mandatory power in the case of territories held under mandate by a member of the United Nations, and shall be approved as provided for in Articles 83 and 85.

Article 80—1. Except as may be agreed upon in individual trusteeship agreements made in accordance with the provisions of this chapter, placing each territory under the trusteeship system, and until such agreements have been concluded, nothing in this chapter shall be construed in or of itself to alter in any manner the rights whatsoever of any states or any peoples or the terms of existing international instruments to which members of the United Nations may respectively be parties.

2. Paragraph 1 of this article shall not be interpreted as giving grounds for delay or postponement of the negotiation and conclusion of such agreements for placing mandated and other territories under the trusteeship system as provided for in Article 77.

Article 81—The trusteeship agreement shall in each case include the terms under which the trust territory will be administered and designate the authority which shall exercise the administration of the trust territory. Such authority, hereafter called the administering authority, may be one or more states or the United Nations itself.

Article 82—There may be designated, in any trusteeship agreement, a strategic area or areas which may include part or all of the trust territory to which the agreement applies, without prejudice to any special agreement or agreements made under Article 43.

Article 83—1. All functions of the United Nations relating to strategic areas, including the approval of the terms of the trusteeship agreements and of their alteration or amendment, shall be exercised by the Security Council.

2. The basic objectives set forth in Article 76 shall be applicable to the people of each strategic area.

3. The Security Council shall, subject to the provisions of the trusteeship agreements and without prejudice to security considerations, avail itself of the assistance of the Trusteeship Council to perform those functions of the United Nations under the trusteeship system relating to political, economic, social and educational matters in the strategic areas.

Article 84—It shall be the duty of the administering authority to insure that the trust territory shall play its part in the maintenance of international peace and security. To this end the administering authority may make use of volunteer forces, facilities, and assistance from the trust territory in carrying out the obligations toward the Security Council undertaken in this regard by the administering authority, as well as for local defense and the maintenance of law and order within the trust territory.

Article 85—1. The functions of the United Nations with regard to trusteeship agreements for all areas not designated as strategic, including the approval of the terms of the trusteeship agreements and of their alteration or amendment, shall be exercised by the General Assembly.

2. The Trusteeship Council, operating under the authority of the General Assembly, shall assist the General Assembly in carrying out these functions.

CHAPTER XIII

THE TRUSTEESHIP COUNCIL COMPOSITION

Article 86—1. The Trusteeship Council shall consist of the following members of the United Nations:

(a) Those members administering trust territories;

(b) Such of those members mentioned by name in Article 23 as are not administering trust territories; and

(c) As many other members elected for three-year terms by the General Assembly as may be necessary to insure that the total number of members of the Trusteeship Council is equally divided between those members of the United Nations which administer trust territories and those which do not.

2. Each member of the Trusteeship Council shall designate one specially qualified person to represent it therein.

FUNCTIONS AND POWERS

Article 87—The General Assembly and, under its authority, the Trusteeship Council, in carrying out their functions, may:

(a) Consider reports submitted by the administering authority;

(b) Accept petitions and examine them in consultation with the administering authority;

(c) Provide for periodic visits to the respective trust territories at times agreed upon within the administering authority; and

(d) Take these and other actions in conformity with the terms of the trusteeship agreements.

Article 88—The Trusteeship Council shall formulate a questionnaire on the political, economic, social and educational advancement of the inhabitants of each trust territory, and the administering authority for each trust territory within the competence of the General Assembly shall make an annual report to the General Assembly upon the basis of such questionnaire.

VOTING

Article 89—1. Each member of the Trusteeship Council shall have one vote.

2. Decisions of the Trusteeship Council shall be taken by a majority of the members present and voting.

PROCEDURE

Article 90—1. The Trusteeship Council shall adopt its own rules of procedure, including the method of selecting its president.

2. The Trusteeship Council shall meet as required in accordance with its rules, which shall include provisions for the convening of meetings on the request of a majority of its members.

Article 91—The Trusteeship Council shall, when appropriate, avail itself of the assistance of the Economic and Social Council and of the specialized agencies in regard to matters with which they are respectively concerned.

CHAPTER XIV

THE INTERNATIONAL COURT OF JUSTICE

Article 92—The International Court of Justice shall be the principal judicial organ of the United Nations. It shall function in accordance with the annexed statute, which is based upon the statute of the Permanent Court of International Justice and forms an integral part of the present chapter.

Article 93—1. All members of the United Nations are ipso facto parties to the statute of the International Court of Justice.

2. A State which is not a member of the United Nations may become party to the statute of the International Court of Justice on conditions to be determined in each case by the General Assembly upon recommendation of the Security Council.

Article 94—1. Each member of the United Nations undertakes to comply with the decision of the International Court of Justice in any case to which it is a party.

2. If any party to a case fails to perform the obligations incumbent upon it under a judgment rendered by the court, the other party may have recourse to the Security Council, which may, if it deems necessary, make recommendations or decide upon measures to be taken to give effect to the judgment.

Article 95—Nothing in the present Charter shall prevent members of the United Nations from entrusting the solution of their differences to other tribunals by virtue of agreements already in existence or which may be concluded in the future.

Article 96—1. The General Assembly or the Security Council may request the International Court of Justice to give an advisory opinion on any legal question.

2. Other organs of the United Nations, and specialized agencies which may at any time be so authorized by the General Assembly, may also request advisory opinions of the court on legal questions arising within the scope of their activities.

CHAPTER XV

THE SECRETARIAT

Article 97—There shall be a Secretariat comprising a Secretary General and such staff as the organization may require. The Secretary General shall be appointed by the General Assembly on the recommendation of the Security Council. He shall be the chief administrative officer of the organization.

Article 98—The Secretary General shall act in that capacity in all meetings of the General Assembly, of the Security Council, of the Economic and Social Council and of the Trusteeship Council, and shall perform such other functions as are entrusted to him by these organs. The Secretary General shall make an annual report to the General Assembly on the work of the organization.

Article 99—The Secretary General may bring to the attention of the Security Council any matter which in his opinion may threaten the maintenance of international peace and security.

Article 100—1. In the performance of their duties the Secretary General and the staff shall not seek or receive instructions from any Government or from any other authority external to the organization. They shall refrain from any action which might reflect on their position as international officials responsible only to the organization.

2. Each member of the United Na-

tions undertakes to respect the exclusively international character of the responsibilities of the Secretary General and the staff, and not to seek to influence them in the discharge of their responsibilities.

Article 101—1. The staff shall be appointed by the Secretary General under regulations established by the General Assembly.

2. Appropriate staffs shall be permanently assigned to the Economic and Social Council, the Trusteeship Council, and, as required, to other organs of the United Nations. These staffs shall form a part of the Secretariat.

3. The paramount consideration in the employment of the staff and in the determination of the conditions of service shall be the necessity of securing the highest standards of efficiency, competence and integrity. Due regard shall be paid to the importance of recruiting the staff on as wide a geographical basis as possible.

CHAPTER XVI

MISCELLANEOUS PROVISIONS

Article 102—1. Every treaty and every international agreement entered into by any member of the United Nations after the present Charter comes into force shall as soon as possible be registered with the Secretariat and published by it.

2. No party to any such treaty or international agreement which has not been registered in accordance with the provisions of Paragraph 1 of this article may invoke that treaty or agreement before any organ of the United Nations.

Article 103—In the event of a conflict between the obligations of the members of the United Nations under the present Charter and any other international obligations to which they are subject, their obligations under the present Charter shall prevail.

Article 104—The organization shall enjoy in the territory of each of its members such legal capacity as may be necessary for the exercise of its functions and the fulfillment of its purposes.

Article 105—1. The organization shall enjoy in the territory of each of its members such privileges and immunities as

are necessary for the fulfillment of its purposes.

2. Representatives of the members of the United Nations and officials of the organization shall similarly enjoy such privileges and immunities as are necessary for the independent exercise of their functions in connection with the organization.

3. The General Assembly may make recommendations with a view to determine the details of the application of Paragraphs 1 and 2 of this article or may propose conventions to the members of the United Nations for this purpose.

CHAPTER XVII

TRANSITIONAL SECURITY ARRANGEMENTS

Article 106—Pending the coming into force of such special agreements referred to in Article 43, as in the opinion of the Security Council enable it to begin the exercise of its responsibilities under Article 42, the parties to the four-nation declaration signed at Moscow, Oct. 30, 1943, and France, shall, in accordance with the provisions of Paragraph 5 of that declaration, consult with one another and, as occasion requires, with other members of the organization with a view to such joint action on behalf of the organization as may be necessary for the purpose of maintaining international peace and security.

Article 107—Nothing in the present Charter shall invalidate or preclude action in relation to any state which during the second World War has been an enemy of any signatory to the present Charter, taken or authorized as a result of that war by the governments having responsibility for such action.

CHAPTER XVIII

AMENDMENTS

Article 108—Amendments to the present Charter shall come into force for all members of the organization when they have been adopted by a vote of two-thirds of the members of the General Assembly and ratified in accordance with their respective constitutional processes by two-thirds of the members of the United Nations, including all the permanent members of the Security Council.

Article 109—1. A general conference of the members of the United Nations for the purpose of reviewing the present Charter may be held at a date and place to be fixed by a two-thirds vote of the General Assembly and by a vote of any seven members of the Security Council. Each member of the United Nations shall have one vote in the conference.

2. Any alteration of the present Charter recommended by a two-thirds vote of the conference shall take effect when ratified in accordance with their respective constitutional processes by two-thirds of the members of the United Nations including all the permanent members of the Security Council.

3. If such a conference has not been held before the tenth annual session of the General Assembly following the coming into force of the present Charter the proposal to call such a conference shall be placed on the agenda of that session of the General Assembly, and the conference shall be held if so decided by a majority vote of the members of the General Assembly and by a vote of any seven members of the Security Council.

CHAPTER XIX

RATIFICATION AND SIGNATURE

Article 110—1. The present Charter shall be ratified by the signatory states in accordance with their respective constitutional processes.

2. The ratifications shall be deposited with the Government of the United States of America, which shall notify all the signatory states of each deposit as well as the Secretary General of the organization when he has been elected.

3. The present Charter shall come into force upon the deposit of ratifications by the Republic of China, France, the Union of Soviet Socialist Republics, the United Kingdom of Great Britain and Northern Ireland, and the United States of America, and by a majority of the other signatory states.

4. The states signatory to the present Charter which ratify it after it has come into force will become original members of the United Nations on the date of the deposit of their respective ratifications.

Article 111—The present Charter, of which the Chinese, English, French, Russian and Spanish texts are equally authentic, shall remain deposited in the archives of the Government of the United States of America. Duly certified copies thereof shall be transmitted by that Government to the Governments of the other signatory states.

In faith whereof the representatives of the United Nations have signed the present Charter.

Done in the city of San Francisco the twenty-sixth day of June, one thousand nine hundred and forty-five.

North Atlantic Treaty[1]

PREAMBLE

The parties to this treaty reaffirm their faith in the purposes and principles of the Charter of the United Nations and their desire to live in peace with all peoples and all governments.

They are determined to safeguard the freedom, common heritage and civilization of their peoples, founded on the principles of democracy, individual liberty and the rule of law.

They seek to promote stability and well-being in the North Atlantic area.

They are resolved to unite their efforts for collective defense and for the preservation of peace and security.

They therefore agree to this North Atlantic Treaty:

ARTICLE I

The parties undertake, as set forth in the Charter of the United Nations, to settle any international disputes in which they may be involved by peaceful means in such a manner that international peace and security, and justice, are not endangered, and to refrain in their international relations from the threat or use of force in any manner inconsistent with the purposes of the United Nations.

ARTICLE II

The parties will contribute toward the further development of peaceful and friendly international relations by strengthening their free institutions, by bringing about a better understandng of the principles upon which these institutions are founded, and by promoting conditions of

[1] Ratified by the Senate, July 21, 1949; went into effect August 24, 1949. The signatories of the treaty are: United States, Canada, Great Britain, France, Belgium, the Netherlands, Luxemburg, Norway, Denmark, Iceland, Italy and Portugal.

stability and well-being. They will seek to eliminate conflict in their international economic policies and will encourage economic collaboration between any or all of them.

ARTICLE III

In order more effectively to achieve the objectives of this treaty, the parties, separately and jointly, by means of continuous and effective self-help and mutual aid, will maintain and develop their individual and collective capacity to resist armed attack.

ARTICLE IV

The parties will consult together whenever, in the opinion of any of them, the territorial integrity, political independence or security of any of the parties is threatened.

ARTICLE V

The parties agree that an armed attack against one or more of them in Europe or North America shall be considered an attack against them all; and consequently they agree that, if such an armed attack occurs, each of them, in exercise of the right of individual or collective self-defense recognized by Article 51 of the Charter of the United Nations, will assist the party or parties so attacked by taking forthwith, individually and in concert with the other parties, such action as it deems necessary, including the use of armed force, to restore and maintain the security of the North Atlantic area.

Any such armed attack and all measures taken as a result thereof shall immediately be reported to the Security Council. Such measures shall be terminated when the Security Council has taken the measures necessary to restore and maintain international peace and security.

ARTICLE VI

For the purpose of Article 5 an armed attack on one or more of the parties is deemed to include an armed attack on the territory of any of the parties in Europe or North America, on the Algerian Departments of France, on the occupation forces of any party in Europe, on the islands under the jurisdiction of any party in the North Atlantic area north of the Tropic of Cancer or on the vessels or aircraft in this area of any of the parties.

ARTICLE VII

This treaty does not affect, and shall not be interpreted as affecting, in any way the rights and obligations under the Charter of the parties which are members of the United Nations, or the primary responsibility of the Security Council for the maintenance of international peace and security.

ARTICLE VIII

Each party declares that none of the international engagements now in force between it and any other of the parties or any third state is in conflict with the provisions of this treaty, and undertakes not to enter into any international engagement in conflict with this treaty.

ARTICLE IX

The parties hereby establish a Council, on which each of them shall be represented, to consider matters concerning the implementation of this treaty. The Council shall be so organized as to be able to meet promptly at any time. The Council shall set up such subsidiary bodies as may be necessary; in particular it shall establish immediately a Defense Committee which shall recommend measures for the implementation of Articles 3 and 5.

ARTICLE X

The parties may, by unanimous agreement, invite any other European state in a position to further the principles of this treaty and to contribute to the security of the North Atlantic area to accede to this treaty. Any state so invited may become a party to the treaty by depositing its instru-

ment of accession with the Government of the United States of America. The Government of the United States of America will inform each of the parties of the deposit of each such instrument of accession.

ARTICLE XI

This treaty shall be ratified and its provisions carried out by the parties in accordance with their respective constitutional processes. The instruments of ratification shall be deposited as soon as possible with the Government of the United States of America, which will notify all the other signatories of each deposit. The treaty shall enter into force between the states which have ratified it as soon as the ratifications of the majority of the signatories, including the ratifications of Belgium, Canada, France, Luxemburg, the Netherlands, the United Kingdom and the United States, have been deposited and shall come into effect with respect to other states on the date of the deposit of their ratifications.

ARTICLE XII

After the treaty has been in force for ten years, or at any time thereafter, the parties shall, if any of them so requests, consult together for the purpose of reviewing the treaty, having regard for the factors then affecting peace and security in the North Atlantic area, including the development of universal as well as regional arrangements under the Charter of the United Nations for the maintenance of international peace and security.

ARTICLE XIII

After the treaty has been in force for twenty years, any party may cease to be a party one year after its notice of denunciation has been given to the Government of the United States of America, which will inform the governments of the other parties of the deposit of each notice of denunciation.

ARTICLE XIV

This treaty, of which the English and French texts are equally authentic, shall be deposited in the archives of the Government of the United States of America. Duly certified copies thereof will be transmitted by that government to the governments of the other signatories.

In witness whereof, the undersigned plenipotentiaries have signed this treaty. Done at Washington, the fourth day of April, 1949.

Presidents and Vice-Presidents of the United States

No.	President	Party	Years in Office	Vice-President
1	George Washington	Fed.	1789–1797	John Adams
2	John Adams	Fed.	1797–1801	Thomas Jefferson
3	Thomas Jefferson	Dem.–Rep.	1801–1809	Aaron Burr / George Clinton
4	James Madison	Dem.–Rep.	1809–1817	George Clinton / Elbridge Gerry
5	James Monroe	Dem.–Rep.	1817–1825	Daniel D. Tompkins
6	John Q. Adams	Dem.–Rep.	1825–1829	John C. Calhoun
7	Andrew Jackson	Dem.	1829–1837	John C. Calhoun / Martin Van Buren
8	Martin Van Buren	Dem.	1837–1841	Richard M. Johnson
9	Wm. H. Harrison	Whig	1841–1841	John Tyler
10	John Tyler[1]	Whig	1841–1845	
11	James K. Polk	Dem.	1845–1849	George M. Dallas
12	Zachary Taylor	Whig	1849–1850	Millard Fillmore
13	Millard Fillmore[1]	Whig	1850–1853	
14	Franklin Pierce	Dem.	1853–1857	William R. King
15	James Buchanan	Dem.	1857–1861	J. C. Breckinridge
16	Abraham Lincoln	Rep.	1861–1865	Hannibal Hamlin / Andrew Johnson
17	Andrew Johnson[1]	Rep.	1865–1869	
18	Ulysses S. Grant	Rep.	1869–1877	Schuyler Colfax / Henry Wilson
19	Rutherford B. Hayes	Rep.	1877–1881	Wm. A. Wheeler
20	James A. Garfield	Rep.	1881–1881	Chester A. Arthur
21	Chester A. Arthur[1]	Rep.	1881–1885	
22	Grover Cleveland	Dem.	1885–1889	Thomas A. Hendricks
23	Benjamin Harrison	Rep.	1889–1893	Levi P. Morton
24	Grover Cleveland	Dem.	1893–1897	Adlai E. Stevenson
25	William McKinley	Rep.	1897–1901	Garrett A. Hobart / Theodore Roosevelt
26	Theodore Roosevelt[1]	Rep.	1901–1909	Chas. W. Fairbanks
27	William H. Taft	Rep.	1909–1913	James S. Sherman
28	Woodrow Wilson	Dem.	1913–1921	Thomas R. Marshall
29	Warren G. Harding	Rep.	1921–1923	Calvin Coolidge
30	Calvin Coolidge[1]	Rep.	1923–1929	Charles G. Dawes
31	Herbert Hoover	Rep.	1929–1933	Charles Curtis
32	Franklin D. Roosevelt	Dem.	1933–1945	John Nance Garner / Henry Agard Wallace / Harry S. Truman
33	Harry S. Truman[1]	Dem.	1945–	Alben W. Barkley

[1] Promoted from the Vice-Presidency on the death of the President.

34. Eisenhower
35. Kennedy
36. Johnson

Qualifications for Voting in the Forty-Eight States

State	Min. Length of U.S. Citizenship	Residence[1] State	County	District	Date Literacy Test Adopted	Poll Tax[2]
Alabama	....	2 yr.	1 yr.	3 mo.	1946	yes
Arizona	....	1 yr.	1 mo.	1 mo.	1912	...
Arkansas	5 yr.	1 yr.	6 mo.	1 mo.	....	yes
California	1 yr.	1 yr.	3 mo.	40 da.	....	...
Colorado	1 yr.	1 yr.	3 mo.	10 da.	....	...
Connecticut	....	1 yr.	....	6 mo.[3]	1855	...
Delaware	1 yr.	1 yr.	3 mo.	1 mo.	1897	...
Florida	....	1 yr.	6 mo.	....	....	...
Georgia[4]	....	1 yr.	6 mo.	....	1877	...
Idaho	....	6 mo.	1 mo.	....	....	...
Illinois	....	1 yr.	3 mo.	1 mo.	....	...
Indiana	....	6 mo.	2 mo.[5]	1 mo.	....	...
Iowa	....	6 mo.	2 mo.	10 da.	....	...
Kansas	....	6 mo.	1 mo.	1 mo.	....	...
Kentucky	....	1 yr.	6 mo.	2 mo.	....	...
Louisiana	....	2 yr.	1 yr.[6]	3 mo.[7]	....	...
Maine	....	6 mo.	....	3 mo.	1892	...
Maryland	....	1 yr.	6 mo.	1 da.	....	...
Massachusetts	....	1 yr.	....	6 mo.[3]	....	...
Michigan	....	6 mo.	20 da.	20 da.[3]	....	...
Minnesota	3 mo.	6 mo.	6 mo.	1 mo.	....	...
Mississippi	....	2 yr.	1 yr.	1 yr.	....	...
Missouri	....	1 yr.	2 mo.	2 mo.	....	...
Montana	....	1 yr.	1 mo.	1 mo.[8]	....	...
Nebraska	....	6 mo.	40 da.	10 da.	....	...
Nevada	....	6 mo.	1 mo.	10 da.[8]	....	...
New Hampshire	6 mo.	6 mo.	6 mo.	6 mo.	1905	yes
New Jersey	....	1 yr.	5 mo.	....	....	...
New Mexico	....	1 yr.	3 mo.	1 mo.	....	...
New York	3 mo.	1 yr.	4 mo.	1 mo.	1921	...
North Carolina	1 yr.	1 yr.	4 mo.	....	1901	...
North Dakota	....	1 yr.	3 mo.	1 mo.	....	...
Ohio	....	1 yr.	40 da.	40 da.[8]	....	...
Oklahoma	....	1 yr.	6 mo.	1 mo.[8]	....	...
Oregon	....	6 mo.	....	....	1924	...
Pennsylvania	1 mo.	1 yr.	....	2 mo.	....	...
Rhode Island	....	2 yr.	....	6 mo.[3]	....	...
South Carolina	....	2 yr.	1 yr.	4 mo.	1895	yes
South Dakota	5 yr.	1 yr.	3 mo.	1 mo.[8]	....	...
Tennessee	....	1 yr.	6 mo.	1 mo.	....	yes
Texas	....	1 yr.	6 mo.	....	....	yes
Utah	3 mo.	1 yr.	4 mo.	2 mo.	....	...
Vermont	....	1 yr.	3 mo.	3 mo.[9]	....	...
Virginia	1 yr.	1 yr.	6 mo.	1 mo.	1902	yes
Washington	....	1 yr.	3 mo.	1 mo.	....	...
West Virginia	....	1 yr.	2 mo.	1 mo.	....	...
Wisconsin	....	1 yr.	....	10 da.	....	...
Wyoming	....	1 yr.	1 mo.	10 da.	1889	...

[1] Registration of all or part of the voters is required in most states. No registration is required in Arkansas, North Dakota and Texas. In Connecticut, registration is permanent. In Vermont, name must be on check-list. [2] Although poll or head taxes are levied in several other states, those listed make payment of the tax a condition for voting. [3] City or town. [4] Minimum voting age is 18; in all other states, minimum age is 21. [5] Township. [6] Parish. [7] Ward. [8] Precinct. [9] To vote for representatives to General Assembly.

The States of the Federal Union

States	Capital	Entered Union
Alabama	Montgomery	1819
Arizona	Phoenix	1912
Arkansas	Little Rock	1836
California	Sacramento	1850
Colorado	Denver	1876
Connecticut	Hartford	1788
Delaware	Dover	1787
Florida	Tallahassee	1845
Georgia	Atlanta	1788
Idaho	Boise	1890
Illinois	Springfield	1818
Indiana	Indianapolis	1816
Iowa	Des Moines	1846
Kansas	Topeka	1861
Kentucky	Frankfort	1792
Louisiana	Baton Rouge	1812
Maine	Augusta	1820
Maryland	Annapolis	1788
Massachusetts	Boston	1788
Michigan	Lansing	1837
Minnesota	St. Paul	1858
Mississippi	Jackson	1817
Missouri	Jefferson City	1821
Montana	Helena	1889
Nebraska	Lincoln	1867
Nevada	Carson City	1864
New Hampshire	Concord	1788
New Jersey	Trenton	1787
New Mexico	Santa Fe	1912
New York	Albany	1788
North Carolina	Raleigh	1789
North Dakota	Bismarck	1889
Ohio	Columbus	1803
Oklahoma	Oklahoma City	1907
Oregon	Salem	1859
Pennsylvania	Harrisburg	1787
Rhode Island	Providence	1790
South Carolina	Columbia	1788
South Dakota	Pierre	1889
Tennessee	Nashville	1796
Texas	Austin	1845
Utah	Salt Lake City	1896
Vermont	Montpelier	1791
Virginia	Richmond	1788
Washington	Olympia	1889
West Virginia	Charleston	1863
Wisconsin	Madison	1848
Wyoming	Cheyenne	1890

Washington's Farewell Address

To the people of the United States:

FRIENDS AND FELLOW CITIZENS: The period for a new election of a citizen to administer the executive government of the United States being not far distant, and the time actually arrived when your thoughts must be employed in designating the person who is to be clothed with that important trust, it appears to me proper, especially as it may conduce to a more distinct expression of the public voice, that I should now apprise you of the resolution I have formed, to decline being considered among the number of those, out of whom a choice is to be made.

I beg you, at the same time, to do me the justice to be assured, that this resolution has not been taken, without a strict regard to all the considerations appertaining to the relation which binds a dutiful citizen to his country; and that in withdrawing the tender of service which silence in my situation might imply, I am influenced by no diminution of zeal for your future interest, no deficiency of grateful respect for your past kindness; but am supported by a full conviction that the step is compatible with both.

The acceptance of, and continuance hitherto in the office to which your suffrages have twice called me, have been a uniform sacrifice of inclination to the opinion of duty, and to a deference for what appeared to be your desire. I constantly hoped that it would have been much earlier in my power, consistently with motives which I was not at liberty to disregard, to return to that retirement from which I had been reluctantly drawn. The strength of my inclination to do this, previous to the last election, had even led to the preparation of an address to declare it to you; but mature reflection on the then perplexed and critical posture of our affairs with foreign nations, and the unanimous advice of persons entitled to my confidence, impelled me to abandon the idea.

I rejoice that the state of your concerns, external as well as internal, no longer renders the pursuit of inclination incompatible with the sentiment of duty or propriety; and am persuaded, whatever partiality may be retained for my services, that in the present circumstances of our country, you will not disapprove my determination to retire.

The impressions with which I first undertook the arduous trust, were explained on the proper occasion. In the discharge of this trust, I will only say that I have, with good intentions, contributed towards the organization and administration of the government, the best exertions of which a very fallible judgment was capable. Not unconscious in the outset, of the inferiority of my qualifications, experience, in my own eyes, perhaps still more in the eyes of others, has strengthened the motives to diffidence of myself; and, every day, the increasing weight of years admonishes me more and more, that the shade of retirement is as necessary to me as it will be welcome. Satisfied that if any circumstances have given peculiar value to my services they were temporary, I have the consolation to believe that, while choice and prudence invite me to quit the political scene, patriotism does not forbid it.

In looking forward to the moment which is to terminate the career of my political life, my feelings do not permit me to suspend the deep acknowledgment of that debt of gratitude which I owe to my beloved country, for the many honors it has conferred upon me; still more for the steadfast confidence with which it has supported me; and for the opportunities I have thence enjoyed of manifesting my inviolable attachment, by service faithful and persevering, though in usefulness unequal to my zeal. If benefits have resulted to our country from these services, let it always be remembered to your praise, and as an instructive example in our annals, that under circumstances in which the passions, agitated in every direction, were liable to mislead amidst appearances sometimes dubious, vicissitudes of fortune often discouraging—in situations in which not unfrequently, want of success has countenanced the spirit of criticism—the constancy of your support was the essential prop of the efforts, and a guarantee of the plans, by which they were effected. Profoundly penetrated with this idea, I shall carry it with me to my grave, as a strong incitement to unceasing vows that heaven may continue to you the choicest tokens of its beneficence—that your union and brotherly affection may be perpetual—that the free constitution, which is the work of your hands, may be sacredly maintained—that its administration in every department may be stamped with wisdom and virtue—that, in fine, the happiness of the people of these states, under the auspices of liberty, may be made complete by so careful a preservation, and so prudent a use of this blessing, as will acquire to them the glory of recommending it to the applause, the affection and adoption of every nation which is yet a stranger to it.

Here, perhaps, I ought to stop. But a solicitude for your welfare, which cannot end but with my life, and the apprehension of danger, natural to that solicitude, urge me, on an occasion like the present, to offer to your solemn contemplation, and to recommend to your frequent review, some sentiments which are the result of much reflection, of no inconsiderable observation, and which appear to me all important to the permanency of your felicity as a people. These will be offered to you with the more freedom, as you can only see in them the disinterested warnings of a parting friend, who can possibly have no personal motive to bias his coun-

sel. Nor can I forget, as an encouragement to it, your indulgent reception of my sentiments on a former and not dissimilar occasion.

Interwoven as is the love of liberty with every ligament of your hearts, no recommendation of mine is necessary to fortify or confirm the attachment.

The unity of government which constitutes you one people, is also now dear to you. It is justly so; for it is a main pillar in the edifice of your real independence; the support of your tranquillity at home; your peace abroad; of your safety; of your prosperity; of that very liberty which you so highly prize. But as it is easy to foresee that, from different causes and from different quarters much pains will be taken, many artifices employed, to weaken in your minds the conviction of this truth, as this is the point in your political fortress against which the batteries of internal and external enemies will be most constantly and actively (though often covertly and insidiously) directed; it is of infinite moment, that you should properly estimate the immense value of your national union to your collective and individual happiness; that you should cherish a cordial, habitual, and immovable attachment to it; accustoming yourselves to think and speak of it as the palladium of your political safety and prosperity; watching for its preservation with jealous anxiety; discountenancing whatever may suggest even a suspicion that it can, in any event, be abandoned; and indignantly frowning upon the first dawning of every attempt to alienate any portion of our country from the rest, or to enfeeble the sacred ties which now link together the various parts.

For this you have every inducement of sympathy and interest. Citizens by birth, or choice, of a common country, that country has a right to concentrate your affections. The name of American, which belongs to you in your national capacity, must always exalt the just pride of patriotism, more than any appellation derived from local discriminations. With slight shades of difference, you have the same religion, manners, habits, and political principles. You have, in a common cause, fought and triumphed together; the independence and liberty you possess, are the work of joint counsels, and joint efforts, of common dangers, suffering and successes.

But these considerations, however powerfully they addressed themselves to your sensibility, are greatly outweighed by those which apply more immediately to your interest.—Here, every portion of our country finds the most commanding motives for carefully guarding and preserving the union of the whole.

The *north*, in an unrestrained intercourse with the *south*, protected by the equal laws of a common government, finds in the productions of the latter, great additional resources of maritime and commercial enterprise, and precious materials of manufacturing industry.—The *south* in the same intercourse, benefiting by the same agency of the *north*, sees its agriculture grow and its commerce expand. Turning partly into its own channels the seamen of the *north*, it finds its particular navigation invigorated; and while it contributes, in different ways, to nourish and increase the general mass of the national navigation, it looks forward to the protection of a maritime strength, to which itself is unequally adapted. The *east*, in a like intercourse with the *west*, already finds, and in the progressive improvement of interior communications by land and water, will more and more find a valuable vent for the commodities which it brings from abroad, or manufactures at home. The *west* derives from the *east* supplies requisite to its growth and comfort—and what is perhaps of still greater consequence, it must of necessity owe the *secure* enjoyment of indispensable *outlets* for its own productions, to the weight, influence, and the future maritime strength of the Atlantic side of the Union, directed by an indissoluble community of interest as *one nation.* Any other tenure by which the *west* can hold this essential advantage, whether derived from its own separate strength; or from an apostate and unnatural connection with any foreign power, must be intrinsically precarious.

While then every part of our country thus feels an immediate and particular interest in union, all the parts combined cannot fail to find in the united mass of means and efforts, greater strength, greater resource, proportionably greater security from external danger, a less frequent interruption of their peace by foreign nations; and, what is of inestimable value, they must derive from union, an exemption from those broils and wars between themselves, which so frequently afflict neighboring countries not tied together by the same government; which their own rivalship alone would be sufficient to produce, but which opposite foreign alliances, attachments, and intrigues, would stimulate and embitter. Hence likewise, they will avoid the necessity of those overgrown military establishments, which under any form of government are inauspicious to liberty, and which are to be regarded as particularly hostile to republican liberty. In this sense it is, that your union ought to be considered as a main prop of your liberty, and that the love of the one ought to endear to you the preservation of the other.

These considerations speak a persuasive language to every reflecting and virtuous mind and exhibit the continuance of the union as a primary object of patriotic desire. Is there a doubt whether a common government can embrace so large a sphere? let experience solve it. To listen to mere speculation in such a case were criminal. We are authorized to hope that a proper organization of the whole, with the auxiliary agency of governments for the respective subdivisions, will afford a happy issue to the experiment. It is well worth a fair and full experiment. With such powerful and obvious motives to union, affecting all parts of our country, while experience shall not have demonstrated its impracticability, there will always be reason to distrust the patriotism of those who, in any quarter, many endeavor to weaken its hands.

In contemplating the causes which may disturb our Union, it occurs as matter of serious concern, that any ground should have been furnished for characterizing parties by *geographical* discriminations,—*northern* and *southern*—*Atlantic* and *western;* whence designing men may endeavor to excite a belief that there is a real difference of local interests and views. One of the expedients of party to acquire influence within particular districts, is to misrepresent the opinions and aims of other districts. You cannot shield yourselves too much against the jealousies and heart burnings which spring from these misrepresentations; they tend to render alien to each other those who ought to be bound together by fraternal affection. The inhabitants of our western country have lately had a useful lesson on this head; they have seen, in the negotiation by the executive, and in the unanimous ratification by the senate of the treaty with Spain, and in the universal satisfaction at the event throughout the United States, a decisive proof how unfounded were the suspicions propagated among them of a policy in the general government and in the Atlantic states, unfriendly to their interests in regard to the Mississippi. They have been witnesses to the formation of two treaties, that with Great Britain and that with Spain, which secure to them everything they could desire, in respect to our foreign relations, towards confirming their prosperity. Will it not be their wisdom to rely for the preservation of these advantages on the union by which they were procured? Will they not henceforth be deaf to those advisers, if such they are, who would sever them from their brethren and connect them with aliens?

To the efficacy and permanency of your Union, a government for the whole is indispensable. No alliances, however strict, between the parts can be an adequate substitute; they must inevitably experience the infractions and interruptions which all alliances, in all times, have experienced. Sensible of this momentous truth, you have improved upon your first essay, by the adoption of a constitution of government, better calculated than your former, for an intimate union, and for the efficacious management of your common concerns. This government, the offspring of our own choice, uninfluenced and unawed, adopted upon full investigation and mature deliberation, completely free in its principles, in the distribution of its powers, uniting security with energy, and maintaining within itself a provision for its own amendment, has a just claim to your confidence and your support. Respect for its authority, compliance with its laws, acquiescence in its measures, are duties enjoined by the fundamental maxims of true liberty. The basis of our political systems is the right of the people to make and to alter their constitutions of government.—But the constitution which at any time exists, until changed by an explicit and authentic act of the whole people, is sacredly obligatory upon all. The very idea of the power, and the right of the people to establish government, presuppose the duty of every individual to obey the established government.

All obstructions to the execution of the laws, all combinations and associations under whatever plausible character, with the real design to direct, control, counteract, or awe the regular deliberations and action of the constituted authorities, are destructive of this fundamental principle, and of fatal tendency.—They serve to organize faction, to give it an artificial and extraordinary force, to put in the place of the delegated will of the nation the will of the party, often a small but artful and enterprising minority of the community; and, according to the alternate triumphs of different parties, to make the public administration the mirror of the ill concerted and incongruous projects of faction, rather than the organ of consistent and wholesome plans digested by common councils, and modified by mutual interests.

However combinations or associations of the above description may now and then answer popular ends, they are likely in the course of time and things, to become potent engines, by which cunning, ambitious, and unprincipled men, will be enabled to subvert the power of the people, and to usurp for themselves the reins of government; destroying afterwards the very engines which have lifted them to unjust dominion.

Towards the preservation of your government and the permanency of your present happy state, it is requisite, not only that you steadily discountenance irregular opposition to its acknowledged authority, but also that you resist with care the spirit of innovation upon its principles, however specious the pretext. One method of assault may be to effect, in the forms of the constitution, alterations which will impair the energy of the system; and thus to undermine what cannot be directly overthrown. In all the changes to which you may be involved, remember that time and habit are at least as necessary to fix the true character of governments, as of other human institutions:—that experience is the surest standard by which to test the real tendency of the existing constitution of a country:—that facility in changes, upon the credit of mere hypothesis and opinion, exposes to perpetual change from the endless variety of hypothesis and opinion: and remember, especially, that for the efficient management of your common interests in a country so extensive as ours, a government of as much vigor as is consistent with the perfect security of liberty is indispensable. Liberty itself will find in such a government, with powers properly distributed and adjusted, its surest guardian. It is, indeed, little else than a name, where the government is too feeble to withstand the enterprises of faction, to confine each member of the society within the limits prescribed by the laws, and to maintain all in the secure and tranquil enjoyment of the rights of person and property.

I have already intimated to you the danger of parties in the state, with particular references to the founding of them on geographical discrimination. Let me now take a more comprehensive view, and warn you in the most solemn manner against the baneful effects of the spirit of party generally.

This spirit, unfortunately, is inseparable from our nature, having its root in the strongest passions of the human mind.— It exists under different shapes in all governments, more or less stifled, controlled, or repressed; but in those of the popular form it is seen in its greatest rankness, and is truly their worst enemy.

The alternate domination of one faction over another, sharpened by the spirit of revenge natural to party dissension, which in different ages and countries has perpetrated the most horrid enormities, is itself a frightful despotism. But this leads at length to a more formal and permanent despotism. The disorders and miseries which result, gradually incline the minds of men to seek security and repose in the absolute power of an individual; and, sooner or later, the chief of some prevailing faction, more able or more fortunate than his competitors, turns this disposition to the purpose of his own elevation on the ruins of public liberty.

Without looking forward to an extremity of this kind (which nevertheless ought not to be entirely out of sight) the common and continual mischiefs of the spirit or party are sufficient to make it the interest and duty of a wise people to discourage and restrain it.

It serves always to distract the public councils, and enfeeble the public administration. It agitates the community with ill founded jealousies and false alarms; kindles the animosity of one part against another; foments occasional riot and insurrection. It opens the door to foreign influence and corruption, which finds a facilitated access to the government itself through the channels of party passions. Thus the policy and the will of one country are subjected to the policy and will of another.

There is an opinion that parties in free countries are useful checks upon the administration of the government, and serve to keep alive the spirit of liberty. This within certain limits is probably true; and in governments of a monarchial cast, patriotism may look with indulgence, if not with favor upon the spirit of party. But in those of the popular character, in governments purely elective, it is a spirit not to be encouraged. From their natural tendency, it is certain there will always be enough of that spirit for every salutary purpose. And there being constant danger of excess, the effort ought to be, by force of public opinion, to mitigate and assuage it. A fire not to be quenched, it demands a uniform vigilance to prevent it bursting into a flame, lest instead of warming, it should consume.

It is important likewise, that the habits of thinking in a free country should inspire caution in those intrusted with its administration, to confine themselves within their respective constitutional spheres, avoiding in the exercise of the powers of one department, to encroach upon another. The spirit of encroachment tends to consolidate the powers of all the departments in one, and thus to create, whatever the form of government, a real despotism. A just estimate of that love of power and proneness to abuse it which predominate in the human heart, is sufficient to satisfy us of the truth of this position. The necessity of reciprocal checks in the exercise of political power, by dividing and distributing it into different depositories and constituting each the guardian of the public weal against invasion of the others, has been evinced by experiments ancient and modern; some of them in our country and under our own eyes.—To preserve them must be as necessary as to institute them. If, in the opinion of the people, the distribution or modification of the constitutional powers be in any particular wrong, let it be corrected by an amendment in the way which the constitution designates.—But let there be no change by usurpation, for though this, in one instance, may be the instrument of good, it is the customary weapon by which free governments are destroyed. The precedent must always greatly overbalance in permanent evil any partial or transient benefit which the use can at any time yield.

Of all the dispositions and habits which lead to political prosperity, religion and morality are indispensable supports. In vain would that man claim the tribute of patriotism, who should labor to subvert these great pillars of human happiness, these firmest props of the duties of men and citizens. The mere politician, equally with the pious man, ought to respect and to cherish them. A volume could not trace all their connections with private and public felicity. Let it simply be asked, where is the security for property, for reputation, for life, if the sense of religious obligation *desert* the oaths which are the instruments of investigation in courts of justice? And let us with caution indulge the supposition that morality can be maintained without religion. Whatever may be conceded to the influence of refined education on minds of peculiar structure, reason and experience both forbid us to expect, that national mo-

rality can prevail in exclusion of religious principle.

It is substantially true, that virtue or morality is a necessary spring of popular government. The rule, indeed extends with more or less force to every species of free government. Who that is a sincere friend to it can look with indifference upon attempts to shake the foundation of the fabric?

Promote, then, as an object of primary importance, institutions for the general diffusion of knowledge. In proportion as the structure of a government gives force to public opinion, it should be enlightened.

As a very important source of strength and security, cherish public credit. One method of preserving it is to use it as sparingly as possible, avoiding occasions of expense by cultivating peace, but remembering, also, that timely disbursements, to prepare for danger, frequently prevent much greater disbursements to repel it; avoiding likewise the accumulation of debt, not only by shunning occasions of expense, but by vigorous exertions, in time of peace, to discharge the debts which unavoidable wars may have occasioned, not ungenerously throwing upon posterity the burden which we ourselves ought to bear. The execution of these maxims belongs to your representatives, but it is necessary that public opinion should cooperate. To facilitate to them the performance of their duty, it is essential that you should practically bear in mind, that towards the payment of debts there must be revenue; that to have revenue there must be taxes, that no taxes can be devised which are not more or less inconvenient and unpleasant; that the intrinsic embarrassment inseparable from the selection of the proper object (which is always a choice of difficulties), ought to be a decisive motive for a candid construction of the conduct of the government in making it, and for a spirit of acquiescence in the measures for obtaining revenue, which the public exigencies may at any time dictate.

Observe good faith and justice towards all nations; cultivate peace and harmony with all. Religion and morality enjoin this conduct, and can it be that good policy does not equally enjoin it? It will be worthy of a free, enlightened, and, at no distant period, a great nation, to give to mankind the magnanimous and too novel example of a people always guided by an exalted justice and benevolence. Who can doubt but, in the course of time and things, the fruits of such a plan would richly repay any temporary advantages which might be lost by a steady adherence to it; can it be that Providence has not connected the permanent felicity of a nation with its virtue? The experiment, at least is recommended by every sentiment which ennobles human nature. Alas! is it rendered impossible by its vices?

In the execution of such a plan, nothing is more essential than that permanent, inveterate antipathies against particular nations and passionate attachments for others, should be excluded; and that in place of them, just and amicable feelings towards all should be cultivated. The nation which indulges towards another an habitual hatred, or an habitual fondness, is in some degree a slave. It is a slave to its animosity or to its affection, either of which is sufficient to lead it astray from its duty and its interest. Antipathy in one nation against another disposes each more readily to offer insult and injury, to lay hold of slight causes of umbrage, and to be haughty and intractable when accidental or trifling occasions of dispute occur. Hence, frequent collisions, obstinate, envenomed, and bloody contests. The nation, prompted by ill will and resentment, sometimes impels to war the government, contrary to the best calculations of policy. The government sometimes participates in the national propensity, and adopts through passion what reason would reject; at other times, it makes the animosity of the nation subservient to projects of hostility, instigated by pride, ambition, and other sinister and pernicious motives. The peace often, sometimes perhaps the liberty of nations, has been the victim.

So likewise, a passionate attachment of one nation for another produces a variety of evils. Sympathy for the favorite nation, facilitating the illusion of an imaginary common interest, in cases where no real common interest exists, and infusing into one the enmities of the other, betrays the former into a participation in the quarrels and wars of the latter, without adequate inducements or justifications. It leads also to concessions, to the favorite nation, of privileges denied to others, which is apt doubly to injure the nation making the concessions, by unnecessary parting with what ought to have been retained, and by exciting jealousy, ill will, and a disposition to retaliate in the parties from whom equal privileges are withheld; and it gives to ambitious, corrupted or deluded citizens who devote themselves to the favorite nation, facility to betray or sacrifice the interests of their own country, without odium, sometimes even with popularity; gilding with the appearances of a virtuous sense of obligation, a commendable deference for public opinion, or a laudable zeal for public good, the base or foolish compliances of ambition, corruption, or infatuation.

• As avenues to foreign influence in innumerable ways, such attachments are particularly alarming to the truly enlightened and independent patriot. How many opportunities do they afford to tamper with domestic factions, to practice the arts of seduction, to mislead public opinion, to influence or awe the public councils!— Such an attachment of a small or weak, towards a great and powerful nation, dooms the former to be the satellite of the latter.

Against the insidious wiles of foreign influence (I conjure you to believe me fellow citizens), the jealousy of a free people ought to be *constantly* awake; since history and experience prove, that foreign influence is one of the most baneful foes of republican government. But that jealousy, to be useful, must be impartial, else it becomes the instrument of the very influence to be avoided, instead of a defense against it. Excessive partiality for one foreign nation and excessive dislike for another, cause those whom they actuate to see danger only on one side, and serve to veil and even second the arts of influence on the other. Real patriots, who may resist the intrigues of the favorite, are liable to become suspected and odious; while its tools and dupes usurp the applause and confidence of the people, to surrender their interests.

The great rule of conduct for us, in regard to foreign nations, is, in extending our commercial relations, to have with them as little *political* connection as possible. So far as we have already formed engagements, let them be fulfilled with perfect good faith:—Here let us stop.

Europe has a set of primary interests, which to us have none, or a very remote relation. Hence, she must be engaged in frequent controversies, the causes of which are essentially foreign to our concerns. Hence, therefore, it must be unwise in us to implicate ourselves, by artificial ties, in the ordinary vicissitudes of her politics, or the ordinary combinations and collusions of her friendships or enmities.

Our detached and distant situation invites and enables us to pursue a different course. If we remain one people, under an efficient government, the period is not far off when we may defy material injury from external annoyance; when we may take such an attitude as will cause the neutrality we may at any time resolve upon, to be scrupulously respected; when belligerent nations, under the impossibility of making acquisitions upon us, will not lightly hazard the giving us provocation, when we may choose peace or war, as our interest, guided by justice, shall counsel.

Why forego the advantages of so peculiar a situation? Why quit our own to stand upon foreign ground? Why, by interweaving our destiny with that of any part of Europe, entangle our peace and prosperity in the toils of European ambition, rivalship, interest, humor, or caprice?

It is our true policy to steer clear of permanent alliance with any portion of the foreign world; so far, I mean, as we are now at liberty to do it; for let me not be understood as capable of patronizing infidelity to existing engagements. I hold the maxim no less applicable to public than private affairs, that honesty is always the best policy. I repeat it, therefore, let those engagements be observed in their genuine sense. But in my opinion, it is unnecessary, and would be unwise to extend them.

Taking care always to keep ourselves by suitable establishments, on a respectable defensive posture, we may safely trust to temporary alliances for extraordinary emergencies.

Harmony, and a liberal intercourse with all nations, are recommended by policy, humanity, and interest. But even our commercial policy should hold an equal and impartial hand; neither seeking nor granting exclusive favors or preferences; consulting the natural course of things; diffusing and diversifying by gentle means the streams of commerce, but forcing nothing; establishing with powers so disposed, in order to give trade a stable course, to define the rights of our merchants, and to enable the government to support them, conventional rules of intercourse, the best that present circumstances and mutual opinion will permit, but temporary, and liable to be from time to time abandoned or varied as experience and circumstances shall dictate; constantly keeping in view, that it is folly in one nation to look for disinterested favors from another; that it must pay with a portion of its independence for whatever it may accept under that character; that by such acceptance, it may place itself in the condition of having given equivalents for nominal favors, and yet of being reproached with ingratitude for not giving more. There can be no greater error than to expect, or calculate upon real favors from nation to nation. It is an illusion which experience must cure, which a just pride ought to discard.

In offering to you, my countrymen, these counsels of an old and affectionate friend, I dare not hope they will make the strong and lasting impression I could wish; that they will control the usual current of the passions, or prevent our nation from running the course which has hitherto marked the destiny of nations, but if I may even flatter myself that they may be productive of some partial benefit, some occasional good; that they may now and then recur to moderate the fury of party spirit, to warn against the mischiefs of foreign intrigue, to guard against the impostures of pretended patriotism; this hope will be a full recompense for the solicitude for your welfare by which they have been dictated.

How far, in the discharge of my official duties, I have been guided by the principles which have been delineated, the public records and other evidences of my conduct must witness to you and to the world. To myself, the assurance of my own conscience is, that I have, at least, believed myself to be guided by them.

In relation to the still subsisting war in Europe; my proclamation of the 22d of April, 1793, is the index to my plan. Sanctioned by your approving voice, and by that of your representatives in both houses of congress, the spirit of that measure has continually governed me, uninfluenced by any attempts to deter or divert me from it.

After deliberate examination, with the aid of the best lights I could obtain, I was well satisfied that our country, under all the circumstances of the case, had a right to take, and was bound in duty and interest, to take a neutral position. Having taken it, I determined, as far as should depend upon me, to maintain it with moderation, perseverance and firmness.

The considerations which respect the right to hold this conduct, it is not necessary on this occasion to detail. I will only observe that, according to my understanding of the matter, that right, so far from being denied by any of the belligerent powers, has been virtually admitted by all.

The duty of holding a neutral conduct may be inferred, without anything more, from the obligation which justice and humanity impose on every nation, in cases in which it is free to act, to maintain inviolate the relations of peace and amity towards other nations.

The inducements of interest for observing that conduct will best be referred to your own reflections and experience. With me a predominant motive has been to endeavor to gain time to our country to settle and mature its yet recent institutions, and to progress, without interruption, to that degree of strength, and consistency which is necessary to give it, humanly speaking, the command of its own fortunes.

Though in reviewing the incidents of my administration, I am unconscious of intentional error, I am nevertheless too sensible of my defects not to think it probable that I may have committed many errors. Whatever they may be, I fervently beseech the Almighty to avert or mitigate the evils to which they may tend. I shall also carry with me the hope that my country will never cease to view them with indulgence; and that, after forty-five years of my life dedicated to its service, with an upright zeal, the faults of incompetent abilities will be consigned to oblivion, as myself must soon be to the mansions of rest.

Relying on its kindness in this as in other things, and actuated by that fervent love towards it, which is so natural to a man who views in it the native soil of himself and his progenitors for several generations; I anticipate with pleasing expectation that retreat in which I promise myself to realize without alloy, the sweet enjoyment of partaking, in the midst of my fellow citizens, the benign influence of good laws under a free government—the ever favorite object of my heart, and the happy reward, as I trust, of our mutual cares, labors and dangers.

GEO. WASHINGTON

Index

488

Acknowledgments

The publishers take this opportunity to express appreciation for the generous assistance of the following individuals and organizations in the work of preparing and illustrating the author's original manuscript and producing it in book form.

The numerous originals and prints which appear throughout the text were located and reproduced through the courteous co-operation of H. Maxson Holloway, Curator; Adele Rathbun, Custodian of Prints; and Walter Krutz, Photographer, of the Chicago Historical Society, of which Paul M. Angle is the Director.

The "Pictograms" and charts used to highlight the significant trends discussed in the later chapters were made available by the United States News Publishing Corporation from the files of *U.S. News and World Report*, a weekly magazine on national and international affairs, published at Washington, D.C.

Selected "Graphicharts" prepared by artist Tom P. Barrett were reprinted with permission of the *Chicago Sun-Times*. Prints of original paintings which record dramatic scenes from American history were furnished by the John Hancock Mutual Life Insurance Company of Boston, Massachusetts. Prints of a number of fine line drawings were provided by the Intertype Corporation of Brooklyn, New York. The design of the end papers of this book was adapted from one of the Intertype Corporation's drawings.

Appreciation is expressed to the following for permission to reproduce pictorial properties: National Industrial Conference Board, Woodward Governor Company, United Nations Department of Public Information, Great American Group of Insurance Companies, *Holiday* Magazine, John M. Haass Lithography Company, Union Pacific Railroad, George B. Allen, Kay Pictures, Cecil and Presbrey, Inc., United States Fire Insurance Company, Parker-Allston Associates, Kaywoodie Company, Town Hall, Inc., General Motors Corporation, Portland Cement Association, *The American Weekly*, United States Army, United States Marine Corps, United States Navy, Acme Newspictures, Bettmann Archive, Litchfield Studio, Caterpillar Tractor Company, *Scene* Magazine, Underwood and Underwood, Higgins Industries, Inc., J. I. Case Company, Eastern Airlines, Parke, Davis and Company.

Panel illustrations which introduce each of the eight units are original drawings by artist John Merryweather. Apart from one reproduction, the maps appearing in this book were prepared by Arthur E. Burke, Head of the Illustration Department, American Technical Society, assisted by members of his staff. Editorial preparation and correlation of text and illustrations were supervised by J. R. Dalzell, Managing Editor, and T. W. Tanaka, Senior Editor, of the American Technical Society. Assisting were Editorial Department members Loretta Fakkema Scholten, who copyedited the manuscript, and R. J. Sullivan, who wrote the illustration legends.

THE PUBLISHERS